Wills, Trusts, and Estate Administration for Paralegals

Jennifer Montante, Esq.

Mohave Community College and Nevada State College

Boston   Columbus   Indianapolis   New York   San Francisco   Upper Saddle River
Amsterdam   Cape Town   Dubai   London   Madrid   Milan   Munich   Paris   Montréal   Toronto
Delhi   Mexico City   São Paulo   Sydney   Hong Kong   Seoul   Singapore   Taipei   Tokyo

This book is dedicated to Gay Perotto and Eugene Parrs of Parrs, Perotto & Magee, LLP in Rochester, New York. Thank you for being the best at what you do and for taking the time to teach me.

Editorial Director: Vernon Anthony
Acquisitions Editor: Gary Bauer
Editorial Assistant: Kevin Cecil
Director of Marketing: David Gesell
Marketing Manager: Mary Salzman
Senior Marketing Coordinator: Alicia Wozniak
Senior Marketing Assistant: Les Roberts
Senior Managing Editor: JoEllen Gohr
Project Manager: Linda Cupp
Procurement Specialist: Deidra Skahill
Art Director: Jayne Conte

Cover Designer: Bruce Kenselaar
Cover Image: bikeriderlondon/Shutterstock; Alexander Raths/Shutterstock; Jamie Grill/Getty Images
Media Project Manager: April Cleland
Full-Service Project Management: Revathi Viswanathan/PreMediaGlobal USA, Inc.
Composition: PreMediaGlobal USA, Inc.
Printer/Binder: LSC Communications
Cover Printer: LSC Communications
Text Font: Goudy 11/13

Credits and acknowledgments borrowed from other sources and reproduced, with permission, in this textbook appear on the appropriate page within text.

Microsoft® and Windows® are registered trademarks of the Microsoft Corporation in the U.S.A. and other countries. Screen shots and icons reprinted with permission from the Microsoft Corporation. This book is not sponsored or endorsed by or affiliated with the Microsoft Corporation.

Many of the designations by manufacturers and sellers to distinguish their products are claimed as trademarks. Where those designations appear in this book, and the publisher was aware of a trademark claim, the designations have been printed in initial caps or all caps.

Library of Congress Cataloging-in-Publication Data

Montante, Jennifer, author.
   Wills, trusts, and estate administration for paralegals / Jennifer Montante, Esq., Mohave Community College and Nevada State College.—First edition.
      pages cm
   Includes index.
   ISBN-13: 978-0-13-215129-0
   ISBN-10: 0-13-215129-4
   1. Estate planning—United States.   2. Wills—United States.   3. Trusts and trustees—United States.
   4. Executors and administrators—United States.   5. Inheritance and succession—United States.
   6. Legal assistants—United States—Handbooks, manuals, etc.   I. Title.
   KF750.M66 2015
   346.7305'2—dc23

                                        2013037103

4 2020

ISBN 10:   0-13-215129-4
ISBN 13: 978-0-13-215129-0

BRIEF CONTENTS

CONTENTS

CHAPTER 16

Remedies for Improper
Administration   417

PREFACE

What makes this textbook unique? It employs the use of the following **Hypothetical Family**, introduced in Chapter 1:

HYPOTHETICAL FAMILY _____

Shirley Smith, age 82, is a widow with two surviving children: Jane Smith and Robert Smith. A third child, Mark Smith, passed away and left one surviving child: Mark Smith, Jr.

Jane Smith was never married but has two adult children: John Smith and Susan Smith-Thompson. John and Susan are both married with minor children of their own.

Robert Smith is married to Mary Smith. They have three minor children: Roberta Smith, Ryan Smith, and Rachael Smith.

The Hypothetical Family, like all families, undergoes ups and downs and life changes that are depicted in the chapter figures throughout the text. The figures tell the family's story while depicting a wide array of estate planning and probate documents. Students can track what happens to the Hypothetical Family using an accompanying Hypothetical Family Project Worksheet in order to determine who owns what property at the conclusion of the text.

This book is designed to provide a comprehensive overview of estate planning and probate in a manner that is straightforward and easy to read and understand. Paralegal and legal studies students at the undergraduate level do not need to know everything there is to know about estate planning and probate (yet). This book presents material in a logical fashion, beginning with basic estate planning and property concepts, followed by more advanced concepts and drafting techniques before delving into probate. Every chapter begins with a real-life scenario to illustrate how the content of the chapter is relevant to every day practice in this field. The activities at the end of the chapter are designed to reinforce students' understanding of the concepts taught in the chapter, to provide students with opportunities to research their own state law, and to provide drafting opportunities that are comparable to tasks they are likely to do in a real law office. Finally, unlike other textbooks, this one **provides all of the legal forms necessary to complete the drafting assignments**, making life easier for professors and students alike.

■ CHAPTER ORGANIZATION AND FEATURES

This book is organized into two parts and can be taught either in one semester or two. Teaching from this text over the course of two semesters allows for more in-depth coverage of each chapter and the exercises that follow.

Part One comprehensively covers estate planning and gives students a solid foundation of underlying concepts that they will need if they work in this field. At the most basic level, it can be said that Part One deals with clients' needs while they are still alive. **Part Two** covers estate administration, the necessary steps to take after someone has passed away. Part Two teaches students how to analyze the facts of a case to determine what process is needed, if any probate is needed at all. Students also learn to draft all of the major forms required for an informal probate proceeding. When finished with Part One and Part Two, students will appreciate just how important good document drafting is to ensure that what happens to their client's estate and loved ones after the client passes away is what he or she wanted.

This text aimed to have a light and upbeat, positive tone to make reading easy and enjoyable. The objective is to not only help students learn the information, but also learn how to use it when working out in the field.

■ CHAPTER FEATURES

Chapters are designed to introduce students to the topic, presenting basic information as a foundation before more advanced concepts. Most chapters contain the following features:

- **Chapter Objectives** to briefly familiarize students with the concepts they should be learning in each chapter. Chapter objectives are also helpful for instructors when preparing course packages and course syllabi.
- **A Real-Life Scenario** at the beginning of the chapter to pique interest in the topic and illustrate how the topic may arise in real life.
- **Figures throughout each chapter** illustrate text content with actual sample documents. The majority of the figures are based on the Hypothetical Family and students can track what occurs in the figures using the accompanying Hypothetical Family Project Worksheet, which is posted online at the companion website.
- **A Conclusion** summarizes the key points of each chapter.
- **End of Chapter Exercises** are organized into the following.

  Concept Review and Reinforcement
  - *Key Terms* provide students with the opportunity to review important vocabulary in each chapter.
  - *Review Questions* provide students with the opportunity to make sure that they understand basic concepts and information covered in each chapter.

  Building Your Paralegal Skills
  - *Critical Thinking* Exercises provide students with the opportunity to analyze the situation provided and apply legal concepts from the chapter to the facts of the given case to come up with a proposed solution.
  - *Paralegal Practice* gives students the opportunity to research or draft documents in a manner comparable to what they will see when working in a law office. Form templates are provided for every assignment.
  - *Cases for Consideration* give students the opportunity to read and consider relevant case law and its interpretation. Instructors can also utilize this section as an opportunity to teach students how to brief cases, which is a valuable paralegal skill.

■ ALTERNATE VERSIONS

Wills, Trusts, and Estate Administration for Paralegals is available in various eBook formats, including CourseSmart and Adobe Reader. *CourseSmart* is an exciting new choice for students looking to save money. As an alternative to purchasing the printed textbook, students can purchase an electronic version of the same content. With a *CourseSmart eTextbook*, students can search the text, make notes online, print out reading assignments that incorporate lecture notes, and bookmark important passages for later review. For more information, or to purchase access to the *CourseSmart eTextbook*, visit **www.coursesmart.com**.

■ RESOURCES FOR INSTRUCTORS

Instructor's Manual

Includes content outlines for classroom discussion, teaching suggestions, and answers to end-of-chapter questions from the text.

MyTest

This computerized test generation system gives you maximum flexibility in preparing tests. It can create custom tests and print scrambled versions of a test at one time, as well as build tests randomly by chapter, level of difficulty, or question type. The software also allows online testing and record-keeping and the ability to add problems to the database. This test bank can also be delivered formatted for use in popular learning management platforms, such as BlackBoard, WebCT, Moodle, Angel, and eCollege. Visit www.PearsonMyTest.com to begin building your tests.

PowerPoint Lecture Presentation

Lecture presentation screens for each chapter are available online.

To access instructor resources, go to **www.pearsonhighered.com/irc**, where you can register for an instructor access code. Within 48 hours of registering you will receive a confirming e-mail including an instructor access code. Once you have received your code, locate your text in the online catalog and click on the Instructor Resources button on the left side of the catalog product page. Select a supplement and a login page will appear. Once you have logged in, you can access instructor material for all Pearson Education textbooks.

■ PEARSON ONLINE COURSE SOLUTIONS

Wills, Trusts, and Estate Administration for Paralegals is supported by online course solutions that include interactive learning modules, a variety of assessment tools, videos, simulations, and current event features. Go to www.pearsonhighered.com or contact your local representative for the latest information.

■ ACKNOWLEDGMENTS

Many thanks to my editor, Gary Bauer, for seeing the potential in me to complete this project and giving me the opportunity to do so. Thanks also to Linda Cupp for her help with manuscript review and development.

I also wish to acknowledge and thank Mohave Community College for giving me the opportunity to take part in designing a new paralegal program at the college, which in turn led to my writing this book. Thank you to my students, for showing me what works and what doesn't in the classroom and for voicing your likes and dislikes.

■ REVIEWERS

Steven C. Kempisty, Bryant and Stratton College, Liverpool

Jennifer A. Jenkins, South College, Tennessee

Clint Davis, Trinity Valley Community College

Ruth Ann Hall, University of Alabama

Hannah Barnhorn, National College, Dayton

Carina Aguirre, Platt College

Teri Fields, Clayton State University

John Whitehead, Kilgore College

Belinda Clifton, IIA College

Robert Donley, Central Penn College

Jameka Ellison, Everest College

Beth Pless, Northeast Wisconsin Technical College

Cathy Trecek, Iowa Western Community College

Robert J. Glidewell, Pulaski Technical College

Bruce A. Moseley, Amarillo College

Annalinda Ragazzo, Bryant and Stratton College, Rochester

Bobby (Buzz) Wheeler, Highline Community College

Charles Splawn, Horry Georgetown Technical College

Joy O'Donnell, Pima Community College

Laura Alfano, Virginia College Online

ABOUT THE AUTHOR

Jennifer Montante is a practicing attorney who is licensed in New York, Florida, Arizona, and Nevada. Her primary areas of practice are estate planning and probate, bankruptcy, and social security disability. Montante was resident faculty of the paralegal program at Mohave Community College from 2007–2010 and has since taught as associate faculty for Mohave Community College and Nevada State College.

Introduction to Estate Planning: The Purpose of and Need for a Will

CHAPTER 1

A REAL-LIFE SCENARIO

A new client sat down before her attorney and declared: "I need a living will." The attorney replied calmly, in statement form: "Okay, you need a document to express your intention not to be kept alive artificially and to appoint someone to make medical decisions on your behalf." The client was belligerent. "NO, I need a document leaving everything to my children when I die. A *living will!*"

© Jennifer Montante

[You may or may not recognize at this point that the client was not aware of the difference between a living will and a last will and testament (or "will"). These documents are commonly confused. That's okay, because this textbook will provide you with a solid comprehension of estate planning and probate, and you will soon be well versed in using the different terms.]

The attorney patiently went on to explain that she would be preparing a complete estate plan on the client's behalf, which would include not only a will and a living will, but also a power of attorney and a health care power of attorney. The client was irate: "I don't need an *estate plan*; I need a living will! Your secretary said that you could prepare a living will for me!" Luckily, the attorney was experienced at handling clients with these types of misconceptions. They were able to move forward and form a comprehensive estate plan. In the end, the client was happy and had an estate plan that she understood.

CHAPTER OBJECTIVES:

1. Understand the purpose of executing a Last Will and Testament (will).

2. Discuss the purpose of estate planning and list the possible components.

3. Categorize assets as either real property or personal property.

4. Describe the requirement of capacity with respect to will execution.

5. Differentiate between testate and intestate succession.

6. Distinguish between probate assets and non-probate assets.

■ INTRODUCTION

The previous example illustrates some common misconceptions that people have with respect to the purposes of various estate planning documents. It further demonstrates that the term "estate plan" is commonly misunderstood and as a result may have negative connotations for some people. It is all too common for clients to believe that they need a certain document because that is the word they have heard most often, or read about on the Internet, or were told about by friends. However, it is the job of the attorney and the paralegal to be able to explain the difference, to identify the needs of the client, and to determine what documents can be used to accomplish those ends. Keep in mind that paralegals must work under the supervision of an attorney and may not give legal advice. However, they can interact with clients and draft legal documents for the attorney to review. Paralegals have a very important job and are crucial to the smooth operation of many law offices across the country. Your review and mastery of this textbook is the first step in the direction of working as a wills, trusts, and estates paralegal.

Key Words and Definitions

A **Last Will and Testament**, or "**will**," is a written document that leaves the estate of the individual who signed the will to the named persons or entities. A will only takes effect upon the maker's death, and can be revoked or amended any time with the maker is still alive. A will usually appoints an executor (or personal representative, depending on the state) to manage the estate and carry out the directions in the will. In addition, a will may nominate guardians of minor children, and may even give funeral and/or burial instructions in some states. Since the terms are sometimes confused, it is important to know the difference between a will and a **living will**, which is a written expression of a person's wishes to be allowed to die a natural death and not be kept alive by heroic or artificial methods.

Figure 1.1 depicts Jane Smith's will. Under the will, Jane Smith leaves her estate to her two children.

Figure 1.2 depicts Jane Smith's living will. Note that the living will discusses medical issues during the life of the maker, whereas the will disposes of property after the maker's death.

A person makes an **estate plan** to provide for his or her lifetime physical and financial needs, as well as the distribution of his or her estate upon death. Most estate planning is done with the assistance of an attorney. An estate plan may include a will and/or a trust, a living will, a health care proxy, and a power of attorney, as well as other documents. However, the primary component of most estate plans is a will.

The focus of some people's estate plans is on avoiding probate at their death. **Probate** is a general term for the entire process of administration of estates of dead persons, including those without wills, with court supervision. In the context of a probate proceeding, the individual who passed away is often referred to as "the **decedent**."

NOTE: The figures included in Chapter 1 and throughout the remainder of this text are based primarily on the following hypothetical family.

Pay close attention to how assets are transferred to different family members via various forms of estate planning and administration to determine who owns which assets at the conclusion of the text.

Will
A written document that leaves the estate of the individual who signed the will to the named persons or entities.

Living Will
A written expression of a person's wishes to be allowed to die a natural death and not be kept alive by heroic or artificial methods.

Estate Plan
A plan made to provide for the maker's physical and financial needs during lifetime, as well as the distribution of their estate upon death.

Probate
A general term for the entire process of administration of estates of dead persons, including those without wills, with court supervision.

Decedent
The dead person.

HYPOTHETICAL FAMILY

Shirley Smith, age 82, is a widow with two surviving children: Jane Smith and Robert Smith. A third child, Mark Smith, passed away and left one surviving child: Mark Smith, Jr.

Jane Smith was never married but has two adult children: John Smith and Susan Smith-Thompson. John and Susan are both married with minor children of their own.

Robert Smith is married to Mary Smith. They have three minor children: Roberta Smith, Ryan Smith, and Rachael Smith.

The assets owned by a decedent can be divided into two main types of property: real property and personal property. **Real property** is all land, structures, firmly attached and integrated equipment, anything growing on the land, and all interests in the property. Real property is immovable. **Personal property** includes all movable assets or things that are not real property and also includes intangible property.

The following table lists some examples:

Real Property	Personal Property
• House	• Clothing
• Vacant Land	• Furniture
• Building	• Automobile
• Life Estate	• Money

A paralegal needs to have a comprehensive understanding of property before he or she can effectively assist clients with estate planning. The topic of property is covered fully in Chapter 2.

Real Property
All land, structures, and firmly attached and integrated equipment, anything growing on the land, and all interests in the property. Real property is immovable.

Personal Property
Includes all movable assets, or things, that are not classified as real property; includes both tangible and intangible property.

Figure 1.1 The following is a sample will of a single female named Jane Smith. Note that the primary purpose of this document is to distribute the testatrix's property after her death.

LAST WILL AND TESTAMENT

I, **JANE SMITH**, of the CITY OF SAMPLE, COUNTY OF SAMPLE COUNTY, STATE OF SAMPLE STATE, do hereby make, publish and declare the following to be my Last Will and Testament, hereby revoking all former Wills and Codicils made by me.

I. I direct that all my debts and funeral expenses be paid and I further authorize my Executor, in its discretion, to prepay any mortgage or other installment indebtedness.

II. I give and bequeath to my children, JOHN SMITH and SUSAN SMITH (hereinafter referred to as "my children"), all of my clothing, jewelry, personal effects, household goods, furniture, furnishings, automobiles and all other tangible personal property which I may own at the time of my death, to be divided among them as they shall agree. If my children are unable to agree as to the recipient of any article, that article, as well as any articles not selected, shall be sold and the proceeds added to my residuary estate.

III. All the rest, residue and remainder of my property, real, personal and mixed, of every name and nature, and wheresoever situate, I give, devise and bequeath in equal shares to my children, with the share of any deceased child to be paid to the child's issue, per stirpes; or in default of issue, to my surviving issue, per stirpes.

IV. I give to my Executor hereinafter named, and to the successor, the following powers and discretions, in addition to those vested in or imposed upon them or either of them by law:

A. To mortgage, sell, convey, exchange or otherwise deal with or dispose of any real or personal property for cash or on credit (including the right to accept a purchase money mortgage as part of the purchase price); to retain as part of the estate any and all securities and property in the form originally received, whether or not it is then income producing and regardless of any rule requiring diversification of investments; to invest and reinvest in any stocks, bonds, shares in mutual funds or authorized common trust funds, or other securities or property, whether real or personal, which my Executor may deem safe and for the best interests of the estate, without being limited to investments authorized by law for the investment of trust funds; to hold title to any and all securities and other investments either in my Executor's name or in the name of a nominee; to borrow money from itself or others on terms my Executor may deem best, and to pledge any property of the estate as security for the repayment thereof; and to make distributions in cash or in kind, or partly in each to the beneficiaries entitled thereto.

B. If any beneficiary or legatee entitled to receive a part of my estate shall be under twenty-one (21) years of age, I authorize and empower my Executor to designate his or her parent, or some other appropriate adult person or trust company, as custodian for the beneficiary or legatee under the Sample State Uniform Transfers to Minors Act until age twenty-one (21), and to distribute the share of the beneficiary or legatee to the designated custodian. A receipt from the custodian shall fully release my Executor.

V. I direct that all inheritance, succession and estate taxes of every kind payable with respect to any property includable in my gross taxable estate, whether or not passing under this my Will, shall be paid out of my residuary estate, and shall not be apportioned.

VI. I hereby nominate, constitute and appoint JOHN SMITH as Executor of this my Last Will and Testament, but if he fails to survive me, or renounces, or fails to qualify, or upon his death, resignation or disqualification, I nominate and appoint SUSAN SMITH as Executrix. I direct that no bond or other security shall be required of my Executor.

VII. The masculine gender, whenever used herein, shall include the feminine, the feminine shall include the masculine; the neuter shall include both the masculine and feminine; and the singular shall include the plural wherever necessary or appropriate.

IN WITNESS WHEREOF, I have hereunto subscribed my name and affixed my seal this 27th day of December, 2011.

Jane Smith
_____
JANE SMITH

We, whose names are hereto subscribed, do certify that on the 27th day of December, 2011, the Testatrix, JANE SMITH, subscribed her name to this instrument, in our presence and in the presence of each of us, and at the same time in our

Figure 1.1 (continued)

presence and hearing, declared the same to be her Last Will and Testament, and requested us, and each of us, to sign our names thereto as witnesses to the execution thereof, which we hereby do in the presence of the Testatrix and of each other.

Michael Pearson _____ residing at *1001 Reed Drive, Sample City, Sample State 12345* _____

Maggy Pearson _____ residing at *1001 Reed Drive, Sample City, Sample State 12345* _____

AFFIDAVIT OF
ATTESTING WITNESSES

STATE OF SAMPLE STATE)
COUNTY OF SAMPLE COUNTY) SS:

_____ *Michael Pearson* and *Maggy Pearson*, being duly sworn, say

We are acquainted with JANE SMITH. The signature at the end of the instrument dated December 27, 2011 and declared by her to be her Last Will was made by her at City of Sample, State of Sample State, in the presence of each of the undersigned.

At the time of signing of this Will, JANE SMITH declared the instrument to which her signature had been affixed to be her Will and we, and each of us, signed our names thereto at the end thereof at that time and at her request and in her presence.

At the time of the execution of the instrument JANE SMITH was over the age of eighteen (18) years, of sound mind and memory, not under any restraint, and competent in every respect to make a Will.

At the time of execution, JANE SMITH could read, write and converse in the English language, and was not suffering from defects of sight, hearing, or speech or any other physical or mental impairment that could affect her capacity to make a valid Will.

The Will was not executed in counterparts.

Michael Pearson _____
Witness

Maggy Pearson _____
Witness

STATE OF SAMPLE STATE}
COUNTY OF SAMPLE COUNTY} ss:

On the 27th day of December in the year 2011 before me, the undersigned, a Notary Public in and for said State, personally appeared Michael Pearson and Maggy Pearson, the subscribing witnesses to the foregoing instrument, with whom I am personally acquainted, who being by me duly sworn, did depose and say that Michael Pearson resides at 1001 Reed Drive, Sample State and Maggy Pearson resides at 1001 Reed Drive, Sample State; that they know JANE SMITH to be the individual described in and who executed the foregoing instrument; that said subscribing witnesses were present and saw said JANE SMITH execute the same; and that said witnesses at the same time subscribed their names as witnesses thereto, and acknowledged to me that they executed the same in their capacities, and that by their signatures on the instrument, the individual(s) or the person upon behalf of which the individual(s) acted, executed the instrument.

Lila P. Legal _____
Notary Public

LILA P. LEGAL Notary Public, State of Sample Sample County My Commission Expires May 10, 2012

Figure 1.2 The following is a sample living will for Jane Smith. Note that the purpose of this document is discussed under paragraph 2.

SAMPLE LIVING WILL

I, **JANE SMITH**, having an address at 123 Oak Street, Sample City, Sample State 12345, and an adult of sound and disposing mind and memory, not acting under duress, menace, fraud or undue influence of any person, do make, publish and declare this to be my Living Will to supplement all other wills I may execute and to be used in the event that I am unconscious or mentally incapacitated and, at the same time, have a catastrophic medical condition.

1. **Declaration of Intent.**

   I realize that, when I am conscious and functioning normally with full mental facilities, I have a legal right to accept or reject medical treatment offered to me by doctors, hospitals or other medical instrumentalities. It is my intent with this Living Will to express my commitment and to designate persons who are legally empowered to act for me when I am unconscious or mentally incapacitated, with full authority from me to make medical decisions for me and to accept or reject medical treatment. I rely on the common law and desire that this Living Will be enforced even if I am in a state of the United States that has not adopted specific statutes related to the enforcement of Living Wills.

   Further, my objective in executing this Living Will is to allow persons appointed by me in this document to withdraw medical care and administer pain-killing drugs when two doctors determine that my brain is no longer functioning or is irrevocably damaged, or when disease or accident places me in a condition where I am irrevocably dying, or when disease or accident has impaired my mind and body where I can no longer function as a normal human being. I intend that this document be effective at all times and in every place in this world.

2. **Purpose.**

   The purpose of this Living Will is to prevent my remaining assets from being used to unnecessarily prolong my life, so that they may be used instead to benefit my spouse and children, if any, and other heirs and devisees who benefit from my worldly estate. Also, I desire to avoid the heartache to my loved ones of an extended illness and to avoid additional pain and suffering to myself through whatever senses remain. In the unlikely event that this instrument may not be legally binding in the jurisdiction where I may be terminally ill, then you who care for me will, I hope, feel morally bound to follow its mandate. It is my decision, not yours, and it is made after careful consideration.

3. **Instruction.**

   If it is ever determined by competent medical evidence, to the satisfaction of the persons designated below, that my body is substantially damaged, deteriorated, destroyed or in a tenuous condition through accident, illness or age, and that I have reached the point where there is no reasonable expectation of recovery from physical or mental disability even with the aid of artificial means or heroic measures, such as respirators, transfusions, electric shock treatments, or instruments to prolong heartbeat (i.e. code arrest mechanisms, artificial respirators, heart massage by manual or mechanical methods, drugs of potent nature), intravenous feedings, or other measures, I request that all such life-prolonging means and measures be withdrawn or withheld from my body so that I may die with dignity. I further request that medication be mercifully administered to me for terminal suffering, even if it hastens the moment of death. I do not fear death as much as I fear the indignity of deterioration, dependence and hopeless pain.

   I consider myself in a tenuous condition if I have an incurable or irreversible physical condition that, in reasonable medical probability, will result in death unless extraordinary medical measures are used. I consider as extraordinary medical measures all medication, surgical procedures, mechanical or electrical devices that will sustain, restore or supplant a vital bodily function. A measure is extraordinary if employing it would not offer a reasonable medical probability of returning me to cognitive, sapient existence and would serve only to postpone the moment of death. I do not consider medical or surgical procedures to alleviate pain or discomfort prohibitive procedures under this Living Will.

4. **Mechanics of Implementation.**

   In order to implement the Living Will, my family physician along with one consulting physician shall make a finding that

   4.a I am unconscious, mentally incompetent or deranged, senile, insane or otherwise in an abnormal mental condition where I am not reasonably able to make decisions of my own.

Figure 1.2 (continued)

4.b Through accident, disease, nervous system, or otherwise, I have an irreversible condition resulting in (1) a brain that is dead, (2) a brain that is damaged to the point where I will not be able to reasonably enjoy a normal life, (3) a body with damaged organs or parts that will prevent me from enjoying the quality of productive life to which I am accustomed, or (4) a combination of all of these which will prevent me from enjoying the productive life to which I am accustomed.

If my family physician is not available, then two attending physicians may concur with the consulting physician in the finding. If three physicians are not immediately available, then two may concur.

The findings of the physicians will be written on my patient chart, or on a dated piece of paper to be placed in my patient file.

Thereupon the representative I have first designated in this Living Will shall concur and evidence that concurrence in writing on the patient chart or otherwise on the dated paper with the physicians' written findings. If my first designated representative or the next is not readily available then whichever one is the most readily available shall sign an affirmation of the decision.

If my representative is not physically available, concurrence may be affirmed by (1) two witnesses over the phone, with those witnesses evidencing the consent by writing this in the patient chart or on the dated paper concerning the physicians' written findings, or (2) by telegram or other means used for transmitting the written language, and a copy of this shall be placed in my medical files.

Once these findings and my representative's decisions have been thus memorialized, I shall be placed in a private room. My family and friends shall be summoned. The physician shall give me no further medical care or life aids such as food and water, except that morphine and other pain-killing or tranquilizing drugs shall be liberally administered even if they accelerate the moment of death. My family and friends shall be left alone with me, except for a doctor or nurse who will assist in keeping my physically clean and presentable until the moment of my passing.

If my doctors or representatives are unaware of these mechanics, I consent to any reasonable alternative method. My purpose in detailing these mechanics is to assist in providing my physicians and representatives with a reasonable method of carefully documenting what they have done to avoid later misunderstanding.

The findings of my doctors and the decision of my representative, once written, shall not be subject to attack by anyone at any later date.

5. **Persons Designated to Make Decisions.**

I give the following persons, singly in the order indicated or acting together, the power to make this decision:

Primary Decision Maker:

ROBERT SMITH, residing at 125 Oak Street, Sample City, Sample State 12345.

Alternate Decision Maker:

JOHN SMITH, residing at 234 Sunny Lane, Sample City, Sample State 12345.

Neither the attending physician nor the hospital is required to determine the reason for the absence of persons I may have listed first in the order of priority above. Whichever one of my family representatives who appears will take the responsibility of making an effort to locate the persons designated with higher priority. However, I trust in the judgment of all the persons named and, if they are unable to contact the person of higher priority, I will trust any of the persons named above who are there to make the necessary decisions. I know that whoever makes the decisions will have made every effort to notify all the other persons to obtain their concurrence and, if they cannot contact them within the time required by the emergency or if they cannot get concurrence of all parties, they have the authority to and will make the necessary decisions.

These persons are given a special power of attorney to act for me during any incapacity to make all decisions with regard to my medical treatment that I could have make had I been conscious and mentally able. I designate these persons also as my guardians ad litem and guardians of my person to sign all documents and bring any legal proceeding that may be necessary to exercise the power and authority vested in them by this Living Will, including the power to bring court proceedings for injunctive relief, damages, or other relief necessary to carry out my wishes expressed in this Living Will. It is my intent that the persons designated act quickly and without the necessity of court proceedings; however, if any doctor, hospital or other medical institution fails to carry out the instructions of my Living Will and the decisions of the persons I have designated to carry out my instructions, then the persons designated to make the decisions are directed to bring immediate court proceedings to enforce

(continued)

Figure 1.2 (continued)

---

this Living Will. I direct that this Living Will be implemented by the persons designated and the attending doctors acting together without the necessity of consulting courts, administrative bodies or hospital committees.

6. **Protection for Persons Designated and Those Assisting.** As further evidence of my convictions as expressed in this Living Will, I direct that the assets of my estate and my insurance be used to hold harmless from any liability the persons designated and any doctor, hospital or other medical instrumentality that assists in carrying out (a) my instructions expressed in this Living Will and (b) the decision and instructions of the persons designated by me to carry out my instructions.

My estate and my insurance shall also be committed to pay any attorney's fees, court costs or any other expenses associated with court proceedings to carry out my instructions expressed in this Living Will and the decisions of the persons I have designated to carry out these wishes and to defend anyone who assists in carrying out these instructions. All doctors, medical personnel, hospitals and other medical instrumentalities shall not be liable for any act complying with this Living Will in good faith, except acts of gross negligence or willful misconduct.

IN WITNESS WHEREOF, I have signed this document this date: <u>December 27</u>, 2011.

Jane Smith
_____
JANE SMITH

Acknowledgement of Witnesses:

This instrument was on the above date signed by the above-named Signator in our presence and published and declared to be the Signator's Living Will. At the Signator's request and in the presence of the Signator and of each other, we have signed below as witnesses thereto. WE ALSO AFFIRM THAT WE ARE NOT RELATED TO THE SIGNATOR BY BLOOD OR MARRIAGE AND ARE NOT INVOLVED WITH THE MEDICAL CARE OF THE SIGNATOR.

Michael Pearson
_____
Witness Signature
Michael Pearson
_____
Witness Name (Printed)

1001 Reed Drive
_____
Sample City, Sample State 12345
_____

Witness Address

Maggy Pearson
_____
Witness Signature
Maggy Pearson
_____
Witness Name (Printed)

1001 Reed Drive
_____
Sample City, Sample State 12345
_____

Witness Address

■ THE PURPOSE OF AND NEED FOR A WILL

In life, some people are careful planners, while others fly by the seat of their pants, letting life "happen" to them. Regardless of which category they fall in during life, most people would prefer to have some control over what happens upon their death. A common concern is to make sure family members and loved ones are well cared for. Others may wish to donate their estate to a charity that they believe in. Some may want to avoid estate or inheritance taxes. Finally, some may just want to ensure that the state does not get their belongings. Whatever your main concern is, most agree that it is better to get to *choose* what you want to happen to your belongings when you are no longer around. The most popular way for a person to direct the distribution of property following his or her death is by executing a will.

A **will** is a written document that directs the distribution of the creator's property upon his or her death. A will is important not only as a written declaration of how assets should be distributed, but also as the mechanism by which legal title to property is transferred. A man who executes a will is known as a **testator**; a female who executes a will is known as a **testatrix**. A will is an **ambulatory** document, meaning that it is fully revocable and subject to change during the maker's lifetime. A will becomes irrevocable upon the death of the testator and also becomes effective at that time.

When an individual dies with a will, he or she is said to die **testate**. A person who dies testate with a valid will is afforded a voice after his or her death to direct any and all of the following:

- How personal property is distributed
- How real property is distributed
- Creation of a testamentary trust, if desired
- Who is appointed to carry out the testator's written intentions (the personal representative or executor)
- Who is appointed as guardian to care for the decedent's minor children, if applicable
- How estate and inheritance taxes are to be paid, if applicable
- In some states, funeral arrangements and organ donation

Wealth Distribution

The primary purpose of a will is to allow individuals to distribute their property as they choose upon death. When someone dies intestate, or without a will, state law determines who inherits the decedent's property and in what amounts and proportions. This is often not the distribution the deceased person would have intended. Therefore, the paramount reason most people execute a will is to direct how their assets are to be distributed upon death.

Creation of a Testamentary Trust

In some instances, a testator may not want a beneficiary to receive his or her entire share outright and all in one lump sum. This can be for a variety of reasons, including but not limited to that the beneficiary is a minor and the assets need to be protected until the age of majority; that the beneficiary lacks capacity to manage his or her own financial affairs; or that a trust is desirable for tax planning reasons (to eliminate or reduce estate taxes).

A testator may chose to create a testamentary trust to set parameters for the care and control of assets, as well as the distribution of the trust assets—in what amounts and for what purposes. A trust is a legal agreement in which legal title to property is transferred to a trustee, who then manages the property for the beneficiaries. A **testamentary trust** is a trust that is drafted as part of the testator's will and only becomes effective upon the testator's death.

Appointment of a Personal Representative

Since a will takes effect after the death of the testator, there must be a live person to give effect to the directions expressed in the will. A personal representative, or executor, is appointed under the will to administer the decedent's estate and carry out the terms of the will.

Appointment of a Guardian for Minor Children

A primary concern for individuals with minor children is who will take care of their children if they die before their children are grown. A **guardian** is a person

Testator
A man who executes a will.
Testatrix
A female who executes a will.
Ambulatory
Revocable or subject to change.
Testate
To die with a valid will.

Testamentary Trust
A trust that is drafted as part of the testator's will and only becomes effective upon the testator's death.

who is appointed to care for and manage the minor's person, the minor's property, or both person and property until the child reaches the legal age of majority, or is otherwise legally emancipated. A testator can appoint a guardian for the minor children under the will, thus dispensing with the requirement that the guardian post bond in order to expedite the court process of being appointed to care for the minor children. If a guardian is not appointed under the will and there is no surviving parent, any party wishing to be appointed for this position will have to go through a separate, formal court proceeding for this purpose that will take more time, expense, and legal fees than if the person was appointed under the will. This is discussed more fully in Chapter 9.

Payment of Estate Taxes

When a person dies, the estate is subject to taxation in the form of state and federal estate taxes, as well as inheritance taxes in some states. An apportionment clause can be included in a will to allocate the tax burden of the beneficiaries in a will. When there is no will, or no apportionment clause is included in the will, state law will determine the method by which the taxes must be paid (often placing the tax burden on the beneficiaries). A tax apportionment clause can spread the burden differently as the testator sees fit.

Funeral Arrangements and Organ Donation

In some states, it is customary for a testator to express his or her preferences with respect to burial or cremation, funeral arrangements, and organ donation within the will. Doing so may be comforting to the testator because he or she then knows that these intentions are listed in the will and are unlikely to be missed or overlooked. In other states, it is considered inappropriate and even incorrect to discuss these preferences within a will, as legal effect will not be given to the testator's intentions in the will under state law.

Be aware that a client may strongly wish to include these preferences within the will, but the directions may or may not be followed by family members upon the testator's death. Practically speaking, funeral arrangements are often made by family members during a time of immense grief and they may or may not be aware of the testator's wishes when the arrangements are made. Often, the will is not located until weeks after the decedent is gone, and even if it is, the family may or may not read the will until after the funeral. Many of these issues and concerns can be alleviated if clients make prepaid funeral arrangements and simply note the existence of those arrangements under the will.

Bequest
A gift of personal property under a will.

Devise
A gift of real property under a will.

Legacy
A gift of personal property or money to a beneficiary (legatee) of a will. A legacy technically does not include real property (which is a "devise"), but usually refers to any gift from the estate of one who died.

Beneficiary
(of a will): A person entitled to receive property under a will or to whom the decedent's property is given or distributed.

■ THE IMPLICATIONS OF DYING WITHOUT A WILL

Dying without a will has many implications for the heirs and intended beneficiaries of the decedent. As was discussed above, a decedent who leaves behind a valid will is said to die testate and the decedent's property will be distributed in accordance with the terms of the will. A testate decedent may distribute property under his or her will in a number of different ways. A **bequest** is a gift of personal property under a will. A **devise** is a gift of real property under a will. A **legacy** is a testamentary gift of money. A **beneficiary** (of a will) is a person entitled to receive property under a will or to whom the decedent's property is given or distributed.

A decedent who dies without a valid will is said to die **intestate**. When a person dies intestate, their property passes according to state laws called **intestate succession statutes**.

Intestate
To die without a valid will.
Intestate Succession Statutes
State laws that determine who will inherit the property of a person who dies without a valid will.

Consider the following examples:

EXAMPLE 1

The client from the Real-Life Scenario at the beginning of this chapter is a widow with no children of her own. She is very close with her next-door neighbor of 40 years and wants to leave her estate to her neighbor when she passes away. She has expressed this to her attorney. Unfortunately, the client passes away suddenly before signing the will that the attorney drafted. Since she died intestate, the widow's estate will pass in accordance with her state's intestacy laws to her nearest living relatives, and her neighbor will inherit nothing from the estate.

▶ **DISCUSSION POINT:** As Example 1 illustrates, it is generally preferable to choose who will inherit from one's estate, rather than die intestate and let the state's default provisions apply. This is another very good reason to execute a valid will.

EXAMPLE 2

Matt Smith and Sarah Clark live together as boyfriend and girlfriend in State X for 15 years. They reside at 123 Robin Street and share all expenses jointly. However, since Sarah has owned the house since before she and Matt met, it is still titled solely in her name when she dies in a tragic automobile accident. Sarah is only 41 years old at the time of her death and has never executed a will. Although Sarah's intention was that Matt would keep the house if anything ever happened to her, he has no legal relationship to her at the time of her death. Therefore, the house will pass instead to Sarah's closest relatives under intestacy.

▶ **DISCUSSION POINT:** What could Sarah Clark have done differently to make sure that Matt would not lose the home in the event of her death? Discuss all of the different options you can think of.

EXAMPLE 3

John Jacobs loses his job and begins to fall behind on his credit card payments. Some of his accounts go into collection and John is concerned that creditors will begin to sue him. John transfers his home into his brother's name in an attempt to avoid having judgment liens filed against his home. John's intention is to transfer the house back once his financial situation improves.

Five years pass and John not only gains meaningful employment but also climbs steadily out of debt.

Unfortunately, John and his brother, Jess Jacobs, never get around to transferring the home back into John's name. Jess Jacobs passes away with John's house still titled in his name. Jess is married to Irene Jacobs at the time of his death. Irene hates John because John once dated Irene's best friend in high school and dumped her, breaking her heart. Irene vows that John will never get his house back.

▶ **DISCUSSION POINT:** When John Jacobs transferred his house to Jess Jacobs, what could Jess Jacobs have done to protect John's interest in the home?

■ REQUIREMENTS AND FORMALITIES

The examples included above are but a brief introduction to this topic and illustrate how important it is to have a will. However, not everyone has the ability to execute a legally valid will. There are specific requirements and formalities that one must observe to execute a valid will. To "execute" a will means to sign it in such a way that it will be legally effective. These issues are discussed below.

Capacity

Legal Capacity
The age of majority at which a person acquires the capacity to make a valid will. Majority age is eighteen (18) in most states, but is age twenty-one (21) in a minority of states.

Sound Mind
Having the mental capacity to execute a document, such as a will. Sound mind is the normal condition of the human mind, not impaired by insanity or other mental disorders.

In order to execute a will, a person must be of legal capacity and "of sound mind." **Legal capacity** is the age of majority at which a person acquires the capacity to make a valid will. Majority age is eighteen (18) in most states, but is age twenty-one (21) in a minority of states. What it means to be "of **sound mind**" is to have the mental ability to make a valid will. Sound mind is the normal condition of the human mind, not impaired by insanity or other mental disorders.

Execution of Will

Holographic Will
A will that is written completely in the handwriting of the testator and signed and dated by the maker. Witnesses may or may not be required, depending on state law.

The requirements for due execution of a will vary by state, but most states require that, at a minimum, the will be written, signed and dated by the maker, and attested and signed by two witnesses. Some states require that there be three witnesses. A few states allow **holographic wills**, which are completely handwritten wills, signed and dated by the maker. Witnesses may or may not be required, depending on state law. States that do *not* allow holographic wills will completely disregard the handwritten last wishes of a decedent.

It is extremely important to note that state law varies and you must check with the requirements in your state. In order to be legally valid, a will must be properly executed pursuant to the laws of the state in which it is made. That is why it is a very poor idea to purchase will forms such as those sold at stationery stores or online. A will is a very important document—too important to leave to chance whether it will be upheld in a court of law after one's death. We will discuss the requirements of will execution in much greater detail in Chapter 5.

■ PROBATE ASSETS V. NON-PROBATE ASSETS

Probate Assets

Probate Assets
The property of the decedent that must be distributed through a probate proceeding in a court of law.

Even when a probate is required after a person dies, it is possible that not all of the decedent's assets will go through probate. **Probate assets** are those that are distributed through a probate proceeding in a court of law. Generally speaking, probate assets are assets that are in the sole name of the decedent at the time of death. Perhaps the most common probate asset is a separate bank account, titled solely in the name of the decedent. Another example of a probate asset is a vehicle titled only in the decedent's name. If the decedent had a will, the probate assets will pass as directed under the will. If the decedent did not have a will, the assets will pass to the decedent's heirs at law. This will be considered more fully in Chapter 5.

Non-Probate Assets

Non-probate assets are assets that pass to the intended beneficiary by operation of law independent of the provisions of a will or a probate proceeding. The most common ways this happens is by title or by beneficiary designation.

Non-Probate Assets
Property that passes to a decedent's intended beneficiaries by operation of law, independent of the provisions of a will or a probate proceeding.

By Title

An asset that is held in joint title will generally pass to the survivor at the first death. For example, if John and Sue are co-owners of a joint bank account and John passes away, the bank account legally belongs to Sue. Therefore, if a probate proceeding is initiated to administer John's estate, the joint bank account will not be a part of it because it is a non-probate asset. Further, if John has a will directing that the account pass to Sally, that provision will have no effect on the account, which will still pass by title to Sue.

By Beneficiary Designation

Some types of property allow the owner to appoint a beneficiary to receive the property upon the owner's death. Life insurance is one of the most common assets to pass by beneficiary designation. The beneficiary appointed to receive the life insurance upon the principal's death receives the proceeds by operation of law (via the beneficiary designation), so the insurance proceeds are a non-probate asset. Pay-on-death (POD) and transfer-on-death (TOD) accounts are other examples of non-probate assets that pass by beneficiary designation. Upon the death of the owner, these types of bank accounts pass to the beneficiary designated to receive the account. Finally, retirement accounts pass by beneficiary designation and so also are non-probate assets.

The only exception to the general rule that property that passes by beneficiary designation is a non-probate asset is when the beneficiary appointed is the decedent's estate. The owner of the asset may choose to appoint their estate as beneficiary if they want the asset to pass pursuant to their will and go through probate. This will be discussed more fully in Chapter 5.

For Review:

Probate Assets	Non-Probate Assets
• Real property titled solely in the decedent's name	• Joint bank account
• Real property held as tenants in common with two or more owners	• Life insurance payable to a beneficiary
• Bank account solely in the decedent's name	• Real property titled as joint tenants with rights of survivorship
• Vehicle titled solely in the decedent's name	• Retirement account
• Life insurance payable to decedent's estate	• POD or TOD account

■ CONCLUSION

This chapter introduced you to some very basic concepts in connection with estate planning. These concepts will be expanded on in much greater detail in later chapters. The idea you should take with you from this chapter is that it is generally preferable to take the time to create an estate plan to ensure that your wishes are carried out, rather than leaving things to chance, or to your state's intestacy statutes. An estate plan commonly includes a will, living will, health care proxy, and power of attorney, and sometimes a trust.

In order to execute a will, a person must have capacity and be of sound mind. Each state has its own requirements for the proper execution of a will. Items that pass through probate pursuant to a will or the state's intestacy statute are probate assets. Assets that pass by title outside of probate are non-probate assets. These assets can be further divided into the following categories: real property and personal property. Personal property is movable; real property is immovable. An understanding of property concepts is needed before a paralegal can effectively assist with estate planning. Therefore, Chapter 2 provides a comprehensive overview of basic property law.

CONCEPT REVIEW AND REINFORCEMENT

KEY TERMS

Will 2	Testatrix 9	Intestate 11
Living Will 2	Ambulatory 9	Intestate Succession Statutes 11
Estate Plan 2	Testate 9	Legal Capacity 12
Probate 2	Testamentary Trust 9	Sound Mind 12
Decedent 2	Bequest 10	Holographic Will 12
Real Property 3	Devise 10	Probate Assets 12
Personal Property 3	Legacy 10	Non-Probate Assets 13
Testator 9	Beneficiary 10	

REVIEW QUESTIONS

1. Compare and contrast a will with a living will.
2. Describe some of the common reasons people choose to execute a will.
3. What are the requirements to execute a valid will?
4. What does it mean to die *testate*?
5. What are some of the implications of dying intestate?
6. What are some of the common components of an estate plan?
7. List five examples of personal property.
8. Define real property and list some common examples.
9. Describe what it means to go through probate.
10. Compare probate assets with non-probate assets.

BUILDING YOUR PARALEGAL SKILLS

CRITICAL THINKING EXERCISES

1. Do you think it is important to have an estate plan? Why or why not?
2. Classify the following items into the appropriate category of property (real or personal):
   - couch
   - bank account
   - vacant lot
   - bed
   - shed
   - truck
   - tractor
   - commercial building

3. Jim passed away, leaving behind his wife, Sue, and his son, Ralph. Determine whether each of the following assets is a probate asset or a non-probate asset:
   - POD account payable to Ralph
   - Life estate payable to "my estate"
   - Car titled "Jim and/or Sue"
   - Retirement account appointing Ralph as beneficiary.

4. Poor Mary has Alzheimer's disease in its advanced stages. She usually knows her own name, but does not recognize any of her family members or friends. Do you think she has capacity to execute a will? Why or why not?

PARALEGAL PRACTICE

Review the following memorandums directed from the supervising attorney to you, the paralegal. Each memorandum discusses a situation with a client and requests your assistance in researching the matter. You must report back with your findings, as directed in the memorandum.

1. _____

MEMORANDUM
To: Paralegal
From: Supervising Attorney
Client: Sue Smith
Re: Form Will

Today I met with a client whose mother recently passed away. The decedent, Sue Smith, did not employ the assistance of an attorney in drafting a will. She instead purchased a form online. Shortly before her death, she filled in the blanks and signed and dated the will. She did not have any witnesses sign the will. Most of the will was typewritten, except for where the decedent wrote in the names of her children.

Please research your state law to determine whether Sue Smith's will was validly executed so as to be admissible to probate. Report your findings and your conclusion in the form of a return memorandum to the supervising attorney.

2. _____

MEMORANDUM
To: Paralegal
From: Supervising Attorney
Client: Matthew Stone
Re: Holographic Will

Today I met with the son of Matthew Stone, who recently passed away. Mr. Stone behind a holographic will that was entirely handwritten and signed and dated by Mr. Stone. There were also two witnesses' signatures.

Please research your state law to determine whether holographic wills are legal. Further, research the requirements for due execution of a holographic will. Determine whether Mr. Stone's will was validly executed so as to be admissible to probate. Report your findings and your conclusion in the form of a return memorandum to the supervising attorney.

3. _____

MEMORANDUM
To: Paralegal
From: Supervising Attorney
Client: Joe Fox
Re: Intestacy Statute

We have been hired as counsel for the estate of Joe Fox. Mr. Fox died intestate. Please locate and print a copy of our state's intestacy statute so that it can be added to the file and referenced later.

The Pearson Course Companion website contains the following additional resources:

- **Forms for Paralegal Practice Activities**
- Chapter Objectives
- Online Study Guide (Containing Multiple Choice and True/False Questions)

- Web Exercises
- Hypothetical Family and Accompanying Project Worksheet

www.pearsonhighered.com/careers

CASE FOR CONSIDERATION

CASE #1:

IN RE ESTATE OF MARVIN NASH, DECEASED
SUPREME COURT OF TEXAS

220 S.W.3d 914; 2007 Tex. LEXIS 318; 50 Tex. Sup. J. 649
September 28, 2006, Argued
April 20, 2007, Delivered

JUDGES: CHIEF JUSTICE JEFFERSON delivered the opinion of the Court.

OPINION BY: Wallace B. Jefferson

OPINION

While death is certain, divorce is not. In this case, the testator anticipated the former but did not prepare for the latter. His will-executed while he was married and designating his then-spouse as primary beneficiary-remained unchanged when he died, notwithstanding his divorce some two years earlier. The Legislature addressed devises in favor of former spouses by enacting Probate Code section 69, which provides that if a testator divorces after executing a will, provisions that favor the former spouse must be read as if the former spouse predeceased the testator. The question presented here is whether a contingent bequest to the testator's former stepdaughter is a provision favoring his former spouse. We conclude it is not and affirm the court of appeals' judgment.

I

Background

Marvin and Vicki Nash were married at the time he executed his will in 1994. Vicki was named the primary

beneficiary, and Shelley Tedder (Vicki's daughter and Nash's then-stepdaughter) was named contingent beneficiary. The relevant provisions of Nash's will are set out below:

Disposition of Residue

I give, devise and bequeath all of the rest and residue of my estate, of every kind and character, real, personal and mixed, but not including any property over which I have a power of appointment, unto my beloved wife, VICKI LYNN NASH, in fee simple forever, if she survives me by thirty (30) days.

First Alternate Disposition of Residue

In the event that my wife and I die at the same time or in the event that she does not survive me by thirty (30) days or in the event that my wife should predecease me, then and in either of these events, I give, devise and bequeath all of the rest and residue of my estate, of every kind and character, real, personal and mixed, but not including any property over which I have a power of appointment unto my beloved step-child, SHELLEY RENE TEDDER.

Marvin and Vicki Nash divorced on July 8, 2002. When Nash died on April 29, 2004, he had made no changes to the will he executed some ten years earlier. Both Vicki Nash and Shelley Tedder survived Marvin Nash.

Nash's nephew, Russell Nash, filed an application for independent administration, stating that Marvin died intestate and providing the names of Marvin's two other heirs at law: Marvin's brother, Leroy Nash; and Marvin's mother, Pat Nash.[1] The application stated that Nash and Vicki were divorced at the time of Nash's death, that Nash never adopted Tedder, and that the trial court should therefore partition Nash's estate among his heirs.

[1]Both Pat and Leroy Nash waived their right to be appointed administrators of Marvin's estate and requested that Russell Nash be appointed as independent administrator.

On May 25, 2004, the trial court granted Russell's application and ordered the clerk to issue letters of independent administration to Russell. Two days later, Tedder opposed Russell's application and sought to probate Nash's will herself. Tedder claimed that Nash left a valid will that had never been revoked and that she, as the contingent beneficiary, was the alternate independent executrix. After a hearing, the trial court stayed the letters of administration. Russell, Pat, and Leroy Nash opposed the probate of Nash's will and sought a declaratory judgment that Tedder take nothing. The trial court admitted Nash's will to probate, issued letters testamentary to Tedder, and declared that Tedder was entitled to Nash's entire estate.[2] Pat and Leroy Nash appealed. The court of appeals reversed the trial court's judgment in part, holding that Marvin Nash's estate descends to his heirs at law because the requisite condition precedent for Shelley Tedder to inherit under Nash's will never occurred. 164 S.W.3d 856, 857. We granted Tedder's petition for review. 49 Tex. Sup. J. 509 (Apr. 21, 2006).

[2]The trial court found that, although a new will had been prepared for Marvin Nash in 2003, he did not execute it before he died.

II

Discussion

Before 1997, Probate Code section 69(a) provided:

(a) If, after making a will, the testator is divorced [**5] or the testator's marriage is annulled, all provisions in the will in favor of the testator's former spouse, or appointing such spouse to any fiduciary [*917] capacity under the will or with respect to the estate or person of the testator's children, shall be null and void and of no effect unless the will expressly provides otherwise.

Act of May 24, 1995, 74th Leg., R.S., ch. 642, § 2, 1995 Tex. Gen. Laws 3516, 3516, *amended by* Act of May 22, 1997, 75th Leg., R.S., ch. 1302, § 5, 1997 Tex.

Gen. Laws 4954, 4955-56. In 1997, the Legislature added the phrase "must be read as if the former spouse failed to survive the testator," so that the statute now provides, in relevant part:

(a) If, after making a will, the testator is divorced or the testator's marriage is annulled, all provisions in the will in favor of the testator's former spouse, or appointing such spouse to any fiduciary capacity under the will or with respect to the estate or person of the testator's children, *must be read as if the former spouse failed to survive the testator*, and shall be null and void and of no effect unless the will expressly provides otherwise.

TEX. PROB. CODE § 69(a) (emphasis added); Act of May 22, 1997, 75th Leg., R.S., ch. 1302, § 5, 1997 Tex. Gen. Laws 4954, 4955-56.

Tedder contends that the Legislature's 1997 amendments govern all contingent bequests; that is, that the entire will should be read "as if the former spouse failed to survive the testator." She argues that, absent such a construction, the 1997 language adds nothing to the statute, which already provided that bequests in favor of a former spouse would be "null and void and of no effect." She also points to *Calloway v. Estate of Gasser*, 558 S.W.2d 571, 575-76 (Tex. Civ. App.—Tyler 1977, writ ref'd n.r.e.), in which the court held that, after divorce, the will should be construed and given effect as though the former spouse had predeceased the testatrix, "thereby passing the decedent's estate to the contingent beneficiaries." Tedder argues that the Legislature's 1997 amendments were intended to codify *Calloway*.

The Nashes contend that section 69 applies only to provisions that favor the former spouse. Because the contingent bequest to Tedder does not favor Marvin Nash's former spouse, the will must be construed as written. Vicki Nash did not predecease Marvin, so the contingent bequest did not become operative, and the estate passes to Marvin Nash's heirs at law.

We agree with the Nashes. When construing a statute, our primary objective is to determine the Legislature's intent which, when possible, we discern from the plain meaning of the words chosen. *State v. Shumake*, 199 S.W.3d 279, 284, 49 Tex. Sup. Ct. J. 769 (Tex. 2006); *City of San Antonio v. City of Boerne*, 111 S.W.3d 22, 25, 46 Tex. Sup. Ct. J. 848 (Tex. 2003). If a statute is clear and unambiguous, we apply its words according to their common meaning without resort to rules of construction or extrinsic aids. *Fitzgerald v. Advanced Spine Fixation Sys., Inc.*, 996 S.W.2d 864, 865-66, 42 Tex. Sup. Ct. J. 985 (Tex. 1999).

The language of the pre-1997 versions of section 69 was clear despite the more recent phrase added by the Legislature: those provisions in a will that favor a former spouse are of no effect. *See, e.g., Smith v. Smith,* 519 S.W.2d 152, 154 (Tex. Civ. App.—Dallas 1975, writ ref'd) (stating that section 69's policy objective is to give effect to the testator's intentions regarding the disposition of his property). The 1997 language— "must be read as if the former spouse failed to survive the testator"—does nothing more than restate the "null and void and of no effect" statutory text. TEX. PROB. CODE § 69(a). While we recognize that we should avoid, when possible, creating statutory language as surplusage, *Sultan v. Mathew,* 178 S.W.3d 747, 751, 49 Tex. Sup. Ct. J. 97 (Tex. 2005), there are times when redundancies are precisely what the Legislature intended, *see In re City of Georgetown,* 53 S.W.3d 328, 336, 44 Tex. Sup. Ct. J. 434 (Tex. 2001) (noting that statutory redundancies may mean that "the Legislature repeated itself out of an abundance of caution, for emphasis, or both").

Our interpretation of section 69 is consistent with the manner in which the courts of appeals interpreted section 69 prior to the 1997 amendments. The Houston and Eastland courts held that contingent bequests (similar to the one at issue here) failed when the former spouse had not actually predeceased the testator, despite section 69. *See McFarlen v. McFarlen,* 536 S.W.2d 590, 591-92 (Tex. Civ. App.—Eastland 1976, no writ) (noting that "[s]ection 69 . . . merely provides that provisions in a will favoring the testator's divorced spouse are a nullity, not the entire will"); *Volkmer v. Chase,* 354 S.W.2d 611, 615 (Tex. Civ. App.—Houston 1962, writ ref'd n.r.e.) (holding that contingent bequest in favor of two of testator's three children failed because contingency-that former spouse predecease testator-had not occurred). Similarly, in *Formby v. Bradley,* 695 S.W.2d 782, 783-84 (Tex. App.—Tyler 1985, writ ref'd n.r.e.), the Tyler court of appeals held that section 69 did not trigger a contingency based on the simultaneous death of the testator and his former spouse, so that the appellee (a third party) was not entitled to serve as independent executrix. And though in *Calloway,* the Tyler court of appeals held that section 69 allowed the estate in question to pass to the named contingent beneficiaries in the will, the court was careful to distinguish its holding from both *Volkmer* and *McFarlen* on the case's facts. *Calloway,* 558 S.W.2d at 576-77.[3] While Tedder asserts that the 1997 amendments were intended to codify *Calloway,* it is difficult to imagine the Legislature would have waited twenty years to incorporate that holding. As the court of appeals noted, "[t]he Legislature could have revised the Probate Code to require that the entire will be read as though the former spouse had predeceased the testator, but it did not do so." 164 S.W.3d at 860 (emphasis omitted).

[3]The court of appeals noted "a considerable difference between the wording of the wills in those two cases and the wording of the will in the instant case." *Calloway,* 558 S.W.2d at 576-77.

Because section 69 affects only those provisions in a will that favor the divorced spouse, the other provisions remain undisturbed. Here, Nash's will devised all of his property to his (now divorced) wife, unless: (1) they died at the same time; (2) she failed to survive him by thirty days; or (3) she predeceased him. Only then would Nash's property pass to Vicki's daughter, Shelley Tedder. None of those three contingencies has occurred.

III

Conclusion

Probate Code section 69 requires that only those provisions in a will that favor a former spouse be read as if she predeceased the testator. The contingent bequest to Tedder is not such a provision, and section 69's language does not govern that bequest. Accordingly, Tedder does not take under the will, and Nash's estate passes according to the laws of descent and distribution. *See* TEX. PROB. CODE ch. 2. We affirm the court of appeals' judgment. TEX. R. APP. p. 60.2(a).

Wallace B. Jefferson

Chief Justice

OPINION DELIVERED: April 20, 2007

Case Questions

1. Did Marvin Nash change his will after he was divorced?
2. Who were the parties to this case, and what were their respective positions?
3. Was the stepchild entitled to inherit the testator's estate? Why or why not?
4. What does this case illustrate with respect to the purpose and need for a will?

Case Comment:

Note that the <u>Nash</u> case above was decided on April 20, 2007. Thereafter, the Texas Legislature responded by amending Section 69 of the Texas Probate Code to plainly state what the court interpreted it to mean in Nash. Following is the statute as amended on August 11, 2007.

Texas Probate Code - Section 69. Voidness Arising From Divorce
§ 69. VOIDNESS ARISING FROM DIVORCE.

(a) If, after making a will, the testator is divorced or the testator's marriage is annulled, all provisions in the will in favor of the testator's former spouse, or appointing such spouse to any fiduciary capacity under the will or with respect to the estate or person of the testator's children, must be read as if the former spouse failed to survive the testator, and shall be null and void and of no effect unless the will expressly provides otherwise.

(b) A person who is divorced from the decedent or whose marriage to the decedent has been annulled is not a surviving spouse unless, by virtue of a subsequent marriage, the person is married to the decedent at the time of death.

Acts 1955, 54th Leg., p. 88, ch. 55, eff. Jan. 1, 1956. Amended by
Acts 1979, 66th Leg., p. 1746, ch. 713, § 12, eff. Aug. 27, 1979;
Acts 1995, 74th Leg., ch. 642, § 2, eff. Sept. 1, 1995;
Acts 1997, 75th Leg., ch. 1302, § 5, eff. Sept. 1, 1997.

Section: 69 Last modified: August 11, 2007

CHAPTER 2

Property

A REAL-LIFE SCENARIO

Megan consulted with an attorney due to the recent death of her father. Megan was an only child and her father died without a will (intestate). The only probate asset was a home that her father and mother had owned jointly. However, the decedent had divorced Megan's mother about twenty years before, and the divorce decree directed that the home be sold and the proceeds split between the parties. Although all those years had passed, the couple had never followed through on the terms of the divorce decree and the property was still held in joint name. To make matters worse, Megan and her mother were not on speaking terms and Megan's mother thought that property was all hers. Why? Because the last recorded deed listed the parties as joint tenants with rights of survivorship and she was the survivor. Megan thought that this was very unfair and that she should inherit her father's share of the home as his sole heir.

© Jennifer Montante

To complicate matters further, Megan's mother got her hands on a death certificate and had the decedent's name removed from the property! Megan had quite a challenge ahead of her, but with her attorney's assistance, was successful at recapturing her father's share of the property and transferring it to herself as his sole heir. By the time you complete this chapter and the accompanying activities, you should be able to describe why Megan was successful at recapturing her father's share of the property.

CHAPTER OBJECTIVES:

1. Define personal property and list examples.

2. Define real property and list examples.

3. Categorize assets as either real property or personal property.

4. Understand the different forms in which title to property may be held.

5. Distinguish among fee simple, life estate, and tenancy for years.

6. List and describe the various types of deeds.

■ INTRODUCTION

You may be wondering what property has to do with estate planning and probate. The answer: everything! If there is no property to worry about, there is little or no need for estate planning and no probate will be required. Therefore, in order to assist clients in these areas, you need to have a solid understanding of property law, including the different types of property, forms of property, estates, how property may be transferred, and more. You will likely study this as a separate topic in much greater detail. However, this chapter will provide you with the basic foundation that you need in order to draft estate planning and probate documents under the supervision of an attorney.

■ REAL PROPERTY V. PERSONAL PROPERTY

Key Terms and Definitions

Real Property
All land, structures, firmly attached and integrated equipment, anything growing on the land, and all interests in the property. Real property is immovable.

Fixture
Personal property that is so permanently attached to real property that it becomes part of the real property.

Personal Property
Includes all movable assets, or things, that are not classified as real property; includes both tangible and intangible property.

The assets owned by a decedent can be divided into two main types of property: real property and personal property. **Real property** is all land, structures, firmly attached and integrated equipment, anything growing on the land, and all interests in the property. Real property is immovable. A **fixture** is a piece of personal property that has been attached to real estate in such a way as to be part of the premises, and whose removal would do harm to the building or land. Thus, a fixture is transformed from a movable asset (personal property) to an integral part of the real property. Generally, fixtures added by a tenant, such as a lighting fixture, heater, or other item that is bolted, screwed, or nailed into the wall, ceiling, or floor cannot be removed or may only be removed at the tenant's expense for necessary repair. Landlord-tenant contracts typically specify how fixtures are to be treated, and the contract terms will prevail if there is a question about whether or not something may be removed at the end of the lease or term.

Personal property includes all movable assets, or things, that are not real property. Clothing, cars, planes, and trains are all personal property. Cash is personal property. Although animals are alive and have thoughts and feelings, they are considered personal property under the law.

Personal property includes **tangible** objects that you can touch and feel, such as a doll or a basketball, as well as **intangible** items that do not have a physical form, such as a patent or a copyright.

Following are some examples:

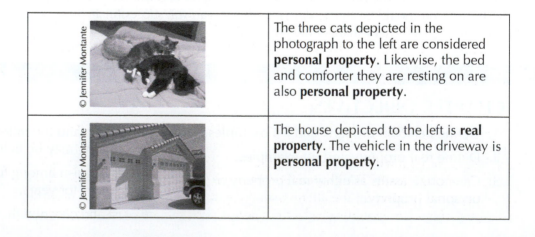

© Jennifer Montante	The three cats depicted in the photograph to the left are considered **personal property**. Likewise, the bed and comforter they are resting on are also **personal property**.
© Jennifer Montante	The house depicted to the left is **real property**. The vehicle in the driveway is **personal property**.

	The car depicted to the left is **personal property**. The title evidencing owner-ship of the Mustang is also **personal property**.
	The backyard, block fence, and moun-tain view in the photo to the left are all **real property**.
	The ceiling fan depicted to the left was considered personal property before it was installed. However, since it is now attached to the ceiling of a home, it is considered a **fixture** that is a part of the real property (the home). ✓ Note that if the fan is removed, it will no longer be a fixture and will regain its former status as personal property.

For Review:

Real Property	Personal Property
• House	• Clothing
• Vacant Land	• Furniture
• Building	• Automobile
• Mountain	• Money
• Storage Shed	• Pets

◼ FORMS OF PROPERTY OWNERSHIP

Fee Simple

When you think of owning property, your mind most likely envisions absolute and total ownership. This is known as owning property in **fee simple**, which is absolute title to land, free of any other claims against the title. One can sell fee simple property or pass it to another by will or inheritance. When you purchase a piece of property pursuant to a warranty deed, you own the property in fee simple. However, fee simple is not the only interest that can be passed by a grantor to a grantee.

Fee Simple
The greatest and most absolute estate that anyone can have in land.

Life Estate

Sometimes, a grantor desires to allow someone the use of a property only for that person's lifetime, known as a life estate. A **life estate** is given to a person by deed or by gift under a will with the idea that that person's interest in the property will cease upon death. The property may then be passed to a another person, the remainder beneficiary. In the alternative, the grantor may retain a right of rever-sion, meaning that upon the death of the person with the life estate, the property

Life Estate
A tenancy that allows a person to own real property for his or her lifetime only.

will revert back to the grantor or the grantor's heirs. The following are examples of the creation of a life estate:

> **Example 1** *"I give to my sister, Sally Smith, a life estate in my property on ABC Street, and upon her death, the property shall pass to my son, John Jones."* (Here, the property passes to John Jones when Sally passes away.)
>
> **Example 2** *"I give to my sister, Sally Smith, a life estate in my property on ABC Street."* (Here, the property reverts back to the grantor upon Sally's death.)

Tenancy in Common

Tenancy in Common
Ownership in property by two or more persons in which each owner has an undivided interest in the property without right of survivorship.

A **tenancy in common** is title taken to property by two or more persons in which each person has an undivided interest in the property and all have an equal right to use the property, even if the percentages of interest are not equal. Parties to a tenancy in common are known as "cotenants." Cotenants are each entitled to use all of the property, so one cotenant cannot force another cotenant to pay rent. Further, if a parcel of real property owned in this manner is rented out to a non-cotenant, the rent must be divided among the cotenants in proportion to their ownership interest.

> **Example 1** Tony and Sarah own 111 ABC Street as tenants in common, but Tony owns 60% and Sarah owns 40%. They decide to rent the house out to Joe for $1,000 per month. Tony is entitled to $600 and Sarah is entitled to $400 per month.
>
> **Example 2** Joe gets evicted and Sarah decides that she would like to move in to 111 ABC Street. Tony tells Sarah that she has to pay him $600 per month. Sarah is not fooled and informs Tony that she can live there rent free as one of the cotenants.

One advantage of a tenancy in common is that there is no survivorship interest, so individual cotenants can sell or transfer their interest to whomever they choose.

> **Example 3** Sarah wants to leave her interest in 111 ABC Street to her daughter. Sarah's will states: *"I give, devise, and bequeath 111 ABC Street to my daughter, Abigail."* Sarah passes away. Since Sarah did not own all of 111 ABC Street, she can only leave the interest she has in the property. The result is that Tony owns 60% and Abigail owns 40%.

It is noteworthy that when property is transferred to two or more persons and it is not specified in the deed or other instrument how title is to be taken, the law in many states holds that the title will automatically pass as a tenancy in common as the statutory default. This is because the law does not favor joint tenancies, which will be discussed next.

Joint Tenancy

Joint Tenancy
Title to property held by more than one person with a right of survivorship.

A **joint tenancy** is a form of property ownership where each party owns an undivided interest in the entire property and a right to use and enjoy all of it, but with a survivorship interest, which means that when one joint tenant dies, the other (or others) have title to the whole property. This is also commonly referred to as a "joint tenancy with right of survivorship," but there is always a right of survivorship where there is a joint tenancy. For parties desiring to leave their interest in a shared piece of property to each other, joint tenancy can accomplish this without requiring the property to go through probate. While the procedure in different states and jurisdictions may vary, the survivor generally must file the death certificate of the deceased joint tenant with an "affidavit of death of joint tenant" in order to terminate the joint tenancy and have the records updated to reflect that the survivor is the sole owner of the property.

Parties who do not want their property interest to pass to the survivor upon death should not select a joint tenancy. A bequest of property held in joint tenancy will fail if the person making the bequest passes away before the other joint tenant. This is because the surviving joint tenant will automatically inherit the property by right of survivorship and the deceased is left with no interest to give or leave to a third party. In other words, the gift will fail.

Tenancy by the Entirety

Tenancy by the entirety is a form of property ownership shared by husbands and wives where both have the right to the entire property and, upon the death of one spouse, the surviving spouse enjoys title to the whole property by right of survivorship. One benefit of this form of property ownership is that the surviving spouse enjoys a stepped-up basis upon the death of the other spouse, meaning that the survivor's tax basis for the property will be increased to reflect the value of the property at the time of the decedent's death. A tax accountant should be consulted for assistance in calculating the basis for the property.

Tenancy by the entirety is not a valid form of property ownership in all states. Community property states do not recognize tenancies by the entirety and are discussed below.

Community Property

Community property is the concept that all income and assets acquired by a husband and wife during the marriage, with a few exceptions, belong equally to the husband and wife. Specific gifts and inheritances acquired by one spouse during the marriage or owned prior to the marriage are considered separate property. Separate property is excluded from community property valuation unless it can be shown that the owning spouse commingled the separate property with the community property or made a gift of the separate property to the community.

This concept can be traced back to Spain and was originally intended to protect rich women from losing everything if their husbands left them. States that currently abide by community property laws include Alaska, Arizona, California, Idaho, Louisiana, New Mexico, Nevada, Texas, and Washington. In most community property states, the surviving spouse acquires the deceased spouse's interest in the real property upon the death of the spouse. State law must always be consulted on a case-by-case basis in order to ascertain community property rights in your state.

The state of Wisconsin is a **marital property state** and has laws similar to community property laws, but not the same. Under Wisconsin's Marital Property Act, enacted in 1986, marital property includes all income and possessions a couple acquires after the "determination date" (with certain exceptions). The determination date is the latest of the couple's marriage day; the date when they both took up residence in Wisconsin; or January 1, 1986. Further details are beyond the scope of this text.

■ DEEDS

A **deed** is a written document that transfers title to or an interest in real property from one person to another person or persons. The person making the transfer of real property is the **grantor**; the person receiving the interest in the real property is the **grantee**. The deed must contain a description of the real property being

Tenancy by the Entirety
A form of property ownership shared by husbands and wives where both have the right to the entire property and, upon the death of one spouse, the surviving spouse enjoys title to the whole property by right of survivorship.

Community Property
A method of holding property acquired during marriage in which each spouse owns one-half of the property outright. Community property is currently valid in: Alaska, Arizona, California, Idaho, Louisiana, New Mexico, Nevada, Texas, and Washington. Wisconsin has a similar law known as "marital property law."

Marital Property State
Under Wisconsin's Marital Property Act, enacted in 1986, marital property includes all income and possessions a couple acquires after the "determination date" (with certain exceptions). The determination date is the latest of the couple's marriage day; the date when they both took up residence in Wisconsin; or January 1, 1986.

Deed
A written document that transfers title or an interest in real property from one person to another person or persons.

Grantor
The person making the transfer of real property in a deed.

Grantee
The person receiving the interest in the real property in a deed.

Warranty Deed
A deed to real property which guarantees that the seller has clear title to the property, and that title can be transferred or conveyed to the buyer.

transferred, name the grantor and the grantee, and be signed and dated by the grantor, whose signature must be acknowledged before a notary public. After execution, the deed should be immediately sent for recording to the county recorder in the county where the property is located. The recordation provides record title for the property and puts others on notice that the transfer has been made.

As always, *check your state's law* to see whether there are additional requirements, such as having one or more witnesses present to sign the deed.

Two main types of deeds are commonly used: the warranty deed and the quitclaim deed. We will also consider the grant deed, the personal representative's deed, and the beneficiary deed.

Warranty Deed

A **warranty deed** is a deed to real property that guarantees that the grantor has clear title to the property, and that title can be transferred or conveyed to the grantee. The grantor further warrants and guarantees that he or she will defend the grantee's title to the property should a question arise in the future. A warranty deed is the strongest of deeds and the most favorable to the grantee. Warranty deeds are used in connection with the sale of real estate because buyers expect that sellers have clear title to the property they are selling.

Figure 2.1 depicts a warranty deed transferring title from a married couple to a third party who purchased the property. The grantee is Jane Smith, from the Hypothetical Family introduced in Chapter 1. She purchased her home from John and Mary Jones several years ago and the deed was executed to transfer title into Jane's name.

Figure 2.1 Warranty Deed

When Recorded Mail To:
Jane Smith
123 Oak Street
Sample City, Sample State 12345

Above Space For Recorder's Use

WARRANTY DEED

GRANTORS

John Jones
Mary Jones
123 Second Street
Second Town, Sample State 98765

GRANTEE

Jane Smith
123 Oak Street
Sample City, Sample State 12345

Property Legal Description: LOTS FOURTEEN (14) and FIFTEEN (15), BLOCK "R," OAK VIEW, TRACT NO. 1051, according to the plat thereof, recorded November 20, 1967 at Fee No. 34553, in the office of the Recorder of Sample County, Sample State.

Figure 2.1 (continued)

Mailing Address: 123 Oak Street, Sample City, Sample State 12345

For valuable consideration, Grantors

Convey to Grantee all right, title, and interest of Grantors in Subject Real Property together with all rights and privileges appurtenant or to become appurtenant to Subject Real Property on effective date;

Covenant that Grantors are seized of Subject Real Property and that the Grantee shall quietly enjoy Subject Real Property;

Warrant the title against all persons whomsoever, subject to matters above set forth, and warrant that Grantors will execute or procure any further necessary assurance of title.

Grantors further covenant for Grantee and successors of Grantee their further assurance of this grant and of the aforesaid warranties and covenants.

WITNESS Grantors' hands this 5th day of May, 2010.

John Jones
_____
John Jones, Grantor

Mary Jones
_____
Mary Jones, Grantor

NOTARY ACKNOWLEDGMENT

STATE OF: SAMPLE }

COUNTY OF: SAMPLE }

On this 5th day of May, 2010, before me, the undersigned, a notary public in and for said state personally appeared JOHN JONES and MARY JONES personally known to me (or proved to me on the basis of satisfactory evidence) to be the persons whose names are subscribed to the within instrument and acknowledged to me that they executed the same in their authorized capacities, and that by their signatures on the instrument the persons or entity upon behalf of which the persons acted, executed instrument.

WITNESS my hand and official seal.

Lila P. Legal
_____
Notary Public

> **LILA P. LEGAL**
> Notary Public, State of Sample
> Sample County
> My Commission Expires May 10, 2012

Quitclaim Deed

A **quitclaim deed** is a deed to real property which transfers to the grantee only whatever interest the grantor has in the property. There are no warranties made about the nature of the grantor's title—the grantor is merely transferring whatever interest he or she has, if any. For this reason, quitclaim deeds are the weakest of deeds. Generally, quitclaim deeds are used to transfer property from one family member to another, into a revocable trust, or between spouses in connection with a divorce. Quitclaim deeds do not warrant good title to the property.

Figure 2.2 depicts a quitclaim deed conveying title from both spouses to one spouse. The first grantor is John Smith, from the Hypothetical Family introduced

Quitclaim Deed
A deed to real property that transfers to the grantee only whatever interest the grantor has in the property.

in Chapter 1. John and his wife, Jasmine Smith, conveyed the property to Jasmine Smith, alone, as grantee when they were having marital problems. They later reconciled but did not remember to transfer the property back into both names.

Figure 2.2 Quitclaim Deed

THIS INDENTURE *made the 26ᵗʰ day of July, 2012*

BETWEEN, John Smith and Jasmine Smith, husband and wife, residing at 234 Sunny Lane, Sample City, Sample State 12345, *parties of the first part*

AND **Jasmine Smith,** residing at 234 Sunny Lane, Sample City, Sample State 12345, *party of the second part*

WITNESSETH, *that the party of the first part, in consideration of One Dollar 00/100 ($1.00) paid by the party of the second part, does hereby remise, release and quitclaim unto the party of the second part, the heirs or successors and assigns of the party of the second part, forever,*

ALL THAT TRACT OR PARCEL OF LAND, situated in the Town of Sample State, with a legal description as follows: LOT TWO (2), HOLIDAY SHORES, INC., TRACT 150, according to the plat thereof, recorded June 10, 1965, at Fee No. 150925 in the office of the County Recorder of Sample County, Sample State.

The Lot is of the dimensions as shown on said map.

SUBJECT TO and together with all covenants, easements and restrictions of record affecting said premises.

BEING AND INTENDING to convey the same premises conveyed to John Smith and Jasmine Smith, husband and wife, the party of the first part by Deed dated January 10, 1995 and recorded on January 12, 1995 in the Sample County Clerk's Office in Book 1995 of Deeds at page 23.

TAX ACCOUNT NO.:	123-45-678
TAX MAILING ADDRESS:	234 Sunny Lane, Sample City, Sample State 12345
PROPERTY ADDRESS:	234 Sunny Lane, Sample City, Sample State 12345

TOGETHER *with the appurtenances and all the estate and rights of the Party of the first part in and to said premises,*

TO HAVE AND TO HOLD *the premises herein granted unto the party of the second part, the heirs, or successors and assigns forever. The word "party" shall be construed as if it read "parties" whenever the sense of this indenture so requires.*

This deed is subject to the trust provisions of Section 13 of the Lien Law.

WITNESS WHEREOF, *the party of the first part has duly executed this deed the day and year first above written.*

In Presence of

John Smith
_____
John Smith

Jasmine Smith
_____
Jasmine Smith

STATE OF SAMPLE   )

COUNTY OF SAMPLE) ss.:

On the 26ᵗʰ day of July in the year 2012 before me, the undersigned, personally appeared **John Smith**, personally known to me or proved to me on the basis of satisfactory evidence to be the individual whose name is subscribed to the within instrument and acknowledged to me that he executed the same in his capacity, and that by his signature on the instrument, the individual, or the person upon behalf of which the individual acted, executed the instrument.

Lila P. Legal
_____
Notary Public

Figure 2.2 (continued)

LILA P. LEGAL
Notary Public, State of Sample
Sample County
My Commission Expires May 10, 2016

STATE OF SAMPLE)

COUNTY OF SAMPLE) ss.:

On the 26th day of July in the year 2012 before me, the undersigned, personally appeared **Jasmine Smith**, personally known to me or proved to me on the basis of satisfactory evidence to be the individual whose name is subscribed to the within instrument and acknowledged to me that she executed the same in her capacity, and that by her signature on the instrument, the individual, or the person upon behalf of which the individual acted, executed the instrument.

Lila P. Legal
Notary Public

LILA P. LEGAL
Notary Public, State of Sample
Sample County
My Commission Expires May 10, 2012

RECORD & RETURN TO:
Pearson & Pearson, Attorneys-At-Law
1001 Reed Drive
Sample County, Sample State 12345

Grant Deed

A **grant deed** is a deed that transfers title to real property from a grantor to a grantee. A grant deed is generally a warranty deed. The difference lies in the fact that a grant deed is usually used in connection with a gift of property or a transfer between family members, whereas a warranty deed is used in connection with a sale of real property. The difference between a grant deed and a quitclaim deed is that the grant deed warrants that the grantor actually owned the title to transfer, while a quitclaim deed only transfers whatever interest the grantor owned, which could be no interest at all.

Figure 2.3 depicts a married couple conveying property into their family trust using a grant deed. The parties are Robert and Mary Smith, from the Hypothetical Family.

Grant Deed
A deed that transfers title to real property from a grantor to a grantee. A grant deed is generally a warranty deed.

Personal Representative's or Executor's Deed

Sometimes a personal representative or executor of an estate has to transfer real property from the estate to one or more beneficiaries. This is accomplished by executing a **personal representative's deed** or an executor's deed, depending on the jurisdiction. The terms are synonymous and basically interchangeable, except that it is customary to use the term accepted in one's jurisdiction.

Personal Representative's Deed
A deed in which the personal representative of an estate is the grantor and is transferring real property to the decedent's heirs or devisees.

Figure 2.3 Grant Deed

When Recorded Mail To:
Robert & Mary Smith
125 Oak Street
Sample City, Sample State 12345

Above Space For Recorder's Use

GRANT DEED

KNOW ALL MEN BY THESE PRESENTS THAT

FOR VALUABLE CONSIDERATION OF TEN DOLLARS ($10.00), and other good and valuable consideration, cash in hand paid, the receipt and sufficiency of which is hereby acknowledged, Robert Smith and Mary Smith hereinafter referred to as "Grantors," do hereby grant unto Robert Smith and Mary Smith as Trustees of The Robert & Mary Smith Family Trust, hereinafter "Grantees," the following lands and property, together with all improvements located thereon, lying in the County of Sample, State of Sample, to wit:

Legal Description: **LOT SEVENTEEN (17), BLOCK "R," OAK VIEW, TRACT NO. 1051, according to the plat thereof, recorded November 20, 1967 at Fee No. 34553, in the office of the Recorder of Sample County, Sample State.**

Physical Address: 125 Oak Street, Sample City, Sample State 12345

LESS AND EXCEPT all oil, gas and minerals, on and under the above described property owned by Grantors, if any, which are reserved by Grantors.

SUBJECT TO all easements, rights-of-way, protective covenants and mineral reservations of record, if any.

GRANTORS do for Grantors and Grantors' heirs, personal representatives, executors and assigns forever hereby covenant with Grantees that Grantors are lawfully seized in fee simple of said premises; that the premises are free from all encumbrances, unless otherwise noted above; that Grantors have a good right to sell and convey the same as aforesaid; and to forever warrant and defend the title to the said lands against all claims whatever.

TO HAVE AND TO HOLD to the said Grantees, their heirs, personal representatives, executors and assigns forever.

WITNESS Grantors' hands this 9th day of January, 2010.

Robert Smith
Robert Smith, Grantor

Mary Smith
Mary Smith, Grantor

NOTARY ACKNOWLEDGMENT

STATE OF: SAMPLE }

COUNTY OF: SAMPLE }

On this 9th day of January, 2010, before me, the undersigned, a notary public in and for said state personally appeared JOHN SMITH and MARY SMITH, personally known to me (or proved to me on the basis of satisfactory evidence) to be the persons whose names are subscribed to the within instrument, and acknowledged to me that they executed the same in their authorized capacities, and that by their signatures on the instrument the persons or entity upon behalf of which the persons acted executed the instrument.

WITNESS my hand and official seal.

Lila P. Legal
Notary Public

> **LILA P. LEGAL**
> Notary Public, State of Sample
> Sample County
> My Commission Expires May 10, 2012

Figure 2.4 depicts an executor's deed conveying title from the Estate of Richard Rich to the beneficiary, John Smith, from the Hypothetical Family. Richard Rich was a friend of John's father who never had any children of his own. When he passed away, he left his vacant lot to John.

Figure 2.4 Executor's Deed

THIS INDENTURE, made the 15th day of March, 2011,

BETWEEN

SUSAN W. RICH, residing at 345 First Street, Sample Town, Sample State 12345, as Executrix of the **Estate of Richard Rich,** late of the Town of Sample, Sample State, *party of the first part,*

AND

JOHN SMITH, residing at 234 Sunny Lane, Sample City, Sample State 12345, *party of the second part:*

WITNESSETH *That the party of the first part, to whom Letters Testamentary were issued by the Surrogate's Court, Sample County, Sample State on January 23, 2011, and by virtue of the power and authority to her given in and by the said last Will and Testament, and/or by Article 11 of the Estates, Powers and Trusts Law, and in consideration of Zero and 00/100 Dollars ($-0-) lawful money of the United States to her paid by the party of the second part, does hereby grant and release to the party of the second part, their distributees and assigns forever,*

ALL THAT TRACT OR PARCEL OF LAND, situated in the Town of Sample State, with a legal description as follows: LOT R-48, GIFT STREET, INC., TRACT 100, according to the map thereof, recorded June 11, 1977, in Liber 500 of Deeds, at page 320 in the office of the County Recorder of Sample County, Sample State.

Said Lot No. R-48 is of the dimensions as shown on said map.

TOGETHER WITH the benefits and subject to the burdens and obligations of restrictions, easements, agreements and rights of way of record, including Declaration of Covenants, Conditions and Restrictions recorded in the Sample County Clerk's Office in Liber 500 of Deeds, page 347.

BEING AND INTENDING to convey the same premises conveyed to Richard Rich by Warranty Deed dated October 10, 1980 and recorded in the Sample County Clerk's Office on October 10, 1980 in Liber 350 of Deeds at page 302.

TAX ACCOUNT NO:	333-44-678
TAX MAILING ADDRESS:	234 Sunny Lane, Sample City, Sample State 12345
PROPERTY ADDRESS:	888 GIFT STREET, SAMPLE TOWN, SAMPLE STATE 12348

TOGETHER *with all right, title and interest, if any, of the party of the first part in and to any streets and roads abutting the above described premises to the center line thereof.*

TOGETHER *with the appurtenances of said party of the first part **and also** all the estate which the said decedent held at the time of his decease, in said premises, **And also** the estate therein, which the party of the first part has or had power to convey or dispose of, whether individually, or by virtue of said Will or otherwise.*

TO HAVE AND TO HOLD *the premises herein granted unto the party of the second part, their heirs, distributees and assigns forever.*

AND *the party of the first part covenants that it has not done or suffered anything whereby the said premises have been encumbered in any way whatever, except as aforesaid.*

The word "party" shall be construed to read "parties" whenever the sense of this indenture so requires.

That, in compliance with Section 13 of the Lien Law, the grantor will receive consideration for this conveyance and will hold the right to receive such consideration as a trust fund to be applied first for the purposes of paying the cost of the

---

(continued)

Figure 2.4 (continued)

improvement and will apply the same first to the payment of the cost of the improvement before using any part of the total of the same for any other purpose.

IN WITNESS WHEREOF, *the party of the first part duly executed this deed the day and year first above written.*

In Presence of

Susan W. Rich
SUSAN W. RICH, EXECUTRIX OF
THE ESTATE OF RICHARD. RICH

STATE OF SAMPLE STATE)

COUNTY OF SAMPLE) ss.:

On <u>March 15,</u> 2011, before me, the undersigned, personally appeared **Susan W. Rich, as Executrix of the Estate of RICHARD RICH,** known to me or proved to me on the basis of satisfactory evidence to be the individual whose name is subscribed to the within instrument and acknowledged to me that she executed the same in her capacity, and that by her signature on the executed instrument, the individual, or the estate or person on behalf of which the individual acted, executed the instrument.

Lila P. Legal
Notary Public

> **LILA P. LEGAL**
> Notary Public, State of Sample
> Sample County
> My Commission Expires May 10, 2012

RECORD & RETURN TO:
Pearson & Pearson, Attorneys-At-Law
1001 Reed Drive
Sample City, Sample State 12345

Beneficiary Deed

Beneficiary Deed
A deed executed while the grantor is alive that takes effect only upon the death of the grantor.

A **beneficiary deed** is a deed executed while the grantor is alive that takes effect only upon the death of the grantor. During the lifetime of the grantor, the property remains titled in the grantor's name. Only after the grantor dies does title to the property pass to the beneficiary. The transfer of title after the death of the grantor is generally accomplished by recording an original death certificate with the county recorder in the county where the real property is located. This is a simple and inexpensive process.

There are several advantages to using a beneficiary deed to transfer real property. First, the use of a beneficiary deed allows the property to stay in the grantor's name while he or she is alive. Second, a beneficiary deed transfers property upon the death of the grantor without the necessity of going through probate. Third, beneficiary deeds are revocable during the lifetime of the grantor. Fourth, beneficiary deeds can be used in conjunction with other estate planning to avoid probate.

Not all states allow the use of beneficiary deeds to transfer real property. Check your state's law to determine whether the use of beneficiary deeds is permitted in your jurisdiction.

Figure 2.5 depicts a beneficiary deed executed by Shirley Smith, the matriarch of the Hypothetical Family. Shirley executed the deed in favor of her only daughter, Jane Smith, at Jane's behest, because she was angry that Robert and Mary spent the Christmas holiday out of town with Mary's family that year.

Figure 2.5 Beneficiary Deed

When Recorded Mail To:
Pearson & Pearson, Attorneys-At-Law
1001 Reed Drive
Sample County, Sample State 12345

Mail Tax Bills & Assessments To:
Shirley Smith
121 Oak Street
Sample City, Sample State 12345

Above Space For Recorder's Use

BENEFICIARY DEED

KNOW ALL MEN BY THESE PRESENTS THAT

I, SHIRLEY SMITH (owner), residing at 121 Oak Street, Sample City, Sample State 12345, hereby convey to JANE SMITH (grantee beneficiary) effective on my death the following described real property:

Legal Description: **LOT THIRTEEN (13), BLOCK "R," OAK VIEW, TRACT NO. 1051, according to the plat thereof, recorded November 20, 1967 at Fee No. 34553, in the office of the Recorder of Sample County, Sample State.**

Physical Address: 121 Oak Street, Sample City, Sample State 12345

If a grantee beneficiary predeceases the owner, the conveyance to that grantee beneficiary shall either (choose one):

[ ] Become null and void.

[*S.S.*] Become part of the estate of the grantee beneficiary.

This deed is exempt from the affidavit and fee requirement under Sample Revised Statutes §11-1134(B)(8).

WITNESS Grantor's hand this 27th day of December, 2011.

Shirley Smith
Shirley Smith, Grantor

NOTARY ACKNOWLEDGMENT

STATE OF SAMPLE   }

COUNTY OF SAMPLE   }

On this 27th day of December, 2011, before me, the undersigned, a notary public in and for said state personally appeared SHIRLEY SMITH, personally known to me (or proved to me on the basis of satisfactory evidence) to be the person whose name is subscribed to the within instrument, and acknowledged to me that he/she executed the same in her authorized capacity, and that by her signature on the instrument the person, or entity upon behalf of which the person acted, executed the instrument.

(continued)

Figure 2.5 (continued)

WITNESS my hand and official seal.

Lila P. Legal
_____
Notary Public

> **LILA P. LEGAL**
> Notary Public, State of Sample
> Sample County
> My Commission Expires May 10, 2012

More About Deeds

As you can see, there are many different types of deeds that can be used to transfer title to real property. It is important for a paralegal to recognize when each type of deed can be used and what type of deed is most appropriate under the specific circumstances of each client's case. Consider the following examples.

EXAMPLE 1

Mabel Mansfield inherited a 2-acre parcel of land from her late husband, John. Mabel is unsure whether her husband had clear title to the property because she recalls some issues years back where they were contacted by a third party claiming that the grantor who conveyed the property to John did not really own the land. Mabel wants to transfer the property to her grandson, John Mansfield, III, in case it has value.

▶ **DISCUSSION POINT:** What type of deed should Mabel use, and why?

EXAMPLE 2

Mr. and Mrs. Johnson purchase 146 Lakefront Drive from Mr. and Mrs. James for $250,000. Mr. and Mrs. James assure the Johnsons that title is free and clear.

▶ **DISCUSSION POINT:** What type of deed should the Johnsons demand, and why?

EXAMPLE 3

Sally Davis is appointed as personal representative of her mother's estate. Her mother owned three pieces of land and directed that one property pass to each of her three children under her will.

▶ **DISCUSSION POINT:** How can Sally accomplish the property transfers that were directed under her mother's will?

■ TREATMENT OF PROPERTY AFTER DEATH

Now that you have gone over the basics of property, it is appropriate to review how property is treated in the context of a probate proceeding. This knowledge is also important when you assist clients with estate planning. It is important to make sure that clients understand that non-probate assets will not pass to the beneficiaries named in their will. Sometimes, reviewing their assets and discussing whom they wish to leave their estate to will prompt clients to adjust the beneficiary designations on their non-probate assets.

Probate Assets

Even when a person dies and a probate is required, it is possible that not all of the decedent's assets will go through probate. **Probate assets** are those that are distributed through a probate proceeding in a court of law. Generally speaking, probate assets are assets that are in the sole name of the decedent at the time of death. Common examples of property that would pass through probate are a separate bank account, titled solely in the name of the decedent, and a car titled only in the decedent's name. If the decedent had a will, the probate assets will pass as directed under the will. If the decedent did not have a will, the assets will pass to the decedent's heirs under the state's intestacy statutes.

Probate Assets
The property of the decedent that must be distributed through a probate proceeding in a court of law.

Non-Probate Assets

Non-probate assets are assets that pass to the intended beneficiary by operation of law independent of the provisions of a will or a probate proceeding. The most common ways this happens is by title or by beneficiary designation.

Non-Probate Assets
Property that passes to a decedent's intended beneficiaries by operation of law, independent of the provisions of a will or a probate proceeding.

By Title

An asset that is held in joint title will generally pass to the survivor at the first death. For example, if John and Sue are co-owners of a joint bank account and John passes away, the bank account legally belongs to Sue. Therefore, if a probate proceeding is initiated to administer John's estate, the joint bank account will not be a part of it because it is a non-probate asset. Further, if John has a will directing that the account pass to Sally, that provision will have no effect on the account, which will still pass by title to Sue.

By Beneficiary Designation

Some types of property allow the owner to appoint a beneficiary to receive the property upon the owner's death. Life insurance is one of the most common assets to pass by beneficiary designation. The beneficiary appointed to receive the life insurance upon the principal's death receives the proceeds by operation of law (via the beneficiary designation); thus, the insurance proceeds are a non-probate asset. Pay-on-Death (POD) and Transfer-on-Death (TOD) accounts are other examples of non-probate assets that pass by beneficiary designation. Upon the death of the owner, these types of bank accounts pass to the beneficiary designated to receive the account. Finally, retirement accounts pass by beneficiary designation and so are non-probate assets.

The only exception to the general rule that property that passes by beneficiary designation is a non-probate asset is when the beneficiary appointed is the decedent's estate. The owner of the asset may choose to appoint the estate as beneficiary if the owner wants the asset to pass pursuant to the will and go through probate. For example, the owner of a life insurance policy may direct that the life insurance be paid to his estate and then direct under his will that the proceeds of the policy be used to pay off the mortgage on a parcel of real property before the property is distributed to the beneficiary.

For Review:

Probate Assets	Non-Probate Assets
• Real property titled solely in the decedent's name	• Joint bank account
• Real property held as tenants in common with two or more owners	• Life insurance payable to a beneficiary
• Bank account solely in the decedent's name	• Real property titled as joint tenants with rights of survivorship
• Vehicle titled solely in decedent's name	• Retirement account
• Life insurance payable to decedent's estate	• POD or TOD account

■ CONCLUSION

This chapter provided an overview of the two main types of property: real and personal. You learned about the different ways in which title to property may be held, including fee simple, life estate, tenancy in common, joint tenancy, tenancy by the entirety, and community property. We also discussed the different types of deeds and when they may be used. Finally, we discussed the transfer of property after death via probate and non-probate transfers. Having a thorough understanding of property law is necessary in order to effectively work as a paralegal in an estate planning law firm. Further, you must be very familiar with property law in order to assist with probate administration.

CONCEPT REVIEW AND REINFORCEMENT

KEY TERMS

LABEL GAME

© Jennifer Montante

Part I. Label each identified item in the picture below as either real property or personal property.

Part II. Select the item that you believe most closely matches the definition of a fixture.

   1. **Window:** _____

   2. **Fireplace:** _____

   3. **Couch:** _____

   4. **Wall:** _____

   5. **Cat:** _____

   6. **Television:** _____

   7. **Clock:** _____

REVIEW QUESTIONS

1. Compare and contrast personal property with real property.
2. Which type of deed contains the most promises and is the strongest deed?
3. What is the name of the party to a deed who receives an interest in real property?
4. What type of deed transfers property from an estate to the decedent's heirs or devisees?
5. What type of deed is executed while the grantor is alive but takes effect only upon death?
6. If given the choice, would you prefer to receive a warranty deed or a quitclaim deed, and why?
7. Describe property ownership in states where spouses own property through tenancy by the entirety.
8. Describe how married couples own property in community property states.
9. Which type of property interest allows a person to possess real property only for his or her lifetime?
10. List and describe at least three different types of deeds discussed in this chapter.

BUILDING YOUR PARALEGAL SKILLS

CRITICAL THINKING EXERCISES

1. Do you think it is important to understand property law before you assist clients with estate planning and probate? Why or why not?

2. John sells his house to Sam using a store-bought contract. The contract is silent regarding fixtures. Discuss whether or not you believe each of these items constitutes a fixture.

   - patio barbeque
   - chandelier
   - refrigerator
   - ceiling fan
   - above-ground pool
   - installed garbage disposal
   - mounted microwave oven

3. Mark owns a car, a bank account, a house, and a CD and wants to leave everything to his only child, Rebecca. He wants to avoid probate by making these items non-probate assets. Discuss how Mark can accomplish this.

4. Barbara and Sally are sisters and decide to purchase a cottage together to enjoy as a family. Barbara has two children and Sally has three children. Both Barbara and Sally want to leave their share of the cottage to their children upon their demise. How would you recommend that Barbara and Sally hold title to the property? Discuss why you selected that choice.

5. Paul and Sarah are siblings and decided to purchase a vacation home in Colorado because they enjoy skiing so much. Paul has no children and wants to leave the home to Sarah at his death. Sarah has two children and wants to leave the vacation home to them. Discuss how Paul and Sarah should hold title to the property, and what else they may need to do to accomplish their respective wishes.

PARALEGAL PRACTICE

Review these memoranda directed from the supervising attorney to you, the paralegal. Each memorandum discusses a situation with a client and requests your assistance in researching the matter. You must then report back with your findings, as directed in the memorandum.

1. _____

MEMORANDUM
To: Paralegal
From: Supervising Attorney
Client: Ned Matthews
Re: Quitclaim Deed

Today I met with Ned Matthews regarding some quitclaim deeds that he needs drafted. I want to make sure that our deed forms comply with all of the statutory requirements.

Please research our state's law to determine the statutory requirements for the drafting and execution of a quitclaim deed in our state. Report your findings and your conclusion in the form of a return memorandum to me. Be sure to cite the statute and include a copy for me to review.

2. _____

MEMORANDUM
To: Paralegal
From: Supervising Attorney
Client: Ned Matthews
Re: Quitclaim Deed

Now that you have researched the statutory formalities, please draft a quitclaim deed conveying Matthew's home at 123 Creed Street, Smalltown, Sample State 12345 to his friend, Clint Brooks. The property's legal description is LOT 2-B, CREED ESTATES, TRACT 4042-G, according to the plat recorded at Fee No. 99-12345. Be sure to update the dates on the deed to the current year.

3. _____

MEMORANDUM
To: Paralegal
From: Supervising Attorney
Client: Joe Fox
Re: Personal Representative's Deed

We were hired as counsel for the estate of Joe Fox. Mr. Fox died intestate. Mr. Fox's heirs are his two children, Melissa Smith and Megan Fox. Please draft a personal representative's deed conveying 789 Sound Street, Sample Town, Sample State 45678 to Mr. Fox's children. Melissa Smith is serving as personal representative of the estate.

ONLINE RESOURCES

The Pearson Course Companion website contains the following additional resources:
- **Forms for Paralegal Practice Activities**
- Chapter Objectives

- Online Study Guide (Containing Multiple Choice and True/False Questions)
- Web Exercises www.pearsonhighered.com /careers

CASES FOR CONSIDERATION

CASE #1:

JOHN M. PRICE V. SAMUEL C. KING.

44 Kan. 639; 25 p. 43
July, 1890, Decided
OPINION BY: VALENTINE

OPINION

The opinion of the court was delivered by VALENTINE, J.: This was an action in the nature of ejectment, brought in the district court of Atchison county to recover certain real estate. The plaintiff, John M. Price, claims under a certain deed of conveyance, a quitclaim deed, executed to R. F. Smith by the three executors of Courtlandt Palmer's estate, to wit: Courtlandt Palmer, Jr., Charles P. Palmer and Henry Draper, and by the sole executrix of Charles Gould's estate, to wit, Henrietta S. Gould, and a certain quitclaim deed from Smith and wife to himself, together with certain other facts and circumstances which he claims create in himself an estate in the property,

either legal or equitable, or both. The defendant, Samuel C. King, claims the property under certain tax deeds executed to him by the county clerk of Atchison county, and also by virtue of being in the actual possession and occupancy of the property. With respect to nearly all the property the judgment of the court below was in favor of the defendant and against the plaintiff, upon the ground, principally, that it was not shown, even *prima facie*, that the plaintiff ever had any title or estate, either legal or equitable, in or to the property.

The deed under which the plaintiff claims was evidently intended by all the parties thereto to be the deed only of the aforesaid executors and executrix, executed in the capacity only of executors and executrix, and not executed in any other capacity, or by any other person or persons. All the evidence upon the subject tends to show this. The deed was indorsed on its back, "executors' deed." It was executed in the name of the executors and executrix as such. It was signed by them as executors and executrix. It was witnessed by the subscribing witnesses to the same effect; and it was also acknowledged by the grantors only as executors and executrix; and as a matter of fact, according to all the extrinsic evidence upon the subject, the grantors intended to execute the deed only as executors and executrix, and afterward with the desire and wish of all the parties it was confirmed by the surrogate's court of the city and county of New York and state of New York as the deed of the executors and executrix; and afterward, at the instance of the plaintiff and Smith, authenticated copies of the wills under which the executors and executrix attempted to execute the deed and the proceedings of the said surrogate's court showing the probate of the wills, etc., were filed and recorded in the office of the probate court of Atchison county, Kansas—the county in which the land supposed to have been conveyed, including the land in controversy, is situated. And further, each of the parties executing the aforesaid deed was actually an executor or executrix, and all together they were all the executors and the only executrix of the Palmer and Gould estates; and one of such executors, Henry Draper, had no possible interest in the property supposed to be conveyed, except as executor, and as the husband of one of the heirs and devisees; and the grantors mentioned in the deed included the names of only three of the heirs or devisees, and there were three of the heirs and devisees of the Palmer estate and the six heirs of the Gould estate who were not mentioned in the deed as grantors or otherwise.

If the foregoing deed shall be construed to be only the deed of the foregoing executors and executrix, then it must unquestionably be held to be absolutely null and void as a conveyance; and we think it must be so construed and so held. No one of the executors or the executrix *as such* had any title or estate in or to any part of the property. The wills under which they attempted to act did not give to them or to any one or more of them any title or estate in or to the property as executors or executrix. Nor did such wills confer upon them or upon any one or more of them, or upon anyone else, any power or authority to sell or convey the property or any part thereof, or to alienate the same in any manner whatever. Nor did any court ever attempt to give to them or to any person or persons any such power or authority; and there was always

an abundance of personal property on hand belonging to each estate with which to meet all demands that might be presented against such estate. Hence, no fact existed authorizing any court to grant any such power or authority. The plaintiff, however, claims that even if the aforesaid deed is void as a conveyance, and even if for that reason the plaintiff has no *legal* title to the property in controversy, still that under all the facts of the case and in equity, he has the paramount *equitable* title thereto. Now in what does the plaintiff's equities or his equitable title consist? His title, so far as any writing is concerned, is founded solely upon a quitclaim deed to himself from Smith, the grantee of the aforesaid executors and executrix, and hence so far as his written title is concerned, he claims only under a quitclaim deed from a party, Smith, whose title was founded upon a void executors' and executrix's deed, which also was and is only a quitclaim deed; and under a quitclaim deed the grantee therein cannot claim to be a *bona fide* purchaser or holder of the property or an equitable owner thereof, as against outstanding equities in other claimants of the property. (*Johnson v. Williams*, 37 Kan. 179.) Indeed, the grantee in a quitclaim deed gets nothing except what his grantor in fact owned at the time of the execution of the deed, which in the present case was nothing, as the executors and executrix, as such, owned nothing in the present case. And such a deed will not estop the maker thereof from afterward purchasing or acquiring an outstanding adverse title or interest in or to the property and holding it as against his grantee. (*Simpson v. Greeley*, 8 Kan. 586, 597, 598; *Bruce v. Luke*, 9 id. 201, 207, *et seq.*; *Scoffins v. Grandstaff*, 12 id. 469, 470; *Young v. Clippinger*, 14 id. 148, 150; *Ott v. Sprague*, 27 id. 624; *Johnson v. Williams*, 37 id. 180, 181.)

It is possible that there might be cases where a party claiming only under a quitclaim deed would have equities beyond the mere terms of his quitclaim deed, but we do not think that this case falls within any of such cases. It is possible where a party purchases real estate and pays a full consideration therefor and takes only a quitclaim deed as a conveyance that his claim of title to the property should be treated at least with favor, but such is not this case. The real estate claimed by the plaintiff to have been conveyed in this present case was worth at the time of its supposed conveyance from $10,000 to $12,000, with an incumbrance on it for taxes amounting to from $300 to $500; and yet the plaintiff's grantor, Smith, paid only $225 for such real estate—less than one-fortieth of the actual value of the property; and the plaintiff, in fact as well as presumptively, knew all this. Also, where there is fraud on the part of the vendor or a mutual mistake of the parties or some accident intervening, it is possible that the holder of a quitclaim deed might obtain equities beyond the terms of his deed: for instance, where the deed is defective or does not fully express what the parties intended that it should express, equity might reform it or might consider it as reformed so as to make it express or accomplish what both the parties intended that it should express and accomplish. But that is not this case. The deed in the present case is just what the parties intended that it should be, and if it were changed in its form or effect in any particular, it would be what the parties intended it should not be. It is true that Smith desired a different kind of deed, and at the instance of Smith two different deeds were sent to the agent of the grantors for execution, but they refused to execute the same, and would not execute any other or different kind of deed than the one which they did in fact execute, and the negotiations with reference to the matter were going on and pending between the parties for about eight months before any final agreement was reached; and after all the parties were well informed as to the facts, Smith finally agreed to take and knowingly did take the very deed which is now in controversy in this case and afterward paid the aforesaid $225 for the same. He took it knowing what it was, and that he could not obtain any other or different kind of deed. And the plaintiff knew the same. There was no fraud, no concealment, no misrepresentation, no deception on the part of the grantors or their agents, and no mistake with reference to the facts on the part of anyone. A quitclaim deed was executed by the grantors merely as executors and executrix, and all the parties knew it; and this quitclaim deed really conveyed nothing, leaving the entire title to the property in the heirs and devisees. By this deed Smith got nothing, and he conveyed nothing to the plaintiff by his quitclaim deed to the plaintiff. And the facts were not such as to create or vest such equities or equitable title in the plaintiff that he may now disturb the rights of the defendant, who holds and claims by a separate and independent title adverse to both the plaintiff and his grantors.

There are also cases where an agent or trustee attempts to bind his principal, but from some lack of authority or from irregularity he fails to do so, and in effect binds himself. But such is not this case. The executors and executrix in this case did not attempt to bind any person. They merely quitclaimed any interest which they might have as executors and executrix in the property; and as before stated, no party was deceived or defrauded or mistaken as to the facts, but all were fully and completely cognizant of the same. Smith got all he purchased or paid for when he got his quitclaim deed. He did not purchase or pay for the individual rights of any person. Of course in the beginning there was some talk of conveying the title to the property, and Smith at all times desired that such should be the case, but the executors and executrix refused, and consented only to quitclaim as to any interest which they might possibly have in the property as executors and executrix. They did not agree to sell or convey any interest which they or others might have in the property in any other capacity; and in the capacity of executors and executrix they will probably never dispute the plaintiff's title. Indeed, all the parties will at all times admit that Smith got by his quitclaim deed and conveyed to the plaintiff by another quitclaim deed all interest which the executors and executrix ever possessed in the property, which in fact was nothing.

The defendant makes the claim that no title passed to Smith or to the plaintiff, for the further reason that neither the wills nor the probate thereof, nor any of the proceedings of the surrogate's court of the city and county of New York, were filed or recorded in the office of the probate court of Atchison county, Kansas—the county in which the land in controversy is situated—until long after the aforesaid deed from the executors and executrix to Smith and the deed from Smith to the plaintiff were executed, delivered, accepted, and recorded. The first of the foregoing deeds was executed in New York on June 24, 1880. It was transmitted to Kansas on July 8, 1880, but on account of disputes between the parties it was not accepted by Smith until about February 7, 1881, when it was accepted by him, paid for, and then recorded in the office of the register of deeds. It was confirmed in the surrogate's court of the city and county of New York on May 23, 1881. The deed from Smith to the plaintiff was executed on June 25, 1881, and was recorded on July 5, 1881. The wills were never probated in Kansas, and no proceedings with reference thereto were ever had in Kansas until April 1, 1882, when authenticated copies of the wills and the records of the proceedings of the aforesaid surrogate's court were filed and recorded in the office of the probate court of Atchison county, Kansas. Now it is claimed by the defendant that no will can be effectual to pass title to real estate unless the same has been probated or recorded in Kansas according to the statutes of Kansas; and §§ 24 and 29 of the act relating to wills, and § 1 of chapter 102 of the laws of 1879 (Gen. Stat. of 1889, P 2932), are referred to as sustaining this claim. Said § 29 reads as follows:

"SEC. 29. No will shall be effectual to pass real or personal estate unless it shall have been duly admitted to probate, or recorded, as provided in this act."

Upon the foregoing facts and statutes referred to it is claimed by the defendant that no title had ever passed to anyone under the wills when the foregoing deeds were executed and delivered, and therefore that no title could have passed to Smith or to the plaintiff because of the wills or otherwise when the foregoing deeds were executed, for at that time neither the executors, nor the executrix, nor the devisees, nor anyone else who might claim title under the wills, had any such title under the same to pass to anyone; and that as both such deeds were merely quitclaim deeds, which could not operate to pass future acquired titles, no title could ever subsequently have passed under them—and the cases heretofore cited are referred to as authority for such claim. With reference to these claims of the defendant just mentioned we shall express no opinion, as we do not think it is necessary for the decision of this case.

We decide in this case, however, the following: The first quitclaim deed executed by the executors and executrix to Smith did not, of itself, and at the time it was executed, convey to Smith any title or interest in or to the property described in the deed, for at that time the grantors, as executors and executrix, had no such title or interest to convey, nor any power or authority to convey any such title or interest; and nothing afterward passed under such deed or by virtue of its terms, for it was only a quitclaim deed; and such is and always has been the law with respect to quitclaim deeds. And nothing at any time passed by virtue of any of or all the facts and circumstances taking place prior to, contemporaneous with and subsequent to the execution of the deed, for no fraud, deception, concealment, mistake of facts or accident occurred or intervened, and it was not the intention of the parties that anything but the interest of the executors and executrix as such, or the interest which they might have had the power to convey, should pass. And we might further say, that a party can never obtain, by way of estoppel or ratification or otherwise, what it was never expected or intended that he should obtain.

Finding that the plaintiff's supposed legal title, founded upon the aforesaid quitclaim deeds, is void, and not finding any equities in favor of the plaintiff sufficient to create an equitable title, we think the judgment of the court below is correct. There are a few other questions presented in this case, but we do not think that they need comment. The plaintiff may pay the taxes due on the two lots adjudged to him at any time, and may then obtain the possession thereof.

The judgment of the court below will be affirmed. All the Justices concurring.

Case Questions

1. Why did the plaintiff believe that he owned the property?
2. How did the defendant acquire title to the property?
3. What was this court's holding, and what was the reason for its holding?

CASE #2:

GEORGE C. MACK, APPELLEE, V. ERNEST F. TREDWAY, APPELLANT

244 Iowa 240; 56 N.W.2d 678
January 13, 1953

JUDGES: Wennerstrum, J. All Justices concur.
OPINION BY: WENNERSTRUM

OPINION

Plaintiff brought an action to establish and quiet title to certain real estate situated in Buena Vista County, Iowa. He claims title by reason of a quitclaim deed which he received from the only child of a former owner. The defendant denied that the plaintiff held title to the property and claims that he is the equitable owner by reason of a contract entered into between D. G. LaGrange, as agent, and the defendant, as purchaser. The trial court found that the plaintiff was the record titleholder of the real estate here involved by reason of the quitclaim deed previously referred to and also held that the defendant had failed to show any agency or authority on the part of D. G. LaGrange to sell and convey the real estate and that by reason thereof the defendant had failed to establish any valid claim of title to said real estate. Thereafter a motion for new trial was submitted to the trial court which was overruled. The defendant has appealed.

Etta Heller originally purchased the property here involved from J. H. LaGrange and his wife on July 21, 1921. Etta Heller died intestate on April 7, 1942, leaving her surviving husband, George Heller, and one married daughter, Velma Irene Boyd. George Heller died a widower and intestate on February 27, 1943. His only heir was Velma Irene Boyd. There was no administration had upon the estates of Etta and George Heller and it is asserted that sole title to the real estate vested in the daughter, Velma Irene Boyd, upon the death of her father. It is claimed by the appellant, Ernest F. Tredway, that D. G. LaGrange received in or about March 1944 a quitclaim deed from Velma Irene Boyd which was never recorded. The testimony relative to this claimed deed will be commented upon later. On March 17, 1944, D. G. LaGrange, as agent, entered into a written contract with appellant-Tredway, as purchaser, for the sale of the real estate here involved for a consideration of $250, payable $3.00 a month beginning May 1, 1944, with like payments each month to and including July 1, 1945, at which time the balance due was to be paid and conveyance made provided the seller was able to furnish a merchantable title. This contract was recorded. At the time it was executed the appellant entered into possession of the property and so continued down to the date of the trial. He made payments on the contract which totaled $52 and on June 29, 1945, he tendered to D. G. LaGrange the sum of $200 as the claimed balance of the purchase price. This tender was refused.

On September 25, 1948, Velma Irene Boyd and her husband executed a quitclaim deed to George C. Mack, the appellee. This deed was recorded in the office of the county recorder of Buena Vista County on October 20, 1948. The appellee claims title to the real estate superior to the rights of the appellant by virtue of the quitclaim deed received by him. Notice and demand that the appellant execute a quitclaim deed to the appellee was served on Tredway on November 22, 1948 (section 649.5, 1946 Code). By virtue of the fact that the appellant refused to execute such a deed the appellee commenced on April 20, 1949, the action which has resulted in this appeal.

In connection with the claim that Velma Irene Boyd conveyed title to D. G. LaGrange in 1944 by reason of a quitclaim deed which was never recorded, the following facts should be noted. An attorney who originally represented the appellant in this action testified at the time of the submission of a motion for new trial that he had conferred with Velma Irene Boyd in Sioux City, Iowa, on December 3, 1949. He testified in part as follows:

"I asked her about the contract between LaGrange and Tredway and she knew nothing about it, so I opened my file and showed it to her. I stated that Mr. Tredway said Don LaGrange told him in 1944 he had a deed from Velma Boyd but she denied it when I asked her. I pointed out to her that if she had given a subsequent quitclaim deed it wouldn't prejudice her and we wanted to find out the correct situation. I did not subpoena her as a witness at the original trial. I felt I had tried long enough on that direction."

Velma Irene Boyd gave an affidavit, which was attached to the petition for new trial, wherein she stated that, "* * * with my knowledge, authority and consent, D. G. LaGrange, my agent, entered into a written contract with Ernest F. Tredway of Storm Lake, Iowa, by which contract he sold the real estate above described in my behalf to Ernest F. Tredway, for the consideration of two hundred fifty dollars ($250.00) payable at the rate of three dollars ($3.00) per month * * *."

In this affidavit no mention is made of a quitclaim deed having been given by Velma Irene Boyd to D. G. LaGrange. In fact, the affidavit shows that D. G. LaGrange was acting as her agent. However, in connection with the evidence presented at the time of the submission of the petition for new trial, Velma Irene Boyd testified to her knowledge D. G. LaGrange was then deceased. She further testified: "I executed a quitclaim deed to D. G. LaGrange in, I think, the spring of March of 1944." In connection with the deed given by Velma Irene Boyd to George Mack she testified: "I never talked to anyone else except to Mack, the plaintiff in this action. He came up and sent some lawyer with him. He came to the produce house and I went out and signed the paper that the lawyer brought in."

Despite the testimony just set forth, Mrs. Boyd then continued her testimony and stated:

"I don't think Mr. Mack was with the lawyer. The lawyer stated that he was representing George Mack and he would like to have a quitclaim deed and they were going to see D. G. LaGrange, but he didn't explain it to me. I signed it and went back to work. After I signed it he gave me $15.00. * * * Mr. Mack came to my house and I wouldn't let him in. The lawyer came up and asked if I had given a quitclaim deed to Mr. LaGrange and I said I don't have to answer that. This

Mr. Mack personally stated he was living on the property and would lose it if I didn't sign a quitclaim deed. I had already signed a quitclaim deed.

"When I signed the quitclaim deed to Mr. Mack, I saw the lawyer first. That is the time I was paid $15.00 and that is the time he came and asked me if I signed a quitclaim deed to LaGrange and I wouldn't answer. I don't know if it was Mr. Mack.

"Later and following the execution of this quitclaim deed, I talked to Mr. Perry, Tredway's lawyer and Mr. Tredway. That is the first time I ever saw them. That was a little over a year ago. I was not asked by Mr. Perry or Mr. Tredway to appear as a witness previous to the trial of this case and I was not subpoenaed. Mr. Perry did not discuss with me the matter of the quitclaim deed to Mr. Mack but we did discuss the quitclaim deed to Mr. LaGrange in 1944."

On cross-examination she further testified: "Mr. Tredway and Mr. Perry called on me a little over a year ago and discussed this case with me. I talked freely with them. I didn't know about the contract existing between Tredway and Don LaGrange."

In connection with the quoted statement last set forth attention is called to the affidavit of Velma Irene Boyd wherein, as previously stated, she asserted that D. G. LaGrange, her agent, had entered into a written contract with Ernest F. Tredway with her knowledge, authority and consent.

In the contract which was entered into by D. G. LaGrange it was not set forth for whom LaGrange was the agent. And the authority of the agent to make the contract is nowhere shown in the record at the time of the entry of the original decree. It is true that in the submission of the petition for a new trial the affidavit of Velma Irene Boyd and her testimony indicate she had given some authority to LaGrange. However, as disclosed by the quoted portions of the record heretofore set forth, there is much in the way of contradictory statements made by Mrs. Boyd.

A further fact which should be noted and which raises considerable doubt relative to the claimed deed from Mrs. Boyd to LaGrange is the following portion of the contract between LaGrange and Tredway:

"It is agreed that the above payments shall be made as rental of said premises but when good title can be furnished then said payments may be applied as a part of the purchase price. It is agreed that the vendor shall institute proper proceedings to obtain title to said premises at an early a date as is practicable, and this contract is subject to the rights of redemption of any parties who have an equitable interest in the premises."

It should be further noted that while appellant-Tredway was in possession of the premises he paid all the taxes including back taxes for the year 1938 down to and including 1943, at which time the premises had been sold for taxes. He also paid on October 28, 1946, the amount of $117.28, which payment was necessary for the redemption of the property from tax sale. In addition to subsequent taxes paid, the appellant also paid $100 for a sewer assessment and $33 for a water connection permit.

The trial court in its conclusions of law held that George C. Mack, the appellee herein, is now the record titleholder of said premises; that his title is subject to a claim and lien in favor of the appellant-defendant, Ernest F. Tredway, for all moneys expended by him for taxes, sewer assessment and a water connection permit with interest on such payments at five per cent from the date each was paid; that the appellee's title is subject to the rights of the appellant to possession of said property until removed therefrom in the manner contemplated and as provided by law; that the appellant has failed to show any agency or authority on the part of D. G. LaGrange to convey the property under the contract and has consequently failed to establish any valid claim or title to said property.

The trial court in ruling on appellant's petition for new trial made this statement: "In connection with the petition the court had the benefit of the testimony of Velma Irene Boyd, and after listening to her testimony and reading her affidavit the court is of the opinion little or no credence can be accorded her testimony and nothing would be gained by granting a new trial."

We believe the trial court was justified in the comment made. It is also our conclusion that under the entire record that court properly held that the title of George C. Mack was superior and paramount to that of the appellant.

I. The appellant in formal terms asserts as a basis for reversal that the trial court erred in ruling that the appellee is now the record title owner of the real estate; in ruling that the appellant had failed to establish any valid claim to the title to said property; and in overruling appellant's petition for a new trial. However, the appellant's contention may be summarized by quoting from his brief as follows:

"The instant case, then, boils down simply to this. When Velma Irene Boyd gave a quitclaim deed to D. G. LaGrange in 1944, she divested herself of all of her interest in the property, and her interest was admittedly the full and complete title. This deed was not recorded, but the new owner, LaGrange, had the full right to contract for the sale of the property to appellant—even though the contract refers to him by the unfortunate term, 'agent.'"

The appellant's last assertion might have some merit if the evidence supported it. It is very apparent to us by a review of the evidence, a limited portion of which we have set forth, that it does not support appellant's claim.

II. It is appellant's contention that when in 1948 the appellee took from Velma Irene Boyd a quitclaim deed he took only the interest then owned by her, of which appellant claims she had none. It is true as held in Junkin v. McClain, 221 Iowa 1084, 1096, 1097, 265 N.W. 362, that in the receiving and accepting of a quitclaim deed the appellee-grantee took it with notice of prior equities, whatever they may be. See also Steele & Son v. Sioux Valley Bank, 79 Iowa 339, 347, 44 N.W. 564, 7 L. R. A. 524, 18 Am. St. Rep. 370; Duntz v. Ames Cemetery Assn., 192 Iowa 1341, 1345, 186 N.W. 443; Howell v. Howell, 211 Iowa 70, 75, 232 N.W. 816. It is our conclusion that the quitclaim deed given to the appellee was not burdened by equities sufficient to prevent the passing of title.

Such equities that the appellant had were properly preserved for him by the trial court in its decree. A quitclaim deed is effectual to convey whatever interest the grantor has in the property sought to be conveyed. 16 Am. Jur., Deeds, section 330, page 624. It is also stated in 26 C. J. S., Deeds, section 118, page 415, as follows:

"The title to realty may be as effectually transferred by a quitclaim deed as by any other form of conveyance and such a deed will convey whatever title or interest the grantor may have at the time it is given."

There is no satisfactory evidence that Velma Irene Boyd had conveyed whatever title she had prior to the giving of the quitclaim deed to the appellee. Besides, we believe the equities and the evidence support the appellee's contention.

III. The granting of a new trial is within the sound discretion of the trial court. We will not interfere unless there is an abuse of discretion. We find no justification for us to say that the trial court abused its discretion in refusing to grant a new trial. We also hold the original decree was properly entered.—Affirmed.

Case Questions

1. How did the plaintiff acquire title to the property?
2. How did the defendant acquire title to the property?
3. What was the issue in this case?
4. What was this court's ruling?
5. Why did this court rule the way that it did?

FORMS TO ACCOMPANY PARALEGAL PRACTICE

Disclaimer: The forms provided to aid students in completing the Paralegal Practice activities assigned in each chapter have been modified as samples to familiarize students with what each form commonly looks like and are not intended to be used as actual forms for any state.

INSTRUCTIONS: The forms are provided in Microsoft Word format and employ the use of Stop Codes (such as SC1, SC2, SC3, and so on). Stop Codes are used in place of the form sections that must be updated with case-by-case information, such as SC1 for the client's name, SC3 for the client's address, and so on. What each Stop Code represents can be inferred by reading the surrounding text on the form. By using the FIND & REPLACE tool on the Microsoft toolbar, the students can replace the Stop Codes with the information provided in the Paralegal Practice activity to complete each assignment. Students must also fill in any blank lines on each form with the appropriate information from the activity and then proofread the document prior to turning in their work.

The following forms are included following this section and will be posted online for students to access to complete the Paralegal Practice activities for this chapter:

- PP Form 2.2—Quitclaim Deed
- PP Form 2.3—Personal Representative's Deed

PP Form 2.2—Quitclaim Deed

When Recorded Mail To:
SC2
Sc4

Above Space For Recorder's Use

GRANTOR:
SC1
Sc3

GRANTEE:
SC2
Sc4

QUITCLAIM DEED

KNOW ALL MEN BY THESE PRESENTS THAT:

FOR VALUABLE CONSIDERATION OF TEN DOLLARS ($10.00), and other good and valuable consideration, cash in hand paid, the receipt and sufficiency of which is hereby acknowledged SC1, hereinafter referred to as "Grantor," does hereby release, remise, and forever quitclaim to SC2, hereinafter "Grantee," the following land and property, together with all improvements located thereon, lying in the County of Sample County, State of Sample, to wit:

Legal Description:_____

Physical Address: Sc3

SUBJECT TO existing taxes, assessments, reservations in patents, encumbrances, covenants, conditions, restrictions, rights of way, easements, obligations and liabilities as may as may appear of record, if any.

TO HAVE AND TO HOLD the said interest in the above described property unto and to the use and benefit of the Grantees and their successors in interest forever; and that neither I nor my heirs or assigns shall have nor make any claims or demand upon said property interest, other than the interest granted herein.

This deed is exempt from the affidavit and fee requirement under Sample Revised Statutes §42-1614(B)(8).

WITNESS Grantor's hand this _____ day of _____, 2014.

_____

SC1, Grantor

NOTARY ACKNOWLEDGMENT

STATE OF SAMPLE   }

COUNTY OF SAMPLE   }

On this _____ day of _____, 2014, before me, the undersigned, a notary public in and for said state personally appeared SC1, personally known to me (or proved to me on the basis of satisfactory evidence) to be the person whose name is subscribed to the within instrument and acknowledged to me that he executed the same in his authorized capacity, and that by his signature on the instrument the person, or entity upon behalf of which the person acted, executed the instrument.

WITNESS my hand and official seal.

_____

Notary Public

My Commission Expires:

_____

PP Form 2.3—Personal Representative's Deed

When Recorded Return To:
Pearson & Pearson, Attorneys-At-Law
1001 Reed Drive
Sample County, Sample State 12345
Attorneys for Personal Representative

Mail Tax Assessments To:
SC3
[Insert Address]

IN THE SUPERIOR COURT OF THE STATE OF SAMPLE
IN AND FOR THE COUNTY OF SAMPLE

In the Matter of the Estate of SC1, Deceased.	Case No. PB-2014-_____ **PERSONAL REPRESENTATIVE'S DEED OF DISTRIBUTION**

The undersigned Personal Representative, SC2, in order to make distribution of the property of this Estate in compliance with Title 14 of Sample Revised Statutes, hereby assigns, transfers and releases to **SC3**, a distributee of the Estate, whose address is _____ [Insert Address of Beneficiary], all right, title and interest of decedent in and to the following described property:

LEGAL DESCRIPTION: _____

PHYSICAL ADDRESS: _____

DATED this __ day of _____ , 2014.

_____
SC2

STATE OF SAMPLE   )

) ss.

County of SAMPLE   )

The foregoing instrument was acknowledged before me this day of _____, 2014, by SC2, as Personal Representative of the Estate of Sc1.

_____
Notary Public

My Commission Expires:

_____

Meeting with an Estate Planning Client: Components of a Basic Estate Plan

CHAPTER 3

A REAL-LIFE SCENARIO

Mrs. Oak, a frail and elderly widow, arrived at the attorney's office for an estate planning consultation accompanied by her hearty and boisterous daughter, Cindy. Cindy assisted Mrs. Oak to her seat across the table from the lawyer and sat down next to her mother. A mere thirty seconds into the consultation, it was obvious to the attorney that Cindy was controlling and likely asserting an undue influence over her mother. She was interjecting into the conversation when it was not appropriate and was speaking for Mrs. Oak out of turn. The attorney politely explained the importance of speaking with Mrs. Oak directly and in confidence and buzzed the secretary to help escort Cindy to the waiting room. Mrs. Oak looked relieved and Cindy did, in fact, leave the room for the duration of the consultation.

© Jennifer Montante

CHAPTER OBJECTIVES:

1. List and describe the components of a typical estate plan.

2. Prepare an estate planning checklist to be used for client interviews.

3. Interview an estate planning client to obtain the necessary information for document drafting.

4. Organize client information to be used for the appropriate estate planning documents.

5. Draft basic estate planning documents for attorney review.

■ INTRODUCTION

Most clients come into the attorney's office with a preconceived notion of what they need. That preconceived notion may be that they need a will, that they need a living trust, that they need a living will (not knowing what the term means), or any variety of other ideas. Their preconceived notion may come from a friend, family member, or neighbor; from the Internet; from television; or from a variety of other sources. More likely than not, the source of the client's information lacks the legal background and experience to make a proper determination about what the client does or does not need. The attorney's job is to find out what the client has, what the client wants, and what the client needs. Further, as the foregoing Real-Life Scenario illustrates, the attorney also must make sure that clients can express their wishes free from the undue influence of others. As an experienced paralegal, you will be able to assist the attorney and the firm's clients with this process.

Estate planning is a very important area of law for paralegals to understand and generally a very pleasant field to work in. While paralegals cannot give legal advice, they can provide great assistance to attorneys with respect to gathering and organizing information from clients and drafting documents for the attorney's review. Estate planning documents are of great importance to clients and may be life altering when unexpected future events arise in clients' lives.

Most attorneys that do estate planning also assist clients with probate proceedings. As a result, legal professionals may develop relationships with clients as they assist them over the years with their initial **estate plan**, as well as changes to that plan when life events occur, and eventually, with probate proceedings. Paralegals working in the areas of estate planning and probate may enjoy a higher level of client interaction than that which commonly takes place in some other areas of law. The relationships that are built with estate planning and probate clients can be very fulfilling for legal professionals.

■ COMPONENTS OF AN ESTATE PLAN

It is important to identify the components of an estate plan. A comprehensive estate plan includes more than just a will. A comprehensive estate plan does more than just dispose of one's worldly possessions upon their demise. Ideally, an estate plan should prepare for every contingency with respect to one's person and one's property *both* during life *and* after death. We will discuss the latter first.

After Death

In addition to the living will and health care proxy, or living will health care power of attorney, and financial power of attorney used during the client's lifetime, clients need to dispose of their assets following their death. This is most commonly accomplished by executing a **Last Will and Testament**, or "will." A **will** is a written document that leaves the estate of the individual who signed the will to the named persons or entities. A will only disposes of property following the maker's death and can be revoked or amended at any time while the maker is still alive.

In addition to disposing of one's assets, a will is useful to ensure that minor children are provided for by appointing a guardian to be legally responsible for them if they lose their parents. Further, some states permit individuals to appoint guardians over themselves under their will in the event they become incapacitated and in need of a guardian. In this respect, the will may be used during the testator's lifetime to aid in appointment of the guardian. Finally, some states permit testators to give instructions regarding their funeral and the disposal of their

Estate Plan
A plan made to provide for the maker's physical and financial needs during lifetime, as well as the distribution of the maker's estate upon death.

Last Will and Testament (Will)
A written document that leaves the estate of the individual who signed the will to the named persons or entities.

remains under their will. Note that state law varies greatly and you must check the law in your state to determine whether it is permissible to give funeral and burial or cremation instructions under a will.

As has been discussed in previous chapters, disposing of assets by will often requires a probate proceeding. **Probate** is a general term for the entire process of administering a decedent's estate with court supervision, and may include intestate estates (those of individuals without wills). Some clients desire to avoid probate and wish to dispose of their assets using a living trust instead. A living trust takes effect immediately upon execution and is discussed below.

During Lifetime

Every estate plan should include a living will, a health care proxy, and a power of attorney. All of these documents are effective during the signer's lifetime. A **living will** is a written expression of a person's wishes to be allowed to die a natural death and not be kept alive by heroic or artificial methods. Other names for a living will are directive to physicians, health care declaration, and medical directive. Living wills often direct the extent and type of medical treatment persons wish to receive if they are in a persistent vegetative state (PVS). A **persistent vegetative state (PVS)** is a condition of patients with severe brain damage in whom a coma has progressed to a state of wakefulness without detectable awareness. It is a diagnosis of some uncertainty in that it deals with a syndrome.

A **health care proxy** is a written statement authorizing an agent or surrogate to make medical treatment decisions for another in the event of the other's inability to do so. A heath care proxy does not take effect until or unless the person becomes unable to make personal medical decisions. A **living will and health care proxy** combines the two forms into one by expressing the person's wishes to be allowed to die a natural death as well as appointing an agent to make medical treatment decisions on the person's behalf.

Most states use the terms living will, health care proxy, and/or a combination of the two for these purposes, but some states use a health care power of attorney in place of a health care proxy. For example, New York State uses a combined living will and health care proxy, whereas Arizona law provides for a separate living will and health care power of attorney. Arizona's **health care power of attorney** enables the principal to appoint an agent to make medical decisions when the principal is incapacitated. Note that the health care power of attorney applies to medical decisions, not financial decisions.

A **power of attorney** is a legal document that authorizes another person to act as the grantor's attorney-in-fact and agent. For all intents and purposes, this means that the appointed individual has the authority to stand in the shoes of the original party and to manage the party's financial affairs. Probably the most common use of a power of attorney is to allow the appointed individual to write checks for the payment of bills and household expenses for the grantor. While in some states there is both a financial power of attorney and a health care power of attorney, the majority of states use the term "power of attorney" only to refer to financial matters. Therefore, for purposes of this chapter, assume that the phrase "power of attorney" refers only to a financial power of attorney.

A living will and health care proxy or living will and health care power of attorney and financial power of attorney are all effective only during the client's lifetime and cease being effective upon the client's death.

A **living trust**, also called an inter vivos trust—*inter vivos* is Latin for "within one's life"—is a trust that is created and becomes effective during the lifetime of the trustor(s) [also called settlor(s)]. Living trusts commonly provide that trustors

---

Probate
A general term for the entire process of administration of estates of dead persons, including those without wills, with court supervision.

Living Will
A written expression of a person's wishes to be allowed to die a natural death and not be kept alive by heroic or artificial methods.

Persistent Vegetative State (PVS)
A condition of patients with severe brain damage in whom a coma has progressed to a state of wakefulness without detectable awareness.

Health Care Proxy
A written statement authorizing an agent or surrogate to make medical treatment decisions for another in the event of the other's inability to do so.

Living Will and Health Care Proxy
A document that combines a living will and a health care proxy into one form, expresses the principal's wishes to be allowed to die a natural death, and appoints an agent to make medical treatment decisions on the principal's behalf.

Health Care Power of Attorney
A power of attorney for medical decisions; in it, the principal appoints an agent to make medical decisions when the principal is incapacitated.

Power of Attorney
A legal document that authorizes another person to act as the grantor's attorney-in-fact and agent; execution before a notary public is nearly always required.

Living Trust
Also called an inter vivos trust, (*inter vivos* is Latin for "within one's life") is a trust that is created and becomes effective during the lifetime of the trustor(s) [also called settlor(s)].

Revocable Living Trust
A trust created by a written declaration during the lifetime of the creator that can be amended or revoked during the creator's lifetime.

receive the benefits of the trust during their lifetimes; a distribution to the beneficiaries occurs following the death of the last trustor to die. **Revocable living trusts** are commonly used in estate planning and can be amended or revoked during the lifetime of the trustor(s) in accordance with the provisions in the initial trust document. In order to be effective, property must be placed into the trust with title handed over to the trustee. In order to effectively circumvent probate, virtually all of the client's assets must be placed into the trust to be distributed pursuant to the terms therein. Any assets that are not placed into the trust will either pass by operation of law to a designated beneficiary or co-owner or will have to go through probate.

EXAMPLE 1 _____

Mary and Tom Jones execute a living trust titled the "Jones Family Living Trust" and need to fund the trust with assets. Mary and Tom are the trustees of the trust. Their bank account is currently titled in their joint names. They will need to re-title their bank account as follows: "Tom Jones and Mary Jones, as Trustees of the Jones Family Living Trust." This designation reflects that the bank account is owned by the trust and that the trustees are responsible for administering the trust.

Pour-over Will
A will that leaves the testator's assets to a living trust, to be administered pursuant to the terms thereof.

When used in estate planning, living trusts must be accompanied by what legal professionals call a pour-over will. A **pour-over will** can be used by a person who has already executed a trust, and leaves all remaining property to the trust. The purpose of a pour-over will is to ensure that any assets that were left out of the trust will be placed into the trust and distributed in accordance with the terms provided in the trust. If probate assets were left out of the trust, a probate of the pour-over will is required in order to turn the missed assets over to the trustee for distribution pursuant to the trust terms. The reason for the name of this type of will is self-evident; like a pitcher pouring water into a glass, this will literally pour any assets that were missed into the trust.

Lawyers may be found guilty of malpractice if they assist a client by drafting a living trust but neglect to also draft a pour-over will. The pour-over will is meant to be there as a safeguard and must be executed after the execution of the living trust. This may seem like a picky requirement, but it is an important technicality. There has to be a trust in place to receive assets before a client can make the bequest to the trust under their will. If we go back to the previous analogy, there must be a glass (the trust) before water (the assets) can be poured into it.

■ INTERVIEWING THE CLIENT

Interviewing the client can be extremely pleasant in many circumstances. Estate planning and probate are generally non-adversarial areas of law. You are on the client's side, helping them to meet their objectives.

However, some clients do find it extremely emotional and difficult to even contemplate their eventual demise or the demise of those whom they love. Such clients must be treated with great care and delicacy. If you are unable to sympathize with emotional clients, this may not be the best area of law for you to work in. Just as many people fear and dread going to the doctor, some clients dread going to see a lawyer to discuss estate planning. Some are even superstitious that something may happen to them once they draft a will. Be aware that there is the potential for a broad range of feelings and attitudes in estate planning.

It is possible that you, as an experienced paralegal, will be assigned to do the client interview. If you are doing the interview alone, you may gather all of the client's information, but you must refrain from giving any legal advice. This means that you can take down clients' information and what they say they want, but you cannot tell clients what they *need*—you have to leave that to the attorney.

■ CHECKLIST

When interviewing the client it is extremely important to be thorough. A good way to make sure you address every point that needs to be addressed is to have a checklist. The checklist will ensure that you address every point even if you get off track or ask questions out of order. Very rarely does a client simply allow you to follow your own line of questions without changing the subject or bringing up other issues. Therefore, having a checklist is very beneficial.

The items that need to be included on the checklist will vary, to some extent, in accordance with state law. For example, some states allow individuals to express what they want to happen to their body under their will. Other states do not honor such intentions expressed under a will. Another example that varies by state is the appointment of a guardian under one's will. Normally, a will does not take effect until death but some states will honor the testator's express intentions regarding the appointment of a guardian under their will should the need for a guardian arise.

INTERVIEWING TIPS

- Maintain good eye contact with the client to show you are engaged and listening.
- Use a checklist to make sure all pertinent questions are asked.
- If asked a question that requires legal advice, do not answer the question even if you are sure you know the answer (doing so would be unauthorized practice of law). Instead, let the client know that you have noted the question and that the attorney will be in contact to provide the answer.

The following are some suggestions of things that should always be included on a checklist:

- ✓ Client's name, date of birth, and address
- ✓ Marital status
- ✓ Marital history
- ✓ Children's names and addresses
- ✓ Other beneficiaries' names and addresses
- ✓ Names of any deceased children and whether client has any children now living
- ✓ Names of any estranged family members and any family members whom client is disinheriting
- ✓ Family tree
- ✓ Complete list of assets (including real and personal property)
- ✓ To whom client wants to leave the estate
- ✓ Whom client wants to appoint as guardian of client's minor children, if any
- ✓ Whom client want to appoint as personal representative

The following are some additional items that may be required and/or customarily requested in some states:

- Social security number(s)
- Children's social security numbers
- Whether the client wants to be buried or cremated
- Appointment of a guardian of the client's person

Discuss with your supervising attorney whether the above information is necessary or appropriate to request from clients in your state. Many law firms use a client intake sheet when meeting with estate planning clients for the first time. Figure 3.1 contains an example of a very basic estate planning intake sheet to be completed by the client.

Figure 3.1 Estate Planning Intake Sheet

DATE: _____

Full Name: _____

Spouse's Name: _____ or N/A

Address: _____

_____

Home Phone: ( )_____

Cell Phone: ( )_____

Email Address:_____@_____

Please answer the following eleven questions prior to your consultation.

1. What is your marital status?

   Married or Single or Divorced or Widowed

2. Are you a resident of this state? Yes or No

3. Do you currently have an estate plan? Yes or No

   If yes, please provide details: _____

4. How many children do you have? _____

5. List the full name and birth date of each child.

Name of Child	Birth Date of Child

6. What documents do you think you want drafted? _____

7. Provide any additional information you think we should know.

_____

_____

_____

CONSULTATION CHECKLIST (To Be Completed by Interviewer):

- Real Property: _____
- IRA/401K: _____
- Insurance Policies: _____
- Bank Accounts: _____
- Stocks/Bonds: _____
- CDs: _____
- Disinheriting: _____
- Buried or Cremated: _____

ADDITIONAL NOTES:

Figure 3.2 depicts a very extensive estate planning intake sheet to be completed by the client.

Figure 3.2 Estate Planning Worksheet

PERSONAL INFORMATION

Client's Full Legal Name _____

Birth date _____ SS# _____ U.S. Citizen? _____

Home Address City State Zip _____

Home Telephone Cell Phone Number Business Telephone _____

Occupation Employer _____

Business Address City State Zip _____

E-mail Address _____ It is okay to communicate with me via my E-mail address.

☐ Divorced: Date of Dissolutions _____ ☐ Widowed: Date of Death _____

☐ Single ☐ Life Partner _____

Spouse's Full Legal Name _____

Birth date _____ SS# _____ US Citizen? _____

Home Address City State Zip _____

Home Telephone Cell Phone Number Business Telephone _____

Occupation Employer _____

Business Address City State Zip _____

E-mail Address ☐ It is okay to communicate with me via my E-mail address. _____

☐ Divorced: Date of Dissolution _____ ☐ Widowed: Date of Death _____

☐ Single ☐ Life Partner _____

CHILDREN AND/OR OTHER FAMILY MEMBERS OR BENEFICIARIES

Use full legal name:

Name	Birthdate	Relationship

OTHER RELATIVES:

Parents, Siblings, Others (if appropriate)

Name	Address	Relationship

IMPORTANT FAMILY QUESTIONS

Do you have a will, trust, or other estate planning documents? *Please furnish copies of these documents*	☐ Yes ☐ No
Are you making payments pursuant to a divorce or property settlement order? *Please furnish a copy*	☐ Yes ☐ No
If married, have you and your spouse signed a pre- or post-marriage contract? *Please furnish a copy*	☐ Yes ☐ No
Do you or any of your children or other beneficiaries have disabilities, serious health problems or other special needs? *If yes, please describe below*	☐ Yes ☐ No

Figure 3.2 (continued)

Do you own a business?	☐ Yes ☐ No
Do you own a long-term care (nursing home) insurance policy?	☐ Yes ☐ No
Do you own any property that is not community property?	☐ Yes ☐ No
Do you support any charitable organizations now that you wish to make provisions for at the time of your death? *If so, please explain below.*	☐ Yes ☐ No
Are you (or your spouse) currently the beneficiary of anyone else's trust? *If so, please explain below.*	☐ Yes ☐ No

INCOME/ASSET/LIABILITY INFORMATION

Please list your income/asset/liability information in the appropriate section below.
Attach additional pages, if necessary.

INCOME:

Earned Monthly Income from
Labor: _____

Monthly Social Security Income: _____

Monthly Pension Income: _____

Other Monthly Income: _____

_____

ASSETS:

REAL PROPERTY

Please list any interest in real estate including your family residence, vacation home, time-share or vacant land. (Please list manner in which title held—Joint Tenant, Community Property, Separate Property, Tenant in Common)

General Description and/or Address	Owner	Market Value	Equity

Total _____

PERSONAL PROPERTY

List separately only major personal effects such as jewelry, collections, antiques, furs, and all other valuable non-business personal property. *(Indicate type below and give a lump sum value for miscellaneous, less valuable items.)*

Type or Owner	Owner	Market Value

Total _____

Figure 3.2 (continued)

BANK AND SAVINGS ACCOUNTS

Checking Account "CA," Savings Account "SA," Certificate of Deposit "CD," Money Market "MM" (*indicate type below*). Do not include IRAs or 401(k)s here

Name of Institution and account no.	Type	Owner	Amount

Total _____

Note: If account is in your name (or your spouse's name) for the benefit of a minor, please specify and give minor's name.

STOCKS AND BONDS TYPE

List any and all stocks and bonds you own. If held in a brokerage account, lump them together under each account. (*Indicate type below.*)

Stocks, Bonds or Investment Accounts	Type	Acct. No.	Owner	Amount

Total _____

LIFE INSURANCE POLICES AND ANNUITIES

Term, whole life, split dollar, group life, annuity. **ADDITIONAL INFORMATION:** Insurance company, type, face amount (death benefit), whose life is insured, who owns the policy, the current beneficiaries, who pays the premium, and who is the life insurance agent.

_____

_____

_____

_____

Total _____

RETIREMENT PLANS

Pension (P), Profit Sharing (PS), H.R. 10, IRA, SEP. 401(K). **ADDITIONAL INFORMATION:** Describe the type of plan, the plan name, the current value of the plan, beneficiary designation and any other pertinent information.

_____

_____

_____

_____

Total _____

Figure 3.2 (continued)

BUSINESS INTERESTS

General and limited partnerships, sole proprietorships, privately owned corporations, professional corporations, oil interests, farm and ranch interests.

ADDITIONAL INFORMATION: Give a description of the interests, who has each interest, your ownership in the interests, and the estimated value of the interests.

_____

_____

_____

_____

Total _____

MONEY OWED TO YOU

Mortgages or promissory notes payable to you, or other money owed to you.

Date of Note	Maturity Date	Owed To	Current Balance

Total _____

ANTICIPATED INHERITANCE, GIFT, OR LAWSUIT JUDGMENT

Gifts or inheritances that you expect to receive at some time in the future, or money that you anticipate receiving through a judgment in a lawsuit. **Describe in appropriate detail**.

Description

_____

_____

_____

_____

Total estimated value _____

OTHER ASSETS

Other property is any property that you have that does not fit into any listed category.

Type	Owner	Value

Total _____

Figure 3.2 (continued)

SUMMARY OF VALUES

Amount*

ASSETS	Client's	Other's	Total Value
Real Property			
Furniture and Personal Effects			
Bank and Savings Accounts			
Stocks and Bonds `			
Life Insurance and Annuities			
Retirement Plans			
Business Interests			
Money Owed to You			
Anticipated Inheritance, Etc.			
Other Assets			
Total Assets:			

DESIGNATION INFORMATION

PERSONS TO ACT FOR YOU IF YOU ARE UNABLE TO SERVE AS GUARDIAN FOR MINOR CHILDREN

If you have any children under the age of 18, list in order of preference who would raise them and love them in a manner as close as possible to the way you would.

Name	Address and Phone Number	Relationship

TEMPORARY GUARDIAN FOR MINOR CHILDREN

Name	Address and Phone Number	Relationship

FINANCIAL DECISION MAKERS—POST-DEATH TRUSTEE

After your death, whom do you want making decisions regarding the management and distribution of your assets to your beneficiaries?

Name	Address and Phone Number	Relationship

(continued)

Figure 3.2 (continued)

HEALTH CARE DECISION MAKERS

HEALTH CARE: If you were unable to make decisions for yourself, whom would you want to make decisions for you with regard to your medical treatment?

Name	Address and Phone Number	Relationship
_____	_____	_____
_____	_____	_____
_____	_____	_____
_____	_____	_____
_____	_____	_____
_____	_____	_____

Do you want to provide that the moment of your death not be unnecessarily prolonged by artificial means or measures?	☐ Yes ☐ No
Do you want to provide that your organs and tissues be made available for transplant purposes?	☐ Yes ☐ No
Do you want to provide that your organs and tissues be made available for medical research?	☐ Yes ☐ No

---

Figure 3.3 depicts an estate planning checklist to be completed by the interviewing attorney or paralegal.

Figure 3.3

Date: _____

A. Client's and client's family's statistical information
   1. *Client:*
      Name:
      Address:
      Phone numbers:
      Social security number:
      Date of birth:
      Employer/income:
   2. *Spouse:*
      Name:
      Address:
      Phone numbers:
      Social security number:
      Date of birth:
      Employer/income:
      Date of marriage:
   3. *Children* (obtain statistical information for all children):
      Name:
      Address:
      Date of birth:
      Children who are married:
      Grandchildren:

Figure 3.3 (continued)

Children who are not children of the current spouse:

a. Who is the other parent?

b. Are there any children who have died?

c. Did they have any children?

d. Do you have any stepchildren?

4. *Other relatives:*

a. Parents (if appropriate):

Name:

Address:

Relationship:

b. Siblings:

Name:

Address:

Relationship:

c. Others (if appropriate):

Name:

Address:

Relationship:

5. *Prior marriage:*

Name:

Date marriage ended:

How marriage ended:

6. *Miscellaneous personal background:*

a. Relatives:

(1) Minors?

(2) Disabled? How?

(3) Disinherited? Why?

b. Documents:

(1) Prior will? Date?

(2) Trust?

(3) Prenuptial agreement?

c. Client:

(1) Health?

(2) Mental competence?

(3) Voluntarily acting?

B. Financial information

1. *Assets:*

a. Home:

Value:

Mortgage/liens:

Title:

b. Other real estate:

Addresses:

Value:

Mortgage/liens:

Title:

Figure 3.3 (continued)

    c. Bank accounts:
       Type:
       Where:
       Value:
       Title:
    d. Securities:
       Type:
       Where:
       Value:
       Title:
    e. Automobiles:
       Make:
       Model:
       Value:
       Title:
    f. Receipt of or anticipated substantial gift or inheritance?
       From whom?
       Value:
    g. Collectibles, artwork, antiques:
       Type:
       Where located:
       Value:
       Title:
    h. Other personal property:
       Type:
       Where located:
       Value:
       Title:
    i. Life insurance:
       Name of company:
       Type of policy:
       Title:
       Beneficiary:
       Insured's name:
       Value:
    j. Retirement plans:
       Type:
       Where located (company):
       Beneficiary:
       Value:
2. Debts:
  Creditors:
  Secured by party?
  Amount:

Figure 3.3 (continued)

> C. Client's plan
>   1. Will?
>   2. Codicil?
>   3. Trust?
>   4. Power of attorney?
>   5. Power of attorney for health care?
>   6. Living will?
>   7. To make gifts while living?

■ ORGANIZE THE INFORMATION

Once you have done the client interview and gathered the client's information, it is time to organize the information and utilize it to develop an estate plan. Determining which types of legal documents should be used for a given client is a job for the supervising attorney, since paralegals cannot make legal determinations or give legal advice.

■ DEVELOP AN ESTATE PLAN

Living Will

The attorney will take the client's information and, together with the clients, determine which combination of documents will best accomplish their needs and objectives. As previously discussed, most estate plans include a living will and a health care proxy, or a combination thereof. Clients must determine whom to appoint as their health care agent to make medical decisions on their behalf if they cannot make the decisions on their own. It is also extremely advisable that clients select an **alternate agent** so that if the first selection is unable to serve, there is someone else ready to take the job. If the agent appointed to serve is unable to do so and there is no appointed alternate, a guardianship proceeding will be necessary; the court will appoint a guardian who can make health care decisions on behalf of the incapacitated party.

Alternate Agent
An agent selected after the principal's first choice so that if the first selected agent is unavailable, there is someone else appointed to perform as agent.

Power of Attorney

Most estate plans will also include a power of attorney. The bulk of clients will execute a durable power of attorney that becomes effective immediately upon signing and remains effective after the client becomes incapacitated. However, there are situations where it may be advisable to use a *springing power of attorney* instead. A springing power of attorney becomes effective only upon determination by a doctor that the principal is incapacitated. One time when a springing power of attorney might be used is when the client does not have a close

Ethical Points to Remember

- Paralegals *can* prepare documents under the supervision of an attorney.
- Paralegals cannot give legal advice.
- Advising a client about which documents are needed constitutes giving legal advice.
- When a non-attorney gives legal advice, it is considered unauthorized practice of law, or *UPL*.
- Consequences for UPL can include civil liability, as well as fines and other penalties.

PARALEGAL PRACTICE TIPS

- *Always be sure to confirm the spelling of the client's name and the names of the client's family members. Do not be afraid to ask for the spelling if the client's handwriting is illegible.*
- *Always be sure to use the client's full legal name when drafting documents unless otherwise advised by your supervising attorney. If a client has written down that his name is "Joe," it is safe to assume that his legal name is probably Joseph. However, you should confirm this with the client before drafting any documents.*
- *Always proofread your documents and check the spelling of all names prior to giving your work to the attorney to review. Your supervising attorney will be checking for legal inaccuracies and may not notice a name misspelling if a common alternate spelling is used. Such mistakes are easily fixed but embarrassing and reflect poorly on the firm when pointed out by the client.*

loved one and is appointing someone only out of necessity—i.e., because he or she has to appoint someone and the appointee is better than anyone else the client can think of. In that instance, the principal does not have anyone whom he or she trusts implicitly, but recognizes that it is necessary to have a document in place appointing *someone* should it be needed. Another variation of this scenario is when widowed or divorced clients do not totally trust their children and do not want them having immediate access to their funds. However, the same clients *would* want their children to act as attorneys-in-fact should they truly become incapacitated. In such a case, a springing power of attorney may be the best choice because it appoints an agent in the event one is truly needed at a future point in time.

Will or Revocable Living Trust with Pour-over Will

The big decision to be made often focuses on whether the client will simply have a will, or instead will have a pour-over will and a revocable living trust ("living trust"). In some jurisdictions it is fairly customary to use the latter option; in other jurisdictions, only very wealthy clients or those with unusual circumstances opt to have a living trust.

Tax planning can be done using either document, so the necessity of tax planning is generally *not* the determining factor for whether a will or a living will with a pour-over will should be used.

The majority of clients seeking a living trust desire to avoid probate. Correct utilization of a living trust and pour-over will to accomplish this option requires that virtually all of the client's assets be re-titled into the name of the trust. For clients with a lot of assets, this can be a daunting task. If an asset is missed, or not put into the trust, it can result in the necessity of a probate proceeding just to transfer the asset into the trust to be distributed pursuant to the trust terms. If clients are not well organized or are elderly and have difficulty getting around, the use of a living trust may not be ideal.

If a married couple with wills has only joint assets, a probate proceeding will not be necessary upon the first death. Clients should be made aware of this fact because it can impact their decision on whether a living trust is really desirable.

Cost can also be an influential factor for some clients. Living trusts are more complex than wills and require several accompanying forms; therefore, they are more costly to prepare than wills alone.

Finally, some parties have blended families or families where the children do not get along. Trustees of living trusts are not under court supervision and can breach their fiduciary duties and do "whatever they want" with the trust funds. The other beneficiaries are then left with suing as their only possible recourse. If the children do not all get along or if trust is a factor, clients may opt for a will to ensure that that written directives are, in fact, followed following the client's death.

■ ETHICAL CONCERNS UNIQUE TO ESTATE PLANNING

Due to the fact that estate planning involves the lifetime management and distribution upon death of clients' assets, there are a number of ethical concerns that can arise. Sadly, greed can bring out the worst in people. The following ethical issues are largely unique to this area of the law.

Avoiding Undue Influence by Family Members

In the Real-Life Scenario at the beginning of this chapter, the client's daughter accompanied the client to the consultation and was attempting to exert influence over her mother's estate planning choices. The attorney quickly identified what was going on and put a stop to it. In the given example, everything worked out because the client seemed relieved and the daughter backed down. However, situations like this occur far too often and do not always end well.

Attorneys owe a duty as advisors to their clients to help them to achieve their own individual objectives, free from the influence and control of others. However, a new client does not always feel comfortable with the attorney at first and may want the moral support of having a close relative with them in the consultation. Estate planning can, after all, be an emotional topic for many. Therefore, the attorney must engage in a balancing act to factor in these different considerations.

If the client clearly wants the family member there and the family member politely sits and listens while the client talks, the attorney may feel comfortable that the person is just there as moral support and that there is no undue influence. If, on the other hand, the client has several children and is indicating that he or she wants to leave the entire estate to the accompanying child while excluding the others, this is a strong indication that there may be undue influence. As a paralegal, you should be aware of and on guard against the possibility of undue influence by family members. If you notice or observe something that makes you uncomfortable, be sure to bring it to the attention of your supervising attorney, who will ultimately decide how to handle the situation.

Caregiver Concerns

With a growing aging population and so many people spreading out and living in different states, many elderly people today rely on assistance from caregivers. Those who do rely on aid from caregivers may also receive rides from their caregivers to everywhere they need to go—including the lawyer's office. Be very cautious whenever a client arrives accompanied by a caregiver; make sure that the caregiver does not appear to be exerting influence or control over the elderly client. Do not allow the caregiver to accompany the client into the room to consult with the attorney. If clients express a wish to leave their estate or even a portion of it to their caregivers, this should raise a red flag. A nominal gift for the caregiver with the balance to family members may be appropriate if prompted solely by the client, with the caregiver being unaware. However, if the client is seeking to leave the entire estate or a large portion of it to the caregiver, this can be an indication that the caregiver is exerting undue influence or engaging in elder abuse; that the client lacks mental capacity to sign legal documents; or both. **Elder abuse** is a growing problem in the United States and is any form of mistreatment that results in harm or loss to an older person. In response to this problem, many states have enacted elder abuse laws to protect against the exploitation of vulnerable adults and punish those who abuse the elderly. It is important for attorneys and other legal staff to be aware of these special concerns when a client has a close relationship with a caregiver and seeks to include the caregiver on estate planning documents.

Elder Abuse
Any form of mistreatment that results in harm or loss to an older person

Gifting to Attorney or Staff Is Unethical

It is highly unethical for an attorney or other legal professional to request or accept a testamentary or lifetime gift from a client. (This excludes nominal gifts given by clients to legal professionals, such as flowers or candy during the holiday season.) Wills must not be drafted to include monetary bequests to the attorney or other staff members, whether it is the client's idea or not. In the rare circumstance where there is, in fact, a close personal relationship between a client and the attorney or a staff member and the client insists on making a gift, the client should be directed to have an independent attorney draft the will so that there is no chance of undue influence, control, or self-dealing by the recipient attorney or staff member.

■ CONCLUSION

In conclusion, the client interview is a time not only to develop a rapport with the client, but also to gather all of the essential information and get a feel for the client's needs and objectives. There are a number of ethical concerns that can arise during the client interview, and it is important for legal professionals to make sure that others are not unduly influencing the client. If the supervising attorney is not in the meeting, the paralegal should refrain from telling the client what documents are needed, because this can be construed as giving legal advice, which is prohibited when done by a non-attorney. The attorney can then analyze the information and see what combination of documents best meets the client's needs in order to develop a comprehensive estate plan. The various components of an estate plan are discussed in much greater detail in later chapters.

CONCEPT REVIEW AND REINFORCEMENT

KEY TERMS

Estate Plan   50
Last Will and Testament   50
Probate   51
Living Will   51
Persistent Vegetative State
   (PVS)   51

Health Care Proxy   51
Living Will and Health Care
   Proxy   51
Health Care Power of
   Attorney   51
Power of Attorney   51

Living Trust   51
Revocable Living Trust   52
Pour-over Will   52
Alternate Agent   63
Elder Abuse   65

REVIEW QUESTIONS

1. Is it a good idea to appoint more than one agent on a living will? Why or why not?
2. What is the purpose of executing a power of attorney?
3. What is the difference between a regular durable power of attorney and a springing power of attorney?
4. List the possible components of an estate plan.
5. Explain when a revocable living trust might be used.
6. Describe a paralegal's role in providing estate planning assistance to a client.

7. What do the ethical rules prohibit a paralegal from doing?
8. What document must accompany a revocable living trust?
9. Is it permissible for clients to give gifts to attorneys or other legal staff members?
10. What concerns may arise when a third party accompanies a client to the initial estate planning consultation?

BUILDING YOUR PARALEGAL SKILLS

CRITICAL THINKING EXERCISES

1. A client walks into the office when the attorney is out and says that he wants to execute a living will to leave everything to his children. Do you see any problems with this? How might you handle the situation?

2. Describe a scenario in which it would be more appropriate to use a springing power of attorney than a durable power of attorney.
3. If an elderly gentleman arrived at your office for an estate planning consultation holding the hand of his 30-year-old "caregiver," how would you handle the situation? What would you think and do?

PARALEGAL PRACTICE

1. _____

MEMORANDUM

To: Paralegal
From: Supervising Attorney
Client: N/A
Re: Estate Planning Checklist

We are doing a lot of estate planning and it would be very helpful to have a checklist to be used as a guideline for client interviews. Please prepare a checklist in draft form and send it to me.

2. _____

MEMORANDUM

To: Paralegal
From: Supervising Attorney
Client: N/A
Re: Estate Planning Intake Form

Our office would really benefit from having an intake form to pass out to new estate planning clients. The clients could then write some of the needed information on the form before the consultation.

Please prepare the document.

CASE FOR CONSIDERATION

CASE #1:

THE STATE OF SOUTH CAROLINA

In the Supreme Court

_____

John Doe, Alias, Petitioner,

v.

Charles M. Condon, Attorney General for the State of South Carolina, Respondent.

_____

IN THE ORIGINAL JURISDICTION

_____

Opinion No. 25138
Submitted May 23, 2000—Filed June 5, 2000

_____

PER CURIAM: Petitioner sought to have the Court accept this matter in its original jurisdiction to determine whether certain tasks performed by a non-attorney employee in a law firm constitute the unauthorized practice of law. Specifically, Petitioner asks (1) whether it is the unauthorized practice of law for a paralegal employed by an attorney to conduct informational seminars for the general public on wills and trusts without the attorney being present; (2) whether it is the unauthorized practice of law for a paralegal employed by an attorney to meet with clients privately at the attorney's office, answer general questions about wills and trusts, and gather basic information from clients; and (3) whether a paralegal can receive compensation from the paralegal's law firm/employer through a profit-sharing arrangement based upon the volume and type of cases the paralegal handles. The Office of the Attorney General filed a return opposing the petition for original jurisdiction.

The Court invoked its original jurisdiction to determine whether the paralegal's activities constituted the unauthorized practice of law, and, pursuant to S.C. Code Ann. § 14-3-340 (1976), John W. Kittredge was appointed as referee to make findings of fact and conclusions of law concerning this matter. A hearing was held and the referee issued proposed findings and recommendations.

We adopt the referee's findings and recommendations attached to this opinion and hold that a non-lawyer employee conducting unsupervised legal presentations for the public and answering legal questions for the public or for clients of the attorney/employer engages in the unauthorized practice of law. *See State v. Despain*, 319 S.C. 317, 460 S.E.2d 576 (1995). We further hold that a proposed fee arrangement which compensates non-lawyer employees based upon the number and volume of cases the non-lawyer employee handles for an attorney violates the ethical rules against fee-splitting with non-lawyer employees. Rule 5.4 of the Rules of Professional Conduct, Rule 407, SCACR.

THE STATE OF SOUTH CAROLINA

In the Supreme Court

IN THE ORIGINAL JURISDICTION

of the Supreme Court

John Doe, Alias, Petitioner,

v.

Charles M. Condon, Attorney General for the State of South Carolina Respondent.

PROPOSED FINDINGS AND RECOMMENDATIONS OF THE REFEREE

This is a declaratory judgment action in the Supreme Court's original jurisdiction. The Court referred this matter to me as Referee. Petitioner, a paralegal, has submitted a generalized list of tasks he wishes to perform and has inquired whether performing them constitutes the unauthorized practice of law. Petitioner also seeks a determination of the propriety of his proposed fee splitting arrangement with his attorney-employer. Despite my repeated offers for an evidentiary hearing, neither party requested a hearing. The record before me is sufficient to address and resolve whether the activities in question constitute the unauthorized practice of law.

I find that a paralegal conducting unsupervised legal presentations for the public and answering legal questions from the audience engages in the unauthorized practice of law. Further, I find that a paralegal meeting individually with clients to answer estate planning questions engages in the unauthorized practice of law. Finally, I find the proposed fee arrangement is improper and violates the ethical prohibition against fee splitting.

BACKGROUND

Petitioner submitted the following questions to the Court:

1. Is it the unauthorized practice of law for a paralegal employed by an attorney to conduct educational seminars for the general public, to disseminate general information about wills and trusts, including specifically a fair and balanced emphasis on living trusts, including answering general questions, without the attorney being present at the seminar as long as the seminar is sponsored by the attorney's law firm and the attorney has reviewed and approved the format, materials and presentation to be made for content, truthfulness and fairness?

2. Is it the unauthorized practice of law for a paralegal employed by an attorney to meet with clients privately in the law office for the purpose of answering general questions about wills, trusts, including specifically living trusts, and estate planning in general,

and to gather basic information from said clients for such purposes as long as it is done under the attorney's direction, and the clients have a follow-up interview and meeting with the attorney who would have primary responsibility for legal decisions?

3. Can a paralegal receive compensation from the law firm he is employed by, through a profit-sharing arrangement, which would be based upon the volume and type of cases the paralegal handled?

DISCUSSION

To protect the public from unsound legal advice and incompetent representation, South Carolina, like other jurisdictions, limits the practice of law to licensed attorneys. *S.C. Code Ann.* § 40-5-310 (1976). While case law provides general guidelines as to what constitutes the practice of law, courts are hesitant to define its exact boundaries. Thus, the analysis in 'practice of law' cases is necessarily fact-driven. The Supreme Court has specifically avoided addressing hypothetical situations, preferring instead to determine what constitutes the unauthorized practice of law on a case by case basis. *In Re Unauthorized Practice of Law Rules Proposed by the South Carolina Bar*, 309 S.C. 304, 422 S.E.2d 123 (S.C. 1992). I find that Petitioner's proposed actions constitute the unauthorized practice of law and that the proposed fee agreement violates the ethical prohibition against fee splitting.

Our Supreme Court has set forth a succinct standard of the proper role of paralegals:

The activities of a paralegal do not constitute the practice of law as long as they are limited to work of a preparatory nature, such as legal research, investigation, or the composition of legal documents, which enable the licensed attorney-employer to carry a given matter to a conclusion through his own examination, approval or additional effort. *Matter of Easler*, 275 S.C. 400, 272 S.E.2d 32, 33 (S.C. 1980).

While the important support function of paralegals has increased through the years, the *Easler* guidelines stand the test of time. As envisioned in *Easler*, the paralegal plays a supporting role to the supervising attorney. Here, the roles are reversed. The attorney would support the paralegal. Petitioner would play the lead role, with no meaningful attorney supervision and the attorney's presence and involvement only surfaces on the back end. Meaningful attorney supervision must be present throughout the process. The line between what is and what is not permissible conduct by a non-attorney is oftentimes "unclear" and is a potential trap for the unsuspecting client. *State v. Buyers Service Co.. Inc.*, 292 S.C. 426, 357 S.E.2d. 15, 17 (S.C. 1987).

The conduct of the paralegal contemplated here clearly crosses the line into the unauthorized practice of law. It is well settled that a paralegal may not give legal advice, consult, offer legal explanations, or make legal recommendations. *State v. Despain*, 319 S.C. 317, 460 S.E.2d 576 (S.C. 1995).

A. EDUCATIONAL SEMINARS

Petitioner intends to conduct unsupervised "wills and trusts" seminars for the public, "emphasizing" living trusts during the course of his presentation. Petitioner also plans to answer estate planning questions from the audience. I find Petitioner's proposed conduct constitutes the unauthorized practice of law.

I find, as other courts have, that the very structure of such "educational" legal seminars suggests that the presenter will actually be giving legal advice on legal matters. *See, In Re Mid America Living Trust Assoc. Inc.*, 927 S.W. 2d 855 (Mo. 1996); *People v. Volk*, 805 P.2d 1116 (Colo. 1991); *Oregon State Bar v. John H. Miller & Co.*, 385 P.2d 181 (Or. 1963). At the very least, Petitioner will implicitly advise participants that they require estate planning services. Whether a will or trust is appropriate in any given situation is a function of legal judgment. To be sure, advising a potential client on his or her need for a living trust (or other particular estate planning instrument or device) fits squarely within the practice of law. These matters cry out for the exercise of professional judgment by a licensed attorney. Thus, in conducting these informational seminars, Petitioner would engage in the unauthorized practice of law as a non-attorney offering legal advice.

Petitioner plans to answer "general" questions during his presentation. I have reviewed the Estate Planning Summary submitted by Petitioner and his attorney-employer. This summary sets forth the subject matter to be covered by the paralegal. Petitioner would present information on, among other things, revocable trusts, irrevocable living trusts, credit shelter trusts, qualified terminable interest property trusts, charitable remainder trusts, qualified personal residence trusts, grantor retained annuity trusts, grantor retained unitrusts and charitable lead trusts. It is difficult to imagine such specific estate planning devices eliciting "general" questions or a scenario in which the exercise of legal judgment would not be involved. It is, after all, a legal seminar, apparently for the purpose of soliciting business.[1] To suggest that some "plan" would anticipate all possible questions with predetermined nonlegal responses is specious. And so complex is this area of law that many states, including South Carolina, have established stringent standards for an attorney to receive the designation of "specialist" in Estate Planning and Probate Law. SCACR, Part IV, Appendices D and E. This is the practice of law.

I fully recognize the prevailing popularity of "financial planners" and others "jump[ing] on the estate planning bandwagon." (Estate Planning Summary submitted by Petitioner's attorney employer, p. 1). This trend in no way affects the decision before the Court. This paralegal would not be presenting the estate planning seminar as a financial planner. This seminar would be conspicuously sponsored by the paralegal's attorney-employer. The attorney's law firm is prominently displayed in the brochure submitted, e.g., name, address, telephone number, and "Firm Profile." In promoting the law firm and representing to the public the "legal" nature of the seminar, neither the paralegal nor his attorney-employer can escape the prohibition against the unauthorized practice of law.

B. INITIAL CLIENT INTERVIEW

Petitioner intends to gather client information and answer general estate planning questions during his proposed "initial client interviews." While Petitioner may properly compile client information, Petitioner may not answer estate planning questions. *See Matter of Easler*, supra. Petitioner's answering legal questions would constitute the unauthorized practice of law for the reasons stated above. While the law firm in which

Petitioner is employed plans to direct clients to an attorney for "follow-up" consultations, a paralegal may not give legal advice in any event. Moreover, permissible preparatory tasks must be performed while under the attorney's supervision. The proposed after the fact attorney review comes too late.

C. COMPENSATION

Petitioner's law firm intends to compensate him based upon the volume and types of cases he "handles." A paralegal, of course, may not "handle" any case.[2] This fee arrangement directly violates Rule 5.4 of the Rules of Professional conduct, SCACR 407.[3] This limitation serves to "discourage the unauthorized practice of law by lay persons and to prevent a non-lawyer from acquiring a vested pecuniary interest in an attorney's disposition of a case that could possibly take preeminence over a client's best interest." *Matter of Anonymous Member of the S.C. Bar*, 295 S.C. 25, 26, 367 S.E.2d 17, 18 (S.C. 1998). This compensation proposal arrangement coupled with Petitioner's desire to market the law firm's services via the educational seminars and meet individually with clients creates a situation ripe for abuse. Indeed, the proposal by Petitioner presents the very evil Rule 5.4 was designed to avoid. Accordingly, I find Petitioner's proposed compensation plan violates both the letter and the spirit of Rule 5.4 prohibiting fee splitting with non-attorneys.

Recommendations

1. Offering legal presentations for the general public constitutes the practice of law.
2. Answering estate planning questions in the context of legal seminars or in private client interviews constitutes the practice of law.
3. Fee sharing arrangements with non-attorneys based on volume and cases "handled" by a paralegal violates Rule 5.4, Rules of Professional Conduct, SCACR 407.

RESPECTFULLY SUBMITTED.

John W. Kittredge Referee

Case Questions

1. Does offering estate planning seminars constitute the practice of law in South Carolina?
2. Discuss how this case impacts paralegals doing estate planning work in South Carolina.
3. Do you agree with the results of this case? Why or why not?

FORMS TO ACCOMPANY PARALEGAL PRACTICE

Students are instructed to prepare their own forms in this chapter's assignments, so there are no accompanying forms for this chapter.

CHAPTER 4

Advance Directives

A REAL-LIFE SCENARIO

In great distress, the daughter of a sixty-year-old man called an attorney. Her father was in the hospital, unconscious, with a wide variety of very serious ailments. The client lived in Colorado; her father lived in Arizona. There were also three other children, all living in other states. The man apparently did not take care of himself physically, and also had not bothered to execute any estate planning documents. He did not have a living will or a power of attorney. This presented two problems: the children were not permitted to make medical decisions or financial decisions on the sick man's behalf.

The doctors were providing care, but the children were given very limited information about the man's health status. Further, although there was money in the bank with which his medical bills and mortgage could have been paid, no one was able to access the money. In order to take care of their father and save his assets, the four children each had to pitch in and take turns paying his bills each month until the client could be appointed as guardian and conservator. The family also had to front over three thousand dollars ($3,000) for legal fees to pay for the guardianship

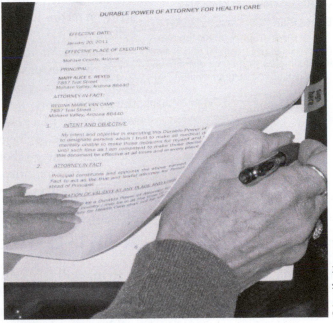

© Jennifer Montante

CHAPTER OBJECTIVES:

1. Define advance directive.
2. Understand the purpose of executing a living will.
3. Understand the purpose of executing a health care proxy.
4. Describe why living wills and health care proxies are often combined into one form.
5. Understand the purpose of executing a power of attorney.
6. Describe the different types of powers of attorney.
7. List the powers that are commonly granted under a power of attorney.
8. Discuss the reasons why a principal may wish to revoke a power of attorney.
9. Describe what it means to be a fiduciary.
10. Describe the difference between a living will and a power of attorney.

and conservatorship proceeding. The financial difficulty placed upon the four children could have been avoided if the man had executed a living will and health care proxy and a power of attorney, which are simple and readily available legal documents. No value can be placed on the time, effort, turmoil, and heartache that the man would have saved his family by executing advance directives.

■ INTRODUCTION

The foregoing example demonstrates the need to have advance directives in place. **Advance directives** are documents used to inform family, friends, and medical personnel about the kind of medical care and treatment a person desires if he or she becomes terminally ill or otherwise incapacitated and to appoint a person to make sure those wishes are carried out. Every **estate plan** should include both a living will and health care proxy and a power of attorney. The purpose of a living will and health care proxy is to declare one's desire not to be kept alive through artificial means and to appoint an agent to make medical decisions on the signer's behalf.

A power of attorney is a legal document that authorizes another person to act as the grantor's attorney-in-fact and agent. For all intents and purposes, this means that the appointed individual has the authority to stand in the shoes of the original party and to manage his or her financial affairs. Probably the most common use of a power of attorney is to allow the appointed individual to write checks for the payment of bills and household expenses for the grantor. While in some states there is both a financial power of attorney and a health care power of attorney, the majority of states use the term "power of attorney" only to refer to financial matters. Therefore, for purposes of this chapter, assume that "power of attorney" is referring only to a financial power of attorney.

■ LIVING WILL AND HEALTH CARE PROXY

A **living will** is a written expression of a person's wishes to be allowed to die a natural death and not be kept alive by heroic or artificial methods. Other names for a living will are directive to physicians, health care declaration, and medical directive. Living wills often direct the extent and type of medical treatment a person wishes to receive if he or she is in a persistent vegetative state (PVS). A **persistent vegetative state (PVS)** is a condition of patients with severe brain damage in whom a coma has progressed to a state of wakefulness without detectable awareness. It is a diagnosis of some uncertainty in that it deals with a syndrome. Figure 4.1 contains a sample living will for Shirley Smith from the Hypothetical Family. Under her living will, Shirley appoints Robert Smith as her health care agent and Jane Smith as her alternate agent.

A **health care proxy** is a written statement authorizing an agent or surrogate to make medical treatment decisions for another in the event of the other's inability to do so. A health care proxy does not take effect until or unless the person becomes unable to make his or her own medical decisions. A **living will and health care proxy** combines the two forms into one by expressing the person's wishes to be allowed to die a natural death AND appointing an agent to make medical treatment decisions on the person's behalf. For example, New York State uses a living will and health care proxy similar to the one depicted in Figure 4.2.

Most states use the terms "living will," "health care proxy," and/or a combination of the two for these purposes, but some states use a health care power of

Advance Directives
Documents used to inform family, friends, and medical personnel about the kind of medical care and treatment a person desires if he or she becomes terminally ill or otherwise incapacitated and to appoint a person to make sure those wishes are carried out.

Estate Plan
A plan made to provide for the maker's physical and financial needs during lifetime, as well as the distribution of the maker's estate upon death.

Living Will
A written expression of a person's wishes to be allowed to die a natural death and not be kept alive by heroic or artificial methods.

Persistent Vegetative State (PVS)
A condition of patients with severe brain damage in whom a coma has progressed to a state of wakefulness without detectable awareness. It is a diagnosis of some uncertainty in that it deals with a syndrome.

Health Care Proxy
A written statement authorizing an agent or surrogate to make medical treatment decisions for another in the event of the other's inability to do so.

Living Will and Health Care Proxy
A legal document that combines a living will with a health care proxy into one form by expressing the principal's wishes to be allowed to die a natural death and appointing an agent to make medical treatment decisions on the principal's behalf.

Figure 4.1 Sample Living Will

I, **SHIRLEY SMITH**, having an address at 121 Oak Street, Sample City, Sample State 12345, and an adult of sound and disposing mind and memory, not acting under duress, menace, fraud or undue influence of any person, do make, publish and declare this to be my Living Will to supplement all other wills I may execute and to be used in the event that I am unconscious or mentally incapacitated and, at the same time, have a catastrophic medical condition.

1. Declaration of Intent.

I realize that, when I am conscious and functioning normally with full mental facilities, I have a legal right to accept or reject medical treatment offered to me by doctors, hospitals or other medical instrumentalities. It is my intent with this Living Will to express my commitment and to designate persons who are legally empowered to act for me when I am unconscious or mentally incapacitated, with full authority from me to make medical decisions for me and to accept or reject medical treatment. I rely on the common law and desire that this Living Will be enforced even if I am in a state of the United States that has not adopted specific statutes related to the enforcement of Living Wills.

Further, my objective in executing this Living Will is to allow persons appointed by me in this document to withdraw medical care and administer pain-killing drugs when two doctors determine that my brain is no longer functioning or is irrevocably damaged, or when disease or accident places me in a condition where I am irrevocably dying, or when disease or accident has impaired my mind and body where I can no longer function as a normal human being with a standard of life which would not endear me to other human beings. I intend that this document be effective at all times and in every place in this world.

2. Purpose.

The purpose of this Living Will is to prevent my remaining assets from being used to unnecessarily prolong my life, so that they may be used instead to benefit my spouse and children, if any, and other heirs and devisees who benefit from my worldly estate. Also, I desire to avoid the heartache to my loved ones of an extended illness and to avoid additional pain and suffering to myself through whatever senses remain. In the unlikely event that this instrument may not be legally binding in the jurisdiction where I may be terminally ill, then you who care for me will, I hope, feel morally bound to follow its mandate. It is my decision, not yours, and it is made after careful consideration.

3. Instruction.

If it is ever determined by competent medical evidence, to the satisfaction of the persons designated below, that my body is substantially damaged, deteriorated, destroyed or in a tenuous condition through accident, illness or age, and that I have reached the point where there is no reasonable expectation of recovery from physical or mental disability even with the aid of artificial means or heroic measures, such as respirators, transfusions, electric shock treatments, or instruments to prolong heart beat (i.e. code arrest mechanisms, artificial respirators, heart massage by manual or mechanical methods, drugs or potent nature), intravenous feedings, or other measures, I request that all such life-prolonging means and measures be withdrawn or withheld from my body so that I may die with dignity. I further request that medication be mercifully administered to me for terminal suffering, even if it hastens the moment of death. I do not fear death as much as I fear the indignity of deterioration, dependence and hopeless pain.

I consider myself in a tenuous condition if I have an incurable or irreversible physical condition that, in reasonable medical probability, will result in death unless extraordinary medical measures are used. I consider as extraordinary medical measures all medication, surgical procedures, mechanical or electrical devices that will sustain, restore or supplant a vital bodily function. A measure is extraordinary if employing it would not offer a reasonable medical probability of returning me to cognitive, sapient existence and would serve only to postpone the moment of death. I do not consider medical or surgical procedures to alleviate pain or discomfort prohibitive procedures under this Living Will.

4. Mechanics of Implementation.

In order to implement the Living Will, my family physician along with one consulting physician shall make a finding that

4.a. I am unconscious, mentally incompetent or deranged, senile, insane or otherwise in an abnormal mental condition where I am not reasonably able to make decisions of my own.

4.b. Through accident, disease, nervous system, or otherwise, I have an irreversible condition resulting in (1) a brain that is dead, (2) a brain that is damaged to the point where I will not be able to reasonably enjoy a normal life, (3) a body with damaged organs or parts that will prevent me from enjoying the quality of productive life to which I am accustomed, or (4) a combination of all of these which will prevent me from enjoying the productive life to which I am accustomed.

(continued)

Figure 4.1 (continued)

If my family physician is not available, then two attending physicians may concur with the consulting physician in the finding. If three physicians are not immediately available, then two may concur.

The findings of the physicians will be written on my patient chart, or on a dated piece of paper to be placed in my patient file.

Thereupon the representative I have first designated in this Living Will shall concur and evidence that concurrence in writing on the patient chart or otherwise on the dated paper with the physicians written findings. If my first designated representative or the next is not readily available then whichever one is the most readily available shall sign an affirmation of the decision.

If my representative is not physically available, concurrence may be affirmed by (1) two witnesses over the phone, with those witnesses evidencing the consent by writing this in the patient chart or on the dated paper concerning the physicians written findings, or (2) by telegram or other means used for transmitting the written language, and a copy of this shall be placed in my medical files.

Once these findings and my representative's decisions have been thus memorialized, I shall be placed in a private room. My family and friends shall be summoned. The physician shall give me no further medical care or life aids such as food and water, except that morphine and other pain-killing or tranquilizing drugs shall be liberally administered even if they accelerate the moment of death. My family and friends shall be left alone with me, except for a doctor or nurse who will assist in keeping my physically clean and presentable until the moment of my passing.

If my doctors or representatives are unaware of these mechanics, I consent to any reasonable alternative method. My purpose in detailing these mechanics is to assist in providing my physicians and representatives with a reasonable method of carefully documenting what they have done to avoid later misunderstanding.

The findings of my doctors and the decision of my representative, once written, shall not be subject to attack by anyone at any later date.

5. **Persons Designated to Make Decisions.**

I give the following persons, singly in the order indicated or acting together, the power to make this decision:

Primary Decision Maker:

ROBERT SMITH, residing at 125 Oak Street, Sample City, Sample State 12345.

Alternate Decision Maker:

JANE SMITH, residing at 123 Oak Street, Sample City, Sample State 12345.

Neither the attending physician nor the hospital is required to determine the reason for the absence of persons I may have listed first in the order of priority above. Whichever one of my family representatives appears will take the responsibility of making an effort to locate the persons designated with higher priority. However, I trust in the judgment of all the persons named and, if they are unable to contact the person of higher priority, I will trust any of the persons named above who are there to make the necessary decisions. I know that whoever makes the decisions will have made every effort to notify all the other persons to obtain their concurrence and, if they cannot contact them within the time required by the emergency or if they cannot get concurrence of all parties, they have the authority to and will make the necessary decisions.

These persons are given a special power of attorney to act for me during any incapacity to make all decisions with regard to my medical treatment that I could have make had I been conscious and mentally able. I designate these persons also as my guardians ad litem and guardians of my person to sign all documents and bring any legal proceeding that may be necessary to exercise the power and authority vested in them by this Living Will, including the power to bring court proceedings for injunctive relief, damages, or other relief necessary to carry out my wishes expressed in this Living Will. It is my intent that the persons designated act quickly and without the necessity of court proceedings; however, if any doctor, hospital or other medical institution fails to carry out the instructions of my Living Will and the decisions of the persons I have designated to carry out my instructions, then the persons designated to make the decisions are directed to bring immediate court proceedings to enforce this Living Will. I direct that this Living Will be implemented by the persons designated and the attending doctors acting together without the necessity of consulting courts, administrative bodies or hospital committees.

6. **Protection for Persons Designated and those Assisting.**

As further evidence of my convictions as expressed in this Living Will, I direct that the assets of my estate and my insurance be used to hold harmless form any liability the persons designated and any doctor, hospital or other medical instrumentality that assists in carrying out (a) my instructions expressed in this Living Will and (b) the decision and instructions of the persons designated by me to carry out my instructions.

Figure 4.1 (continued)

My estate and my insurance shall also be committed to pay any attorney's fees, court costs or any other expenses associated with court proceedings to carry out my instructions expressed in this Living Will and the decisions of the persons I have designated to carry out these wishes and to defend anyone who assists in carrying out these instructions. All doctors, medical personnel, hospitals and other medical instrumentalities shall not be liable for any act complying with this Living Will in good faith, except acts of gross negligence or willful misconduct.

IN WITNESS WHEREOF, I have signed this document this date: __December 27__, 2011.

Shirley Smith
_____
SHIRLEY SMITH

ACKNOWLEDGEMENT OF WITNESSES

Michael Pearson
_____
Witness Signature
Michael Pearson
_____
Witness Name (Printed)

1001 Reed Drive
_____
Sample City, Sample State 12345
_____

Witness Address

Maggy Pearson
_____
Witness Signature
Maggy Pearson
_____
Witness Name (Printed)

1001 Reed Drive
_____
Sample City, Sample State 12345
_____

Witness Address

This instrument was on the above date signed by the above-named Signator in our presence and published and declared to be the Signator's Living Will. At the Signator's request and in the presence of the Signator and in the presence of each other, we have signed below as witnesses thereto. WE ALSO AFFIRM THAT WE ARE NOT RELATED TO THE SIGNATOR BY BLOOD OR MARRIAGE AND ARE NOT INVOLVED WITH THE MEDICAL CARE OF THE SIGNATOR.

Figure 4.2 Sample Living Will and Health Care Proxy for Joe Client

If I am persistently unconscious, or if I am brain dead, or if there is no reasonable expectation of my recovery from a seriously incapacitating or terminal illness or condition, or if I am suffering from a disease or condition in which thought, purposeful action, social interaction, and awareness of self and environment are absent, I direct that my attending physician and other health care suppliers withhold or withdraw medical procedures that merely sustain life or prolong the dying process. Such procedures include, among others, heart-lung resuscitation, antibiotics, dialysis, mechanical ventilator, chemotherapy, radiation therapy, and all other "life-prolonging" medical or surgical procedures that are merely intended to keep me alive without reasonable hope of improving my condition or curing my illness or injury.

_____

_____

PLEASE NOTE: If, at some future time, you are suffering from one of the terminal conditions described above and cannot make decisions for yourself, Sample State law prohibits withholding artificial nutrition and hydration from you, unless you have already made your wishes known.
    IF I CANNOT EAT OR DRINK ENOUGH BECAUSE OF MY IRREVERSIBLE MEDICAL CONDITIONS (**INITIAL** ONE OF THE FOLLOWING):

_____ I DO

_____ I DO NOT

WANT ARTIFICIAL NUTRITION (INTRAVENOUS OR TUBE FEEDING) AND HYDRATION (INTRAVENOUS FLUIDS) FORCED UPON ME.

_____

_____

(continued)

Figure 4.2 (continued)

I also direct that I be given medical treatment to relieve pain or to provide comfort, even if such treatment might shorten my life, suppress my appetite or my breathing, or be habit forming.

I value life and the dignity of life. I ask only that my dying be not unreasonably prolonged, nor the dignity of life destroyed. I do not fear death so much as I fear the indignity of deterioration, dependence, hopeless pain and useless extravagance.

I appoint _____ as my Health Care Agent to make and/or participate in all decisions related to my health care, treatment, hospitalization, rehabilitation, convalescence, and custody, to the fullest extent permitted by Sample State law (whenever I am unable to do so by reason of physical or mental infirmity). Further, my Health Care Agent should be permitted complete and unlimited access to my person during all periods of care, treatment, hospitalization, rehabilitation, convalescence and custody, wheresoever it may take place. In the event that such access is limited by medical necessity, my Health Care Agent shall be accorded first priority access.

I direct that my Health Care Agent shall be permitted to request the disclosure of medical services provided to me or to request copies of my entire medical records, or a portion or summary thereof, for any purpose that my Health Care Agent deems appropriate. This authorization shall remain in effect until my death or until such time that this document is revoked.

I further appoint my Health Care Agent as my Surrogate pursuant to Article 29B of the Public Health Law of the State of Sample State, to make decisions regarding cardiopulmonary resuscitation in the event of my incapacity to do so.

I hereby designate my Health Care Agent as my guardian of the person in the event I shall become incompetent to manage myself or my affairs, and there shall be no need for the judicial appointment of a guardian of my person to insure that these health care decisions of mine are carried out.

Dated at _____, Sample State this_____ day of _____, 2012.

_____,
JOE CLIENT

We declare that JOE CLIENT is personally known to us, appears to be of sound mind, and signed willingly and free from duress. This document was signed, in our presence, and we have signed as witnesses in the presence of each other, this _____ day of _____ 2012. Neither witness is appointed as agent by this document.

_____ residing at _____

_____ residing at _____

attorney in place of a health care proxy. Nevada and Arizona both use a health care power of attorney to appoint a person's agent to make medical decisions. You can see how this can be confusing for the average individual, who generally thinks of a power of attorney as a document authorizing someone to make *financial* decisions on another person's behalf. This will be discussed more fully below.

Purposes of a Living Will

The primary purposes of executing a living will are often: 1) to preserve the principal's assets for family members, and 2) to avoid unnecessary suffering on the part of loved ones.

Sample purpose language from a living will is as follows: "*The purpose of this Living Will is to prevent my remaining assets from being used to unnecessarily prolong my life, so that they may be used instead to benefit my spouse and children, if any, and other heirs and devisees who benefit from my worldly estate. Also, I desire to avoid the heartache to my loved ones of an extended illness and to avoid additional pain and suffering to myself through whatever senses remain. In the unlikely event that this instrument may not be legally binding in the jurisdiction where I may be terminally ill, then you who care for me will, I hope, feel morally bound to follow its mandate. It is my decision, not yours, and it is made after careful consideration."*

The famous Terry Schiavo case illustrates the terrible heartache that family members may go through if a loved one becomes ill or is injured and falls into a persistent vegetative state without having signed a living will to express whether or not he or she wishes to be kept alive by artificial measures. This is a personal decision, best made by each individual by executing this simple, but important, legal document. Another important legal document is a power of attorney, discussed below.

■ POWERS OF ATTORNEY

Key Terms and Definitions

A **power of attorney** is a written document that authorizes one person to act as an agent for another. The person granting the power under a power of attorney is called the "principal" or the "grantor," depending upon the state in which the document is executed. A **principal** is person who authorizes another, as an agent, to represent him or her. The individual appointed under a power of attorney is called the **attorney-in-fact** and/or agent. An **agent** is a person or business authorized to act on another's behalf. The attorney-in-fact in a position of trust and must act in the best interest of the principal pursuant to the power of attorney. He or she has a **fiduciary duty** to uphold as the agent of the principal. A **fiduciary** is a person to whom property or power is entrusted for the benefit of another.

Powers

Powers of attorney are also commonly called "statutory powers of attorney" because a state's statutes often provide a sample of what a power of attorney should look like in that state. Further, there are standard enumerated powers that may

Familiar Case for Consideration

> ### THE TERRY SCHIAVO CASE
>
> The Terry Schiavo case is perhaps one of the most pungent examples of the consequences of failing to execute a living will and health care proxy (or comparable documents in your state). In February 1990, Schiavo collapsed in her home from respiratory and cardiac arrest, resulting in extensive brain damage. Prior to her collapse, Schiavo was an active, healthy, employed young woman.
>
> Schiavo was diagnosed as being in a persistent vegetative state, and was institutionalized for over 15 years. Her husband, Michael Schiavo, and her parents, the Schindlers, engaged in a long court battle over whether Schiavo should be removed from the feeding tubes that kept her alive. It was Michael's position that Terry did not wish to be kept alive under these conditions; her parents believed she should be kept alive endlessly. Schiavo did not have a living will expressing her intentions. The court finally adopted Michael's position regarding Schiavo's end-of-life wishes. After many appeals and valiant legislative efforts to prevent the removal of the feeding tubes, the feeding tubes were ordered to be removed on March 18, 2005 (CNN, 2005). (Schiavo later died of dehydration following the removal of the feeding tubes.)

Power of Attorney
A person who authorizes another, as an agent, to represent him or her.

Principal
A person who authorizes another, as an agent, to represent him or her.

Attorney-in-Fact
The person appointed under a power of attorney to act as the principal's agent.

Agent
A person or business authorized to act on another's behalf.

Fiduciary Duty
A duty or responsibility required of a fiduciary that arises out of a position of loyalty and trust.

Fiduciary
A person in a position of loyalty and trust, such as an executor, administrator, guardian, attorney-in-fact, or trustee; also a person to whom property or power is entrusted for the benefit of another.

Power
A legal ability, capacity, or authority.

be conferred, in whole or in part, under a validly executed power of attorney. A **power** is defined as a legal ability, capacity, or authority.

Following are some of the standard and customary powers granted to an attorney-in-fact and agent.

The power to conduct or deal with:

- Real estate transactions;
- Personal property transactions;
- Bond, share and commodity transactions;
- Banking transactions;
- Business operating transactions;
- Insurance transactions;
- Estate transactions;
- Claims and litigation;
- Personal relationships and affairs;
- Benefits from military service;
- Records, reports, and statements;
- Retirement benefit transactions;
- Making gifts to the principal's spouse, children, and more remote descendants, in any amount, to each of such persons in any year;
- Tax matters;
- All other matters;
- Full and unqualified authority to the attorney(s)-in-fact to delegate any or all of the foregoing powers to any person or persons whom the attorney-in-fact shall select;
- Making gifts of the principal's property to others and to charitable organizations in the pattern the principal has used in his or her lifetime;
- To prepare, sign, and file all tax returns required by law; to prepare, sign, and file refund claims and to collect tax refunds; to sign agreements extending the statute of limitations in all tax matters; to represent the principal before any taxing authority or any court in connection with any tax matters;
- To make or change all beneficiary designations, withdrawals, rollovers, transfers, elections, and waivers under law regarding employee benefit plans and individual retirement accounts, whether as plan participant, beneficiary, IRA owner, or spouse of a participant, including without limitation the waiver of qualified joint and survivor annuity and qualified pre-retirement survivor annuity benefits as provided in IRC §417;
- To authorize any distribution, transfer, or rollover from all qualified plans and IRAs;
- To conduct Medicaid and Medicare planning and transactions, including claims, litigation, and settlements;
- To make transfers to any trust that the principal has created; to amend or revoke, in whole or in part, any revocable trust the principal has created, regardless of any disability or incompetency; to make withdrawals from any revocable trust the principal has created;
- To request the disclosure of medical services provided by the principal's physicians or other medical staff or request copies of the principal's entire medical records or a portion thereof for any purpose that the attorney-in-fact deems appropriate or solely upon the request of the attorney-in-fact; and
- To engage in all insurance transactions, exercise all rights with respect to insurance, designate or change the beneficiary on life insurance policies.

Depending upon the state, the principal may be required to initial the blank or the box next to each of the enumerated powers. In order to minimize the burden on the principal, some states include a space where the principal can initial one time but select all of the powers. This may not seem like a big deal to a healthy reader. However, many elderly or ill clients have great difficulty writing and this eases their burden. Other states simply include all of the listed powers without any requirement of selection by the principal.

■ TYPES OF POWERS OF ATTORNEY

General Durable Power of Attorney

The first sample power of attorney provided in this chapter is a **durable** power of attorney, in that it remains in effect after the principal becomes incapacitated. Note the following language, found on page 4 of Sample 1:

Durable
Indicates that a power of attorney will remain in effect after the principal becomes incapacitated.

> "THIS POWER OF ATTORNEY SHALL NOT BE AFFECTED BY MY SUBSEQUENT DISABILITY OR INCOMPETENCE."

This is very important because, in most instances, the primary purpose of executing a power of attorney is to ensure that the principal has appointed someone to manage his or her financial affairs in the event the principal becomes incapacitated. Therefore, most powers of attorney are executed as durable powers of attorney.

It is very important to note that while a durable power of attorney remains in effect after the principal becomes incapacitated, it takes effect *immediately* upon execution. Therefore, while the attorney-in-fact may not need to use the power of attorney for years to come, he or she has the legal authority to use it right away. Therefore, it is crucial that the principal appoint someone whom he or she trusts to carry out this responsibility properly. Generally speaking, that means that the appointee can be trusted to not use the document until and unless it is necessary to do so.

Some people are not comfortable with relinquishing immediate power and control to another individual while they still have capacity to manage their own affairs. Those people may choose to execute a durable power of attorney effective at a future time. Figure 4.3 displays a general durable power of attorney executed by Shirley Smith from the Hypothetical Family.

Figure 4.3 General Durable Power of Attorney

Effective Date:
<u>December 27, 2011</u>
Effective Place of Execution:
Sample County, Sample State

PRINCIPAL:
SHIRLEY SMITH
121 Oak Street
Sample City, Sample State 12345

(continued)

Figure 4.3 (continued)

AGENT (ATTORNEY-IN-FACT):

JANE SMITH

123 Oak Street
Sample City, Sample State 12345

Successor Agents. If any Agent named by me shall die, become incompetent, resign or refuse to accept the office of Agent, I name the following as successor to such Agent:

ROBERT SMITH, residing at 125 Oak Street, Sample City, Sample State 12345.

NOTICE: THE POWERS GRANTED BY THIS DOCUMENT ARE BROAD AND SWEEPING. THEY ARE EXPLAINED IN THE UNIFORM STATUTORY FORM POWER OF ATTORNEY ACT. IF YOU HAVE ANY QUESTIONS ABOUT THESE POWERS, OBTAIN COMPETENT LEGAL ADVICE. THIS DOCUMENT DOES NOT AUTHORIZE ANYONE TO MAKE MEDICAL AND OTHER HEALTH-CARE DECISIONS FOR YOU. YOU MAY REVOKE THIS POWER OF ATTORNEY IF YOU LATER WISH TO DO SO.

THE POWERS YOU GRANT BELOW ARE EFFECTIVE EVEN IF YOU BECOME DISABLED OR INCOMPETENT.

I, **SHIRLEY SMITH**, residing at 121 Oak Street, Sample City, Sample State 12345, appoint **JANE SMITH** residing at 123 Oak Street, Sample City, Sample State 12345, as my Agent (attorney-in-fact) to act for me in any lawful way with respect to the following subjects:

TO GRANT ALL OF THE FOLLOWING POWERS:

A. **Property transactions.** To lease, sell, mortgage, purchase, exchange, and acquire, and to agree, bargain, and contract for the lease, sale, purchase, exchange, and acquisition of, and to accept, take, receive, and possess any interest in real property whatsoever, on such terms and conditions, and under such covenants, as my Agent shall deem proper; and to maintain, repair, tear down, alter, rebuild, improve manage, insure, move, rent, lease, sell, convey, subject to liens, mortgages, and security deeds, and in any way or manner deal with all or any part of any interest in real property whatsoever, including specifically, but without limitation, real property lying and being situated in the State of Sample, under such terms and conditions, and under such covenants, as my Agent shall deem proper and may for all deferred payments accept purchase money notes payable to me and secured by mortgages or deeds to secure debt, and may from time to time collect and cancel any of said notes, mortgages, security interests, or deeds to secure debt.

B. **Tangible personal property transactions.** To lease, sell, mortgage, purchase, exchange, and acquire, and to agree, bargain, and contract for the lease, sale, purchase, exchange, and acquisition of, and to accept, take, receive, and possess any personal property whatsoever, tangible or intangible, or interest thereto, on such terms and conditions, and under such covenants, as my Agent shall deem proper; and to maintain, repair, improve, manage, insure, rent, lease, sell, convey, subject to liens or mortgages, or to take any other security interests in said property which are recognized under the Uniform Commercial Code as adopted at that time under the laws of the State of Sample or any applicable state, or otherwise hypothecate (pledge), and in any way or manner deal with all or any part of any real or personal property whatsoever, tangible or intangible, or any interest therein, that I own at the time of execution or may thereafter acquire, under such terms and conditions, and under such covenants, as my Agent shall deem proper.

C. **Stock and bond transactions.** To purchase, sell, exchange, surrender, assign, redeem, vote at any meeting, or otherwise transfer any and all shares of stock, bonds, or other securities in any business, association, corporation, partnership, or other legal entity, whether private or public, now or hereafter belonging to me.

D. **Commodity and option transactions.** To organize or continue and conduct any business which term includes, without limitation, any farming, manufacturing, service, mining, retailing or other type of business operation in any form, whether as a proprietorship, joint venture, partnership, corporation, trust or other legal entity; operate, buy, sell, expand, contract, terminate or liquidate any business; direct, control, supervise, manage or participate in the operation of any business and engage, compensate and discharge business managers, employees, agents, attorneys, accountants and consultants; and, in general, exercise all powers with respect to business interests and operations which the principal could if present and under no disability.

E. **Banking and other financial institution transactions.** To make, receive, sign, endorse, execute, acknowledge, deliver and possess checks, drafts, bills of exchange, letters of credit, notes, stock certificates, withdrawal receipts and deposit instruments relating to accounts or deposits in, or certificates of deposit of banks, savings and loans, credit unions, or other institutions or associations. To pay all sums of money, at any time or times, that

Figure 4.3 (continued)

may hereafter be owing by me upon any account, bill of exchange, check, draft, purchase, contract, note, or trade acceptance made, executed, endorsed, accepted, and delivered by me or for me in my name, by my Agent. To borrow from time to time such sums of money as my Agent may deem proper and execute promissory notes, security deeds or agreements, financing statements, or other security instruments in such form as the lender may request and renew said notes and security instruments from time to time in whole or in part. To have free access at any time or times to any safe deposit box or vault to which I might have access.

F. **Business operating transactions.** To conduct, engage in, and otherwise transact the affairs of any and all lawful business ventures of whatever nature or kind that I may now or hereafter be involved in.

G. **Insurance and annuity transactions.** To exercise or perform any act, power, duty, right, or obligation, in regard to any contract of life, accident, health, disability, liability, or other type of insurance or any combination of insurance; and to procure new or additional contracts of insurance for me and to designate the beneficiary of same; provided, however, that my Agent cannot designate himself or herself as beneficiary of any such insurance contracts.

H. **Estate, trust, and other beneficiary transactions.** To accept, receipt for, exercise, release, reject, renounce, assign, disclaim, demand, sue for, claim and recover any legacy, bequest, devise, gift or other property interest or payment due or payable to or for the principal; assert any interest in and exercise any power over any trust, estate or property subject to fiduciary control; establish a revocable trust solely for the benefit of the principal that terminates at the death of the principal and is then distributable to the legal representative of the estate of the principal; and, in general, exercise all powers with respect to estates and trusts which the principal could exercise if present and under no disability; provided, however, that the Agent may not make or change a will and may not revoke or amend a trust revocable or amendable by the principal or require the trustee of any trust for the benefit of the principal to pay income or principal to the Agent unless specific authority to that end is given.

I. **Claims and litigation.** To commence, prosecute, discontinue, or defend all actions or other legal proceedings touching my property, real or personal, or any part thereof, or touching any matter in which I or my property, real or personal, may be in any way concerned. To defend, settle, adjust, make allowances, compound, submit to arbitration, and compromise all accounts, reckonings, claims, and demands whatsoever that now are, or hereafter shall be, pending between me and any person, firm, corporation, or other legal entity, in such manner and in all respects as my Agent shall deem proper.

J. **Personal and family maintenance.** To hire accountants, attorneys at law, consultants, clerks, physicians, nurses, agents, servants, workmen, and others and to remove them, and to appoint others in their place, and to pay and allow the persons so employed such salaries, wages, or other remunerations, as my Agent shall deem proper.

K. **Benefits from Social Security, Medicare, Medicaid, or other governmental programs, or military service.** To prepare, sign and file any claim or application for Social Security, unemployment or military service benefits; sue for, settle or abandon any claims to any benefit or assistance under any federal, state, local or foreign statute or regulation; control, deposit to any account, collect, receipt for, and take title to and hold all benefits under any Social Security, unemployment, military service or other state, federal, local or foreign statute or regulation; and, in general, exercise all powers with respect to Social Security, unemployment, military service, and governmental benefits, including but not limited to Medicare and Medicaid, which the principal could exercise if present and under no disability.

L. **Retirement plan transactions.** To contribute to, withdraw from and deposit funds in any type of retirement plan (which term includes, without limitation, any tax qualified or nonqualified pension, profit sharing, stock bonus, employee savings and other retirement plan, individual retirement account, deferred compensation plan and any other type of employee benefit plan); select and change payment options for the principal under any retirement plan; make rollover contributions from any retirement plan to other retirement plans or individual retirement accounts; exercise all investment powers available under any type of self-directed retirement plan; and, in general, exercise all powers with respect to retirement plans and retirement plan account balances which the principal could if present and under no disability.

M. **Tax matters.** To prepare, to make elections, to execute and to file all tax, social security, unemployment insurance, and informational returns required by the laws of the United States, or of any state or subdivision thereof, or of any foreign government; to prepare, to execute, and to file all other papers and instruments which the Agent shall think to be desirable or necessary for safeguarding of me against excess or illegal taxation or against penalties imposed for claimed violation of any law or other governmental regulation; and to pay, to compromise, or to contest or to apply for refunds in connection with any taxes or assessments for which I am or may be liable.

(continued)

Figure 4.3 (continued)

THIS POWER OF ATTORNEY SHALL BE CONSTRUED AS A GENERAL DURABLE POWER OF ATTORNEY.

THIS **POWER OF ATTORNEY IS EFFECTIVE IMMEDIATELY AND WILL CONTINUE UNTIL IT** IS REVOKED.

THIS POWER OF ATTORNEY SHALL BE CONSTRUED AS A GENERAL DURABLE POWER OF ATTORNEY AND SHALL CONTINUE TO BE EFFECTIVE EVEN IF I BECOME DISABLED, INCAPACITATED, OR INCOMPETENT.

Authority to Delegate. My Agent shall have the right by written instrument to delegate any or all of the foregoing powers involving discretionary decision-making to any person or persons whom my Agent may select, but such delegation may be amended or revoked by any agent (including any successor) named by me who is acting under this power of attorney at the time of reference.

Right to Compensation. My Agent shall be entitled to reasonable compensation for services rendered as agent under this power of attorney.

Choice of Law. This power of attorney will be governed by the laws of the state of Sample without regard for conflicts of laws principles. It was executed in the state of Sample and is intended to be valid in all jurisdictions of the United State of America and all foreign nations.

I am fully informed as to all the contents of this form and understand the full import of this grant of powers to my Agent. I agree that any third party who receives a copy of this document may act under it. Revocation of the power of attorney is not effective as to a third party until the third party learns of the revocation. I agree to indemnify the third party for any claims that arise against the third party because of reliance on this power of attorney.

I, SHIRLEY SMITH, the principal, sign my name to this power of attorney this 27th day of December, 2011, and, being first duly sworn, do declare to the undersigned authority that I sign and execute this instrument as my power of attorney and that I sign it willingly, or willingly direct another to sign for me, that I execute it as my free and voluntary act for the purposes expressed in the power of attorney and that I am eighteen years of age or older, of sound mind and under no constraint or undue influence.

Shirley Smith
—————————————————
SHIRLEY SMITH, Principal

I, MICHAEL PEARSON, the witness, sign my name to the foregoing power of attorney being first duly sworn and do declare to the undersigned authority that the principal signs and executes this instrument as the principal's power of attorney and that the principal signs it willingly, or willingly directs another to sign for the principal, and that I, in the presence and hearing of the principal, sign this power of attorney as witness to the principal's signing and that to the best of my knowledge the principal is eighteen years of age or older, of sound mind and under no constraint or undue influence.

Michael Pearson
—————————————————
Witness

NOTARY ACKNOWLEDGMENT

The state of SAMPLE
County of SAMPLE

Subscribed, sworn to and acknowledged before me by SHIRLEY SMITH, the principal, and subscribed and sworn to before me by <u>Michael Pearson</u>, witness, this <u>27th</u> day of December, 2011.
WITNESS my hand and official seal.

Lila P. Legal
—————————————————
Notary Public

| LILA P. LEGAL |
| Notary Public, State of Sample |
| Sample County |
| My Commission Expires May 10, 2012 |

Durable Power of Attorney Effective at a Future Time

A durable power of attorney effective at a future time does not take effect until a future event occurs. Generally, it means that the attorney-in-fact's powers do not take effect until a physician has certified that the principal is incapacitated and unable to manage his or her own affairs. These documents are often referred to as **springing powers of attorney** by legal professionals because they spring into effect, not upon execution, but upon the principal becoming incapacitated. They are durable because they remain in effect despite the principal's incapacity. Figure 4.4 depicts a sample of a springing power of attorney. Note that the document is still revocable by the principal at any time prior to his becoming incapacitated.

Springing Power of Attorney
A power of attorney that becomes effective upon the occurrence of a specific event at a future time.

Figure 4.4 Sample Springing Power of Attorney

JOE CLIENT
DURABLE GENERAL POWER OF ATTORNEY EFFECTIVE AT A
FUTURE TIME SAMPLE STATE STATUTORY SHORT FORM

Caution: This is an important document. It gives the person whom you designate (your "Agent") broad powers to handle your property during your lifetime, which may include powers to mortgage, sell, or otherwise dispose of any real or personal property without advance notice to you or approval by you. These powers may only be used after a certification that you have become disabled, incapacitated, or incompetent or that some other event has occurred. These powers are explained more fully in Sample State General Obligations Law, Article 5, Title 15, Sections 5-1502A through 1-1506, which expressly permit the use of any other or different form power of attorney.

This document does not authorize anyone to make medical or other health care decisions for you. You may execute a health care proxy to do this.

If there is anything about this form that you do not understand, you should ask your lawyer to explain it to you.

THIS is intended to constitute a POWER OF ATTORNEY EFFECTIVE AT A FUTURE TIME pursuant to Article 5, Title 15 of the Sample State General Obligations Law:

I, **JOE CLIENT**, residing at 123 STREET, SAMPLETOWN, SAMPLE STATE 12345,

do hereby appoint **JANE CLIENT**, residing at 123 STREET, SAMPLETOWN, SAMPLE STATE 12345,

OR

JOHN CLIENT, residing at 456 STREET, SAMPLETOWN, SAMPLE STATE 12345

MY ATTORNEY(S)-IN-FACT TO ACT

[ ] Each agent may **SEPARATELY** act.

[ ] All agents must act **TOGETHER**.

TO TAKE EFFECT upon the occasion of the signing of a written statement **EITHER**

    (I) by a physician or physicians named herein by me at this point:

    Dr.

OR

  (II) if no physician or physicians are named hereinabove, or if the physician or physicians named hereinabove are unable to act, by my regular physician, or by a physician who has treated me within one year preceding the date of such signing, or by a licensed psychologist or psychiatrist, **CERTIFYING** that the following specified events has occurred:

I am suffering from diminished capacity, whether physical or mental, which precludes me from conducting my affairs in a competent manner.

IN MY NAME, PLACE AND STEAD in any way which I myself could do, if I were personally present, with respect to the following matters as each of them are defined in Title 15 of Article 5 of the Sample State General Obligations Law to the extent that I am permitted by law to act through an agent:

(continued)

Figure 4.4 (continued)

(DIRECTIONS: Initial in the blank space to the left of your choice any one or more of the following lettered subdivisions as to which you WANT to give your agent authority. If the blank space to the left of any particular lettered subdivision is NOT initialed NO AUTHORITY WILL BE GRANTED for matters that are included in that subdivision. Alternatively, the letter corresponding to each power you wish to grant may be written or typed in the blank line in subdivision "(Q)", and you may then put your initials in the blank space to the left of subdivision "(Q)" in order to grant each of the powers so indicated.)

[ ] (A) Real estate transactions;

[ ] (B) Chattel and goods transactions;

[ ] (C) Bond, share and commodity transactions;

[ ] (D) Banking transactions;

[ ] (E) Business operating transactions;

[ ] (F) Insurance transactions;

[ ] (G) Estate transactions;

[ ] (H) Claims and litigation;

[ ] (I) Personal relationships and affairs;

[ ] (J) Benefits from military service;

[ ] (K) Records, reports and statements;

[ ] (L) Retirement benefit transactions;

[ ] (M) Making gifts to my spouse, children and more remote descendants, and parents, in any amount, to each of such persons in any year;

[ ] (N) Tax matters;

[ ] (O) All other matters;

[ ] (P) Full and unqualified authority to my attorney(s)-in-fact to delegate any or all of the foregoing powers to any person or persons whom my attorney-in-fact shall select;

[ ] (Q) **Each of the matters identified herein by the following letters: (A) through (X) inclusive.**

[ ] (R) To make gifts of my property to others, including my attorney-in-fact, and to charitable organizations; the attorney-in-fact herein named also has the power to make gifts in the pattern I have used in my lifetime; this authority, however, is not intended nor shall it be construed as a power of appointment

[ ] (S) To prepare, sign, and file all tax returns required by law; to prepare, sign, and file refund claims and to collect tax refunds; to sign agreements extending the statute of limitations in all tax matters; to represent me before any taxing authority or any court in connection with any tax matters;

[ ] (T) To make or change all beneficiary designations, withdrawals, rollovers, transfers, elections and waivers under law regarding employee benefit plans and individual retirement accounts, whether as plan participant, as beneficiary, IRA owner, or as spouse of a participant, including without limitation the waiver of qualified joint and survivor annuity and qualified pre-retirement survivor annuity benefits as provided in IRC §417; to authorize any distribution, transfer, or rollover from all qualified plans and IRAs.

[ ] (U) To conduct Medicaid and Medicare planning and transactions, including claims, litigation and settlements;

[ ] (V) To make transfers to any trust that I have created; to amend or revoke, in whole or in part, any revocable trust I have created, regardless of any disability or incompetency; to make withdrawals from any revocable trust I have created.

[ ] (W) To request the disclosure of medical services provided by my physicians or other medical staff or request copies of my entire medical records or a portion thereof for any purpose that my Attorney-in-Fact deems appropriate or solely upon the request of my Attorney-in-Fact. This power shall include the authority to access records relating to the provision of health care and to make decisions relating to the payment for

Figure 4.4 (continued)

medical and health care services. This authorization shall remain in effect until my death or until such time that this Power of Attorney is revoked by me.

[ ] (X) To engage in all insurance transactions, exercise all rights with respect to insurance, designate or change the beneficiary on life insurance policies, including naming my attorney-in-fact as beneficiary.

THIS POWER OF ATTORNEY SHALL NOT BE AFFECTED BY MY SUBSEQUENT DISABILITY OR INCOMPETENCE.

To induce any third party to act hereunder, I hereby agree that any third party receiving a duly executed copy or facsimile of this instrument may act hereunder, and that revocation or termination hereof shall be ineffective as to such third party unless and until actual notice or knowledge of such revocation or termination shall have been received by such third party, and I for myself and for my heirs, executors, and legal representatives and assigns, hereby agree to indemnify and hold harmless any such third party from and against any and all claims that may arise against such third party by reason of such third party having relied on the provisions of this instrument.

This General Power of Attorney Effective at a Future Time may be revoked by me at any time.

IN WITNESS WHEREOF, I have hereunto signed my name and affixed my seal this _____ day of _____, 2012.

_____
JOE CLIENT

STATE OF SAMPLE STATE}

COUNTY OF SAMPLETOWN} ss:

On the _____ day of _____ in the year 2012 before me, the undersigned, a Notary Public in and for said State, personally appeared **JOE CLIENT**, personally known to me or proved to me on the basis of satisfactory evidence to be the individual whose name is subscribed to the within instrument and acknowledged to me that he executed the same in his capacity, and that by his signature on the instrument, the individual, or the person upon behalf of which the individual acted, executed the instrument.

_____
Notary Public

Limited Powers of Attorney

In contrast to a general durable power of attorney, a **limited power of attorney** may limit the scope of the agent's authority and/or the length of time that the document remains in effect. Here are some common examples:

1. Husband and wife are selling their home. Both are required to sign the deed at the real estate closing. However, husband has a business trip to Japan planned for the closing date. He may sign a limited power of attorney for the single real estate transaction so that his wife can sign on his behalf.
2. Client hires attorney to assist with forming a new corporation. Attorney needs to apply for an Employer Identification Number (EIN) for the client. Client must execute a limited power of attorney authorizing Attorney to correspond with the IRS for the purpose of obtaining the EIN.

■ EXECUTION OF POWERS OF ATTORNEY

Many states require only that the principal execute the document in the presence of a notary public. However, some other states also require the presence of two witnesses. Finally, some states also require that the appointed agent also sign the original power of attorney. This makes a lot of sense because parties later honoring

Limited Power of Attorney
A power of attorney that limits the scope of the agent's authority and/or the length of time that the document remains in effect.

PARALEGAL PRACTICE TIPS

- Keep in mind that the client for whom you are drafting a power of attorney is the PRINCIPAL.
- Keep in mind that most clients should appoint two different people under their power of attorney: 1) their first choice should be currently appointed as

their Attorney-in-Fact and Agent; and also 2) their second choice should be appointed as alternate. This double appointment acts as a contingency plan in the event that the client's first choice is unwilling or unavailable to act when needed. It also prevents clients from having to execute a new document if they later learn that their first choice cannot act on their behalf.

- Husbands and wives will generally appoint each other under their respective powers of attorney. It is still advisable that they appoint alternates. Unfortunately, tragic events do occur where both spouses are affected; for example, a car accident putting both spouses in the hospital.

- Carefully go over the powers listed on your power of attorney document to ensure that clients are comfortable with granting all of the powers and also to ensure that there are not powers missing that need to be added.

the document can compare the signature of the party claiming to be the attorney-in-fact with the signature on the document, helping to reduce the risk of fraud.

■ THIRD-PARTY RELIANCE

Powers of attorney would not be very helpful if third parties refused to rely on them. Imagine you were appointed as your grandmother's attorney-in-fact under a properly executed power of attorney. She has had a stroke and can no longer write, so you need to help her pay her bills. You go to her bank with her power of attorney in hand in order to let them know that you will be writing checks on Grandma's behalf. However, the bank teller says, "Um, how do I know this isn't a forgery? No, I won't honor it." This would certainly present a problem, since Grandma cannot execute a new document after her stroke. In order to avoid this sort of situation, state laws provide that third parties may honor a power of attorney provided it is duly executed in accordance with the laws of that state and that the document has not been revoked. Further, most states have provisions that anyone who wrongfully refuses to honor a valid power of attorney faces civil liability.

■ REVOCATION OF POWERS OF ATTORNEY

If a principal decides that he or she no longer wants the person originally selected as agent to act, the principal may simply destroy the old documents and execute new ones. However, if the principal fears that the appointed agent will act improperly pursuant to the old document, it will also be necessary to execute a revocation of power of attorney removing the attorney-in-fact's authority to act. The statutory requirements for the revocation will nearly always be the same as the requirements for the execution of the power of attorney in that state. A sample revocation of power of attorney appears in Figure 4.5.

After executing the revocation, the principal must distribute it to all parties who were given the revoked power of attorney. In addition, he or she may also wish to record it with the county recorder in order to put the public on notice that the old power of attorney is no longer valid and should not be honored.

■ COST

A power of attorney is a relatively inexpensive and simple document that should be included in every estate plan. If prepared outside of an estate plan, most attorneys would charge only a minimal fee for this document (most likely between $100 and $150). It is not advisable for clients to purchase commercial forms off of the Internet or from stationery stores, as these forms are generally not state specific and may not meet the requirements for due execution in the client's state. Further, clients are unlikely to find out if the form is inadequate until it is too late to execute a new form (i.e., until they are incapacitated).

■ CONSEQUENCES OF BEING WITHOUT A POWER OF ATTORNEY

An individual who becomes unable to handle his or her financial affairs without having executed a power of attorney puts his or her family in a difficult situation. If time is of the essence and bills need to be paid, someone will have to petition

Figure 4.5 Revocation of Power of Attorney

Know all Men by these Presents, That

Whereas, JOE CLIENT

in and by his Powers of Attorney, bearing the date of January 1, 2012 did make, constitute and appoint

JANE CLIENT

As his agent by the aforesaid Power of Attorney as it may more fully and at large appear.

   Now know ye, That JOE CLIENT has revoked, countermanded, annulled and made void, and by these presents does revoke, countermand annul and make void the said Powers of Attorney above mentioned, and all power and authority thereby given, or intended to be given, to the said JANE CLIENT.

   In Witness Whereof, JOE CLIENT has hereunto set his hand and seal the _____ day of _____, 2012 and

                               Sealed and delivered in the presence of _____

                                                                       JOE CLIENT

STATE OF SAMPLE STATE

(COUNTY OF SAMPLETOWN) ss.:

On the _____ day of _____ in the year 2012 before me, the undersigned, personally appeared **JOE CLIENT**, personally known to me or proved to me on the basis of satisfactory evidence to be the individual whose name is subscribed to the within instrument and acknowledged to me that he executed the same in his capacity, and that by his signature on the instrument, the individual, or the person upon behalf of which the individual acted, executed the instrument.

                                                      _____

                                                      NOTARY PUBLIC

---

the court on an emergency basis for appointment as Conservator (see Chapter 9 for more details). This type of court proceeding is extensive and requires that all statutorily required kin be notified of the proceeding. Generally speaking, this includes the individual's spouse, children, and parents. However, you must look to your state statutes to determine those individuals who are entitled to notice of the proceedings in your state. Attorney's fees for preparing a petition for appointment as conservator are likely to start at around $3,000 plus costs, and then go up from there. The person petitioning the court to be appointed generally must front the money for the proceeding, but can later be reimbursed from the ward's estate. A **ward** is a person who has been legally placed under the care of a guardian or a court. When you think of the savings that simply executing a power of attorney can bring, there is really no justification for being without this document.

Ward
A person who has been legally placed under the care of a guardian or a court.

■ CONCLUSION

It is extremely important to execute advance directives to let people know what type of medical treatment one does and does not want in the event of terminal illness and/or incapacity. Likewise, it is also very important to execute a financial power of attorney, which is a relatively simple, but very important, document giving another person authority to manage the principal's financial affairs. Every person who is of sound mind and over the age of majority should execute these documents. The cost of these documents is nominal, but the potential savings in a time of crisis is huge.

CONCEPT REVIEW AND REINFORCEMENT

KEY TERMS

Advance Directives 72	Power of Attorney 77	Durable 79
Estate Plan 72	Principal 77	Springing Power of Attorney 83
Living Will 72	Attorney-in-Fact 77	Limited Power of Attorney 85
Persistent Vegetative State (PVS) 72	Agent 77	Ward 87
Health Care Proxy 72	Fiduciary Duty 77	
Living Will and Health Care Proxy 72	Fiduciary 77	
	Power 78	

REVIEW QUESTIONS

1. When is a power of attorney effective?
2. When does a power of attorney cease being effective?
3. When does a springing power of attorney become effective?
4. What is the purpose of a living will?
5. What is the purpose of a health care power of attorney?
6. List some of the commons powers granted under a power of attorney.
7. If your client no longer trusts the individual he appointed under his power of attorney, what document should be prepared?
8. Describe what it means to be in a persistent vegetative state.
9. What is a fiduciary? Describe in your own words what this means to you.
10. What have states done to ensure that third parties honor power of attorney documents?

BUILDING YOUR PARALEGAL SKILLS

CRITICAL THINKING EXERCISES

1. Tom Smith wants to execute a document stating his wishes with respect to the type of medical attention he desires to receive if he is in a persistent vegetative state. However, he disagrees with some of the language on the standard living will form he obtained. What do you think he should do?
2. Mary Jones is an elderly woman who does not have any close living relatives. She wants to execute a power of attorney so that someone can help her to pay her bills if she no longer is able to. Mary is friends with Nancy Nice, who is fifteen years younger. Mary trusts Nancy to assist her with paying bills, should the need ever arise. However, she does not feel comfortable relinquishing control just yet. What type of document should Mary execute?
3. Make a chart comparing the pros and cons of executing a durable power of attorney versus a springing power of attorney.
4. Jonathan Smith executes a power of attorney appointing his neighbor, Timothy Trick, as his attorney-in-fact. He gives Timothy a copy of the document, and Timothy promises never to use it unless Jonathan becomes incapacitated. A couple of months later, Jonathan and Timothy have a falling out over Jonathan's fence, which is in very bad condition. Jonathan refuses to repair the fence, and Timothy threatens to use the power of attorney to obtain money to fix the fence. Jonathan demands that Timothy give his copy of the power of attorney back. Timothy tells him that it does not matter, because he already made a bunch of copies and distributed them to Jonathan's banks. He also recorded the power of attorney with the county recorder. What should Jonathan do? Provide details.

PARALEGAL PRACTICE

1. _____

MEMORANDUM
To: Paralegal
From: Supervising Attorney
Client: Sally Marie Jacobs
Re: Power of Attorney

Today I met with Sally Jacobs to discuss her estate planning needs. Her address is 123 First Street, Sample Town, Sample State 12345. At this time, she only wants to execute a power of attorney appointing her friend, Susan Johnson, as her agent. They are roommates.

Sally will think about her will and living will and get back to us sometime next week. Please prepare the power of attorney now.

2. _____

MEMORANDUM
To: Paralegal
From: Supervising Attorney
Client: Matthew Meyers
Re: Power of Attorney, Health Care power of attorney, and Living Will

I met with Mr. Meyers today regarding a power of attorney. He wishes to appoint his nephew, Joseph Hertz, but is not comfortable granting him immediate authority. Mr. Meyer's address is 666 Old Way, Sample Town, Sample State 12345. His nephew lives a few doors down the street at #672.

Mr. Meyer's physician is Elizabeth Simpson, M.D., Medical Building, 456 Autumn Road, Suite 2, Sample Town, Sample State 12345.

I advised that Mr. Meyers should also execute a Health Care power of attorney and a living will at this time. He wants to appoint his friend, Elma White, as his agent and his nephew as his alternate agent.

Please prepare the documents for my review.

3. _____

MEMORANDUM
To: Paralegal
From: Supervising Attorney
Client: Robert Spoon
Re: Revocation of Power of Attorney

I met with Robert Spoon today about some problems he has had with his grandson, Nicholas Spoon. He previously appointed Nicholas under his power of attorney on December 1, 2007. He now wishes to revoke the authority. Please prepare the document for my review.

ONLINE RESOURCES

The Pearson Course Companion website contains the following additional resources:
- Forms for Paralegal Practice Activities
- Chapter Objectives
- Online Study Guide (Containing Multiple Choice and True/False Questions)
- Web Exercises www.pearsonhighered.com/careers

CASES FOR CONSIDERATION

SCHEIBLE v. THE JOSEPH L. MORSE GERIATRIC CENTER, INC., ET AL.

988 So.2d 1130
July 30, 2008.
[988 So.2d 1131]

Jack Scarola and Mara Ritchie Poncy Hatfield of Searcy Denney Scarola Barnhart & Shipley, P.A., and Marnie Ritchie Poncy of Legal Aid Society of Palm Beach County, West Palm Beach, for appellant.

Rachel Studley and Michele I. Nelson of Wicker, Smith, O'Hara, McCoy & Ford, P.A., West Palm Beach, for appellee The Joseph L. Morse Geriatric Center, Inc.

SHAHOOD, C.J.

Linda Scheible, as personal representative of the Estate of Madeline Neumann, appeals from the Final Judgment of the trial court in her favor and against the appellee, The Joseph L. Morse Geriatric Center, Inc., and from the trial court's order denying her motion for prejudgment interest. We affirm.

This case arises out of the death of Madeline Neumann at The Joseph L. Morse Geriatric Center, a nursing home, in 1995. Mrs. Neumann was admitted to Morse in December 1992 at the age of 89. At the time, she had an admitting diagnosis of senile dementia and a seizure disorder. At the time of admission, Mrs. Neumann's granddaughter, Linda Scheible, presented Morse with a living will/advance directive previously signed by herself and Mrs. Neumann that stated there were to be no life-prolonging treatments or resuscitative measures taken on Mrs. Neumann's behalf if she had a terminal condition or was in the process of dying. Mrs. Neumann named Linda Scheible as her healthcare surrogate.

On the evening of October 17, 1995, nursing home staff found Mrs. Neumann unresponsive in her bed. She was breathing, but staff could not obtain her vitals. They called 911. EMS arrived, intubated Mrs. Neumann, administered dopamine, and took her to the hospital. During transport, Mrs. Neumann attempted to remove the tubing and her hands were placed in physical restraints. On October 19, 2005, Mrs. Neumann was extubated. She remained in the hospital until her death on October 23, 1995. The immediate cause of death was cardiopulmonary arrest.

Appellant filed a complaint against Morse in August 1997 alleging willful disregard of advance health care directive under chapter 765, Florida Statutes (1995), willful disregard of the federal patient self-determination act, common law intentional battery, and violation of the Nursing Home Resident's Rights Act (section 400.022(1), Florida Statutes (1995)). Appellant later amended the complaint to add a breach of contract claim[1] and add Dr. Jaimy Bensimon and Dr. Jaimy Bensimon, P.A. as defendants, and again later to add a negligence claim. Morse succeeded in getting summary judgment granted as to the health care advance directive count and the violation of the federal patient self-determination act count on the grounds that no private cause of action existed under those statutes.

While the case was proceeding, this court issued its opinion in Beverly Enterprises-Fla., Inc. v. Knowles, 766 So.2d 335 (Fla. 4th DCA 2000), holding that section 400.023, Florida Statutes, provided for the personal representative of a deceased to bring a cause of action for violation of nursing home resident's rights "only when the deprivation or infringement of the resident's rights caused the patient's death." 766 So.2d at 336 (emphasis in original). Morse sought summary judgment based on its argument that in light of Knowles, appellant's claim could not succeed since it did not allege that Morse caused Mrs. Neumann's death and there was no evidence to support that conclusion.

The trial court granted Morse's motion for summary judgment as to violation of nursing home resident's rights, pursuant to Knowles. The Supreme Court of Florida later upheld this court's decision in Knowles, specifically agreeing that section 400.023, Florida Statutes, provides that the personal representative of an estate may bring an action against the nursing home for violation of the patient's bill of rights only when the deprivation or infringement caused the patient's death. Knowles v. Beverly Enters.-Fla., Inc., 898 So.2d 1, 6 (Fla. 2004).

This case went to jury trial on the battery, negligence, and breach of contract counts. The jury returned a verdict finding Dr. Bensimon not liable for battery or negligence, but finding that Morse breached its contract with Mrs. Neumann. The jury awarded $150,000 for breach of contract damages.

Appellants filed a motion for entry of judgment and requested therein that the court attach prejudgment interest to the verdict from the date of loss. Appellants claimed that as a matter of law, such prejudgment interest is an element of pecuniary damages that attaches to a verdict on a claim for breach of contract. Morse opposed the inclusion of prejudgment interest, arguing it should be denied because appellant's claim was essentially for the recovery of unliquidated personal injury damages, appellant did not suffer the loss of a vested property right, and the amount of damages could not be conclusively ascertained prior to trial. The trial court denied appellant prejudgment interest.

Appellant argues that the trial court's ruling was in error because: (1) it concludes that the language of section 400.023, Florida Statutes (1995), "when the cause of death results from the deprivation" to unambiguously require the deprivation to be the cause of death rather than an act which results in the cause of death—thus it deletes words from the statute; (2) it ignores the illogical effect such an interpretation of the phrase has upon the provisions of 400.023(4) which expressly contemplates deprivations of the right to refuse care that result in death; (3) it renders the NHRRA right to refuse care of section 400.022(k), Florida Statutes (1995), meaningless; (4) it creates an unconstitutional requirement; and (5) it discriminates unfairly against those who express their constitutional right to health care self-determination by prohibiting life-prolonging treatment.

Appellant's argument presents a question about causation. The theory begins with the premise that Mrs. Neumann was suffering from respiratory arrest when she was found in a non-responsive state by the nursing home staff. Had her wishes been followed and no resuscitative measures been taken, appellant urges she would have expired naturally from that condition. But since she was provided with the care she did not want, appellant argues the immediate cause of her death was cardiopulmonary arrest. The question is therefore whether one who is already in the process of dying has a cause of action based on allegations that resuscitative measures were taken contrary to their expressed will, and the measures result in a manner of death other than that which would have occurred absent those measures. Appellant therefore characterizes the measures taken that prolonged Mrs. Neumann's life as an intervening cause of her death.

Despite appellant's argument, the holding of this court in Knowles, and the supreme court's opinion affirming it, is that deprivation of the right to refuse health care cannot constitute a legal cause of death for which a plaintiff may sue. In affirming this court's opinion in Knowles, the supreme court made very clear its agreement that "the plain meaning of the language used in the statute indicates that only personal representatives of the estate of a deceased resident whose death resulted from the deprivation or infringement of the decedent's rights may bring an action for damages under the statutory rights scheme." 898 So.2d at 6 (emphasis in original). As already noted, appellant attempts to fit her claim into the holding of Knowles by characterizing the nursing home's violation of the patient's bill of rights as the supervening cause of a different kind of death than Mrs. Neumann otherwise would have experienced. We hold this characterization to be incorrect.

The breach of Mrs. Neumann's rights that appellant alleged in this count is that measures were taken by nursing home staff to keep her alive that she did not want taken. The immediate wrong suffered was therefore akin to "wrongful prolongation of life." As appellee points out, the Supreme Court of Florida has previously approved of the proposition that finders of fact should not engage in such determinations, such as "to weigh the value of impaired life against the value of nonexistence." Kush v. Lloyd, 616 So.2d 415, 423 (Fla. 1992) (affirming district court decision rejecting general damages for "wrongful life" claim due to "existential conundrum" raised by the issue).

We also affirm the other issue raised by appellant, the denial of her motion for prejudgment interest.

While admitting the loss at issue in this case included "something as abstract as the loss of the assurance of a natural death," appellant claims it is still governed by the loss theory described in Argonaut Insurance Co. v. May Plumbing Co., 474 So.2d 212, 215 (Fla. 1985).

Despite appellant's argument under the "loss theory," we hold that the trial court was correct that whether prejudgment interest is allowed depends on the nature of the damages claimed. Therefore, the fact that appellant recovered under a breach of contract theory should not automatically entitle appellant to prejudgment interest if the nature of damages is inappropriate for such interest.

In Aetna Casualty & Surety Co. v. Langel, 587 So.2d 1370 (Fla. 4th DCA 1991), the trial court awarded the plaintiff prejudgment interest on his claim against an uninsured motorist. The trial court did so on the basis that the action was in contract pursuant to the uninsured motorist provisions in the insurance policy rather than a personal injury action. Langel, 587 So.2d at 1373. We held the trial court erred because "although the [plaintiffs'] action was based upon a contract of insurance, it was still essentially one for the recovery of personal injury damages, and, accordingly, the [plaintiffs] were not entitled to pre-judgment interest." Id. at 1373-74 (quoting Cooper v. Aetna Cas. & Surety, 485 So.2d 1367, 1368 (Fla. 2d DCA 1986)); see also United Servs. Auto. Ass'n v. Strasser, 530 So.2d 1026, 1027 (Fla. 4th DCA 1988)(affirming denial of prejudgment interest).

Further, in Alvarado v. Rice, 614 So.2d 498, 499 (Fla. 1993), the Supreme Court of Florida addressed the question, certified to it by this court, whether the claimant in a personal injury action is entitled to interest on past medical expenses. The trial court had denied prejudgment interest, and this court affirmed. Alvarado, 614 So.2d at 499. The supreme court stated:

It is well settled that a plaintiff is entitled to pre-judgment interest when it is determined that the plaintiff has suffered an actual, out-of-pocket loss at some date prior to the entry of judgment. Argonaut Ins. Co. v. May Plumbing Co., 474 So.2d 212, 215 (Fla. 1985). To date, cases recognizing a right to prejudgment interest have all involved the loss of a vested property right.

Id.

The supreme court concluded that unlike the plaintiffs in Argonaut and the other cases cited above, Alvarado had not suffered the loss of a vested property right. Id. at 500. The court approved the decision of this court affirming denial of prejudgment interest. Id. at 501.

The present case is similar to the uninsured motorist case of Langel. Although appellant's action was technically for breach of contract, the damages sought involved unliquidated personal injury damages. See Morales Sand & Soil L.L.C. v. Kendall Props. & Invs., 923 So.2d 1229, 1232 (Fla. 4th DCA 2006)(stating that "[d]amages are liquidated when the proper amount to be awarded can be determined with exactness from the cause of action as pleaded, i.e., from a pleaded agreement between the parties, by an arithmetical calculation or by application of definite rules of law") (quoting Bowman v. Kingsland Dev., Inc., 432 So.2d 660, 662 (Fla. 5th DCA 1983); Air Ambulance Prof'ls, Inc. v. Thin Air, 809 So.2d 28, 31 (Fla. 4th DCA 2002)) (reversing award of prejudgment interest on unliquidated breach of contract damages because "[p]rejudgment interest is allowed on only liquidated claims, that is, sums which are certain, but which the defendant refuses to surrender").

Affirmed.

HAZOURI and DAMOORGIAN, JJ., concur.

Note:

[1]The theory of the breach of contract count was that the living will/advance directive was incorporated into the contract between Mrs. Neumann and Morse for her care.

Case Questions

1. Who did Mrs. Neumann appoint as her health care agent?
2. Explain in your own words why the plaintiff brought this lawsuit.
3. What was the trial court's holding?
4. What was this court's holding, and what was the reason for its holding?

CASE #2:

TENNESSEE FARMERS LIFE REASSURANCE COMPANY

v.

ROSE et al.
239 S.W.3d 743
October 2, 2007.

Paul T. Coleman and Vivian L. Crandall, Knoxville, Tennessee, for the appellant Linda S. Rose.

Jennifer E. Raby, Rockwood, Tennessee, for the appellees, Kristin N. Taylor, Edward R. Langley, Phillip M. Langley, and Ethan E. Langley.

OPINION

CORNELIA A. CLARK, J., delivered the opinion of the court, in which WILLIAM M. BARKER, C.J., and JANICE M. HOLDER, GARY R. WADE, and WILLIAM C. KOCH, JR., JJ., joined.

We granted permission to appeal in this case to determine whether the decedent's durable power of attorney authorized her attorney-in-fact to change the beneficiary of the decedent's life insurance policy. For the reasons stated below, we conclude that the durable power of attorney authorized the attorney-in-fact to change the beneficiary of the policy. Accordingly, we reverse the judgments of the lower courts; however, because our holding does not resolve all of the issues raised in the pleadings, we remand this case to the trial court for further proceedings.

I. SUMMARY OF FACTS & PROCEEDINGS BELOW

On October 20, 1999, Brenda Gail Langley ("Langley") purchased a $50,000 life insurance policy from the plaintiff, Tennessee Farmers Life Reassurance Company ("Tennessee Farmers"). Langley designated three of her four children and one grandchild as the named beneficiaries of the policy; those individuals are Kristin N. Taylor, Edward R. Langley, Phillip M. Langley, and Ethan E. Langley (the child of Edward Langley). The policy provided that the beneficiaries would share equally in the proceeds and also provided that the insured could change the beneficiary/beneficiaries.

On August 21, 2002, Langley executed a durable power of attorney, appointing her sister, Linda S. Rose ("Rose"), as her attorney-in-fact. In pertinent part, the power of attorney provided:

"I BRENDA GAIL LANGLEY... do hereby appoint and constitute LINDA SUE ROSE, my true and lawful attorney for me and in my name and on my behalf:

. . . to transact all insurance business on my behalf, to apply for or continue policies, collect profits, file claims, make demands, enter into compromise and settlement agreements, file suit or actions or take any other action necessary or proper in this regard;. . . .

Giving and granting unto the said LINDA SUE ROSE, my said attorney, full power and authority to do, execute and perform all and every other act and thing whatsoever, without any limitation] whatever and without being confined to the specific acts hereinabove set out, requisite or necessary to be done in and about the premises as fully and to all intents and purposes as I might or could do and I hereby ratify and confirm all that LINDA SUE ROSE, my said attorney, shall lawfully do or cause to be done by virtue of these presents, and for me and in my name and on my

behalf. This power of attorney shall not be affected by any subsequent disability or incapacity of mine if such should occur. It is my express intent that the authority herein conferred upon my said attorney shall be exercisable in all events notwithstanding my subsequent disability or incapacity."

On October 28, 2002, Rose, purportedly acting as Langley's attorney-in-fact, signed a "Customer Service Request" revoking Langley's original designation of beneficiaries (Langley's three children and grandchild) and naming Rose as sole beneficiary. Rose signed the document as "Brenda G. Langley, P.O.A. Linda Rose." The form also was signed by Langley's insurance agent and was submitted to the insurance company.

Langley died on March 29, 2003. Five days later, Rose filed a claim for the proceeds of the policy. In July and early August 2003, the deceased's three children and grandchild filed separate claims for the policy proceeds.

Due to the competing claims for the life insurance proceeds, Tennessee Farmers filed this interpleader action pursuant to Tennessee Rule of Civil Procedure 22.01.1 Tennessee Farmer's complaint named Rose and the four original beneficiaries as defendants. The respective defendants filed answers to the complaint. The original beneficiaries subsequently filed a motion for summary judgment in which they asserted that Rose did not have the authority under the power of attorney to change the beneficiary designation on the policy. Rose responded to the motion, asserting that the power of attorney granted her the power to "transact all insurance business" and "to perform all and every other act and thing whatsoever, without any limitation. . . ." Based upon that language in the power of attorney, Rose argued that she was authorized to change the beneficiary designation to herself.

The trial court granted the original beneficiaries' motion for summary judgment, ruling that Rose "did not have the specific authority under the Durable General Power of Attorney executed by the decedent insured to execute a change of beneficiary form applicable to the life insurance policy at issue." The Court of Appeals, with one judge dissenting, affirmed the trial court's judgment.

Rose filed an application for permission to appeal to this Court. We granted permission to appeal to address the issue of whether the deceased's durable power of attorney authorized her attorney-in-fact to change the beneficiary of her life insurance policy.

II. STANDARD OF REVIEW

The trial court's grant of summary judgment is purely a question of law. Accordingly, our review is de novo, and no presumption of correctness attaches to the lower courts' judgments. Cumulus Broad. Inc. v. Shim, 226 S.W.3d 366, 373 (Tenn. 2007).

III. ANALYSIS

A written power of attorney that states it is not affected by the subsequent disability or incapacity of the principal is a "durable power of attorney." See Tenn. Code Ann. § 34-6-102 (2001). The power of attorney executed by Langley provides that it "shall not be affected" by her subsequent disability or incapacity, if any. Consequently, the instrument at issue is a durable power of attorney, which should be construed in light of the Uniform Durable Power of Attorney Act, Tennessee Code Annotated sections 34-6-101 to -110 (2001) ("the Act").

We begin our analysis by examining two particular sections of the Act, sections 34-6-108 and 34-6-109. Section 34-6-108(a) provides:

Upon the principal clearly expressing an intention to do so within the instrument creating a power of attorney, the language contained in § 34-6-109 may be incorporated into such power of attorney by appropriate reference. The provisions so incorporated shall apply to the attorney-in-fact with the same effect and subject to the same judicial interpretation and control in appropriate cases, as though such language were set forth verbatim in such instrument.

Tenn. Code Ann. § 34-6-108(a) (2001) (emphasis added).

Section 34-6-109 then proceeds to list twenty-two various powers which, pursuant to section 34-6-108, may be incorporated by reference into a durable power of attorney. In pertinent part, section 34-6-109(5) authorizes an attorney-in-fact to "[a]cquire, maintain, cancel or in any manner deal with any policy of life, accident, disability, hospitalization, medical or casualty insurance, and prosecute each claim for benefits due under any policy[.]" (emphasis added.) The words "or in any manner deal with any policy of life . . . insurance" could be interpreted to include the power to change the beneficiary of a life insurance policy. However, those words must be read in pari materia with section 34-6-108(c) which expressly provides:

Nothing contained in this section and § 34-6-109 shall be construed to vest an attorney-in-fact with, or

authorize an attorney-in-fact to exercise, any of the following powers:

(5) Change beneficiary designations on any death benefits payable on account of the death of the principal from any life insurance policy, employee benefit plan, or individual retirement account[.]

Tenn. Code Ann. § 34-6-108(c) (2001).

In light of section 34-6-108(c)(5), the phrase "in any manner deal with any policy of life … insurance" as used in 34-6-109(5) must be read to exclude the power to change the beneficiary of a life insurance policy. Despite section 34-6-108(c)(5)'s exclusion, however, section 34-6-108(b) provides:

Nothing contained in this section and § 34-6-109 shall be construed to limit the power of the principal either to:

1. Grant any additional powers to the attorney-in-fact, including any powers otherwise excluded under subsection (c); or
2. Delete any of the powers otherwise granted in § 34-6-109.

Tenn. Code Ann. § 34-6-108(b) (2001) (emphasis added).

While the foregoing sections are somewhat cumbersome to read, they essentially provide that, in cases in which the provisions of section 34-6-109 are incorporated by reference into the power of attorney, an attorney-in-fact is not authorized to change the beneficiary of the principal's life insurance policy unless the principal has expressly authorized the attorney-in-fact to do so within the power of attorney. The appellees (the original beneficiaries under Langley's policy) rely upon these statutory provisions and argue that Langley's power of attorney did not expressly authorize Rose to change the beneficiary/beneficiaries of Langley's life insurance policy. Thus, they contend that the trial court did not err in granting their motion for summary judgment.

We note that Langley's power of attorney did not mention any provisions of the Act, nor did her power of attorney otherwise clearly express an intention to adopt the language contained in section 34-6-109. For that reason, our resolution of this case does not involve the application of sections 34-6-108 and 34-6-109; instead, the language of Langley's power of attorney solely controls the attorney-in-fact's power, if any, to change the beneficiary of Langley's life insurance policy.

The execution of a power of attorney creates a principal-agent relationship. E.g., Rawlings v. John

Hancock Mut. Life Ins. Co., 78 S.W.3d 291, 296-97 n. 1 (Tenn. Ct. App. 2001). Unless otherwise constrained by law or public policy,[2] a person executing a power of attorney may empower his or her agent to do the same acts, to make the same contracts, and to achieve the same legal consequences as the principal would be personally empowered to do. Restatement (Second) of Agency § 17 (1958); 12 Samuel Williston, Treatise on the Law of Contracts § 35:9, at 188 (Richard A. Lord ed., 4th ed.1999).

The authority of the agent may be couched in general terms and may be as broad as the principal decides to make it. In the absence of specific legal requirements, a power of attorney may be in any form and may be executed in accordance with any recognized common-law method for executing written instruments. Realty Growth Investors v. Council of Unit Owners, 453 A.2d 450, 454 (Del. 1982). "The language of a power of attorney determines the extent of the authority conveyed." Armstrong v. Roberts, 211 S.W.3d 867, 869 (Tex. Ct. App. 2006). The more specific a power of attorney is concerning the performance of particular acts, the more the agent is restricted from performing acts beyond the specific authority granted. In re Estate of Kurrelmeyer, 179 Vt. 359, 895 A.2d 207, 211 (2006); cf. Restatement (Second) of Agency §§ 33 cmt. b & 37(2).

A power of attorney is a written instrument that evidences to third parties the purpose of the agency and the extent of the agent's powers. Lempert v. Singer, 766 F.Supp. 1356, 1360 (D.V.I. 1991); Realty Growth Investors, 453 A.2d at 454; Ho v. Presbyterian Church of Laurelhurst, 116 Or. App. 115, 840 P.2d 1340, 1343 (1992); Schall v. Gilbert, 169 Vt. 627, 741 A.2d 286, 289 (1999). It should be construed using the same rules of construction generally applicable to contracts and other written instruments, except to the extent that the fiduciary relationship between the principal and the agent[3] requires otherwise. In re Trust of Jameison, 300 Mont. 418, 8 P.3d 83, 87 (2000); In re Estate of Littlejohn, 698 N.W.2d 923, 925 (N.D. 2005); Restatement (Second) of Agency § 32.

The legal effect of a written contract or other written instruments is a question of law. In re Trust of Jameison, 8 P.3d at 86-87 (power of attorney); In re Estate of Littlejohn, 698 N.W.2d at 926 (power of attorney); Guiliano v. Cleo, Inc., 995 S.W.2d 88, 95 (Tenn. 1999) (written contract). Thus, powers of attorney should be interpreted according to their plain terms. Muller v. Bank of Am., N.A., 28 Kan. App. 2d 136, 12 P.3d 899, 902 (2000); see Buettner v. Buettner, 183 S.W.3d 354, 359 (Tenn. Ct. App. 2005). There is no room for the construction of a power of attorney that is not ambiguous or uncertain, and whose meaning and portent are perfectly clear. See Geren v. Geren, 29 Kan. App. 2d 565, 29 P.3d 448, 451-52 (2001). However, when the meaning of a power of attorney is unclear or ambiguous, the intention of the principal, at the time of the execution of the power of attorney, should be given effect. Brookfield Prod. Credit Ass'n v. Weisz, 658 S.W.2d 897, 899-900 (Mo. Ct. App. 1983); Restatement (Second) of Agency § 34 cmt. b. While the parol evidence rule applies, Restatement (Second) of Agency § 48, the courts may arrive at the meaning of a power of attorney by considering the five factors identified in Restatement (Second) of Agency section 34.

A formal written instrument that has been carefully drawn can be assumed to spell out the intent of the author with a high degree of particularity. Thus, an instrument like a power of attorney should be subjected to careful scrutiny in order to carry out the intent of the author and no more. There should be neither a "strict" nor a "liberal" interpretation of the instrument, but rather a fair construction that carries out the author's intent as expressed in the instrument. In re Estate of Kurrelmeyer, 895 A.2d at 211; Restatement (Second) of Agency § 34, cmt. h.

Applying the foregoing principles to the specific power of attorney executed by Langley, we hold that the power of attorney authorized Rose to change the beneficiary/beneficiaries of Langley's life insurance policy. In pertinent part, the power of attorney authorized Rose "to transact all insurance business on [Langley's] behalf, to apply for or continue policies, collect profits, file claims, make demands, enter into compromise and settlement agreements, file suit or actions or take any other action necessary or proper in this regard." (emphases added). As stated above, "[t]here is no room for construction of a power of attorney that is not ambiguous or uncertain, and whose meaning and portent are perfectly clear." Langley's power of attorney is neither ambiguous nor uncertain-it grants Rose the authority "to transact all insurance business" and to "take any other action in this regard." There simply is no escaping the significance of the word "all" and the words "take any other action in this regard" in delineating the scope of the insurance business which Rose was authorized to conduct. By authorizing Rose "to transact all insurance business" and "to take any other action in this regard," the power of attorney plainly and unambiguously authorized her to conduct any and all insurance-related business on Langley's behalf, which includes the power to change the beneficiary of Langley's life insurance policy. Just as Rose could have canceled this policy, purchased another one, and named a new beneficiary for the second policy, she had authority to make this change. If we were to construe the words of Langley's power of attorney to exclude the power to change beneficiary designations, we would effectively be rewriting Langley's power of attorney from authorizing Rose to transact "all" insurance business on Langley's behalf to authorizing Rose to transact "nearly all" of Langley's insurance business.[4]

If Langley's power of attorney had incorporated by reference the powers listed in Tennessee Code Annotated section 34-6-109, it would have been necessary for the power of attorney to have used the words "change beneficiary designations" or "change beneficiaries" in order to authorize Rose to make such changes, and the words "to transact all insurance business" would have been insufficient to confer that power on the attorney-in-fact. Langley's power of attorney, however, did not incorporate by reference the powers listed in section 34-6-109, and her power of attorney therefore did not trigger the application of section 34-6-108(c)(5). Therefore, without the limitation of section 34-6-108(c)(5), the words of Langley's power of attorney sufficiently authorized her attorney-in-fact to change her beneficiary designation. This holding, however, does not resolve all the issues arising out of this case.

This case was decided in the trial court on the original beneficiaries' motion for summary judgment. The sole ground raised in that motion was whether Langley's power of attorney authorized Rose to change the life insurance beneficiary. In granting the original beneficiaries' motion for summary judgment, the trial court pretermitted all of the other defenses raised in the original beneficiaries' answer to the complaint. In their answer to the complaint filed by Tennessee Farmers, the original beneficiaries denied that Langley "had the capacity to execute said durable general power of attorney given her physical and mental condition." They went on to allege "that if the decedent did indeed sign said durable general power of attorney, said execution was not of her own free will but was rather the result of the duress, coercion, control and/or undue influence exercised by the defendant Linda [S.] Rose upon the decedent." Their answer also asserted that Rose's action in changing the beneficiary of Langley's life insurance policy to herself "was a violation of [Rose's] fiduciary duty and was done for her sole benefit and to the detriment of the decedent and the decedent's children and grandchild."

Our holding that Langley's power of attorney granted Rose the authority to change the beneficiary designation does not foreclose any of those defenses. See Matlock v. Simpson, 902 S.W.2d 384, 386 (Tenn. 1995) (an attorney-in-fact under an unrestricted power of attorney has a confidential relationship with the principal, and as such, transactions that benefit the agent are looked upon with suspicion); Childress v. Currie, 74 S.W.3d 324, 328 (Tenn. 2002) (where a confidential relationship exists, a transaction which provides a benefit to the dominant party gives rise to a presumption of undue influence that may be rebutted only by clear and convincing evidence of the fairness of the transaction). Instead, our opinion today clarifies that Rose had the legal authority to alter the beneficiary designation. It does not, however, address whether her chosen designation, i.e. to herself, was valid under other principles of law. We therefore conclude that this case should be remanded to the trial court for further proceedings concerning the pretermitted [239 S.W.3d 752] issues. Accordingly, we express no opinion as to the ultimate resolution of the issues arising out of these pretermitted issues.

IV. CONCLUSION

For the reasons stated above, we reverse the judgment of the Court of Appeals and remand to the trial court for further proceedings. The costs on appeal are taxed to appellees, Kristin N. Taylor, Edward R. Langley, Phillip M. Langley, and Ethan E. Langley, for which execution may issue if necessary.

Notes:
[1]Tennessee Rules of Civil Procedure 22.01 provides, in pertinent part: "Persons having claims against the plaintiff may be joined as defendants and required to interplead when their claims are such that the plaintiff is or may be exposed to double or multiple liability."
[2]For example, other jurisdictions have held that a principal may not use a power of attorney to authorize another to create a will on his or her behalf. In re Estate of Garrett, 81 Ark. App. 212, 100 S.W.3d 72, 76 (2003); Smith v. Snow, 106 S.W.3d 467, 470 (Ky. Ct. App. 2002).
[3]Agents acting pursuant to an unrestricted power of attorney have a fiduciary relationship with the principal. See Askew v. Askew, 619 S.W.2d 384, 386 (Tenn. Ct. App. 1981); Restatement (Second) of Agency §§ 33 cmt. b & 39.

[4]The facts of this case illustrate the critical importance of carefully considering, when drafting a durable power of attorney, whether or not to incorporate by reference the various powers listed in Tennessee Code Annotated section 34-6-109.

Case Questions

1. Why did the Supreme Court of Tennessee grant permission to appeal in this case? In other words, what is the issue being considered by the court?
2. How did the trial court rule?
3. Whom did Brenda Gail Langley appoint under her power of attorney?
4. What was the holding in this case?
5. What portion of Langley's power of attorney authorized Linda S. Rose to change the beneficiary designation on the insurance policy?

FORMS TO ACCOMPANY PARALEGAL PRACTICE

Disclaimer: The forms provided to aid students in completing the Paralegal Practice activities assigned in each chapter have been modified as samples to familiarize students with what each form commonly looks like and are not intended to be used as actual forms for any state.

INSTRUCTIONS: The forms are provided in Microsoft Word format and employ the use of Stop Codes (such as SC1, SC2, SC3, and so on). Stop Codes are used in place of the form sections that must be updated with case-by-case information, such as SC1 for the client's name, SC3 for the client's address, and so on. What each Stop Code represents can be inferred by reading the surrounding text on the form. By using the FIND & REPLACE tool on the Microsoft toolbar, the students can replace the Stop Codes with the information provided in the Paralegal Practice activity to complete each assignment. Students must also fill in any blank lines on each form with the appropriate information from the activity and then proofread the document prior to turning in their work.

The following forms are included following this section and will be posted online for students to access to complete the Paralegal Practice activities for this chapter:

- PP Form 6.1—Durable Power of Attorney
- PP Form 6.2.A—Springing Power of Attorney
- PP Form 6.2.B—Health Care Power of Attorney
- PP Form 6.2.C—Living Will
- PP Form 6.3—Revocation of Power of Attorney

PP Form 6.1—Durable Power of Attorney

GENERAL DURABLE POWER OF ATTORNEY

Effective Date: _____ , 2014

Effective Place of Execution:
Sample County, Sample State

PRINCIPAL:
SC1
Sc3

AGENT (ATTORNEY-IN-FACT):
SC2
Sc4

NOTICE: THE POWERS GRANTED BY THIS DOCUMENT ARE BROAD AND SWEEPING. THEY ARE EXPLAINED IN THE UNIFORM STATUTORY FORM POWER OF ATTORNEY ACT. IF YOU HAVE ANY QUESTIONS ABOUT THESE POWERS, OBTAIN COMPETENT LEGAL ADVICE. THIS DOCUMENT DOES NOT AUTHORIZE ANYONE TO MAKE MEDICAL AND OTHER HEALTH-CARE DECISIONS FOR YOU. YOU MAY REVOKE THIS POWER OF ATTORNEY IF YOU LATER WISH TO DO SO.

THE POWERS YOU GRANT BELOW ARE EFFECTIVE EVEN IF YOU BECOME DISABLED OR INCOMPETENT.

I, **SC1**, residing at Sc3, appoint **SC2** residing at Sc4, as my Agent (attorney-in-fact) to act for me in any lawful way with respect to the following subjects:

TO GRANT ALL OF THE FOLLOWING POWERS:

(N) **Property transactions.** To lease, sell, mortgage, purchase, exchange, and acquire, and to agree, bargain, and contract for the lease, sale, purchase, exchange, and acquisition of, and to accept, take, receive, and possess any interest in real property whatsoever, on such terms and conditions, and under such covenants, as my Agent shall deem proper; and to maintain, repair, tear down, alter, rebuild, improve manage, insure, move, rent, lease, sell, convey, subject to liens, mortgages, and security deeds, and in any way or manner deal with all or any part of any interest in real property whatsoever, including specifically, but without limitation, real property lying and being situated in the State of Sample, under such terms and conditions, and under such covenants, as my Agent shall deem proper and may for all deferred payments accept purchase money notes payable to me and secured by mortgages or deeds to secure debt, and may from time to time collect and cancel any of said notes, mortgages, security interests, or deeds to secure debt.

(O) **Tangible personal property transactions.** To lease, sell, mortgage, purchase, exchange, and acquire, and to agree, bargain, and contract for the lease, sale, purchase, exchange, and acquisition of, and to accept, take, receive, and possess any personal property whatsoever, tangible or intangible, or interest thereto, on such terms and conditions, and under such covenants, as my Agent shall deem proper; and to maintain, repair, improve, manage, insure, rent, lease, sell, convey, subject to liens or mortgages, or to take any other security interests in said property which are recognized under the Uniform Commercial Code as adopted at that time under the laws of the State of Sample or any applicable state, or otherwise hypothecate (pledge), and in any way or manner deal with all or any part of any real or personal property whatsoever, tangible or intangible, or any interest therein, that I own at the time of execution or may thereafter acquire, under such terms and conditions, and under such covenants, as my Agent shall deem proper.

(P) **Stock and bond transactions.** To purchase, sell, exchange, surrender, assign, redeem, vote at any meeting, or otherwise transfer any and all shares of stock, bonds, or other securities in any business, association, corporation, partnership, or other legal entity, whether private or public, now or hereafter belonging to me.

(Q) **Commodity and option transactions.** To organize or continue and conduct any business which term includes, without limitation, any farming, manufacturing, service, mining, retailing or other type of business operation in any form, whether as a proprietorship, joint venture, partnership, corporation, trust or other legal entity; operate, buy, sell, expand, contract, terminate or liquidate any business; direct, control, supervise, manage or participate in the operation of any business and engage, compensate and discharge business managers, employees, agents, attorneys, accountants and consultants; and, in general, exercise all powers with respect to business interests and operations which the principal could if present and under no disability.

(R) **Banking and other financial institution transactions.** To make, receive, sign, endorse, execute, acknowledge, deliver and possess checks, drafts, bills of exchange, letters of credit, notes, stock certificates, withdrawal receipts and deposit instruments relating to accounts or deposits in, or certificates of deposit of banks, savings and loans, credit unions, or other institutions or associations. To pay all sums of money, at any time or times, that may hereafter be owing by me upon any account, bill of exchange, check, draft, purchase, contract, note, or trade acceptance made, executed, endorsed, accepted, and delivered by me or for me in my name, by my Agent. To borrow from time to time such sums of money as my Agent may deem proper and execute promissory notes, security deeds or agreements, financing statements, or other security instruments in such form as the lender may request and renew said notes and security instruments from time to time in whole or in part. To have free access at any time or times to any safe deposit box or vault to which I might have access.

(S) **Business operating transactions.** To conduct, engage in, and otherwise transact the affairs of any and all lawful business ventures of whatever nature or kind that I may now or hereafter be involved in.

(T) **Insurance and annuity transactions.** To exercise or perform any act, power, duty, right, or obligation, in regard to any contract of life, accident, health, disability, liability, or other type of insurance or any combination of insurance; and to procure new or additional contracts of insurance for me and to designate the beneficiary of same; provided, however, that my Agent cannot designate himself or herself as beneficiary of any such insurance contracts.

(U) **Estate, trust, and other beneficiary transactions.** To accept, receipt for, exercise, release, reject, renounce, assign, disclaim, demand, sue for, claim and recover any legacy, bequest, devise, gift or other property interest or payment due or payable to or for the principal; assert any interest in and exercise any power over any trust, estate or property subject to fiduciary control; establish a revocable trust solely for the benefit of the principal that terminates at the death of the principal and is then distributable to the legal representative of the estate of the principal; and, in general, exercise all powers with respect to estates and trusts which the principal could exercise if present and under no disability; provided, however, that the Agent may not make or change a will and may not revoke or amend a trust revocable or amendable by the principal or require the trustee of any trust for the benefit of the principal to pay income or principal to the Agent unless specific authority to that end is given.

(V) **Claims and litigation.** To commence, prosecute, discontinue, or defend all actions or other legal proceedings touching my property, real or personal, or any part thereof, or touching any matter in which I or my property, real or personal, may be in any way concerned. To defend, settle, adjust, make allowances, compound, submit to arbitration, and compromise all accounts, reckonings, claims, and demands whatsoever that now are, or hereafter shall be, pending between me and any person, firm, corporation, or other legal entity, in such manner and in all respects as my Agent shall deem proper.

(W) **Personal and family maintenance.** To hire accountants, attorneys at law, consultants, clerks, physicians, nurses, agents, servants, workmen, and others and to remove them, and to appoint others in their place, and to pay and allow the persons so employed such salaries, wages, or other remunerations, as my Agent shall deem proper.

(X) **Benefits from Social Security, Medicare, Medicaid, or other governmental programs, or military service.** To prepare, sign and file any claim or application for Social Security, unemployment or military service benefits; sue for, settle or abandon any claims to any benefit or assistance under any federal, state, local or foreign statute or regulation; control, deposit to any account, collect, receipt for, and take title to and hold all benefits under any Social Security, unemployment, military service or other state, federal, local or foreign statute or regulation; and, in general, exercise all powers with respect to Social Security, unemployment, military service, and governmental benefits, including but not limited to Medicare and Medicaid, which the principal could exercise if present and under no disability.

(Y) **Retirement plan transactions.** To contribute to, withdraw from and deposit funds in any type of retirement plan (which term includes, without limitation, any tax qualified or nonqualified pension, profit sharing, stock bonus, employee savings and other retirement plan, individual retirement account, deferred compensation plan and any other type of employee benefit plan); select and change payment options for the principal under any retirement plan; make rollover contributions from any retirement plan to other retirement plans or individual retirement accounts; exercise all investment powers available under any type of self-directed retirement plan; and, in general, exercise all powers with respect to retirement plans and retirement plan account balances which the principal could if present and under no disability.

(Z) **Tax matters.** To prepare, to make elections, to execute and to file all tax, social security, unemployment insurance, and informational returns required by the laws of the United States, or of any state or subdivision thereof, or of any foreign government; to prepare, to execute, and to file all other papers and instruments which the Agent shall think to be desirable or necessary for safeguarding of me against excess or illegal taxation or against penalties imposed for claimed violation of any law or other governmental regulation; and to pay, to compromise, or to contest or to apply for refunds in connection with any taxes or assessments for which I am or may be liable.

(continued)

THIS POWER OF ATTORNEY SHALL BE CONSTRUED AS A GENERAL DURABLE POWER OF ATTORNEY. THIS POWER OF ATTORNEY IS EFFECTIVE IMMEDIATELY AND WILL CONTINUE UNTIL IT **IS REVOKED. THIS POWER OF ATTORNEY SHALL BE CONSTRUED AS A GENERAL DURABLE POWER OF ATTORNEY AND SHALL CONTINUE TO BE EFFECTIVE EVEN IF I BECOME DISABLED, INCAPACITATED, OR INCOMPETENT.**

Authority to Delegate. My Agent shall have the right by written instrument to delegate any or all of the foregoing powers involving discretionary decision-making to any person or persons whom my Agent may select, but such delegation may be amended or revoked by any agent (including any successor) named by me who is acting under this power of attorney at the time of reference.

Right to Compensation. My Agent shall be entitled to reasonable compensation for services rendered as agent under this power of attorney.

Successor Agents. If any Agent named by me shall die, become incompetent, resign or refuse to accept the office of Agent, I name the following (each to act alone and successively, in the order named) as successor(s) to such Agent:

SC5, residing at Sc6; then

SC7, residing at Sc8.

Choice of Law. This power of attorney will be governed by the laws of the state of Sample without regard for conflicts of laws principles. It was executed in the state of Sample and is intended to be valid in all jurisdictions of the United States of America and all foreign nations.

I am fully informed as to all the contents of this form and understand the full import of this grant of powers to my Agent.

I agree that any third party who receives a copy of this document may act under it. Revocation of the power of attorney is not effective as to a third party until the third party learns of the revocation. I agree to indemnify the third party for any claims that arise against the third party because of reliance on this power of attorney.

I, SC1, the principal, sign my name to this power of attorney this _____ day of _____, 2014, and, being first duly sworn, do declare to the undersigned authority that I sign and execute this instrument as my power of attorney and that I sign it willingly, or willingly direct another to sign for me, that I execute it as my free and voluntary act for the purposes expressed in the power of attorney and that I am eighteen years of age or older, of sound mind and under no constraint or undue influence.

_____
SC1, Principal

I, _____, the witness, sign my name to the foregoing power of attorney being first duly sworn and do declare to the undersigned authority that the principal signs and executes this instrument as the principal's power of attorney and that the principal signs it willingly, or willingly directs another to sign for the principal, and that I, in the presence and hearing of the principal, sign this power of attorney as witness to the principal's signing and that to the best of my knowledge the principal is eighteen years of age or older, of sound mind and under no constraint or undue influence.

_____
Witness

NOTARY ACKNOWLEDGMENT

The state of SAMPLE
County of SAMPLE

Subscribed, sworn to and acknowledged before me by SC1, the principal, and subscribed and sworn to before me by _____, witness, this _____ day of _____, 2014.

WITNESS my hand and official seal.

_____
Notary Public

_____
Printed Name

PP Form 6.2.A—Springing Power of Attorney

DURABLE POWER OF ATTORNEY EFFECTIVE AT A FUTURE TIME

Pursuant to Sample Revised Statute §14-5501(B)(2)

THIS POWER OF ATTORNEY IS EFFECTIVE ON THE DISABILITY OR INCAPACITY OF THE PRINCIPAL

NOTICE: THE POWERS GRANTED BY THIS DOCUMENT ARE BROAD AND SWEEPING. THEY ARE EXPLAINED IN THE UNIFORM STATUTORY FORM POWER OF ATTORNEY ACT. IF YOU HAVE ANY QUESTIONS ABOUT THESE POWERS, OBTAIN COMPETENT LEGAL ADVICE. THIS DOCUMENT DOES NOT AUTHORIZE ANYONE TO MAKE MEDICAL AND OTHER HEALTH-CARE DECISIONS FOR YOU. YOU MAY REVOKE THIS POWER OF ATTORNEY IF YOU LATER WISH TO DO SO.

PRINCIPAL:
SC1
Sc3

AGENT (ATTORNEY-IN-FACT):
SC2
Sc4

I, **SC1**, residing at SC2, do hereby appoint **SC3**, residing at SC4, **MY ATTORNEY-IN-FACT TO ACT**

TO TAKE EFFECT upon the occasion of the signing of a written

statement **EITHER**

(I) by a physician or physicians named herein by me at this point:

Dr._____

_____

_____

OR

(II) if no physician or physicians are named hereinabove, or if the physician or physicians named hereinabove are unable to act, by my regular physician, or by a physician who has treated me within one year preceding the date of such signing, or by a licensed psychologist or psychiatrist,

CERTIFYING that the following specified event has occurred:
I am suffering from diminished capacity, whether physical or mental, which precludes me from conducting my affairs in a competent manner.

IN MY NAME, PLACE AND STEAD in any way which I myself could do, if I were personally present, with respect to the following matters to the extent that I am permitted by law to act through an agent:

TO GRANT ALL OF THE FOLLOWING POWERS:

(A) Property transactions. To lease, sell, mortgage, purchase, exchange, and acquire, and to agree, bargain, and contract for the lease, sale, purchase, exchange, and acquisition of, and to accept, take, receive, and possess any interest in real property whatsoever, on such terms and conditions, and under such covenants, as my Agent shall deem proper; and to maintain, repair, tear down, alter, rebuild, improve manage, insure, move, rent, lease, sell, convey, subject to liens, mortgages, and security deeds, and in any way or manner deal with all or any part of any interest in real property whatsoever, including specifically, but without limitation, real property lying and being situated in the State of Sample, under such terms and conditions, and under such covenants, as my Agent shall deem proper and may for all deferred payments accept purchase money notes payable to me and secured by mortgages or deeds to secure debt, and may from time to time collect and cancel any of said notes, mortgages, security interests, or deeds to secure debt.

(B) Tangible personal property transactions. To lease, sell, mortgage, purchase, exchange, and acquire, and to agree, bargain, and contract for the lease, sale, purchase, exchange, and acquisition of, and to accept, take,

(continued)

receive, and possess any personal property whatsoever, tangible or intangible, or interest thereto, on such terms and conditions, and under such covenants, as my Agent shall deem proper; and to maintain, repair, improve, manage, insure, rent, lease, sell, convey, subject to liens or mortgages, or to take any other security interests in said property which are recognized under the Uniform Commercial Code as adopted at that time under the laws of the State of Sample or any applicable state, or otherwise hypothecate (pledge), and in any way or manner deal with all or any part of any real or personal property whatsoever, tangible or intangible, or any interest therein, that I own at the time of execution or may thereafter acquire, under such terms and conditions, and under such covenants, as my Agent shall deem proper.

(C) Stock and bond transactions. To purchase, sell, exchange, surrender, assign, redeem, vote at any meeting, or otherwise transfer any and all shares of stock, bonds, or other securities in any business, association, corporation, partnership, or other legal entity, whether private or public, now or hereafter belonging to me.

(D) Commodity and option transactions. To organize or continue and conduct any business which term includes, without limitation, any farming, manufacturing, service, mining, retailing or other type of business operation in any form, whether as a proprietorship, joint venture, partnership, corporation, trust or other legal entity; operate, buy, sell, expand, contract, terminate or liquidate any business; direct, control, supervise, manage or participate in the operation of any business and engage, compensate and discharge business managers, employees, agents, attorneys, accountants and consultants; and, in general, exercise all powers with respect to business interests and operations which the principal could if present and under no disability.

(E) Banking and other financial institution transactions. To make, receive, sign, endorse, execute, acknowledge, deliver and possess checks, drafts, bills of exchange, letters of credit, notes, stock certificates, withdrawal receipts and deposit instruments relating to accounts or deposits in, or certificates of deposit of banks, savings and loans, credit unions, or other institutions or associations. To pay all sums of money, at any time or times, that may hereafter be owing by me upon any account, bill of exchange, check, draft, purchase, contract, note, or trade acceptance made, executed, endorsed, accepted, and delivered by me or for me in my name, by my Agent. To borrow from time to time such sums of money as my Agent may deem proper and execute promissory notes, security deeds or agreements, financing statements, or other security instruments in such form as the lender may request and renew said notes and security instruments from time to time in whole or in part. To have free access at any time or times to any safe deposit box or vault to which I might have access.

(F) Business operating transactions. To conduct, engage in, and otherwise transact the affairs of any and all lawful business ventures of whatever nature or kind that I may now or hereafter be involved in.

(G) Insurance and annuity transactions. To exercise or perform any act, power, duty, right, or obligation, in regard to any contract of life, accident, health, disability, liability, or other type of insurance or any combination of insurance; and to procure new or additional contracts of insurance for me and to designate the beneficiary of same; provided, however, that my Agent cannot designate himself or herself as beneficiary of any such insurance contracts.

(H) Estate, trust, and other beneficiary transactions. To accept, receipt for, exercise, release, reject, renounce, assign, disclaim, demand, sue for, claim and recover any legacy, bequest, devise, gift or other property interest or payment due or payable to or for the principal; assert any interest in and exercise any power over any trust, estate or property subject to fiduciary control; establish a revocable trust solely for the benefit of the principal that terminates at the death of the principal and is then distributable to the legal representative of the estate of the principal; and, in general, exercise all powers with respect to estates and trusts which the principal could exercise if present and under no disability; provided, however, that the Agent may not make or change a will and may not revoke or amend a trust revocable or amendable by the principal or require the trustee of any trust for the benefit of the principal to pay income or principal to the Agent unless specific authority to that end is given.

(I) Claims and litigation. To commence, prosecute, discontinue, or defend all actions or other legal proceedings touching my property, real or personal, or any part thereof, or touching any matter in which I or my property, real or personal, may be in any way concerned. To defend, settle, adjust, make allowances, compound, submit to arbitration, and compromise all accounts, reckonings, claims, and demands whatsoever that now are, or hereafter shall be, pending between me and any person, firm, corporation, or other legal entity, in such manner and in all respects as my Agent shall deem proper.

(J) Personal and family maintenance. To hire accountants, attorneys at law, consultants, clerks, physicians, nurses, agents, servants, workmen, and others and to remove them, and to appoint others in their place, and to pay and allow the persons so employed such salaries, wages, or other remunerations, as my Agent shall deem proper.

(K) Benefits from Social Security, Medicare, Medicaid, or other governmental programs, or military service. To prepare, sign and file any claim or application for Social Security, unemployment or military service benefits; sue for, settle or abandon any claims to any benefit or assistance under any federal, state, local or foreign statute or regulation; control, deposit to any account, collect, receipt for, and take title to and hold all benefits under any Social Security, unemployment, military service or other state, federal, local or foreign statute or regulation; and, in general, exercise all powers with respect to Social Security, unemployment, military service, and governmental benefits, including but not limited to Medicare and Medicaid, which the principal could exercise if present and under no disability.

(L) Retirement plan transactions. To contribute to, withdraw from and deposit funds in any type of retirement plan (which term includes, without limitation, any tax qualified or nonqualified pension, profit sharing, stock bonus, employee savings and other retirement plan, individual retirement account, deferred compensation plan and any other type of employee benefit plan); select and change payment options for the principal under any retirement plan; make rollover contributions from any retirement plan to other retirement plans or individual retirement accounts; exercise all investment powers available under any type of self-directed retirement plan; and, in general, exercise all powers with respect to retirement plans and retirement plan account balances which the principal could if present and under no disability.

(M) Tax matters. To prepare, to make elections, to execute and to file all tax, social security, unemployment insurance, and informational returns required by the laws of the United States, or of any state or subdivision thereof, or of any foreign government; to prepare, to execute, and to file all other papers and instruments which the Agent shall think to be desirable or necessary for safeguarding of me against excess or illegal taxation or against penalties imposed for claimed violation of any law or other governmental regulation; and to pay, to compromise, or to contest or to apply for refunds in connection with any taxes or assessments for which I am or may be liable.

THIS POWER OF ATTORNEY SHALL BE CONSTRUED AS A GENERAL DURABLE POWER OF ATTORNEY THAT IS EFFECTIVE ONLY ON THE DISABILITY OR INCAPACITY OF THE PRINCIPAL.

Authority to Delegate. My Agent shall have the right by written instrument to delegate any or all of the foregoing powers involving discretionary decision-making to any person or persons whom my Agent may select, but such delegation may be amended or revoked by any agent (including any successor) named by me who is acting under this power of attorney at the time of reference.

Right to Compensation. My Agent shall be entitled to reasonable compensation for services rendered as agent under this power of attorney.

Successor Agents. If any Agent named by me shall die, become incompetent, resign or refuse to accept the office of Agent, I name the following (each to act alone and successively, in the order named) as successor(s) to such Agent:

SC5, residing at Sc6; then

SC7, residing at Sc8.

Choice of Law. This power of attorney will be governed by the laws of the state of Sample without regard for conflict of laws principles. It was executed in the state of Sample and is intended to be valid in all jurisdictions of the United States of America and all foreign nations.

I am fully informed as to all the contents of this form and understand the full import of this grant of powers to my Agent. I agree that any third party who receives a copy of this document may act under it. Revocation of the power of attorney is not effective as to a third party until the third party learns of the revocation. I agree to indemnify the third party for any claims that arise against the third party because of reliance on this power of attorney.

I, SC1, the principal, sign my name to this power of attorney this _____ day of _____, 2014, and, being first duly sworn, do declare to the undersigned authority that I sign and execute this instrument as my power of attorney and that I sign it willingly, or willingly direct another to sign for me, that I execute it as my free and voluntary act for the purposes expressed in the power of attorney and that I am eighteen years of age or older, of sound mind and under no constraint or undue influence.

_____

SC1, Principal

I, _____, the witness, sign my name to the foregoing power of attorney being first duly sworn and do declare to the undersigned authority that the principal signs and executes this instrument as the principal's power of attorney and that the principal signs it willingly, or willingly directs another to sign for the principal, and that I, in the presence and hearing of the principal, sign this power of attorney as witness to the principal's signing

(*continued*)

and that to the best of my knowledge the principal is eighteen years of age or older, of sound mind and under no constraint or undue influence.

_____
Witness

NOTARY ACKNOWLEDGMENT

The state of SAMPLE
County of SAMPLE

Subscribed, sworn to and acknowledged before me by SC1, the principal, and subscribed and sworn to before me by _____, witness, this _____ day of _____, 2014.

WITNESS my hand and official seal.

_____
Notary Public

PP Form 6.2.B—Health Care Power of Attorney

DURABLE POWER OF ATTORNEY FOR HEALTH CARE

Effective Date: _____, 2014

Effective Place of Execution: Sample County, Sample

PRINCIPAL:
SC1
Sc3

ATTORNEY-IN-FACT:
SC2
Sc4

1. INTENT AND OBJECTIVE.

   My intent and objective in executing this Durable Power of Attorney for Health Care is to designate persons whom I trust to make all medical decisions for me when I am mentally unable to make those decisions for myself and to care for me in every way until such time as I am competent to make those decisions for myself. I intend that this document be effective at all times and in every place in the world.

2. ATTORNEY-IN-FACT.

   Principal constitutes and appoints the above named person as primary Attorney-in-Fact to act as the true and lawful attorney for Principal and in the name place and stead of Principal.

3. DECLARATION OF VALIDITY AT ANY PLACE AND UNDER ANY CIRCUMSTANCES.

   I declare this to be a Durable Power of Attorney for Health Care under the provisions of any state or country I may be in at the time of my incapacity and that this Durable Power of Attorney for Health Care shall not be affected or revoked by the disability of the Principal.

4. APPOINTMENT OF SUCCESSOR ATTORNEY-IN-FACT.

   I appoint the above named person as my primary Attorney-in-Fact. If the person designated above cannot make health care decisions for me, I designate the following person(s) to act instead in the priority order indicated:

   SC5, residing at Sc6; then
   SC7, residing at Sc8.

5. <u>GENERAL STATEMENT OF POWERS.</u>

I specifically authorize said person to make health care decisions for me, if I become incapable of giving informed consent with respect to

5.a. Requesting, receiving, and reviewing any information, verbal or written, regarding my physical condition or mental health, including, but not limited to, medical and hospital records;

5.b. Consenting to disclosure my medical records;

5.c. Consenting, refusing to consent, and withdrawing consent to any treatment or care, which is meant to maintain, treat or diagnose a physical or mental condition;

5.d. Consenting to withdrawal or withholding treatment that would keep me alive;

5.e. Disposing of my body or body parts as may be permitted by the laws of the state or country where I may be incapacitated; and

5.f. Making all decisions concerning whether I have an autopsy performed and the extent of that autopsy if so chosen.

6. <u>SPECIFIC POWERS.</u>

I expressly authorize my attorney-in-fact to

6.a. **Employ and Discharge Others.** Employ and discharge physicians, psychiatrists, dentists, nurses, therapists and other professionals that you, as Agent, may deem necessary for my physical, mental and emotional well-being, and to pay them or any of them reasonable compensation.

6.b. **Consent or Refuse Consent to My Medical Care.** Give or withhold consent to my medical care, surgery or other medical procedures or tests; to arrange for my hospitalization, convalescent care or home care, which I or you, as my agent, may have previously allowed or consent to which may have been guided in making such decisions by what I have told you about my personal preferences regarding such care. Based on those same preferences, you may also summon paramedics or other emergency medical personnel and seek emergency treatment for me or choose not to do so as you deem appropriate, given my wishes and my medical status at the time of the decision. You are authorized when dealing with hospitals and physicians to sign documents titled or purporting to be a "Refusal to Permit Treatment" and "Leaving Hospital against Medical Advice" as well as any necessary waivers of or releases from liability required by the hospitals or to implement my wishes regarding medical treatment or non-treatment.

6.c. **Consent or Refuse Consent to My Psychiatric Care.** Upon the execution of a certificate by two independent psychiatrists who have examined me, who are licensed to practice in the state of my residence and in whose opinions I am in immediate need of hospitalization because of mental disorders, alcoholism or drug abuse; to arrange for voluntary admission to appropriate hospital or institution for treatment of the diagnosed problem or disorder; to arrange for private psychiatric and psychological treatment of me; to refuse consent for any such hospitalization, institutionalization and private treatment, withdraw or change consent to such hospitalization, institutionalization and private treatment which I or you, as my Agent, may have given at an earlier time.

6.d. **Refuse My Life-Prolonging Procedures.** Request that aggressive medical therapy not be instituted or be discontinued including (but not limited to) cardiopulmonary resuscitation, the implantation of a cardiac pacemaker, renal dialysis, parenteral feeding, the use of respirators or ventilators, blood transfusions, nasogastric tube use, intravenous feeding, endotracheal tube use, antibiotics, and organ transplants. You should try to discuss the specifics of any such decision with me if I am able to communicate with you in any manner, even by blinking my eyes. If I am unconscious, comatose, senile or otherwise unreachable by such communication, you should make the decision guided primarily by any preferences that I may have previously expressed and secondarily by the information given by the physicians treating me as to my medical diagnosis and prognosis. You may specifically request and concur with the writing of "no-code" (DO NOT RESUSCITATE) order by the attending or treating physician.

6.e. **Provide Me Relief from Pain.** Consent to and arrange for the administration of pain-relieving drugs of any type or other surgical or medical procedures calculated to relieve my pain, even though their use may lead to permanent physical damage, addiction or even hasten the moment of (but not intentionally cause) my death. You may also consent to and arrange for unconventional pain-relief therapies such as biofeedback, guided imagery relaxation therapy, acupuncture or cutaneous stimulation and other therapies which you or I believe may be helpful to me.

7. <u>THIRD-PARTY RELIANCE.</u>

For the purpose of inducing any physician, hospital, bank, broker, custodian, insurer, lender, transfer agent, taxing authority, governmental agency or other party to act in accordance with the powers granted in this document, I hereby represent, warrant and agree that

(continued)

7.a. If this document is revoked or amended for any reason, I, my estate, my heirs, successors, and assigns will hold such party or parties harmless from any loss suffered or liability incurred by such party or parties in acting in accordance with this document prior to that parties receipt of written notice of any such termination or amendment.

7.b. The powers conferred on you by this document may be exercised by you alone and your signature or act under the authority granted in this document may be accepted by third parties as fully authorized by me and with the same force and effect as if I were personally present, competent, and acting on my own behalf.

7.c. No person who acts in reliance upon any representation you make as to the scope of your authority granted under this document shall incur any liability to me, my estate, my heirs, successors or assigns for permitting you to exercise any such power, nor shall any person who deals with you be responsible to determine or ensure the proper applications of funds or property.

7.d. You shall have the right to seek appropriate court orders mandating acts which you deem appropriate in third party refuses to comply with actions taken by you which are authorized by this document or enjoining acts by third parties which you have not authorized. In addition, you may bring legal action against any third party who fails to comply with actions I have authorized you to take and demand damages, including punitive damages, on my behalf for such noncompliance.

8. <u>BROAD INTERPRETATION.</u>

I give and grant unto you, as Agent and attorney-in-fact, full power and authority to do and perform all and every act and thing whatsoever requisite and necessary to be done in and about the premises, as fully to all intents and purposes as I might or could do if personally present, hereby ratifying and confirming all that you, as attorney-in-fact and Agent, shall lawfully do or cause to be done by virtue of these presents.

9. <u>EFFECT OF RECORDATION.</u>

If this Power is recorded, it may be revoked only by an instrument revoking the same duly acknowledged by me and recorded in the same country or counties in which this Power was originally recorded.

10. <u>DURATION.</u>

This Durable Power of Attorney for Health Care shall be perpetual.

11. <u>REVOCATION.</u>

I revoke any prior Durable Power of Attorney for Health Care. This Durable Power of Attorney for Health Care supplements any General Power of Attorney I have executed to provide for other matters of concern should I be incapacitated and supplements any living will I have executed.

WARNING TO PERSONS EXECUTING THIS DOCUMENT

THIS IS AN IMPORTANT LEGAL DOCUMENT. IT CREATES A DURABLE POWER OF ATTORNEY FOR HEALTH CARE. BEFORE EXECUTING THIS DOCUMENT, YOU SHOULD KNOW THESE IMPORTANT FACTS:

THIS DOCUMENT GIVES THE PERSON YOU DESIGNATE AS YOUR ATTORNEY-IN-FACT THE POWER TO MAKE HEALTH CARE DECISIONS FOR YOU, SUBJECT TO ANY LIMITATIONS OR STATEMENT OF YOUR DESIRES THAT YOU INCLUDE IN THIS DOCUMENT. THE POWER TO MAKE HEALTH CARE DECISIONS FOR YOU MAY INCLUDE CONSENT, REFUSAL OF CONSENT OR WITHDRAWAL OF CONSENT TO ANY CARE, TREATMENT, SERVICE OR PROCEDURE TO MAINTAIN, DIAGNOSE OR TREAT A PHYSICAL OR MENTAL CONDITION. YOU MAY STATE IN THIS DOCUMENT ANY TYPES OF TREATMENT OR PLACEMENTS THAT YOU DO NOT DESIRE.

THE PERSON YOU DESIGNATE IN THIS DOCUMENT HAS A DUTY TO ACT CONSISTENT WITH YOUR DESIRES AS STATED IN THIS DOCUMENT OR OTHERWISE MADE KNOWN OR, IF YOUR DESIRES ARE UNKNOWN, TO ACT IN YOUR BEST INTEREST.

EXCEPT AS YOU OTHERWISE SPECIFY IN THIS DOCUMENT THE POWER OF THE PERSON YOU DESIGNATE TO MAKE HEALTH CARE DECISIONS FOR YOU MAY INCLUDE THE POWER TO GIVE CONSENT TO YOUR DOCTOR TO WITHHOLD TREATMENT THAT WOULD KEEP YOU ALIVE.

UNLESS YOU SPECIFY A SHORTER PERIOD OF TIME, THIS POWER WILL EXIST FROM THE DATE YOU EXECUTE THIS DOCUMENT UNTIL THE EXPIRATION DATE SET FORTH IN THE CAPTION. IF YOU ARE UNABLE TO MAKE HEALTH CARE DECISIONS FOR YOURSELF AT THE TIME THIS SEVEN-YEAR PERIOD ENDS THIS POWER WILL CONTINUE TO EXIST UNTIL SUCH TIME YOU BECOME ABLE TO MAKE THOSE DECISIONS.

NOTWITHSTANDING THIS DOCUMENT, YOU HAVE THE RIGHT TO MAKE MEDICAL AND OTHER HEALTH CARE DECISIONS FOR YOURSELF AS LONG AS YOU CAN GIVE INFORMED CONSENT WITH RESPECT TO THE

PARTICULAR DECISION, IN ADDITION, NO TREATMENT MAY BE GIVEN TO YOU OVER YOUR OBJECTION AND, ANY HEALTH CARE NECESSARY TO KEEP YOU ALIVE MAY NOT BE ADMINISTERED IF YOU OBJECT.

YOU HAVE THE RIGHT TO REVOKE THE APPOINTMENT OF THE PERSON DESIGNATED IN THIS DOCUMENT BY NOTIFYING THAT PERSON OF THE REVOCATION ORALLY OR IN WRITING.

YOU HAVE THE RIGHT TO REVOKE THE AUTHORITY GRANTED TO THE PERSON DESIGNATED IN THIS DOCUMENT TO MAKE HEALTH CARE DECISIONS FOR YOU BY NOTIFYING THE TREATING PHYSICIAN, HOSPITAL OR OTHER HEALTH CARE PROVIDER ORALLY OR IN WRITING.

THE PERSON DESIGNATED IN THIS DOCUMENT TO MAKE HEALTH CARE DECISIONS FOR YOU HAS THE RIGHT TO EXAMINE YOUR MEDICAL RECORDS AND TO CONSENT TO THEIR DISCLOSURE UNLESS YOU LIMIT THIS RIGHT IN THIS DOCUMENT.

IF THERE IS ANYTHING IN THIS DOCUMENT THAT YOU DO NOT UNDERSTAND, YOU SHOULD ASK A LAWYER TO EXPLAIN IT TO YOU.

THIS POWER OF ATTORNEY WILL NOT BE VALID FOR MAKING HEALTH CARE DECISIONS UNLESS IT IS EITHER (L) SIGNED BY TWO QUALIFIED WITNESSES WHO ARE PERSONALLY KNOWN TO YOU AND WHO ARE PRESENT WHEN YOU SIGN OR ACKNOWLEDGE YOUR SIGNATURE OR (2) ACKNOWLEDGED BEFORE A NOTARY PUBLIC.

IN WITNESS WHEREOF, I have signed this document this date _____, 2014.

_____
SC1

NOTARY ACKNOWLEDGMENT

STATE OF SAMPLE
COUNTY OF SAMPLE

On this _____ day of _____, 2014, before me, the undersigned, a notary public in and for said state personally appeared SC1 personally known to me (or proved to me on the basis of satisfactory evidence) to be the person whose name is subscribed to the within instrument and acknowledged to me that she executed the same in her authorized capacity, and that by her signature on the instrument the person or entity upon behalf of which the persons acted, executed instrument. WITNESS my hand and official seal.

_____
Notary Public

SIGNATURE OF WITNESSES

_____   _____
Witness Signature

                                         _____

                                         _____

_____   _____
Witness Name (Printed)   Witness Address

_____   _____
Witness Signature

                                         _____

                                         _____

_____   _____
Witness Name (Printed)   Witness Address

(continued)

PP Form 6.2.C—Living Will

LIVING WILL

I, **SC1**, having an address at Sc3, and an adult of sound and disposing mind and memory, not acting under duress, menace, fraud or undue influence of any person, do make, publish and declare this to be my Living Will to supplement all other wills I may execute and to be used in the event that I am unconscious or mentally incapacitated and, at the same time, have a catastrophic medical condition.

1. DECLARATION OF INTENT.

   I realize that, when I am conscious and functioning normally with full mental facilities, I have a legal right to accept or reject medical treatment offered to me by doctors, hospitals or other medical instrumentalities. It is my intent with this Living Will to express my commitment and to designate persons who are legally empowered to act for me when I am unconscious or mentally incapacitated, with full authority from me to make medical decisions for me and to accept or reject medical treatment. I rely on the common law and desire that this Living Will be enforced even if I am in a state of the United States that has not adopted specific statutes related to the enforcement of Living Wills.

   Further, my objective in executing this Living Will is to allow persons appointed by me in this document to withdraw medical care and administer pain-killing drugs when two doctors determine that my brain is no longer functioning or is irrevocably damaged, or when disease or accident places me in a condition where I am irrevocably dying, or when disease or accident has impaired my mind and body where I can no longer function as a normal human being with a standard of life which would not endear me to other human beings. I intend that this document be effective at all times and in every place in this world.

2. PURPOSE.

   The purpose of this Living Will is to prevent my remaining assets from being used to unnecessarily prolong my life, so that they may be used instead to benefit my spouse and children, if any, and other heirs and devisees who benefit from my worldly estate. Also, I desire to avoid the heartache to my loved ones of an extended illness and to avoid additional pain and suffering to myself through whatever senses remain. In the unlikely event that this instrument may not be legally binding in the jurisdiction where I may be terminally ill, then you who care for me will, I hope, feel morally bound to follow its mandate. It is my decision, not yours, and it is made after careful consideration.

3. INSTRUCTION.

   If it is ever determined by competent medical evidence, to the satisfaction of the persons designated below, that my body is substantially damaged, deteriorated, destroyed or in a tenuous condition through accident, illness or age, and that I have reached the point where there is no reasonable expectation of recovery from physical or mental disability even with the aid of artificial means or heroic measures, such as respirators, transfusions, electric shock treatments, or instruments to prolong heart beat (i.e. code arrest mechanisms, artificial respirators, heart massage by manual or mechanical methods, drugs or potent nature), intravenous feedings, or other measures, I request that all such life-prolonging means and measures be withdrawn or withheld from my body so that I may die with dignity. I further request that medication be mercifully administered to me for terminal suffering, even if it hastens the moment of death. I do not fear death as much as I fear the indignity of deterioration, dependence and hopeless pain.

   I consider myself in a tenuous condition if I have an incurable or irreversible physical condition that, in reasonable medical probability, will result in death unless extraordinary medical measures are used. I consider as extraordinary medical measures all medication, surgical procedures, mechanical or electrical devices that will sustain, restore or supplant a vital bodily function. A measure is extraordinary if employing it would not offer a reasonable medical probability of returning me to cognitive, sapient existence and would serve only to postpone the moment of death. I do not consider medical or surgical procedures to alleviate pain or discomfort prohibitive procedures under this Living Will.

4. MECHANICS OF IMPLEMENTATION.

   In order to implement the Living Will, my family physician along with one consulting physician shall make a finding that

4.a. I am unconscious, mentally incompetent or deranged, senile, insane or otherwise in an abnormal mental condition where I am not reasonably able to make decisions of my own.

4.b. Through accident, disease, nervous system, or otherwise, I have an irreversible condition resulting in (1) a brain that is dead, (2) a brain that is damaged to the point where I will not be able to reasonably enjoy a normal life, (3) a body with damaged organs or parts that will prevent me from enjoying the quality of productive life to which I am accustomed, or (4) a combination of all of these which will prevent me from enjoying the productive life to which I am accustomed.

If my family physician is not available, then two attending physicians may concur with the consulting physician in the finding. If three physicians are not immediately available, then two may concur.

The findings of the physicians will be written on my patient chart, or on a dated piece of paper to be placed in my patient file.

Thereupon the representative I have first designated in this Living Will shall concur and evidence that concurrence in writing on the patient chart or otherwise on the dated paper with the physicians written findings. If my first designated representative or the next is not readily available then whichever one is the most readily available shall sign an affirmation of the decision.

If my representative is not physically available, concurrence may be affirmed by (1) two witnesses over the phone, with those witnesses evidencing the consent by writing this in the patient chart or on the dated paper concerning the physicians written findings, or (2) by telegram or other means used for transmitting the written language, and a copy of this shall be placed in my medical files.

Once these findings and my representative's decisions have been thus memorialized, I shall be placed in a private room. My family and friends shall be summoned. The physician shall give me no further medical care or life aids such as food and water, except that morphine and other pain killing or tranquilizing drugs shall be liberally administered even if they accelerate the moment of death. My family and friends shall be left alone with me, except for a doctor or nurse who will assist in keeping my physically clean and presentable until the moment of my passing.

If my doctors or representatives are unaware of these mechanics, I consent to any reasonable alternative method. My purpose in detailing these mechanics is to assist in providing my physicians and representatives with a reasonable method of carefully documenting what they have done to avoid later misunderstanding.

The findings of my doctors and the decision of my representative, once written, shall not be subject to attack by anyone at any later date.

5. PERSONS DESIGNATED TO MAKE DECISIONS.

I give the following persons, singly in the order indicated or acting together, the power to make this decision:**Primary Decision Maker:**

SC2, residing at Sc4.

Alternate Decision Maker(s):
SC5, residing at Sc6; then
SC7, residing at Sc8.

Neither the attending physician nor the hospital is required to determine the reason for the absence of persons I may have listed first in the order of priority above. Whichever one of my family representatives appears will take the responsibility of making an effort to locate the persons designated with higher priority. However, I trust in the judgment of all the persons named and, if they are unable to contact the person of higher priority, I will trust any of the persons named above who are there to make the necessary decisions. I know that whoever makes the decisions will have made every effort to notify all the other persons to obtain their concurrence and, if they cannot contact them within the time required by the emergency or if they cannot get concurrence of all parties, they have the authority to and will make the necessary decisions.

These persons are given a special power of attorney to act for me during any incapacity to make all decisions with regard to my medical treatment that I could have make had I been conscious and mentally able. I designate these persons also as my guardians ad litem and guardians of my person to sign all documents and bring any legal proceeding that may be necessary to exercise the power and authority vested in them by this Living Will, including the power to bring court proceedings for injunctive relief, damages, or other relief necessary to carry

(continued)

out my wishes expressed in this Living Will. It is my intent that the persons designated act quickly and without the necessity of court proceedings; however, if any doctor, hospital or other medical institution fails to carry out the instructions of my Living Will and the decisions of the persons I have designated to carry out my instructions, then the persons designated to make the decisions are directed to bring immediate court proceedings to enforce this Living Will. I direct that this Living Will be implemented by the persons designated and the attending doctors acting together without the necessity of consulting courts, administrative bodies or hospital committees.

6. PROTECTION FOR PERSONS DESIGNATED AND THOSE ASSISTING.

As further evidence of my convictions as expressed in this Living Will, I direct that the assets of my estate and my insurance be used to hold harmless form any liability the persons designated and any doctor, hospital or other medical instrumentality that assists in carrying out (a) my instructions expressed in this Living Will and (b) the decision and instructions of the persons designated by me to carry out my instructions.

My estate and my insurance shall also be committed to pay any attorney's fees, court costs or any other expenses associated with court proceedings to carry out my instructions expressed in this Living Will and the decisions of the persons I have designated to carry out these wishes and to defend anyone who assists in carrying out these instructions. All doctors, medical personnel, hospitals and other medical instrumentalities shall not be liable for any act complying with this Living Will in good faith, except acts of gross negligence or willful misconduct.

IN WITNESS WHEREOF, I have signed this document this date: _____, 2014.

_____
SC1

ACKNOWLEDGEMENT OF WITNESSES

This instrument was on the above date signed by the above-named Signator in our presence and published and declared to be the Signator's Living Will. At the Signator's request and in the presence of the Signator and in the presence of each other, we have signed below as witnesses thereto. WE ALSO AFFIRM THAT WE ARE NOT RELATED TO THE SIGNATOR BY BLOOD OR MARRIAGE AND ARE NOT INVOLVED WITH THE MEDICAL CARE OF THE SIGNATOR. At the time of signing, the Signator appeared to be of sound mind and free from duress.

_____   _____
Witness Signature   _____

_____

_____   _____
Witness Name (Printed)   Witness Address

_____   _____
Witness Signature   _____

_____

_____

_____   _____
Witness Name (Printed)   Witness Address

PP Form 6.3—Revocation of Power of Attorney

REVOCATION OF POWER OF ATTORNEY

Know all Men by these Presents, That

Whereas, SC1

in and by his Powers of Attorney, bearing the date of _____ did make, constitute and appoint

SC2

As his agent by the aforesaid Power of Attorney as it may more fully and at large appear.

Now know ye, That SC1 has revoked, countermanded, annulled and made void, and by these presents does revoke, countermand annul and make void the said Powers of Attorney above mentioned, and all power and authority thereby given, or intended to be given, to the said

SC2.

In Witness Whereof, SC1 has hereunto set his hand and seal the _____ day of _____, 2014 and

Sealed and delivered in the presence of

_____

SC1

STATE OF SAMPLE STATE)

COUNTY OF SAMPLE) ss.:

On the _____ day of _____ in the year 2014 before me, the undersigned, personally appeared **SC1**, personally known to me or proved to me on the basis of satisfactory evidence to be the individual whose name is subscribed to the within instrument and acknowledged to me that he/she executed the same in his/her capacity, and that by his/her signature on the instrument, the individual, or the person upon behalf of which the individual acted, executed the instrument.

_____

Notary Public

WHEN RECORDED RETURN TO:
Pearson & Pearson, Attorneys-At-Law
1001 Reed Drive
Sample County, Sample State 12345

CHAPTER 5

Last Wills and Testaments

A REAL-LIFE SCENARIO

A family of 10 with all adult children watched as their beloved father passed away over the course of a few days. The father was still competent to express his wishes until the last day—the day of his demise. The family dynamics were less than perfect. The one common thread was that all, or nearly all, of the members loved their father. However, love for each other and their mother was another story. The fighting began as children arrived from a variety of states with their own ideas about what should happen and who should inherit.

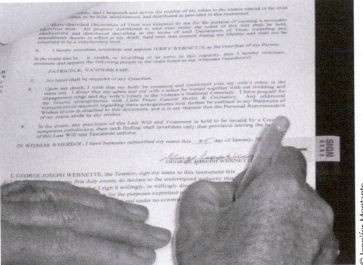

© Jennifer Montante

The father was truly concerned about his wife's well-being after he was gone, for one son had a criminal history and yet was the mother's favorite. The father was worried that the bad seed would wipe the mother out as soon as he had access to the family assets. He would inevitably attain access because his mother would deny him nothing.

The father called his attorney and she was kind enough to come to the hospital and to bring with her a tape recorder to record his wishes. Another trusted son from out-of-state brought along a camcorder and also recorded his father's intentions. The recordings were approximately one hour long. The children's mother was present and did not object to her husband's intentions at the time he was expressing them. The attorney left the hospital and drew

CHAPTER OBJECTIVES:

1. Understand the purpose of executing a Last Will and Testament.

2. Describe the necessary requirements for a valid will.

3. Discuss the different types of wills.

4. Identify the common articles in wills.

5. Determine what clauses are necessary to carry out a client's specific wishes.

6. Explain what holographic and nuncupative wills are.

up a will that included a trust for the wife in order to preserve the assets and provide for her during the remainder of her lifetime. Using her legal training and knowledge, the attorney determined that the use of a trust was the best way to provide for the wife and keep the assets out of the reach of the bad seed.

The next day, the attorney went to the hospital with the will in hand to deliver it to her client. Although she had an appointment, when the attorney arrived, the client was asleep and the family members were absent. As a result, she left the will in an envelope with the nurses to deliver to the wife for her husband to execute. Rather than give her husband the will, she told him each time he asked for it that the attorney never brought it. Several children observed their father's requests and their mother's denials and did not learn until after their father died that the attorney had, in fact, dropped off the will. The wife effectively prevented her husband from signing a written will prior to his death.

Thereafter, two of the children attempted to probate the nuncupative (oral) recorded will as the last will and testament of the decedent. Nuncupative wills were not flatly prohibited by state statute, nor were they provided for. A lengthy court battle ensued.

■ INTRODUCTION

Key Terms and Definitions

Will
A written document that leaves the estate of the individual who signed the will to the named persons or entities.

A **last will and testament**, or **will**, is a written document that leaves the estate of the individual who signed the will to the named persons or entities. A will only disposes of property following the maker's death, and can be revoked or amended at any time while the maker is still alive.

The primary purpose of executing a will is to control the disposition of one's assets after death. Many are concerned with making sure their family members and other loved ones are well cared for. Others wish to donate their estate to a charity or another worthy cause.

In addition to disposing of one's assets, a will is useful to ensure that minor children are provided for by appointing a guardian to be legally responsible for them if they lose their parents. Further, some states permit individuals to appoint guardians over themselves under their will in the event they become incapacitated and in need of a guardian. In this respect, the will may be used during the testator's lifetime to aid in appointment of the guardian. Finally, some states permit testators to give instructions regarding their funeral and the disposal of their remains under their will. *Note* that state law varies greatly and you must check the law in your state to determine whether it is permissible to give funeral and burial or cremation instructions under a will.

Intestate
To die without a valid will.

A decedent who dies without a valid will is said to die **intestate**. When individuals die intestate, their property passes according to their state's intestacy laws, called **intestate succession statutes**. Intestate succession statutes are in place to ensure that the close family members of those who do not execute a will are still provided for upon the loss of their loved one. However, it is generally preferable to choose who will inherit from one's estate, rather than let the state's default provisions apply. This is one very good reason to execute a valid will.

Intestate Succession Statutes
State laws that determine who will inherit the property of a person who dies without a valid will.

Probate
A general term for the entire process of administration of estates of dead persons, including those without wills, with court supervision.

As has been discussed in previous chapters, disposing of assets by will often requires a probate proceeding. **Probate** is a general term for the entire process of administering a decedent's estate with court supervision, and may include intestate estates (those without wills).

■ REQUIREMENTS FOR DUE EXECUTION OF A WILL

Capacity

In order to execute a will, a person must have legal capacity and be of sound mind. **Legal capacity** is the age of majority at which a person acquires the capacity to make a valid will. Majority age is eighteen (18) in most states, but is age twenty-one (21) in a minority of states. What it means to be "of **sound mind**" is to have the mental ability to make a valid will. Sound mind is the normal condition of the human mind, not impaired by insanity or other mental disorders. The individual executing the will must have capacity at the time they execute the will, but the will execution can take place during a "lucid moment." For example, an elderly woman with early-onset dementia is still very coherent in the morning hours but becomes more confused as the day progresses and she gets tired. Circumstances dictate that this woman should meet with her estate planning attorney during the morning hours when she is most alert. If the woman is capable of reading and understanding the will at the time she signs it, the will is properly executed with respect to capacity.

Legal Capacity
The age of majority at which a person acquires the capacity to make a valid will. Majority age is eighteen (18) in most states, but is twenty-one (21) in a minority of states.

Sound Mind
Having the mental capacity to execute a document, such as a will. Sound mind is the normal condition of the human mind, not impaired by insanity or other mental disorders.

Execution of Will

A **testator** is a man who executes a will; a **testatrix** is a female who executes a will. In some states, it is now customary to use the term "testator" for both genders. The requirements for due execution of a will vary by state, but most states require that, at a minimum, the will is written, signed and dated by the maker, and attested and signed by two witnesses. Some states require that there be three witnesses. **Attestation** is the act of witnessing a signature for the purpose of declaring that the will was properly signed and declared by the signer to be his or her signature.

Testator
A man who executes a will.
Testatrix
A female who executes a will.

Attestation
The act of witnessing a signature for the purpose of declaring that the will was properly signed and declared by the signer to be his or her signature.

■ WRITTEN WILLS

There are a number of different types of written wills that you will hear about in an estate planning office. The following descriptions are intended to orient you to the basic terminology.

You may have heard of the term "simple will." You may think this means the will was simple to draft. However, "simple will" is a misnomer. Simple wills need not be simple in that they can contain complex provisions pertaining to multiple beneficiaries. However, **simple wills** generally do not include tax planning language and for that reason are referred to as "simple" by legal professionals. Tax planning is often done to reduce tax liability upon death for sizeable estates. Simple wills do not contain tax planning language. The next several figures display a number of common simple wills.

Simple Will
A phrase used by legal professionals to indicate a will that does not include tax planning language.

Figure 5.1 depicts the will of a single female. It is the second will executed by Jane Smith from the Hypothetical Family and depicts a simple will leaving everything to adult beneficiaries.

Figure 5.2 depicts the will of a married female with minor children. The testatrix is Jasmine J. Smith, who is the wife of John Smith from The Hypothetical Family. Since there are minor children involved, this will includes additional provisions that were not present in Figure 5.1. First, the will provides that the share of any minor child be held in a Uniform Transfers to Minors Account until the child reaches age 21. Second, the will appoints a guardian for the minor children.

Figure 5.1 Last Will and Testament

I, **JANE SMITH**, of the CITY OF SAMPLE, COUNTY OF SAMPLE COUNTY, STATE OF SAMPLE STATE, do hereby make, publish and declare the following to be my Last Will and Testament, hereby revoking all former Wills and Codicils made by me.

I. I direct that all my debts and funeral expenses be paid and I further authorize my Executor, in its discretion, to prepay any mortgage or other installment indebtedness.

II. I give and bequeath to my children, JOHN SMITH and SUSAN SMITH, and my nephew, MARK SMITH, JR., all of my clothing, jewelry, personal effects, household goods, furniture, furnishings, automobiles and all other tangible personal property which I may own at the time of my death, to be divided among them as they shall agree. If my beneficiaries are unable to agree as to the recipient of any article, that article, as well as any articles not selected, shall be sold and the proceeds added to my residuary estate.

III. All the rest, residue and remainder of my property, real, personal and mixed, of every name and nature, and wheresoever situate, I give, devise and bequeath in equal shares to JOHN SMITH, SUSAN SMITH, and MARK SMITH, JR., or all to the survivors of them.

IV. I give to my Executor hereinafter named, and to the successor, the following powers and discretions, in addition to those vested in or imposed upon them or either of them by law:

    A. To mortgage, sell, convey, exchange or otherwise deal with or dispose of any real or personal property for cash or on credit (including the right to accept a purchase money mortgage as part of the purchase price); to retain as part of the estate any and all securities and property in the form originally received, whether or not it is then income producing and regardless of any rule requiring diversification of investments; to invest and reinvest in any stocks, bonds, shares in mutual funds or authorized common trust funds, or other securities or property, whether real or personal, which my Executor may deem safe and for the best interests of the estate, without being limited to investments authorized by law for the investment of trust funds; to hold title to any and all securities and other investments either in my Executor's name or in the name of a nominee; to borrow money from itself or others on terms my Executor may deem best, and to pledge any property of the estate as security for the repayment thereof; and to make distributions in cash or in kind, or partly in each to the beneficiaries entitled thereto.

    B. If any beneficiary or legatee entitled to receive a part of my estate shall be under twenty-one (21) years of age, I authorize and empower my Executor to designate his or her parent, or some other appropriate adult person, or trust company, as custodian for the beneficiary or legatee under the Sample State Uniform Transfers to Minors Act until age twenty-one (21), and to distribute the share of the beneficiary or legatee to the designated custodian. A receipt from the custodian shall fully release my Executor.

V. I direct that all inheritance, succession and estate taxes of every kind payable with respect to any property includable in my gross taxable estate, whether or not passing under this my Will, shall be paid out of my residuary estate, and shall not be apportioned.

VI. I hereby nominate, constitute and appoint JOHN SMITH as Executor of this my Last Will and Testament, but if he fails to survive me, or renounces, or fails to qualify, or upon his death, resignation or disqualification, I nominate and appoint SUSAN SMITH as Executrix. I direct that no bond or other security shall be required of my Executor.

VII. The masculine gender, whenever used herein, shall include the feminine, the feminine shall include the masculine; the neuter shall include both the masculine and feminine; and the singular shall include the plural wherever necessary or appropriate.

IN WITNESS WHEREOF, I have hereunto subscribed my name and affixed my seal this 25th day of February, 2012.

Jane Smith

_____

JANE SMITH

We, whose names are hereto subscribed, do certify that on the 25th day of *February*, 2012, the Testatrix, JANE SMITH, subscribed her name to this instrument, in our presence and in the presence of each of us, and at the same time in our presence and hearing, declared the same to be her Last Will and Testament, and requested us, and each

Figure 5.1 (continued)

of us, to sign our names thereto as witnesses to the execution thereof, which we hereby do in the presence of the Testatrix and of each other.

Michael Pearson _____ residing at *1001 Reed Drive, Sample City, Sample State 12345* _____

Maggy Pearson _____ residing at *1001 Reed Drive, Sample City, Sample State 12345* _____

AFFIDAVIT OF ATTESTING WITNESSES

STATE OF SAMPLE STATE)
COUNTY OF SAMPLE COUNTY) SS:

_____ *Michael Pearson* _____ and _____ *Maggy Pearson* _____ , being duly sworn say:

We are acquainted with JANE SMITH. The signature at the end of the instrument dated February 25, 2012 declared by her to be her Last Will, was made by her at City of Sample, State of Sample State, in the presence of each of the undersigned.

At the time of signing Will, JANE SMITH declared the instrument to which her signature had been affixed to be her Will and we, and each of us, signed our names thereto at the end thereof at that time and at her request and in her presence.

At the time of the execution of the instrument JANE SMITH was over the age of 18 years, of sound mind and memory, and not under any restraint and competent in every respect to make a Will.

At the time of execution, JANE SMITH could read, write and converse in the English language, and was not suffering from defects of sight, hearing, or speech or any other physical or mental impairment that could affect her capacity to make a valid Will.

The Will was not executed in counterparts.

Michael Pearson _____
Witness

Maggy Pearson _____
Witness

STATE OF SAMPLE STATE}
COUNTY OF SAMPLE COUNTY} ss:

On the 25th day of February in the year 2011 before me, the undersigned, a Notary Public in and for said State, personally appeared Michael Pearson and Maggy Pearson, the subscribing witnesses to the foregoing instrument, with whom I am personally acquainted, who being by me duly sworn, did depose and say that Michael Pearson resides at 1001 Reed Drive, Sample State and Maggy Pearson resides at 1001 Reed Drive, Sample State; that they know JANE SMITH to be the individual described in and who executed the foregoing instrument; that said subscribing witnesses were present and saw said JANE SMITH execute the same; and that said witnesses at the same time subscribed their names as witnesses thereto, and acknowledged to me that they executed the same in their capacities, and that by their signatures on the instrument, the individual(s) or the person upon behalf of which the individual(s) acted, executed the instrument.

Lila P. Legal _____
Notary Public

LILA P. LEGAL
Notary Public, State of Sample
Sample County
My Commission Expires May 10, 2012

(continued)

Figure 5.2 LAST WILL AND TESTAMENT of **JASMINE J. SMITH**

I, **JASMINE J. SMITH**, of the CITY OF SAMPLE, COUNTY OF SAMPLE, STATE OF SAMPLE, do hereby make, publish and declare the following to be my Last Will and Testament, hereby revoking all former Wills and Codicils made by me.

I. I direct that all my just legal debts and funeral expenses be paid, and I further authorize my Personal Representative, in its discretion, to prepay any mortgage or other installment indebtedness.

II. I am married to JOHN SMITH (hereinafter referred to as "my husband"). The following are my children: ADAM J. SMITH and LILLIAN J. SMITH.

III. I give and bequeath to my husband all of my clothing, jewelry, personal effects, household goods, furniture, furnishings, automobiles, and all other tangible personal property which I may own at the time of my death to be his absolutely, provided he survives me.

IV. If my husband does not survive me, then I direct that my children, ADAM J. SMITH AND LILLIAN J. SMITH, may select from the foregoing those articles he or she may wish to retain, and I hereby give and bequeath to each child the articles selected. If my children are unable to agree as to the recipient of any article, that article, along with any articles not selected, shall be sold and the proceeds added to my residuary estate.

V. All the rest, residue and remainder of my property, real, personal and mixed, of every name and nature and wheresoever situate, I give, devise and bequeath to my husband, if he survives me.

VI. If my husband does not survive me, I give, devise and bequeath all the rest, residue and remainder of my estate in equal shares to my children, ADAM J. SMITH and LILLIAN J. SMITH, per stirpes; provided, however, that the share of any child under the age of twenty-one (21) shall be held in a separate account under the Sample Uniform Transfers to Minors Act (UTMA) until age twenty-one (21). I nominate and appoint Jane Smith as Custodian of any UTMA account created hereunder for the benefit of my child(ren).

VII. If my husband and I shall die under circumstances that there is not sufficient evidence to determine the order of our deaths, then it shall be presumed that I survived him, and my estate shall be administered and distributed, in all respects, in accordance with this presumption.

VIII. I give to my Personal Representative, hereinafter named, and to the successor, the following powers and discretions, in addition to those vested in or imposed upon them or either of them by law:

A. To mortgage, sell, convey, exchange or otherwise deal with or dispose of any real or personal property for cash or on credit (including the right to accept a purchase money mortgage as part of the purchase price); to retain as part of the estate any and all securities and property in the form originally received, whether or not it is then income producing and regardless of any rule requiring diversification of investments; to invest and reinvest in any stocks, bonds, shares in mutual funds or authorized common trust funds, or other securities or property, whether real or personal, which my Personal Representative may deem safe and for the best interests of the estate, without being limited to investments authorized by law for the investment of trust funds; to hold title to any and all securities and other investments either in my Personal Representative's name or in the name of a nominee; to borrow money from itself or others on terms my Personal Representative may deem best, and to pledge any property of the estate as security for the repayment thereof; and to make distributions in cash or in kind, or partly in each, to the beneficiaries entitled thereto.

B. If any beneficiary or legatee entitled to receive a part of my estate shall be under twenty-one (21) years of age, I authorize and empower my Personal Representative to designate his or her parent, or some other appropriate adult person, or trust company, as custodian for the beneficiary or legatee under the Sample Uniform Transfers to Minors Act until the beneficiary or legatee reaches age twenty-one (21), and to distribute the share of the beneficiary or legatee to the designated custodian. A receipt from the custodian shall fully release my Personal Representative from all liability and accountability to the legatee or beneficiary.

IX. I direct that all inheritance, succession, and estate taxes of every kind payable with respect to any property includable in my gross taxable estate, whether or not passing under this my Will, shall be paid out of my residuary estate and shall not be apportioned.

X. If my husband fails to survive, I nominate, constitute and appoint JANE SMITH as Guardian of my minor children. I direct that no bond or other security shall be required of the Guardian of my minor children.

Figure 5.2 (continued)

XI. I hereby nominate, constitute, and appoint my husband as Personal Representative of this my Last Will and Testament; but if he fails to survive me, or renounces, or fails to qualify, or upon his death, resignation or disqualification, I nominate and appoint JANE SMITH as Personal Representative hereof. I direct that no bond or other security shall be required of my Personal Representative.

XII. I hereby nominate, constitute and appoint JOHN SMITH as the Guardian of my Person. In the event that JOHN SMITH is unable or unwilling to so serve in this capacity, then I hereby nominate, constitute and appoint JANE SMITH as my Alternate Guardian. I direct that no bond or other security shall be required of my Guardian.

XIII. The masculine gender, whenever used herein, shall include the feminine; the feminine shall include the masculine; the neuter shall include both the masculine and feminine; and the singular shall include the plural, wherever necessary or appropriate.

IN WITNESS WHEREOF, I have hereunto subscribed my name this 31st day of May, 2011.

Jasmine J. Smith
_____
JASMINE J. SMITH

I, JASMINE J. SMITH, the Testatrix, sign my name to this instrument this 31st day of May , 2011, and being first duly sworn, do declare to the undersigned authority that I sign and execute this instrument as my will and that I sign it willingly, or willingly direct another to sign for me, that I execute it as my free and voluntary act for the purposes expressed in that document and that I am eighteen years of age or older, of sound mind and under no constraint or undue influence.

Jasmine J. Smith
_____
Testatrix

We, Michael Pearson, Maggy Pearson, the witnesses, sign our names to this instrument being first duly sworn and do declare to the undersigned authority that the testator signs and executes this instrument as his/her will and that he/she signs it willingly, or willingly directs another to sign for him/her, and that each of us, in the presence and hearing of the testator, signs this will as witness to the testator's signing and that to the best of our knowledge the testator is eighteen years of age or older, of sound mind and under no constraint or undue influence.

Michael Pearson
_____
Witness

Maggy Pearson
_____
Witness

The State of Sample}
County of Sample}

Subscribed, sworn to and acknowledged before me by JASMINE J. SMITH, the Testatrix, and subscribed and sworn to before me by Michael Pearson and Maggy Pearson , witnesses, this 31st day of May, 2011.

Lila P. Legal
_____
Notary Public

| LILA P. LEGAL |
| Notary Public, State of Sample |
| Sample County |
| My Commission Expires May 10, 2012 |

Will With Testamentary Trust

When testators have minor children, they commonly wish to set up a trust fund for the benefit of their children during minority. The trust can authorize the appointed trustee to make distributions for the children's health, maintenance and support, as well as for other needs, such as an education, a wedding, or even a down payment for a home. Figure 5.3 contains a will with a testamentary trust for the husband of Susan Smith (now Susan Smith-Thompson) from the Hypothetical Family. Since the couple is young and may still have more children, the will is drafted generically to leave everything to their children as a group. This permits the couple to have more children without the necessity of later updating their will. The will directs that the share of each child who is then under the age of 30 be held in a separate, equal trust share for the benefit of each child.

Figure 5.3 Last Will and Testament

I, **ARTHUR THOMPSON**, of the CITY OF SAMPLE, COUNTY OF SAMPLE, STATE OF SAMPLE, do hereby make, publish and declare the following to be my Last Will and Testament, hereby revoking all former Wills and Codicils made by me.

I. I direct that all my debts and funeral expenses be paid, and I further authorize my Executor, in its discretion, to prepay any mortgage or other installment indebtedness.

II. I give and bequeath to my wife, SUSAN SMITH-THOMPSON (hereinafter referred to as "my wife"), all of my clothing, jewelry, personal effects, household goods, furniture, furnishings, automobiles and all other tangible personal property which I may own at the time of my death to be hers absolutely, provided she survives me.

III. If my wife does not survive me, then I direct that each of my surviving children may select from the foregoing those articles he or she may wish to retain, and I hereby give and bequeath to each child the articles selected. If my children are unable to agree as to the recipient of any article, I authorize and direct my Executor to make the decision. If, in the sole judgment of my Executor, any child is too young to make a prudent selection, I authorize my Executor to make a selection on behalf of the child. If any of my children is a minor at the time of delivery of any articles, I authorize my Executor, in its discretion, to deliver the articles either directly to the child, or to the child's guardian, or to the person having the care and custody of the child, and a duly executed receipt from the child or guardian or other person shall constitute a complete acquittance to my Executor with respect to the bequest. Any articles not selected shall be sold and the proceeds added to my residuary estate.

IV. All the rest, residue and remainder of my property, real, personal and mixed, of every name and nature, and wheresoever situate, I give, devise and bequeath to my wife, if she survives me.

V. If my wife does not survive me, I give, devise and bequeath all the rest, residue and remainder of my estate to my Trustee, hereinafter named, in trust for the following uses and purposes:

A. I direct my Trustee to divide my said residuary estate into such number of equal shares as shall provide one (1) such equal share for each of my children as shall then be living and one (1) such equal share for the then living issue (collectively), per stirpes, of each of my issue as shall not then be living, and after making such division, my Trustee shall:

1. Pay and distribute the equal share so provided for the then living issue (collectively), per stirpes, of each deceased issue of mine; provided however, that if any such issue shall be under the age of twenty-one (21) years, I authorize my Trustee to hold the issue's share in trust, paying or applying to the use and benefit of the issue so much of the income and principal as my Trustee may deem needed for the issue's comfortable support, maintenance and education, other available income considered, and accumulating any unused income, but all remaining principal and accumulated income shall be paid to the issue upon attaining twenty-one (21), or in the event of his or her prior death, it shall be paid to his or her estate.

2. Pay and distribute the equal share so provided for each then living child of mine who shall have attained the age of thirty (30) years, outright and free of trust.

Figure 5.3 (continued)

3. One such equal share shall be held in trust for the benefit of each child of mine who is then living and shall not have attained the age of thirty (30) years. With respect to each such part:

   a. My Trustee shall pay to the beneficiary so much of the net income of such part, together with such amounts from principal as my Trustee, in its discretion, shall deem necessary or advisable to provide adequately for the beneficiary's health, support, maintenance, education, and medical emergencies, after taking into account all other available income. Undistributed income shall be accumulated and added to principal.

   b. I particularly desire that each of my children shall have the opportunity for a college education and professional or post-graduate study, if they so desire. Accordingly, I expressly authorize my Trustee to make advances of principal as my Trustee, in its sole and absolute discretion, shall deem necessary or advisable for the purpose of financing a college or post-graduate education as each of the beneficiaries may wish to pursue, even though the advances may completely exhaust the trust.

   c. I particularly desire that each of my children shall have the opportunity to have an automobile, if they so desire. Accordingly, I expressly authorize my Trustee to make any advances of principal as it, in its sole and absolute discretion, shall deem necessary and advisable to provide for each beneficiary's purchase of an automobile.

   d. I particularly desire that each of my children shall have the opportunity to have a wedding, if they so desire. Accordingly, I expressly authorize my Trustee to make any advances of principal as it, in its sole and absolute discretion, shall deem necessary and advisable to provide for each beneficiary's wedding.

   e. I particularly desire that each of my children shall have the opportunity to purchase a home, if they so desire. Accordingly, I expressly authorize my Trustee to make any advances of principal as it, in its sole and absolute discretion, shall deem necessary and advisable to provide for each beneficiary's down payment for a home.

   f. I authorize and direct my Trustee to pay and distribute one-half (1/2) of the remaining principal of such part and any undistributed income of his or her trust to the beneficiary upon attaining twenty-five (25) years of age.

   g. I authorize and direct my Trustee to pay and distribute the entire remaining principal of such part and any undistributed income of his or her trust to the beneficiary upon attaining thirty (30) years of age.

   h. If the beneficiary should die before reaching thirty (30) years of age, the entire remaining principal of his or her part shall be paid to his or her issue then living, per stirpes; or, in default of such issue, to my issue then living, per stirpes; provided, however, that if the issue is a beneficiary of a trust created hereunder, his or her share shall be added to the trust to be held and administered pursuant to the terms thereof.

4. My Trustee's decision with respect to any advances of principal pursuant to this Article shall be final and binding on all persons interested in the trust, and shall not be subject to judicial review.

VI. If my wife and I shall die under circumstances that there is not sufficient evidence to determine the order of our deaths, then it shall be presumed that I survived her and my estate shall be administered and distributed, in all respects, in accordance with this presumption.

VII. I give to my Executor and to my Trustee hereinafter named, and to the successor or successors of either, the following powers and discretions, in addition to those vested in or imposed upon them or either of them by law:

A. To mortgage, sell, convey, exchange or otherwise deal with or dispose of any real or personal property for cash or on credit (including the right to accept a purchase money mortgage as part of the purchase price); to lease any property for periods longer or shorter than the probable duration of any trust; to retain as part of the estate or trust any and all securities and property in the form originally received, including securities of or issued by any corporate executor or trustee, whether or not it is then income producing and regardless of any rule requiring diversification of investments; to invest and reinvest in any stocks, bonds, shares in mutual funds or authorized common trust funds, or other securities or property, whether real or personal, which my Executor or Trustee may deem safe and for the best interests of the estate or trust, without being limited to investments authorized by law for the investment of trust funds;

(continued)

Figure 5.3 (continued)

to hold title to any and all securities and other investments either in my Executor's or Trustee's name or in the name of a nominee; to borrow money from itself or others on terms my Executor or Trustee may deem best, and to pledge any property of the estate or trust as security for the repayment thereof; to hold two or more trusts or other funds in one or more consolidated funds, in which the separate trusts as funds shall have undivided interests; to determine as to every sum received (including stock dividends or the distribution of securities), whether the same is principal or income, or what part thereof is principal or income, and as to every expense or disbursement incurred or made by it, whether the same should be borne by the principal or income, or in what share by each; and to make distributions in cash or in kind, or partly in each, including undivided interests, even though shares be composed differently.

B. In case any income or principal of the trust becomes payable to a person under twenty-one (21) years of age, or to a person under legal disability, or to a person not adjudicated incompetent but who, by reason of illness or mental or physical disability, is in the opinion of my Trustee, unable to administer properly the income or principal, then the income or principal may be paid out by my Trustee in any one or more of the following ways as it deems best: (a) directly to the beneficiary; (b) to the guardian or custodian of the beneficiary; (c) to any relative of the beneficiary or to any other person with whom the beneficiary may be living, for the care, comfort, support, maintenance, education and welfare of the beneficiary; (d) by my Trustee using income or principal directly for the care, comfort, support, maintenance education and welfare of the beneficiary.

C. In determining the amounts of principal to be used for the benefit of any of my infant children during minority, it is my desire that my Trustee first consult with the guardian of the person of my children, and I direct that my Trustee shall be fully protected with respect to any payment made in reliance upon information received from the guardian. The final determination as to the appropriateness of using principal for the benefit of any infant child shall rest with my Trustee.

D. I expressly authorize my Trustee to receive and execute receipts for the proceeds of any life insurance policies on my life which may become payable to my Trustee; and I direct that a receipt executed by my Trustee shall fully discharge the respective insurance companies from all liability and responsibility with respect to the payment and use of the proceeds of the policies. If my Trustee's claim to any insurance proceeds is contested, whether by the insurance company or by any other claimant, my Trustee shall have full power and authority to settle, compromise or otherwise collect, or to enforce by legal action, any contested policy, paying the expenses of the action out of the trust estate. My Trustee's decision with respect to any contested claim shall be final and conclusive upon all parties interested in this trust.

E. I further expressly authorize my Trustee to purchase any assets from my Executor at the value established for the assets in the Federal Estate Tax proceeding in my estate, and/or to loan to my Executor sums as may be needed to pay any and all taxes and administration expenses. Loans may be made with or without security, and with or without interest, and upon other terms and conditions as my Executor and Trustee may agree. The authority hereby granted shall be exercised notwithstanding that my Executor and Trustee are one and the same person or corporation.

F. If at any time during the administration of any trust herein created, the Trustee, in its absolute discretion, deems the continuation thereof to be uneconomical and not in the best interests of the beneficiary or beneficiaries thereof, the Trustee, in its absolute discretion, is authorized to terminate the same and distribute the assets, free of the Trust, to the current income beneficiary or beneficiaries in the proportions in which they are entitled to the income therefrom.

G. If any beneficiary or legatee entitled to receive a part of my estate shall be under twenty-one (21) years of age, I authorize and empower my Executor or Trustee, as the case may be, to designate his or her parent, or some other appropriate adult person, or trust company, as custodian for the beneficiary or legatee under the Sample Uniform Transfers to Minors Act until age twenty-one (21), and to distribute the share of the beneficiary or legatee to the designated custodian. A receipt from the custodian shall fully release my Executor or Trustee from all liability and accountability to the legatee or beneficiary.

H. I expressly authorize my Trustee to merge any trust created hereunder with any other trust created by me or my spouse under will or agreement, which property shall be held, administered and distributed in accordance with the provisions of the trust; provided, however, that this power shall apply only if the trust to which the distribution would be made is substantially identical in form and content to the trust described herein, and for the same beneficiaries.

Figure 5.3 (continued)

I. No individual Trustee of any trust herein created shall be authorized to exercise any power herein to make any discretionary distribution of either income or principal to himself or herself, or to make discretionary allocations in his or her own favor between principal and income; and no individual Trustee shall be authorized to exercise any power herein to distribute income or principal to or for the benefit of any person whom he or she is legally obligated to support. These powers may be exercised by the remaining Trustee who is not so disqualified.

VIII. I direct that all inheritance, succession and estate taxes of every kind payable with respect to any property includable in my gross taxable estate, whether or not passing under this my Will, shall be paid out of my residuary estate, and shall not be apportioned.

IX. If my wife does not survive me, I nominate, constitute and appoint JANE SMITH as guardian of the person of each infant child of mine; but if JANE SMITH fails to survive me, or fails to qualify for any reason, then I nominate and appoint BARBARA THOMPSON as guardian. I direct that no bond or other security shall be required of either of them, in any jurisdiction, for the faithful performance of their duties.

X. I hereby nominate, constitute and appoint my wife as Executrix of this my Last Will and Testament; but if she fails to survive me, or renounces, or fails to qualify, or upon her death, resignation or disqualification, I nominate and appoint JANE SMITH as Executor hereof. If both my wife and JANE SMITH are unable to serve as Executor, I nominate and appoint BARBARA THOMPSON as Executor. I hereby nominate, constitute and appoint JANE SMITH as Trustee of the trusts herein created. I nominate and appoint BARBARA THOMPSON as alternate Trustee. I direct that no bond or other security shall be required of my Executor or Trustee.

XI. The masculine gender, whenever used herein shall include the feminine, the feminine shall include the masculine; the neuter shall include both the masculine and feminine; and the singular shall include the plural wherever necessary or appropriate.

IN WITNESS WHEREOF, I have hereunto subscribed my name this *4th* day of *March*, 2012.

Arthur Thompson
ARTHUR THOMPSON

We, whose names are hereto subscribed, do certify that on the *4th* day of *March*, 2012, the Testator, ARTHUR THOMPSON, subscribed his name to this instrument, in our presence and in the presence of each of us, and at the same time in our presence and hearing, declared the same to be his Last Will and Testament, and requested us, and each of us, to sign our names thereto as witnesses to the execution thereof, which we hereby do in the presence of the Testator and of each other.

Michael Pearson _____ residing at *1001 Reed Drive, Sample City, Sample State 12345* _____

Maggy Pearson _____ residing at *1001 Reed Drive, Sample City, Sample State 12345* _____

AFFIDAVIT OF ATTESTING WITNESSES

STATE OF SAMPLE STATE)
COUNTY OF SAMPLE COUNTY) SS:

_____ *Michael Pearson* _____ and _____ *Maggy Pearson* _____, being duly sworn say:

We are acquainted with ARTHUR THOMPSON. The signature at the end of the instrument dated March 4, 2012 declared by her to be her Last Will, was made by him at City of Sample, State of Sample State, in the presence of each of the undersigned.

At the time of signing Will, ARTHUR THOMPSON declared the instrument to which her signature had been affixed to be her Will and we, and each of us, signed our names thereto at the end thereof at that time and at her request and in his presence.

At the time of the execution of the instrument ARTHUR THOMPSON was over the age of 18 years, of sound mind and memory, and not under any restraint and competent in every respect to make a Will.

(continued)

Figure 5.3 (continued)

At the time of execution, ARTHUR THOMPSON could read, write and converse in the English language, and was not suffering from defects of sight, hearing, or speech or any other physical or mental impairment that could affect her capacity to make a valid Will.
The Will was not executed in counterparts.

Michael Pearson
—————————————————
                                    Witness

Maggy Pearson
—————————————————
                                    Witness

STATE OF SAMPLE STATE}
COUNTY OF SAMPLE COUNTY} ss:

On the 4<u>th</u> day of <u>March</u> in the year 2012 before me, the undersigned, a Notary Public in and for said State, personally appeared <u>Michael Pearson</u> and <u>Maggy Pearson</u>, the subscribing witnesses to the foregoing instrument, with whom I am personally acquainted, who being by me duly sworn, did depose and say that <u>Michael Pearson</u> resides at <u>1001 Reed Drive</u>, Sample State and <u>Maggy Pearson</u> resides at <u>1001 Reed Drive</u>, Sample State; that they know ARTHUR THOMPSON to be the individual described in and who executed the foregoing instrument; that said subscribing witnesses were present and saw said ARTHUR THOMPSON execute the same; and that said witnesses at the same time subscribed their names as witnesses thereto, and acknowledged to me that they executed the same in their capacities, and that by their signatures on the instrument, the individual(s) or the person upon behalf of which the individual(s) acted, executed the instrument.

Lila P. Legal
—————————————————
Notary Public

> LILA P. LEGAL
> Notary Public, State of Sample
> Sample County
> My Commission Expires May 10, 2012

Pour-Over Will

Some clients desire to avoid probate and wish to dispose of their assets using a living trust instead of a will. A **living trust**, also called an inter vivos trust (*inter vivos* is Latin for "within one's life"), is a trust that is created and becomes effective during the lifetime of the trustor(s) [also called settlor(s)]. Living trusts commonly provide that the trustors receive the benefits of the trust during their lifetimes, followed by a distribution to beneficiaries following the death of the last trustor to die. **Revocable living trusts** are commonly used in estate planning and can be amended or revoked during the lifetime of the trustor(s) in accordance with the provisions in the initial trust document. In order to be effective, property must be placed into the trust with title handed over to the trustee. In order to effectively circumvent probate, all of the trustor's assets must either be placed into the trust to be distributed pursuant to the terms therein or pass to beneficiaries by operation of law. Any assets that are not transferred into the trust prior to the trustor's death will either pass by operation of law to a designated beneficiary or co-owner, or will have to go through probate.

When used in estate planning, living trusts must be accompanied by what legal professionals call a pour-over will. A **pour-over Will** is appropriate for a person who has already executed a trust and leaves all remaining property to the trust.

Living Trust
Also called an inter vivos trust (*inter vivos* is Latin for "within one's life"), it is a trust that is created and becomes effective during the lifetime of the trustor(s) [also called settlor(s)].

Revocable Living Trust
A trust created by a written declaration during the lifetime of the creator that can be amended or revoked during the creator's lifetime.

Pour-over Will
A will that leaves the testator's assets to a living trust, to be administered pursuant to the terms thereof.

The purpose of a pour-over will is to ensure that any assets that were left out of the trust will be placed into the trust and distributed in accordance with the terms provided in the trust. If probate assets were left out of the trust, a probate of the pour-over will is required in order to turn the asset over to the trustee for distribution pursuant to the trust terms. The reason for the name of this type of will is self-evident; like a pitcher pouring water into a glass, this will literally pours any assets that were missed into the trust.

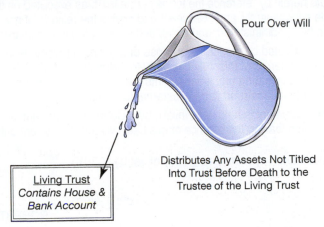

Pour Over Will

Distributes Any Assets Not Titled
Into Trust Before Death to the
Trustee of the Living Trust

Living Trust
*Contains House &
Bank Account*

Figure 5.4 contains the Pour-over Will of Robert Smith, from the Hypothetical Family. In his will, Robert leaves everything to the Robert & Mary Smith Family Trust.

Figure 5.4 Pour-Over Will Of Robert Smith

I, ROBERT SMITH, residing at 125 Oak Street, Sample City, Sample State 12345, which I hereby declare to be my place of domicile, being of sound mind and memory and disposing disposition, do make, publish and declare this to be my Last Will and Testament, thus revoking any and all previous Wills and their codicils which I have made previously.

I AM MARRIED TO: MARY SMITH

THE FOLLOWING ARE MY CHILDREN: RALPH SMITH & RYAN SMITH.

1. I give the entire residue of my estate to the trustee then in office under that trust designated as THE ROBERT & MARY SMITH FAMILY TRUST, dated January 9, 2010, of which I am a Settlor. I direct that the residue of my estate shall be added to, administered, and distributed as part of that trust, according to the terms of the trust and any amendment made to it before my death. To the extent permitted by law, it is not my intent to create a separate trust by this will or to subject the trust or the property added to it by the will to the jurisdiction of the probate court.

2. I direct that inheritance, death and estate taxes, including interest and penalties thereon, becoming due by reason of my death, with respect to property other than property held in trust or property taxed to my estate as a generation-skipping transfer, be paid preferably out of my residuary estate passing under this Will to the extent thereof, but may be paid out of the trust receiving distribution of my residuary estate passing under this Will if the Trustee deems it appropriate. Any such taxes, and interest and penalties thereon, attributable to trust property or property taxed as a generation-skipping transfer shall be paid out of the respective property so taxed by the person or persons having custody of such property or by the person or persons receiving distribution of such property. The determination of the amount of tax due by my residuary estate shall be made as if trust property where a pro rata share of my estate and as if no property classified as a generation-skipping transfer were taxed to my estate.

3. I hereby nominate, constitute and appoint MARY SMITH as the Personal Representative of this will. In the event she is unable or unwilling to so serve in this capacity, then I nominate, constitute and appoint JANE SMITH as Personal Representative hereof. I nominate, constitute and appoint JASMINE SMITH as alternate Personal Representative if JANE SMITH is unable or unwilling to serve.

(continued)

Figure 5.4 (continued)

The Personal Representative shall have full power and authority to carry out the provisions of the Will, including the power to manage and operate during the probate of my estate, any property and any business belonging to my estate.

4. No bond shall be required of any Personal Representative.

5. If the disposition in paragraph 1, above, is inoperative or is invalid for any reason, or if the trust referred to in paragraph 1, above, fails or is revoked, I incorporate herein by reference the terms of that trust, as executed on this date, without giving effect to any amendments made subsequently, and I bequeath and devise the residue of my estate to the trustee named in the trust as trustee, to be held, administered, and distributed as provided in this instrument.

The above-described Declaration of Trust was executed by me for the purpose of creating a revocable inter vivos trust. All property distributed to said trust under the terms of this will shall be held, administered and distributed according to the terms of said Declaration of Trust, including any amendments thereto in effect at my death. Said trust was created during my lifetime and shall not be construed to be a testamentary trust.

6. In the event, any provision of this Last Will and Testament is held to be invalid by a Court of competent jurisdiction, then such finding shall invalidate only that provision leaving the balance of this Last Will and Testament enforce.

IN WITNESS WHEREOF, I have hereunto subscribed my name this 9th day of January, 2010.

Robert Smith
_____
ROBERT SMITH

I, ROBERT SMITH, the Testator, sign my name to this instrument this 9th day of January, 2010, and being first duly sworn, do declare to the undersigned authority that I sign and execute this instrument as my will and that I sign it willingly, or willingly direct another to sign for me, that I execute it as my free and voluntary act for the purposes expressed in that document and that I am eighteen years of age or older, of sound mind and under no constraint or undue influence.

Robert Smith
_____
Testator

We, Michael Pearson and Maggy Pearson, the witnesses, sign our names to this instrument being first duly sworn and do declare to the undersigned authority that the testator signs and executes this instrument as his/her will and that he/she signs it willingly, or willingly directs another to sign for him/her, and that each of us, in the presence and hearing of the testator, signs this will as witness to the testator's signing and that to the best of our knowledge the testator is eighteen years of age or older, of sound mind and under no constraint or undue influence.

Michael Pearson
_____
Witness

Maggy Pearson
_____
Witness

The State of Sample}
County of Sample}

Subscribed, sworn to and acknowledged before me by ROBERT SMITH, the Testator, and subscribed and sworn to before me by Michael Pearson and Maggy Pearson, witnesses, this 9th day of January, 2010.

Lila P. Legal
_____
Notary Public

| LILA P. LEGAL |
| Notary Public, State of Sample |
| Sample County |
| My Commission Expires May 10, 2012 |

All of the foregoing wills are simple wills in that they do not include tax planning language.

Tax Planning Will

Some clients have amassed a significant amount of wealth that they will not dispose of during their lifetime. The goal of these clients is usually to preserve as much wealth as possible for their children and future generations. Tax planning wills may be used to minimize or completely avoid estate tax upon an individual's death when drafted by competent legal professionals in compliance with federal and state tax laws.

Estate tax is a tax on your right to transfer property at death. It is computed based on an accounting of everything you own or have certain interests in as of your date of death. The value used is the fair market value at the time of death, rather than what you paid for the items. The total of all items is your **gross estate**. Any available deductions are subtracted from your gross estate in order to arrive at your taxable estate. Then, the value of lifetime taxable gifts is added to the taxable estate figure and the tax is computed. Finally, the tax is reduced by the amount of the available unified credit. The unified credit can be thought of as providing for an "exemption equivalent" or exempted value with respect to the sum of the taxable estate and the taxable gifts during lifetime. For a person dying during 2006, 2007, or 2008, the applicable exclusion amount was $2,000,000, so if the sum of the taxable estate plus the adjusted taxable gifts made during lifetime equaled $2,000,000 or less, there was no federal estate tax to pay. The amount of the unified credit rose to $3.5 million in 2009, was repealed for 2010, was $5 million in 2011 and $5.12 million in 2012, then went back down to $1 million in 2013. Luckily, this complicated tax applies only to roughly two percent (2%) of all Americans. This and additional information are available from the Internal Revenue Service at http://www.irs.gov.

Although federal estate tax applies to a small percentage of Americans, states may impose an additional state estate tax. States that impose estate tax may begin taxing at lower levels of wealth, thereby necessitating tax planning for state estate tax reasons, if not federal estate tax reasons.

Complicated tax planning techniques may be used in wills (or trusts) in order to reduce estate tax liability and preserve as much of the estate as possible for the beneficiaries or heirs. However, these methods are beyond the scope of this text. If you work for an office that does tax planning, be aware that tax laws change frequently and continuing education is necessary for attorneys and paralegals practicing in that field.

Estate Tax
A tax on the right to transfer property at death; based on an accounting of everything one owns or has certain interests in as of the date of death.

Gross Estate
The value at the time of a decedent's death of all of the decedent's property, real or personal, tangible or intangible, wherever situated

■ REQUIRED WILL COMPONENTS

In order to execute a valid will, a person must be over the age of majority and of sound mind. The additional requirements for due execution of a written will vary by state statute. However, they generally require the following:

- *Publication Clause:* The testator must clearly identify himself or herself as the maker of the will and state that a will is being made. The second requirement is usually satisfied by having the words "Last Will and Testament" on the document.
- *Revocation Clause:* The testator must state that he or she revokes all prior wills and codicils (amendments to wills). If the revocation clause is missing, a subsequent will may only revoke the earlier version to the extent that they are inconsistent. Consult with your state statutes for specific rules.
- *Capacity:* The testator must demonstrate that he or she has capacity to execute the will and does so freely and willingly.

- *Identification of Family or Heirs:* The will must identify the heirs of the testator.
- *Signature at End:* The testator must sign at the end of the will. Failure to sign at the end may result in provisions appearing after the testator's signature being ignored or invalidated.
- *Due Execution:* The testator must sign and date the will in the presence of witnesses. Most states require two witnesses, but some may require three witnesses. Many states require that the witnesses be disinterested, meaning that they are not beneficiaries under the will.
- *Self-Proving Affidavit:* Many states have a statutory affidavit that may be attached to wills so that the witnesses do not have to be located or testify in order to probate the will. The affidavit usually includes notarization of the testator's and witnesses' signatures.

■ COMMON WILL ARTICLES

In addition to the more standard provisions in wills, there are a number of articles that are commonly used to accomplish more specific goals. There are many options, but samples of some of the common provisions are included below.

Memorandum as to Personal Effects

For example, rather than spelling out many bequests of personal effects, testators may, depending on state law, be permitted to leave a separate memorandum as to who should receive their personal items. The following is a sample article leaving personal effects pursuant to a memorandum that can be written, signed, and dated by the testator and left with the will.

> I direct that all of my clothing, jewelry, personal effects, household goods, furniture, furnishings, automobiles and all other tangible personal property which I may own at the time of my death be distributed in accordance with the Memorandum which I have left with this my Will. Any articles not included in my Memorandum shall be divided among my children as they shall agree.

Gifts to Beneficiaries

Legacy
A gift of personal property or money to a beneficiary (legatee) of a will. A legacy technically does not include real property (which is a "devise"), but usually refers to any gift from the estate of one who died.

Bequest
A gift of personal property under a will.

Conditional Bequest
A gift under a will that will take place only if a particular event has occurred by the time the maker of the will dies.

Executory Bequest
A bequest that provides for a gift to a beneficiary upon the happening of a specified event, such as when the beneficiary graduates from college or marries.

Specific Bequest
A gift in a will of a specified article to a certain person or persons.

Some testators may have very specific desires about the type and form of gifts to beneficiaries. Some of the most common types of gifts follow. A **legacy** is a gift of personal property or money to a beneficiary (legatee) of a will. A legacy technically does not include real property (which is a "devise"), but usually refers to any gift from the estate of one who died. "Legacy" is synonymous with the word "bequest." A **bequest** is a gift of personal property under the terms of a will. Bequests are not always outright. A **conditional bequest** is a gift under a will that will take place only if a particular event has occurred by the time the maker of the will dies. An **executory bequest** provides for a gift to a beneficiary upon the happening of a specified event, such as when the beneficiary graduates from college or marries. A bequest can be of specific assets or of the residue (what is left after all specific gifts have been made).

A **specific bequest** is a gift of specific tangible personal property or money under a will. For example,

1. I give and bequeath my figurine collection to my daughter, TINA BLACK.
2. I give and bequeath all of my jewelry in equal shares to my daughters, TINA BLACK and SUSAN RIVERS.
3. I give and bequeath my 1988 Camaro to my nephew, RALPH PETERS.
4. I give and bequeath my Picasso paintings to my son, RYAN RIVERS.

5. I give and bequeath the sum of One Thousand Dollars ($1,000.00) to my niece, SHEILA GRANT.

A **devise** is a gift of a real property interest under a will. For example,

1. I give, devise, and bequeath my real property located at 123 Cabin Lane, Dansville, New York, to my son, SAMUEL PETERS, provided he survives me.
2. I give, devise, and bequeath a life estate in my residential real property located in Tampa, Florida, to my partner, ROBERT MATTHEWS; provided, however, that he is required to pay for all utilities, property taxes, and insurance for the property while he resides there. Upon the death of Robert Matthews or his failure to reside at the property for six consecutive months, whichever occurs first, I give, devise and bequeath the property to my son, SAMUEL PETERS, provided he is then living.

Residuary Clause

After all other bequests have been made, whatever assets remain in the testator's estate (the "residue") are distributed pursuant to a residuary clause. For example,

- I give, devise, and bequeath all the rest, residue, and remainder of my estate, whether real, personal, or mixed, and wheresoever situate, to my husband, provided he survives me. If my husband fails to survive me, I give, devise, and bequeath all the rest, residue, and remainder of my estate to my sister, SAMANTHA PETERSON; or if she fails to survive, to my niece, JESSICA PETERSON.
- All the rest, residue and remainder of my property, real, personal and mixed, of every name and nature and wheresoever situate, I give, devise and bequeath in equal shares to my children, ANDREW M. ROBINSON and DAVID A. ROBINSON, or all to the survivor of them.

No Contest Provision

When a testator desires to disinherit an heir, that heir may potentially object to the probate of the will in order to "take back" their inheritance. A testator may include a **no contest** or **in terrorem clause** in order to prevent the disinherited individual from contesting the probate of the will, resulting in delays and additional administrative expenses for the estate. **In terrorem** is Latin for "in [order to] frighten" and is a legal term for giving a warning, usually to prevent the filing of a lawsuit. Again, some states do not honor such clauses, while other states view their inclusion in a will as an absolute bar to any contest. The following is a sample no contest clause:

> If any beneficiary or distributee hereunder objects to the probate of any part or all of this Will on any ground, or shall otherwise object to any term or provision thereof, or shall institute, join in or carry on any action or proceeding to invalidate, set aside or modify any term or provision hereof, or seeks to prevent any term or provision thereof from being given effect according to its express terms, the legacy, devise or other disposition to such beneficiary under this Will shall be deemed revoked, and the property such beneficiary or distributee would otherwise have received shall be distributed in the same manner and to the same persons as if such beneficiary or distributee had predeceased me.

Note that the foregoing paragraph implies that the disinherited individual was to receive something of value under the will to begin with. Typically, this clause follows or accompanies a nominal monetary bequest to the person the testator desires to disinherit. For example, the testator may leave the person $1.00 or $10.00 and include the no contest provision to prevent him or her from contesting the nominal bequest.

Option to Purchase Property

When the testator orders that the real property be sold, he or she may also give designated beneficiaries or heirs the first option to purchase the property. The following is a sample purchase option clause:

> However, I grant to each of my children, or any combination of them, the first option to purchase the real property in cash at its fair market value, as determined for estate tax purposes. In lieu of paying cash, my child or children electing to purchase the real property may do so by reducing his, her or their shares of my residuary estate to which they would otherwise receive under Article _____ hereof, but not below zero. Fair market value shall be determined by a qualified appraiser selected by the Executor. The appraisal shall be obtained as soon as practical after the appointment of the Executor of my estate. The cost of the appraisal shall be paid by the estate. This option must be exercised in writing and delivered to the Executor prior to the option's expiration. The first option to purchase shall expire one hundred twenty (120) days after the appointment of the Executor of my estate.

Life Estate in Property

Some testators may choose to allow an individual to live in their home for that individual's lifetime, prior to giving the property to someone else. The following is a sample of what such a clause might look like:

> I give and devise to JOHN SMITH, my residential real property located at 123 City Street, Sample City, Sample State; provided, however, that CINDY JONES shall have life use of the premises, subject to the conditions set forth herein. If JOHN SMITH predeceases me, his/her interest in said property shall pass to his/her issue, per stirpes.
>
> After my death, CINDY JONES shall have full life use of the premises without the necessity of paying rent; however she shall pay the costs of property and fire insurance, utilities and water charges. She shall also pay the costs of ordinary repair and maintenance expenses up to a cost of $100 per repair, including by way of example but not limited to, replacement of broken windows and the repair of minor plumbing leaks in respect thereof; however, the total annual cumulative repair and maintenance expenses for which the life tenant is responsible shall not exceed $1,000 per year. CINDY JONES shall be required to provide the remainderman with proof of payment of the property and fire insurance on an annual basis, which policy(s) shall name the remainderman as the loss payee. If CINDY JONES dies, or fails to maintain the residence as provided herein, or permanently moves from the premises, or fails to continually occupy it for period of six months, her life interest in the property created hereby shall terminate. In the event that CINDY JONES cannot maintain the residence as provided herein or pay the insurance or the utilities, I direct that she be entitled to six months notice from the remainderman owner of the property to vacate the premises. I direct that CINDY JONES shall not be required to furnish a bond or other security and she shall not be liable for any depreciation of my interest in said property or be obligated to replace any part thereof which may be consumed or destroyed.

Testamentary Trust
A trust that is drafted as part of the testator's will and only becomes effective upon the testator's death.

Testamentary Trust for Adult Child

A **testamentary trust** is a trust that is established following the testator's death pursuant to the terms of the will. The following is a sample article creating a trust for one adult child of the testator, where the other children received their shares outright:

The equal share so provided for my son/daughter, JOE NOTRUST (hereinafter the "beneficiary"), shall pass to my Trustee, hereinafter named, to be held in trust for his/her benefit, for the following uses and purposes:

1. My Trustee shall pay to the beneficiary so much of the net income of such part, together with such amounts from principal as my Trustee, in its sole discretion, shall deem necessary or advisable to provide adequately for the beneficiary's health, support, maintenance, education, and medical emergencies, after taking into account all other available resources. Undistributed income shall be accumulated and added to principal.
2. I authorize my Trustee, in its sole discretion, to terminate the trust and distribute the entire remaining principal and interest from the trust to the beneficiary, but my Trustee shall not be required to do so.
3. If the beneficiary fails to survive, or fails to survive through the termination of the trust, I direct my Trustee to pay and distribute the share so provided to the beneficiary's then living issue, per stirpes; or in default of issue, to my surviving issue, per stirpes.
4. My Trustee's decision with respect to any distributions of income or principal pursuant to this Article shall be final and binding on all persons interested in the trust, and shall not be subject to judicial review.

Figure 5.5 is a chart containing a plain-language version of the language creating the foregoing testamentary trust:

Attorney as Executor

Some clients do not have many close family members or friends whom they trust to appoint as executor. Such an individual may wish to appoint an attorney as their

Figure 5.5

1. My Trustee shall pay to the beneficiary so much of the net income of such part, together with such amounts from principal as my Trustee, in its sole discretion, shall deem necessary or advisable to provide adequately for the beneficiary's health, support, maintenance, education, and medical emergencies, after taking into account all other available resources. Undistributed income shall be accumulated and added to principal.	The Trustee has the sole discretion and authority to determine how much to distribute to the beneficiary to provide for the beneficiary's listed needs. The Trustee is to take into account the beneficiary's other available resources when determining how much to distribute. If the Trustee does not distribute all of the income from the trust to the beneficiary, the interest gets added to the principal balance of the trust.
2. I authorize my Trustee, in its sole discretion, to terminate the trust and distribute the entire remaining principal and interest from the trust to the beneficiary, but my Trustee shall not be required to do so.	The Trustee has the authority to terminate the trust and distribute the funds to the beneficiary, if he or she so chooses.
3. If the beneficiary fails to survive, or fails to survive through the termination of the trust, I direct my Trustee to pay and distribute the share so provided to the beneficiary's then living issue, per stirpes; or in default of issue, to my surviving issue, per stirpes.	If the beneficiary dies, the trust funds are to be distributed to the beneficiary's issue, per stirpes (*See* Chapter 3 for definitions). If the beneficiary has no issue, the balance of the trust is to be distributed to the Testator's issue, per stirpes.
4. My Trustee's decision with respect to any distributions of income or principal pursuant to this Article shall be final and binding on all persons interested in the trust, and shall not be subject to judicial review.	The Trustee's decisions regarding distributions from the trust are final and are not reviewable by a court.

ETHICAL Points to Remember

- Advising a client regarding the legality of terms in a will constitutes giving legal advice.
- Paralegals *cannot* give legal advice.
- Paralegals can prepare documents under the supervision of an attorney but must defer all legal questions to the supervising attorney to avoid the Unauthorized Practice of Law (UPL).
- The inclusion of terms that are not legally enforceable in a will reflects poorly on the drafting attorney and law firm and could potentially lead to future claims of malpractice by clients or heirs.
- **Malpractice** is an act or continuing conduct of a professional which does not meet the standard of professional competence and results in provable damages to his/her client. Such an error or omission may be through negligence, ignorance (when the professional should have known), or intentional wrongdoing.

executor. The permissibility of this depends on state law. However, in the state of New York it is permissible for an attorney to probate an estate and be compensated for that and to be compensated as executor, provided the appropriate language appears in the will. The view is that the role of attorney and the role of executor are two separate, distinct roles that both require time and effort. Some states take a very different position on this, so a will should not be drafted appointing an attorney as executor without first consulting state law. A sample attorney/executor authorization clause is as follows:

> I hereby authorize my Executor to receive the statutory commission for executors, as well as attorney fees for estate administration at the attorney's standard and customary fee schedule in effect at the time of my death.

Testimonium Clause

Testimonium clause
Also called a signature clause, this clause appears immediately above the testator's signature to establish the end of the will by presenting the testator's signature and affixing the date of the will's execution.

A **testimonium clause**, also called a *signature clause*, appears immediately above the testator's signature. The purpose of this clause is to establish the end of the will by presenting the testator's signature and affixing the date of the will's execution. For example:

- IN WITNESS WHEREOF, I have hereunto subscribed my name this _____ day of _____, 2014.

  (SEAL)
  _____
  JODY JACOBS

- IN TESTIMONY WHEREOF, I have set my hand and seal to this my Last Will & Testament consisting of five (5) typewritten pages this _____ day of _____, 2014.

  (SEAL)
  _____
  JODY JACOBS

■ HOLOGRAPHIC WILL

Holographic Will
A will that is written completely in the handwriting of the testator and signed and dated by the maker. Witnesses may or may not be required, depending on state law.

A few states allow **holographic wills**, which are completely handwritten wills, signed and dated by the maker. Witnesses may or may not be required, depending on state law. States that do *not* allow holographic wills generally disregard the handwritten last wishes of a decedent.

It is extremely important to note that state law varies and you must check with the requirements in your state. In order to be legally valid, a will must be properly executed pursuant to the laws of the state in which it is made. That is why it is a very poor idea to purchase will forms such as those sold at stationery stores or online. Generic will forms do not conform to the requirements of due execution in every state. A will is a very important document—too important to leave it to chance whether it will be upheld in a court of law after one's death.

Figure 5.6 contains Arizona Revised Statutes sections that outline the requirements for due execution of a regular will and a holographic will in the state of Arizona.

Figure 5.6 Requirements for Due Execution of Regular and Holographic Will in Arizona

14-2502. Execution; witnessed wills; holographic wills from Chapter 2, Article 5 from TITLE 14 - TRUSTS, ESTATES AND PROTECTIVE PROCEEDINGS. Phoenix, AZ: Arizona State Legislature.

A. Except as provided in sections 14-2503, 14-2506 and 14-2513, a will shall be:
   1. In writing.
   2. Signed by the testator or in the testator's name by some other individual in the testator's conscious presence and by the testator's direction.
   3. Signed by at least two people, each of whom signed within a reasonable time after that person witnessed either the signing of the will as described in paragraph 2 or the testator's acknowledgment of that signature or acknowledgment of the will.

B. Intent that the document constitute the testator's will can be established by extrinsic evidence, including, for holographic wills under section 14-2503, portions of the document that are not in the testator's handwriting.

14-2503. Holographic will

A will that does not comply with section 14-2502 is valid as a holographic will, whether or not witnessed, if the signature and the material provisions are in the handwriting of the testator.

Discussion Questions for Figure 5.6

1. What are the requirements for due execution of a will in Arizona?
2. What are the requirements for due execution of a holographic will in Arizona?
3. How do the requirements in Arizona compare to the requirements for due execution of a will in your State?

■ NUNCUPATIVE WILL

A **nuncupative will** is a will that has been delivered orally to witnesses, as opposed to being written down and executed with the usual formalities. Only a minority of states honor nuncupative wills, and those that do generally have strict requirements about when nuncupative wills are permitted.

Usually, nuncupative wills are only permitted during a person's last illness, or when death is imminent, when there is no time to execute a formal will. Other requirements may include that there be three witnesses present, that the oral declarations be reduced to writing shortly thereafter, and there may be a limit on the dollar amount that may pass by oral will. It is important to research your state's statutes to determine whether a nuncupative will may be honored and, if so, under what circumstances. Even if nuncupative wills are permitted, it is wise to execute a written will whenever possible.

Nuncupative Will
A will that has been delivered orally to witnesses, as opposed to being written down and executed with the usual formalities.

■ CHANGING OR REVOKING A WILL

Although wills should be drafted to provide for as many contingencies as possible (for example, by having contingent beneficiaries and appointing one or more alternate agents), clients' lives change as time passes by. When the changes in a client's life are significant (such as a divorce, the death of a beneficiary), the client's will may become out of date and must be revoked or revised.

Methods of will revocation are the following:

- By physical act
- By operation of law
- By subsequent writing

■ *Revocation by physical act* may occur by burning, tearing, canceling (usually by writing "cancelled" across each page of the will), obliterating or shredding, or otherwise destroying the will. The will revocation must be performed by the testator and should never be done by the attorney or a legal staff member.

■ *Revocation by operation of law* may occur under state statute by the subsequent marriage or divorce of the testator after executing the will. This means that the testator does not have to know about it or agree to the revocation.

■ *Revocation by subsequent writing* is the best way to revoke a will. Most wills expressly state that they revoke all prior wills and codicils of the testator. This clause is commonly found at the very beginning of the new will. Failure to put in a revocation clause may have the effect of making the new will a codicil to the old one.

Codicil
A written amendment to a person's will, which must be executed with the same formalities as the original will (i.e. dated, signed and witnessed) and must reference the will it amends.

A **codicil** is a written amendment to a person's will, which must be executed with the same formalities as the original will (i.e., dated, signed, and witnessed) and must reference the will it amends. A codicil can add to, subtract from, or modify the terms of the original will. When the person dies, both the will and the codicil are submitted for approval by the probate court and form the basis for administration of the decedent's estate. Prior to the use of computers, codicils were an effective way to update a will because less typing was required, resulting in less cost for the client and less risk of there being a mistake made. Now, however, with the use of computers and where law firms normally have all documents saved for many years to come, it is normally prudent to simply update the client's will, rather than do a codicil. When codicils are used, they should always be designated as the First Codicil to Last Will and Testament, Second Codicil to Last Will and Testament, etc.

Figure 5.7 displays the First Codicil to the Last Will and Testament of Robert Smith, from the Hypothetical Family. Robert specifically requested that his attorney prepare a codicil because he decided that he would not want his wife to serve as personal representative but did not want her to know he was changing his will at that time. He intended to leave it in another safe place where it would be found, should he pass away.

Figure 5.7 First Codicil

I, **ROBERT SMITH**, of the CITY OF SAMPLE, COUNTY OF SAMPLE, STATE OF SAMPLE, having heretofore made my Last Will and Testament, dated January 9, 2010 and published in the presence of Michael Pearson and Maggy Pearson as witnesses, do hereby make, publish and declare this to be a First Codicil thereto:

FIRST: I hereby revoke the provisions of Paragraph 3, and direct that the following be substituted in its place:

I hereby nominate, constitute and appoint JOHN SMITH as the Personal Representative of this will. In the event he is unable or unwilling to so serve in this capacity, then I nominate, constitute and appoint JANE SMITH as Personal Representative hereof. I nominate, constitute and appoint JASMINE SMITH as alternate Personal Representative if both JOHN SMITH and JANE SMITH are unable or unwilling to serve.

The Personal Representative shall have full power and authority to carry out the provisions of the Will, including the power to manage and operate during the probate of my estate, any property and any business belonging to my estate.

SECOND: Except as hereby amended, and subject to the amendments herein contained, I hereby ratify, confirm and republish my said Last Will and Testament in all respects.

IN WITNESS WHEREOF, I have hereunto subscribed my name this 6th day of February, 2012.

Figure 5.7 (continued)

Robert Smith
ROBERT SMITH

I, ROBERT SMITH, the Testator, sign my name to this instrument this 6ᵗʰ day of February, 2012, and being first duly sworn, do declare to the undersigned authority that I sign and execute this instrument as the First Codicil to my will and that I sign it willingly, or willingly direct another to sign for me, that I execute it as my free and voluntary act for the purposes expressed in that document and that I am eighteen years of age or older, of sound mind and under no constraint or undue influence.

Robert Smith
Testator

We, Michael Pearson and Maggy Pearson, the witnesses, sign our names to this instrument being first duly sworn and do declare to the undersigned authority that the testator signs and executes this instrument as his/her will and that he/she signs it willingly, or willingly directs another to sign for him/her, and that each of us, in the presence and hearing of the testator, signs this First Codicil to will as witness to the testator's signing and that to the best of our knowledge the testator is eighteen years of age or older, of sound mind and under no constraint or undue influence.

Michael Pearson
Witness

Maggy Pearson
Witness

The State of Sample}
County of Sample}

Subscribed, sworn to and acknowledged before me by ROBERT SMITH, the Testator, and subscribed and sworn to before me by Michael Pearson and Maggy Pearson, witnesses, this 6ᵗʰ day of February, 2012.

Lila P. Legal
Notary Public

> **LILA P. LEGAL**
> Notary Public, State of Sample
> Sample County
> My Commission Expires May 10, 2012

■ CONCLUSION

In conclusion, there is much to know when it comes to drafting a will. Although people may be able to draft their own wills, it is generally not advisable, and indeed highly likely, that necessary formalities will be missed when the will is executed. Clients who really care about what happens after their demise will get assistance from a competent lawyer to ensure that their wishes are properly expressed in a valid written will. Paralegals can play a central role in this process by drafting the will for the attorney's approval. In addition to written wills, some states honor holographic (handwritten) wills and/or nuncupative (oral) wills. If you intend to work for a law firm that does estate planning work, it is wise to become familiar with the laws pertaining to wills in the state(s) in which the law firm practices.

CONCEPT REVIEW AND REINFORCEMENT

KEY TERMS

Will   114

Intestate   114

Intestate Succession
   Statutes   114

Probate   114

Legal Capacity   115

Sound Mind   115

Testator   115

Testatrix   115

Attestation   115

Simple Will   115

Living Trust   124

Revocable Living Trust   124

Pour-over Will   124

Estate Tax   127

Gross Estate   127

Legacy   128

Bequest   128

Conditional Bequest   128

Executory Bequest   128

Specific Bequest   128

Devise   129

No Contest Clause   129

Testamentary Trust   130

Testimonium clause   132

Holographic Will   132

Nuncupative Will   133

Codicil   134

REVIEW QUESTIONS

1. Explain what it means to be "of sound mind."
2. What is legal capacity?
3. What type of will accompanies a living trust?
4. What is the purpose of a tax planning will?
5. What are the requirements for due execution of a will?
6. What is the purpose of an in terrorem clause?
7. What is a legacy?
8. What is a devise?
9. Explain what a conditional bequest is.
10. What is a publication clause?
11. What does a revocation clause do?
12. Describe a nuncupative will.
13. Explain what a holographic will is.
14. How can a will be revoked?
15. How can a will be amended?

BUILDING YOUR PARALEGAL SKILLS

CRITICAL THINKING EXERCISES

1. John wants his sister to be able to live in his home for the remainder of her life, but ultimately wants the home to pass to his three children: Ross, Maggy, and Brooke. Draft a clause that accomplishes John's goals.
2. If a client's assets are sufficient in size that there will be state estate tax but not federal estate tax, should the client have a tax planning will? Why or why not?
3. Poor Denny Crane has Alzheimer's disease in its advanced stages. He usually knows his own name, but does not recognize any of his family members or friends, other than his best friend, Alan Shore. Do you think he has capacity to execute a will? Why or why not?

PARALEGAL PRACTICE

Review each memorandum directed from the supervising attorney to you, the paralegal. The memorandum will discuss a situation with a client and request your assistance in researching the matter. You must then report back with your findings, as directed in the memorandum.

1. _____

MEMORANDUM
To: Paralegal
From: Supervising Attorney
Client: Rachael C. Carson
Re: Will for Single Female
_____

Today I met with Rachael Carson. Rachael is divorced and has two adult children: Bridgett & Madeline Carson. Neither daughter is married. Rachael wants to leave everything in equal shares to her children, or all to the survivor of them. She wants to appoint Bridgett as Personal Representative and Madeline as alternate. There will be no third alternate. Please prepare a draft of the will for my review.

2. _____

MEMORANDUM
To: Paralegal
From: Supervising Attorney
Client: Jennifer K. Jones
Re: Will for Married Female
_____

Today I met with Jennifer Jones regarding a will. Her husband is currently out of the country for an extended business trip and will come back and consult regarding his will in a few months. Jennifer wants to leave everything to her husband, Kevin M. Jones, and then in equal shares to her children, Sally L. Thomas, Susan J. Jones, and Mark L. Jones, per stirpes. Appoint Kevin as Personal Representative, Sally as first alternate, and Susan as second alternate. Jennifer's state of residence permits her to appoint a guardian of her person under the will and also permits instructions regarding her preference for burial or cremation. She wants to appoint Kevin as guardian and Susan as alternate. Her preference is to be cremated. Please prepare a draft of the will for my review.

3. _____

MEMORANDUM
To: Paralegal
From: Supervising Attorney
Client: Matthew Price
Re: Draft a Will
_____

We were hired as counsel for Matthew Price. Mr. Price has two adult sons: Matthew Price, Jr. and Timothy Price. He wishes to leave his personal effects pursuant to a written statement, which he will leave with his will. The remainder of his estate will pass in equal shares to his sons, per stirpes. Appoint Matthew Price, Jr. as personal representative and Timothy as alternate. Please prepare a draft of the will for my review.

4. _____

MEMORANDUM
To: Paralegal
From: Supervising Attorney
Client: Sue Smith
Re: Form Will
_____

Today I met with a client whose mother recently passed away. The decedent, Sue Smith, did not employ the assistance of an attorney in drafting a will. She instead purchased a form online. Shortly before her death, she filled in the blanks and signed and dated the will. She did not have any witnesses sign the will. The will was typewritten, except where the decedent wrote in the names of her children.

Please research your state's law to determine whether Sue Smith's will was validly executed so as to be admitted to probate. Report your findings and your conclusion in the form of a return memorandum to the supervising attorney.

5. _____

MEMORANDUM

To: Paralegal
From: Supervising Attorney
Client: Matthew Stone
Re: Holographic Will

Today I met with the son of Matthew Stone, who recently passed away. Mr. Stone left behind a holographic will that was entirely handwritten and signed and dated by Mr. Stone. There were also two witnesses' signatures.

Please research your state's law to determine whether holographic wills are legal. Further, research the requirements for due execution of a holographic will. Determine whether Mr. Stone's will was validly executed so as to be admitted to probate. Report your findings and your conclusion in the form of a return memorandum to the supervising attorney.

ONLINE RESOURCES

The Pearson Course Companion website contains the following additional resources:
- **Forms for Paralegal Practice Activities**
- Chapter Objectives
- Online Study Guide (Containing Multiple Choice and True/False Questions)
- Web Exercises www.pearsonhighered.com/careers

CASES FOR CONSIDERATION

CASE #1:

LAWSON V. MORRISON, ET AL.

2 U.S. 286
July 1792, Session, U.S. Supreme Court

OPINION

CHEW, President, delivered his opinion, in general terms, in affirmance of the sentence of the Register's Court.

M'KEAN, Chief Justice. There has been no case or precedent cited, which comes up to this, in all its parts; but there are several cases, which depended upon the same principle.

Before the statute of 29 Car. 2 ch. 3. Wills in England might be revoked by any express words, without writing; and so it was in Pennsylvania, until altered by positive law; but in England, since that statute, and in Pennsylvania, since the act of Assembly, of the 4th of Anne, "concerning the probates of written and nuncupative Wills, and for confirming devises of lands," Wills of lands must be revoked by writing, accompanied with solemnities similar to those necessary for making the Wills. Here, latter Wills of lands, or a writing, revoking a former Will, must be proved by two or more credible witnesses; and no Testament, or Will in writing, for personal estate, can be revoked by words, except the same be committed to writing and read to the testator, is allowed by him, and proved by two witnesses at least. Besides these actual revocations, there are other acts of the testator, which have always been considered as revocations, because contrary to, or inconsistent with, the Will, and evidencing an alteration of intention; as a deed in fee; or a lease for years to the same devisee, to commence after the testator's death; a subsequent marriage and birth of a child, cancelling, obliterating or destroying the Will, and such like. These are termed, "implied, constructive, or legal, revocations," and still subsist as they were before the act of Assembly, or the statute of frauds. Cro. I. 49. Carth. 81. But all presumptive revocations may be encountered by evidence, and rebutted by other circumstances. Cowp. 53. Doug. 37.

It has been often determined, that a Will, revoked by a subsequent Will, but not cancelled, was re-established by the cancellation of the subsequent Will. 1 Show. 537. Shaw. P.C. 146. 1 Will. 345. 2 Vern. 741. S.C. Prec. Chan. 459. S.C. 4. Burr. 2512. Cowp. 86. 92. Doug. 40. 2 Blackst. 937. 3 Mod. 204. Salk. 592. 3 Mod.

There are, however, some particular circumstances, in this case, besides the general question.

It appears, that the appellant had lived in the neighborhood of the testatrix when she made the Will of 1779; that the legatees in that Will were chiefly the same as in the present, but some legacies were larger, on account of the money being then depreciated, and that Oliver Anderson was expressly requested by the testatrix to take care of the Will of 1775, left the last should get into the hands of the appellant, or be lost. On the other hand, it does not appear what became of the Will of 1779, after it was sent and delivered to the testatrix, whether it was destroyed by her, or any other person,— but it cannot be found. It does not appear, wherein the Will of 1779 differed from the present one nor what alteration was thereby made in particular, only that there were partial alterations, and there were no executors named in it.

In this view of the case, I am of opinion, that the mere circumstance of making the Will of 1779, is not virtually a revocation of the former, the contents being unknown, and it not appearing to have been in esse at her death, but rather the contrary, and that she had cancelled or destroyed it. No other person was interested in its destruction, from anything I can discover, except the appellant, or his brother, who were not in America; and charity will induce a presumption, that she herself destroyed it. If this is the fact, the first Will is not thereby revoked, as neither could be complete Wills, until the death of the testatrix, and her destroying it had the same effect as if it had never existed, unless it had been clearly proved, that she did it with an intention to die intestate. Should a contrary opinion hold, to wit, that the first Will was revoked, at the instant the second was executed, yet the cancelling of the second by the Testatrix herself is a revival of the first, if undestroyed. Cowp. 92 Harwood v. Goodright.

Here is a good subsisting Will properly attested: There is no way to defeat it, but by proving it was revoked by another Will, subsisting at the death of the Testatrix, or that she cancelled the latter Will, so revoking all former ones, with a mind to die intestate. And as the appellant has failed in such proof, I concur with the President, that the Will of 1775 must stand; and that the sentence of the Register's Court be affirmed, with double costs.

THE COURT concurring, the sentence of the Register's Court was, accordingly, affirmed, with double costs.[1]

---

[1]See ant. p. 266. Boudinot et al. Executors against Bradford.

Case Questions

1. How must wills in Pennsylvania be revoked?
2. Which will was found to stand?
3. What was this court's holding, and what was the reason for its holding?

CASE #2:

IN THE MATTER OF THE ESTATE OF MUDER, DECEASED.

159 Ariz. 173; 765 P.2d 997
December 6, 1988, Supreme Court of Arizona.

OPINION BY: CAMERON

OPINION

I. JURISDICTION

Respondent seeks review of the decision and opinion of the court of appeals, which reversed the trial court's admission of Edward Frank Muder's will to probate. We have jurisdiction pursuant to Ariz. Const. art. 6 § 5(3), A.R.S. § 12-120.24 and Ariz. R. Civ. App. p. 23.

II. ISSUE

We must determine whether the purported will is a valid holographic will pursuant to A.R.S. § 14-2503.

III. FACTS

Edward Frank Muder died on 15 March 1984. In September 1986, Retha Muder, the surviving spouse, submitted a purported will dated 26 January 1984 to the probate court. The purported will was on a preprinted will form set forth as Exhibit A.

The daughters of Edward Muder by a previous wife contested the will. They were unsuccessful in the trial court and appealed to the court of appeals. A divided court of appeals reversed. *In re Estate of Muder*, 156 Ariz. 326, 751 P.2d 986 (1988). We granted Retha Muder's petition for review.

IV. WAS THE DOCUMENT A VALID WILL UNDER A.R.S. § 14-2502?

The right to make a will did not exist at common law. It is a statutory right. 1 W. Bowe & D. Parker, *Page on the Law of Wills* at 62-63 (1960). Because the legislature has the power to withhold or to grant the right to make a will, its exercise may be made subject to such regulations and requirements as the legislature pleases. *In re Estate of Wilkins*, 54 Ariz. 218, 221, 94 P.2d 774, 775 (1939).

It is apparent that this was not a proper formal will pursuant to statute because only one witness signed.

> Except as provided for holographic wills, ... every will shall be in writing signed by the testator or in the testator's name by some other person in the testator's presence and by his direction, and shall be signed by *at least two* persons each of whom witnessed either the signing or the testator's acknowledgment of the signature or of the will.

A.R.S. § 14-2502 (emphasis added).

Also, the document does not meet the requirements for a self-proved will. The self-proving affidavit does not state that the testator signed or acknowledged his signature, or the will, in the presence of witnesses. A.R.S. § 14-2504; See In re Estate of Mackaben, 126 Ariz. 599, 601, 617 P.2d 765, 767 (App. 1980).

We agree with the court of appeals that the will is not valid under the formal will statute, A.R.S. § 14-2502.

V. IS THE DOCUMENT A VALID HOLOGRAPHIC WILL?

To serve as a will, the document must indicate that the testator had **testamentary intent**. *In re Estate of Blake v. Benza*, 120 Ariz. 552, 553, 587 P.2d 271, 272 (App. 1978); *see also In re Estate of Harris*, 38 Ariz. 1, 296 p. 267 (1931). **Testamentary intent** requires that the writing, together with whatever extrinsic evidence may be admissible, establish that the testator intended such writing to dispose of his property upon his death. *Blake*, 120 Ariz. at 553, 587 P.2d at 272.

Because this will fails under A.R.S. § 14-2502, it is only valid if it can be considered a holographic will under the statute that provides:

> A will which does not comply with § 14-2502 is valid as a holographic will, whether or not witnessed, if the signature and the material provisions are in the handwriting of the testator.

A.R.S. § 14-2503. This section was enacted in 1973 and replaced the previous holographic will statute that stated:

> A holographic will is one entirely written and signed by the hand of the testator himself.

Attestation by subscribing witnesses is not necessary in the case of a holographic will.

A.R.S. § 14-123 (1956).

Under the previous statute, no printed matter was allowed on the document. Litigation resulted because often a testator would write his holographic will on paper containing printed letterheads. Such printed matter was obviously not in the testator's handwriting. To avoid the harsh result of denying such holographic wills admission to probate, courts created the "surplusage theory." This theory held that the statutory words "wholly" or "entirely" were satisfied when the material provisions of the will were "wholly" or "entirely" in the handwriting of the testator, and that other written or printed material could accordingly be disregarded as surplusage. Arizona adopted the surplusage theory to preserve the validity of such holographic wills. See In re Estate of Schuh, 17 Ariz. App. 172, 173, 496 P.2d 598, 599 (1972); see also In re Estate of Morrison, 55 Ariz. 504, 510, 103 P.2d 669, 672 (1940) (it was important that the testamentary part of the will be wholly written by the testator and signed by him).

With the increased use of printed will forms, states with statutes similar to our previous statute requiring that a holographic will be entirely in the handwriting of the testator, applied the surplusage theory to the printed will forms by disregarding the printed matter and then looking to see if what was left made sense and could be considered a valid will. See Estate of Black, 30 Cal.3d 880, 641 P.2d 754, 181 Cal. Rptr. 222 (1982); Succession of Burke, 365 So.2d 858 (La.Ct.App.1978); Watkins v. Boykin, 536 S.W.2d 400 (Tex.Civ.App.1976); see also In re Estate of Johnson, 129 Ariz. 307, 630 P.2d 1039 (App.1981).

California considered this issue because its statute required that a holographic will must be entirely written, dated, and signed by the hand of the testator himself and that any matter printed that was incorporated in the will provisions had to be considered part of the will. Estate of Black, 30 Cal.3d 880, 883, 641 P.2d 754, 755, 181 Cal. Rptr. 222, 223 (1982). The will in Black was a document that was handwritten on three pages of a partially preprinted stationer's form. Id. The court upheld the will by finding that none of the incorporated material was either material to the substance of the will or essential to its validity as a testamentary disposition. Id. at 885, 641 P.2d at 757, 181 Cal. Rptr. at 225. As Justice Richardson stated:

No sound purpose or policy is served by invalidating a holograph where every statutorily required element of the will is concededly expressed in the testatrix' own handwriting and where her **testamentary intent** is clearly revealed in the words as she wrote them. Frances Black's sole mistake was her superfluous utilization of a small portion of the language of the preprinted form. Nullification of her carefully expressed testamentary purpose because of such error is unnecessary to preserve the sanctity of the statute.

Black, 30 Cal.3d at 888, 641 P.2d at 759, 181 Cal. Rptr. at 227.

We believe that our legislature, in enacting the present statute, [HN5] A.R.S. § 14-2503, intended to allow printed portions of the will form to be incorporated into the handwritten portion of the holographic will as long as the **testamentary intent** of the testator is clear and the protection afforded by requiring the material provisions be in the testator's handwriting is present.

Indeed, our statute states:

B. The underlying purposes and policies of this title are:

...

2. To discover and make effective the intent of a decedent in distribution of his property.

A.R.S. § 14-1102(B)(2).

In the instant case, there is no question as to the testator's intent. We hold that a testator who uses a preprinted form, and in *his own handwriting* fills in the blanks by designating his beneficiaries and apportioning his estate among them and signs it, has created a valid holographic will. Such handwritten provisions may draw testamentary context from both the printed and the handwritten language on the form. We see no need to ignore the preprinted words when the testator clearly did not, and the statute does not require us to do so.

We find the words of an early California decision persuasive:

If testators are to be encouraged by a statute like ours to draw their own wills, the courts should not adopt upon purely technical reasoning a construction which would result in invalidating such wills ...

In re Soher's Estate, 78 Cal. 477, 482, 21 p. 8, 10 (1889) (quoted with approval by Estate of Black, 30 Cal.3d 880, 884, 641 P.2d 754, 756, 181 Cal. Rptr. 222, 224 (1982)).

VI. RELIEF

We vacate the opinion of the court of appeals and affirm the judgment of the trial court admitting the will to probate.

DISSENT BY: MOELLER

DISSENT

MOELLER, Justice, dissenting.

As the majority correctly notes, there is no common law right to make a will. To be entitled to probate, a document must meet the applicable statutory criteria. The majority opinion of the court of appeals and Judge Haire's persuasive special concurrence amply demonstrate that the document in this case does not comply with Arizona's holographic will statute, A.R.S. § 14-2503. The statute is clear: in a holographic will the "signature and the material provisions" must be in the handwriting of the testator. The majority reads into the statute a provision that printed portions of a form may be "incorporated" into the handwritten provisions so as to meet the statutory requirements. I am unable to discern such expansiveness in the statute. Neither was the court of appeals in the recent case of *In re Estate of Johnson,* 129 Ariz. 307, 630 P.2d 1039 (App.1981), which was decided under the identical statute and in which we denied review. *Johnson,* if followed, compels the conclusion that the instrument in this case is not a valid holographic will; however, the majority opinion neither discusses, distinguishes, or disapproves of *Johnson.*

I am sympathetic to the majority's desire to give effect to a decedent's perceived **testamentary intent**. However, the legislature has chosen to require that **testamentary intent** be expressed in certain deliberate ways before a document is entitled to be probated as a will. Whether the holographic will statute should be amended to take into account the era of do-it-yourself legal forms is a subject within the legislative domain. I suspect the ad hoc amendment engrafted on the statute in this case will prove to be more mischievous than helpful. Because I believe there has been no compliance with the statute on holographic wills, I respectfully dissent.

Case Questions

1. What was the issue in this case?
2. What was this court's holding, and what was the reason for its holding?
3. Why did the dissenting judge disagree with the majority opinion?

FORMS TO ACCOMPANY PARALEGAL PRACTICE

Disclaimer: The forms provided to aid students in completing the Paralegal Practice activities assigned in each chapter have been modified as samples to familiarize students with what each form commonly looks like and are not intended to be used as actual forms for any state.

INSTRUCTIONS: The forms are provided in Microsoft Word format and employ the use of Stop Codes (such as SC1, SC2, SC3, and so on). Stop Codes are used in place of the form sections that must be updated with case-by-case information, such as SC1 for the client's name, SC3 for the client's address, and so on. What each Stop Code represents can be inferred by reading the surrounding text on the form. By using the FIND & REPLACE tool on the Microsoft toolbar, the students can replace the Stop Codes with the information provided in the Paralegal Practice activity to complete each assignment. Students must also fill in any blank lines on each form with the appropriate information from the activity and then proofread the document prior to turning in their work.

The following forms are included following this section and will be posted online for students to access to complete the Paralegal Practice activities for this chapter:

- PP Form 5.1—Simple Will for Single Female
- PP Form 5.2—Simple Will for Married Female
- PP Form 5.3—Simple Will for Single Male

PP Form 5.1—Simple Will for Single Female
LAST WILL AND TESTAMENT OF SC1

I, **SC1**, of the CITY OF SAMPLE, COUNTY OF SAMPLE, STATE OF SAMPLE, do hereby make, publish and declare the following to be my Last Will and Testament, hereby revoking all former Wills and Codicils made by me.

I. I direct that all my just legal debts and funeral expenses be paid, and I further authorize my Personal Representative, in its discretion, to prepay any mortgage or other installment indebtedness.

II. I give and bequeath to my children, SC2 (hereinafter referred to as "my children"), all of my clothing, jewelry, personal effects, household goods, furniture, furnishings, automobiles, and all other tangible personal property which I may own at the time of my death, to be divided among them as they shall agree. If my children are unable to agree as to the recipient of any article, that article, along with any articles not selected, shall be sold and the proceeds added to my residuary estate.

III. All the rest, residue and remainder of my property, real, personal and mixed, of every name and nature and wheresoever situate, I give, devise and bequeath in equal shares to my children, SC2, or all to the survivor(s) of them.

IV. I give to my Personal Representative, hereinafter named, and to the successor, the following powers and discretions, in addition to those vested in or imposed upon them or either of them by law:

A. To mortgage, sell, convey, exchange or otherwise deal with or dispose of any real or personal property for cash or on credit (including the right to accept a purchase money mortgage as part of the purchase price); to retain as part of the estate any and all securities and property in the form originally received, whether or not it is then income producing and regardless of any rule requiring diversification of investments; to invest and reinvest in any stocks, bonds, shares in mutual funds or authorized common trust funds, or other securities or property, whether real or personal, which my Personal Representative may deem safe and for the best interests of the estate, without being limited to investments authorized by law for the investment of trust funds; to hold title to any and all securities and other investments either in my Personal Representative's name or in the name of a nominee; to borrow money from itself or others on terms my Personal Representative may deem best, and to pledge any property of the estate as security for the repayment thereof; and to make distributions in cash or in kind, or partly in each, to the beneficiaries entitled thereto.

B. If any beneficiary or legatee entitled to receive a part of my estate shall be under twenty-one (21) years of age, I authorize and empower my Personal Representative to designate his or her parent, or some other appropriate adult person, or trust company, as custodian for the beneficiary or legatee under the Sample Uniform Transfers to Minors Act until the beneficiary or legatee reaches age twenty-one (21), and to distribute the share of the beneficiary or legatee to the designated custodian. A receipt from the custodian shall fully release my Personal Representative from all liability and accountability to the legatee or beneficiary.

V. I direct that all inheritance, succession, and estate taxes of every kind payable with respect to any property includable in my gross taxable estate, whether or not passing under this my Will, shall be paid out of my residuary estate and shall not be apportioned.

VI. I hereby nominate, constitute, and appoint SC3 Personal Representative of this my Last Will and Testament; but if SC3 fails to survive me, or renounces, or fails to qualify, or upon his death, resignation or disqualification, I nominate and appoint SC4 as Personal Representative hereof. If both SC3 and SC4 are unwilling or unavailable to serve, I nominate, constitute and appoint SC5 as alternate Personal Representative hereof. I direct that no bond or other security shall be required of my Personal Representative.

VII. The masculine gender, whenever used herein, shall include the feminine; the feminine shall include the masculine; the neuter shall include both the masculine and feminine; and the singular shall include the plural, wherever necessary or appropriate.

IN WITNESS WHEREOF, I have hereunto subscribed my name this _____ day of _____, 2014.

_____
SC1

I, SC1, the Testatrix, sign my name to this instrument this _____ day of _____, 2014, and being first duly sworn, do declare to the undersigned authority that I sign and execute this instrument as my will and that I sign it willingly, or willingly direct another to sign for me, that I execute it as my free and voluntary act for the purposes expressed in that document and that I am eighteen years of age or older, of sound mind and under no constraint or undue influence.

_____
Testatrix

(continued)

We, _____ and _____, the witnesses, sign our names to this instrument being first duly sworn and do declare to the undersigned authority that the testator signs and executes this instrument as his/her will and that he/she signs it willingly, or willingly directs another to sign for him/her, and that each of us, in the presence and hearing of the testator, signs this will as witness to the testator's signing and that to the best of our knowledge the testator is eighteen years of age or older, of sound mind and under no constraint or undue influence.

_____
Witness

_____
Witness

The State of Sample}

County of Sample}

Subscribed, sworn to and acknowledged before me by SC1, the Testatrix, and subscribed and sworn to before me by _____ and _____, witnesses, this _____ day of _____, 2014.

_____
Notary Public

My Commission Expires:

PP Form 5.2—Simple Will for Married Female
LAST WILL AND TESTAMENT OF SC1

I, **SC1**, of the CITY OF SAMPLE, COUNTY OF SAMPLE, STATE OF SAMPLE, do hereby make, publish and declare the following to be my Last Will and Testament, hereby revoking all former Wills and Codicils made by me.

I. I direct that all my just legal debts and funeral expenses be paid, and I further authorize my Personal Representative, in its discretion, to prepay any mortgage or other installment indebtedness.

II. I am married to SC2 (hereinafter referred to as "my husband"). The following are my children: SC3.

III. I give and bequeath to my husband all of my clothing, jewelry, personal effects, household goods, furniture, furnishings, automobiles, and all other tangible personal property which I may own at the time of my death to be his absolutely, provided he survives me.

IV. If my husband does not survive me, then I direct that my children, SC3, may select from the foregoing those articles he or she may wish to retain, and I hereby give and bequeath to each child the articles selected. If my children are unable to agree as to the recipient of any article, that article, along with any articles not selected, shall be sold and the proceeds added to my residuary estate.

V. All the rest, residue and remainder of my property, real, personal and mixed, of every name and nature and wheresoever situate, I give, devise and bequeath to my husband, if he survives me.

VI. If my husband does not survive me, I give, devise and bequeath all the rest, residue and remainder of my estate in equal shares to my children, SC3, per stirpes.

VII. If my husband and I shall die under circumstances that there is not sufficient evidence to determine the order of our deaths, then it shall be presumed that I survived him, and my estate shall be administered and distributed, in all respects, in accordance with this presumption.

VIII. I give to my Personal Representative, hereinafter named, and to the successor, the following powers and discretions, in addition to those vested in or imposed upon them or either of them by law:

A. To mortgage, sell, convey, exchange or otherwise deal with or dispose of any real or personal property for cash or on credit (including the right to accept a purchase money mortgage as part of the purchase price); to retain as part of the estate any and all securities and property in the form originally received, whether or not it is then income producing and regardless of any rule requiring diversification of investments; to invest and reinvest in any stocks, bonds, shares in mutual funds or authorized common trust funds, or other securities or property, whether real or personal, which my Personal Representative may deem safe and for the best interests of the estate, without being limited to investments authorized by law for the investment of trust funds; to hold title to any and all securities and other investments either in my Personal Representative's name or in the name of a nominee; to borrow money from itself or others on terms my Personal Representative may deem best, and to pledge any property of the estate as security for the repayment thereof; and to make distributions in cash or in kind, or partly in each, to the beneficiaries entitled thereto.

B. If any beneficiary or legatee entitled to receive a part of my estate shall be under twenty-one (21) years of age, I authorize and empower my Personal Representative to designate his or her parent, or some other appropriate adult person, or trust company, as custodian for the beneficiary or legatee under the Sample Uniform Transfers to Minors Act until the beneficiary or legatee reaches age twenty-one (21), and to distribute the share of the beneficiary or legatee to the designated custodian. A receipt from the custodian shall fully release my Personal Representative from all liability and accountability to the legatee or beneficiary.

IX. I direct that all inheritance, succession, and estate taxes of every kind payable with respect to any property includable in my gross taxable estate, whether or not passing under this my Will, shall be paid out of my residuary estate and shall not be apportioned.

X. I hereby nominate, constitute, and appoint my husband as Personal Representative of this my Last Will and Testament; but if he fails to survive me, or renounces, or fails to qualify, or upon his death, resignation or disqualification, I nominate and appoint SC4 as Personal Representative hereof. If both my husband and SC4 are unwilling or unavailable to serve, I nominate, constitute and appoint SC5 as alternate Personal Representative hereof. I direct that no bond or other security shall be required of my Personal Representative.

XI. I hereby nominate, constitute and appoint SC2 as the Guardian of my Person. In the event that SC2 is unable or unwilling to so serve in this capacity, then I hereby nominate, constitute and appoint SC4 as my Alternate Guardian. *No bond shall be required of any Guardian.*

XII. Upon my death, I direct that my body be (choose one) buried/cremated. Any additional instructions or requests regarding these arrangements may further be outlined in my Statement of Wishes if one is attached to this document, and it is my request that the Personal Representative of my estate abide by my wishes.

XIII. The masculine gender, whenever used herein, shall include the feminine; the feminine shall include the masculine; the neuter shall include both the masculine and feminine; and the singular shall include the plural, wherever necessary or appropriate.

IN WITNESS WHEREOF, I have hereunto subscribed my name this _____ day of _____, 2014.

_____
SC1

I, SC1, the Testatrix, sign my name to this instrument this _____ day of _____, 2014, and being first duly sworn, do declare to the undersigned authority that I sign and execute this instrument as my will and that I sign it willingly, or willingly direct another to sign for me, that I execute it as my free and voluntary act for the purposes expressed in that document and that I am eighteen years of age or older, of sound mind and under no constraint or undue influence.

_____
Testatrix

We, _____ and _____, the witnesses, sign our names to this instrument being first duly sworn and do declare to the undersigned authority that the testator signs and executes this instrument as his/her will and that he/she signs it willingly, or willingly directs another to sign for him/her, and that each of us, in the presence and hearing of the testator, signs this will as witness to the testator's signing and that to the best of our knowledge the testator is eighteen years of age or older, of sound mind and under no constraint or undue influence.

_____
Witness

_____
Witness

(continued)

The State of Sample}

County of Sample}

Subscribed, sworn to and acknowledged before me by SC1, the Testatrix, and subscribed and sworn to before me by
_____ and _____, witnesses, this _____ day of _____, 2014.

_____
Notary Public

My Commission Expires:

PP Form 5.3—Simple Will for Single Male
LAST WILL AND TESTAMENT OF SC1

I, **SC1**, of the CITY OF SAMPLE, COUNTY OF SAMPLE, STATE OF SAMPLE, do hereby make, publish and declare the following to be my Last Will and Testament, hereby revoking all former Wills and Codicils made by me.

I. I direct that all my just legal debts and funeral expenses be paid, and I further authorize my Personal Representative, in its discretion, to prepay any mortgage or other installment indebtedness.

II. I am single and have the following children: SC2 (hereinafter referred to as "my children").

III. Pursuant to Sample Revised Statute §14-2513, I may leave with this, my Last Will and Testament, a statement, either handwritten or signed by myself, directing that certain items of tangible personal property be distributed to certain named individuals. I hereby direct my Personal Representative to be bound by the provisions of said statement. My Personal Representative may assume no such statement exists if none is found within thirty (30) days after my death.

IV. All the rest, residue and remainder of my property, real, personal and mixed, of every name and nature and wheresoever situate, I give, devise and bequeath in equal shares to my children, SC2, per stirpes.

V. I give to my Personal Representative, hereinafter named, and to the successor, the following powers and discretions, in addition to those vested in or imposed upon them or either of them by law:

A. To mortgage, sell, convey, exchange or otherwise deal with or dispose of any real or personal property for cash or on credit (including the right to accept a purchase money mortgage as part of the purchase price); to retain as part of the estate any and all securities and property in the form originally received, whether or not it is then income producing and regardless of any rule requiring diversification of investments; to invest and reinvest in any stocks, bonds, shares in mutual funds or authorized common trust funds, or other securities or property, whether real or personal, which my Personal Representative may deem safe and for the best interests of the estate, without being limited to investments authorized by law for the investment of trust funds; to hold title to any and all securities and other investments either in my Personal Representative's name or in the name of a nominee; to borrow money from itself or others on terms my Personal Representative may deem best, and to pledge any property of the estate as security for the repayment thereof; and to make distributions in cash or in kind, or partly in each, to the beneficiaries entitled thereto.

B. If any beneficiary or legatee entitled to receive a part of my estate shall be under twenty-one (21) years of age, I authorize and empower my Personal Representative to designate his or her parent, or some other appropriate adult person, or trust company, as custodian for the beneficiary or legatee under the Sample Uniform Transfers to Minors Act until the beneficiary or legatee reaches age twenty-one (21), and to distribute the share of the beneficiary or legatee to the designated custodian. A receipt from the custodian shall fully release my Personal Representative from all liability and accountability to the legatee or beneficiary.

VI. I direct that all inheritance, succession, and estate taxes of every kind payable with respect to any property includable in my gross taxable estate, whether or not passing under this my Will, shall be paid out of my residuary estate and shall not be apportioned.

VII. I hereby nominate, constitute, and appoint SC3 Personal Representative of this my Last Will and Testament; but if SC3 fails to survive me, or renounces, or fails to qualify, or upon his death, resignation or disqualification, I nominate and appoint SC4 as Personal Representative hereof. I direct that no bond or other security shall be required of my Personal Representative.

VIII. The masculine gender, whenever used herein, shall include the feminine; the feminine shall include the masculine; the neuter shall include both the masculine and feminine; and the singular shall include the plural, wherever necessary or appropriate.

IN WITNESS WHEREOF, I have hereunto subscribed my name this _____ day of _____, 2014.

_____
SC1

I, SC1, the Testator, sign my name to this instrument this _____ day of _____, 2014, and being first duly sworn, do declare to the undersigned authority that I sign and execute this instrument as my will and that I sign it willingly, or willingly direct another to sign for me, that I execute it as my free and voluntary act for the purposes expressed in that document and that I am eighteen years of age or older, of sound mind and under no constraint or undue influence.

_____
Testator

We, _____ and _____, the witnesses, sign our names to this instrument being first duly sworn and do declare to the undersigned authority that the testator signs and executes this instrument as his/her will and that he/she signs it willingly, or willingly directs another to sign for him/her, and that each of us, in the presence and hearing of the testator, signs this will as witness to the testator's signing and that to the best of our knowledge the testator is eighteen years of age or older, of sound mind and under no constraint or undue influence.

_____
Witness

_____
Witness

The State of Sample}

County of Sample}

Subscribed, sworn to and acknowledged before me by SC1, the Testator, and subscribed and sworn to before me by _____ and _____, witnesses, this _____ day of _____, 2014.

_____
Notary Public

My Commission Expires:

Testamentary and Non-Testamentary Trusts

CHAPTER 6

A REAL-LIFE SCENARIO

Mr. and Mrs. Johnson were an elderly couple who had married late in life. Mr. Johnson had five children from a previous marriage. Mrs. Johnson had no children of her own but was close to her niece and nephew. The couple executed a revocable living trust and put their brokerage account, which was the bulk of their estate, into the trust.

Mr. Johnson passed away first. Mrs. Johnson allegedly made changes to the trust after Mr. Johnson's passing. Mr. Johnson's children were told that the brokerage account was to go to them after Mrs. Johnson passed away but were not given a copy of the trust. When the wife finally passed away, her niece presented herself to the five children as the trustee of the trust and wrote them each a check that bounced. The amounts of the checks did not even come close to adding up the account's balance. The children contacted the bank holding the brokerage account and the bank froze the account. The purported trustee had to open a probate in order to get the account unfrozen and transfer the funds to the beneficiaries. She denied having a copy of the trust, but alleged she was

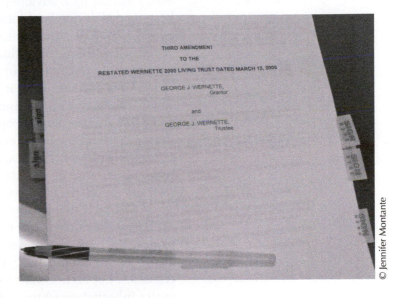

© Jennifer Montante

CHAPTER OBJECTIVES:

1. Understand the purpose of executing a trust.

2. Describe the purpose of a spendthrift clause.

3. List and describe the different types of trusts.

4. Discuss the benefits of choosing a revocable living trust as an estate planning tool.

5. Discuss circumstances under which it may be in a client's best interest to have a testamentary trust, rather than an inter vivos trust.

doing what she was supposed to under the trust terms. The bank lost its copy of the trust. With no trust agreement to be found, the estate should have passed under intestacy to Mrs. Smith's heirs: her niece and nephew. However, there were allegations of serious wrongdoing and breach of fiduciary duty on the part of the niece-trustee. Perhaps that is why she opened the probate to distribute a portion of the trust account to Mr. Johnson's children. The children hired an attorney and litigation ensued. However, neither side had concrete proof of what had transpired.

■ INTRODUCTION

The foregoing scenario illustrates some of the potential downfalls of putting one's assets into a revocable living trust in order to avoid probate. In the example, Mrs. Johnson took advantage of the fact that the trust was revocable and could be amended during her lifetime and made changes to the trust after her husband passed, which negatively affected his offspring. Further, Mrs. Johnson's niece was appointed as trustee but refused to give the beneficiaries a copy of the trust, claiming she could not find it. To make matters worse, the bank was required to have a copy of the trust but lost it and could not provide the beneficiaries with a copy. There was no court supervising the trust administration to oversee the trustee and make sure she was acting properly pursuant to the trust terms. Only after a probate was opened did the beneficiaries even have an opportunity to contest what had transpired and seek the trustee's removal from office. All allegations were speculative, at best, since no one could produce the actual trust document. Of course, this scenario represents what could happen in the worst of cases. There are instances when revocable living trusts are used seamlessly without any problems whatsoever.

Trusts are one possible tool in your toolbox when assisting clients with estate planning. There are many different types of trusts that serve a variety of purposes. Trusts are commonly used when clients want to provide for one or more beneficiaries, but do not want to give the beneficiaries control of or access to their entire inheritance. Often, clients establish a trust in order to preserve assets for future generations. Trusts may also be used to protect assets from the reach of creditors. A **spendthrift clause** is a provision in a trust or will that states that if a prospective beneficiary has pledged to turn over his or her inheritance to a third party, the trustee or executor shall not honor such a pledge.

Trusts can be created independently or pursuant to the terms of a last will and testament. Trusts that are created during the lifetime of the creator are known as **inter vivos trusts**. Inter vivos trusts can be drafted so that they are either revocable or irrevocable during the lifetime of the creator. Trusts created under a will are **testamentary trusts**. These two main types of trusts are discussed more fully below.

Trust Elements

Every type of trust must contain the following five components in order to be valid:

1. A trustor/donor/settlor (the creator of the trust);
2. A trustee;
3. Trust property;
4. One or more beneficiaries; and
5. A trust purpose.

Spendthrift Clause
A provision in a trust or will that states that if a prospective beneficiary has pledged to turn over his or her inheritance to a third party, the trustee or executor shall not honor such a pledge.

Inter Vivos Trust (also known as a Living Trust)
A trust created by a written declaration during the lifetime of the creator.

Testamentary Trust
A trust that is drafted as part of the testator's will and only becomes effective upon the testator's death.

If any of the foregoing five components is missing, the trust will fail. The trustor, who is also sometimes known as the grantor or settlor, is the creator of the trust as a method for holding, investing, and distributing the trust property to named beneficiaries. A trustor may create a trust for many different reasons, including but not limited to the following: tax savings; to have the trust property managed by someone other than the trustor; to prevent the creditors of a beneficiary from reaching the trust funds; and to prevent a beneficiary from getting his or her share outright. The trust property is also known as res, corpus, principal, assets, fund, and estate. Trust property includes any property that can be freely transferred from one person to another—both personal property and real property. The trustee of a trust holds legal title to the property in the trust and manages the property for the benefit of the beneficiaries of the trust. The beneficiaries of the trust hold **equitable title** to trust property, meaning that they have the right to use and enjoy the property.

■ TWO MAIN TYPES OF TRUSTS

Testamentary Trusts

A testamentary trust is a trust that is established following the testator's death pursuant to the terms of the will. The designated assets are transferred to the trustee to hold in trust for the benefit of the named beneficiaries until the **terminating event** (the event that triggers the trust termination) occurs.

Often, the terminating event is *age*.

Terminating Event
The event that triggers trust termination.

EXAMPLE 1 _____

"I direct my Trustee to hold said assets in trust for the benefit of my children until my youngest living child reaches the age of twenty-five (25). At that time, the trust shall terminate and the then remaining assets shall be distributed outright in equal shares to my children."

EXAMPLE 2 _____

"I direct my Trustee to create three separate, equal trust shares for the benefit of each of my three children: Thomas Jones, Megan Jones, and Rachael Jones. Each trust share shall terminate upon the child's attaining the age of thirty (30)."

However, another common terminating event is *death*.

EXAMPLE 3 _____

"If any child fails to survive through the termination of his or her trust, that child's trust shall pass equally into the trusts of my surviving children, as provided herein."

Testamentary trusts can be structured in many different ways. One primary decision the testator must make is whether there should be one single trust for the benefit of all minor children, as is depicted in Figure 6.1, or separate, equal trust shares for the benefit of each child, as is depicted in Figure 6.2.

Figure 6.1 Last Will and Testament

This will creates one single trust for the benefit of all of the testator's children.

LAST WILL AND TESTAMENT

I, **RICHARD JAMES**, of the TOWN OF SAMPLE TOWN, STATE OF SAMPLE STATE, do hereby make, publish and declare the following to be my Last Will and Testament, hereby revoking all former Wills and Codicils made by me.

I. I direct that all my debts and funeral expenses be paid and I further authorize my Executor, in its discretion, to prepay any mortgage or other installment indebtedness.

II. I give and bequeath to my children, CINDY JAMES, JOHN JAMES, and JACOB JAMES (hereinafter referred to as "my children"), all of my clothing, jewelry, personal effects, household goods, furniture, furnishings, automobiles and all other tangible personal property which I may own at the time of my death, to be divided among them as they shall agree. If my children are unable to agree as to the recipient of any article, I authorize and direct my Executor to make the decision. If, in the sole judgment of my Executor, any child is too young to make a prudent selection, I authorize my Executor to make a selection on behalf of the child. If any of my children is a minor at the time of delivery of any articles, I authorize my Executor, in its discretion, to deliver the articles either directly to the child, or to the child's guardian, or to the person having the care and custody of the child, and a duly executed receipt from the child or guardian or other person shall constitute a complete acquittance to my Executor with respect to the bequest. Any articles not selected shall be sold and the proceeds added to my residuary estate.

III. I give, devise and bequeath all the rest, residue and remainder of my estate to my Trustee, hereinafter named, in trust for the following uses and purposes:

A. I direct my Trustee to distribute so much of net income of this trust among my children, CINDY JAMES, JOHN JAMES, AND JACOB JAMES, in amounts and proportions as my Trustee, in its sole discretion, shall deem best. I recognize that one or more of my children may have greater needs than the others, due to circumstances that I cannot anticipate. I, therefore, expressly authorize my Trustee to pay a larger share of the income, or all of it, if necessary, to those children having the greater need.

B. If at any time the income of the trust, together with any other available income, is not adequate for the support, maintenance and education of my children, or for illnesses, emergencies or other financial needs of a particular child or grandchild, I authorize my Trustee, in its sole discretion, to use so much of the principal as it may deem necessary or advisable for these purposes. Advances of principal shall be made according to need, as determined by my Trustee, and without regard to equality of distribution.

C. I particularly desire that each of my children shall have the opportunity for a college education and professional or postgraduate study, if they so desire. Accordingly, I expressly authorize my Trustee to make advances of principal as my Trustee, in its sole and absolute discretion, shall deem necessary or advisable for the purpose of financing college or post-graduate education as each of the beneficiaries may wish to pursue, even though the advances may completely exhaust the trust.

D. My Trustee's decision with respect to any advances of principal pursuant to this Article shall be final and binding on all persons interested in the trust, and shall not be subject to judicial review.

E. When my youngest living child reaches THIRTY (30) years of age, I direct my Trustee to pay the remaining trust property in equal shares to my children, CINDY JAMES, JOHN JAMES, AND JACOB JAMES, with the share of any deceased child to be paid to the child's issue, per stirpes, or, in default of issue, to my surviving issue, per stirpes; provided, however, that if the issue is a beneficiary of a trust created hereunder, his or her share shall be added to the trust to be held and administered pursuant to the terms thereof.

F. If any grandchild of mine to whom a share of principal is to be distributed as herein provided is under twenty-one (21) years of age, I authorize my Trustee to hold the grandchild's share in trust, paying or applying to the use and benefit of the grandchild so much of the income and principal as my Trustee may deem needed for the grandchild's comfortable support, maintenance and education, other available income considered, and accumulating any unused income, but all remaining principal and accumulated income shall be paid to the grandchild upon attaining age twenty-one (21), or in the event of his or her prior death, it shall be paid to his or her estate.

Figure 6.1 (continued)

IV. I give to my Executor and to my Trustee hereinafter named, and to the successor or successors of either, the following powers and discretions, in addition to those vested in or imposed upon them or either of them by law:

A. To mortgage, sell, convey, exchange or otherwise deal with or dispose of any real or personal property for cash or on credit (including the right to accept a purchase money mortgage as part of the purchase price); to lease any property for periods longer or shorter than the probable duration of any trust; to retain as part of the estate or trust any and all securities and property in the form originally received, including securities of or issued by any corporate executor or trustee, whether or not it is then income producing and regardless of any rule requiring diversification of investments; to invest and reinvest in any stocks, bonds, shares in mutual funds or authorized common trust funds, or other securities or property, whether real or personal, which my Executor or Trustee may deem safe and for the best interests of the estate or trust, without being limited to investments authorized by law for the investment of trust funds; to hold title to any and all securities and other investments either in my Executor's or Trustee's name or in the name of a nominee; to borrow money from itself or others on terms as my Executor or Trustee may deem best, and to pledge any property of the estate or trust as security for the repayment thereof; to hold two or more trusts or other funds in one or more consolidated funds, in which the separate trusts as funds shall have undivided interests; to determine as to every sum received (including stock dividends or the distributions of securities), whether the same is principal or income, or what part thereof is principal or income, and as to every expense or disbursement incurred or made by it, whether the same should be borne by the principal or income, or in what share by each; and to make distributions in cash or in kind, or partly in each, including undivided interests, even though shares be composed differently.

B. In case any income or principal of the trust becomes payable to a person under twenty-one (21) years of age, or to a person under legal disability, or to a person not adjudicated incompetent but who, by reason of illness or mental or physical disability, is in the opinion of my Trustee, unable to administer properly the income or principal, then the income or principal may be paid out by my Trustee in any one or more of the following ways as it deems best: (a) directly to the beneficiary; (b) to the guardian, committee, conservator or custodian of the beneficiary; (c) to any relative of the beneficiary or to any other person with whom the beneficiary may be living, for the care, comfort, support, maintenance, education and welfare of the beneficiary; (d) by my Trustee using income or principal directly for the care, comfort, support, maintenance, education and welfare of the beneficiary.

C. I expressly authorize my Trustee to receive and execute receipts for the proceeds of any life insurance policies on my life which may become payable to my Trustee; and I direct that a receipt executed by my Trustee shall fully discharge the respective insurance companies from all liability and responsibility with respect to the payment and use of the proceeds of the policies. If my Trustee's claim to any insurance proceeds is contested, whether by the insurance company or by any other claimant, my Trustee shall have full power and authority to settle, compromise or otherwise collect, or to enforce by legal action, any contested policy, paying the expenses of the action out of the trust estate. My Trustee's decision with respect to any contested claim shall be final and conclusive upon all parties interested in this trust.

D. I further expressly authorize my Trustee to purchase any assets from my Executor at the value established for the assets in the Federal Estate Tax proceeding in my estate, and/or to loan to my Executor sums as may be needed to pay any and all taxes and administration expenses. The loans may be made with or without security, and with or without interest, and upon other terms and conditions as my Executor and Trustee may agree. The authority hereby granted shall be exercised notwithstanding that my Executor and Trustee are one and the same person or corporation.

E. If at any time during the administration of any trust herein created, the Trustee, in its absolute discretion, deems the continuation thereof to be uneconomical and not in the best interests of the beneficiary or beneficiaries thereof, the Trustee, in its absolute discretion, is authorized to terminate the same and distribute the assets, free of the Trust, to the current income beneficiary or beneficiaries in the proportions in which they are entitled to the income there from.

F. If any beneficiary or legatee entitled to receive a part of my estate shall be under twenty-one (21) years of age, I authorize and empower my Executor or Trustee, as the case may be, to designate his or her parent, or some other appropriate adult person, or trust company, as custodian for the beneficiary or legatee under the Sample State Uniform Transfers to Minors Act until age twenty-one (21), and to distribute the share of the beneficiary or legatee to the designated custodian. A receipt from the custodian shall fully release my Executor or Trustee from all liability and accountability to the legatee or beneficiary.

G. I expressly authorize my Trustee to merge any trust created hereunder with any other trust created by me under will or agreement, which property shall be held, administered and distributed in accordance with the provisions of

(*continued*)

Figure 6.1 (continued)

the trust; provided, however, that this power shall apply only if the trust to which the distribution would be made is substantially identical in form and content to the trust described herein, and for the same beneficiaries.

H. If any party to any proceeding relating to my estate or any trust established hereunder shall be under a disability by reason of infancy or incompetency, and there is another party without any disability to the proceeding with the same interest as the person under a disability, it shall not be necessary to serve the person under a disability with process in the proceeding, and he shall be deemed to be virtually represented therein as provided by law by the other person who is served with process, and the person under the disability shall be bound in all respects by any Decree or Judgment entered in the proceeding.

I. No individual Trustee of any trust herein created shall be authorized to exercise any power herein to make any discretionary distribution of either income or principal to himself or herself, or to make discretionary allocations in his or her own favor between principal and income; and no individual Trustee shall be authorized to exercise any power herein to distribute income or principal to or for the benefit of any person whom he or he is legally obligated to support. These powers may be exercised by the remaining Trustee who is not so disqualified.

VI. I direct that all inheritance, succession and estate taxes of every kind payable with respect to any property includable in my gross taxable estate, whether or not passing under this my Will, shall be paid out of my residuary estate, and shall not be apportioned.

VII. If my daughter's mother cannot serve as guardian, or if she fails to survive me, or fails to qualify for any reason, then I nominate and appoint LILA JAMES as guardian. If LILA JAMES cannot serve as guardian, or if he fails to survive me, or fails to qualify for any reason, I nominate and appoint MARK JAMES as guardian. I direct that no bond or other security shall be required of either of them, in any jurisdiction, for the faithful performance of their duties.

VIII. I hereby nominate, constitute and appoint LILA JAMES as Executrix of this my Last Will and Testament; but if she fails to survive me, or renounces, or fails to qualify, or upon her death, resignation or disqualification, I nominate and appoint MARK JAMES as Executor hereof. I hereby nominate, constitute and appoint LILA JAMES as Trustee of the trust herein; but if she fails to survive me, or renounces, or fails to qualify, or upon her death, resignation or disqualification, I nominate and appoint MARK JAMES as Trustee. I direct that no bond or other security shall be required of my Executor or Trustees.

IX. The masculine gender, whenever used herein, shall include the feminine, the feminine shall include the masculine; the neuter shall include both the masculine and feminine; and the singular shall include the plural wherever necessary or appropriate.

IN WITNESS WHEREOF, I have hereunto subscribed my name this ___ day of_____ 2013.

_____
RICHARD JAMES

We whose names are hereto subscribed, do certify that on the _____ day of_____ 2013, the Testator, RICHARD JAMES, subscribed his name to this instrument, in our presence and in the presence of each of us, and at the same time in our presence and hearing, declared the same to be his Last Will and Testament, and requested us, and each of us, to sign our names thereto as witnesses to the execution thereof, which we hereby do in the presence of the Testator and of each other.

_____ residing at _____

_____ residing at _____

AFFIDAVIT OF ATTESTING WITNESSES

_____ and _____ , being duly sworn, say:

We are acquainted with RICHARD JAMES. The signature at the end of the instrument dated _____ 2013, declared by him to be his Last Will, was made by him at Rochester, State of Sample State, in the presence of each of the undersigned.

Figure 6.1 (continued)

At the time of signing the Will, RICHARD JAMES declared the instrument to which his signature had been affixed to be his Will and we, and each of us, signed our names thereto at the end thereof at that time and at his request and in his presence.

At the time of the execution of the instrument RICHARD JAMES was over the age of 18 years, of sound mind and memory, and not under any restraint and competent in every respect to make a Will.

At the time of execution, RICHARD JAMES could read, write and converse in the English language, and was not suffering from defects of sight, hearing or speech, or any other physical or mental impairment, which would affect his capacity to make a valid Will.

The Will was not executed in counterparts.

_____
Witness

_____
Witness

STATE OF SAMPLE STATE)

COUNTY OF SAMPLE) SS:

On the _____ day of _____ in the year 2013 before me, the undersigned, a Notary Public in and for said State, personally appeared _____ and _____, the subscribing witnesses to the foregoing instrument, with whom I am personally acquainted, who, being by me duly sworn, did depose and say that _____ resides at _____, Sample State and _____ resides at _____, Sample State; that they know RICHARD JAMES to be the individual described in and who executed the foregoing instrument; that said subscribing witnesses were present and saw said RICHARD JAMES execute the same; and that said witnesses at the same time subscribed their names as witnesses thereto, and acknowledged to me that they executed the same in their capacities, and that by their signatures on the instrument, the individual, or the person upon behalf of which the individual acted, executed the instrument.

_____
LILA P. LEGAL
Notary Public, State of Sample
Sample County
My Commission Expires May 10, 2012

Figure 6.2 contains a will with a testamentary trust for Susan Smith (now Susan Smith-Thompson) from the Hypothetical Family. The will directs that the share of each child who is then under the age of 30 be held in a *separate, equal trust share* for the benefit of that child.

The testator appoints the trustee of the testamentary trust under the will. This appointment is generally made in the same paragraph where the testator appoints the executor or personal representative. The following sample language has been extracted from Figure 6.1:

VIII. I hereby nominate, constitute and appoint LILA JAMES as Executrix of this my Last Will and Testament; but if she fails to survive me, or renounces, or fails to qualify, or upon her death, resignation or disqualification, I nominate and appoint MARK JAMES as Executor hereof. I hereby nominate, constitute and appoint LILA JAMES as Trustee of the trust herein; but if she fails to survive me, or renounces, or fails to qualify, or upon her death, resignation or disqualification, I nominate and appoint MARK JAMES as Trustee. I direct that no bond or other security shall be required of my Executor or Trustees.

Figure 6.2 Last Will and Testament

I, **Susan Smith-Thompson**, of the CITY OF SAMPLE, COUNTY OF SAMPLE, STATE OF SAMPLE, do hereby make, publish and declare the following to be my Last Will and Testament, hereby revoking all former Wills and Codicils made by me.

I. I direct that all my debts and funeral expenses be paid, and I further authorize my Executor, in its discretion, to prepay any mortgage or other installment indebtedness.

II. I give and bequeath to my husband, ARTHUR THOMPSON (hereinafter referred to as "my husband"), all of my clothing, jewelry, personal effects, household goods, furniture, furnishings, automobiles and all other tangible personal property which I may own at the time of my death to be his absolutely, provided he survives me.

III. If my husband does not survive me, then I direct that each of my surviving children may select from the foregoing those articles he or she may wish to retain, and I hereby give and bequeath to each child the articles selected. If my children are unable to agree as to the recipient of any article, I authorize and direct my Executor to make the decision. If, in the sole judgment of my Executor, any child is too young to make a prudent selection, I authorize my Executor to make a selection on behalf of the child. If any of my children is a minor at the time of delivery of any articles, I authorize my Executor, in its discretion, to deliver the articles either directly to the child, or to the child's guardian, or to the person having the care and custody of the child, and a duly executed receipt from the child or guardian or other person shall constitute a complete acquittance to my Executor with respect to the bequest. Any articles not selected shall be sold and the proceeds added to my residuary estate.

IV. All the rest, residue and remainder of my property, real, personal and mixed, of every name and nature, and wheresoever situate, I give, devise and bequeath to my husband, if he survives me.

V. If my husband does not survive me, I give, devise and bequeath all the rest, residue and remainder of my estate to my Trustee, hereinafter named, in trust for the following uses and purposes:

A. I direct my Trustee to divide my said residuary estate into such number of equal shares as shall provide one (1) such equal share for each of my children as shall then be living and one (1) such equal share for the then living issue (collectively), per stirpes, of each of my issue as shall not then be living, and after making such division, my Trustee shall

1. Pay and distribute the equal share so provided for the then living issue (collectively), per stirpes, of each deceased issue of mine; provided however, that if any such issue shall be under the age of twenty-one (21) years, I authorize my Trustee to hold the issue's share in trust, paying or applying to the use and benefit of the issue so much of the income and principal as my Trustee may deem needed for the issue's comfortable support, maintenance and education, other available income considered, and accumulating any unused income, but all remaining principal and accumulated income shall be paid to the issue upon attaining twenty-one (21), or in the event of his or her prior death, it shall be paid to his or her estate.

2. Pay and distribute the equal share so provided for each then living child of mine who shall have attained the age of thirty (30) years, outright and free of trust.

3. One such equal share shall be held in trust for the benefit of each child of mine who is then living and shall not have attained the age of thirty (30) years. With respect to each such part:

   a. My Trustee shall pay to the beneficiary so much of the net income of such part, together with such amounts from principal as my Trustee, in its discretion, shall deem necessary or advisable to provide adequately for the beneficiary's health, support, maintenance, education, and medical emergencies, after taking into account all other available income. Undistributed income shall be accumulated and added to principal.

   b. I particularly desire that each of my children shall have the opportunity for a college education and professional or post-graduate study, if they so desire. Accordingly, I expressly authorize my Trustee to make advances of principal as my Trustee, in its sole and absolute discretion, shall deem necessary or advisable for the purpose of financing a college or post-graduate education as each of the beneficiaries may wish to pursue, even though the advances may completely exhaust the trust.

   c. I particularly desire that each of my children shall have the opportunity to have an automobile, if they so desire. Accordingly, I expressly authorize my Trustee to make any advances of principal as it, in its sole and absolute discretion, shall deem necessary and advisable to provide for each beneficiary's purchase of an automobile.

   d. I particularly desire that each of my children shall have the opportunity to have a wedding, if they so desire. Accordingly, I expressly authorize my Trustee to make any advances of principal as it, in its sole and absolute discretion, shall deem necessary and advisable to provide for each beneficiary's wedding.

Figure 6.2 (continued)

e. I particularly desire that each of my children shall have the opportunity to purchase a home, if they so desire. Accordingly, I expressly authorize my Trustee to make any advances of principal as it, in its sole and absolute discretion, shall deem necessary and advisable to provide for each beneficiary's down payment for a home.

f. I authorize and direct my Trustee to pay and distribute one-half (1/2) of the remaining principal of such part and any undistributed income of his or her trust to the beneficiary upon attaining twenty-five (25) years of age.

g. I authorize and direct my Trustee to pay and distribute the entire remaining principal of such part and any undistributed income of his or her trust to the beneficiary upon attaining thirty (30) years of age.

h. If the beneficiary should die before reaching thirty (30) years of age, the entire remaining principal of his or her part shall be paid to his or her issue then living, per stirpes; or, in default of such issue, to my issue then living, per stirpes; provided, however, that if the issue is a beneficiary of a trust created hereunder, his or her share shall be added to the trust to be held and administered pursuant to the terms thereof.

4. My Trustee's decision with respect to any advances of principal pursuant to this Article shall be final and binding on all persons interested in the trust, and shall not be subject to judicial review.

VI. If my husband and I shall die under circumstances that there is not sufficient evidence to determine the order of our deaths, then it shall be presumed that I survived him and my estate shall be administered and distributed, in all respects, in accordance with this presumption.

VII. I give to my Executor and to my Trustee hereinafter named, and to the successor or successors of either, the following powers and discretions, in addition to those vested in or imposed upon them or either of them by law:

A. To mortgage, sell, convey, exchange or otherwise deal with or dispose of any real or personal property for cash or on credit (including the right to accept a purchase money mortgage as part of the purchase price); to lease any property for periods longer or shorter than the probable duration of any trust; to retain as part of the estate or trust any and all securities and property in the form originally received, including securities of or issued by any corporate executor or trustee, whether or not it is then income producing and regardless of any rule requiring diversification of investments; to invest and reinvest in any stocks, bonds, shares in mutual funds or authorized common trust funds, or other securities or property, whether real or personal, which my Executor or Trustee may deem safe and for the best interests of the estate or trust, without being limited to investments authorized by law for the investment of trust funds; to hold title to any and all securities and other investments either in my Executor's or Trustee's name or in the name of a nominee; to borrow money from itself or others on terms my Executor or Trustee may deem best, and to pledge any property of the estate or trust as security for the repayment thereof; to hold two or more trusts or other funds in one or more consolidated funds, in which the separate trusts as funds shall have undivided interests; to determine as to every sum received (including stock dividends or the distribution of securities), whether the same is principal or income, or what part thereof is principal or income, and as to every expense or disbursement incurred or made by it, whether the same should be borne by the principal or income, or in what share by each; and to make distributions in cash or in kind, or partly in each, including undivided interests, even though shares be composed differently.

B. In case any income or principal of the trust becomes payable to a person under twenty-one (21) years of age, or to a person under legal disability, or to a person not adjudicated incompetent but who, by reason of illness or mental or physical disability, is in the opinion of my Trustee, unable to administer properly the income or principal, then the income or principal may be paid out by my Trustee in any one or more of the following ways as it deems best: (a) directly to the beneficiary; (b) to the guardian or custodian of the beneficiary; (c) to any relative of the beneficiary or to any other person with whom the beneficiary may be living, for the care, comfort, support, maintenance, education and welfare of the beneficiary; (d) by my Trustee using income or principal directly for the care, comfort, support, maintenance education and welfare of the beneficiary.

C. In determining the amounts of principal to be used for the benefit of any of my infant children during minority, it is my desire that my Trustee first consult with the guardian of the person of my children, and I direct that my Trustee shall be fully protected with respect to any payment made in reliance upon information received from the guardian. The final determination as to the appropriateness of using principal for the benefit of any infant child shall rest with my Trustee.

D. I expressly authorize my Trustee to receive and execute receipts for the proceeds of any life insurance policies on my life which may become payable to my Trustee; and I direct that a receipt executed by my Trustee shall fully discharge the respective insurance companies from all liability and responsibility with respect to the payment and

(continued)

Figure 6.2 (continued)

use of the proceeds of the policies. If my Trustee's claim to any insurance proceeds is contested, whether by the insurance company or by any other claimant, my Trustee shall have full power and authority to settle, compromise or otherwise collect, or to enforce by legal action, any contested policy, paying the expenses of the action out of the trust estate. My Trustee's decision with respect to any contested claim shall be final and conclusive upon all parties interested in this trust.

E. I further expressly authorize my Trustee to purchase any assets from my Executor at the value established for the assets in the Federal Estate Tax proceeding in my estate, and/or to loan to my Executor sums as may be needed to pay any and all taxes and administration expenses. Loans may be made with or without security, and with or without interest, and upon other terms and conditions as my Executor and Trustee may agree. The authority hereby granted shall be exercised notwithstanding that my Executor and Trustee are one and the same person or corporation.

F. If at any time during the administration of any trust herein created, the Trustee, in its absolute discretion, deems the continuation thereof to be uneconomical and not in the best interests of the beneficiary or beneficiaries thereof, the Trustee, in its absolute discretion, is authorized to terminate the same and distribute the assets, free of the Trust, to the current income beneficiary or beneficiaries in the proportions in which they are entitled to the income therefrom.

G. If any beneficiary or legatee entitled to receive a part of my estate shall be under twenty-one (21) years of age, I authorize and empower my Executor or Trustee, as the case may be, to designate his or her parent, or some other appropriate adult person, or trust company, as custodian for the beneficiary or legatee under the Sample Uniform Transfers to Minors Act until age twenty-one (21), and to distribute the share of the beneficiary or legatee to the designated custodian. A receipt from the custodian shall fully release my Executor or Trustee from all liability and accountability to the legatee or beneficiary.

H. I expressly authorize my Trustee to merge any trust created hereunder with any other trust created by me or my spouse under will or agreement, which property shall be held, administered and distributed in accordance with the provisions of the trust; provided, however, that this power shall apply only if the trust to which the distribution would be made is substantially identical in form and content to the trust described herein, and for the same beneficiaries.

I. No individual Trustee of any trust herein created shall be authorized to exercise any power herein to make any discretionary distribution of either income or principal to himself or herself, or to make discretionary allocations in his or her own favor between principal and income; and no individual Trustee shall be authorized to exercise any power herein to distribute income or principal to or for the benefit of any person whom he or she is legally obligated to support. These powers may be exercised by the remaining Trustee who is not so disqualified.

VIII. I direct that all inheritance, succession and estate taxes of every kind payable with respect to any property includable in my gross taxable estate, whether or not passing under this my Will, shall be paid out of my residuary estate, and shall not be apportioned.

IX. If my husband does not survive me, I nominate, constitute and appoint JANE SMITH as guardian of the person of each infant child of mine; but if JANE SMITH fails to survive me, or fails to qualify for any reason, then I nominate and appoint BARBARA THOMPSON as guardian. I direct that no bond or other security shall be required of either of them, in any jurisdiction, for the faithful performance of their duties.

X. I hereby nominate, constitute and appoint my husband as Executor of this my Last Will and Testament; but if he fails to survive me, or renounces, or fails to qualify, or upon his death, resignation or disqualification, I nominate and appoint JANE SMITH as Executrix hereof. If both my husband and JANE SMITH are unable to serve as Executor, I nominate and appoint BARBARA THOMPSON as Executrix. I hereby nominate, constitute and appoint JANE SMITH as Trustee of the trusts herein created. I nominate and appoint BARBARA THOMPSON as alternate Trustee. I direct that no bond or other security shall be required of my Executor or Trustee.

XI. The masculine gender, whenever used herein shall include the feminine, the feminine shall include the masculine; the neuter shall include both the masculine and feminine; and the singular shall include the plural wherever necessary or appropriate.

IN WITNESS WHERE OF, I have hereunto subscribed my name this 4th day of March, 2012.

Susan Smith-Thompson
_____
SUSAN SMITH-THOMPSON

Figure 6.2 (continued)

We, whose names are hereto subscribed, do certify that on the *4*th day of *March*, 2012, the Testatrix, SUSAN SMITH-THOMPSON, subscribed her name to this instrument, in our presence and in the presence of each of us, and at the same time in our presence and hearing, declared the same to be her Last Will and Testament, and requested us, and each of us, to sign our names thereto as witnesses to the execution thereof, which we hereby do in the presence of the Testatrix and of each other.

Michael Pearson _____ residing at *1001 Reed Drive, Sample City, Sample State 12345* _____

Maggy Pearson _____ residing at *1001 Reed Drive, Sample City, Sample State 12345* _____

AFFIDAVIT OF ATTESTING WITNESSES

STATE OF SAMPLE STATE   )
COUNTY OF SAMPLE COUNTY) SS:

____*Michael Pearson*____ and ____*Maggy Pearson*____ , being duly sworn, say:

We are acquainted with SUSAN SMITH-THOMPSON. The signature at the end of the instrument dated *March 4*, 2012 declared by her to be her Last Will, was made by her at City of Sample, State of Sample State, in the presence of each of the undersigned.

At the time of signing Will, SUSAN SMITH-THOMPSON declared the instrument to which her signature had been affixed to be her Will and we, and each of us, signed our names thereto at the end thereof at that time and at her request and in his presence.

At the time of the execution of the instrument SUSAN SMITH-THOMPSON was over the age of 18 years, of sound mind and memory, and not under any restraint and competent in every respect to make a Will.

At the time of execution, SUSAN SMITH-THOMPSON could read, write and converse in the English language, and was not suffering from defects of sight, hearing, or speech or any other physical or mental impairment that could affect her capacity to make a valid Will.

The Will was not executed in counterparts.

Michael Pearson _____
Witness

Maggy Pearson _____
Witness

STATE OF SAMPLE STATE   }
COUNTY OF SAMPLE COUNTY } SS:

On the 4th day of March in the year 2012 before me, the undersigned, a Notary Public in and for said State, personally appeared Michael Pearson and Maggy Pearson, the subscribing witnesses to the foregoing instrument, with whom I am personally acquainted, who being by me duly sworn, did depose and say that Michael Pearson resides at 1001 Reed Drive, Sample State and Maggy Pearson resides at 1001 Reed Drive, Sample State; that they know SUSAN SMITH-THOMPSON to be the individual described in and who executed the foregoing instrument; that said subscribing witnesses were present and saw said SUSAN SMITH-THOMPSON execute the same; and that said witnesses at the same time subscribed their names as witnesses thereto, and acknowledged to me that they executed the same in their capacities, and that by their signatures on the instrument, the individual(s) or the person upon behalf of which the individual(s) acted, executed the instrument.

Lila P. Legal _____
Notary Public

LILA P. LEGAL
Notary Public, State of Sample
Sample County
My Commission Expires May 10, 2012

Living Trust
Also called an inter vivos trust (*inter vivos* is Latin for "within one's life"), is a trust that is created and becomes effective during the lifetime of the trustor(s) [also called settlor(s)].

Trustor, Donor, or Settlor
The creator of a trust.

Trustee
The person or entity who holds the assets (corpus) of the trust and manages the trust and its assets pursuant to the trust's terms.

Trust Corpus (Latin for "body")
The principal of the trust, usually comprising money, securities, and other assets.

In the foregoing example, Lila James is appointed both as executrix (a female executor) and as trustee of the testamentary trust. If Lila James cannot serve for any reason, Mark James is appointed as alternate executor and trustee. The will further directs that these fiduciaries are not required to post a bond with the court in order to serve in the appointed capacities.

Non-Testamentary Trusts

An **inter vivos trust** (also known as a **living trust**) is a trust created by a written declaration during the lifetime of the creator. The creator of a trust may be known as a **trustor, donor**, or **settlor**, depending on the jurisdiction in which the trust is created. Trustor is the term used primarily in the western states.

The property is then placed with the trustee and distribution takes place in accordance with the terms of the trust. The **trustee** is the person or entity who holds the assets (corpus) of the trust and manages the trust and its assets pursuant to the trust's terms. Often, the trustor acts as trustee during his or her lifetime and is also the beneficiary of the trust during his or her lifetime. Upon the death of the trustor or settlor, the successor trustee takes over and the trust either terminates or continues for the benefit of the remainder beneficiaries, depending on the trust's terms. The trustee's powers and duties are discussed in greater detail in Chapter 8.

Required Components

In order to be valid, a trust must be funded with some type of property. The **trust corpus** (Latin for "body") is the principal of the trust, usually comprising money, securities, and other assets. The trust property must be delivered to the trustee to administer in accordance with the trust terms. **Trust property**, or corpus, is also sometimes known as the res, principal, fund, assets, and estate.

The requirements for trust execution vary by state, but generally the trustor's signature and date at the end of the trust document are required. The trustor usually must execute the trust before a notary public. Some states also require the presence of one or two witnesses, whose signatures may also need to be notarized.

With respect to testamentary trusts, the will containing the trust must be executed properly in order for a valid trust to be created following the testator's death. There must also be adequate assets in the probate estate with which to fund the testamentary trust, or a provision directing that a non-probate asset may be used to fund the trust. For example, life insurance payable upon the testator's death may be used to fund a testamentary trust if the beneficiary designation for the life insurance also reflects this intention.

EXAMPLE 1 _____

Mary Smith executes a will on January 10, 2010. The will contains a testamentary trust for the benefit of Mary's daughter, Nancy Smith. Mary intends to fund the trust for her daughter using a $50,000 life insurance policy. Mary's intentions will be carried out if the beneficiary designation on her life insurance policy reads as follows: *"To the testamentary trust created under my Last Will & Testament dated 11/10/2010."*

EXAMPLE 2

Michael Masters executes a will on January 10, 2010. The will contains two testamentary trusts: one for Michael's wife and one for Michael's son, Michael Masters, Jr. Michael intends to fund the trust for his son using a $50,000 life insurance policy. He does not want that money to go to his wife. The beneficiary designation on the life insurance should read as follows: *"To the testamentary trust created under my Last Will & Testament dated 11/10/2010 for the benefit of my son, Michael Masters, Jr."* In this instance, it would be insufficient to simply designate the policy *"to the testamentary trust created under my Last Will & Testament dated 11/10/2010"* because more than one testamentary trust is created under the will.

■ REVOCABLE LIVING TRUSTS AS AN ALTERNATIVE TO PROBATE

Many clients are interested in avoiding probate. **Probate** is a general term for the entire process of administration of estates of dead persons, including those without wills, with court supervision. Probate has a nasty societal stigma resulting from a combination of the media and negative stories that people have heard. Contrary to popular belief, many probate cases go very smoothly. However, a primary motivation for some is to avoid the expense (i.e., attorney's fees) of a probate proceeding, as well as the length of time it takes to go through probate (generally ranging from six months to two years). Clients may opt for a revocable living trust with a pour-over will to avoid the necessity of a probate proceeding following their death. However, competent legal counsel is needed to assist clients in weighing the pros and cons of using a revocable living trust as an alternative to probate.

Probate
A general term for the entire process of administration of estates of dead persons, including those without wills, with court supervision.

Revocable Living Trust

A **revocable living trust** is a trust created by a written declaration during the lifetime of the creator. The fact that this type of trust is revocable means that the trustor reserves the right to amend or revoke the trust during his or her lifetime. Note that the term "living trust" is often used to denote a revocable living trust and means the same thing. (An **irrevocable trust** generally may not be amended after execution. However, many states do allow an irrevocable trust to be revoked if all of the living beneficiaries consent to the revocation.)

In order to avoid probate, all would-be probate assets must be retitled into the name of the trust following the execution of the trust and for the remainder of the trustor's lifetime. Any asset that is not transferred into the trust may necessitate a probate proceeding, thereby negating the purpose of the trust in the first place (to avoid probate). Once again, **probate assets** are those which are distributed through a probate proceeding in a court of law. Generally speaking, probate assets are assets that are in the sole name of the decedent at the time of death. Common examples are bank accounts, vehicles, and property held solely in the decedent's name. Assets that pass by title or beneficiary designation are generally not re-titled into the name of the trust; however, they must be looked at carefully to ensure that the designations match the client's intentions.

Revocable Living Trust
A trust created by a written declaration during the lifetime of the creator that can be amended or revoked during the creator's lifetime.

Irrevocable Trust
A trust that cannot be amended after execution by the trust creator.

Probate Assets
The property of the decedent that must be distributed through a probate proceeding in a court of law.

EXAMPLE 1 _____

John & Carol Robinson are convinced that they want to avoid probate at all costs. They have a modest estate comprising a home, two cars, a joint bank account, and CDs that are only in Carol's name. They execute the Robinson Family Trust (which is a revocable living trust) on December 30, 2011, and appoint themselves as co-trustees. They also execute a pour-over will and other estate planning documents. In addition, their attorney prepares a deed transferring the family home "To John Robinson and Carol, Robinson, as Trustees of the Robinson Family Trust." The deed is properly executed and recorded. After executing the trust, John & Carol follow their attorney's advice and go directly to the Department of Motor Vehicles and retitle the cars into the name of the trust. After that, they tuck their documents into

a drawer and forget about them until Nancy passes away in an automobile accident several months later.

What happens? Is probate avoided at Nancy's death?

Analysis: To answer, we must review how the assets are titled upon Nancy's death. The house and the cars are already in the trust. The joint bank account will pass by operation of law to John. The CDs are only in Carol's name, so a probate will be needed to transfer them into the trust so that they can be distributed pursuant to the trust's terms.

Answer: No, probate is not avoided at Nancy's death.

EXAMPLE 2 _____

The scenario is the same as in Example 1, except that it is John that dies in the car accident, not Nancy. Nancy does not do anything or change anything with her documents or her assets following John's death. Nancy dies five years later. Now what happens?

Analysis: As in Example 1, we must review how the assets are titled upon Nancy's death. The house and

the cars are already in the trust. The joint bank account became Nancy's at John's death—whether or not legal title was changed—since Nancy was the surviving account holder. The CDs are also only in Carol's name. The bank account and the CDs need to be transferred into the trust.

Answer: Once again, probate is not avoided at Nancy's death.

Resolution for Examples 1 & 2: Probate could have been avoided by retitling the bank account and the CDs into the name of the trust immediately following trust execution.

With a revocable living trust, the trustor usually acts as trustee during his or her lifetime and is also the beneficiary of the trust during his or her lifetime. Upon the death of the trustor or settlor, a successor trustee takes over and the trust either terminates or continues for the benefit of the remainder beneficiaries.

Pour-over Will

Pour-over Will
A will that leaves the testator's assets to a living trust, to be administered pursuant to the terms thereof.

Proper drafting requires that clients have a pour-over will, in addition to a revocable living trust. The function of a pour-over will is to direct that any asset that was missed, or not transferred into the trust, pass into the trust to be administered pursuant to the terms thereof. If the pour-over will has to be employed to transfer assets into the trust after the trustor's death, a probate proceeding will be required.

Continuing with Example 1, the pour-over wills for John and Carol Robinson would contain language substantially similar to the following:

"I give, devise, and bequeath all the rest, residue and remainder of my estate to the Robinson Family Trust U/A (Under Agreement) dated December 30, 2011, of which I am a Trustor. I direct that the residue of my estate shall be added to, administered, and distributed as part of that trust, according to the terms of the trust and any amendment made to it before my death. To the extent permitted by law, it is not my intent to create a separate trust by this will or to subject the trust or the property added to it by the will to the jurisdiction of the probate court."

A sample revocable living trust and a pour-over will are included in Figures 6.3 and 6.4, respectively. Figure 6.3 depicts the Robert & Mary Smith Family Trust executed by Robert and Mary Smith from the Hypothetical Family.

Figure 6.3 Robert & Mary Smith Family Trust

ROBERT & MARY SMITH FAMILY TRUST

U/A DATED JANUARY 9, 2010

by

Robert Smith and Mary Smith

Settlors
and

ROBERT SMITH and MARY SMITH

Co-Trustees
Name of Trust: ROBERT & MARY SMITH FAMILY TRUST

TABLE OF CONTENTS

(continued)

Figure 6.3 (continued)

DECLARATION OF TRUST

DECLARATION OF TRUST, made as of this 9th day of <u>January</u>, 2010, between ROBERT SMITH and MARY SMITH, having an address at 125 Oak Street, Sample City, Sample State 12345, as Settlors (hereinafter referred to as the "Settlors"), and ROBERT SMITH and MARY SMITH, having an address of 125 Oak Street, Sample City, Sample State 12345, as Trustees (hereinafter referred to as the "Trustee").

WITNESSETH

WHEREAS, the Settlors desire to create a revocable trust with the sum of ONE DOLLAR ($1.00) together such monies, securities and other assets as the Trustee hereafter may hold or acquire hereunder (said amount and other monies, securities and assets, together with any additions thereto received pursuant to the Settlor's Last Will and Testament or otherwise, being hereinafter referred to as the "trust estate"), for the purposes and upon the terms and conditions hereinafter set forth.

NOW, THEREFORE, in consideration of the covenants herein contained and other valuable consideration, the receipt and sufficiency of which hereby are acknowledged, the Settlors hereby transfer and deliver to the Trustees as and for the trust estate the amount of ONE DOLLAR ($1.00), to hold the same, and any other property which the Trustee hereafter may acquire,

IN TRUST, for the purposes and upon the terms and conditions hereinafter set forth:

ARTICLE FIRST

Directions of Settlors

The Trustee shall hold, manage, invest and reinvest the trust estate, shall collect the income therefrom, and shall pay any part or all of the income and principal to whomever the Settlors from time to time may direct in writing.

Until the Settlors hereafter may direct to the contrary, the net income shall be paid to the Settlors on a monthly basis.

Any income not so paid or applied shall be accumulated and added to the principal of this trust at least quarter-annually.

ARTICLE SECOND

Disability of Settlors

If at any time one of the Settlors shall be under any legal disability or shall be unable to manage his or her affairs properly by reason of illness or mental or physical disability (as such incapacity is defined in this Agreement), (whether or not a court of competent jurisdiction has declared the Settlors incompetent or mentally ill or has appointed a legal representative for the Settlor), the remaining initial Co-Trustee shall act as sole trustee and may pay or apply so much or all of the net income and the principal of the trust estate as the Co-Trustee deems necessary or advisable for the health, education, maintenance or support of both Settlors. Any income not so paid or applied shall be accumulated and added to the principal of this trust at least quarter-annually.

If at any time BOTH Settlors shall be under any legal disability or shall be unable to manage properly their affairs by reason of illness or mental or physical disability (as such incapacity is defined in this Agreement) (whether or not a court of competent jurisdiction has declared the Settlors incompetent or mentally ill or has appointed a legal representative for the Settlors), the successor Trustee may pay or apply so much or all of the net income and the principal of the trust estate as the successor Trustee deems necessary or advisable for the health, education, maintenance or support of the Settlors. Any income not so paid or applied shall be accumulated and added to the principal of this trust at least quarter-annually.

In making any payment hereunder, the successor Trustee may consider, but shall not be required to consider, the income and other resources of the Settlors. No such payment shall be charged upon a subsequent division of the trust estate against the principal of any share which may be set apart for any beneficiary hereunder.

Figure 6.3 (continued)

ARTICLE THIRD

Death of the Settlors

Upon the death of the first Settlor, this Trust shall continue for the benefit of the second Settlor. Upon the death of the second Settlor, the remaining trust property shall be paid outright and free of trust in equal shares to the Settlors' children, or all to the survivors of them.

ARTICLE FOURTH

Distributions to Minors or Incompetents

In any case in which the Trustee is authorized or directed by any provision of this Agreement to pay or distribute income or principal to any person who shall be a minor or incompetent, the Trustee, in the sole discretion of the Trustee and without authorization of any court, may pay or distribute the whole or any part of such income or principal to such minor or incompetent personally, or may apply the whole or any part thereof directly to the health, education, maintenance or support of such minor or incompetent, or may pay or distribute the whole or any part thereof to the guardian, committee, conservator or other legal representative, wherever appointed, of such minor or incompetent or to the person with whom such minor or incompetent may from time to time reside, or in the case of a minor, may pay or distribute the whole or any part thereof to a custodian for such minor under any gifts to minors or transfers to minors act. Evidence of such payment or distribution or the receipt therefor by the person to whom any such payment or distribution is made shall be a full discharge of the Trustee from all liability with respect thereto, even though the Trustee may be such person.

The Trustee, in the sole discretion of the Trustee, may defer payment or distribution of any or all income or principal to which a minor may be entitled until such minor shall attain the age of twenty-one (21) years, or to make such payment or distribution at any time and from time to time, during the minority of such minor, holding the whole or the undistributed portion thereof as a separate fund vested in such minor but subject to the power in trust hereby given to the Trustee to administer and invest such fund and to use the income or principal thereof for the benefit of such minor as if such fund were held in trust hereunder. No bond or other security and no periodic accounts shall be required with respect to such fund, and the same shall be subject to commission as if it were a separate trust fund. The Trustee shall pay and distribute any balance of such fund to such minor when such minor shall attain the age of twenty-one (21) years. Except as is herein above provided, if such minor shall die before attaining the age of twenty-one (21) years, the Trustee shall pay and distribute such balance to the executors, administrators, or legal representatives of the estate of such minor.

The word "minor", wherever used in this Article FOURTH, shall mean any person who has not attained the age of twenty-one (21) years.

ARTICLE FIFTH

Payment of Debts

Upon the death of each of the Settlors, the Trustee may pay from the principal of the trust estate the amount of any estate or death taxes, by whatever name called, imposed under the laws of any jurisdiction by reason of the Settlor's death, whether in respect of property passing under this Agreement or the Settlor's last will and testament or otherwise, and the amount of all of the debts which the Settlor's estate must pay, the expenses of their last illnesses and funeral, and the expenses of administering their estate. The Trustee may rely upon the written certification of the executors, administrators, or legal representatives of the Settlor's estate as to the amount of any such tax, debt or expense, without any duty to inquire as to the correctness thereof, and, in its discretion, may make payment thereof either to said executors, administrators, or legal representatives or to the taxing authority or person to whom such amount is owed.

ARTICLE SIXTH

Settlors' Right to Revoke or Amend

The Settlors reserve the right, at any time and without the consent of any person or notice to any person other than the Trustee, to amend or revoke in whole or in part this Agreement or any trust created hereunder, including the right to change the terms or beneficiaries thereof, by delivering to the Trustee written notice of such amendment or revocation

(continued)

Figure 6.3 (continued)

signed by the Settlors. No amendment of this Agreement, however, shall increase the obligations or reduce the commissions of the Trustee without the consent of the Trustee. Upon any such revocation, the Trustee shall deliver to the Settlors all property in the possession or control of the Trustee with respect to any trust which has been revoked and shall execute and deliver any instruments necessary to release any interest of the Trustee in such property. The sale or other disposition by the Settlors of the whole or any part of the trust estate held hereunder shall constitute as to such whole or part a revocation of this Agreement and the trust or trusts affected thereby.

The Settlors reserves the power and right during the life of the Settlors to collect any rent, interest or other income which may accrue from the trust estate and, in her sole discretion, to accumulate such income as a trust asset or to pay such income to the Settlors individually and not in any fiduciary capacity. The Settlors further reserves the power and right during life of the Settlors to mortgage or pledge all or any part of the trust estate as collateral for any loan.

ARTICLE SEVENTH

Powers of Trustee

In the administration of any property, real or personal, at any time forming a part of the trust estate, including accumulated income, and in the administration of any trust created hereunder, the Trustee, in addition to and without limitation of the powers conferred on trustees under Sample Law, shall have the following powers to be exercised in the sole discretion of the Trustee, except as otherwise expressly provided in this Agreement:

(a) To retain such property for any period, whether or not the same is of the character permissible for investments by fiduciaries under any applicable law, and without regard to the effect any such retention may have upon the diversity of investments;

(b) To sell, transfer, exchange, convert or otherwise dispose of, or grant options with respect to, such property, at public or private sale, with or without security, in such manner, at such times, for such prices, and upon such terms and conditions as the Trustee may deem advisable;

(c) To invest and reinvest in common or preferred stocks, securities, investment trusts, mutual funds, regulated investment companies, bonds and other property, real or personal, foreign or domestic, including any undivided interest in any one or more common trust funds, whether or not such investments be of the character permissible for investments by fiduciaries under any applicable law, and without regard to the effect any such investment may have upon the diversity of investments;

(d) To render liquid the trust estate or any trust created hereunder in whole or in part, at any time and from time to time, and to hold unproductive property, cash or readily marketable securities of little or no yield for such period as the Trustee may deem advisable;

(e) To lease any such property beyond the period fixed by statute for leases made by fiduciaries and beyond the duration of any trust created hereunder;

(f) To join or become a party to, or to oppose, any reorganization, readjustment, recapitalization, foreclosure, merger, voting trust, dissolution, consolidation or exchange, and to deposit any securities with any committee, depository or trustee, and to pay any fees, expenses and assessments incurred in connection therewith, and to charge the same to principal, and to exercise conversion, subscription or other rights, and to make any necessary payments in connection therewith, or to sell any such privileges;

(g) To vote in person at meetings of stock or security holders and adjournments thereof, and to vote by general or limited proxy with respect to any stock or securities;

(h) To hold stock and securities in the name of a nominee without indicating the trust character of such holding, or unregistered or in such form as will pass by delivery, or to use a central depository and to permit registration in the name of a nominee;

(i) To initiate or defend, at the expense of the trust estate, any litigation relating to this Agreement or any property of the trust estate which the Trustee considers advisable, and to pay, compromise, compound, adjust, submit to arbitration, sell or release any claims or demands of the trust estate or any trust created hereunder against others or of others against the same as the Trustee may deem advisable, including the acceptance of deeds of real property in satisfaction of notes, bonds and mortgages, and to make any payments in connection therewith which the Trustee may deem advisable;

(j) To borrow money for any purpose from any source, including any trustee at any time acting hereunder, and to secure the repayment of any and all amounts so borrowed by mortgage or pledge of any property;

Figure 6.3 (continued)

(k) To possess, manage, develop, subdivide, control, partition, mortgage, lease or otherwise deal with any and all real property; to satisfy and discharge or extend the term of any mortgage thereof; to execute the necessary instruments and covenants to effectuate the foregoing powers, including the giving or granting of options in connection therewith; to make repairs, replacements and improvements, structural or otherwise, or abandon the same if deemed to be worthless or not of sufficient value to warrant keeping or protecting; to abstain from the payment of real estate taxes, assessments, water charges and sewer rents, repairs, maintenance and upkeep of the same; to permit to be lost by tax sale or other proceeding or to convey the same for a nominal consideration or without consideration; to set up appropriate reserves out of income for repairs, modernization and upkeep of buildings, including reserves for depreciation and obsolescence, and to add such reserves to principal and, if the income from the property itself should not suffice for such purposes, to advance out of other income any sums needed therefor, and advance any income of the trust for the amortization of any mortgage on property held in the trust;

(l) To purchase from the legal representatives of the estate of the Settlors or from the trustees of any trust established by the Settlors any property constituting a part of such estate or trust at its fair market value and to make loans for adequate consideration to such legal representatives or trustees, upon such terms and conditions as the Trustee may determine in the sole discretion of the Trustee;

(m) To carry insurance of the kinds and in the amounts which the Trustee considers advisable, at the expense of the trust estate, to protect the trust estate and the Trustee personally against any hazard;

(n) To make distribution of the trust estate or of the principal of any trust created hereunder in cash or in kind, or partly in kind, and to cause any distribution to be composed of cash, property or undivided fractional shares in property different in kind from any other distribution, and to determine the fair valuation of the property so allocated, with or without regard to the tax basis; to hold the principal of separate trusts in a consolidated fund and to invest the same in solido; to split trusts for purposes of allocating GST exemptions (within the meaning of Section 2642(a) of the Internal Revenue Code); and to merge any trusts which have substantially identical terms and beneficiaries, and to hold them as a single trust;

(o) To employ and pay the compensation of accountants, attorneys, experts, investment counselors, custodians, agents and other persons or firms providing services or advice, irrespective of whether the Trustee may be associated therewith; to delegate discretionary powers to such persons or firms; and to rely upon information or advice furnished thereby or to ignore the same, as the Trustee in its discretion may determine;

(p) To execute and deliver any and all instruments or writings which it may deem advisable to carry out any of the foregoing powers; and

(q) To exercise all such rights and powers and to do all such acts and enter into all such agreements as persons owning similar property in their own right might lawfully exercise, do or enter into.

Except as otherwise provided herein, the Trustee may determine, when there is reasonable doubt or uncertainty as to the applicable law or the relevant facts, which receipts of money or other assets should be credited to income or principal, and which disbursements, commissions, assessments, fees and other expenses should be charged to income or principal. Any distributions or dividends payable in the stock of a corporation, and rights to subscribe to securities or rights other than cash declared or issued by a corporation, shall be dealt with as principal. The proceeds from the sale, redemption or other disposition, whether at a profit or loss, and regardless of the tax treatment thereof, of any property constituting principal, including mortgages and real estate acquired through foreclosure or otherwise, shall normally be dealt with as principal, but the Trustee may allocate a portion of any such proceeds to income if the property disposed of produced no income or substantially less than the current rate of return on trust investments, or if the Trustee shall deem such action advisable for any other reason. The Trustee may (but are not directed to) allocate receipts and disbursements between income and principal in accordance with Sample law. The preceding provisions of this paragraph shall not be deemed to authorize any act by the Trustee which may be a violation of any law prohibiting the accumulation of income.

No person who deals with any Trustee hereunder shall be bound to see to the application of any asset delivered to such Trustee or to inquire into the authority for, or propriety of, any action taken or not taken by such Trustee.

Notwithstanding anything to the contrary contained herein, during such time as any current or possible future beneficiary of any trust created hereunder (other than the Settlors) may be acting as a Trustee hereunder, such person shall be disqualified from exercising any power to make any discretionary distributions of income or principal to himself or herself (unless the discretion to make such distributions is limited by an ascertainable standard within the meaning of Section 2041(b)(1)(A) of the Internal Revenue Code), or to satisfy any of his or her legal obligations, or to make discretionary allocations of receipts or disbursements as between income and principal. No Trustee who is a current

(continued)

Figure 6.3 (continued)

or possible future beneficiary of any trust hereunder (other than the Settlors) shall participate in the exercise of any powers of the Trustee which would cause such beneficiary to be treated as the owner of trust assets for tax purposes.

No Trustee shall be liable for acts or omissions in administering the trust estate or any trust created by this Agreement, except for that Trustee's own actual fraud, gross negligence or willful misconduct. If any Trustee becomes liable as Trustee to any other person who is not a beneficiary in connection with any matter not within the Trustee's control and not due to the Trustee's actual fraud, gross negligence or willful misconduct, such Trustee shall be fully indemnified and held harmless by the trust estate and any trust created hereunder giving rise to such liability, as the case may be, against and in respect of any damages that such Trustee may sustain, including without limitation attorneys' fees. No successor Trustee shall incur any liability, by reason of qualifying as a Trustee hereunder, for the acts or omissions of any predecessor Trustee.

The Trustee is authorized, but not required, to accept any property transferred to the Trustee by any person during such person's lifetime or by such person's last will and testament. Any property so transferred to, and accepted by, the Trustee shall become a part of such trust or trusts created by this Agreement as such person shall direct and may be commingled with the other property in the trust or trusts to which such property has been added and shall be held, administered and disposed of as a part of such trust or trusts.

ARTICLE EIGHTH

Appointment of Trustee

The Settlors appoint ROBERT SMITH and MARY SMITH as Co-Trustees hereunder. Upon the death, resignation, or incapacity (as hereinafter defined) of both initial Co-Trustees, the Settlors hereby appoint JANE SMITH to act as successor Trustee hereunder. If JANE SMITH is unable or unwilling to serve as successor Trustee, then the Settlors appoint JASMINE SMITH as successor Co-Trustee.

A Settlor shall be deemed incapacitated upon receipt by the successor Trustee of a certificate signed by a medical doctor stating that in the opinion of such doctor the Settlor is either mentally or physically incapable of attending to his or her affairs. The successor Trustee shall indicate acceptance of her offices as Trustee by giving personally, or by mail, a written acceptance of the appointment and written agreement to act as Trustee, duly acknowledged, to the primary income beneficiary. The Successor Trustee shall be authorized to exercise all the powers, privileges and discretions conferred on the Trustee hereunder, and shall not be obligated to inquire into or be liable for any act or omission of any Trustee who shall have served prior to their qualification as successor or substituted Trustee. Further, the Successor Trustee shall only be responsible to administer assets listed in Schedule A hereof which are actually received by the Successor Trustee, as well as any other assets actually coming into the hands of the Successor Trustee.

The Successor Trustee shall have full authority to take whatever steps are necessary to collect and take possession of all the trust assets held by the original Trustee regardless of the location of said assets and regardless of whether said assets are held in the form of real estate, bank accounts, stocks or bonds, mutual funds, brokerage investment accounts or similar investments, for purposes herein set forth.

Any corporation resulting from any merger, consolidation or conversion to which a corporate Trustee may be a party, or any corporation otherwise succeeding generally to all or a greater part of the assets or business of such corporate Trustee, shall be deemed the successor to such corporate Trustee without the execution or filing of any paper or any further action on the part of any party hereto or beneficiary hereunder.

The term "Trustee" wherever used herein shall mean the trustee in office from time to time. Any such trustee shall have the same rights, powers, duties, authority and privileges, whether or not discretionary, as if originally appointed hereunder.

No bond, surety or other security shall be required of any Trustee acting hereunder for the faithful performance of the duties of Trustee, notwithstanding any law of any State or other jurisdiction to the contrary.

The Trustee shall be entitled to receive as Trustee such compensation as shall be set forth in the published Schedule of Compensation of the corporate Trustee in effect when such compensation is payable.

ARTICLE NINTH

Accounts of Trustee

The Trustee, at any time and from time to time, may render to the Settlors an account of the acts and transactions of the Trustee with respect to the income and principal of any trust created hereunder, from the date of the creation of such

Figure 6.3 (continued)

trust or from the date of the last previous account of the Trustee. After the death of the Settlors, the Trustee, at any time and from time to time, may render an account to the living person or persons who are entitled, at the time of such account, to receive all or a portion of the income of the trusts herein created. The approval of any person of full age, or a guardian or parent of a minor or incompetent person, to whom an account is rendered shall, as to all matters stated therein, be final and binding upon him or such minor or incompetent person, or any persons claiming through him or such minor or incompetent person, as the case may be. A person of full age, or a guardian or parent of a minor or incompetent person, to whom an account is rendered shall be deemed to have approved the account if he assents to the account in writing or if he does not communicate to the Trustee his written objections to the account within sixty days after the receipt of the account (provided the account was accompanied by a notice of said sixty day period within which to raise objections).

The Settlors shall have full power and authority on behalf of all persons interested in any trust hereunder, whether such interest relates to income or principal, to settle any account of the Trustee. Such settlement shall be final and binding upon all persons so interested in such trust. Upon such settlement, the Trustee shall be fully and completely discharged and released from all further liability with respect to acts and transactions set forth in the account so settled.

The Trustee shall not be required at any time to file any account in any court, nor shall the Trustee be required to have any account judicially settled. Nothing herein, however, shall be construed as limiting the right of the Trustee to seek a judicial settlement of any account.

ARTICLE TENTH

Representation of Persons Under Disability

In any proceeding relating to any trust hereunder, it shall not be necessary to serve process upon, or to make a party to the proceeding, any person under a disability if another party to the proceeding who is not under a disability has the same interest as the person under a disability. The written approval by all of the then living adult beneficiaries of any trust hereunder relating to the administration of such trust, whether the same relates to an accounting or any other action taken or omitted or proposed to be taken or omitted by the Trustee, shall be deemed to be the approval of and shall be binding upon all beneficiaries of such trust including those who are minors or are not yet born at the time of such action.

ARTICLE ELEVENTH

Simultaneous Death

If any beneficiary under this Agreement shall die simultaneously with the Settlors or any other person upon whose death such beneficiary shall become entitled to receive either income or principal under this Agreement, or in such circumstances as to render it difficult or impracticable to determine who predeceased the other, then for purposes of this Agreement such beneficiary shall be deemed to have predeceased the Settlors or such other person. The provisions of this Agreement shall be construed as aforesaid, notwithstanding the provisions of any applicable law establishing a different presumption of order of death or providing for survivorship for a fixed period as a condition of inheritance of property.

ARTICLE TWELFTH

Rights of Beneficiaries Are Not Assignable

No disposition, charge or encumbrance on the income or principal of any trust established hereunder shall be valid or binding upon the Trustee. No beneficiary shall have any right, power or authority to assign, transfer, encumber or otherwise dispose of such income or principal or any part thereof until the same shall be paid to such beneficiary by the Trustee. No income or principal shall be subject in any manner to any claim of any creditor of any beneficiary or liable to attachment, execution or other process of law prior to its actual receipt by the beneficiary.

ARTICLE THIRTEENTH

Construction

The validity and construction of this Agreement and the trusts created hereunder shall be governed by the laws of the State of Sample.

(continued)

Figure 6.3 (continued)

Any provision herein which refers to a statute, rule, regulation or other specific legal reference which is no longer in effect at the time said provision is to be applied shall be deemed to refer to the successor, replacement or amendment to such statute, rule, regulation or other reference, if any, and shall be interpreted in such a manner so as to carry out the original intent of said provision.

For purposes of this Agreement, the disability or incapacity of an individual (including the Settlors or any Trustee) shall be conclusively established by a written statement signed by such individual's then attending physician and filed with the records of any trust established hereunder attesting that, in such physician's opinion, such individual is unable to manage his or her affairs. Such written statement shall be conclusive evidence of such fact, and any third party may rely on same in dealing with any trust established hereunder and shall not be obliged to inquire whether such individual is no longer under such disability or incapacity at the time of such dealings.

Wherever used in this Agreement and the context so requires, the masculine shall include the feminine and the singular shall include the plural, and vice versa.

The captions in this Agreement are for convenience of reference, and they shall not be considered when construing this Agreement.

ARTICLE FOURTEENTH

Binding Effect

This Agreement shall extend to and be binding upon the heirs, executors, administrators, successors and assigns of the undersigned Settlors and upon the Trustee acting hereunder.

ARTICLE FIFTEENTH

Short Name

This Agreement and the trusts created hereunder may be referred to, in any other instrument, by the name: "ROBERT & MARY SMITH FAMILY TRUST." Any transfers to this Agreement or any trust hereunder may refer to the aforesaid name or to "ROBERT SMITH and MARY SMITH, as Co-Trustees under the ROBERT & MARY SMITH FAMILY TRUST," with or without specifying any change in Trustee or any amendment to this Agreement.

IN WITNESS WHEREOF, this Agreement has been duly executed as of the date first above written.

Robert Smith
ROBERT SMITH, Settlor

Mary Smith
MARY SMITH, Settlor

Robert Smith
ROBERT SMITH, Trustee

Mary Smith
MARY SMITH, Trustee

This Trust was signed in the presence of us who, at the request and in the presence of Settlor and in the presence of each other, have signed the same as witnesses thereto.

Michael Pearson	1001 Reed Drive
Witness Signature	Sample City, Sample State 12345
Witness Name (Printed)	Witness Address
Maggy Pearson	1001 Reed Drive
Witness Signature	Sample City, Sample State 12345
Witness Name (Printed)	Witness Address

Figure 6.3 (continued)

ACKNOWLEDGMENT OF ROBERT SMITH AND MARY SMITH, SETTLORS & TRUSTEES

STATE OF SAMPLE
COUNTY OF SAMPLE

On this 9th day of January, 2010, this instrument was acknowledged before me by ROBERT SMITH and MARY SMITH, who acknowledged themselves to be the Settlors and Trustees of Robert & Mary Smith Family Trust, dated March 13, 2010, and that they, being authorized to so do, executed the within instrument for the purposes therein contained by signing for that Trust as such Settlors.

IN WITNESS WHEREOF, I hereunto set my hand and official seal.

Lila P. Legal
Notary Public

> **LILA P. LEGAL**
> Notary Public, State of Sample
> Sample County
> My Commission Expires May 10, 2012

ACKNOWLEDGMENT OF WITNESSES

STATE OF SAMPLE
COUNTY OF SAMPLE

On this 9th day of January, 2010, this instrument was acknowledged before me, a Notary Public, by Michael Pearson and Maggy Pearson, the above witnesses, who personally appeared before me, are personally known to me, and whose names are subscribed to this instrument and acknowledged that they executed the same for the purposes contained therein.

IN WITNESS WHEREOF, I hereunto set my hand and official seal.

Lila P. Legal
Notary Public

> **LILA P. LEGAL**
> Notary Public, State of Sample
> Sample County
> My Commission Expires May 10, 2012

Figure 6.4 contains the Pour-over Will of Mary Smith, from the Hypothetical Family. Under her will, Mary leaves everything to the Robert & Mary Smith Family Trust.

Additional Documents

In addition to the trust itself and the pour-over will, other documents may be needed to fund the trust. For example, any real property must be transferred by deed into the name of the trust. Cars, trucks, boats, and other personal property with a title must be re-titled into the name of the trust. Any bank accounts or

Figure 6.4 Pour-Over Will of Mary Smith

I, MARY SMITH, residing at 125 Oak Street, Sample City, Sample State 12345, which I hereby declare to be my place of domicile, being of sound mind and memory and disposing disposition, do make, publish and declare this to be my Last Will and Testament, thus revoking any and all previous Wills and their codicils which I have made previously.

I AM MARRIED TO ROBERT SMITH

THE FOLLOWING ARE MY CHILDREN:
RALPH SMITH & RYAN SMITH

1.   I give the entire residue of my estate to the trustee then in office under that trust designated as THE ROBERT & MARY SMITH FAMILY TRUST, dated January 9, 2010, of which I am a Settlor. I direct that the residue of my estate shall be added to, administered, and distributed as part of that trust, according to the terms of the trust and any amendment made to it before my death. To the extent permitted by law, it is not my intent to create a separate trust by this will or to subject the trust or the property added to it by the will to the jurisdiction of the probate court.

2.   I direct that inheritance, death and estate taxes, including interest and penalties thereon, becoming due by reason of my death, with respect to property other than property held in trust or property taxed to my estate as a generation-skipping transfer, be paid preferably out of my residuary estate passing under this Will to the extent thereof, but may be paid out of the trust receiving distribution of my residuary estate passing under this Will if the Trustee deems it appropriate. Any such taxes, and interest and penalties thereon, attributable to trust property or property taxed as a generation-skipping transfer shall be paid out of the respective property so taxed by the person or persons having custody of such property or by the person or persons receiving distribution of such property. The determination of the amount of tax due by my residuary estate shall be made as if trust property where a pro rata share of my estate and as if no property classified as a generation-skipping transfer were taxed to my estate.

3.   I hereby nominate, constitute and appoint ROBERT SMITH as the Personal Representative of this will. In the event he is unable or unwilling to so serve in this capacity, then I nominate, constitute and appoint JANE SMITH as Personal Representative hereof. I nominate, constitute and appoint JASMINE SMITH as alternate Personal Representative if JANE SMITH is unable or unwilling to serve.

The **Personal Representative** shall have full power and authority to carry out the provisions of the Will, including the power to manage and operate during the probate of my estate, any property and any business belonging to my estate.

4.   No bond shall be required of any Personal Representative.

5.   If the disposition in paragraph 1, above, is inoperative or is invalid for any reason, or if the trust referred to in paragraph 1, above, fails or is revoked, I incorporate herein by reference the terms of that trust, as executed on this date, without giving effect to any amendments made subsequently, and I bequeath and devise the residue of my estate to the trustee named in the trust as trustee, to be held, administered, and distributed as provided in this instrument.

The above-described Declaration of Trust was executed by me for the purpose of creating a revocable inter vivos trust. All property distributed to said trust under the terms of this will shall be held, administered and distributed according to the terms of said Declaration of Trust, including any amendments thereto in effect at my death. Said trust was created during my lifetime and shall not be construed to be a testamentary trust.

6.   In the event, any provision of this Last Will and Testament is held to be invalid by a Court of competent jurisdiction, then such finding shall invalidate only that provision leaving the balance of this Last Will and Testament enforce.

IN WITNESS WHEREOF, I have hereunto subscribed my name this 9th day of January, 2010.

Mary Smith
_____
MARY SMITH

I, MARY SMITH, the Testatrix, sign my name to this instrument this 9th day of January, 2010, and being first duly sworn, do declare to the undersigned authority that I sign and execute this instrument as my will and that I sign it willingly, or willingly direct another to sign for me, that I execute it as my free and voluntary act for the purposes expressed in that document and that I am eighteen years of age or older, of sound mind and under no constraint or undue influence.

Mary Smith
_____
Testatrix

Figure 6.4 (continued)

We, <u>Michael Pearson</u> and <u>Maggy Pearson</u>, the witnesses, sign our names to this instrument being first duly sworn and do declare to the undersigned authority that the Testatrix signs and executes this instrument as her will and that she signs it willingly, or willingly directs another to sign for her, and that each of us, in the presence and hearing of the Testatrix, signs this will as witness to the Testatrix's signing and that to the best of our knowledge the Testatrix is eighteen years of age or older, of sound mind and under no constraint or undue influence.

Michael Pearson
_____
Witness

Maggy Pearson
_____
Witness

The State of Sample }
County of Sample   }

Subscribed, sworn to and acknowledged before me by MARY SMITH, the Testatrix, and subscribed and sworn to before me by <u>Michael Pearson</u> and <u>Maggy Pearson</u>, witnesses, this <u>9</u>th day of <u>January</u> 2010.

Lila P. Legal
_____
Notary Public

> **LILA P. LEGAL**
> Notary Public, State of Sample
> Sample County
> My Commission Expires May 10, 2012

---

brokerage accounts must also be re-titled into the name of the trust. General personal property, such as the contents of the trust creator's home, may be transferred into the trust using a **bill of sale**. A sample bill of sale is shown in Figure 6.5.

Bill of Sale
A document used to transfer personal property, such as the contents of the trust creator's home, into the trust.

Figure 6.5 Bill of Sale to Trust Personal Property and Household Goods

Date: 1/9/2010

BUYERS:
Robert Smith & Mary Smith
125 Oak Street
Sample City, Sample State 12345,
As Trustees of the Robert & Mary Smith Family Trust dated January 9, 2010.

SELLERS:
Robert Smith & Mary Smith
125 Oak Street
Sample City, Sample State 12345

Address and Location of Property Sold: 125 Oak Street, Sample City, Sample State 12345

Property Sold: The Property Sold shall consist of all right, title, and interest of seller in, and to, all household furnishings, fixtures, equipment, works of art, silverware, chinaware, artifacts, collections, musical instruments, antiques, jewelry, furs, and all personal property, and personal effects, including but not limited to items described in Exhibit A attached hereto

Figure 6.5 (continued)

and made part hereof located in or about the residence of sellers at the above stated address as of this date and as may be hereinafter acquired in this residence or in later acquired residences of seller.

Conveyance: For valuable consideration, receipt of which is acknowledged, Sellers sells and conveys to Buyer the Property Sold, to have and to hold the Property Sold to Buyer and the heirs, executors, administrators and assigns of Buyer forever, and Seller and the heirs, executors, administrators and assigns of Seller warrant to defend the sale of the Property Sold unto Buyer, against all and every person whomsoever lawfully claiming or to claim the same.

IN WITNESS WHEREOF, Buyer has duly executed this Bill of Sale on January 9, 2010.

Robert Smith
_____
Robert Smith

Mary Smith
_____
Mary Smith

NOTARY ACKNOWLEDGMENT

STATE OF SAMPLE
COUNTY OF SAMPLE

On this 9th day of January, 2010, before me, the undersigned, a notary public in and for said state personally appeared ROBERT SMITH and MARY SMITH personally known to me (or proved to me on the basis of satisfactory evidence) to be the persons whose names are subscribed to the within instrument and acknowledged to me that they executed the same in their authorized capacities, and that by their signatures on the instrument the persons or entity upon behalf of which the persons acted, executed instrument.

WITNESS my hand and official seal.

Lila P. Legal
_____
Notary Public

| **LILA P. LEGAL** |
| Notary Public, State of Sample |
| Sample County |
| My Commission Expires May 10, 2012 |

Potential Disadvantages of Using a Revocable Living Trust as an Alternative to Probate

At this point, you may be wondering why anyone would opt *not* to execute a revocable living trust and pour-over will as an alternative to probate. Immediate expense, additional requirements, family dynamics, and the cost of probate in your jurisdiction are among the other factors that should be considered when making this choice.

Immediate Expense

The cost of preparing a revocable living trust with all necessary accompanying documents is significantly higher than that of a basic estate plan with a simple will. It takes much more time to draft the former than the latter, and the attorney's fee will be appropriately higher due to the additional work involved.

A careful review of the figures in this chapter reveals the difference in the level of complexity associated with drafting a revocable living trust, as opposed to a basic will.

Additional Requirements

Diligence is required on the part of the trustors to make sure that all assets are transferred into the trust following the trust execution. In addition, as the trustors experience life changes and buy and sell assets, they must be certain to title all newly acquired property into the trust. Oftentimes, even people who initially fund the trust correctly forget to continue doing so as they purchase new things in the years that follow. As has been exemplified throughout this chapter, if assets are not properly titled into the trust, probate will not be avoided.

Family Dynamics

Family dynamics also warrant major consideration when making estate planning decisions. As the real-life scenario at the beginning of this chapter illustrates, there are times when a potential trustee may not be 100% trustworthy. Often, when a second (or third) marriage is involved, there are step-parents and step-siblings that may not trust each other or get along. The trustee of a trust has wide authority to dispose of the trust property. Although the trustee is legally obligated to follow the terms of the trust, some trustees fail to do so. The only recourse for the other beneficiaries is to seek legal assistance, which may mean a court battle. It is also difficult to recapture assets or funds that have been misappropriated or spent, even if a judgment has been obtained. In summary, as the old adage goes, if there is any doubt whether the family members can get along, "it's better safe than sorry." The relatively nominal expense of an ordinary probate proceeding with the benefit of court supervision is certainly preferable over having a family battle in probate litigation, and likely spending tens of thousands of dollars on attorney's fees.

Cost of Probate

Probate is not always costly. Some states (including many of the eastern states) have more rigid requirements for probate proceedings, thereby making the process more costly. However, many other states have streamlined the probate process, making it quite inexpensive. For example, Texas and Arizona both have fairly quick and easy probate processes. Further still, most states have shortened proceedings available for small estates, or estates that meet specific statutory criteria and are below a certain dollar amount. Therefore, if the cost of a possible future probate proceeding in your client's state is nominal, it may not make economic sense to try to avoid a probate, particularly when the client's assets are modest.

■ ADDITIONAL TRUSTS AND TRUST CLAUSES

Spendthrift Clause

As was mentioned above, a **spendthrift clause** is a provision in a trust or will that states that if a prospective beneficiary has pledged to turn over his or her inheritance to a third party, the trustee or executor shall not honor such a pledge. The practical effect of including this clause is to preclude the beneficiaries' creditors from reaching the contents of the trust prior to trust termination. If a terminating event occurs and the indebted beneficiary receives his or her share outright and free of trust, the creditors will then be able to attach to any money received by the beneficiary. The inclusion of a spendthrift clause is desirable when there are concerns that one or more beneficiaries may have credit problems or may need to file bankruptcy in the future. If the beneficiary is unlikely to ever be solvent or cease being a spendthrift (one who spends money unwisely and wastefully), a **spendthrift trust** may be created to provide funds for the beneficiary's maintenance and support and at the same time secure trust assets against his improvidence or incapacity. When drafted as a trust, as opposed to included as a clause in a trust, a spendthrift trust is unlikely to provide for a final distribution to the spendthrift and likely instead to provide only a lifetime income stream to the beneficiary, with the balance paid to a remainder beneficiary upon the spendthrift's death.

Spendthrift Trust
A trust created to provide a fund for the maintenance of a beneficiary and at the same time to secure it against the beneficiary's improvidence or incapacity.

Trusts for Minors

Another common reason to form a trust, whether within a revocable living trust or a testamentary trust, is to provide for one's children or grandchildren during minority. There are many potential problems when minor children inherit money. These problems range from the child wasting the money due to immaturity, to the very real possibility that other parties may take advantage of the beneficiary by "borrowing" the money or stealing it outright.

EXAMPLE

Shawn's father died testate following a work-related accident. Under the will, Shawn received a large inheritance at age nineteen and had it promptly stolen by a roommate. The roommate was convicted of the crime and spent time in jail, but paid only a very small portion back to the victim through restitution. This tragedy could have been avoided if Shawn's father had created a testamentary trust to keep Shawn's inheritance in trust and under the supervision of a trustee until Shawn reached a more mature number of years.

Sprinkling Trust (also called "spraying trust")
A trust in which the income or principal is distributed among members of a designated class in amounts and proportions determined by the trustee's discretion.

A **sprinkling trust** (also called "spraying trust") is one in which the income or principal is distributed among members of a designated class in amounts and proportions determined by the trustee's discretion. When trusts are established for the benefit of minor children, separate, equal trusts may be created, or one sprinkling trust may be created for the benefit of all of the children until the youngest child reaches a designated age. A sprinkling trust may make more sense when there are modest estate assets and where children may have unequal needs because the trustee is afforded discretion to spend more money on those with the greater need.

Pet Trust
A trust created to ensure that a pet is cared for upon the disability or death of the owner by ordering payments to a designated caregiver on a regular basis. Pet trusts are governed by state law and usually continue for the life of the pet or 21 years, whichever occurs first.

Pet Trust

Animal lovers are rightfully concerned about what will happen to their beloved pets after they are no longer around to take care of them. As of April 2011, 45 states had enacted Companion Animal (Pet) Trust Laws allowing people to establish trusts for the benefit of their animals (Animal Legal and Historical Center, 2011). Following are statutes from two different states permitting the creation of a pet trust to care for one's animals.

Kansas

Chapter 58a: Kansas Uniform Trust Code

Article 4: Creation, Validity, Modification, And Termination of Trust

Statute 58a-408: Trust for care of animal. (a) A trust may be created to provide for the care of an animal alive during the settlor's lifetime. The trust terminates upon the death of the animal or, if the trust was created to provide for the care of more than one animal alive during the settlor's lifetime, upon the death of the last surviving animal.

(b) A trust authorized by this section may be enforced by a person appointed in the terms of the trust or, if no person is so appointed, by a person appointed by the court. A person having an interest in the welfare of the animal may request the court to appoint a person to enforce the trust or to remove a person appointed.

(c) Property of a trust authorized by this section may be applied only to its intended use, except to the extent the court determines that the value of the trust property exceeds the amount required for the intended use. Except as otherwise provided in the terms of the trust, property not required for the intended use may be distributed to the settlor, if then living, otherwise to the settlor's successors in interest.

History: L. 2002, ch. 133, § 29; Jan. 1, 2003.

Nevada

NRS 163.0075 Validity of trust providing for care of one or more animals.

1. A trust created for the care of one or more animals that are alive at the time of the settlor's death is valid. Such a trust terminates upon the death of all animals covered by the terms of the trust. A settlor's expression of intent must be liberally construed in favor of the creation of such a trust.

2. Except as otherwise provided in this subsection, property of a trust described in subsection 1 may not be used in a manner inconsistent with its intended use. Except as otherwise directed by the terms of the trust, if a court determines that the value of a trust described in subsection 1 exceeds the amount required to care for the animal beneficiary, the excess amount must be distributed to the person who would have taken the trust property if the trust had terminated on the date of the distribution.

3. The intended use of a trust described in subsection 1 may be enforced by the trustee or, if a trustee was not designated, by a person appointed by the court to act as the trustee. A person having a demonstrated interest in the welfare of the animal beneficiary may petition the court for an order to appoint himself or herself as trustee or to remove the trustee. The court shall give preference for appointment to a person who demonstrates such an interest.

(Added to NRS by 2001, 958)

Note the similarity between Kansas and Nevada's statutes. Both statutes allow for the creation of a pet trust for the benefit one or more of the settlor's pets and both provide that the trust will terminate upon the death of the last surviving animal. However, Kansas permits the trust to be created for animals alive during the settlor's lifetime, whereas Nevada provides that the animals must be alive at the settlor's death in order for the trust to be valid.

Tax Planning Trusts for Spouse

There are also specific types of trusts that can be created for the benefit of a surviving spouse in order to reduce estate tax liability upon each of the first and the second deaths. There have been recent changes to the tax law that may affect the use of bypass trusts, such as disclaimer and credit shelter trusts, which have been traditionally and widely used to reduce estate tax liability for married couples. A **bypass trust** is an estate planning device whereby a designated portion of a deceased spouse's estate passes to a trust for the benefit of the surviving spouse, rather than passing outright to the surviving spouse, thereby reducing the likelihood that the surviving spouse's estate will be subject to federal estate tax. Further details about tax planning trusts are beyond the scope of this chapter.

Special Needs Trust

A **special needs trust** is created to ensure that beneficiaries who are disabled or mentally ill can enjoy the use of property that is intended to be held for their benefit, while also preventing such beneficiaries from losing access to essential government benefits. These complex trusts must be created in careful compliance with federal and state law in order to successfully avoid the loss of benefits. Special needs trusts are often drafted for elderly individuals in order to become or remain eligible for Medicaid and other health care, nursing home care, or long-term care that the beneficiary may need.

Charitable Remainder Trust

A **charitable remainder trust** is a trust in which the trustor or a beneficiary receives the income from the trust for a time period (usually for life) and then the remainder of the trust is given to charity. A **charitable remainder annuity trust** is similar to a charitable remainder trust except that instead of receiving income from the trust, the beneficiary receives a fixed amount of income from the trust in at least annual installments and after death, the balance is given to charity. In order to qualify for a tax deduction under the Internal Revenue Code, the remainder must pass to a qualified charity or other tax-exempt institution for which the taxpayer can claim an income tax reduction. These trusts may be used both to fulfill the altruistic intentions of the trustor and to reduce tax liability.

When a testator or a trustor makes a gift to a charity under a will or trust and it subsequently becomes impossible or impracticable to apply the gift to the particular named charity, the equity court may order the gift to be applied to another charity "as near as possible" to the designated charity, pursuant to the **cy pres doctrine**. Cy *pres* means "as near as possible."

■ FIDUCIARY DUTIES OF TRUSTEES

Along with all of their statutory and documentary powers, fiduciaries have fundamental duties to uphold. **Fiduciary duties** include the duties of loyalty, disclosure, accounting, and obedience. The duty of loyalty means that since the trustee is the legal owner of the trust property, he or she is prevented from taking advantage of the legal ownership to use the trust property for his or her own benefit. The trustee must act in good faith when entering into transactions on behalf of

---

Bypass Trust
An estate planning device whereby a designated portion of a deceased spouse's estate passes to a trust for the benefit of the surviving spouse, rather than passing outright to the surviving spouse, thereby reducing the likelihood that the surviving spouse's estate will be subject to federal estate tax.

Special Needs Trust
A trust created to ensure that a beneficiary who is disabled or mentally ill can enjoy the use of property that is intended to be held for his or her benefit while also preventing the beneficiary from losing access to essential government benefits.

Charitable Remainder Trust
A trust in which the trustor or a beneficiary receives the income from the trust for a time period (usually for life) and then the remainder of the trust is given to charity.

Charitable Remainder Annuity Trust
A trust in which the beneficiary receives a fixed amount of income from the trust in at least annual installments and, after death, the balance is given to charity.

Cy Pres Doctrine
When a testator or a trustor makes a gift to a charity under a will or trust and it subsequently becomes impossible or impracticable to apply the gift to the particular named charity, the equity court may order the gift to be applied to another charity "as near as possible" to the designated charity.

Fiduciary Duties
The duty of an agent to act in the principal's best interests.

the trust and must also invest trust assets prudently. The trustee also has a duty to keep the beneficiaries of the trust reasonably informed concerning the trust administration and material facts for the beneficiaries to protect their interests, and also must account to the beneficiaries for how the trust assets are administered and distributed. The duty of obedience requires the trustee to follow the terms of the trust document while administering the trust, thereby carrying out the trust creator's intent.

■ CONCLUSION

The two main types of trusts are inter vivos trusts and testamentary trusts. Inter vivos trusts are created during the lifetime of the creator and take effect immediately. Testamentary trusts are created pursuant to a will after the testator's death.

Many clients choose to execute a revocable living trust and a pour-over will to avoid the necessity of a probate proceeding following their death. However, that choice may not be the best choice for all clients. In particular, if the clients do not have someone they can trust to do the job of a trustee or if the beneficiaries do not get along, a will may be the better choice. Careful attention must be paid to all clients' individual situations to determine which vehicle will best suit their specific needs.

There are a wide variety of additional types of trusts that can be created to serve a variety of purposes, including trusts for minors, tax planning trusts, special needs trusts, and charitable remainder trusts. In conclusion, trusts are a useful estate planning tool that can serve a variety of purposes.

CONCEPT REVIEW AND REINFORCEMENT

KEY TERMS

Spendthrift Clause 150	Probate 161	Pet Trust 176
Inter Vivos Trust 150	Revocable Living Trust 161	Bypass Trust 178
Testamentary Trust 150	Irrevocable Trust 161	Special Needs Trust 178
Terminating Event 151	Probate Assets 161	Charitable Remainder Trust 178
Living Trust 160	Pour-over Will 162	Charitable Remainder Annuity Trust 178
Trustor, Donor, Settlor 160	Bill of Sale 173	
Trustee 160	Spendthrift Trust 176	Cy Pres Doctrine 178
Trust Corpus 160	Sprinkling Trust 176	Fiduciary Duties 178

REVIEW QUESTIONS

1. When does an inter vivos trust get funded?
2. When does a testamentary trust become effective?
3. Discuss the purpose of a spendthrift clause.
4. What is the purpose of a bill of sale?
5. List some of the main events that may trigger trust termination.
6. Describe the purpose of a pet trust.
7. Explain when a special needs trust might be used.
8. What document should always accompany a revocable living trust?
9. Describe a charitable remainder trust.
10. Describe the main fiduciary duties required of trustees.

BUILDING YOUR PARALEGAL SKILLS

CRITICAL THINKING EXERCISES

1. Tony Lucas recently remarried. He has three minor children from his first marriage. Tony's new wife has two grown children who dislike Tony and his children. Tony wants to provide for his new wife, but also wants to make sure his own children are provided for if he passes away. How do you recommend Tony accomplish these goals? Fully explain the reasoning for your answer.

2. Mary Jones is an elderly woman who does not have any close living relatives. Mary is friends with Nancy Nice, who is 15 years younger. Mary wants to leave the bulk of her estate to Nancy, and a small portion in trust for Nancy's young daughter, age ten 10. What document(s) should Mary execute, and what provisions do you recommend be included therein?

PARALEGAL PRACTICE

Review each memorandum directed from the supervising attorney to you, the paralegal. The memorandum will discuss a situation with a client and request your assistance in researching the matter or drafting the document(s) requested. You must then report back with your findings, as directed in the memorandum.

1. _____

MEMORANDUM
To: Paralegal
From: Supervising Attorney
Client: Mark Moore
Re: Testamentary Trust

Today I met with Mark Moore to discuss his estate planning needs. His address is 978 Maple Street, SampleTown, SampleState 12345. Unfortunately, Mark just lost his wife to cancer. Mark has three small children. He is very close with his sister, Samantha Moore. He wants to create one trust for the benefit of his children. The trust will terminate when the youngest child reaches age 23. Mark is appointing his sister as personal representative and trustee. Please draft the will for my review.

2. _____

MEMORANDUM
To: Paralegal
From: Supervising Attorney
Client: Samantha Moore
Re: Revocable Living Trust and Pour-Over Will

Today I also met with Mark Moore's sister, Samantha Moore, to discuss her estate plan. She is unmarried and does not have many assets, but desires to avoid probate. Please draft a revocable living trust. I have already prepared the pour-over will. Mark Moore will be the primary residuary beneficiary and will receive everything outright and free of trust. If Mark fails to survive, Samantha will leave everything to Mark's children, per stirpes. If any child is under the age of 21, that child's share will be held in a Uniform Transfers to Minors Account until the majority age. Appoint Sally Moore as Custodian of any UTMA account created under the trust.

Samantha will appoint herself as trustee, Mark Moore as first alternate, and Sally Moore as second alternate trustee. Under the will, Samantha will appoint Mark as personal representative and Sally as alternate. Please prepare the trust for my review.

CASE FOR CONSIDERATION

CASE #1:

MATTER OF DR. ROBERT VON TAUBER, 2011-365773/A (11-15-2011)

2011 NY Slip Op 52095(U)
2011-365773/A.
Surrogate's Court of the City of New York,
Nassau County.
Decided November 15, 2011.

[NOTE: This case is unpublished as indicated by the issuing court.]

Farrell, Fritz, P.C., Uniondale, NY (attorney for petitioner).

Attorney General of the State of New York, New York, NY.

EDWARD W. MCCARTY, III., J.

Before the court are two petitions for the application of cy pres (EPTL 8-1.1) to a revocable inter vivos trust.

Petitioners are the co-trustees of the "DR. ROBERT VON TAUBER AND OLGA VON TAUBER, M.D., REVOCABLE TRUST" dated October 28, 1993 and amended February 3, 1994.

The court has jurisdiction to entertain a petition under EPTL 8-1.1 in connection with an inter vivos trust, pursuant to SCPA 209 subdivision [6] and Article VI §12 [d] of the Constitution of the State of New York (*Matter of Kramer*, 20 Misc 3d 383 [Sur Ct, Nassau County 2008]; *In re Fleet Nat'l Bank*; 20 Misc 3d 879 [Sup Ct, Albany County 2008]).

Venue is predicated upon the location of the assets of the trust in financial institutions in Nassau County (SCPA 207).

The first petition seeks the application of cy pres to Article "FIRST" section 8 subsection B of the trust which provides:

The sum of Two Hundred Thousand ($200,000) Dollars to be held by my Trustee, in further trust, to create and fund the *DR. ROBERT AND OLGA VON TAUBER FOUNDATION* and the annual income thereof shall be distributed to a needy minor individual or individuals that reside in the Town of Huntington and who by letter and other proof shows his or her need for monetary support for continuing their education and who is selected by my Trustee for such annual distribution.

The sum available to fund the trust is $200,000.00. The trustees contend that this is inadequate to fund and administer a foundation over any substantial period of time. They propose to distribute the funds to Long Island Community Foundation, Division of Community Funds, Inc., to establish a fund entitled "Dr. Robert and Olga Von Tauber Funds." The fund would be administered as an institutional endowment fund for college scholarships. The recipients would be high school students residing in the Town of Huntington who demonstrate financial need. It is anticipated that the trustees will work with the existing scholarship committees at high schools in Huntington. The Attorney General has appeared in this proceeding and raises no objection to the proposed plan.

When literal compliance with the terms of a charitable gift are impracticable, the court can direct the application of the funds in a manner which will most effectively carry out the charitable purpose (*Sherman v Richmond Hose Co. No. 2*, 230 NY 462 [1921]; *Trustees of Sailors' Snug Harbor in the City of New York v Carmody*, 211 NY 286 [1914]).

The requirements for the application of cy pres are that (1) the trust is charitable in nature, (2) the language of the instrument when read in light of all attendant circumstances must indicate a general charitable intent, and (3) the particular purpose for which the trust was created has failed or become impracticable (*Matter of Othmer*, 185 Misc 2d 122

[Sur Ct, Kings County 2000]). A trust for the advancement of education is charitable in nature (*Russell v Allen*, 107 US 163 [1883]; *Matter of Post*, 2 A.D.3d 1091 [3d Dep. 2003]). The terms of the gift and the fact that there are several charitable gifts indicates a charitable intent (*Matter of Othmer*, 12 Misc 3d 414 [Sur Ct, Kings County 2006]).

The court is satisfied that the expense of administering an independent foundation would significantly reduce the funds available for scholarships, thereby frustrating the intent of the grantors. Where the funds are not sufficient to accomplish the precise directions of the grantor, the application of cy pres is appropriate (*Matter of MacDowell*, 217 NY 454 [1916]).

Where the purpose of a charitable gift has several components, the proposed plan under cy pres must satisfy each of them, if practicable (*Matter of Scott*, 8 NY2d 419 [1960]; *Matter of Mary Holbrook Russell Mem. Scholarship Fund*, 189 Misc 2d 198 [Sur Ct, Nassau County 2001]). Here, the plan of the trustees satisfies the grantor's requirements that the gift be applied (1) to provide scholarships, (2) for high school students, (3) residing in the Town of Huntington, (4) who require financial assistance to attend college.

The court therefore approves distribution of the trust funds allocated to this trust provision in accordance with the plan presented by the trustees.

The second petition is for the application of cy pres to Article "FIRST" subsection (10) (iii) of the trust which provides that 25% of the remainder is to be held in further trust as follows:

"…to establish, in perpetuity, an endowment and to use the annual net income thereof to fund a fellowship for the advanced study of Psychiatry in the Department of Psychiatry and Behavioral Science, School of Medicine, SUNY, Stony Brook.

The Trustee shall determine the amount of the annual net income that shall be distributed to the fellow; and, income not distributed shall be accumulated and added to principal.

A fellowship search committee shall be appointed by the department chair; such committee to consist of not less than three (3) members. The committee will select a new fellow annually and such fellow will hold the fellowship for a period of one (1) year.

A fellowship candidate shall have completed at least three (3) years of basic psychiatric residency training and shall demonstrate a desire, in the judgment of the search committee, to make a contribution to a better understanding of psychiatric illness and treatment. The fellow shall be memorialized in perpetuity and shall be known as "the Dr. Robert von Tauber and Olga von Tauber, M.D., Fellow in Psychiatric Medicine."

The Health and Sciences Center at Stony Brook has informed the trustees that the funds available (approximately $266,000.00) are insufficient to establish a fellowship. In addition, the rules of the University prohibit the Department from offering an unaccredited fellowship. The fact that the gift is in conflict with the medical school's guidelines warrants a modification of the terms of the trust (*In re Trustees of Columbia University in City of New York*, 27 Misc 3d 1205[A] [Sur Ct, Nassau County 2010]).

After consultation with the University, the trustees propose to establish a fund entitled "The Robert Von Tauber and Olga Von Tauber Fund." The fund is to be administered by the Department of Psychiatry and Behavioral Sciences at the Stony Brook University School of Medicine for the benefit of fourth year medical students and fellows. The Attorney General appears in this proceeding and does not oppose the plan.

The plan of the trustees does not affect a change of the charitable institution nor does it significantly alter the classification of the recipients. Therefore, it more closely resembles an administrative change, which can be effectuated under the doctrine of equitable deviation (EPTL 8-1.1, *see Matter of Wilson*, 59 NY2d 461 [1983]). The plan meets the higher standards imposed under the doctrine of cy pres, as well (*see In re Trustees of Columbia University in City of New York*, 27 Misc 3d 1205[A] [Sur Ct, Nassau County 2010]).

The Court approves distribution of the funds applicable to the gift of part of the residuary estate to Stony Brook University in accordance with the proposed plan of the trustees.

Settle decree.

Case Questions

1. What type of trust was at issue in the above case?
2. What was the purpose of the first petition?
3. How did the court apply the doctrine of cy pres to the first petition?
4. What was the purpose of the second petition?
5. How did the court apply the doctrine of cy pres to the second petition?
6. Do you agree with the court's ruling? Why or why not?

FORMS TO ACCOMPANY PARALEGAL PRACTICE

> Disclaimer: The forms provided to aid students in completing the Paralegal Practice activities assigned in each chapter have been modified as samples to familiarize students with what each form commonly looks like and are not intended to be used as actual forms for any state.

INSTRUCTIONS: The forms are provided in Microsoft Word format and employ the use of Stop Codes (such as SC1, SC2, SC3, and so on). Stop Codes are used in place of the form sections that must be updated with case-by-case information, such as SC1 for the client's name, SC3 for the client's address, and so on. What each Stop Code represents can be inferred by reading the surrounding text on the form. By using the FIND & REPLACE tool on the Microsoft toolbar, the students can replace the Stop Codes with the information provided in the Paralegal Practice activity to complete each assignment. Students must also fill in any blank lines on each form with the appropriate information from the activity and then proofread the document prior to turning in their work.

The following forms are included after this section and will be posted online for students to access to complete the Paralegal Practice activities for this chapter:

- PP Form 6.1—Simple Will for Single Male with 1 Trust for Children
- PP Form 6.2—Revocable Living Trust (1 Grantor)

PP Form 6.1—Simple Will for Single Male with 1 Trust for Children

LAST WILL AND TESTAMENT

I, **SC1**, of the TOWN OF SAMPLE, COUNTY OF SAMPLE, STATE OF SAMPLE, do hereby make, publish and declare the following to be my Last Will and Testament, hereby revoking all former Wills and Codicils made by me.

I. I direct that all my debts and funeral expenses be paid and I further authorize my Executor, in its discretion, to prepay any mortgage or other installment indebtedness.

II. I give and bequeath to my children, SC4 (hereinafter referred to as "my children"), all of my clothing, jewelry, personal effects, household goods, furniture, furnishings, automobiles and all other tangible personal property which I may own at the time of my death, to be divided among them as they shall agree. If my children are unable to agree as to the recipient of any article, I authorize and direct my Executor to make the decision. If, in the sole judgment of my Executor, any child is too young to make a prudent selection, I authorize my Executor to make a selection on behalf of the child. If any of my children is a minor at the time of delivery of any articles, I authorize my Executor, in its discretion, to deliver the articles either directly to the child, or to the child's guardian, or to the person having the care and custody of the child, and a duly executed receipt from the child or guardian or other person shall constitute a complete acquittance to my Executor with respect to the bequest. Any articles not selected shall be sold and the proceeds added to my residuary estate.

(continued)

III. I give, devise and bequeath all the rest, residue and remainder of my estate to my Trustee, hereinafter named, in trust for the following uses and purposes:

A. I direct my Trustee to distribute so much of net income of this trust among my children, SC4, in amounts and proportions as my Trustee, in its sole discretion, shall deem best. I recognize that one or more of my children may have greater needs than the others, due to circumstances that I cannot anticipate. I, therefore, expressly authorize my Trustee to pay a larger share of the income, or all of it, if necessary, to those children having the greater need.

B. If at any time the income of the trust, together with any other available income, is not adequate for the support, maintenance and education of my children, or for illnesses, emergencies or other financial needs of a particular child or grandchild, I authorize my Trustee, in its sole discretion, to use so much of the principal as it may deem necessary or advisable for these purposes. Advances of principal shall be made according to need, as determined by my Trustee, and without regard to equality of distribution.

C. I particularly desire that each of my children shall have the opportunity for a college education and professional or post-graduate study, if they so desire. Accordingly, I expressly authorize my Trustee to make advances of principal as my Trustee, in its sole and absolute discretion, shall deem necessary or advisable for the purpose of financing college or post-graduate education as each of the beneficiaries may wish to pursue, even though the advances may completely exhaust the trust.

D. My Trustee's decision with respect to any advances of principal pursuant to this Article shall be final and binding on all persons interested in the trust, and shall not be subject to judicial review.

E. When my youngest living child reaches THIRTY (30) years of age, I direct my Trustee to pay the remaining trust property in equal shares to my children, SC4, with the share of any deceased child to be paid to the child's issue, per stirpes, or, in default of issue, to my surviving issue, per stirpes; provided, however, that if the issue is a beneficiary of a trust created hereunder, his or her share shall be added to the trust to be held and administered pursuant to the terms thereof.

F. If any grandchild of mine to whom a share of principal is to be distributed as herein provided is under twenty-one (21) years of age, I authorize my Trustee to hold the grandchild's share in trust, paying or applying to the use and benefit of the grandchild so much of the income and principal as my Trustee may deem needed for the grandchild's comfortable support, maintenance and education, other available income considered, and accumulating any unused income, but all remaining principal and accumulated income shall be paid to the grandchild upon attaining age twenty-one (21), or in the event of his or her prior death, it shall be paid to his or her estate.

IV. I give to my Executor and to my Trustee hereinafter named, and to the successor or successors of either, the following powers and discretions, in addition to those vested in or imposed upon them or either of them by law:

A. To mortgage, sell, convey, exchange or otherwise deal with or dispose of any real or personal property for cash or on credit (including the right to accept a purchase money mortgage as part of the purchase price); to lease any property for periods longer or shorter than the probable duration of any trust; to retain as part of the estate or trust any and all securities and property in the form originally received, including securities of or issued by any corporate executor or trustee, whether or not it is then income producing and regardless of any rule requiring diversification of investments; to invest and reinvest in any stocks, bonds, shares in mutual funds or authorized common trust funds, or other securities or property, whether real or personal, which my Executor or Trustee may deem safe and for the best interests of the estate or trust, without being limited to investments authorized by law for the investment of trust funds; to hold title to any and all securities and other investments either in my Executor's or Trustee's name or in the name of a nominee; to borrow money from itself or others on terms as my Executor or Trustee may deem best, and to pledge any property of the estate or trust as security for the repayment thereof; to hold two or more trusts or other funds in one or more consolidated funds, in which the separate trusts as funds shall have undivided interests; to determine as to every sum received (including stock dividends or the distributions of securities), whether the same is principal or income, or what part thereof is principal or income, and as to every expense or disbursement incurred or made by it, whether the same should be borne by the principal or income, or in what share by each; and to make distributions in cash or in kind, or partly in each, including undivided interests, even though shares be composed differently.

B. In case any income or principal of the trust becomes payable to a person under twenty-one (21) years of age, or to a person under legal disability, or to a person not adjudicated incompetent but who, by reason of illness or mental or physical disability, is in the opinion of my Trustee, unable to administer properly the income or principal, then the income or principal may be paid out by my Trustee in any one or more of the following ways as it deems best: (a) directly to the beneficiary; (b) to the guardian, committee, conservator or custodian of the beneficiary; (c) to any relative of the beneficiary or to any other person with whom the beneficiary may be living, for the care, comfort, support, maintenance, education and welfare of the beneficiary; (d) by my Trustee using income or principal directly for the care, comfort, support, maintenance, education and welfare of the beneficiary.

C. I expressly authorize my Trustee to receive and execute receipts for the proceeds of any life insurance policies on my life which may become payable to my Trustee; and I direct that a receipt executed by my Trustee shall fully discharge the respective insurance companies from all liability and responsibility with respect to the payment and use of the proceeds of the policies. If my Trustee's claim to any insurance proceeds is contested, whether by the insurance company or by any other claimant, my Trustee shall have full power and authority to settle, compromise or otherwise collect, or to enforce by legal action, any contested policy, paying the expenses of the action out of the trust estate. My Trustee's decision with respect to any contested claim shall be final and conclusive upon all parties interested in this trust.

D. I further expressly authorize my Trustee to purchase any assets from my Executor at the value established for the assets in the federal estate tax proceeding in my estate, and/or to loan to my Executor sums as may be needed to pay any and all taxes and administration expenses. The loans may be made with or without security, and with or without interest, and upon other terms and conditions as my Executor and Trustee may agree. The authority hereby granted shall be exercised notwithstanding that my Executor and Trustee are one and the same person or corporation.

E. If at any time during the administration of any trust herein created, the Trustee, in its absolute discretion, deems the continuation thereof to be uneconomical and not in the best interests of the beneficiary or beneficiaries thereof, the Trustee, in its absolute discretion, is authorized to terminate the same and distribute the assets, free of the Trust, to the current income beneficiary or beneficiaries in the proportions in which they are entitled to the income therefrom.

F. If any beneficiary or legatee entitled to receive a part of my estate shall be under twenty-one (21) years of age, I authorize and empower my Executor or Trustee, as the case may be, to designate his or her parent, or some other appropriate adult person, or trust company, as custodian for the beneficiary or legatee under the Sample Uniform Transfers to Minors Act until age twenty-one (21), and to distribute the share of the beneficiary or legatee to the designated custodian. A receipt from the custodian shall fully release my Executor or Trustee from all liability and accountability to the legatee or beneficiary.

G. I expressly authorize my Trustee to merge any trust created hereunder with any other trust created by me under will or agreement, which property shall be held, administered and distributed in accordance with the provisions of the trust; provided, however, that this power shall apply only if the trust to which the distribution would be made is substantially identical in form and content to the trust described herein, and for the same beneficiaries.

H. If any party to any proceeding relating to my estate or any trust established hereunder shall be under a disability by reason of infancy or incompetency, and there is another party without any disability to the proceeding with the same interest as the person under a disability, it shall not be necessary to serve the person under a disability with process in the proceeding, and he shall be deemed to be virtually represented therein as provided by law by the other person who is served with process, and the person under the disability shall be bound in all respects by any Decree or Judgment entered in the proceeding.

I. No individual Trustee of any trust herein created shall be authorized to exercise any power herein to make any discretionary distribution of either income or principal to himself or herself, or to make discretionary allocations in his or her own favor between principal and income; and no individual Trustee shall be authorized to exercise any power herein to distribute income or principal to or for the benefit of any person whom he or he is legally obligated to support. These powers may be exercised by the remaining Trustee who is not so disqualified.

V. I direct that all inheritance, succession and estate taxes of every kind payable with respect to any property includable in my gross taxable estate, whether or not passing under this my Will, shall be paid out of my residuary estate, and shall not be apportioned.

VI. If my daughter's mother cannot serve as guardian, or if she fails to survive me, or fails to qualify for any reason, then I nominate and appoint SC6 as guardian. If SC6 cannot serve as guardian, or if he fails to survive me, or fails to qualify for any reason, I nominate and appoint SC7 as guardian. I direct that no bond or other security shall be required of either of them, in any jurisdiction, for the faithful performance of their duties.

VII. I hereby nominate, constitute and appoint SC8 as Executrix of this my Last Will and Testament; but if she fails to survive me, or renounces, or fails to qualify, or upon her death, resignation or disqualification, I nominate and appoint SC9 as Executrix hereof. I hereby nominate, constitute and appoint SC8 as Trustee of the trust herein; but if she fails to survive me, or renounces, or fails to qualify, or upon her death, resignation or disqualification, I nominate and appoint SC9 as Trustee. I direct that no bond or other security shall be required of my Executor or Trustees.

(continued)

VIII. The masculine gender, whenever used herein, shall include the feminine, the feminine shall include the masculine; the neuter shall include both the masculine and feminine; and the singular shall include the plural wherever necessary or appropriate.

IN WITNESS WHEREOF, I have hereunto subscribed my name this ____ day of _____ 2014.

_____
SC1

We whose names are hereto subscribed, do certify that on the _____ day of_____ 2014, the Testator, SC1, subscribed his name to this instrument, in our presence and in the presence of each of us, and at the same time in our presence and hearing, declared the same to be his Last Will and Testament, and requested us, and each of us, to sign our names thereto as witnesses to the execution thereof, which we hereby do in the presence of the Testator and of each other.

_____ residing at _____

_____ residing at _____

AFFIDAVIT OF ATTESTING WITNESSES

_____ and _____ being duly sworn say:

We are acquainted with SC1. The signature at the end of the instrument dated _____ 2014, declared by him to be his Last Will, was made by him at Rochester, State of Sample, in the presence of each of the undersigned.

At the time of signing the Will, SC1 declared the instrument to which his signature had been affixed to be his Will and we, and each of us, signed our names thereto at the end thereof at that time and at his request and in his presence.

At the time of the execution of the instrument SC1 was over the age of 18 years, of sound mind and memory, and not under any restraint and competent in every respect to make a Will.

At the time of execution, SC1 could read, write and converse in the English language, and was not suffering from defects of sight, hearing or speech, or any other physical or mental impairment, which would affect his capacity to make a valid Will.

The Will was not executed in counterparts.

_____
Witness

_____
Witness

STATE OF SAMPLE   )

COUNTY OF SAMPLE) SS:

On the _____ day of _____ in the year 2014 before me, the undersigned, a Notary Public in and for said State, personally appeared _____ and _____, the subscribing witnesses to the foregoing instrument, with whom I am personally acquainted, who, being by me duly sworn, did depose and say that _____ resides at _____, Sample and _____ resides at _____, Sample; that they know SC1 to be the individual described in and who executed the foregoing instrument; that said subscribing witnesses were present and saw said SC1 execute the same; and that said witnesses at the same time subscribed their names as witnesses thereto, and acknowledged to me that they executed the same in their capacities, and that by their signatures on the instrument, the individual, or the person upon behalf of which the individual acted, executed the instrument.

_____
Notary Public

PP Form 6.2—Revocable Living Trust (1 Grantor)

SC1 TRUST
U/A DATED _____
by
SC1

Grantor
and
SC1

Trustee
Name of Trust: SC1 TRUST
Date: _____

TABLE OF CONTENTS

DECLARATION OF TRUST

DECLARATION OF TRUST, made as of this ____ day of _____, 2014, between SC1, having an address at Sc2, as Grantor (hereinafter referred to as the "Grantor"), and SC1, having an address of Sc2, as Trustee (hereinafter referred to as the "Trustee").

WITNESSETH

WHEREAS, the Grantor wish to create a revocable living trust and to fund the trust with assets;
THEREFORE, the Grantor hereby creates the SC1 TRUST as follows:

ARTICLE FIRST

Directions of Grantor

The Trustee shall hold, manage, invest and reinvest the trust estate, shall collect the income therefrom, and shall pay any part or all of the income and principal to whomever the Grantor from time to time may direct in writing.

(continued)

Until the Grantor hereafter may direct to the contrary, the net income shall be paid to the Grantor on a monthly basis.

Any income not so paid or applied shall be accumulated and added to the principal of this trust at least quarter-annually.

ARTICLE SECOND

Disability of Grantor

If at any time the Grantor shall be under any legal disability or shall be unable to manage his affairs properly by reason of illness or mental or physical disability (as such incapacity is defined in this Agreement), (whether or not a court of competent jurisdiction has declared the Grantor incompetent or mentally ill or has appointed a legal representative for the Grantor), the successor trustee shall act as sole trustee and may pay or apply so much or all of the net income and the principal of the trust estate as the Trustee deems necessary or advisable for the health, maintenance and support of the Grantor. Any income not so paid or applied shall be accumulated and added to the principal of this trust at least quarter-annually.

In making any payment hereunder, the successor Trustee may consider, but shall not be required to consider, the income and other resources of the Grantor. No such payment shall be charged upon a subsequent division of the trust estate against the principal of any share which may be set apart for any beneficiary hereunder.

ARTICLE THIRD

Death of the Grantor

Upon the death of the Grantor, this Trust shall terminate and the then remaining trust property shall be paid outright and free of trust in equal shares to the Grantor's named child: SC3; or if SC3 is not then living, to his issue, per stirpes. The share of any issue under the age of twenty-one shall be held in a separate Sample Uniform Transfers to Minors Account until age twenty-one. The Grantor hereby appoints SC4 as Custodian of any UTMA accounts created for the issue of SC3.

ARTICLE FOURTH

Distributions To Minors Or Incompetents

In any case in which the Trustee is authorized or directed by any provision of this Agreement to pay or distribute income or principal to any person who shall be a minor or incompetent, the Trustee, in the sole discretion of the Trustee and without authorization of any court, may pay or distribute the whole or any part of such income or principal to such minor or incompetent personally, or may apply the whole or any part thereof directly to the health, education, maintenance or support of such minor or incompetent, or may pay or distribute the whole or any part thereof to the guardian, committee, conservator or other legal representative, wherever appointed, of such minor or incompetent or to the person with whom such minor or incompetent may from time to time reside, or in the case of a minor, may pay or distribute the whole or any part thereof to a custodian for such minor under any gifts to minors or transfers to minors act. Evidence of such payment or distribution or the receipt therefor by the person to whom any such payment or distribution is made shall be a full discharge of the Trustee from all liability with respect thereto, even though the Trustee may be such person.

The Trustee, in the sole discretion of the Trustee, may defer payment or distribution of any or all income or principal to which a minor may be entitled until such minor shall attain the age of twenty-one (21) years, or to make such payment or distribution at any time and from time to time, during the minority of such minor, holding the whole or the undistributed portion thereof as a separate fund vested in such minor but subject to the power in trust hereby given to the Trustee to administer and invest such fund and to use the income or principal thereof for the benefit of such minor as if such fund were held in trust hereunder. No bond or other security and no periodic accounts shall be required with respect to such fund, and the same shall be subject to commission as if it were a separate trust fund. The Trustee shall pay and distribute any balance of such fund to such minor when such minor shall attain the age of twenty-one (21) years. Except as is herein above provided, if such minor shall die before attaining the age of twenty-one (21) years, the Trustee shall pay and distribute such balance to the executors, administrators, or legal representatives of the estate of such minor.

The word "minor," wherever used in this Article FOURTH, shall mean any person who has not attained the age of twenty-one (21) years.

ARTICLE FIFTH

Payment of Debts

Upon the death of each of the Grantor, the Trustee may pay from the principal of the trust estate the amount of any estate or death taxes, by whatever name called, imposed under the laws of any jurisdiction by reason of the Grantor's death, whether in respect of property passing under this Agreement or the Grantor's last will and testament or otherwise, and the amount of all of the debts which the Grantor's estate must pay, the expenses of their last illnesses and funerals, and the expenses of administering their estate. The Trustee may rely upon the written certification of the executors, administrators, or legal representatives of the Grantor's estate as to the amount of any such tax, debt or expense, without any duty to inquire as to the correctness thereof, and, in its discretion, may make payment thereof either to said executors, administrators, or legal representatives or to the taxing authority or person to whom such amount is owed.

ARTICLE SIXTH

Grantor's Right To Revoke Or Amend

The Grantor reserve the right, at any time and without the consent of any person or notice to any person other than the Trustee, to amend or revoke in whole or in part this Agreement or any trust created hereunder, including the right to change the terms or beneficiaries thereof, by delivering to the Trustee written notice of such amendment or revocation signed by the Grantor. No amendment of this Agreement, however, shall increase the obligations or reduce the commissions of the Trustee without the consent of the Trustee. Upon any such revocation, the Trustee shall deliver to the Grantor all property in the possession or control of the Trustee with respect to any trust which has been revoked and shall execute and deliver any instruments necessary to release any interest of the Trustee in such property. The sale or other disposition by the Grantor of the whole or any part of the trust estate held hereunder shall constitute as to such whole or part a revocation of this Agreement and the trust or trusts affected thereby.

The Grantor reserves the power and right during the life of the Grantor to collect any rent, interest or other income which may accrue from the trust estate and, in her sole discretion, to accumulate such income as a trust asset or to pay such income to the Grantor individually and not in any fiduciary capacity. The Grantor further reserves the power and right during life of the Grantor to mortgage or pledge all or any part of the trust estate as collateral for any loan.

ARTICLE SEVENTH

Powers of Trustee

In the administration of any property, real or personal, at any time forming a part of the trust estate, including accumulated income, and in the administration of any trust created hereunder, the Trustee, in addition to and without limitation of the powers conferred on trustees under Sample Law, shall have the following powers to be exercised in the sole discretion of the Trustee, except as otherwise expressly provided in this Agreement:

(a) To retain such property for any period, whether or not the same is of the character permissible for investments by fiduciaries under any applicable law, and without regard to the effect any such retention may have upon the diversity of investments;

(b) To sell, transfer, exchange, convert or otherwise dispose of, or grant options with respect to, such property, at public or private sale, with or without security, in such manner, at such times, for such prices, and upon such terms and conditions as the Trustee may deem advisable;

(c) To invest and reinvest in common or preferred stocks, securities, investment trusts, mutual funds, regulated investment companies, bonds and other property, real or personal, foreign or domestic, including any undivided interest in any one or more common trust funds, whether or not such investments be of the character permissible for investments by fiduciaries under any applicable law, and without regard to the effect any such investment may have upon the diversity of investments;

(d) To render liquid the trust estate or any trust created hereunder in whole or in part, at any time and from time to time, and to hold unproductive property, cash or readily marketable securities of little or no yield for such period as the Trustee may deem advisable;

(e) To lease any such property beyond the period fixed by statute for leases made by fiduciaries and beyond the duration of any trust created hereunder;

(continued)

(f) To join or become a party to, or to oppose, any reorganization, readjustment, recapitalization, foreclosure, merger, voting trust, dissolution, consolidation or exchange, and to deposit any securities with any committee, depository or trustee, and to pay any fees, expenses and assessments incurred in connection therewith, and to charge the same to principal, and to exercise conversion, subscription or other rights, and to make any necessary payments in connection therewith, or to sell any such privileges;

(g) To vote in person at meetings of stock or security holders and adjournments thereof, and to vote by general or limited proxy with respect to any stock or securities;

(h) To hold stock and securities in the name of a nominee without indicating the trust character of such holding, or unregistered or in such form as will pass by delivery, or to use a central depository and to permit registration in the name of a nominee;

(i) To initiate or defend, at the expense of the trust estate, any litigation relating to this Agreement or any property of the trust estate which the Trustee considers advisable, and to pay, compromise, compound, adjust, submit to arbitration, sell or release any claims or demands of the trust estate or any trust created hereunder against others or of others against the same as the Trustee may deem advisable, including the acceptance of deeds of real property in satisfaction of notes, bonds and mortgages, and to make any payments in connection therewith which the Trustee may deem advisable;

(j) To borrow money for any purpose from any source, including any trustee at any time acting hereunder, and to secure the repayment of any and all amounts so borrowed by mortgage or pledge of any property;

(k) To possess, manage, develop, subdivide, control, partition, mortgage, lease or otherwise deal with any and all real property; to satisfy and discharge or extend the term of any mortgage thereof; to execute the necessary instruments and covenants to effectuate the foregoing powers, including the giving or granting of options in connection therewith; to make repairs, replacements and improvements, structural or otherwise, or abandon the same if deemed to be worthless or not of sufficient value to warrant keeping or protecting; to abstain from the payment of real estate taxes, assessments, water charges and sewer rents, repairs, maintenance and upkeep of the same; to permit to be lost by tax sale or other proceeding or to convey the same for a nominal consideration or without consideration; to set up appropriate reserves out of income for repairs, modernization and upkeep of buildings, including reserves for depreciation and obsolescence, and to add such reserves to principal and, if the income from the property itself should not suffice for such purposes, to advance out of other income any sums needed therefor, and advance any income of the trust for the amortization of any mortgage on property held in the trust;

(l) To purchase from the legal representatives of the estate of the Grantor or from the trustees of any trust established by the Grantor any property constituting a part of such estate or trust at its fair market value and to make loans for adequate consideration to such legal representatives or trustees, upon such terms and conditions as the Trustee may determine in the sole discretion of the Trustee;

(m) To carry insurance of the kinds and in the amounts which the Trustee considers advisable, at the expense of the trust estate, to protect the trust estate and the Trustee personally against any hazard;

(n) To make distribution of the trust estate or of the principal of any trust created hereunder in cash or in kind, or partly in kind, and to cause any distribution to be composed of cash, property or undivided fractional shares in property different in kind from any other distribution, and to determine the fair valuation of the property so allocated, with or without regard to the tax basis; to hold the principal of separate trusts in a consolidated fund and to invest the same in solido; to split trusts for purposes of allocating GST exemptions (within the meaning of Section 2642(a) of the Internal Revenue Code); and to merge any trusts which have substantially identical terms and beneficiaries, and to hold them as a single trust;

(o) To employ and pay the compensation of accountants, attorneys, experts, investment counselors, custodians, agents and other persons or firms providing services or advice, irrespective of whether the Trustee may be associated therewith; to delegate discretionary powers to such persons or firms; and to rely upon information or advice furnished thereby or to ignore the same, as the Trustee in its discretion may determine;

(p) To execute and deliver any and all instruments or writings which it may deem advisable to carry out any of the foregoing powers; and

(q) To exercise all such rights and powers and to do all such acts and enter into all such agreements as persons owning similar property in their own right might lawfully exercise, do or enter into.

Except as otherwise provided herein, the Trustee may determine, when there is reasonable doubt or uncertainty as to the applicable law or the relevant facts, which receipts of money or other assets should be credited to income or principal, and which disbursements, commissions, assessments, fees and other expenses should be charged to income or principal. Any distributions or dividends payable in the stock of a corporation, and rights to subscribe to securities or rights other than cash declared or issued by a corporation, shall be dealt with as principal. The proceeds from the sale, redemption or other disposition, whether at a profit or loss, and regardless of the tax treatment thereof, of any property constituting principal, including mortgages and real estate acquired through foreclosure or otherwise, shall normally be dealt with as principal, but the Trustee may allocate a portion of any such proceeds to income if the property disposed of produced no income or substantially less than the current rate of return on trust investments, or if the Trustee shall deem such action advisable for any other reason. The Trustee may (but are not directed to) allocate receipts and disbursements between income and principal in accordance with Sample law. The preceding provisions of this paragraph shall not be deemed to authorize any act by the Trustee that may be a violation of any law prohibiting the accumulation of income.

No person who deals with any Trustee hereunder shall be bound to see to the application of any asset delivered to such Trustee or to inquire into the authority for, or propriety of, any action taken or not taken by such Trustee.

Notwithstanding anything to the contrary contained herein, during such time as any current or possible future beneficiary of any trust created hereunder (other than the Grantor) may be acting as a Trustee hereunder, such person shall be disqualified from exercising any power to make any discretionary distributions of income or principal to himself or herself (unless the discretion to make such distributions is limited by an ascertainable standard within the meaning of Section 2041(b)(1)(A) of the Internal Revenue Code), or to satisfy any of his or her legal obligations, or to make discretionary allocations of receipts or disbursements as between income and principal. No Trustee who is a current or possible future beneficiary of any trust hereunder (other than the Grantor) shall participate in the exercise of any powers of the Trustee which would cause such beneficiary to be treated as the owner of trust assets for tax purposes.

No Trustee shall be liable for acts or omissions in administering the trust estate or any trust created by this Agreement, except for that Trustee's own actual fraud, gross negligence or willful misconduct. If any Trustee becomes liable as Trustee to any other person who is not a beneficiary in connection with any matter not within the Trustee's control and not due to the Trustee's actual fraud, gross negligence or willful misconduct, such Trustee shall be fully indemnified and held harmless by the trust estate and any trust created hereunder giving rise to such liability, as the case may be, against and in respect of any damages that such Trustee may sustain, including without limitation attorneys' fees. No successor Trustee shall incur any liability, by reason of qualifying as a Trustee hereunder, for the acts or omissions of any predecessor Trustee.

The Trustee is authorized, but not required, to accept any property transferred to the Trustee by any person during such person's lifetime or by such person's last will and testament. Any property so transferred to, and accepted by, the Trustee shall become a part of such trust or trusts created by this Agreement as such person shall direct and may be commingled with the other property in the trust or trusts to which such property has been added and shall be held, administered and disposed of as a part of such trust or trusts.

ARTICLE EIGHTH

Appointment of Trustee

The Grantor appoints SC1 as Trustee hereunder. Upon the death, resignation, or incapacity (as hereinafter defined) of the initial Trustee, the Grantor hereby appoints SC5 to act as successor Trustee hereunder. If SC5 is unable or unwilling to serve as successor Trustee, then the Grantor appoints his son, SC6, as second successor Trustee.

The Grantor shall be deemed incapacitated upon receipt by the successor Trustee of a certificate signed by a medical doctor stating that in the opinion of such doctor the Grantor is either mentally or physically incapable of attending to her affairs. The successor Trustee shall indicate acceptance of his or her offices as Trustee by giving personally, or by mail, a written acceptance of the appointment and written agreement to act as Trustee, duly acknowledged, to the primary income beneficiary. The Successor Trustee shall be authorized to exercise all the powers, privileges and discretions conferred on the Trustee hereunder, and shall not be obligated to inquire into or be liable for any act or omission of any Trustee who shall have served prior to qualification as successor or substituted Trustee. Further, the Successor Trustee shall only be responsible to administer assets listed in Schedule A hereof which are actually received by the Successor Trustee, as well as any other assets actually coming into the hands of the Successor Trustee.

The Successor Trustee shall have full authority to take whatever steps are necessary to collect and take possession of all the trust assets held by the original Trustee regardless of the location of said assets and regardless of whether said assets are held in the form of real estate, bank accounts, stocks or bonds, mutual funds, brokerage investment accounts or similar investments, for purposes herein set forth.

(continued)

Any corporation resulting from any merger, consolidation or conversion to which a corporate Trustee may be a party, or any corporation otherwise succeeding generally to all or a greater part of the assets or business of such corporate Trustee, shall be deemed the successor to such corporate Trustee without the execution or filing of any paper or any further action on the part of any party hereto or beneficiary hereunder.

The term "Trustee" wherever used herein shall mean the trustee in office from time to time. Any such trustee shall have the same rights, powers, duties, authority and privileges, whether or not discretionary, as if originally appointed hereunder.

No bond, surety or other security shall be required of any Trustee acting hereunder for the faithful performance of the duties of Trustee, notwithstanding any law of any State or other jurisdiction to the contrary.

The Trustee shall be entitled to receive as Trustee such compensation as shall be set forth in the published Schedule of Compensation of the corporate Trustee in effect when such compensation is payable.

ARTICLE NINTH

Accounts of Trustee

The Trustee, at any time and from time to time, may render to the Grantor an account of the acts and transactions of the Trustee with respect to the income and principal of any trust created hereunder, from the date of the creation of such trust or from the date of the last previous account of the Trustee. After the death of the Grantor, the Trustee, at any time and from time to time, may render an account to the living person or persons who are entitled, at the time of such account, to receive all or a portion of the income of the trusts herein created. The approval of any person of full age, or a guardian or parent of a minor or incompetent person, to whom an account is rendered shall, as to all matters stated therein, be final and binding upon him or such minor or incompetent person, or any persons claiming through him or such minor or incompetent person, as the case may be. A person of full age, or a guardian or parent of a minor or incompetent person, to whom an account is rendered shall be deemed to have approved the account if he assents to the account in writing or if he does not communicate to the Trustee his written objections to the account within sixty days after the receipt of the account (provided the account was accompanied by a notice of said sixty day period within which to raise objections).

The Grantor shall have full power and authority on behalf of all persons interested in any trust hereunder, whether such interest relates to income or principal, to settle any account of the Trustee. Such settlement shall be final and binding upon all persons so interested in such trust. Upon such settlement, the Trustee shall be fully and completely discharged and released from all further liability with respect to acts and transactions set forth in the account so settled.

The Trustee shall not be required at any time to file any account in any court, nor shall the Trustee be required to have any account judicially settled. Nothing herein, however, shall be construed as limiting the right of the Trustee to seek a judicial settlement of any account.

ARTICLE TENTH

Representation of Persons Under Disability

In any proceeding relating to any trust hereunder, it shall not be necessary to serve process upon, or to make a party to the proceeding, any person under a disability if another party to the proceeding who is not under a disability has the same interest as the person under a disability. The written approval by all of the then living adult beneficiaries of any trust hereunder relating to the administration of such trust, whether the same relates to an accounting or any other action taken or omitted or proposed to be taken or omitted by the Trustee, shall be deemed to be the approval of and shall be binding upon all beneficiaries of such trust including those who are minors or are not yet born at the time of such action.

ARTICLE ELEVENTH

Simultaneous Death

If any beneficiary under this Agreement shall die simultaneously with the Grantor or any other person upon whose death such beneficiary shall become entitled to receive either income or principal under this Agreement, or in such circumstances as to render it difficult or impracticable to determine who predeceased the other, then for purposes of this Agreement such beneficiary shall be deemed to have predeceased the Grantor or such other person. The provisions of this Agreement shall be construed as aforesaid, notwithstanding the provisions of any applicable law establishing a different presumption of order of death or providing for survivorship for a fixed period as a condition of inheritance of property.

ARTICLE TWELFTH

Rights of Beneficiaries Are Not Assignable

No disposition, charge or encumbrance on the income or principal of any trust established hereunder shall be valid or binding upon the Trustee. No beneficiary shall have any right, power or authority to assign, transfer, encumber or otherwise dispose of such income or principal or any part thereof until the same shall be paid to such beneficiary by the Trustee. No income or principal shall be subject in any manner to any claim of any creditor of any beneficiary or liable to attachment, execution or other process of law prior to its actual receipt by the beneficiary.

ARTICLE THIRTEENTH

Construction

The validity and construction of this Agreement and the trusts created hereunder shall be governed by the laws of the State of Sample.

Any provision herein which refers to a statute, rule, regulation or other specific legal reference which is no longer in effect at the time said provision is to be applied shall be deemed to refer to the successor, replacement or amendment to such statute, rule, regulation or other reference, if any, and shall be interpreted in such a manner so as to carry out the original intent of said provision.

For purposes of this Agreement, the disability or incapacity of an individual (including the Grantor or any Trustee) shall be conclusively established by a written statement signed by such individual's then attending physician and filed with the records of any trust established hereunder attesting that, in such physician's opinion, such individual is unable to manage his or her affairs. Such written statement shall be conclusive evidence of such fact, and any third party may rely on same in dealing with any trust established hereunder and shall not be obliged to inquire whether such individual is no longer under such disability or incapacity at the time of such dealings.

Wherever used in this Agreement and the context so requires, the masculine shall include the feminine and the singular shall include the plural, and vice versa.

The captions in this Agreement are for convenience of reference, and they shall not be considered when construing this Agreement.

ARTICLE FOURTEENTH

Binding Effect

This Agreement shall extend to and be binding upon the heirs, executors, administrators, successors and assigns of the undersigned Grantor and upon the Trustee acting hereunder.

ARTICLE FIFTEENTH

Short Name

This Agreement and the trusts created hereunder may be referred to, in any other instrument, by the name "SC1 TRUST." Any transfers to this Agreement or any trust hereunder may refer to the aforesaid name or to "SC1, as Trustee under the SC1 TRUST," with or without specifying any change in Trustee or any amendment to this Agreement.

IN WITNESS WHEREOF, this Agreement has been duly executed as of the date first above written.

_____
SC1, Grantor

_____
SC1, Trustee

(continued)

This Trust was signed in the presence of us who, at the request and in the presence of Grantor and in the presence of each other, have signed the same as witnesses thereto.

_____
Witness Signature

_____
Witness Name (Printed)

_____
Witness Signature

_____
Witness Name (Printed)

_____
_____

_____
Witness Address

_____
_____

_____
Witness Address

ACKNOWLEDGMENT OF SC1, GRANTOR & TRUSTEE

STATE OF SAMPLE
COUNTY OF SAMPLE

On this _____ day of _____, 2014, this instrument was acknowledged before me by SC1 , who acknowledged themselves to be the Grantor and the Trustee of the SC1 TRUST, dated _____, 2014, and that they, being authorized to so do, executed the within instrument for the purposes therein contained by signing for that Trust as such Grantor and Trustee.

IN WITNESS WHEREOF, I hereunto set my hand and official seal.

_____
Notary Public

ACKNOWLEDGMENT OF WITNESSES

STATE OF SAMPLE
COUNTY OF SAMPLE

On this _____ day of _____, 2014, this instrument was acknowledged before me, a Notary Public, by _____ and _____, the above witnesses, who personally appeared before me, are personally known to me, and whose names are subscribed to this instrument and acknowledged that they executed the same for the purposes contained therein.

IN WITNESS WHEREOF, I hereunto set my hand and official seal.

_____
Notary Public

CHAPTER 7

Guardianships and Conservatorships

A REAL-LIFE SCENARIO

An elderly widow, the mother of five children, lived in California. The widow's youngest son lived in her home with her, while the other four children lived in Arizona. The youngest son had a criminal record and an ongoing drug problem, but still could do no wrong in his mother's eyes. He routinely took her ATM card each month the day after her social security was deposited and took most of her money. He would then "borrow" the card at other times during the month, making withdrawals that resulted in overdraft fees being assessed by the bank. The widow's two daughters had a hard time reaching their mother by telephone and also got the sense when speaking to her that something was not right. They went to California to visit their mother and found her home to be in a filthy state with damage done to the interior by their youngest brother. They went to the bank with their mother and learned from the teller what was happening with the withdrawals. They immediately helped their mother to get the account changed so that their brother would no longer have access to the funds and moved their mother to Arizona to spend equal time living with each of them. Since their mother had not executed a power of attorney and no longer

© Alexander Raths/Fotolia

CHAPTER OBJECTIVES:

1. Understand the purpose of a guardianship.
2. Understand the purpose of a conservatorship.
3. Describe the process by which a guardian or conservator is appointed.
4. Discuss the powers and the fiduciary duties conferred upon guardians and conservators.
5. Discuss circumstances where a guardian and conservatorship may be necessary.
6. Explain how the necessity of petitioning for a guardianship may be prevented.
7. Explain how the necessity of petitioning for a conservatorship may be prevented.

had capacity to sign a power of attorney, the daughters petitioned the court to appoint them as co-guardians and co-conservators in order to manage their mother's affairs.

■ INTRODUCTION

The foregoing scenario is exemplary of an all-too-common occurrence. As people age, it is sad that many lose the mental capacity to effectively manage their own affairs. If prior appointments have not been made under a living will and a power of attorney, a guardianship and conservatorship may be necessary in order for a loved one to step in and take care of an aging family member.

Key Terms and Definitions

Guardian
The one who legally has the care and management of the person, property, or both of a minor or incompetent.

Guardianship
The legal process by which a guardian is appointed.

Guardian Ad Litem
A guardian appointed by a court to protect a minor who brings or defends a lawsuit.

Conservator
One who legally has the care and management of the property, but not the person, of someone who is incompetent.

Conservatorship
The legal process by which a conservator is appointed.

Ward
A person who has been legally placed under the care of a guardian or a court.

Fiduciary Duty
A duty or responsibility required of a fiduciary that arises out of a position of loyalty and trust.

Fiduciary
A person in a position of loyalty and trust, such as an executor, administrator, guardian, attorney-in-fact, or trustee; also a person to whom property or power is entrusted for the benefit of another.

A **guardian** is one who legally has the care and management of the person, property, or both of a minor or incompetent. A **guardianship** is the legal process by which a guardian is appointed. A **guardian ad litem** is a guardian appointed by a court to protect a minor who brings or defends a lawsuit.

A **conservator** is one who legally has the care and management of the property, but not the person, of someone who is incompetent. A **conservatorship** is the legal process by which a conservator is appointed. Guardians and conservators have a fiduciary duty to act in the best interest of the ward. The **ward** is the incompetent individual for whom a legal representative is being sought.

A **fiduciary duty** is a duty or responsibility required of a fiduciary that arises out of a position of loyalty and trust. A **fiduciary** is a person in a position of loyalty and trust, such as an executor, administrator, guardian, attorney-in-fact, or trustee. Fiduciary duties are discussed fully in Chapter 8.

An individual petitioning to be appointed as a guardian will very commonly also simultaneously petition to be appointed as conservator so that he or she can manage both the ward and the ward's property. However, some states allow a guardian to also manage the property of a ward or incompetent up to a limited dollar amount or value without also having to be appointed as conservator. This is to avoid unnecessary expense and work for the petitioner when the ward's assets are of nominal value.

■ NATURAL GUARDIANS OF MINOR CHILDREN

Parents are naturally the guardians of their biological and adopted children during minority and are morally responsible for their children's care and development. Under case law and statutory law, the power to make health and financial decisions on behalf of their children is legally conferred on parents. By way of example, Figure 7.1 depicts §744.301 of the 2012 Florida Statutes, pertaining to parents as the natural guardians of their own children.

Notice that under §744.301(2), a parent acting as guardian of a minor child in Florida can collect, receive, manage, and dispose of funds from a variety of sources up to an aggregate total of $15,000.00 without any formal appointment by the court or necessity of posting a bond. For example, Myra Minor is injured in a car accident in Tampa, Florida, and, luckily, is not seriously injured. The insurance company offers Myra's parents $8,000.00 in full settlement of all of her claims. Her parents can accept the settlement and administer the funds on Myra's

Figure 7.1 2012 Florida Statutes §744.301, Natural Guardians

(1) The parents jointly are the natural guardians of their own children and of their adopted children, during minority. If one parent dies, the surviving parent remains the sole natural guardian even if he or she remarries. If the marriage between the parents is dissolved, the natural guardianship belongs to the parent to whom sole parental responsibility has been granted, or if the parents have been granted shared parental responsibility, both continue as natural guardians. If the marriage is dissolved and neither parent is given parental responsibility for the child, neither may act as natural guardian of the child. The mother of a child born out of wedlock is the natural guardian of the child and is entitled to primary residential care and custody of the child unless the court enters an order stating otherwise.

(2) Except as otherwise provided in this chapter, on behalf of any of their minor children, and without appointment, authority, or bond if the amounts received in the aggregate do not exceed $15,000, natural guardians may:

    (a) Settle and consummate a settlement of any claim or cause of action accruing to any of their minor children for damages to the person or property of any minor children;

    (b) Collect, receive, manage, and dispose of the proceeds of any settlement;

    (c) Collect, receive, manage, and dispose of any real or personal property distributed from an estate or trust;

    (d) Collect, receive, manage, and dispose of and make elections regarding the proceeds from a life insurance policy or annuity contract payable to, or otherwise accruing to the benefit of, the child; and

    (e) Collect, receive, manage, dispose of, and make elections regarding the proceeds of any benefit plan as defined in s. 710.102, of which the minor is a beneficiary, participant, or owner.

(3) In addition to the authority granted in subsection (2), natural guardians are authorized, on behalf of any of their minor children, to waive and release, in advance, any claim or cause of action against a commercial activity provider, or its owners, affiliates, employees, or agents, which would accrue to a minor child for personal injury, including death, and property damage resulting from an inherent risk in the activity.

    (a) As used in this subsection, the term "inherent risk" means those dangers or conditions, known or unknown, which are characteristic of, intrinsic to, or an integral part of the activity and which are not eliminated even if the activity provider acts with due care in a reasonably prudent manner. The term includes, but is not limited to:

        1. The failure by the activity provider to warn the natural guardian or minor child of an inherent risk; and

        2. The risk that the minor child or another participant in the activity may act in a negligent or intentional manner and contribute to the injury or death of the minor child. A participant does not include the activity provider or its owners, affiliates, employees, or agents.

    (b) To be enforceable, a waiver or release executed under this subsection must, at a minimum, include the following statement in uppercase type that is at least 5 points larger than, and clearly distinguishable from, the rest of the text of the waiver or release:

NOTICE TO THE MINOR CHILD'S NATURAL GUARDIAN

READ THIS FORM COMPLETELY AND CAREFULLY. YOU ARE AGREEING TO LET YOUR MINOR CHILD ENGAGE IN A POTENTIALLY DANGEROUS ACTIVITY. YOU ARE AGREEING THAT, EVEN IF (name of released party or parties) USES REASONABLE CARE IN PROVIDING THIS ACTIVITY, THERE IS A CHANCE YOUR CHILD MAY BE SERIOUSLY INJURED OR KILLED BY PARTICIPATING IN THIS ACTIVITY BECAUSE THERE ARE CERTAIN DANGERS INHERENT IN THE ACTIVITY WHICH CANNOT BE AVOIDED OR ELIMINATED. BY SIGNING THIS FORM YOU ARE GIVING UP YOUR CHILD'S RIGHT AND YOUR RIGHT TO RECOVER FROM (name of released party or parties) IN A LAWSUIT FOR ANY PERSONAL INJURY, INCLUDING DEATH, TO YOUR CHILD OR ANY PROPERTY DAMAGE THAT RESULTS FROM THE RISKS THAT ARE A NATURAL PART OF THE ACTIVITY. YOU HAVE THE RIGHT TO REFUSE TO SIGN THIS FORM, AND (name of released party or parties) HAS THE RIGHT TO REFUSE TO LET YOUR CHILD PARTICIPATE IF YOU DO NOT SIGN THIS FORM.

    (c) If a waiver or release complies with paragraph (b) and waives no more than allowed under this subsection, there is a rebuttable presumption that the waiver or release is valid and that any injury or damage to the minor child arose from the inherent risk involved in the activity.

        (1) To rebut the presumption that the waiver or release is valid, a claimant must demonstrate by a preponderance of the evidence that the waiver or release does not comply with this subsection.

(continued)

Figure 7.1 (continued)

> (2) To rebut the presumption that the injury or damage to the minor child arose from an inherent risk involved in the activity, a claimant must demonstrate by clear and convincing evidence that the conduct, condition, or other cause resulting in the injury or damage was not an inherent risk of the activity.
>
> (3) If a presumption under this paragraph is rebutted, liability and compensatory damages must be established by a preponderance of the evidence.
>
> (d) Nothing in this subsection limits the ability of natural guardians, on behalf of any of their minor children, to waive and release, in advance, any claim or cause of action against a noncommercial activity provider, or its owners, affiliates, employees, or agents, to the extent authorized by common law.
>
> (4) All instruments executed by a natural guardian for the benefit of the ward under the powers specified in this section are binding on the ward. The natural guardian may not, without a court order, use the property of the ward for the guardian's benefit or to satisfy the guardian's support obligation to the ward.

behalf without the necessity of a court proceeding. If, on the other hand, Myra's older brother, Bart Minor, was very seriously injured in the same automobile accident and the insurance company offered $200,000.00 to settle all claims, Bart's parents could not accept or administer the funds without being appointed by the court as guardians ad litem. A **guardian ad litem** is a guardian appointed by a court to protect a minor who brings or defends a lawsuit. Figure 7.2 depicts the applicable Florida statute.

Most states have similar limitations on the dollar amount that parents can administer on behalf of their minor children based solely on their position as natural guardians without further appointment by the court in their jurisdiction. If the set dollar amount is exceeded, then a parent must petition to be appointed as a guardian ad litem, if a lawsuit is involved, or as a conservator, if the minor is otherwise in receipt of substantial funds. A parent who needs to apply for a conservatorship would do so using the same court process that is discussed later in this chapter.

Figure 7.2 2012 Florida Statutes §744.3025, Claims of Minors

> (1) (a) The court may appoint a guardian ad litem to represent the minor's interest before approving a settlement of the minor's portion of the claim in any case in which a minor has a claim for personal injury, property damage, wrongful death, or other cause of action in which the gross settlement of the claim exceeds $15,000.
>
> (b) The court shall appoint a guardian ad litem to represent the minor's interest before approving a settlement of the minor's claim in any case in which the gross settlement involving a minor equals or exceeds $50,000.
>
> (c) The appointment of the guardian ad litem must be without the necessity of bond or notice.
>
> (d) The duty of the guardian ad litem is to protect the minor's interests as described in the Florida Probate Rules.
>
> (e) A court need not appoint a guardian ad litem for the minor if a guardian of the minor has previously been appointed and that guardian has no potential adverse interest to the minor. A court may appoint a guardian ad litem if the court believes a guardian ad litem is necessary to protect the interests of the minor.
>
> (2) Unless waived, the court shall award reasonable fees and costs to the guardian ad litem to be paid out of the gross proceeds of the settlement.

■ GUARDIANSHIP AND/OR CONSERVATORSHIP FOR MINOR CHILDREN

Appointment of a Guardian and Conservator for Minor Children

Of course, there are a variety of circumstances where a nonparent may need to petition the court to be appointed as guardian and/or conservator of a minor child. Sometimes, both parents are still alive but are incapacitated or otherwise unavailable to rear their children. Unfortunate circumstances warranting these proceedings include drug and alcohol abuse, imprisonment, mental illness, child abuse, and downright abandonment by the parents. When Child Protective Services (CPS) becomes involved in a case, they seek to place the children with other close relatives. In many states of the United States **Child Protective Services (CPS)** is the name of the governmental agency in that responds to reports of child abuse or neglect. Most CPS agencies fulfill most or all of the following functions: provide services to children and families in their own homes; place children in foster care; provide services to children in foster care to help transition them into adulthood; and place children in adoptive homes. Figure 7.3 contains the 2012 Florida statute, §744.3021, providing for the appointment of guardians for minor children.

Child Protective Services (CPS)
In many states of the United States, the name of a governmental agency that responds to reports of child abuse or neglect.

Appointment of Guardian and Conservator for Minor Children Under a Will

As was discussed in earlier chapters, one motivating factor for executing a will is to provide for the testator's minor children. Whether the minors reside in a one-parent or a two-parent home, it is very prudent to make arrangements in the event of a worst-case scenario. Parents may nominate a guardian and conservator under their last will and testament to serve without bond and care for any minor children in the event that the parents do not survive until the children are grown. Sample language is as follows:

> "In the event my wife predeceases me, I nominate, constitute, and appoint Sally Wisdom as Guardian and Conservator of my minor children. If Sally Wisdom is unwilling or unavailable to serve, I nominate and appoint Rebecca Wisdom to serve as alternate Guardian and Conservator. I direct that no bond shall be required of my Guardian and Conservator in any jurisdiction for the faithful performance of their duties."

Figure 7.3 2012 Florida Statutes §744.3021, Guardians of Minors

(1) Upon petition of a parent, brother, sister, next of kin, or other person interested in the welfare of a minor, a guardian for a minor may be appointed by the court without the necessity of adjudication pursuant to s. 744.331. A guardian appointed for a minor, whether of the person or property, has the authority of a plenary guardian.

(2) A minor is not required to attend the hearing on the petition for appointment of a guardian, unless otherwise directed by the court.

(3) In its discretion, the court may appoint an attorney to represent the interests of a minor at the hearing on the petition for appointment of a guardian.

As with any other appointment under a will, the person nominated must still petition the court to be legally appointed to serve as a guardian and/or conservator. However, making the nomination under the will is advantageous over doing nothing for a number of reasons. First, it reflects the parent's wishes and judgment with respect to whom is most fit to care for the parent's children. Second, in most instances (and preferably in all instances), the parent has consulted with the individual they are nominating as guardian and/or conservator and so the person has been made aware of this contingency plan and has consented to the nomination. Third, the waiver of bond under the will is preferable because it means the person can be appointed irrespective of financial situation and that will not have to go through the trouble or the process of posting a bond before being allowed to serve. Finally, the court will normally give priority for appointment to a petitioner who was nominated under a will over any applicant who was not. Figure 7.4 contains the 2012 Florida statute, §744.3046, which outlines

Figure 7.4 2012 Florida Statutes §744.3046, Preneed Guardian for Minor

(1) Both parents, natural or adoptive, if living, or the surviving parent, may nominate a preneed guardian of the person or property or both of the parent's minor child by making a written declaration that names such guardian to serve if the minor's last surviving parent becomes incapacitated or dies. The declarant or declarants may also name an alternate to the guardian to act if the designated preneed guardian refuses to serve, renounces the appointment, dies, or becomes incapacitated after the death of the last surviving parent of the minor.

(2) The written declaration must reasonably identify the declarant or declarants and the designated preneed guardian and must be signed by the declarant or declarants in the presence of at least two attesting witnesses present at the same time. The written declaration must also provide the following information for each minor child named in such declaration: the full name as it appears on the birth certificate or as ordered by a court, date of birth, and social security number, if any.

(3) The declarant must file the declaration with the clerk of the court. When a petition for incapacity of the last surviving parent or the appointment of a guardian upon the death of the last surviving parent is filed, the clerk shall produce the declaration.

(4) Production of the declaration in a proceeding to determine incapacity of the last surviving parent, or in a proceeding to appoint a guardian upon the death of the last surviving parent, constitutes a rebuttable presumption that the designated preneed guardian is entitled to serve as guardian. The court is not bound to appoint the designated preneed guardian if the designated preneed guardian is found to be unqualified to serve as guardian.

(5) The preneed guardian shall assume the duties of guardian immediately upon an adjudication of incapacity of the last surviving parent or the death of the last surviving parent.

(6) If the preneed guardian refuses to serve, a written declaration appointing an alternate preneed guardian constitutes a rebuttable presumption that the alternate preneed guardian is entitled to serve as guardian. The court is not bound to appoint the alternate preneed guardian if the alternate preneed guardian is found to be unqualified to serve as guardian.

(7) Within 20 days after assumption of duties as guardian, a preneed guardian shall petition for confirmation of appointment. If the court finds the preneed guardian to be qualified to serve as guardian, appointment of the guardian must be confirmed. Each guardian so confirmed shall file an oath in accordance with s. 744.347 and shall file a bond, if the court requires a bond. Letters of guardianship must then be issued in the manner provided in s. 744.345.

(8) The clerk shall maintain all declarations filed pursuant to this section until:

   (a) A petition for incapacity of the last surviving parent is filed or petition for the appointment of a guardian upon the death of the last surviving parent is filed as provided in subsection (3); or

   (b) All minor children named in the declaration have reached the age of majority.

the requirements in Florida for parents to appoint a preneed guardian for minor children in the event of the death or incapacity of both parents.

The next section of this chapter illustrates what must be done in order for a guardian and/or a conservator of a minor to be appointed by the court.

■ PROCEDURE FOR APPOINTMENT OF GUARDIAN AND CONSERVATOR FOR A MINOR

The person seeking appointment (the petitioner) as guardian and/or conservator has to complete the appropriate initial paperwork to be filed with the court. A **petitioner** is one who presents a formal, written application to a court, officer, or legislative body that requests action on a certain matter.

The initial court paperwork is likely to include the following:

- Petition for Appointment as Guardian and/or Conservator
- Affidavit of Person to Be Appointed
- Consent of Parent and Waiver of Notice (if applicable)
- Consent to Appointment and Waiver of Notice (if applicable, from family members with equal right to appointment)
- Letters of Appointment and Acceptance of Appointment
- Order of Appointment
- Order to Guardian/Conservator and Acknowledgment

The foregoing list contains the most commonly required forms, but specific requirements vary by state. Note that in instances where the minor child's parents are still alive but are unable to care for the minor, it is desirable to have the parents consent to the petitioner's appointment by filling out a Consent of Parent and Waiver of Notice form. For example, if a minor child has one living parent but the parent is too ill to care for the child, he or she may consent to the appointment of a family member to become the child's guardian and caregiver. However, if there are surviving parents but the parents do not consent to the petitioner's appointment, there is likely to be a court battle in which the judge will decide what is in the best interests of the minor child under the circumstances. Figure 7.5 is the Petition for Appointment filed by Jane Smith, from the Hypothetical Family, asking to be appointed as guardian and conservator of her nephew, Mark Smith, Jr., following the untimely death of Mark's parents in a car accident.

In addition to the Petition, Jane Smith was also required to complete the Affidavit depicted in Figure 7.6 demonstrating that she was qualified to seek appointment as Mark's guardian and conservator.

Figure 7.5 Petition for Appointment

```
1001 Reed Drive
Sample County, Sample State 12345
(928) 788-1234
(928) 788-1235 (Facsimile)
michael.pearson@pearsonlaw.com
Attorney for Petitioner
```

(continued)

Figure 7.5 (continued)

IN THE SUPERIOR COURT OF THE STATE OF SAMPLE
IN AND FOR THE COUNTY OF SAMPLE

In The Matter of the Guardianship and/or)   Case No.: GC-2008-1009
Conservatorship of:)
)
MARK SMITH, JR.,)   **PETITION FOR PERMANENT APPOINTMENT OF**
A Minor.)   **GUARDIAN AND/OR CONSERVATOR OF A MINOR**
)
)
)

REQUIRED INFORMATION ABOUT PETITIONER,
UNDER OATH OR AFFIRMATION

1. INFORMATION ABOUT ME (The Petitioner):
Name: Jane Smith
Street Address: 123 Oak Street
City, State, Zip: Sample City, Sample State 12345
Telephone: (928) 321-4153   Date of Birth: 09-13-1963

✓ I am related by blood to the person who needs a guardian and/ or conservator ("the minor").
(If applicable) HOW I am related to the minor: <u>I am his aunt</u>.

2. INFORMATION ABOUT THE MINOR WHO NEEDS A GUARDIAN AND/ OR CONSERVATOR. The minor is called the proposed ward (for the guardianship) and proposed protected person (for the conservatorship):
Name: Mark Smith, Jr.
Street Address: 123 Oak Street
City, State, Zip: Sample City, Sample State 12345
Telephone: (928) 321-4153
Date of Birth: 02-10-1993
The Minor is ☐ married or ☒ unmarried.
Mother's Name: Maya Smith (Deceased)
Mother's Address: Not Applicable
Father's Name: Mark Smith (Deceased)
Father's Address: Not Applicable

3. PERSON(S) ENTITLED TO NOTICE of this Court matter under Sample law. S.R.S. § 14-5207 for guardians, and § 14-5405 for conservators, and to whom I will give notice of this case.
MOTHER (Not Applicable- Deceased)
FATHER (Not Applicable- Deceased)
THE MINOR (If over 14):
Mark Smith, Jr.
123 Oak Street
Sample City, Sample State 12345
<u>OTHER PERSON ENTITLED TO NOTICE:</u>
Name   Address   Relationship to Minor

A. Shirley Smith, 121 Oak Street, Sample City, Sample State 12345, Grandmother
B. Robert Smith, 125 Oak Street, Sample City, Sample State 12345, Uncle

Figure 7.5 (continued)

4. ASSETS OF THE MINOR I SAY NEEDS GUARDIAN AND/OR MINOR CONSERVATOR
   (Check one box)

   ☐ The minor who needs a guardian and/or conservator has no substantial assets or income. No bond by petitioner is <u>required: OR</u>

   ☒ The minor who needs a guardian and/or conservator has assets and/or annual income in the approximate amount of $0.00.

   Explain: <u>The minor is the contingent beneficiary of a life insurance policy in the amount of $100,000.00.</u>

5. PERSON TO BE APPOINTED GUARDIAN AND/OR CONSERVATOR (Complete this section only if the person is a different person than Petitioner):

   <u>Same as above.</u>

   ☒ The person to be appointed guardian and/or conservator is related by blood to the minor who needs a guardian and/or conservator. If "yes" above. HOW is the person to be appointed guardian and/or conservator related to the minor? <u>Aunt.</u>

6. INFORMATION REGARDING GUARDIANSHIP AND/OR CONSERVATORSHIP to the best of my knowledge (check one box):

   ☒ No guardian and/or conservator has been appointed by Will or by any Court Order, and no Court proceedings and pending for such appointment:

         OR,

   ☐ Someone has been appointed guardian and/or conservator or Court proceedings and pending. Explain who, when, in what court, and if the appointee is guardian and/or conservator):

   _____

7. PARENTAL RIGHTS. All parental rights of custody regarding the minor have been suspended or terminated by:

   ☐ Written consent of the parent(s) to the guardianship and/or conservatorship. (Notarized copy must be attached)

   ☐ Abandonment of the minor for at least six (6) months prior to the filing of this Petition.

   ☐ Prior court order **(You must provide the Court with a certified copy of the order.)**

   ☒ Other Circumstances: (Explain)

   <u>The minor's parents both passed away in a tragic car accident on June 10, 2008.</u>

8. REASONS FOR CONSERVATORSHIP: (Check one or more of the boxes if applicable) The minor needs a conservator because

   ☒ The minor owns money or property that requires management or protection that cannot be otherwise provided.

   ☒ The minor may have business affairs that may be jeopardized or prevented by his or her minority.

   ☒ The minor needs funds for his or her support and education and protection is necessary or desirable to obtain or provide funds.

9. REASONS FOR REQUESTED PERSON TO BE APPOINTED GUARDIAN AND/OR CONSERVATOR: (Check one or more of the boxes that you think apply to the relationship of the proposed guardian and/or conservator to the person you say requires a guardian):

   ☒ Proposed appointee was selected by the minor, who is at least 14 years old and who has sufficient mental capacity to make an intelligent choice.

   ☐ Proposed appointee is the spouse of the minor.

   ☐ Proposed appointee is the parent of the minor.

   ☒ Proposed appointee is a relative of the minor and has had care and custody of the minor for the last 6 months prior to filing this Petition.

   ☐ Proposed appointee was chosen to be the guardian by someone who is caring for the minor or is paying benefits for the minor.

   ☐ Proposed appointee is a person selected by the Will of a deceased parent

(continued)

Figure 7.5 (continued)

☐ Proposed appointee is a public fiduciary, a professional guardian, a conservator, or the Sample Veteran's Service Commission.

☐ The proposed appointee is not related by blood to the minor and the person will submit a full set of fingerprints to the court required by S.R.S. § 14-5206.

☐ Written consent of the parents to the conservatorship.

10. REASONS I AM ASKING FOR A GUARDIANSHIP AND/OR CONSERVATORSHIP ORDER: The appointment of a guardian and/or conservator for the minor is necessary or desirable to provide continuing care and supervision of the minor and is in the best interests of the minor because

(Explain):

The minor's parents both passed away in a tragic car accident on June 10, 2008. We have a very close family and his closest surviving relatives are his grandmother, Shirley Smith, and his uncle, Robert Smith, who have both agreed that I should be appointed as Guardian and Conservator. Mark Smith, Jr. is very close to my two children and has been residing in my home since his parents' death. He has further expressed that he desires I be appointed for this position.

REQUIRED STATEMENTS TO THE COURT, UNDER OATH OR AFFIRMATION: (Note: All of these statements must be true and you must check the box for each statement to indicate to the Court that each statement is true, or you cannot file this Petition.)

11. ☒ TRUE   This Court is the proper Venue for this case because the minor who needs a guardian and/or conservator lives or is present in this county.

12. ☒ TRUE   The person who is requested to be the guardian and/or conservator has completed the required document called Affidavit of Person to be Appointed as Guardian and/or Conservator and is filing the Affidavit with this Petition as required by Sample law, S.R.S. § 14-5106, and/or § 14-5410.

REQUESTS TO THE COURT FOR AN ORDER, UNDER OATH OR AFFIRMATION:

1. Schedule a hearing to determine if a guardianship and/or conservatorship is appropriate;
2. After Petitioner gives notice of the hearing to all interested persons and to those required by law, hold a hearing to determine if the court should order a guardianship and/or conservatorship;
3. Appoint a permanent guardian and/or conservator of the minor; and
4. Make any other orders the Court decides are in the best interests of the minor.

OATH OR AFFIRMATION

STATE OF SAMPLE

COUNTY OF SAMPLE

I, the Petitioner, declare under penalty of perjury, that I have read this Petition. All the statements in the Petition are true and correct and complete to the best of my knowledge and belief.

DATE: *July 22, 2008*

Jane Smith
_____
JANE SMITH

SWORN TO OR AFFIRMED before me this 22nd day of July 2008 by JANE SMITH.

Lila P. Legal
_____
Notary Public

LILA P. LEGAL Notary Public, State of Sample Sample County My Commission Expires May 10, 2012

Figure 7.6 Affidavit of Person to be Appointed

Pearson & Pearson, Attorneys-At-Law
1001 Reed Drive
Sample County, Sample State 12345
(928) 788-1234
(928) 788-1235 (Facsimile)
michael.pearson@pearsonlaw.com
Attorney for Petitioner

IN THE SUPERIOR COURT OF THE STATE OF SAMPLE
IN AND FOR THE COUNTY OF SAMPLE

In the Matter of the Guardianship and/or conservatorship of))) MARK SMITH, JR.,) A Minor.)	Case No.: GC-2009-1009 **AFFIDAVIT OF PERSON TO BE APPOINTED** **GUARDIAN AND/OR CONSERVATOR**

INSTRUCTIONS: The person who wants to be appointed the guardian and/or conservator must answer each statement as TRUE or FALSE. Each answer that is false must be explained in writing in an attachment to this Affidavit.

STATEMENT MADE UNDER OATH TO THE COURT; Sample law S.R.S. § 14-5100 requires the person seeking appointment to answer the following items. This document must be filed with the Petition for Appointment of Guardian and/or Conservator.

1. ☒ True or ☐ False.   I have not been convicted of a felony in any jurisdiction.

2. ☒ True or ☐ False.   I have not acted as a guardian and/or conservator for another person for at least three years before I filed this Petition.

3. ☒ True or ☐ False.   I know and understand the powers and duties I would have as a guardian and/or conservator.

4. ☒ True or ☐ False.   I have not had a power of attorney for anyone for at least three years before I filed this Petition.

5. ☒ True or ☐ False.   I am not, to the best of my knowledge, listed in the Child Abuse Registry at the Office of the Sample Attorney General.

6. ☒ True or ☐ False.   To the best of my knowledge, no business in which I have an interest is listed in the Child Abuse Registry at the Office of the Sample Attorney General.

7. ☒ True or ☐ False.   Sample law requires that a guardian and/or conservator file an annual report/ accounting with the court. If I have been a guardian/conservator before, I filed the required documents either on time or within 3 months of receiving a notice from the court that the report/ accounting was due.

8. ☒ True or ☐ False.   I have never been removed by the Court as a guardian and/or conservator.

9. ☒ True or ☐ False.   The nature of my relationship to the proposed minor or protected person is: I am his aunt.

10. ☒ True or ☐ False.   I met the proposed minor under the following circumstances: I am his aunt.

11. ☒ True or ☐ False.   I have never received anything of value greater than a total of one hundred dollars in any one year by gift, or will, or inheritance from an individual or the estate of an individual to whom I was not related by blood or marriage and for whom I served at any time as guardian and/or conservator, trustee, or attorney-in-fact.

12. ☒ True or ☐ False.   No business in which I have an interest has ever received anything of value greater than a total of one hundred dollars in any one year by gift, or will, or inheritance from an individual or the estate of an individual to whom I am not related by blood or marriage and for whom I served at any time as guardian and/or conservator, trustee, or attorney-in-fact.

13. ☒ True or ☐ False.   To the best of my knowledge, I am not named as a personal representative, trustee, beneficiary, or other type of beneficiary for any individual to whom I am not related by blood or marriage and for whom I have ever served as guardian and/or conservator, trustee, or attorney-in-fact.

(continued)

Figure 7.6 (continued)

14. ☒ True or ☐ False.   To the best of my knowledge, no business in which I have an interest is named as a personal representative, trustee, beneficiary, or other type of beneficiary for any individual to whom I am not related by blood or marriage and for whom I have ever served as guardian and/or conservator, trustee, or attorney-in-fact.

15. ☒ True or ☐ False.   I have no interest in any business that provides housing, health care, nursing care, residential care, assisted living, home health services, or comfort care services to any individual.

OATH OF THE PERSON SEEKING TO BE APPOINTED AS GUARDIAN AND/OR CONSERVATOR:

STATE OF SAMPLE   )
SAMPLE COUNTY   ) ss.

I have read, understood, and completed the above statements and the attached document. Everything I have said is true and correct to the best of my knowledge, information, and belief.

Signature: *Jane Smith* _____

SWORN TO OR AFFIRMED before me this 22nd day of July 2008 by JANE SMITH.

Lila P. Legal _____
Notary Public

> **LILA P. LEGAL**
> Notary Public, State of Sample
> Sample County
> My Commission Expires May 10, 2012

In addition, Jane Smith signed the acceptance portion of the Letters of Permanent Guardian and Conservator and Acceptance of Appointment depicted in Figure 7.7 and filed them with the court prior to being appointed and in contemplation of her petition being approved.

Figure 7.7 Letters and Acceptance of Appointment

Pearson & Pearson, Attorneys-At-Law
1001 Reed Drive
Sample County, Sample State 12345
(928) 788-1234
(928) 788-1235 (Facsimile)
michael.pearson@pearsonlaw.com
Attorney for Petitioner

IN THE SUPERIOR COURT OF THE STATE OF SAMPLE IN AND FOR THE COUNTY OF SAMPLE

In the Matter of the Guardianship and/or Conservatorship of:	) Case No.: GC-2008-1009
	)
	) **LETTERS OF PERMANENT GUARDIAN AND**
MARK SMITH, JR.,	) **CONSERVATOR AND ACCEPTANCE OF LETTERS**
A Minor.	) **OF APPOINTMENT**
	)

Figure 7.7 (continued)

ISSUANCE OF LETTERS:

1. **This person is appointed:** JANE SMITH as permanent guardian and/or conservator for the above captioned minor.
2. **Reason for appointment:** The above-captioned minor is an incapacitated ward and/or protected person.
3. **Length of appointment:** Until further order of this court.
4. **Restrictions** that apply to this permanent appointment, by order of the court: **None.**
5. **Mental Health Care:**

☐ **OUTPATIENT MENTAL HEATH CARE.** The guardian and/or conservator has the authority to consent for the Ward/Incapacitated person to receive outpatient mental health care and treatment.

☐ **INPATIENT MENTAL HEALTH CARE.** The guardian and/or conservator has the authority to place the ward in a level one behavioral health facility for inpatient mental health care and treatment. This authority expires on _____ (date).

DATE: *9/28/2008*.

Rachael Bright
Clerk of the Superior Court

By   *Simon Summers*
Deputy Clerk

ACCEPTANCE OF LETTERS OF APPOINTMENT

STATE OF SAMPLE   )
) ss.
County of Sample   )

I hereby accept the duties of permanent guardian and\or conservator of MARK SMITH, JR. and do so solemnly swear that I will perform these duties according to law.

Jane Smith
Guardian and/or Conservator

SWORN TO OR AFFIRMED before me this 22nd day of July 2008 by JANE SMITH.

Lila P. Legal
Notary Public

| LILA P. LEGAL |
| Notary Public, State of Sample |
| Sample County |
| My Commission Expires May 10, 2012 |

Shortly after filing the case, the court set a hearing date to consider the petition and ascertain whether it was in the best interest of the minor child to have Jane Smith appointed as guardian and conservator of Mark Smith, Jr.

Jane then provided notice of the hearing to all interested parties, including the ward, since the law in her jurisdiction required that she notify the minor if he was over fourteen, and he was age fifteen at the time.

Jane's family members attended the hearing and expressed their support for her appointment as guardian and conservator. The judge quickly determined that a guardianship and conservatorship was necessary and that Jane should be appointed. He then signed the orders depicted in Figures 7.8 and 7.9 and directed the Clerk of the Court to issue the Letters of Appointment, displayed in Figure 7.7.

Figure 7.8 Order of Appointment

Pearson & Pearson, Attorneys-At-Law
1001 Reed Drive
Sample County, Sample State 12345
(928) 788-1234
(928) 788-1235 (Facsimile)
michael.pearson@pearsonlaw.com
Attorney for Petitioner

IN THE SUPERIOR COURT OF THE STATE OF SAMPLE
IN AND FOR THE COUNTY OF MOHAVE

In the Matter of the Guardianship and/or Conservatorship of:	) Case No.: GC-2008-1009
	)
	) **ORDER OF APPOINTMENT OF A PERMANENT**
MARK SMITH, JR.,	) **GUARDIAN AND/OR CONSERVATOR OF A MINOR**
A Minor.	)

The Court has read the sworn or affirmed Petition for Permanent Appointment of a Guardian and/or Conservator of a Minor and held a hearing to determine whether the Court should enter the Order requested in the Petition.

THE COURT FINDS:

1. Petitioner is entitled to file said Petition under S.R.S. §14-5303(A) and §14-5404(A).
2. Petitioner has given Notice of Hearing as required by law, or all interested parties have waived Notice of Hearing.
3. Venue in this county is proper
4. **Guardianship and/or Conservatorship:**

   a. The above-captioned person is an unmarried minor born on February 10, 1993.

   b. ☒ All parental rights of custody have been terminated or suspended by written consent of the parent(s), prior court order, or other circumstances.

   c. ☒ No guardian of the minor has been appointed by Will or any Order of any Court, and no other proceedings for the appointment of a guardian are pending in any other Court.

   d. Appointment of a Conservator is necessary because the minor owns money or property that requires management or protection which cannot otherwise be provided or has or may have business affairs which may be jeopardized or prevented by his or her minority or the minor needs funds for his or her education and protection is necessary or desirable to obtain or provide funds.

   e. A criminal background check has been reviewed and the Court has concluded that it contains nothing to prevent the appointment; *or* X No fingerprint or background check was required.

   f. ☒ JANE SMITH is qualified to serve as guardian and/or conservator for the minor.

IT IS, THEREFORE, ORDERED that (Check boxes that apply).

1. **APPOINTMENT OF GUARDIAN AND/OR CONSERVATOR:** The Court appoints JANE SMITH as permanent guardian and/or conservator for the minor(s) named in the caption above.
2. **BOND:** The guardian and/or conservator will serve without bond, restricted letters to issue to him or her upon acceptance of the appointment, OR

   ☒ Bond is set in the amount of $100,000.00.

Figure 7.8 (continued)

3. **FUNDS:** ☒ The minor's funds are to be deposited in this jurisdiction, in a federally insured, interest bearing account titled "The Estate of (name of minor), by (name of conservator)."

4. **RESTRICTED ACCOUNT:** The account is to be restricted, and no withdrawal of principal or interest shall be permitted by the depository except upon receipt of a certified copy of an Order of this Court authorizing the withdrawal.

5. **REINVESTMENT:** The depository may, however permit reinvestment of the funds within the depository without further Order of the Court so long as the funds remain restricted in the same institution, at the same branch.

6. **PROOF OF RESTRICTED ACCOUNT:** The conservator may only hold funds in a depository which agrees to be bound by the terms of this Order and to make written proof of its agreement to be bound, including such proof of the account, the account number, the amount of the deposit the notarized signature of the depository branch manager, and the agreement not to permit any withdrawal unless it is first provided with a certified copy of this Court's Order permitting the withdrawal.

7. **ESTABLISHING RESTRICTED ACCOUNT:** The __conservator or __attorney for the minor or __attorney for the conservator is responsible for establishing the restricted account and filing the proof required by this Order with the Court within 30 days of this Order.

8. **UNRESTRICTED LETTERS:** Upon entry of the Order, Letters of Guardianship and/or Conservatorship of a Minor shall be issued by the Clerk of the Court, WITHOUT RESTRICTION.

9. ☒ **ACCEPTANCE OF LETTERS:** The guardian and/or conservator shall sign the Acceptance of the Letters under oath, and file the Acceptance with the Clerk of the Court.

10. ☒ **ANNUAL REPORT OF GUARDIAN:** The guardian shall report to the Court *in writing* on the status of the minor and the need to continue the guardianship at least annually by: September 28th (date) as required by S.R.S. §14-5315, by filing the required form with the Clerk of the Court.

11. ☒ **ANNUAL ACCOUNTING OF CONSERVATOR:** ☒ The conservator shall report to the Court for the administration of the protected person's property by filing an accounting on before September 28th and every year thereafter and must petition the Court for approval of the annual accounting as required by S.R.S. § 14-5319. OR __Annual Accounting is waived and is not required to be filed with the court.

12. **CHANGE OF ADDRESS:** The guardian and/or conservator shall immediately notify the Court in writing of any change in the address of himself or herself or of the minor.

13. **OTHER DUTIES UNDER THE LAW:** The duties of the guardian and or/conservator as required by Sample law and as set forth in this Order of Appointment and the Order to Guardian and/or Conservators and Acknowledgement shall continue until the minor turns 18 or until the guardian and/or conservator is discharged from these duties by Order of this Court. The guardian and/or conservator should still petition the Court to officially terminate his or her guties when the minor turns 18 or if the guardianship and/or conservatorship otherwise terminated by operation of law.

14. **IT IS FURTHER ORDERED** to set this matter for internal review to determine compliance by the person appointed with this Order on October 15, 2009, at 9:00 A.M.

DONE IN OPEN COURT this *28th* day of September, 2008.

Harold Shoemaster
Judge of the Superior Court

Figure 7.9 Order to Guardian and Acknowledgment

1001 Reed Drive
Sample County, Sample State 12345
(928) 788-1234
(928) 788-1235 (Facsimile)
michael.pearson@pearsonlaw.com
Attorney for Petitioner

(continued)

Figure 7.9 (continued)

IN THE SUPERIOR COURT OF THE STATE OF SAMPLE
IN AND FOR THE COUNTY OF SAMPLE

In the Matter of the Guardianship and/or Conservatorship of: MARK SMITH, JR., A Minor.	) Case No.: GC-2008-1009)) **ORDER TO GUARDIAN AND ACKNOWLEDGMENT**)))

The welfare and best interest of the person named above ("your ward") are matters of great concern to this Court. By accepting appointment as guardian, you have subjected yourself to the power and supervision of the Court. Therefore, to assist you in the performance of your duties, this order is entered. You are required to be guided by it and comply with its provisions as it relates to your duties as guardian of your ward to your duties as his/her guardian as follows:

1. You have powers and responsibilities similar to those of a parent of a minor child, except that you are not legally obligated to contribute to the support of your ward from your own funds.

2. Unless the order appointing you provides otherwise, your duties and responsibilities include (but are not limited to) making appropriate arrangements to see that your ward's personal needs (such as food, clothing, and shelter) are met.

3. You are responsible for making decisions concerning your ward's educational, social, and religious activities. If your ward is 14 years of age or older, you must take into account the ward's preferences to the extent they are known to you or can be discovered with a reasonable amount of effort.

4. You are responsible for making decisions concerning your ward's medical needs. Such decisions include (but are not limited to) the decision to place your ward in a nursing home or other health care facility and the employment of doctors, nurses, or other professionals to provide for your ward's health care needs. However, you are to use the least restrictive means and environment available that meet your ward's needs.

5. You may arrange for medical care to be provided even if your ward does not wish to have it, **but you may not place your ward in a level one behavioral health facility against your ward's will unless the Court specifically has authorized you to consent to such placement.**

6. You may handle small amounts of money or property belonging to your ward without being appointed conservator. As a general rule, "small amount" means that the ward does not receive income (from all sources) exceeding $10,000 per year, does not accumulate excess funds exceeding that amount, and does not own real property. If more that these amounts come into your possession, or are accumulated by you, you are required to petition the Court for the appointment of a conservator.

7. If you handle any money or property belonging to your ward, you have a duty to do each of the following:

    a. Care for and protect your ward's personal effects;

    b. Apply any monies you receive for your ward's current support, care, and educational needs;

    c. Conserve any excess funds not so spent for your ward's future needs;

    d. Maintain your ward's funds in a separate account, distinct from your own and identified as belonging to the ward;

    e. Maintain records of all of the ward's property received an expended during the period of the guardianship;

    f. Account to your ward or your ward's successors at the termination of the guardianship, if requested; and

    g. Not purchase, lease, borrow, or use your ward's property or money for your benefit or anyone else's, without prior Court approval.

8. You shall not accept any remuneration of any kind for placing your ward in a particular nursing home or other care facility, using a certain doctor, or using a certain lawyer. "Remuneration" includes, but is not limited to, direct or indirect payments of money, "kickbacks," gifts, favors, and other kinds of personal benefits.

9. You will need to obtain a certified copy of the Letters that are issued to you by the Clerk of the Superior Court. Your certified copy is proof of your authority to act as guardian of your ward, and you should have this document available when acting on behalf of your ward. You may need to obtain additional (or updated) copies from time to time for delivery to, or inspection by, the people with whom you are dealing.

Figure 7.9 (continued)

10. You are required to report annually, in writing, with respect to your ward's residence, physical and mental health, whether there still is a need for a guardian, and (if there is no conservator) your ward's financial situation. Your report is due each year on the anniversary date of your appointment. In addition to sending copies to the other persons named in the statute, you are directed to lodge a copy of your annual report with the appropriate Judge of this Court.

11. If your ward's physical address changes, you shall notify the Court by updating the probate information form within three days of learning of the change in your ward's physical address. If your ward dies, you shall notify the Court in writing of the ward's death within ten days of learning that the ward has died.

12. You must be conscious at all times of the needs and best interests of your ward. If the circumstances that made a guardianship necessary should end, you are responsible for petitioning the Court to terminate the guardianship and obtaining your discharge as guardian. Even if the guardianship should terminate by operation of law, you will not be discharged from your responsibilities until you have obtained an order from this Court discharging you.

13. If you should be unable to continue with your duties for any reason, you (or your guardian or conservator, if any) must petition the Court to accept your resignation and appoint a successor. If you should die, your personal representative or someone acting on your behalf must advise the Court and petition for the appointment of a successor.

14. If you have any questions about the meaning of this order or the duties that it and the statutes impose upon you by reason of your appointment as guardian, you should consult an attorney or petition the Court for instructions.

15. If you are not a certified fiduciary and are not related by blood or marriage to the ward, you are not entitled to compensation for your service as the ward's guardian. *See* S.R.S. §14-5651 (J)(I).

This is an outline of some of your duties as a guardian. It is your responsibility to obtain proper legal advice about your duties. Failure to do so may result in personal financial liability for any losses.

WARNING: FAILURE TO OBEY THE ORDERS OF THIS COURT AND THE STATUTORY PROVISIONS RELATING TO GUARDIANS MAY RESULT IN YOUR REMOVAL FROM THE OFFICE AND OTHER PENALTIES. IN SOME CIRCUMSTANCES, YOU MAY BE HELD IN CONTEMPT OF COURT, AND YOU CONTEMPT MAY BE PUNISHED BY CONFINEMENT IN JAIL, FINE, OR BOTH.

DATED this 28th day of September, 2008.

Harold Shoemaster
Judge of the Superior Court

DATE: July 22, 2008

Jane Smith
JANE SMITH

STATE OF SAMPLE)
) ss.
County of Sample)

SUBSCRIBED AND SWORN TO before me this 22nd day of July 2008 by JANE SMITH.

Lila P. Legal
Notary Public

LILA P. LEGAL
Notary Public, State of Sample
Sample County
My Commission Expires May 10, 2012

PARALEGAL PRACTICE TIP

■ *When representing a guardian and/or conservator, make sure they understand the importance of careful record keeping, as they will later have to account to the court and interested parties for every transaction.*

From that point forward, Jane had legal authority to act as guardian and conservator until Mark, Jr. reached the majority age of eighteen. As was directed by the order, Jane filed an annual report in her capacity as guardian. She further filed an annual accounting in her capacity as conservator showing her expenditures of the ward's funds and assets on behalf of the ward. When Mark, Jr., reached majority age, Jane was required to file final reports with the court. Upon approval of her final accounting, Mark, Jr., received the remaining funds from his parents' estate.

The process for appointing a guardian and/or conservator of an incapacitated adult has many similarities and is covered below.

■ OUTLINE OF PROCEDURE FOR GUARDIANSHIP AND CONSERVATORSHIP OF AN ADULT

The court process for appointing a guardian and/or conservator of an adult is very similar to that for a minor, with some additional requirements. As with minors, the process will go more smoothly if a person has already been nominated to serve as guardian and/or conservator. Figure 7.10 is the Florida statute section outlining how an adult may appoint a preneed guardian. Notice that generally the requirements for the written declaration under (2) would be met by a properly executed will containing the appointment of a guardian.

Having a preneed guardian appointed helps the process to go more smoothly, but even an appointed guardian still must be approved by the court. The person seeking appointment (the petitioner) first has to complete the appropriate initial paperwork to be filed with the court.

That paperwork is likely to include a Petition for Appointment of Guardian and/or Conservator for Ward; An Affidavit of Person to Be Appointed; A Motion for Appointment of Attorney for Ward, Medical Professional, and Court Investigator; A Consent to Appointment and Waiver of Notice (if applicable,

Figure 7.10 2012 Florida Statutes §744.3045, Preneed Guardian

1. A competent adult may name a preneed guardian by making a written declaration that names such guardian to serve in the event of the declarant's incapacity.

2. The written declaration must reasonably identify the declarant and preneed guardian and be signed by the declarant in the presence of at least two attesting witnesses present at the same time.

3. The declarant may file the declaration with the clerk of the court. When a petition for incapacity is filed, the clerk shall produce the declaration.

4. Production of the declaration in a proceeding for incapacity shall constitute a rebuttable presumption that the preneed guardian is entitled to serve as guardian. The court shall not be bound to appoint the preneed guardian if the preneed guardian is found to be unqualified to serve as guardian.

5. The preneed guardian shall assume the duties of guardian immediately upon an adjudication of incapacity.

6. If the preneed guardian refuses to serve, a written declaration appointing an alternate preneed guardian constitutes a rebuttable presumption that such preneed guardian is entitled to serve as guardian. The court is not bound to appoint the alternate preneed guardian if the alternate preneed guardian is found to be unqualified to serve as guardian.

7. Within 20 days after assumption of duties as guardian, a preneed guardian shall petition for confirmation of appointment. If the court finds the preneed guardian to be qualified to serve as guardian pursuant to ss. 744.309 and 744.312, appointment of the guardian must be confirmed. Each guardian so confirmed shall file an oath in accordance with s. 744.347 and shall file a bond, if required. Letters of guardianship must then be issued in the manner provided in s. 744.345.

from family members with equal right to appointment); Letters of Appointment and Acceptance; Order of Appointment; and an Order to Guardian/Conservator and Acknowledgment. These are the most common forms, but the requirements vary by state.

Shortly after filing the case, an attorney for the ward will be appointed by the court to determine and advise the court whether it is in the best interest of the ward to have a guardian and/or conservator appointed. A physician will also be appointed to examine the ward to make a determination of whether or not the individual is incapacitated and in need of a guardian and/or conservator. The physician and the attorney for the ward are generally both required to file a report with the court containing their recommendations. The physician for the ward will generally not be required to appear in court; however, the attorney for the ward will be required to appear at the hearing in most jurisdictions.

Once a hearing date is set, the petitioner will have to provide notice of the hearing to all other interested parties, *including the ward*. At the hearing, the judge will review the reports and listed to the proffered testimony and then make a determination whether the petitioner should be appointed. If the judge determines that a guardianship and/or conservatorship is necessary, the Letters will be issued (giving authority to act to the petitioner) and the judge will also sign the orders that were previously lodged with the court.

The appointed party will then have legal authority to act on the ward's behalf. They must also answer to the court on a continuous basis. If appointed as conservator, the party will be required to file regular accountings showing his or her expenditures of the ward's funds and assets on behalf of the ward. The accountings may be required to be filed annually, or more often, depending on state statute and the case itself. The guardianship and/or conservatorship will terminate either upon an adjudication by the court that the ward's incapacity has ended or upon the death of the ward. If the ward passes away, the conservator must continue to safeguard the funds until a personal representative is appointed to administer the ward's estate, at which time the conservator must distribute the assets to the personal representative.

■ AVOIDANCE OF GUARDIANSHIP AND CONSERVATORSHIP FOR AN ADULT

The necessity of going through the guardianship and conservatorship processes for an incompetent adult can be avoided through careful estate planning. A properly executed living will and health care proxy or living will with a health care power of attorney (depending on state law) prevents the need for a guardianship proceeding by appointing a health care agent to make medical decisions in advance, while the principal still has capacity to sign. Should the need for someone to make medical decisions on the principal's behalf arise in the future, he or she is covered and no court proceeding is necessary.

Likewise, a properly executed power of attorney authorizing the attorney-in-fact to make financial decisions on behalf of the principal negates the need for a conservatorship if the document signer later becomes incapacitated. A durable power of attorney is durable because it remains effective after the principal becomes incapacitated.

These relatively simple but very important documents can save clients and their families a whole lot of trouble and money by avoiding the need for a guardianship and conservatorship.

■ CONCLUSION

Guardianship is required when individuals are incompetent to make their own medical decisions and have not previously appointed an agent to make medical decisions on their behalf. A guardianship could also be required if the appointed agent is deceased or unable or unavailable to act. A conservatorship is commonly also necessary along with a guardianship to administer the ward's income and assets. In some jurisdictions, a guardian may be permitted to administer the ward's funds up to a nominal amount without the necessity of a guardianship. A conservatorship for an incapacitated adult can be avoided by executing a valid durable power of attorney.

Guardianships and conservatorships are court processes that serve very important functions in emergency situations where a person is incapacitated and has not previously appointed agents to act on his or her behalf. Guardianships and conservatorships are also required when children become orphaned or their parents become otherwise unfit or unable to care for the minors. Clients of all ages can save themselves and their family members' time, money, and effort by seeking legal counsel while they are healthy to formulate a comprehensive estate plan.

CONCEPT REVIEW AND REINFORCEMENT

KEY TERMS

Guardian 196	Conservator 196	Fiduciary Duty 196
Guardianship 196	Conservatorship 196	Fiduciary 196
Guardian Ad Litem 196	Ward 196	Child Protective Services (CPS) 199

REVIEW QUESTIONS

1. List some of the common forms required to appoint a guardian for a minor child.
2. When might a parent of a child need to petition the court for appointment as guardian ad litem?
3. What is the difference between a guardianship and a conservatorship?
4. What form(s) may be executed prior to incapacity to avoid the necessity of a guardianship proceeding?
5. What form can be executed prior to incapacity to avoid the necessity of a conservatorship?
6. List the forms that are commonly required to appoint a guardian for an incapacitated adult.
7. What is the role of the physician in an adult guardianship proceeding?
8. What is the role of the attorney for the ward in an adult guardianship proceeding?
9. Who must be notified of the court hearing in an adult guardianship proceeding?
10. What are some of the responsibilities of the guardian and conservator to the court after appointment?

PREPARE DOCUMENTS

1. _____

MEMORANDUM

To: Paralegal
From: Supervising Attorney
Client: Susan Smith
Re: Petition for Appointment as Permanent Guardian and Conservator of a Minor

Susan Smith met with me yesterday to discuss concerns about her niece, Katelyn Smith. Katelyn's father (Susan's brother) died tragically in a car accident last month and Susan has been taking care of Katelyn since then. Katelyn's mother has an alcohol addiction and has been in and out of Katelyn's life since shortly after her birth. A conservatorship will be necessary since there was a life insurance policy for Katelyn and wrongful death proceeds are also anticipated. Please draft the Petition for Appointment. (You may fill in any missing information as you see fit.)

2. _____

MEMORANDUM

To: Paralegal
From: Supervising Attorney
Client: Susan Smith
Re: Affidavit of Person to be Appointed as Guardian and Conservator

Please also draft the Affidavit of Person to be Appointed for the Susan Smith case.

3. _____

MEMORANDUM

To: Paralegal
From: Supervising Attorney
Client: Susan Smith
Re: Consent to Appointment and Waiver of Notice

Susan was able to get into contact with Katelyn's mother. Her name is Jessica Graves. She lives at 123 Dizzy Street, Anytown, Anystate, 23455. She will consent to Susan's appointment as Katelyn's guardian and conservator. Please draft the document. (You may fill in any missing information as you see fit.)

ONLINE RESOURCES

The Pearson Course Companion website contains the following additional resources:

- **Forms for Paralegal Practice Activities**
- Chapter Objectives
- Online Study Guide (Containing Multiple Choice and True/False Questions)
- Web Exercises www.pearsonhighered.com/careers

CASES FOR CONSIDERATION

CASE #1:

SOLOMON LEAKE and HAYDEN MAE LEAKE, Plaintiffs, against PHROSKA LEAKE McALISTER, Defendant.

2009 U.S. Dist. LEXIS 63561
July 21, 2009, Decided
July 21, 2009, Filed

OPINION BY: Colleen McMahon

OPINION

MEMORANDUM ORDER

McMahon, J.:

In this action ostensibly brought by two elderly Virginia residents to recover funds allegedly misappropriated from them by their daughter, who is an attorney in New York, the Court is confronted with the need to decide who should serve as plaintiff Solomon Leake's representative under Federal Rule of Civil Procedure 17(c). The Court assumes the parties' familiarity with the underlying facts of this case, and particularly with the Court's memorandum order of July 1, 2009, and memorandum to counsel of July 7, 2009.

A bit of history is in order. The issue of Mr. Leake's competence arose when, on the eve of trial, plaintiffs moved *in limine* under New York's Dead Man's Statute to preclude defendant Phroska Leake McAlister from testifying about certain personal transactions with her father that led to her obtaining money from him. (Dkt. ## 50, 55.) Plaintiffs asserted that the Dead Man's Statute barred Ms. McAlister's testimony because Mr. Leake was not competent to testify about those transactions himself. The Court directed plaintiff to obtain medical testimony on the issue, and plaintiffs' counsel recently provided the Court with the transcript of the May 6, 2009 deposition of Dr. William Yetter, a board certified psychiatrist and one of Mr. Leake's treating physicians. I was also provided with certain medical records of Mr. Leake.

Dr. Yetter testified that Mr. Leake suffers from "dementia, probably of the Alzheimer's type, with a history of delusions." (Vetter Dep. Tr. at 9:7) Medical records indicated that Mr. Leake was originally diagnosed with Alzheimer's some years ago. (Id. at 13:10-18;

30:23-31:7.) Dr. Yetter attended Mr. Leake during the latter's hospitalization from October 10, 2005 through November 22, 2005 at Chesapeake General Hospital (the "Hospital").[1] (Id. at 5:21-23.) When Mr. Leake was admitted to the hospital, Dr. Yetter testified that Mr. Leake was "very confused, very psychotic, very delusional." (Id. at 25:2-3.) According to Dr. Yetter,

> Well, [Mr. Leake] thought he was dead. He would lie in bed looking straight up at the ceiling. Sometimes he would be very profane and threatening, agitated, labile, meaning his moods were up and down.
>
> (Id. at 24:15-18.)

Mr. Leake's Hospital records reflect that, in the days before Mr. Leake was admitted to the Hospital, "he [had] not been eating, kind of manicy, reciting Shakespeare, rambling with flight of ideas, feeling the earth was round and people were going to fall off the edge." (Yetter Dep. Ex. 2 at 4.) The records also indicate that Mr. Leake "has been to Riverdale Hospital for psychiatric care before." (Id.) The circumstances and date of any prior hospitalization is not in the record before this Court.

During Mr. Leake's hospitalization he underwent a CAT scan of his brain, which showed "moderate central and peripheral cortical atrophy; in other words a shrinking of the brain." (Yetter Dep. Tr. at 27:25-28:3.) According to Dr. Vetter, "the fact that he had a shrinkage of his brain was very indicative of an Alzheimer's-looking picture." (Id. at 28:15-18.)

After Mr. Leake was discharged from the Hospital on November 22, 2005, records indicate that Dr. Yetter saw him eight additional times on an outpatient basis. (Id. at 6:2-4.) The dates of those visits were January 17, 2006; March 14, 2006; June 16, 2006; September 22, 2006; July 11, 2007; May 13, 2008; February 23,

---

[1]Dr. Yetter testified that Mr. Leake was an inpatient at the hospital from October 10, 2005 to November 22, 2005. However, Hospital records reflect Mr. Leake's admission date as "10/22/2005" and his discharge date as "11/22/05."

2009; and May 4, 2009. (Id. at 8:19-9:21.) Dr. Yetter's diagnosis of "dementia, probably of the Alzheimer's type, with a history of delusions" has remained consistent during all of Dr. Yetter's examinations of Mr. Leake. (Id. at 9:22-25.)

Dr. Yetter was asked specifically about whether Mr. Leake was competent at this time to testify about the issues in this lawsuit. Dr. Yetter responded, "No, I believe he is too confused." (Id. at 11:20.) Dr. Yetter testified that,

> When I last saw Mr. Leake on May the 4th of 2009, which was two days ago, I did on occasion tell him that I was doing to be giving a deposition over some matters regarding his daughter and funds and such, and he had no knowledge at all of what was going on, that he had done anything in the past, that he had given any powers. He didn't know what really was transpiring at all. I might add, this is very typical as an Alzheimer's patient will progress. This man was allegedly diagnosed back in 1997, according to hospital records, and this would give him approximately a 12-year history now of Alzheimer's, which is fairly remarkable for the Alzheimer's itself in terms of mortality statistics. But I would not expect his memory to have improved and would probably worsen since 1997. But he is not able to recall any kind of financial issues or really recall anything of this nature that's going on today.

(Id. at 13:2-20.) Dr. Yetter also testified that, at Mr. Leake's May 4, 2009, appointment, "he thought it was 1909. He didn't know what day the day was. He did get the month. He still couldn't spell [the word] world backwards, but he could spell world forwards." (Id. at 51:24-52:2.)

Dr. Yetter was not asked whether Mr. Leake was competent for any particular purpose—to testify, to make a will, to execute a power of attorney—on January 14, 2006, the date when the POA was signed. As will be seen, this omission from the deposition proves critically important.

When the Court reviewed Dr. Yetter's deposition transcript, it was apparent not only that Mr. Leake was not competent to testify, but also that he was not competent to continue the prosecution of this action in his own name. (See Dkt. # 56, Mem. and Order, dated 7/1/09.) Moreover, given Dr. Yetter's detailed description of Mr. Leake's delusional mental state in late 2005, and the consistency of his diagnosis in the months following his November 2005 hospitalization, the Court harbored concerns that Mr. Leake might not have been competent to prosecute this action in his own name in 2007, when the lawsuit was filed.

I therefore asked the parties to address what sort of intervention was required under Federal Rule of Civil Procedure 17(c).

At a hearing on July 6, 2009, plaintiffs' attorney advised the Court that another of Mr. Leake's daughters, Sundy Leake, had been given a power of attorney for her father, and proposed that Ms. Leake be appointed to represent her father in this action. (7/6/2009 Hr'g Tr. at 4:1-5:7.) Defendant, who is embroiled in a feud with her mother and sisters (especially Sundy), opposed the appointment of Ms. Leake as her father's representative, although Ms. McAlister concurs that someone should be appointed to represent him. (Id. at 7:20-25.)

At the July 6 hearing, Ms. Leake took the stand and was examined by plaintiffs' attorney and by defendant. The Court also propounded questions.

Ms. Leake, who lives in New York and works as a "medical editor" (id. at 48:5) testified that she has been taking care of her parents, both of whom are now over ninety years old, for several years. According to Ms. Leake, at some point it was determined that something needed to be done to "stop[] the hemorrhaging from what we thought—stopping the hemorrhaging from my father's bank account." (Id. at 12:3-5.) Ms. Leake testified that her mother and sister, Adrianne Leake-Gaylord, had begun to take steps to have a guardian of some sort appointed for her father by a Virginia court (Virginia being her parents' place of residence), but that she (Ms. Leake) aborted that process in favor of having her father execute a power of attorney making her his attorney-in-fact. (Id. at 10:18-11:2; 21:10-14.) When questioned about how she created the power of attorney, Ms. Leake testified that,

> Well, I was pretty desperate. I have a computer at home, basically, and I really was looking for something like a **guardianship** or a **conservatorship** because that's what my mother and sister were attempting to do. They had hired an attorney in Virginia. I even had a conversation with that particular lawyer in Virginia, but I didn't think that was the way to go. It was a matter of expediency and I had to do something immediately. So I went online and found something that I thought would pretty much cover my father's and my parent's [sic] needs.

(Id. at 10:8-112.) So instead of going forward with the legal guardianship process, on January 14, 2006, Ms. Leake obtained her father's signature on the durable power of attorney she downloaded from the internet (the "POA") giving Ms. Leake, and in the alternative her sister Adrianne Leake-Gaylord, his power of attorney.[2]

At the time Mr. Leake executed the POA, he was living in an assisted living facility, where he had been placed after his release from the Hospital. (Id. at 14:20.) According to Ms. Leake, her father was put in an assisted living facility because he "needed help with continuing his medicine schedule, whatever therapies are offered in assisted living." (Id. at 17:20-22.) On January 14, 2006, Ms. Leake took her father on a "day trip" out of this facility to have him sign the POA. (Id. at 14:20.) On that day, Ms. Leake testified, that her father "was subdued. He was medicated," and that "he was OK, again a very sick man who was recovering." (Id. at 15:1; 16:3-4.)

Ms. Leake drove her father to what Ms. Leake described as "a check cashing place" in Hampton, Va. (Id. at 26:11-17.) Ms. Leake testified that the notary working there who notarized the POA was unknown to the family and had never met Mr. Leake or Ms. Sundy Leake before January 14, 2006. (Id. at 20:15-22.) In addition to the notary, Ms. Sundy Leake and plaintiff Hayden Leake were the only people present when Mr. Leake signed the POA. (Id. at 26:1-10.) Adrianne Leake, Mr. Leake's other daughter who was listed as the successor to Ms. Leake in the POA, was not present. (Id. at 26:7-8; 35:2-3.)

Ms. Leake testified that she read the POA to her father and explained to him why he needed to sign it. (Id. at 20:12.) She further testified that her father signed the POA on the second to last page of the fifteen-page document, and placed his initials of every page of the document. (Id. at 11:8-13.) The Court asked Ms. Leake whether it was her "perception that [her] father was at that point *not* competent to manage his affairs?" to which, she answered, "Oh Absolutely." (Id. at 12:8-10) (emphasis added). Later on Ms. Leake was asked by plaintiffs' counsel, Mr. Simon, whether she had a "discussion with her father as to the nature of the document?" and whether, in her opinion, "did [her] father understand what the nature of the document was?" (Id. at 13:16 -21.) Ms. Leake answered both questions, "Yes." (*Id.*)

The Court pressed Ms. Leake for details about her father's mental state on or about January 14, 2006, and about the "discussion" they had on that day, but Ms. Leake's testimony on the subject was vague and insubstantial:

THE COURT: Was he having delusions?

MS. LEAKE: Not at that point.

THE COURT: Were you able to carry [*11] on conversations with him?

MS. LEAKE: Oh, yes.

THE COURT: About what subjects?

MS. LEAKE: About anything and everything. He would question me, of course, about anything and everything. We weren't talking too much politics at that point.

THE COURT: What were you talking about?

MS. LEAKE: Family issues, what we were going to do. Well, my conversations with him was what I was attempting to do, and that was to help get him better so that he could come home—so that he could come home. But what I pretty much needed to do right now was to stabilize the household and make sure that mother was OK and that he was OK and then he would come home. He wanted to come home. I mean, that was the point and I kept telling him, OK, when you are ready and when we have things in place, because I knew that I needed to put things in place in order to support his household.

THE COURT: Did he express a desire to come home?

MS. LEAKE: Yes.

THE COURT: What did he say?

MS. LEAKE: Why can't I come home?

THE COURT: And January, what was the date of this?

MS. LEAKE: January 14, 2006

THE COURT: Did you have conversations with him on this day?

MS. LEAKE: Yes.

THE COURT: About what? I am sorry, but I am somewhat at a loss. I need to assess whether your father was competent to execute a power of attorney on that day.

MS. LEAKE: Yes. Your question, again?

---

[2] Plaintiffs' papers indicate that Ms. Sundy Leake is also the attorney-in-fact for her mother, Hayden Mae Leake. Plaintiffs contend, however, that Mrs. Leake, "despite her advanced age, is fully competent to prosecute this action in her own name. The Court has no evidence to the [*9] contrary.

THE COURT: What did you talk about?

MS. LEAKE: I explained to him what needed to be done.

THE COURT: That's fine. That's what you said. I want to know what he said.

MS. LEAKE: *Well, he wasn't talking much. I mean he wasn't talking a lot. He wasn't talking like the man I had known to talk a lot.*

THE COURT: Did he say anything at all?

MS. LEAKE: He would say, OK, well what do you want me to do, or these are things my father asked me. Well, what do you want me to do? Well, Pop, this is a power of attorney. I would explain to him that I have to manage your household and that this would help me to do that so that I can write the checks so that we can pay the bills. Ok. *So what do you want me to do? Well, I want you to sign here. I want you to look over this document. And he would flip through the pages.*

THE COURT: In your estimation was your father able to read and comprehend the very technical, legal language that is in this document?

MS. LEAKE: I would read him paragraphs of it.

THE COURT: Who was the notary?

MS. LEAKE: The Notary was in Hampton.

THE COURT: Well, her name is Winneta Pollard. Who is she?

MS. LEAKE: I don't know.

THE COURT: She is not someone that dealt with you before?

MS. LEAKE: No.

THE COURT: Someone that had seen your father before?

MS. LEAKE: No, not to my knowledge. I would always attempt to explain everything, as I have said, read paragraphs or point things out to him.

(Id. at 18:4-20:20.) (emphasis added). The Court deems it highly significant that Ms. Sundy Leake refused to opine that her father was able to comprehend the contents of the document she was reading to him. Her testimony about his leafing through the document suggests to the Court that Mr. Leake was not able to read the POA.

After the POA was executed, Ms. Leake took her father back to the assisted living facility. (Id. at 33:12-15.) She also testified that after obtaining her father's

signature on the POA that, "then, I believe, I took over the account." (Id. at 21:2-3.)

It also appears that Ms. Leake—not her father—was the person who initiated contact with Mr. Simon, plaintiffs' counsel, about this lawsuit. Mr. Simon stated at the hearing that Ms. Leake "sought me out, retained me" in her capacity as attorney-in-fact. (Id. at 4:9-10.) Ms. Leake confirmed in her testimony that she was the person that contacted Mr. Simon. (Id. at 21:4-6.)

These circumstances increase, rather than decrease, the Court's concern about Mr. Leake's competence at the time the lawsuit was commenced, and cause me to wonder why Ms. Leake (in her representative capacity) was not named as the plaintiff when this lawsuit was filed. However, that is water under the bridge. The Court wants to go forward and reach the merits of this deeply troubling case, because the allegations here are serious—that an attorney, who at one time held a power of attorney from her father, helped herself to money from his bank account.

I was sufficiently unconvinced by Ms. Leake's testimony on July 6 that I declined Mr. Simon's suggestion that I appoint her as her father's representative at that time. Instead I asked both sides to submit briefs by Friday, July 10, 2009, addressing the question of whether Ms. Leake could serve as Mr. Leake's guardian in this matter, and if not, who should be appointed. I subsequently provided the parties with a memorandum outlining the particular issues to be addressed. (Dkt. # 57.)

Plaintiffs submitted papers as requested. Defendant failed to file anything until yesterday—ten days after the due date, when this opinion was well on the way to being finalized. The response is not focused or suffused with legal argument; it consists of an affirmation (with many gaps) from her brother, Damien Leake, and a number of letters and e-mails that confirm both the intensity of this intra-family dispute and the jockeying that the plaintiffs' children appear to be engaged in concerning their "inheritance." The response increases the Court's concern about this entire situation—including about the fact that this action is pending here in New York.

MR. LEAKE'S COMPETENCY TO EXECUTE THE JANUARY 14, 2006 POWER OF ATTORNEY

Sundy Leake is, in effect, moving for leave to be substituted as party plaintiff for her father in this action. She relies on the POA for authority, and she asserts that her father was competent when he executed that document. The initial question to be addressed is whether Mr. Leake was competent to execute the POA in January 2006.

Mr. Simon, plaintiffs' counsel, correctly points out that a party is presumed competent, and the party asserting incapacity must prove incompetence. See Feiden v. Feiden, 151 A.D.2d 889, 891, 542 N.Y.S.2d 860 (3rd Dep't 1989). It is also correct that even those suffering from a disease of the mind, such as Alzheimer's, are not presumed to be wholly incompetent, id., and "in such cases it must be shown that, because of the affliction, the person was incompetent at the time of the transaction." Matter of Waldron, 240 A.D.2d 507, 508, 659 N.Y.S.2d 290 (2nd Dep't 1997).

However, it is also the law in New York that, "where there is medical evidence of mental illness or a mental defect, the burden shifts to the opposing party to prove by *clear and convincing evidence* that the person executing the document in question possessed the requisite mental capacity." In re Rose S., 293 A.D.2d 619, 620, 741 N.Y.S.2d 84 (2nd Dep't 2002) (emphasis added); McKinney's Public Health Law § 2981; see also Kaminester v. Foldes, 51 A.D.3d 528, 529, 859 N.Y.S.2d 412 (1st Dep't 2008). The medical evidence presently before the court is to the effect that, at the time Mr. Leake signed the power of attorney, (1) he had suffered from Alzheimer's or some form of dementia for almost a decade; (2) he had been admitted to the Hospital not two months earlier with delusions so significant that he thought he was dead; (3) three days after Mr. Leake signed the power of attorney, his physician was still of the opinion that Mr. Leake suffered from "dementia, probably of the Alzheimer's type, with a history delusions" (Yetter Dep. Tr. at 9:2-7); and (4) in May 2009, Mr. Leake "didn't know what was transpiring at all." (Id. at 13:8-9.) In light of this evidence, the burden rests with Ms. Leake to prove, by clear and convincing evidence, that her father had the requisite mental capacity at the time he signed the power of attorney to understand and appreciate the nature and consequences of what he was doing.

Ms. Leake has not satisfied that burden. Her testimony establishes that she removed her father from an assisted living facility on January 14, 2006, and took him to a strange place, where he appeared before a stranger, for the purpose of having him sign a complex legal document. The evidence establishes that Ms. Leake was the person who originated the idea of having her father give her a power of attorney; there is no evidence, other than his signature on

the document, that Mr. Leake had any desire to give his daughter his power of attorney. Indeed, when Ms. Leake was asked by defendant whether her father had asked her to prepare a document giving Ms. Leake his power of attorney, Ms. Leake testified, "No, he didn't ask me that directly, no. *He was in no condition.*" (7/2/2009 Hr'g Tr. at 22:20-23) (emphasis added).

While Ms. Leake's testimony establishes that she read the document to her father, and that he placed his initials and his signature on it in appropriate places, the Court is unconvinced by Ms. Leake's testimony that Mr. Leake had a sufficient understanding of the import of the document. There is no evidence that he asked any questions about it or sought any clarification of its complicated provisions. The fact that his signature and initials appear on the document (and the Court has no reason to believe that they are not Mr. Leake's signature and initials) is far from convincing proof of competence; Ms. Leake specifically declined to assure the Court that her father understood the very technical, legal language of the POA; and the notary who was present did not testify.

It would be entirely consistent with what the Court knows about Mr. Leake's medical history and his condition in the period preceding his signing the POA for me to conclude that this severely impaired and quite elderly man sat quietly and entirely without understanding while the document was read to him, and followed his daughter's instructions that he place his initials and his signature in appropriate places on the document.

The Court would of course prefer to have competent medical evidence about Solomon Leake's mental state in mid-January 2006. Regrettably, Dr. Yetter was not asked at his deposition whether Mr. Leake was competent to understand and appreciate the significance of a durable power of attorney in January 2006; he was only asked those questions about his present mental capacity. The medical evidence that I do have relating to the relevant period does not convince me that Mr. Leake was competent on January 14, 2006.

Movant Sundy Leake argues that Mr. Leake could have been competent on January 14, 2006, because his hospitalization was a temporary "crisis" likely caused by his failure to take prescribed medication She notes that her father's medical records indicate that he was "stable and improved" upon his discharge from the hospital. (See Pls. Mem. at 10-11, citing Yetter Dep. Ex. 2 at 2.) She contends that Mr. Leake would have been competent to execute the POA once he restarted his medications and left the Hospital.

Dr. Yetter did indeed testify that Mr. Leake's failure to medicate properly might have caused him to regress:

> Well, according to my records, it says [Mr. Leake] had not really been taking his medicines. The number one reason why people regress and come in is when they usually don't take their medicines. And one of them that he was taking was Risperdal [sic], which was an antipsychotic, as well as Aricept, which is for Alzheimer's. By not taking those medicines, he could have regressed because of that.

(Yetter Dep. Tr. at 25:15-22.) But this testimony gives the Court no clue whether Mr. Leake was legally competent before he regressed; he could well have been unable to understand things like powers of attorney even before his regression. Indeed, Ms. Sundy Leake testified at the July 6, 2009, hearing that her father had had delusional behavior prior to his 2005 hospitalization. When asked by the Court what happened during the "crisis" that preceded his hospitalization, Ms. Leake testified, "Well, he was having delusions and agitation. He was out there. But it was something that we had seen before, but I was the one who admonished my mother that we have to get him help and she was, of course, very distressed." (7/6/2009 Hr'g Tr. at 17:6-9.) Ms. Leake also testified that her mother had anxiety about having her father at home after his hospitalization because "she was afraid he would go off again." (Id. at 36:15-16.) The Court asked, "Did [Mr. Leake] wander like some of these Alzheimer's patients do, leave the house and walk away?" Ms. Leake answered, "That sort of thing, yes. Disappearing, writing checks to various charities that he couldn't afford." (Id. at 36:17-18.)

Nor does the testimony reveal whether Mr. Leake's improvement following his regression caused him to improve significantly enough to regain legal competence. Clearly Mr. Leake was not legally competent during his hospitalization; he was having delusions so serious that he believed he was dead. Dr. Yetter was not asked what "stable and improved" meant, or whether stabilization meant that Mr. Leake was restored to legal competence (even competence at the low level needed to execute a will or a power of attorney) upon his discharge from the Hospital. Mr. Leake could have improved to the point where he no longer needed to reside in a hospital bed, yet still be far from the point of having capacity to execute complex legal documents.

Plaintiffs also cite to entries made on a form entitled "progress notes" from Mr. Leake's first outpatient visit to Dr. Yetter after he was discharged from the Hospital on January 17, 2006—three days after the POA was executed. These notes, which were apparently prepared by a person named Adams (not by Dr. Yetter), reflect that Mr. Leake was "doing well, [no] voices or problems. Stable since [approximate] October. Daughter reports [no] issues." (Simon Aff'n Ex. D.) Boxes on the form are checked off indicating that Mr. Leake was "well-groomed;" his mood was "normal;" his Global Assessment of Functioning ("GAF") was, on a scale of 1-100, in the "70-80 healthy" range; his progress was "good;" and he was not suicidal or homicidal. (Id.) Based on these entries, plaintiffs argue that the Court should conclude that Mr. Leake was "behaving and functioning normally and rationally" at the time he executed the POA. (Pls. Mem. at 12.)

Unfortunately, the progress notes from the January 17, 2006 outpatient visit are neither clear nor convincing evidence of legal competence. The notes do not appear to have been written by Dr. Yetter (it is "Adam's" signature at the bottom of the form, rather than his own), and Dr. Yetter's deposition testimony about this outpatient visit is to the effect that, during this very visit, the doctor confirmed Mr. Leake's diagnosis "dementia, probably of the Alzheimer's type, with a history of delusions." (Yetter Dep. Tr. at 9:5-7.) The reference to something called Global Assessment of Functioning is entirely unexplained, so I have no idea what it means that Mr. Leake was functioning at a "70-80 healthy" level.

The case cited in support of plaintiffs' argument that Mr. Leake was competent to sign the POA, Matter of Mildred M.J., 43 A.D.3d 1391, 844 N.Y.S.2d 539 (4th Dep't 2007), is readily distinguishable. In that case, one of the daughters of an elderly woman sought to invalidate a power of attorney and health care proxy on the grounds that her mother lacked sufficient capacity to execute such documents. The Fourth Department upheld the determination of the trial court that the power of attorney and the healthy care proxy were validly executed. Id. at 1392. Although the mother suffered from "moderate dementia," both a doctor and a nurse practitioner testified specifically that the mother "would have been able to understand questions such as whom she would like to make her health care decisions if she were unable to do so and whether she would like her grandson to handle her financial affairs." Id. In addition to the medical testimony, the attorneys who witnessed the execution of the documents "testified that, when they met with the [mother] and discussed the documents, she was capable of understanding the nature of the transactions that she was authorizing." Id.

The record before me is far more closely analogous to the record in Matter of Rose S., 293 A.D.2d at 621.

There, petitioner failed to meet his burden of showing that an individual who had been diagnosed with dementia possessed the requisite capacity to execute a health care proxy because, *inter alia*, "the petitioner testified that he explained to Rose what the proxy was for, [but] he failed to establish that he inquired as to her competence.") There is no testimony that anyone inquired whether Mr. Leake understood what was being read to him and, as previously noted, Sundy Leake declined the Court's express invitation to opine on her father's understanding of the technical, legal language of the document.

Another difference between this case and Matter of Mildred M.J. and this case is the extensive medical testimony that Mr. Leake was "very delusional" and lacking competence both before and after the date he signed the POA. Yet no medical professional—Dr. Yetter or anyone else—has opined on the subject of Mr. Leake's capacity to understand and appreciate what it meant to execute a POA on January 14, 2006.

In sum, Ms. Leake has not met her burden of producing "clear and convincing" evidence that Mr. Leake had an interval on January 14, 2006, during which he was legally competent to execute a power of attorney in her favor. The Court declines to permit Ms. Leake to be substituted for her father on the strength of the POA.

THE COURT WILL APPOINT AN INDEPENDENT GUARDIAN UNDER RULE 17(C)

Under Rule 17(c), the Court has the power to appoint a guardian—or make another appropriate order—to protect the interests of an infant or incompetent. Fed. R. Civ. P. 17(c)(2); see Seide v. Prevost, 536 F. Supp. 1121, 1132 (S.D.N.Y. 1982). Faced with evidence of Mr. Leake's mental state, there is no question that someone has to be appointed guardian for Mr. Leake. See, e.g., Ferretti v. River Manor Health Care Ctr., 323 F.3d 196, 201 (2d Cir. 2003); Bender v. Del Valle, No. 05-6459, 2009 U.S. Dist. LEXIS 52549, 2009 WL 1754333, at *2 (S.D.N.Y. June 22, 2009). The only question is who.

The Court appreciates that plaintiffs do not have a great deal of money; indeed, it appears that a concern about the plaintiffs'—and in particular Mr. Leake's—finances underlay Ms. Leake's decision to seek to be appointed her father's attorney-in-fact and the commencement of this lawsuit. However, in light of the emotionally-charged nature of this family dispute and the rancor between the parties—as well as the Court's uneasiness about both the accusations against Ms. McAlister and the circumstances in which Ms. Leake obtained what appears to be a power of attorney from her legally incompetent father—the Court is convinced that it would be in the best interests of Mr. Leake for a non-family member to be appointed his guardian in this matter. To the extent that anything in Ms. McAlister's most recent submission is helpful, it confirms my reluctance to appoint any member of the family to represent his interests.

I am pleased to report that Nancy Ludmerer, Esq., Counsel at the Davis Polk & Wardwell LLP law firm, has agreed to take on the representation of Mr. Leake on a *pro bono* basis. Ms. Ludmerer has extensive litigation experience, including experience representing people with mental illness. See http://www.davispolk.com/lawyers/nancy-ludmered. The Court is confident that Ms. Ludmerer is well-equipped to handle this task.[3]

The Court orders that Ms. Ludmerer act as *guardian ad litem* for Mr. Leake in connection with the instant lawsuit. While the Davis Polk firm is donating her services, I am at present inclined to make Mr. Leake's estate responsible for her expenses. Among other things, I imagine Ms. Ludmerer will give me a clearer picture of the family finances; if it turns out that her ward's estate can incur some payment for her services in addition to expenses, the Court will order that such payment be made.

I have asked Ms. Ludmerer to report to the court by October 7, 2009, on what course of action she finds it most prudent for her ward to pursue in connection with this matter. I direct all members of the Leake family and Mr. Simon to cooperate with any inquiries Ms. Ludmerer makes as she carries out her duties, and to provide all consents and authorizations with respect to medical, psychiatric, hospital, financial, tax, and other records that she may request.

Dated: July 21, 2009

/s/ Colleen McMahon

U.S.D.J

---

[3]Ms. Ludmerer informed the Court that, in January 2008, she was appointed to the New York Departmental Disciplinary Committee of the First Department ("Disciplinary Committee"). The Court is aware that, sometime in 2004, Hayden Leake filed a grievance with the First Department Disciplinary Committee, seeking an accounting of the funds allegedly misappropriated by Ms. McAlister. (See Pls. Pre-trial Mem. P 10.) This grievance was apparently dismissed. (See Defs. Pre-trial Mem). This does not present any barrier to Ms. Ludmerer serving as Mr. Leake's *guardian ad litem*, since Ms. Ludmerer's appointment occurred well after the grievance was dismissed. Ms. Ludmerer will of course recuse herself if another, similar complaint against Ms. McAlister is filed before the Committee.

Case Questions

1. What was the nature of Dr. Yetter's testimony?
2. Why didn't Ms. Leake go forward with the guardianship? What did she do instead?
3. How did Ms. Leake obtain her father's signature on the power of attorney?
4. What was Ms. Leake's burden of proof? Did she meet that burden of proof?
5. Who was appointed as guardian ad litem and on what basis?

CASE #2:

JULIA C. VENOYA, Petitioner, VS. STATE OF CALIFORNIA, et al., Respondent.
No. CIV S-08-1699 DAD P

UNITED STATES DISTRICT COURT FOR THE EASTERN DISTRICT OF CALIFORNIA

2009 U.S. Dist. LEXIS 16805
March 4, 2009, Decided
March 5, 2009, Filed

OPINION BY: DALE A. DROZD

OPINION

ORDER AND FINDINGS AND RECOMMENDATIONS

Shirley V. Remmert, on behalf of petitioner Julia C. Venoya, her mother, has filed an application for a writ of habeas corpus pursuant to 28 U.S.C. § 2254, together with two applications to proceed in forma pauperis.

PRELIMINARY SCREENING

Rule 4 of the Rules Governing Section 2254 Cases allows a district court to dismiss a petition if it "plainly appears from the face of the petition and any exhibits annexed to it that the petitioner is not entitled to relief in the district court. . . ." Rule 4, Rules Governing Section 2254 Cases. The Advisory Committee Notes to Rule 8 indicate that the court may dismiss a petition for writ of habeas corpus at several stages of a case, including "summary dismissal under Rule 4; a dismissal pursuant to a motion by the respondent; a dismissal after the answer and petition are considered; or a dismissal after consideration of the pleadings and an expanded record."

BACKGROUND

According to the application, on July 6, 2004, petitioner Julia C. Venoya appeared at a hearing for a temporary **conservatorship** in San Mateo County Probate Court. She was eighty years old, suffered from cataracts, and could not hear well at the time. The petition alleges that the Public Guardian's Office routinely labeled petitioner as having dementia, but she contends that there is no medical cause for a **conservatorship** of any kind. (Pet. at 5a.) Petitioner challenges various Probate Court orders as a violation of her rights under the United States Constitution, federal law, and state law. (*Id.* at 5a-5l.)

Shortly after the commencement of this action, San Mateo County Deputy Counsel Portor Goltz submitted to this court a letter requesting that the court dismiss this action because Ms. Remmert is not authorized to act on behalf of petitioner, a conserved person. Attorney Goltz explained that the San Mateo County Superior Court found petitioner Julia Venoya incapable of handling her own affairs and imposed a dementia **conservatorship** pursuant to California Probate Code § 2356.5. The Probate Court appointed the San Mateo County Public Guardian as the Conservator of the Person and Estate of Julia Venoya. Attorney Goltz notes that Ms. Remmert is not an attorney and has been deemed a vexatious litigant in both the San Mateo County Superior Court and the United States

District Court for the Northern District of California. (Letter from Portor Goltz, Deputy Counsel, San Mateo County Counsel, to the Hon. Dale A. Drozd, United States District Court for the Eastern District of California (Aug. 18, 2008)).

ANALYSIS

Even assuming for the sake of argument that Ms. Remmert is permitted to act on behalf of petitioner, the undersigned finds that federal habeas corpus jurisdiction does not extend to the situation presented here. Under 28 U.S.C. § 2254(a):

> The Supreme Court, a Justice thereof, a circuit judge, or a district court shall entertain an application for a writ of habeas corpus in behalf of a person in custody pursuant to the judgment of a State court only on the ground that he is in custody in violation of the Constitution or the laws or treaties of the United States.

28 U.S.C. § 2254(a).

Although the Ninth Circuit has not directly addressed whether federal habeas corpus jurisdiction extends to adult **guardianship** cases, the First Circuit has held in a persuasive opinion that it does not. *See Hemon v. Office of Pub. Guardian,* 878 F.2d 13 (1st Cir. 1982). In that case a son had filed an application for writ of habeas corpus seeking to nullify the Office of Public Guardian's status as guardian of his mother. The First Circuit held that a dispute over adult **guardianship** is not within the scope of federal habeas corpus jurisdiction because it involves an area of state domestic relations law. In so concluding, the court explained that the United States Supreme Court has held that the federal habeas corpus statute does not confer jurisdiction to consider a collateral attack on a state court judgment that terminates parental rights because "[t]he federal writ of habeas corpus, representing as it does a profound interference with state judicial systems and the finality of state decisions, should be reserved for those instances in which the federal interest in individual liberty is so strong that it outweighs federalism and finality concerns." *Hemon,* 878 F.2d at 14 (quoting *Lehman v. Lycoming County Children's Services Agency,* 458 U.S. 502, 515-16, 102 S. Ct. 3231, 73 L. Ed. 2d 928 (1982)).

The First Circuit acknowledged that *Lehman* involved child custody and not adult **guardianship**. However, the court determined that the reasoning in *Lehman* extended with full force to disputes involving adult **guardianship**. The court explained that:

> [T]he same concerns about federalism and finality that counsel against federal habeas jurisdiction over child custody disputes also counsel against federal habeas jurisdiction over disputes regarding **guardianship**. The long-standing policy of the federal courts to avoid interference in state domestic relations disputes - for example, by abstaining from asserting federal subject matter jurisdiction over domestic relations matters, - is not limited to the area of child custody, but extends to the entire field of domestic relations. (citations omitted)

878 F.2d at 15. The court concluded that the state courts had adjudicated the question of how to best protect Hemon's mother, so there was no occasion for it to undertake federal review by way of habeas corpus proceedings. *Id.*

In this case, the undersigned agrees with the First Circuit's rationale and finds that the dispute over petitioner's **guardianship** is not within the scope of this federal court's habeas corpus jurisdiction. The San Mateo County Superior Court has determined the most proper way to protect petitioner's rights, and this court declines to allow re-litigation of the matter through federal habeas proceedings. Accordingly, the court will recommend that this action be dismissed.

CONCLUSION

IT IS HEREBY ORDERED that:

1. The Clerk of the Court is directed to randomly assign a United States District Judge to this action; and
2. The Clerk of the Court is directed to send a courtesy copy of these findings and recommendations to Portor Goltz, San Mateo County Deputy Counsel, 400 County Center, Redwood City, CA 94063-1662.

IT IS HEREBY RECOMMENDED that:

1. Petitioner's July 23, 2008 and August 7, 2008 applications to proceed in forma pauperis (Doc. Nos. 2 & 5) be denied;
2. Petitioner's application for a writ of habeas corpus be dismissed; and
3. This action be closed.

These findings and recommendations are submitted to the United States District Judge assigned to the case, pursuant to the provisions of 28 U.S.C. § 636(b)(1). Within twenty days after being served with these findings and recommendations, petitioner may file written objections with the court. The document should be captioned "Objections to Magistrate Judge's Findings and Recommendations." Petitioner is advised that failure to file objections within the specified time may waive the right to appeal the District Court's order. *Martinez v. Ylst*, 951 F.2d 1153 (9th Cir. 1991).

DATED: March 4, 2009.

/s/ Dale A. Drozd

DALE A. DROZD

UNITED STATES MAGISTRATE JUDGE

Case Questions

1. Is this a federal or a state court case?
2. Who was the petitioner in this case and what did she allege?
3. What was the holding (court's decision) in this case?
4. What was the rationale (court's reason) for the holding?

FORMS TO ACCOMPANY PARALEGAL PRACTICE

> **Disclaimer:** The forms provided to aid students in completing the Paralegal Practice activities assigned in each chapter have been modified as samples to familiarize students with what each form commonly looks like and are not intended to be used as actual forms for any state.

INSTRUCTIONS: The forms are provided in Microsoft Word format and employ the use of Stop Codes (such as SC1, SC2, SC3, and so on). Stop Codes are used in place of the form sections that must be updated with case-by-case information, such as SC1 for the client's name, SC3 for the client's address, and so on. What each Stop Code represents can be inferred by reading the surrounding text on the form. By using the FIND & REPLACE tool on the Microsoft toolbar, the students can replace the Stop Codes with the information provided in the Paralegal Practice activity to complete each assignment. Students must also fill in any blank lines on each form with the appropriate information from the activity and then proofread the document prior to turning in their work.

The following forms are included following this section and will be posted online for students to access to complete the Paralegal Practice activities for this chapter:

- PP Form 7.1—Petition for Appointment as Guardian and/or Conservator
- PP Form 7.2—Affidavit of Person to be Appointed as Guardian and/or Conservator
- PP Form 7.3—Consent to Appointment of Guardian and Conservator

PP Form 7.1

Attorney Name, Esq. – State Bar No. _____
LAW FIRM NAME
Address
City, State, Zip Code
Phone Number
Fax Number
Attorney for Petitioner

IN THE SUPERIOR COURT OF THE STATE OF SAMPLE STATE
IN AND FOR THE COUNTY OF SAMPLE COUNTY

In The Matter of the Guardianship and/or Conservatorship of:	)))	Case No.: PB-2014-
_____	))	PETITION FOR PERMANENT APPOINTMENT OF GUARDIAN AND/OR CONSERVATOR OF A MINOR
A Minor	))))))))))	
_____	)	

REQUIRED INFORMATION ABOUT PETITIONER, UNDER OATH OR AFFIRMATION:

1. INFORMATION ABOUT ME (The Petitioner):

   Name: _____

   Street Address:_____

   City, State, Zip:_____

   Telephone: (   ) _____-_____   Date of Birth: ____-_____-_____

   ✓   I am related by blood to the person who needs a guardian and/ or conservator ("the minor")

   (If applicable) HOW I am related to the minor:_____

   (Example:, Grandmother, uncle, aunt, sister, etc.)

2. INFORMATION THE MINOR WHO NEEDS A GUARDIAN AND/ OR CONSERVATOR. The minor is called the proposed ward (for the guardianship) and proposed protected person (for the conservatorship):

   Name:_____

   Street Address:_____

   City, State, Zip:_____

   Telephone: ( )____-_____   Date of Birth: ____-_____-_____

   The Minor is ☐ married or ☐ unmarried.

   Mother's Name:_____

   Mother's Address:_____

   Father's Name:_____

   Father's Address:_____

3. PERSON(S) ENTITLED TO NOTICE of this Court matter under Sample law. SAMPLE STATUTES § 14-5207 for guardians, and § 14-5405 for conservators, and to whom I will give notice of this case.

MOTHER

FATHER

THE MINOR (If over 14)

OTHER PERSON ENTITLED TO NOTICE:

Name	Address	Relationship to Minor
A		
B		
C		
D		

4. ASSETS OF THE MINOR I SAY NEEDS GUARDIAN AND/OR MINOR CONSERVATOR

(Check one box)

☐ The minor who needs a guardian and/or conservator has no substantial assets or income. No bond by petitioner is required: OR.

☐ The minor who needs a guardian and/or conservator has assets and/or annual income in the approximate amount of $_____.

Explain:

_____

_____

_____

5. PERSON TO BE APPOINTED GUARDIAN AND/OR CONSERVATOR (Complete this section only if the person is a different person than Petitioner):

Name:_____

Street Address:_____

City, State, Zip:_____

Telephone: (   )_____-_____   Date of Birth: ____-____-_____

☐ The person to be appointed guardian and/or conservator is related by blood to the minor who needs a guardian and/or conservator. If "yes" above, HOW is the person to be appointed guardian and/or conservator related to the minor?

_____

(Example: grandmother, uncle, sister)

6. INFORMATION REGARDING GUARDIANSHIP AND/OR CONSERVATORSHIP to the best of my knowledge. (check one box):

☐ No guardian and/or conservator has been appointed by Will or by any Court Order, and no Court proceedings and pending for such appointment:

OR,

☐ Someone has been appointed guardian and/or conservator or Court proceedings and pending. Explain who, when, in what court, and if the appointee is guardian and/or conservator):

_____

_____

7. PARENTAL RIGHTS. All parental rights of custody regarding the minor have been suspended or terminated by:

☐ Written consent of the parent(s) to the guardianship and/or conservatorship. (Notarized copy must be attached)

☐ Abandonment of the minor for at least six (6) months prior to the filing of this Petition.

☐ Prior court order (**You must provide the Court with a certified copy of the order.**)

☐ Other Circumstances: (Explain)

_____

_____

_____

(continued)

8. REASONS FOR CONSERVATORSHIP: (Check one or more of the boxes if applicable) the minor needs a conservator because:

☐ The minor owns money or property that required management or protection that cannot be otherwise provided.

☐ The minor may have business affairs that may be jeopardized or prevented by his or her minority.

☐ The minor needs funds for his or her support and education and protection is necessary or desirable to obtain or provide funds.

9. REASONS FOR REQUESTED PERSON TO BE APPOINTED GUARDIAN AND/OR CONSERVATOR: (Check one or more of the boxes that you think apply to the relationship of the proposed guardian and/or conservator to the person you say requires a guardian):

☐ Proposed appointee was selected by the minor who is at least 14 years old and who has sufficient mental capacity to make an intelligent choice.

☐ Proposed appointee is the spouse of the minor

☐ Proposed appointee is the parent of the minor

☐ Proposed appointee is a relative of the minor and has had care and custody of the minor for the last 6 months prior to filing this Petition.

☐ Proposed appointee was chosen to be the guardian by someone who is caring for the minor or is paying benefits for the minor.

☐ Proposed appointee is a person selected by the Will of a deceased parent

☐ Proposed appointee is a public fiduciary, a professional guardian, conservator, or the Sample Veteran's Service Commission.

☐ The proposed appointee is not related by blood to the minor and the person will submit a full set of fingerprints to the court required by SAMPLE STATUTES § 14-5206.

☐ Written consent of the parents to the conservatorship.

10. REASONS I AM ASKING FOR A GUARDIANSHIP AND/OR CONSERVATORSHIP ORDER: The appointment of a guardian and/or conservator for the minor is necessary or desirable to provide continuing care and supervision of the minor and is in the best interests of the minor because:

(**Explain**):

_____

_____

_____

_____

REQUIRED STATEMENTS TO THE COURT, UNDER OATH OR AFFIRMATION: (Note: All of these statements must be true and you must check the box for each statement to indicate to the Court that each statement is true, or you cannot file this Petition.)

11. ☐ TRUE This Court is the proper venue for this case because the minor who needs a guardian and/or conservator lives or is present in this county.

12. ☐ TRUE The person who is requested to be the guardian and/or conservator has completed the required document called Affidavit of Person to be Appointed as Guardian and/or Conservator and is filing the Affidavit with this Petition as required by Sample law, SAMPLE STATUTES § 14-5106, and/or § 14-5410.

REQUESTS TO THE COURT FOR AN ORDER, UNDER OATH OR AFFIRMATION:

1. Schedule a hearing to determine if a guardianship and/or conservatorship is appropriate;

2. After Petitioner gives notice of the hearing to all interested persons and to those required by law, hold a hearing to determine if the court should order a guardianship and/or conservatorship;

3. Appoint a permanent guardian and/or conservator of the minor; and

4. Make any other orders the Court decides are in the best interests of the minor.

OATH OR AFFIRMATION

STATE OF SAMPLE STATE
COUNTY OF SAMPLE

I, the Petitioner, declare under penalty of perjury, that I have read this Petition. All the statements in the Petition are true and correct and complete to the best of my knowledge and belief.

SIGNATURE:_____ DATE: _____

Sworn to or affirmed before me this _____ day of _____, _____

By _____.

My Commission Expires:_____

Notary Public/ Deputy Clerk

PP Form 7.2

Attorney Name, Esq. – State Bar No. _____
LAW FIRM NAME
Address
City, State Zip Code
Phone Number
Fax Number
Attorney for Petitioner

IN THE SUPERIOR COURT OF THE STATE OF SAMPLE STATE
IN AND FOR THE COUNTY OF SAMPLE COUNTY

In the Matter of the Guardianship and/or conservatorship of _____ A Minor	) Case No.: PB-2014-))) **AFFIDAVIT OF PERSON TO BE APPOINTED**) **GUARDIAN AND/OR CONSERVATOR**))))))))

> **INSTRUCTIONS:** The person who wants to be appointed the guardian and/or conservator must answer each statement as TRUE or FALSE. Each answer that is false must be explained in writing in an attachment to this Affidavit.

    STATEMENT MADE UNDER OATH TO THE COURT; Sample law SAMPLE STATUTES § 14-5100 requires the person seeking appointment to answer the following items. This document must be filed with the Petition for Appointment of Guardian and/or Conservator.

13. ☐ True or ☐ False. I have not been convicted of a felony in any jurisdiction.

14. ☐ True or ☐ False. I have not acted as a guardian and/or conservator for another person for at least three years before I filed this Petition.

15. ☐ True or ☐ False. I know and understand the powers and duties I would have as a guardian and/or conservator.

(continued)

16. ☐ True or ☐ False. I have not had a power of attorney for anyone for at least three years before I filed this Petition.

17. ☐ True or ☐ False. I am not, to the best of my knowledge, listed in the Child Abuse Registry at the Office of the Sample Attorney General.

18. ☐ True or ☐ False. To the best of my knowledge, no business in which I have an interest is listed in the Child Abuse Registry at the Office of the Sample Attorney General.

19. ☐ True or ☐ False. Sample law requires that a guardian and/or conservator file an annual report/ accounting with the court. If I have been a guardian/conservator before, I either filed the required documents on time, or within 3 months of receiving a notice from the court that the report/accounting was due.

20. ☐ True or ☐ False. I have never been removed by the Court as a guardian and/or conservator.

21. ☐ True or ☐ False. The nature of my relationship to the proposed minor or protected person is_____ _____

22. ☐ True or ☐ False. I met the proposed minor under the following circumstances: _____ _____ _____

23. ☐ True or ☐ False. I have never revieved anything of value greater than a total of one hundred dollars in any one year by gift, or will, or inheritance from an individual or the estate of an individual to whom I was not related by blood or marriage and for whom I served at any time as guardian and/or conservator, trustee, or attorney-in-fact.

24. ☐ True or ☐ False. No business in which I have an interest has ever received anything of value greater than a total of one hundred dollars in any one year by gift, or will, or inheritance from an individual or the estate of an individual to whom I am not related by blood or marriage and for whom I served at any time as guardian and/or conservator, trustee, or attorney-in-fact.

25. ☐ True or ☐ False. To the best of my knowledge, I am not named as a personal representative, trustee, beneficiary, or other type of beneficiary for any individual to whom I am not related by blood or marriage and for whom I have ever served as guardian and/or conservator, trustee, or attorney-in-fact.

26. ☐ True or ☐ False. To the best of my knowledge, no business in which I have an interest is named as a personal representative, trustee, beneficiary, or other type of beneficiary for any individual to whom I am not related by blood or marriage and for whom I have ever served as guardian and/or conservator, trustee, or attorney-in-fact.

27. ☐ True or ☐ False. I have no interest in any business that provides housing, health care, nursing care, residential care, assisted living, home health services, or comfort care services to any individual.

OATH OF THE PERSON SEEKING TO BE APPOINTED AS GUARDIAN AND/OR CONSERVATOR:

STATE OF SAMPLE   )
MOHAVE SAMPLE   ) ss.

I have read, understood, and completed the above statements and the attached document. Everything I have said is true and correct to the best of my knowledge, information, and belief.

Signature:_____

Subscribed and sworn to before me this _____day of _____, 20_____.

By:_____

My Commission Expires_____

_____

Notary Public/ Deputy Clerk

PP Form 7.3

Attorney Name, Esq. – State Bar No. _____
LAW FIRM NAME
Address
City, State, Zip Code
Phone Number
Fax Number
Attorney for Petitioner

IN THE SUPERIOR COURT OF THE STATE OF SAMPLE STATE
IN AND FOR THE COUNTY OF SAMPLE COUNTY

In the Matter of the Guardianship and/or Conservatorship of:	) Case No.: PB-2014-
	)
	)
	) **CONSENT OF PARENT TO GUARDIANSHIP AND/**
SC1,	) **OR CONSERVATORSHIP OF MINOR CHILD (AND**
A Minor.	) **WAIVER OF NOTICE)**
	)
	)
_____	)

REQUIRED INFORMATION FROM PARENT, UNDER OATH OR AFFIRMATION:

1. **INFORMATION ABOUT ME:**

   Name: _____

   Street Address: _____

   City, State, Zip Code: _____

   Telephone: _____ **Date of Birth:** _____

   I am the natural □ MOTHER or □ FATHER of the minor child(ren) named above, who needs a guardian and/or conservator.

2. I have read the Petition for Permanent Appointment of Guardian and/or Conservator of a Minor and consent to the appointment of (name) _____ to be the guardian of the minor child(ren).

3. □ (Optional) I waive notice of all further proceedings in this matter. I understand that I can reverse this waiver by filing a written document with the court under this court case number declaring that I no longer waive notice of hearings and other court proceedings.

OATH OR AFFIRMATION OF THE PARENT

STATE OF SAMPLE	)
	) ss.
County of SAMPLE	)

I declare, under penalty of perjury that I have read, understood, and completed the above statements. Everything I have said is true and correct to the best of my knowledge, information and belief.

_____

Signature_____ Date_____

SUBSCRIBED AND SWORN TO before me this   day of _____, 2014, by _____.

Notary Public

My Commission Expires:

CHAPTER 8

Fiduciary Powers and Duties

A REAL-LIFE SCENARIO

An elderly man had lived with one of his grown sons for over twenty years. For purposes of this scenario, we will call the man Frank, and his live-in son Frank, Jr. Frank and Frank, Jr., shared many joint assets, including the family home and other real property. Frank had several other children and some of them did not get along. Adam, another son, strongly disliked Frank, Jr.

Unfortunately, Frank and Frank, Jr., both became very ill within weeks of one another. Adam involved an old family friend and neighbor, Mrs. Sharp, who stepped in and began bossing everyone around. Frank signed a new power of attorney appointing Mrs. Sharp. It was unlikely that Frank had capacity to sign anything at the time the document was signed.

© bikeriderlondon/Shutterstock

Shortly thereafter, Frank, Jr., was forcibly removed from the home by Adam and others. Mrs. Sharp began transferring assets that were in joint name to third parties, breaking the joint tenancy with right of survivorship that the Franks had shared. (*See* Chapter 2 to review rules pertaining to real property.) Clearly, Mrs. Sharp was overstepping her role as attorney-in-fact by making transfers that Frank would not have made himself and that were not at his direction. Sadly, Mrs. Sharp breached her fiduciary duty to Frank by performing transfers that were both immoral and illegal under the circumstances.

CHAPTER OBJECTIVES:

1. Understand what it means to be a fiduciary.
2. List the various agents who are known as fiduciaries.
3. Discuss the powers and duties of the different types of fiduciaries.
4. Discuss the relationship between statutory powers and powers conferred by written document.
5. Describe the purpose of the Uniform Fiduciary Act.

■ INTRODUCTION

The foregoing scenario illustrates what can happen when a person errs in judgment and appoints someone who is not trustworthy to act as his or her fiduciary.

Key Terms and Definitions

Fiduciary
A person in a position of loyalty and trust, such as an executor, administrator, guardian, attorney-in-fact, or trustee; also a person to whom property or power is entrusted for the benefit of another.

Guardian
The one who legally has the care and management of the person, property, or both of a minor or incompetent person.

Fiduciary Duty
A duty or responsibility required of a fiduciary that arises out of a position of loyalty and trust.

Fiduciary Capacity
A position of trust; the legal capability of a person or institution (such as a bank) to act as a fiduciary.

A **fiduciary** is a person in a position of loyalty and trust, such as an executor, administrator, **guardian**, attorney-in-fact, or trustee. An alternate definition is that a **fiduciary** is a person to whom property or power is entrusted for the benefit of another. He or she has a **fiduciary duty** to uphold as the agent of the principal. The phrase "**fiduciary capacity**" means a position of trust. Most of the other chapters in this textbook deal with some type of fiduciaries; this chapter addresses the fiduciary powers and duties that those individuals have while doing their jobs.

■ SOURCES OF POWER

The first source of fiduciary power is state statute. Fiduciary powers conferred by state statute are granted automatically to each fiduciary even if the document appointing that fiduciary is silent on the fiduciary's intended powers. The concept is that fiduciaries cannot do their jobs without a certain minimal level of authority or power.

The second source of fiduciary power is the document appointing the fiduciary. Often, grantors or document creators may confer additional powers upon their fiduciaries to ensure that they will have sufficient authority to carry out the creator's intentions. In other instances, a document creator may wish to specifically limit the powers of his or her fiduciary to only those powers that are selected or enumerated. The document appointing the fiduciary can be as expansive and broad or as narrow and limited as the principal desires.

■ COMMON POWERS

Powers of Attorney-in-Fact

Power of Attorney
A legal document that authorizes another person to act as the grantor's attorney-in-fact and agent; execution before a notary public is nearly always required.

Principal (also known as the "Grantor")
A person who authorizes another, as an agent, to represent him or her.

Attorney-in-Fact
The person appointed under a power of attorney to act as the principal's agent.

The person granting the power under a **power of attorney** is called the "principal" or the "grantor," depending upon the state in which the document is executed. A **principal** is person who authorizes another, as an agent, to represent him or her. The individual appointed under a power of attorney is called the **attorney-in-fact** and/or agent. The attorney-in-fact is in a position of trust and must act in the best interest of the principal pursuant to the power of attorney.

The standard and customary powers granted to an attorney-in-fact and agent are enumerated in Figure 8.1.

The power to conduct or deal with the following:

1. Real estate transactions
2. Chattel and goods transactions
3. Bond, share, and commodity transactions
4. Banking transactions
5. Business operating transactions
6. Insurance transactions
7. Estate transactions
8. Claims and litigation

9. Personal relationships and affairs
10. Benefits from military service
11. Records, reports, and statements
12. Retirement benefit transactions
13. Making gifts to the principal's spouse, children, and more remote descendants, in any amount, to each of such persons in any year
14. Tax matters
15. All other matters
16. Making gifts of property to others and to charitable organizations in the pattern the principal has used in the past
17. Preparing, signing, and filing all tax returns required by law; signing agreements extending the statute of limitations in all tax matters; and representing the principal before any taxing authority or any court in connection with any tax matters
18. Making or changing all of the principal's beneficiary designations, withdrawals, rollovers, transfers, elections and waivers under law regarding employee benefit plans and individual retirement accounts, whether as plan participant, beneficiary, IRA owner, or spouse of a participant, including without limitation the waiver of qualified joint and survivor annuity and qualified pre-retirement survivor annuity benefits as provided in IRC §417; and authorizing any distribution, transfer, or rollover from all qualified plans and IRAs
19. Medicaid and Medicare planning and transactions, including claims, litigation and settlements
20. Transferring assets to any trust that the principal has created; amending or revoking, in whole or in part, any revocable trust the principal has created, regardless of any disability or incompetency; and making withdrawals from any revocable trust the principal has created
21. Requesting disclosure of medical services provided by the principal's physicians or other medical staff or requesting copies of the principal's entire medical records or a portion thereof for any purpose that the attorney-in-fact deems appropriate, or solely upon the request of the attorney-in-fact
22. Engaging in all insurance transactions, exercising all rights with respect to insurance, and designating or changing the beneficiary of life insurance policies

In addition, the principal can give to the attorney-in-fact full and unqualified authority to delegate any or all of the foregoing powers to any person or persons whom the attorney-in-fact selects.

Note that a principal can elect to choose all of the matters listed in the document or elect to choose only certain powers. If the document is intended to be

EXAMPLE 1

John Smith is an unmarried, very successful executive who travels often for his career. He is purchasing a piece of real estate in another state for investment purposes but is unable to attend the real estate closing due to other engagements. John's close friend from high school, Peter Parker, was recently laid off and has offered to travel out of state to attend the closing. John trusts Peter to perform this favor but does not feel comfortable appointing Peter as his attorney-in-fact for any other purpose. In this instance, the most appropriate form for John to execute is a limited power of attorney authorizing Peter to perform this real estate transaction only.

ongoing and the person appointed is someone the principal trusts completely, it is generally a good idea to grant the attorney-in-fact as many powers as possible so that the attorney-in-fact can truly step into the shoes of the principal in the event of the principal's subsequent disability or incapacity. On the other hand, there are times when a power of attorney is only needed for a specific and narrow purpose.

Prohibited Use of Power of Attorney

Most importantly, powers granted pursuant to a power of attorney *cease upon the death of the principal*. Therefore, an attorney-in-fact is legally prohibited from using a power of attorney after the principal has died.

Some state statutes may also expressly prohibit an attorney-in-fact from exercising certain powers on behalf of the principal. One power that is prohibited under Arizona law is found under Arizona Revised Statute § 16-102:

Figure 8.1 Standard and Customary Powers of Attorney-in-Fact or Agent

16-102. <u>Power of attorney; prohibited use</u>

A power of attorney or other form of proxy is not valid for use by a person in any procedure or transaction concerning elections, including voter registration, petition circulation or signature, voter registration cancellation, early ballot requests or voting another person's ballot.

Thus, according to Arizona statute, an attorney-in-fact may not use a power of attorney to cast a vote for another person.

Other states have enacted similar statutes.

Powers of Executor or Personal Representative

Executor
A male nominated in a will of a decedent to carry out the terms of the will; a personal representative of the estate.

Executrix
A female nominated in a will to carry out the terms of the will; a personal representative of the estate.

An **executor** is a male nominated in a will of a decedent to carry out the terms of the will as a personal representative of the estate. An **executrix** is a female nominated in a will to carry out the terms of the will. Personal representatives are generally given broad powers to carry out the expressed intentions of the testator or testatrix. As with powers of attorney, default powers are often conferred by state statute. Those powers may be expanded upon in the will if necessary or desirable.

Figure 8.2 is a sample article from a New York will conferring powers on the testator's executor:

Notice that the foregoing article expressly states that the powers granted are *in addition to* those conferred by law. Paragraph A confers additional power with respect to the sale of real property. Paragraph B permits the executor to deliver the share of a minor beneficiary to the child's legal custodian pursuant to the Uniform Transfers to Minors Act.

Duration of Authority

Although a will becomes effective upon the death of the testator, a personal representative's authority does not take effect until the individual has been appointed by the court. Once appointed, a personal representative remains responsible for the estate until the estate has been administered and closed or the personal representative has been otherwise removed or discharged from his or her appointment by the court.

Figure 8.2

VII. I give to my Executor, hereinafter named, and to the successor, the following powers and discretions, in addition to those vested in or imposed upon them or either of them by law:

A. To mortgage, sell, convey, exchange or otherwise deal with or dispose of any real or personal property for cash or on credit (including the right to accept a purchase money mortgage as part of the purchase price); to retain as part of the estate any and all securities and property in the form originally received, whether or not it is then income producing and regardless of any rule requiring diversification of investments; to invest and reinvest in any stocks, bonds, shares in mutual funds or authorized common trust funds, or other securities or property, whether real or personal, which my Executor may deem safe and for the best interests of the estate, without being limited to investments authorized by law for the investment of trust funds; to hold title to any and all securities and other investments either in my Executor's name or in the name of a nominee; to borrow money from itself or others on terms my Executor may deem best, and to pledge any property of the estate as security for the repayment thereof; and to make distributions in cash or in kind, or partly in each, to the beneficiaries entitled thereto.

B. If any beneficiary or legatee entitled to receive a part of my estate shall be under twenty-one (21) years of age, I authorize and empower my Executor to designate his or her parent, or some other appropriate adult person, or trust company, as custodian for the beneficiary or legatee under the New York Uniform Transfers to Minors Act until the beneficiary or legatee reaches age twenty-one (21), and to distribute the share of the beneficiary or legatee to the designated custodian. A receipt from the custodian shall fully release my Executor from all liability and accountability to the legatee or beneficiary.

Powers of Trustee

A **trustee** is a person who holds legal title to property in trust for another. Figure 8.3 depicts a sample article from a will that confers powers on both the executor and the trustee of the testamentary trust. Notice that many more powers are conferred than in Figure 8.2.

Trustee
The person or entity who holds the assets (corpus) of the trust and manages the trust and its assets pursuant to the trust's terms.

Figure 8.3

VII. I give to my Executor and to my Trustee, hereinafter named, and to the successor or successors of either, the following powers and discretions, in addition to those vested in or imposed upon them or either of them by law:

A. To mortgage, sell, convey, exchange or otherwise deal with or dispose of any real or personal property for cash or on credit (including the right to accept a purchase money mortgage as part of the purchase price); to lease any property for periods longer or shorter than the probable duration of any trust; to retain as part of the estate or trust any and all securities and property in the form originally received, including securities of or issued by any corporate executor or trustee, whether or not it is then income producing and regardless of any rule requiring diversification of investments; to invest and reinvest in any stocks, bonds, shares in mutual funds or authorized common trust funds, or other securities or property, whether real or personal, which my Executor or Trustee may deem safe and for the best interests of the estate or trust, without being limited to investments authorized by law for the investment of trust funds; to hold title to any and all securities and other investments either in my Executor's or Trustee's name or in the name of a nominee; to borrow money from itself or others on terms as my Executor or Trustee may deem best, and to pledge any property of the estate or trust as security for the repayment thereof; to hold two or more trusts or other funds in one or more consolidated funds, in which the separate trusts as funds shall have undivided interests; to determine as to every sum received (including stock dividends or the distribution of securities) whether the same is principal or income, or what part thereof is principal or income, and as to every expense or disbursement incurred or made by it, whether the same should be borne by the principal or income, or in what share by each; and to make distributions in cash or in kind, or partly in each, including undivided interests, even though shares be composed differently.

B. In case any income or principal of the trust becomes payable to a person under twenty-one (21) years of age, or to a person under legal disability, or to a person not adjudicated incompetent but who, by reason of illness or mental or physical disability, is, in the opinion of my Trustee, unable to administer properly the income or principal,

(continued)

Figure 8.3 (continued)

then the income or principal may be paid out by my Trustee in any one or more of the following ways, as it deems best: (a) directly to the beneficiary; (b) to the guardian, committee, conservator or custodian of the beneficiary; (c) to any relative of the beneficiary or to any other person with whom the beneficiary may be living for the care, comfort, support, maintenance, education and welfare of the beneficiary; (d) by my Trustee using the income or principal directly for the care, comfort, support, maintenance, education and welfare of the beneficiary.

C. In determining the amounts of principal to be used for the benefit of any of my infant children during minority, it is my desire that my Trustee first consult with the guardian of the person of my children, and I direct that my Trustee shall be fully protected with respect to any payment made in reliance upon information received from the guardian. The final determination as to the appropriateness of using principal for the benefit of any infant child shall rest with my Trustee.

D. I expressly authorize my Trustee to receive and execute receipts for the proceeds of any life insurance policies on my life which may become payable to my Trustee; and I direct that a receipt executed by my Trustee shall fully discharge the respective insurance companies from all liability and responsibility with respect to the payment and use of the proceeds of the policies. If my Trustee's claim to any insurance proceeds is contested, whether by the insurance company or by any other claimant, my Trustee shall have full power and authority to settle, compromise, or otherwise collect, or to enforce by legal action any contested policy, paying the expenses of the action out of the trust estate. My Trustee's decision with respect to any contested claim shall be final and conclusive upon all parties interested in this trust.

E. I further expressly authorize my Trustee to purchase any assets from my Executor at the value established for the assets in the federal estate tax proceeding in my estate, and/or to loan to my Executor sums as may be needed to pay any and all taxes and administration expenses. The loans may be made with or without security, and with or without interest, and upon other terms and conditions as my Executor and Trustee may agree. The authority, hereby granted, shall be exercised, notwithstanding that my Executor and Trustee are one and the same person or corporation.

F. If at any time during the administration of any trust herein created, the Trustee, in its absolute discretion, deems the continuation thereof to be uneconomical and not in the best interests of the beneficiary or beneficiaries thereof, the Trustee, in its absolute discretion, is authorized to terminate the same and distribute the assets, free of the trust, to the current income beneficiary or beneficiaries in the proportions in which they are entitled to the income therefrom.

G. If any beneficiary or legatee entitled to receive a part of my estate shall be under twenty-one (21) years of age, I authorize and empower my Executor or Trustee, as the case may be, to designate his or her parent, or some other appropriate adult person, or trust company, as custodian for the beneficiary or legatee under the New York Uniform Transfers to Minors Act until the beneficiary or legatee attains the age of twenty-one (21), and to distribute the share of the beneficiary or legatee to the designated custodian. A receipt from the custodian shall fully release my Executor or Trustee from all liability and accountability to the legatee or beneficiary.

H. If any party to any proceeding relating to my estate or to any trust established hereunder shall be under a disability by reason of infancy or incompetency, and there is another party without any disability to the proceeding with the same interest as the person under a disability, it shall not be necessary to serve the person under a disability with process in the proceeding, and he shall be deemed to be virtually represented therein as provided by law by the other person who is served with process, and the person under the disability shall be bound in all respects by any Decree or Judgment entered in the proceeding.

I. No individual Trustee of any trust herein created shall be authorized to exercise any power, herein, to make any discretionary distribution of either income or principal to himself or herself, or to make discretionary allocations in his or her own favor between principal and income; and no individual Trustee shall be authorized to exercise any power, herein, to distribute income or principal to or for the benefit of any person whom he or she is legally obligated to support. These powers may be exercised by the remaining Trustee, who is not so disqualified.

Notice that the language found in Figure 8.3 makes it clear that the powers conferred upon the fiduciaries in the document are *in addition to* those provided under the law.

Statutory Powers

Figure 8.4 depicts the statutory powers given to trustees under Rhode Island law.

Figure 8.4

Rhode Island Statutes and Codes **§ 18-4-2 Powers of trustees.** – (a) Every trust, inter vivos or testamentary, previously or subsequently effective, in which no provision is made to the contrary, shall be deemed to give to the trustees or trustee under the trust for the time being, in addition to any other power they may lawfully have, full power in their, his, or her discretion, or if a corporation in the discretion of its duly authorized officer or committee:

(1) To invest and reinvest the trust estate, or any part of it, in real or personal property, foreign or domestic, including, without limiting the generality of the preceding provisions, savings accounts of banks and trust companies and shares of stock or other securities of corporations, building and loan associations, investment trusts, and investment companies, and to vary from time to time the investments of the trust estate;

(2) To exercise discretionary powers of sale, lease, partition by suit or deed, and exchange over the trust estate, or any part of it, whether real or personal property; in case of any sale, to sell at public or private sale, for cash or on credit and together or in parcels; in case of any lease, to lease for a period that the trustees or trustee shall deem advisable, whether terminating during the continuance of the trusts or thereafter; and in case of any partition or in case of any exchange, to give or receive money for equality of partition or exchange;

(3) To appoint a proxy or proxies, with or without power of substitution, to vote shares of a corporation or association included in the trust estate as directed or in a manner that the proxy or proxies shall deem best;

(4) To participate in, assent to, or disapprove any plan for the reorganization, recapitalization, consolidation, merger, winding up, or readjustment of the indebtedness of any corporation or association, and to take any and all action required by reason of participation in the plan; and

(5) Upon the termination of any trust with respect to any portion of the trust estate, to set aside the portion from the remainder of the trust estate; upon the termination of any trust with respect to the entire trust estate, or any part of it, to partition the trust estate into the shares, if any, in which it is distributable; and in connection with the setting aside of any portion or any partition to exercise the power of sale conferred by this section upon the trustees or trustee, and to allocate to any share in or part of the trust estate specific investments at their fair value at the time of allocation as determined by the trustees or trustee acting in good faith.

(6) To donate a conservation easement on any real property in order to obtain the benefit of the estate tax exclusion allowed under §§ 170 and 2031(c), respectively, of the United States Internal Revenue Code of 1986, as amended, if:

(i) Each party who has an interest in the real property that would be affected by the conservation easement consents in writing to the donation, or

(ii) The trust instrument directs, requires or permits a donation of a conservation easement in gross, in which case no consent shall be required.

(b) The trustees or trustee may be authorized by the superior court to execute any or all of the powers set forth in subdivisions (a)(1) to (a)(5) of this section, upon the terms and conditions that the court may deem proper, notwithstanding any provision of any trust instrument which is or may possibly be deemed to be inconsistent with the exercise of any of these powers, if, in the opinion of the court, authority to exercise the power or powers is or may become necessary or desirable to enable the trustees or trustee to properly perform the duties and accomplish the purposes of the trust, the authorization to be granted only upon written application to a justice of the court and upon the notice, if any, that the justice may direct.

Figure 8.4 Discussion Questions:

1. Compare Figure 8.3 with Figure 8.4. List at least one power in Figure 8.3 that is not in Figure 8.4.

2. Find at least one power in Figure 8.4 that is not listed in Figure 8.3

Co-Trustees

Co-trustees serving simultaneously must act unanimously in most jurisdictions. Consider Figure 8.5, a statute from the state of Nevada pertaining to what happens when there are multiple trustees.

Figure 8.5

NRS 163.110 Powers of cotrustees: Exercisable by majority if more than two cotrustees; liability of dissenting cotrustee; unanimous action required if only two cotrustees; petition of interested person.

1. Unless it is otherwise provided by the trust instrument or by court order, any power vested in three or more trustees may be exercised by a majority of the trustees. A trustee who has not joined in exercising a power is not liable to the beneficiaries or to others for the consequences of the exercise of power and a dissenting trustee is not liable for the consequences of an act in which that trustee joined at the direction of the majority trustees, if the trustee expressed his or her dissent in writing to any of his or her cotrustees at or before the time of the joinder.

2. This section does not excuse a cotrustee from liability for inactivity in the administration of the trust nor for failure to attempt to prevent a breach of trust.

3. Except as otherwise authorized in the trust instrument or by order of the court, a power vested in two trustees may only be exercised by unanimous action.

4. If the trustees cannot exercise a power vested in them in a manner permitted by this section, an interested person may petition the court for appropriate instructions pursuant to NRS 164.010 and 164.015.

[10:136:1941; 1931 NCL § 7718.39]—(NRS A 1999, 2368)

Note that in Nevada, where there are two trustees, unanimous action is required. In other words, both trustees must perform all actions on behalf of the trust together—in agreement and in concert. This represents the rule in the majority of states, not only for trustees, but also for other fiduciaries covered in this chapter. This raises drafting considerations that are addressed in the *Paralegal Practice Tips* later in this chapter.

Now examine Ohio's rules for multiple trustees in Figure 8.6.

Under Ohio law, where there are three or more trustees, the trustees may act by majority decision. Interestingly, (G) imposes an additional fiduciary duty on each

Figure 8.6

Ohio Revised Code §5807.03 Cotrustees - delegation - liability.

(A) If there are three or more cotrustees serving, the cotrustees may act by majority decision.

(B) If a vacancy occurs in a cotrusteeship, the remaining cotrustees may act for the trust.

(C) A cotrustee must participate in the performance of a trustee's function unless the cotrustee is unavailable to perform the function because of absence, illness, disqualification under other law, or other temporary incapacity or the cotrustee has properly delegated the performance of the function to another trustee.

(D) If a cotrustee is unavailable to perform duties because of absence, illness, disqualification under other law, or other temporary incapacity and prompt action is necessary to achieve the purposes of the trust or to avoid injury to the trust property, the remaining cotrustee or a majority of the remaining cotrustees may act for the trust.

(E) A trustee may delegate to a cotrustee duties and powers that a prudent trustee of comparable skills could properly delegate under the circumstances. A delegation made under this division shall be governed by section 5808.07 of the Revised Code. Unless a delegation was irrevocable, a trustee may revoke a delegation previously made.

(F) Except as otherwise provided in division (G) of this section, and subject to divisions (C) and (E) of this section, a trustee who does not join in an action of another trustee is not liable for the action.

(G) Except as otherwise provided in this division, each trustee shall exercise reasonable care to prevent a cotrustee from committing a serious breach of trust and to compel a cotrustee to redress a serious breach of trust. A trustee is not required to exercise reasonable care of that nature under this division, and a trustee is not liable for resulting losses, when section 5815.25 of the Revised Code is applicable or there is more than one other trustee and the other trustees act by majority vote.

(H) A dissenting trustee who joins in an action at the direction of the majority of the trustees and who notified any cotrustee of the dissent at or before the time of the action is not liable for the action.

Effective Date: 01-01-2007

---

trustee to "exercise reasonable care to prevent a cotrustee from committing a serious breach of trust and to compel a cotrustee to redress such a breach of trust." In other words, a cotrustee is not only responsible for his or her own actions, but also to watch out for the conduct of co-fiduciaries to ensure that breaches of trust do not occur.

Powers of Guardian

A **guardian** is one who legally has the care and management of the person, property, or both of a minor or incompetent. Figure 8.7 outlines the statutory powers given to guardians in the state of South Carolina.

Figure 8.7

South Carolina Probate Code SECTION 62-5-312. General powers and duties of **guardian**. [SC ST SEC 62-5-312]

(a) A **guardian** of an incapacitated person has the same powers, rights, and duties respecting his ward that a parent has respecting his unemancipated minor child except that a **guardian** is not liable to third persons for acts of the ward solely by reason of the parental relationship. In particular, and without qualifying the foregoing, a **guardian** has the following powers and duties, except as modified by order of the court:

  (1) to the extent that it is consistent with the terms of any order by a court of competent jurisdiction relating to detention or commitment of the ward, he is entitled to custody of the person of his ward and may establish the ward's place of abode within or without this State.

  (2) If entitled to custody of his ward he shall make provision for the care, comfort, and maintenance of his ward and, whenever appropriate, arrange for his training and education. Without regard to custodial rights of the ward's person, he shall take reasonable care of his ward's clothing, furniture, vehicles, and other personal effects and commence protective proceedings if other property of his ward is in need of protection.

  (3) A **guardian** may give any consents or approvals that may be necessary to enable the ward to receive medical or other professional care, counsel, treatment, or service.

  (4) If no conservator for the estate of the ward has been appointed or if the **guardian** is also conservator, he may:

    (i) institute proceedings to compel any person under a duty to support the ward or to pay sums for the welfare of the ward to perform his duty;

    (ii) receive money and tangible property deliverable to the ward and apply the money and property for support, care, and education of the ward; but, he may not use funds from his ward's estate for room and board or services which he, his spouse, parent, or child have furnished the ward unless a charge for the services and/or room and board is approved by order of the court made upon notice to at least one of the next of kin of the ward, if notice is possible. He must exercise care to conserve any excess for the ward's needs.

  (5) A **guardian** is required to report the condition of his ward and of the estate which has been subject to his possession or control, as required by the court or court rule, but at least on an annual basis.

  (6) If a conservator has been appointed, all of the ward's estate received by the **guardian** in excess of those funds expended to meet current expenses for support, care, and education of the ward must be paid to the conservator for management as provided in this Code, and the **guardian** must account to the conservator for funds expended.

(b) Any **guardian** of one for whom a conservator also has been appointed shall control the custody and care of the ward and is entitled to receive reasonable sums for his services and for room and board furnished to the ward as agreed upon between him and the conservator, provided the amounts agreed upon are reasonable under the circumstances. The **guardian** may request the conservator to expend the ward's estate by payment to third persons or institutions for the ward's care and maintenance.

HISTORY: 1986 Act No. 539, § 1.

> **Figure 8.7 Discussion Questions:**
> 1. What powers does a guardian in South Carolina have?
> 2. Does it make a difference whether a conservator has been appointed?
> 3. What provisions are specific to a guardian for an incapacitated adult? What do they provide?

Uniform Fiduciaries Act
An act drafted by the National Conference of Commissioners on Uniform State laws and approved and recommended for enactment in all states in 1922. "The general purpose of the Act is to establish uniform and definite rules in place . . . as to 'constructive notice' of breaches of fiduciary obligations . . . [and to] facilitate the performance by fiduciaries of their obligations, rather than to favor any particular class of persons dealing with fiduciaries."

PARALEGAL PRACTICE TIP

- When drafting documents, it is a good idea for clients to appoint at least one alternate for each type of fiduciary. The alternate performs if the client's first choice is unable to act.
- Clients should consider physical location when appointing their agents. All other factors being equal, it is easier for fiduciaries to perform if they live nearby. For example, Mary Greer has two daughters and trusts them both. Jenna lives down the street from Mary; Megan lives in another state. It makes sense to appoint Jenna as Mary's agent and Megan as the alternate agent because Jenna is close by and it is easier for her to serve.
- Clients should give careful thought to whether it is appropriate to appoint co-fiduciaries. Co-fiduciaries must generally act in concert and it can be difficult if the fiduciaries do not both live nearby or do not see eye to eye.

■ UNIFORM FIDUCIARIES ACT

The **Uniform Fiduciaries Act** was drafted by the National Conference of Commissioners on Uniform State Laws and approved and recommended for enactment in all states in 1922. The purposes of the Act are outlined in the model version as follows:

> "The general purpose of the Act is to establish uniform and definite rules in place of the diverse and indefinite rules now prevailing as to 'constructive notice' of breaches of fiduciary obligations. In some cases there should be no liability in the absence of actual knowledge or bad faith; in others there should be action at peril. In none of the situations here treated is the standard of due care or negligence made the test."

> "The general purpose of the Act is to facilitate the performance by fiduciaries of their obligations, rather than to favor any particular class of persons dealing with fiduciaries. In order to prevent occasional breaches of trust, the courts have sometimes adopted rules which can easily be evaded by a dishonest fiduciary, but which seriously hamper honest fiduciaries in the performance of their obligations. The fact that the English courts have substantially adopted the principles here laid down, and that these principles have worked well in practice, would tend to dissipate any fear that their adoption in this country would result in inadequate protection to beneficiaries."

The following states adopted the Act in some form:

Alabama: Ala. Code § 19-1-1 et seq.

Arizona: Ariz. Rev. Stat. § 14-7501 et seq.

Colorado: Colo. Rev. Stat. § 15-1-101 et seq.

Hawaii: Haw. Rev. Stat. § 556-1 et seq.

Idaho: Idaho Code § 68-301 et seq.

Indiana: Ind. Code § 30-2-4-1 et seq.

Louisiana: La. Rev. Stat. § 9:3801 et seq. . . . Scroll down to "3801" or browser-search for it.

Maryland: Md. Code, Est. & Tr. art., § 15-201 et seq.

Minnesota: Minn. Stat. § 520.01 et seq.

Missouri: Mo. Rev. Stat. § 456.240 et seq. . . . Scroll down to "456.240" or browser-search for it.

Nevada: Nev. Rev. Stat. § 162.010 et seq.

New Jersey: N.J. Stat. § 3B:14-52 et seq.

New York: N.Y. Gen. Bus. Law art. 23-B [§ 359-i et seq.]

North Carolina: N.C. Gen. Stat. § 32-1 et seq.

Ohio: Ohio Rev. Code § 5815.04 et seq. . . . [Uniform Fiduciary Act] Scroll down to § 5815.04.

Tennessee: Tenn. Code § 35-2-101 et seq.

Utah: Utah Code § 22-1-1 et seq.

Wisconsin: Wis. Stats. § 112.01

See http://lawsource.com/also/usa.cgi?usm.

Figure 8.8 is the Uniform Fiduciaries Act as approved by the American Bar Association and recommended for enactment in the states.

Figure 8.8 Uniform Fiduciaries Act

AN ACT CONCERNING LIABILITY FOR PARTICIPATION IN BREACHES OF FIDUCIARY OBLIGATION AND TO MAKE UNIFORM THE LAW WITH REFERENCE THERETO.

Be it enacted

SECTION 1. [Definition of Terms.]

(1) In this act unless the context of subject-matter otherwise requires:

"Bank" includes any person or association of persons, whether incorporated or not, carrying on the business of banking.

"Fiduciary" includes a trustee under any trust, expressed, implied, resulting or constructive, executor, administrator, guardian, conservator, curator, receiver, trustee in bankruptcy, assignee for the benefit of creditors, partner, agent, officer of a corporation, public or private, public officer, or any other person acting in a fiduciary capacity for any person, trust or estate.

"Person" includes a corporation, partnership, or other association, or two or more persons having a joint or common interest.

"Principal" includes any person to whom a fiduciary as such owes an obligation.

(2) A thing is done "in good faith" within the meaning of this act, when it is in fact done honestly, whether it be done negligently or not.

SECTION 2. [Application of Payments Made to Fiduciaries.] A person who in good faith pays or transfers to a fiduciary any money or other property which the fiduciary as such is authorized to receive, is not responsible for the proper application thereof by the fiduciary; and any right or title acquired from the fiduciary in consideration of such payment or transfer is not invalid in consequence of a misapplication by the fiduciary.

SECTION 3. [Registration of Transfer of Securities Held by Fiduciaries.] If a fiduciary in whose name are registered any shares of stock, bonds or other securities of any corporation, public or private, or company or other association, or of any trust, transfers the same, such corporation or company or other association, or any of the managers of the trust, or its or their transfer agent, is not bound to inquire whether the fiduciary is committing a breach of his obligation as fiduciary in making the transfer, or to see to the performance of the fiduciary obligation, and is liable for registering such transfer only where registration of the transfer is made with actual knowledge that the fiduciary is committing a breach of his obligation as fiduciary in making the transfer, or with knowledge of such facts that the action in registering the transfer amounts to bad faith.

SECTION 4. [Transfer of Negotiable Instrument by Fiduciary.] If any negotiable instrument payable or indorsed to a fiduciary as such is indorsed by the fiduciary, or if any negotiable instrument payable or indorsed to his principal is indorsed by a fiduciary empowered to indorse such instrument on behalf of his principal, the indorsee is not bound to inquire whether the fiduciary is committing a breach of his obligation as fiduciary in indorsing or delivering the instrument, and is not chargeable with notice that the fiduciary is committing a breach of his obligation as fiduciary unless he takes the instrument with actual knowledge of such breach or with knowledge of such facts that his action in taking the instrument amounts to bad faith. If, however, such instrument is transferred by the fiduciary in payment of or as security for a personal debt of the fiduciary to the actual knowledge of the creditor, or is transferred in any transaction known by the transferee to be for the personal benefit of the fiduciary, the creditor or other transferee is liable to the principal if the fiduciary in fact commits a breach of his obligation as fiduciary in transferring the instrument.

SECTION 5. [Check Drawn by Fiduciary Payable to Third Person.] If a check or other bill of exchange is drawn by a fiduciary as such, or in the name of his principal by a fiduciary empowered to draw such instrument in the name of his principal, the payee is not bound to inquire whether the fiduciary is committing a breach of his obligation as fiduciary in drawing or delivering the instrument, and is not chargeable with notice that the fiduciary is committing a breach of his obligation as fiduciary unless he takes the instrument with actual knowledge of such breach or with knowledge of such facts that his action in taking the instrument amounts to bad faith. If, however, such instrument is payable to a personal creditor of the fiduciary and delivered to the creditor in payment of or as security for a personal debt of the fiduciary to the actual knowledge of the creditor, or is drawn and delivered in any transaction known by the payee to be for the personal benefit of the fiduciary, the creditor or other payee is liable to the principal if the fiduciary in fact commits a breach of his obligation as fiduciary in drawing or delivering the instrument.

SECTION 6. [Check Drawn by and Payable to Fiduciary.] If a check or other bill of exchange is drawn by a fiduciary as such or in the name of his principal by a fiduciary empowered to draw in the name of his principal by a fiduciary empowered to draw such instrument in the name of his principal, payable to the fiduciary personally, or payable to a third person and by him transferred to the fiduciary, and is thereafter transferred by the fiduciary,

(continued)

Figure 8.8 (continued)

whether in payment of a personal debt of the fiduciary or otherwise, the transferee is not bound to inquire whether the fiduciary is committing a breach of his obligation as fiduciary in transferring the instrument, and is not chargeable with notice that the fiduciary is committing a breach of his obligation as fiduciary unless he takes the instrument with actual knowledge of such breach or with knowledge of such facts that his action in taking the instrument amounts to bad faith.

SECTION 7. [Deposit in Name of Fiduciary as Such.] If a deposit is made in a bank to the credit of a fiduciary as such, the bank is authorized to pay the amount of the deposit or any part thereof upon the check of the fiduciary, signed with the name in which such deposit is entered, without being liable to the principal, unless the bank pays the check with actual knowledge that the fiduciary is committing a breach of his obligation as fiduciary in drawing the check or with knowledge of such facts that its action in paying the check amounts to bad faith. If, however, such a check is payable to the drawee bank and is delivered to it in payment of or as security for a personal debt of the fiduciary to it, the bank is liable to the principal if the fiduciary in fact commits a breach of his obligation as fiduciary in drawing or delivering the check.

SECTION 8. [Deposit in Name of Principal.] If a check is drawn upon the account of his principal in a bank by a fiduciary who is empowered to draw checks upon his principal's account, the bank is authorized to pay such check without being liable to the principal, unless the bank pays the check with actual knowledge that the fiduciary is committing a breach of his obligation as fiduciary in drawing such check, or with knowledge of such facts that its action in paying the check amounts to bad faith. If, however, such a check is payable to the drawee bank and is delivered to it in payment of or as security for a personal debt of the fiduciary to it, the bank is liable to the principal if the fiduciary in fact commits a breach of his obligation as fiduciary in drawing or delivering the check.

SECTION 9. [Deposit in Fiduciary's Personal Account.] If a fiduciary makes a deposit in a bank to his personal credit of checks drawn by him upon an account in his own name as fiduciary, or of checks payable to him as fiduciary, or of checks drawn by him upon an account in the name of his principal if he is empowered to draw checks thereon, or of checks payable to his principal and indorsed by him, if he is empowered to indorse such checks, or if he otherwise makes a deposit of funds held by him as fiduciary, the bank receiving such deposit is not bound to inquire whether the fiduciary is committing thereby a breach of his obligation as fiduciary; and the bank is authorized to pay the amount of the deposit or any part thereof upon the personal check of the fiduciary without being liable to the principal, unless the bank receives the deposit or pays the check with actual knowledge that the fiduciary is committing a breach of his obligation as fiduciary in making such deposit or in drawing such check, or with knowledge of such facts that its action in receiving the deposit or paying the check amounts to bad faith.

SECTION 10. [Deposit in Names of Two or More Trustees.] When a deposit is made in a bank in the name of two or more persons as trustees and a check is drawn upon the trust account by any trustee or trustees authorized by the other trustee or trustees to draw checks upon the trust account, neither the payee nor other holder nor the bank is bound to inquire whether it is a breach of trust to authorize such trustee or trustees to draw checks upon the trust account, and is not liable unless the circumstances be such that the action of the payee or other holder or the bank amounts to bad faith.

SECTION 11. [Act not Retroactive.] The provisions of this act shall not apply to transactions taking place prior to the time when it takes effect.

SECTION 12. [Cases not Provided for in Act.] In any case not provided for in this act the rules of law and equity, including the law merchant and those rules of law and equity relating to trusts, agency, negotiable instruments and banking, shall continue to apply.

SECTION 13. [Uniformity of Interpretation.] This act shall be so interpreted and construed as to effectuate its general purpose to make uniform the law of those states which enact it.

SECTION 14. [Short Title.] This act may be cited as the Uniform Fiduciaries Act.

SECTION 15. [Inconsistent Laws Repealed.] All acts or parts of acts inconsistent with this act are hereby repealed.

SECTION 16. [Time of Taking Effect.] This Act shall take effect [ ].

Figure 8.8 Discussion Questions

1. What were the expressed purposes of the Uniform Fiduciary Act?
2. How does the Uniform Fiduciary Act help fiduciaries to do their job?
3. Does the Uniform Fiduciary Act afford any protection to third parties? Explain your answer.

FIDUCIARY DUTIES

Along with all of the statutory and documentary powers, fiduciaries have fundamental duties to uphold. Fiduciaries are held to a high moral and legal standard and must always act in the best interest of those whom they are appointed to serve. Fiduciary duties include the duties of loyalty, disclosure, accounting, obedience, and more. Fiduciaries are entrusted with the assets and property of others and must be organized, intelligent, honest, and loyal. Fiduciaries must be capable of engaging in business transactions such as making contracts and selling assets. A failure to act in the best interest of those being served is called a **breach of fiduciary duty**. Fiduciaries may potentially be held civilly liable for breaches of duty, acts of negligence, and other failures in service.

CONCLUSION

The agents discussed in prior chapters including health care agents, attorneys-in-fact, executors, trustees, guardians, and conservators, are fiduciaries. *Fiduciaries are individuals who are held in a position of trust and confidence and who must act in the best interest of those whom they are appointed to serve.* A failure to act in the best interest of those being served is a *breach of fiduciary duty.* Fiduciaries may be held liable for breaches of duty, acts of negligence, and other failures. The cases at the end of this chapter illustrate how courts inquire into fiduciary behavior to determine appropriateness.

PARALEGAL PRACTICE TIPS

- When drafting documents for clients, remember that their appointed fiduciaries should NOT be any of the following: minors, incompetent persons, felons, or persons who have or may have a conflict of interest.

Breach of Fiduciary Duty
A failure by a fiduciary to act in the best interest of those being served.

CONCEPT REVIEW AND REINFORCEMENT

KEY TERMS

Fiduciary   234
Guardian   234
Fiduciary Duty   234
Fiduciary Capacity   234
Power of Attorney   234

Principal (also known as the "Grantor")   234
Attorney-in-Fact   234
Executor   236
Executrix   236

Trustee   237
Uniform Fiduciaries Act   242
Breach of Fiduciary Duty   245

REVIEW QUESTIONS

1. List some of the agents who are known as fiduciaries.
2. What are the two sources of fiduciary power?
3. What are some common powers granted under a power of attorney?
4. What are some common powers given to an executor?
5. What are some common powers given to a trustee?
6. List some common powers given to trustees.
7. What is fiduciary capacity?
8. Explain what fiduciary duty means.
9. What is a breach of fiduciary duty?
10. What is the purpose of the Uniform Fiduciaries Act?

BUILDING YOUR PARALEGAL SKILLS

CRITICAL THINKING EXERCISES

1. If you were a state legislator, would you approve the Uniform Fiduciaries Act for approval in full or in part? Which parts would you remove, if any?

2. What type of characteristics would you look for in an individual whom you were contemplating appointing as *your* fiduciary?

PARALEGAL PRACTICE

1. _____

MEMORANDUM
To: Paralegal
From: Supervising Attorney
Client: Not Applicable
Re: Powers of Trustees

I want to make sure that our firm's trust templates are as current as possible. Please research the statutory powers for trustees in our state and print a copy. Review the statutory powers and summarize them for me in the form of a return memorandum with the statutory copy attached to the memo. Finally, think of at least one power a trustee could need to effectively perform his or her duties that you feel is missing from the statutory powers. Draft a proposed paragraph conferring that power to a trustee.

ONLINE RESOURCES

The Pearson Course Companion website contains the following additional resources:
- **Forms for Paralegal Practice Activities**
- Chapter Objectives
- Online Study Guide (Containing Multiple Choice and True/False Questions)
- Web Exercises www.pearsonhighered.com/careers

CASES FOR CONSIDERATION

CASE #1:

DELINA ANDRIOLO, AS EXECUTRIX OF THE ESTATE OF MARY FRIGAULT ET AL. V. KAREN MAINES

2007 Mass. Super. LEXIS 537
December 19, 2007, Decided

OPINION BY: Thomas P. Billings

MEMORANDUM AND ORDER ON DEFENDANT'S MOTION FOR SUMMARY JUDGMENT

The defendant's Motion for Summary Judgment is ALLOWED.

The deposition testimony of Atty. Spino establishes, without contradiction, that when he met with Mary Frigault in late May 2004, and again several days later on May 27 when she executed the Power of Attorney, she was able to understand and carry in mind the nature, situation and extent of her property and her relation to the natural objects of her bounty; was free from delusion resulting from disease or weakness that would or could influence the disposition of her property; and was able to comprehend the nature of the transaction she was undertaking. See *Palmer v. Palmer*, 23 Mass. App. Ct. 245, 250, 500 N.E.2d 1354 (1986). The record similarly establishes that the decisions to put the assets of her 401(k) plan into a trust for the benefit of her granddaughters, to execute a durable power of attorney, and to appoint the defendant as her attorney in fact were Ms. Frigault's alone.

The conclusory statement to the contrary in the affidavit of Lorraine Allain, and her observations and those of the plaintiff that Ms. Frigault was in pain, medicated, and drowsy during the afternoon before the evening on which (after Ms. Allain and the plaintiff had left for the day) she signed the Power of Attorney, are insufficient in the face of the direct, contrary evidence supplied by Spino--to create a genuine issue concerning whether Ms. Frigault lacked the capacity to execute the power of attorney or the declaration of trust, or whether she did so under duress. See *Brogan v. Brogan*, 59 Mass. App. Ct. 398, 402-03, 796 N.E.2d 850 (2003).

Finally, it is undisputed in the record that the defendant, as attorney-in-fact, acted in accordance with her principal's instructions in transferring the assets of the 401(k) plan into the trust established for the granddaughters' benefit, and did not breach her fiduciary duty by self-dealing or otherwise. See *Gagnon v. Coombs*, 39 Mass. App. Ct. 144, 155, 157-58, 654 N.E.2d 54 (1995).

There was therefore no breach of fiduciary duty (Count I), and no conversion (Count II), and the defendant is entitled to judgment as a matter of law.

ORDER

Summary judgment is to enter for the defendant, dismissing the Complaint. The case will remain open, however, pending a final order on the plaintiff's Cross Motion for Sanctions (Paper # 17).

Thomas P. Billings, Associate Justice
Dated: December 19, 2007

Case Questions

1. What was the issue in this case?
2. Did Ms. Frigault (the principal) have capacity when she executed a power of attorney?
3. Did the attorney-in-fact act in accordance with the principal's instructions?
4. Did the attorney-in-fact breach her fiduciary duty to Ms. Frigault? Why or why not?

CASE #2:

ESTATE OF ESTHER M. NICELY, DECEASED

1998 Phila. Ct. Com. Pl. LEXIS 11
September 2, 1998, Decided

OPINION BY: PAWELEC

OPINION

First and Final Account of First Western Trust Services Company, Successor to Beaver Trust Company, and Inez C. Nicely, Attorney-in-Fact for Esther M. Nicely.

Before the court for adjudication is the first and final account of First Western Services Co., successor to Beaver Trust Company and Inez C. Nicely, attorneys-in-fact for Esther M. Nicely. The account is actually stated by First Western Services Company. Inez C. Nicely has refused to join in or sign the account. Instead, acting in her capacity as Executrix of the Estate of Esther M. Nicely, Deceased, Inez C. Nicely has filed Objections to the Bank's accounting as attorney-in-fact.

On May 11, 1988, Esther M. Nicely and her husband, Daniel J. Nicely, executed separate but identical powers of attorney which appointed Beaver Trust Company and their daughter, Inez C. Nicely, as attorneys-in-fact, to act either jointly or individually, as they may agree. Copies of the powers have been admitted into evidence as Exhibits O-13 and O-12 respectively.

Having appointed the Bank and their daughter as attorneys-in-fact, the Nicelys delivered assets valued at more than $1,000,000.00 into the hands of the Bank. These assets included, inter alia: more than $700,000.00 in bank deposits and securities titled in the names of Daniel J. Nicely and Esther M. Nicely, his wife; more than $100,000.00 in bank deposits titled in the names of Daniel and his daughter, Inez; more than $100,000.00 in securities titled in the names of Esther and her daughter, Inez; more than $15,000.00 in securities titled in the names of Daniel and his wife and son, Donald A. Nicely; and, more than $90,000.00 in securities titled in the names of Esther and son, Donald.

Among the securities titled in the names of Daniel J. Nicely and Esther M. Nicely, his wife, and delivered to the Bank, as attorney-in-fact, was a certain Subordinated Capital Note of Colony Savings Bank which bore: an issue date of April 16, 1987; a maturity date of April 16, 1997; a face value of $30,000.00; and, a 12.5% rate of interest. On its reverse side, said Subordinated Capital Note bore the following language,

> "In addition, upon the death of any Noteholder, whether or not the Subordinated Capital Note was held jointly, the Bank, if requested, will redeem any Subordinated Capital Note tendered to it within 180 days of the Noteholder's death by the personal representative of the Noteholder's estate or by the surviving joint holder. Such redemption will be made at 100% of the principal amount plus accrued interest."

Having appointed the Bank and their daughter as attorneys-in-fact, the Nicelys also delivered their original Wills into the hands of the Bank. By his Will, dated August 20, 1985, Daniel J. Nicely, gave all of his estate to his wife, Esther M. Nicely, and, appointed her to act as executrix. In the event of the death of Esther in his lifetime, Daniel made bequests of stock, gave the residue of his estate to his children, Donald Alvin Nicely and Inez C. Nicely, and, appointed Inez

to act as executrix. By her Will, dated August 21, 1985, Esther M. Nicely gave all of her estate to her husband, Daniel J. Nicely, and, appointed him to act as executor. In the event of the death of Daniel in her lifetime, Esther made bequests of stock, gave the residue of her estate to her children, Donald Alvin Nicely and Inez C. Nicely, and appointed Inez to act as executrix.

Daniel J. Nicely died on July 29, 1988 and his Will of August 20, 1985 was duly admitted to probate by the Register of Wills of Beaver County. Because Esther M. Nicely and Inez C. Nicely renounced their rights to administer the decedent's estate, Beaver Trust Company was appointed Administrator d.b.n.c.t.a. of the Estate of Daniel J. Nicely, Deceased. Because there was no change in the titles of the assets which had been delivered to the Bank as attorney-in-fact, Esther M. Nicely became sole owner of those assets which had been titled in the names of herself and her late husband. Acting as Administrator, the Bank filed an Inventory in the Estate of Daniel J. Nicely, Deceased, which Inventory showed a total estate of $46,950.00, consisting of an automobile valued at $2,850.00, and, a Capital Note of First Western Bancorp valued at $44,100.00. On August 1, 1988, acting as attorney-in-fact for Esther M. Nicely, the Bank acknowledged receipt of said Capital Note.

On January 9, 1989, again acting as attorney-in-fact for Esther M. Nicely, the Bank changed the title of the aforementioned Subordinated Capital Note of Colony Savings Bank from Daniel J. and Esther M. Nicely, joint tenants, to Esther M. Nicely, individual. Said Subordinated Capital Note became worthless when, on or about April 5, 1990, the Office of Thrift Supervision of the U.S. Department of the Treasury placed Colony Savings Bank into receivership.

Esther M. Nicely died on November 29, 1994, testate and a resident of Philadelphia. Her Will of August 21, 1985 was duly admitted to probate by the Register of Wills of Philadelphia County who granted Letters Testamentary to her daughter, Inez C. Nicely. Acting as Executrix, Inez C. Nicely has filed numerous objections to the instant account which was filed by the Bank, her co-attorney-in-fact, on March 3, 1995.

The objections are enumerated in three separate filings: 1) Objections to account, 2) Supplemental Objections, and 3) Second Supplemental Objections. They are then restated at pages 2 and 3, and, pages 59 through 63 of her brief. All other objections or claims were withdrawn or waived.

By her Objections and brief, Inez C. Nicely raises the following questions for adjudication:

1. Reimbursement to the Estate of Esther M. Nicely of $187,616.20 plus interest from date of payment for Federal Estate Tax unnecessarily paid caused by breach of First Western's fiduciary duty and negligence. By this Objection, the objectant seeks to surcharge the accountant in the full amount of Federal Estate Tax which was paid on the death of Esther M. Nicely, being $187,616.20, together with interest from the date of payment of such tax, being August 29, 1995. This Objection is premised on the theory that the Bank was negligent and breached its fiduciary duty in failing to inform and advise the principal and her husband, Daniel J. Nicely, of the opportunity to minimize or eliminate the payment of Federal Estate Tax on the death of the surviving spouse. The objectant contends that Esther's estate would have paid no Federal Estate Tax if the accountant had advised the Nicelys to implement a simple estate plan of splitting their assets so that each held the amount of the Unified Credit for Federal Estate Tax purposes in his or her sole name, and, creating trusts of said amounts which trusts would not be in the estate of the surviving spouse on his or her death. The objectant views the bank's failure to give advice on estate planning as negligence and a breach of fiduciary duty which resulted in the unnecessary payment of $187,616.20 in Federal Estate Tax by the estate of the surviving spouse, Esther.

2. Included in 1) above is the overpayment of both Federal Estate Tax and Pennsylvania Inheritance Tax by reason of the breach of the fiduciary duty and negligence of First Western in the failure to disclaim an asset in the amount of $44,100.00 which remained an asset of the principal and unnecessarily included in the Federal and Pennsylvania Estate Tax Returns. By this Objection, the objectant seeks to surcharge the accountant in the amount of $18,643.22, being Federal Estate Tax and Pennsylvania transfer inheritance tax which were paid by the estate of Esther M. Nicely on the aforementioned Capital Note of First Western Bancorp, together with interest from the date of payment of such taxes, being August 29, 1995. Said Capital Note was valued at $44,100.00 on the death of Daniel J. Nicely. Acting as administrator of Daniel's estate, the Bank distributed said Capital Note to itself as attorney-in-fact for Esther. According to the objectant, the inclusion of said Capital Note in Esther's estate resulted in unnecessary payments of $15,888.07 in Federal Estate Tax

and $2,755.15 in Pennsylvania transfer inheritance tax. This Objection is premised on the theory that the Bank was negligent and breached its fiduciary duty in failing to disclaim said Capital Note on behalf of Esther, or, in the alternative, in failing to advise her or her daughter, the co-attorney-in-fact, of the availability of a disclaimer as a means of eliminating the payment of death taxes on said Capital Note on the death of Esther.

3. Reimbursement to the Estate of Esther M. Nicely of $30,000.00 plus interest from March 28, 1990 for the negligent management of the aforementioned Colony Savings Bank Subordinated Capital Note due 4/16/97. Acknowledged as received in the Account but carried erroneously in the Account at p. 27(b) at face value, but which is without value. By this Objection, the objectant seeks to surcharge the accountant in the amount of $30,000.00, together with interest from the last payment of interest on the Colony Note. Objectant argues that the Bank should have redeemed the Colony Note and not had it reissued. This argument is premised on the theory that the accountant, especially considering its financial expertise, knew or should have known that Colony Savings Bank was an unsound financial institution, and, accordingly, this investment was unsound. Further, objectant argues that when the accountant had the Colony Note reissued in the name of Mrs. Nicely instead of redeeming it, the accountant, in fact, made an investment decision for which it is responsible.

4. Reimbursement to the Estate of Esther M. Nicely for overpayment of individual federal income tax of principal for the tax years 1988 through 1993. By this Objection, the objectant seeks to surcharge the accountant in the amount of $868.00, being overpayments of federal income taxes allegedly caused by understatement of the Bank's compensation as deductions on the principal's Forms 1040 for calendar years 1988 to 1993. In its brief, the Bank asserts that $868.00 is a de minimis amount, and, agrees to have said amount deducted from its request for compensation.

5. Reimbursement to the Estate of Esther M. Nicely of interest and penalties paid by reason of the late filing of 1993 and 1994 Personal Property Tax Returns with Philadelphia County. By this Objection, the objectant seeks to surcharge the accountant in the amount of $290.03, being payments of interest and penalties on delinquent payments of Philadelphia Personal Property Taxes

for calendar years 1993 and 1994. In its brief, the Bank asserts that $290.03 is a de minimis amount, and, agrees to have said amount deducted from its request for compensation.

6. Reimbursement to the Estate of Esther M. Nicely for the unnecessary expenses, costs, including attorney fees, incurred by the Estate for the failure of First Western to turnover upon proper demand the assets of the principal following the death of Esther on November 29, 1994 causing expenses of legal proceedings to compel turnover. By this Objection, the objectant seeks to surcharge the accountant in the amount of $7,750.00, being attorney's fees and costs incurred by the objectant in the period December 7, 1994 to March 29, 1995, together with interest from the date of payment of such fees and costs, being April of 1995. The objectant argues that this is a claim for damages sustained by the principal's estate as a result of the allegedly egregious conduct of the Bank in failing and refusing to deliver the assets of the deceased principal to the duly appointed and qualified executrix of her estate.

7. Costs and expenses including attorney fees incurred by the Executrix in the prosecution of the within proceedings to recover from First Western the losses to the estate of the principal caused by the breach of fiduciary duties owed to the principal. By this Objection, the objectant seeks to surcharge the accountant, in an undetermined amount, for counsel fees, costs, expert witness fees and all other expenses of her efforts to prosecute the aforementioned surcharge claims. In her brief, the objectant seeks leave to file a Petition to determine the amount of this surcharge.

8. A denial of the requested termination fee of $16,134.00 because of (a) lack of written fee agreement and (b) the breaches of the fiduciary duties by First Western owed to the principal. In its Petition for Adjudication, the Bank seeks a "termination fee" of $16,134.08, being one (1%) percent of the market value of the principal on the death of Esther M. Nicely, that is, on November 29, 1994. By this Objection, the objectant opposes said claim for a "termination fee".

9. First Western is not entitled to counsel fees, costs and filing fees. By this Objection, the objectant opposes said claims to counsel fees, costs and filing fees. The objectant argues that the Bank did not have to file an account, and, that it did so only to protect its own interests.

Surcharge is a penalty for failure to exercise common prudence, common skill and common caution in the performance of the fiduciary duty and is imposed to compensate beneficiaries for loss caused by a fiduciary's want of due care. *Estate of Dobson*, 490 Pa. 476, 478, 417 A.2d 138; *Presumptions and the Burden of Proof in the Orphans' Court*, (Tredinnick, J.), 7 Fiduc. Rep. 2d 102, 127.

In general, one who seeks to surcharge a fiduciary bears the burden of proving that the trustee breached an applicable fiduciary duty. *Estate of Dobson*, supra; *Estate of Stetson*, 463 Pa. 64, 345 A.2d 679; *Linn Est.*, 435 Pa. 598, 258 A.2d 645; *Maurice Est.*, 433 Pa. 103, 249 A.2d 334. The one seeking the surcharge must prove his or her case by a preponderance of evidence. Further, a "corporate fiduciary is presumed to possess greater competence in the management of estates than a man of ordinary prudence." See *Kelsey Trust*, 12 Fiduc. Rep. 2d, 209. We shall examine the objections in accord with the aforesaid standards.

Objectant contends that when her parents executed their individual powers of attorney designating objectant and the Bank as attorneys-in-fact, they not only empowered these agents to act on their behalf in regard to all the matters enumerated in the powers, but, when the attorneys-in-fact accepted the said designation, a concomitant duty was imposed upon the attorneys-in-fact to affirmatively exercise the enumerated powers set forth in the powers for the benefit of the principals.

Alternatively, objectant contends that by agreeing to act as an agent pursuant to said powers, and, by taking action pursuant to said powers, the Bank assumed an affirmative obligation to use the full range of its expertise, including but not limited to its expertise in estate planning and investment management, for the benefit of the Nicelys.

In support of this theory, counsel for objectant cites much law in his extensive brief. He states "that the Power of Attorney created and established a principal and agency relationship between the parties. *3 Am.Jur. 2d Agency, § 23*; *In Re Shahan*, 429 Pa. Super 91, 631 A.2d 1298 (1993); *In re Miller's Estate*, 19 Pa. D. & C. 141, 7 P.S. §§ 102 and 402. The person holding a power of attorney is known and designated as an 'attorney-in-fact' while the person appointing the attorney-in-fact is generally designated and known as the 'principal'."

Counsel for objectant cites numerous cases dealing with the relationship of agent to principal, and, the duties and obligations of an agent to his principal.

An agency is not a trust. The term "fiduciary," as defined in Section 102 of the Probate, Estates and Fiduciaries Code, 20 Pa.C.S.A. § 102, does not expressly include an "attorney-in-fact" or an "agent." Similarly, the statute under which the Bank has been granted its trust powers does not include "agent" or "attorney-in-fact" within its definition of the term "fiduciary." Nevertheless, it has been recognized that the relationship of agent to principal is a "fiduciary" relationship. *Restatement of Trusts, 2d § 28.*

I find no quarrel with the law as set forth in objectant's brief. However, the cited cases and statutes do not address the seminal issue, i.e. does an attorney-in-fact have an affirmative duty to exercise each and every power which is conferred upon him in a power of attorney? Stated in the alternative: does the enumeration of powers in a power of attorney, in and of itself, impose an affirmative duty upon the attorney-in-fact to exercise each and every one of those powers? Counsel for objectant has cited no precedent, in statute, case law, or legal treatise, which supports the proposition that such an affirmative duty exists. My independent research has likewise failed to find legal precedent for the existence of any such affirmative duty.

Clearly, when a person executes a power of attorney, he designates, empowers and authorizes his attorney-in-fact to act on his behalf. However, standing alone, a power of attorney is not a contract of employment. The mere existence of a power of attorney, without more, imposes no duty to exercise any of the powers which are conferred therein. An attorney-in-fact is only required to perform such actions and provide such services as he agrees or undertakes to perform or provide. The agreement or undertaking may encompass all or only some of the powers which are enumerated in the power of attorney. The agreement or undertaking may be express or implied. It may be written or verbal. It may arise from the conduct of the principal and agent, as in the case where one acts or fails to act in justifiable reliance upon another's action or inaction.

If the agent agrees or undertakes to exercise a power which has been conferred upon him in a power of attorney, then he must act with due care for the benefit of his principal. An agent is a fiduciary with respect to matters within the scope of his agency and is required to act solely for the benefit of his principal in all matters concerned with the agency. *Onorato v. Wissahickon Park, Inc.*, 430 Pa. 416, 244 A.2d 22 (1968). But, again, this is so only in matters in which the agent has agreed or undertaken to act.

Accordingly, I find the argument advanced by objectant to be without merit. An attorney-in-fact does not have an affirmative duty to exercise any of the powers set forth in a power of attorney unless he has agreed or undertaken to do so.

This is the current law and the common experience. It would not be difficult to envision the mischief and difficulties which would ensue if there was an affirmative duty on the part of every attorney-in-fact to exercise every power which is enumerated in every power of attorney. Is an attorney-in-fact obligated to make gifts or create trusts simply because such powers are enumerated in a power of attorney? The answer must be no. What if the principal is sui juris and capable of acting alone? What if the principal's assets and family situation indicate that gifts and trusts are totally unwarranted?

Now, we must examine the facts to determine if there was any agreement or undertaking to act, and, if there was, what were the terms of the agreement or the nature of the undertaking? It is undisputed that the Nicelys executed powers of attorney designating the Bank and their daughter as their attorneys-in-fact and that the Bank agreed to act in this capacity for a fee.

Inez Nicely first approached the Bank for the purpose of getting help for her parents. She testified that when she met with the Bank representative, Coleman Clougherty, she explained that "my father was getting forgetful; we (her parents) needed help with the administration of income, bills; we needed someone to follow the assets, to invest, reinvest; also, we needed income for my parents for the rest of their lives to take care of their financial needs." [NT 320] She further testified that Mr. Clougherty told her that the Bank could certainly take care of paying the bills, receivables, watching over her parents, that they had what they needed, and, that they (the Bank) could take care of the assets they had. They (the Bank) would invest and reinvest. Subsequently, there was a meeting at the home of Mr. and Mrs. Nicely when the powers of attorney were executed and many of the securities and investments were handed over to the Bank as well as the Wills that Mr. and Mrs. Nicely had previously executed.

Mr. Clougherty, the trust officer from the Bank, was present at both of the aforesaid occasions. After the documents were executed, he took possession of many of the assets and the Wills. He testified that 75% to 85% of the assets were in the joint names of Mr. and Mrs. Nicely, and, that the Wills were received as a safekeeping service. [NT 143] He did read the Wills and noted that they were simple Wills leaving everything to the surviving spouse and then to the children.

Mr. Clougherty was responsible for getting the account opened, seeing it was properly set up, and, he became the administrator of the account. During the administration of the account, he determined that a trust might be a more appropriate vehicle for the management of this account. A trust agreement was prepared and sent to Inez Nicely and Donald Nicely, the children, for review and discussion. There was no further action in regard to the trust.

Jo L. Shane, a trust officer who was familiar with the account, also testified. She stated that when the assets were received, a custodian account, without investment advice, was set up. She stated that this was different than a custodian account with an investment advisor and generated lower fees. She stated that the Bank agreed to hold assets, collect income, pay bills, reinvest cash, reinvest funds when financial investments came due and make provisions for the health, welfare and comfort of the Nicelys. She testified that the assets were never reviewed for suitability of investment but they did look to determine if there were sufficient funds to pay bills. She further testified that the assets were never put in street name as they would have been if the Bank were managing them but remained titled as they were when they were received, i.e. in the names of the Nicelys. Many were in the name of husband and wife. Some were titled jointly with one of the children. The Bank did make recommendations to Inez Nicely for the investment of excess cash or when Certificates of Deposit or Treasury bills matured. She further testified that it was her understanding that the investments were to remain the same as they were when they came into the account. [NT 115-117]

In addition, as attorney-in-fact, the Bank arranged and paid for snow removal and lawn care. They arranged for a cleaning service to be provided to the Nicely residence. They arranged for home nursing and personal care for Mr. and Mrs. Nicely when that became necessary. They collected mortgage payments on a mortgage held by the Nicelys.

Richard Markson and Edwin S. Henry testified on behalf of objectant as experts. They opined as to the powers and duties of the Bank under the powers of attorney, and, as to damages which were allegedly caused by the Bank's performance or lack thereof.

There is nothing in the entire record to support a finding that the Bank agreed or undertook to act as an estate planner or trustee for the Nicelys. It did not breach any duty. Nor was it negligent. The Bank was aware of the composition of the Nicely's assets and the dispositive schemes in their wills. Nevertheless, such knowledge did not impose an affirmative obligation on the Bank, as attorney-in-fact, to advise the Nicelys to divide their assets and execute new Wills in order to minimize death taxes. While the Bank may be presumed to have more expertise in the management of assets than the ordinary man, it had no obligation to do more than it agreed or undertook to do. When it acts, the Bank may be judged by a higher standard. But, it was not required to act. Nor is there any evidence that the Nicelys, at the time the powers of attorney were executed, expected more from the Bank than they received. Income was collected, the bills were paid, excess cash was reinvested, and, matters concerning health and welfare were looked after. Accordingly, Objection 1 is dismissed.

Objection 2 contends that the Bank breached its fiduciary duty to disclaim the interest of Mrs. Nicely in the estate of her husband. If this had been done, the funds would have passed directly to the children and would not have remained available to Mrs. Nicely and would not have been in her estate at the time of her death. It is true that the power of attorney, in No. 16, did empower the attorney-in-fact "to disclaim any interest in property" on behalf of the principal. However, I have already determined that there was no affirmative duty on the part of the attorney-in-fact to exercise any of the listed powers unless there was an agreement or undertaking to do so. I have found no agreement that would impose such a duty nor do I find anything that the Bank did pursuant to the "power" that would impose any extended fiduciary duty on the Bank. The Bank, as Mrs. Nicely's attorney-in-fact and custodian of her assets, simply received assets due her from the estate of her husband pursuant to his Will. Accordingly, I find that the Bank did not breach any fiduciary duty nor was it negligent in not disclaiming Mrs. Nicely's interest in her husband's estate. Objection 2 is dismissed.

Objection 3 deals with the $30,000.00 Colony Savings Bank Note which turned out worthless when the Bank was taken over by the Resolution Trust Company. This note was purchased by the Nicelys on April 16, 1987, and held in both their names as joint tenants. It was a 10 year Note and paid interest at the rate of 12.5%. It was one of the assets turned over by the Nicelys to the Bank in May of 1988. The Note paid interest until March of 1990. Thereafter, Colony Bank was taken over by Resolution Trust Company, and, at that time it became worthless. Prior to that, the Note could have been sold if a buyer could be found. The Note by its terms also provided that upon the death of any Note holder, Colony Savings Bank, if requested, would redeem the Note at face value plus accrued interest. Following the death of Mr. Nicely on July 29, 1988, the accountant had the Note reissued by Colony Savings Bank in the name of Mrs. Nicely, the surviving joint tenant.

Objectant argues that the accountant should have redeemed the Colony Savings Bank Note instead of having it reissued.

In support of this objection, objectant offered the testimony of Richard Markson, CFA, as an expert witness and called Jo Shane as of cross examination. Mr. Markson testified that the Bank should have liquidated the security rather than having it reissued. His conclusion was based on the fact that the note paid 12 1/2% interest, which indicated a speculative security [NT 231] and that pursuant to his analysis, Colony Saving had a negative net worth [NT 230]. He also considered the reissuance of the note in the name of Mrs. Nicely to be an investment decision by the Bank. He also testified that his testimony and opinion are based on the assumption that the Bank had been hired to perform, supervise and give management advice. [NT 248]. However, he went on to say that the Bank also violated its duty as custodian in not informing the principal of the available choice, i.e. reissue or redeem. [NT 248]. He agreed that in 1987 and 1988, Colony Savings Bank was a solvent institution. [NT 251]. It was his opinion that the Note was not of investment quality when it was purchased by Mr. Nicely in 1987. [NT 255-256]. However, he went on to opine that even if the Bank had investment supervisory authority over the account, it did not make economic sense to conduct an investigation of the safety of this hard to value investment when it was such a small component of the total assets in the account. [NT 259-262]. In his opinion, if the security does not seem to meet investment guidelines and the size of the holding does not warrant analysis, a sale recommendation is appropriate. [NT 262]

Ms. Shane testified that many of the assets received from the Nicelys were in the joint names of Mr. and Mrs. Nicely. Upon Mr. Nicely's death, they were transferred into the surviving owner's name, including the Colony Savings Bank Note. [NT 127]. The Note had been purchased by Mr. Nicely. It provided a good rate of income. It had paid the interest regularly. It was a small portion of a large portfolio. [NT 127] And, upon consideration of their understanding that the preference was to keep all investments as they were [NT 110], the Bank simply transferred this asset into the sole name of the surviving owner.

Upon consideration of all the evidence, I find that objectant has failed to prove that the accountant was negligent or breached a fiduciary duty in regard to the Colony Savings Bank Note. Objection 3 is dismissed.

Objection 6 concerns counsel fees and costs expended by Inez in getting the Bank to turn the assets over to her in her capacity as executrix of her mother's estate. After the death of Esther Nicely, a dispute arose between Inez and her brother as to who was entitled to certain assets which the Bank had in its possession pursuant to the power of attorney. As a result, the Bank requested authorization from Inez to release $76,000.00 from the power of attorney account to Donald Nicely and to execute a receipt and release in regard to the administration of the power-of-attorney account. The Bank also submitted an accounting of its administration. Said account included a termination fee and additional income fees payable to the Bank. Inez refused to sign the receipt and release and did not agree to the payment of the fees. Instead, she filed a petition to compel the turnover of the assets. The Bank then filed the instant account with the Clerk. After the account had been filed with the Clerk, counsel for Inez and Donald reached an agreement as to how the dispute as to the $76,000.00 should be resolved. After a conference with counsel, I entered an order on May 5, 1995 directing the delivery of the assets and reserving the other questions for determination at the audit of the Bank's account. The order of May 5, 1995 permitted Inez to administer the assets as executrix. It expressly reserved determination of other issues to the instant audit. It did not determine any of the other issues.

In Objection 6, the objectant suggests that the Bank improperly refused to deliver the assets in that it demanded that she, in her capacity as executrix and as an individual, and her brother, execute a receipt, release and indemnification agreement which, in essence, would hold the Bank harmless for its administration of the power-of-attorney account. She argues that this only protected the interest of the Bank and not the interest of the principal.

In determining whether or not the objectant should recover counsel fees and costs for her efforts to compel delivery of the assets, this Court is mindful of the following statements of a panel of our Superior Court in *Estate of Wanamaker*, 314 Pa. Super. 177, 179, 460 A.2d 824 (1983),

"The general rule is that each party to adversary litigation is required to pay his or her own counsel fees. . . . . In the absence of a statute allowing counsel fees, recovery of such fees will be permitted only in exceptional circumstances. . . . ." (citations omitted)

In the matter of *Weiss Estate*, 4 Fiduc. Rep. 2d 71, 77 (O.C. Div. Phila., 1983), Judge Shoyer expressed the opinion that

". . . . the orphans' court, as a court of equity, has always had the power to surcharge a party for counsel fees when it is apparent that the conduct of a party has been the cause of additional legal expenses: *Shollenberger's Appeal*, 21 Pa. 337"

Counsel fees may be awarded as part of taxable costs of a matter, under 42 Pa. C.S.A. Section 2503 (7) and (9), which recognize a right of participants in litigation to receive counsel fees,

"(7) . . . . as a sanction . . . . for dilatory, obdurate or vexatious conduct during the pendency of a matter."; and,
* * * *
"(9) . . . . because the conduct of another party in commencing the matter or otherwise was arbitrary, vexatious or in bad faith."

See *Brenckle v. Arblaster*, 320 Pa. Super. Ct. 87, 466 A.2d 1075 (1983); *Shoemaker Estate*, 6 Fiduc. Rep. 2d 128 (O.C. Div. Allegh. 1986); and, *Garrano Estate*, 11 Fiduc. Rep. 2d, 302 (O.C. Div. Bucks, 1991). *Considering the facts that Esther died on November 29, 1994; that Inez qualified as executrix of her estate on January 4, 1995; that Inez filed her Petition for turnover of assets on February 14, 1995; and, that the Bank filed its account on March 3, 1995, this Court holds that Inez is not entitled to recover the counsel fees and costs* which she seeks in Objection 6. The Bank had every right to file an account and seek confirmation thereof and a discharge from this Court. The Bank acted expeditiously in filing its account. Under the circumstances extant in this matter, this Court holds that the Bank did not engage in dilatory, obdurate or vexatious conduct. Nor did the Bank act in bad faith. Accordingly, the general rule enunciated in *Wanamaker*, supra, applies, and, objectant must pay her own counsel fees and costs incurred in gaining possession of her mother's assets. Objection 6 is dismissed.

In Objection 7 objectant request costs, expenses and counsel fees for this litigation to surcharge the Bank for breach of fiduciary duties. Having found that the Bank did not breach any fiduciary duty; that it did not engage in dilatory, obdurate or vexatious conduct;

and, that it did not act in bad faith, this Court will apply the general rule of *Wanamaker*, supra, and, dismiss Objection 7.

Objection 8 concerns the Bank's request for a "termination fee" of one (1%) percent of the market value of the principal on the death of Esther M. Nicely. It is well settled that a fiduciary or agent claiming a fee or commission has the burden of proving that the said request is fair and reasonable and that it is based on services actually performed and not on some arbitrary formula. *In re Testamentary Trust* etc., 490 Pa. 71, 415 A.2d 37, 42; *Sonovick Estate*, 373 Pa. Super 396, 400, 541 A.2d 374; 373 Pa. Super. 396, 541 A.2d 374, 376. Just as well settled is the principle that fiduciaries are entitled to fair and just compensation for services they perform. The absence of a compensation agreement is not a bar to compensation. The amount of compensation to be awarded is the actual worth of the services rendered. *In Re Reed*, Pa., 467 Pa. 371, 357 A.2d 138.

In the instant matter, there is nothing in writing in regard to fees to be paid to the Bank for its services. No fee agreement was ever executed. Inez testified that fees were never mentioned in either of her two meetings with Mr. Clougherty. [NT 322, 323]. Mr. Clougherty testified that at the first meeting, he told Inez that the Bank would charge six (6%) percent of the income for its services. He did not remember if he told Inez about any fee to be charged to principal nor did he remember if he told her about the Bank's fee schedule. [NT 195]. As to the second meeting with Inez and her father, Daniel J. Nicely, which took place at the Nicely home, Mr. Clougherty testified that Mr. Nicely "asked what it was going to cost," to which he replied, six (6%) percent of the income. [NT 196]. He did not recall saying anything about principal commissions nor did he recall if he gave them a fee schedule. [NT 196].

The statement of proposed distribution states that the Bank received a fee for its services of six (6%) percent of income from the inception of the account in 1988 through 1992. From 1993 through 1995, the Bank received a fee of six (6%) percent of the first $50,000.00 of income and five (5%) percent of income in excess of $50,000.00. There is no explanation anywhere in the record of the reasons or circumstances which brought about this change in compensation. It is undisputed that the Bank received $39,75.00 in income commissions and tax preparation fees. [NT 55] There was no objections to these payments. The Bank is now requesting an additional $16,124.00 as a termination fee. This is one (1%) of the market value of the principal.

Jo L. Shane and Coleman J. Clougherty testified on behalf of the Bank in support of this claim for additional compensation. In addition, Exhibits A-2 and A-3 were received into evidence. A-2 is the fee schedule in effect when the power of attorney account was opened. It provides for a fee of six (6%) percent of the income received by the Agent or custodian with a one (1%) percent fee upon termination of the account." A-3 is a computation of the entries that were made during the tenure of the account and a log showing dates and services that were provided on behalf of the account. Also, included in A-3 are dates and events which occurred after the death of Esther Nicely and concern the present litigation.

Ms. Shane testified that during the administration of this account there were 722 principal entries posted in the Nicely account and 2,108 income entries. She stated much work was required because there were many assets, some held in various combinations of names and in many different institutions. In addition, other services were performed for the Nicelys such as having nurses for the nursing and personal care of Mr. and Mrs. Nicely, arranging for cleaning services, grass cutting, collecting mortgage payments, snow removal, going to the hospital with Mrs. Nicely and arranging for repairs to some realty. [NT 21-26].

In regard to the value of the described services [NT 21-24], Ms. Shane, in her testimony, indicated that they were all performed in the custodian account at a fee of six (6%) percent of income. [NT 24] Subsequently, she stated that the fee schedule was the basis for the fees taken and the requested termination fee. [NT 56, 57] She further testified that the services proved were beyond regular services for a custodian account, that this is supported by the documentation contained in Exhibit A-3, and, thus, the Bank is entitled to the termination fee of $16,124.00 for the services rendered. [NT 57-63]

In summary, the Bank had a fee schedule in effect when the power of attorney was executed. It is undisputed that the Nicelys never executed a fee agreement. According to the record, the only fee discussed with the Nicelys was six (6%) percent of income received. The Bank received this fee and additional fees for the preparation of tax returns. These fees total $39,765. There was no objection to these fees. Clearly the Bank cannot impose its fee agreement on the Nicelys unilaterally. Accordingly, the Bank argues that it performed the regular services pursuant to the custodian account and many extraordinary services which entitle it to the requested compensation. The requested

additional compensation just happens to equal the one (1%) percent termination fee set forth in the Bank's fee schedule.

It is true that the Bank performed many services for the Nicelys. However, when Mr. Clougherty met with the Nicelys, he was aware that Mr. and Mrs. Nicely would need things done for their well being, e.g. "Something as simple as getting someone to cut the grass." The Bank in accepting this account, in essence, agreed to do such things. This does not mean they should not receive compensation for doing these things if it is warranted. We must also note that in administering the account, the Bank really acted in a ministerial fashion. It assumed no responsibility for investments and it proclaimed so throughout these proceedings. Thus, upon consideration of all the services performed by the Bank and the fees already received by the Bank, this Court finds that it is fair and just to award the Bank an additional $5,000.00 in terminal compensation. Said sum of $5,000.00 must be reduced, however, by the "de minimis" amounts which are the subject of Objections 4 and 5. Accordingly, the Bank will receive $3,841.97 in satisfaction of its claim for a termination fee.

Objection 9 concerns the Bank's claims for counsel fees and costs. After the death of Esther Nicely, when differences began to develop between the Bank and objectant in regard to the administration of the power of attorney account, the Bank retained the firm of Reed, Luce, Tosh, McGregor & Wolford of Beaver County. The Bank and objectant were unable to resolve their differences and litigation commenced in Philadelphia County. As litigation in Philadelphia seemed imminent, the Bank retained the firm of Dechert Price & Rhoads. The Reed firm seeks a total of $11,189.00, being $10,040.00 in fees and $1,149.00 in costs, for its representation of the Bank from January 16, 1995 to July 1, 1996. Said sum of $1,149.00 in "costs" includes the sum of $1,000.00 which appears to have been advanced to the Dechert firm. The Dechert firm seeks a total of $21,469.78, being: $16,103.40 in fees and $1,866.38 in costs for its representation of the Bank from February 8, 1995 to July 19, 1996; and, $3,500.00 in estimated fees for its representation of the Bank at hearings on July 30 and 31, 1996. The Bank offered two Exhibits and the testimony of two witnesses in support of the aforementioned claims for counsel fees and costs.

Jo L. Shane testified that the Bank prepared its own form of account and submitted same to the Reed firm, in Beaver County, for review and presentation to a Court. While she could not testify as to the specific work which was done by Reed attorneys, Ms. Shane identified Exhibit "A-4" as the firm's bill for $11,189.00. No Reed attorney testified before this Court. An examination of Exhibit "A-4" shows that it claims $10,040.00 for 100.4 hours of work by two attorneys. Said 100.4 hours of work may be broken down into the following periods, to wit: 49.5 hours spent from January 16, 1995 to March 22, 1995; 15.5 hours spent from April 10, 1995 to June 13, 1995; 7.6 hours spent from June 22, 1995 to November 2, 1995; and, 27.8 hours spent from November 7, 1995 to July 1, 1996.

Ms. Shane testified that the Dechert firm was hired to file the Bank's account in Philadelphia. She identified Exhibit "A-5" as Dechert's bill for $21,469.78. Arthur R.G. Solmssen, Jr., Esquire, a Dechert associate, testified that his firm was retained to resolve disputes which arose on the termination of the Bank's tenure as attorney-in-fact. Mr. Solmssen advised the Bank that the filing of an account, in this Court, was the simplest, easiest and cheapest means of resolving those disputes. The Bank submitted an account for review and filing by the Dechert firm. Mr. Solmssen further testified that his firm spent many hours answering questions from counsel for the executrix. When counsel for the executrix would not be satisfied, the Dechert firm filed the Bank's account and proceeded to audit. An examination of Exhibit "A-5" shows that it claims $19,603.40 for 126.4 hours of work by two attorneys and two paralegals. Exhibit "A-5" is broken down in the following manner, to wit: $3,961.40 for 31 hours spent from February 8 to March 31, 1995; $4,084.00 for 28 hours spent from April 13 to June 19, 1995; $8,058.00 for 47.4 hours spent from November 1, 1995 to July 19, 1996; and, $3,500.00 for 20 hours expected to be spent in preparation for and attendance at two Hearings on July 30 and 31, 1996.

It is fundamental that an attorney seeking compensation has the burden of establishing facts which show that he or she is entitled to such compensation. *Wanamaker Estate, supra.* In *In re Trust Estate of LaRocca,* 431 Pa. 542 , 546, 246 A.2d 337 (1968), our Supreme Court enunciated the facts to be taken into consideration in determining the compensation payable to an attorney. These factors are so well settled and recognized that there is no need to repeat them.

The services performed by the Bank's counsel in this matter fall into four categories. First, the Bank retained counsel when disagreements arose about its management of the power of attorney account.

Attempts to resolve said disagreements led to the preparation, review and filing of the account. Second, counsel represented the Bank in responding to Objections, that is, in resisting requested surcharges. Third, counsel prosecuted the Bank's claim for a termination fee. Fourth, counsel prosecuted the Bank's claim for counsel fees and costs.

Although the matter *sub judice* concerns a dispute between a principal and an agent, the law applicable to the compensation of counsel for fiduciaries is just as applicable here.

A fiduciary has authority to employ counsel and reasonable counsel fees are a just charge against the estate. *Hunter, Vol. 1 - Attorney & Client 1(a), p.206* and cases cited therein. Fees of counsel in successfully representing a fiduciary in resisting a surcharge are properly payable from the estate. *Browarsky Estate,* 437 Pa. 282, 263 A.2d 365; *Wormley Estate,* 359 Pa. 295, 300, 59 A.2d 98. Accordingly, I hold that counsel fees ensuing from representation of the Bank in preparing, reviewing and filing of the account; in resisting the Petition for turnover of assets; and, in resisting requested surcharges, are properly payable from the estate. See *Fiduciary Review,* Feb. 1970, p.2.

However, counsel fees for services rendered in an attempt by the Bank to secure a termination fee and counsel fees are another matter. Clearly, as was stated previously, a fiduciary or agent claiming a fee or commission has the burden of proving that the said request is fair and reasonable and based on services performed. Also, an attorney seeking compensation has the burden of establishing facts that show that he or she is entitled to such compensation. Since they have the burden of substantiating their claims to compensation, in essence, the Bank and its counsel are claimants against the estate.

In prosecuting claims for compensation, a fiduciary and its counsel are subject to the general rule that a party who retains counsel to protect or advance his own interests must pay his own counsel fees. See *Wanamaker Trust,* 30 Fiduc. Rep. 240. Accordingly, I hold that the fees of an attorney employed to substantiate a fiduciary's claim for compensation are not compensable from the estate. *Powers Est.,* 58 Pa. D. & C. 379, 386; *Fiduciary Review,* Aug. 1977, p. 4. In the same vein, time expended by counsel in seeking its own compensation is of no benefit to the fund but only benefits counsel. Accordingly, it is not compensable from the fund.

In determining how much of the requested counsel fees are compensable from the assets of the principal, this Court is cognizant of its own observations in *Conti Estate*, 8 Fiduc. Rep. 2d 272 (1988), to wit,

" . . . . an executor may not substantially increase the legal fees to be paid by the estate by retaining different counsel who duplicate each other's efforts: . . . . If several attorneys are retained to settle the estate, an aggregate of counsel fees charged to the estate should not exceed one reasonable fee for all the services performed: . . . ." (citations omitted)

Having considered the record in this matter, this Court finds that the amount of $20,000.00 represents one reasonable fee for the efforts of the Bank's counsel in preparing, reviewing and filing the account; in resisting the Petition for turnover of assets; and, in resisting requested surcharges. Counsel fees in excess of $20,000.00 are not compensable from the assets of the principal: because they were incurred in the Bank's attempts to secure a termination fee and counsel fees; and, because they represent a duplication of effort of counsel. Having considered the record in this matter, this Court will make the following allocation of allowable fees of counsel for the bank, to wit: $5,000.00 to the firm of Reed, Luce, Tosh, McGregor & Wolford; and, $15,000.00 to the firm of Dechert Price & Rhoads. The awards will be made accordingly.

All Objections having been addressed, the account, as stated to January 30, 1995, that is, before the delivery of assets ordered by Decree of this Court dated May 5, 1995, shows a combined balance of principal and income of $1,371,146.01 which, composed as set forth in the account, together with income received since the filing thereof, if any, is awarded as follows: $3,841.97 to First Western Trust Services Company, in full and final satisfaction of its claim for a termination fee; $5,000.00 to First Western Trust Services Company, in full and final satisfaction of its claim for counsel fees due the firm of Reed, Luce, Tosh, McGregor & Wolford; $149.00 to First Western Trust Services Company, in full and final satisfaction of its claim for costs due the firm of Reed, Luce, Tosh, McGregor & Wolford; $15,000.00 to First Western Trust Services Company, in full and final satisfaction of its claim for counsel fees due the firm of Dechert Price & Rhoads; $1,866.38 to First Western Trust Services Company, in full and final satisfaction of its claim for costs due the firm of Dechert Price & Rhoads; and, the balance then remaining to Inez C. Nicely, Executrix of the Estate of Esther M. Nicely, Deceased.

The above awards to First Western Trust Services Company shall be paid by Inez C. Nicely, Executrix as aforesaid, from the assets of the estate of the deceased principal.

The above awards are made subject to all payments heretofore properly made on account of distribution.

Leave is hereby granted to the accountant to make all transfers and assignments necessary to effect distribution in accordance with this adjudication.

AND NOW, unless exceptions are filed to this adjudication within twenty (20) days, the account, as amended by this Adjudication, is confirmed absolutely.

J.

Case Questions

1. What was the basis for Objection 1 by Inez C. Nicely regarding First Western's breach of fiduciary duty and negligence?
2. How were the awards to First Western Trust Services Company to be paid?
3. What was the outcome of this case?

FORMS TO ACCOMPANY PARALEGAL PRACTICE

Disclaimer: The forms provided to aid students in completing the Paralegal Practice activities assigned in each chapter have been modified as samples to familiarize students with what each form commonly looks like and are not intended to be used as actual forms for any state.

INSTRUCTIONS: The forms are provided in Microsoft Word format and employ the use of Stop Codes (such as SC1, SC2, SC3, and so on). Stop Codes are used in place of the form sections that must be updated with case-by-case information, such as SC1 for the client's name, SC3 for the client's address, and so on.

What each Stop Code represents can be inferred by reading the surrounding text on the form. By using the FIND & REPLACE tool on the Microsoft toolbar, the students can replace the Stop Codes with the information provided in the Paralegal Practice activity to complete each assignment. Students must also fill in any blank lines on each form with the appropriate information from the activity and then proofread the document prior to turning in their work.

The following forms are included following this section and will be posted online for students to access to complete the Paralegal Practice activities for this chapter:

- PP Form 8.1—Memorandum to Attorney

PP Form 8.1

<u>INTEROFFICE MEMORANDUM</u>

TO:	SUPERVISING ATTORNEY
FROM:	[CLICK **HERE** AND TYPE NAME]
SUBJECT:	POWERS OF TRUSTEES
DATE:	10/26/2013
CC:	[CLICK HERE AND TYPE NAME]

Testate v. Intestate Succession

CHAPTER 9

A REAL-LIFE SCENARIO

A client scheduled a probate consultation with an attorney and arrived with her daughter to translate. The client was foreign and recently widowed. She had not been married for long, and was also relatively new to the United States. The client's husband (the decedent) was previously divorced and had two children from his prior marriage. He did not leave a will, and a probate battle ensued between the ex-wife, the sons, and the widow. To make matters more complicated, the decedent had a meager probate estate but did have an insurance policy and an IRA, both of which named the sons as beneficiaries. A lot of time, money, and attorneys' fees could have been avoided if the decedent had opted to execute a will to express his intentions. Instead, the state's intestacy provisions applied and the parties disagreed as to how the assets were to be distributed.

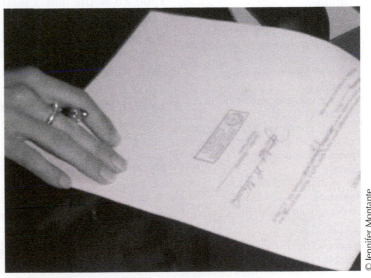

© Jennifer Montante

CHAPTER OBJECTIVES:

1. Define *intestate succession*.
2. Explain how intestate succession works.
3. Analyze an intestate succession statute and apply it to the facts of a given case to determine who the heirs are and how much they will inherit.
4. Discuss why it is beneficial to die testate.
5. Define *escheat* and describe when escheat might take place.
6. Discuss the benefits of doing an unclaimed property search.

■ INTRODUCTION

Scenarios like the foregoing example happen far too often. This chapter will help you to better understand how important it is to execute a will, as well as the implications of dying intestate. The choice of whether or not to execute a will may seem unimportant to a healthy person who is expecting to live a long life. However, life is full of unexpected surprises and the sad truth is that no one knows what may happen tomorrow. If you are truly concerned about those whom you care about, there is only one choice to make.

Key Terms and Definitions

A **Last Will and Testament,** or "**will,**" is a written document that leaves the estate of the individual who signed the will to the named persons or entities. A will only takes effect upon the maker's death, and can be revoked or amended at any time while the maker is still alive. A will usually appoints an **executor** (or personal representative, depending on the state) to manage the estate and carry out the directions in the will. In addition, a will may nominate guardians of minor children, and may even give funeral and/or burial instructions in some states. A male who executes a will is known as a **testator**, whereas a female who executes a will is referred to as a **testatrix**. Likewise, a female executor is properly referred to as an **executrix**. Individuals who die with a will die **testate**. People who do not execute a will prior to passing away die **intestate**.

■ TESTATE SUCCESSION

A decedent who left behind a valid will is said to have died testate; the decedent's property will be distributed to beneficiaries and devisees pursuant to the will. A **beneficiary** of a will is a person entitled to receive property under a will or to whom the decedent's property is given or distributed. The advantages to dying *testate* include having the ability to designate who is to receive one's assets, ensuring that loved ones will be provided for, determining who will serve as personal representative, and lowering the cost of estate administration. Generally speaking, probate proceedings go much more smoothly and cost less in attorneys' fees when the decedent had a will than when the decedent died intestate.

Last Will and Testament

You may have heard of the term "simple will." You may think this means the will was easy to draft, and for that reason, "simple will" is really a misnomer. Simple wills do not have to be simple, in that they can contain complex provisions pertaining to multiple beneficiaries. However, **simple wills** generally do not include tax planning language and for that reason are referred to as "simple" by legal professionals. Tax planning is often done to reduce tax liability upon death for sizeable estates. However, many estates do not meet the minimum threshold for federal or state tax liability and do not require tax planning. A **testamentary trust** is a trust that is established following the testator's death pursuant to the terms of the will.

Figure 9.1 depicts an example of a new simple will executed by Jane Smith from the Hypothetical Family to include her nephew, Mark Smith, Jr., as a beneficiary.

Will
A written document that leaves the estate of the individual who signed the will to the named persons or entities.

Executor
A male nominated in a will of a decedent to carry out the terms of the will; a personal representative of the estate.

Testator
A man who executes a will.

Testatrix
A female who executes a will.

Executrix
A female nominated in a will to carry out the terms of the will; a personal representative of the estate.

Testate
To die with a valid will.

Intestate
To die without a valid will.

Beneficiary
A beneficiary of a will is a person entitled to receive property under a will or to whom the decedent's property is given or distributed.

Simple Will
A phrase used by legal professionals to indicate a will that does not include tax planning language.

Testamentary Trust
A trust that is drafted as part of the testator's will and only becomes effective upon the testator's death.

Figure 9.1

Mark Smith and his wife both passed away in a car accident when Mark Smith, Jr., was an infant. As a result, both Shirley and Jane Smith helped to raise him. After executing her will, Jane Smith realized that to leave Mark Jr. out would be like omitting her own son. Jane also decided that if one of the beneficiaries predeceased her, she wanted that person's share to pass to her surviving beneficiaries, instead of the deceased party's children. She went back to the attorney's office and executed the following will, thereby revoking her prior will.

LAST WILL AND TESTAMENT

I, **JANE SMITH**, of the CITY OF SAMPLE, COUNTY OF SAMPLE COUNTY, STATE OF SAMPLE STATE, do hereby make, publish and declare the following to be my Last Will and Testament, hereby revoking all former Wills and Codicils made by me.

I. I direct that all my debts and funeral expenses be paid and I further authorize my Executor, in its discretion, to prepay any mortgage or other installment indebtedness.

II. I give and bequeath to my children, JOHN SMITH and SUSAN SMITH, and my nephew, MARK SMITH, JR. all of my clothing, jewelry, personal effects, household goods, furniture, furnishings, automobiles and all other tangible personal property which I may own at the time of my death, to be divided among them as they shall agree. If my beneficiaries are unable to agree as to the recipient of any article, that article, as well as any articles not selected, shall be sold and the proceeds added to my residuary estate.

III. All the rest, residue and remainder of my property, real, personal and mixed, of every name and nature, and wheresoever situate, I give, devise and bequeath in equal shares to JOHN SMITH, SUSAN SMITH, and MARK SMITH, JR., or all to the survivors of them.

IV. I give to my Executor hereinafter named, and to the successor, the following powers and discretions, in addition to those vested in or imposed upon them or either of them by law:

A. To mortgage, sell, convey, exchange or otherwise deal with or dispose of any real or personal property for cash or on credit (including the right to accept a purchase money mortgage as part of the purchase price); to retain as part of the estate any and all securities and property in the form originally received, whether or not it is then income producing and regardless of any rule requiring diversification of investments; to invest and reinvest in any stocks, bonds, shares in mutual funds or authorized common trust funds, or other securities or property, whether real or personal, which my Executor may deem safe and for the best interests of the estate, without being limited to investments authorized by law for the investment of trust funds; to hold title to any and all securities and other investments either in my Executor's name or in the name of a nominee; to borrow money from itself or others on terms my Executor may deem best, and to pledge any property of the estate as security for the repayment thereof; and to make distributions in cash or in kind, or partly in each to the beneficiaries entitled thereto.

B. If any beneficiary or legatee entitled to receive a part of my estate shall be under twenty-one (21) years of age, I authorize and empower my Executor to designate his or her parent, or some other appropriate adult person, or trust company, as custodian for the beneficiary or legatee under the Sample State Uniform Transfers to Minors Act until age twenty-one (21), and to distribute the share of the beneficiary or legatee to the designated custodian. A receipt from the custodian shall fully release my Executor.

V. I direct that all inheritance, succession and estate taxes of every kind payable with respect to any property includable in my gross taxable estate, whether or not passing under this my Will, shall be paid out of my residuary estate, and shall not be apportioned.

VI. I hereby nominate, constitute and appoint JOHN SMITH as Executor of this my Last Will and Testament, but if he fails to survive me, or renounces, or fails to qualify, or upon his death, resignation or disqualification, I nominate and appoint SUSAN SMITH as Executrix. I direct that no bond or other security shall be required of my Executor.

VII. The masculine gender, whenever used herein, shall include the feminine, the feminine shall include the masculine; the neuter shall include both the masculine and feminine; and the singular shall include the plural wherever necessary or appropriate.

(continued)

Figure 9.1 (continued)

IN WITNESS WHEREOF, I have hereunto subscribed my name and affixed my seal this *25th* day of *February* 2012.

Jane Smith
_____
JANE SMITH

We, whose names are hereto subscribed, do certify that on the *25th* day of *February*, 2012, the Testatrix, JANE SMITH, subscribed her name to this instrument, in our presence and in the presence of each of us, and at the same time in our presence and hearing, declared the same to be her Last Will and Testament, and requested us, and each of us, to sign our names thereto as witnesses to the execution thereof, which we hereby do in the presence of the Testatrix and of each other.

*Michael Pearson*_____ residing at *1001 Reed Drive, Sample City, Sample State 12345*_____

*Maggy Pearson*_____ residing at *1001 Reed Drive, Sample City, Sample State 12345*

AFFIDAVIT OF
ATTESTING WITNESSES

STATE OF SAMPLE STATE   )
COUNTY OF SAMPLE COUNTY   ) SS:

____*Michael Pearson*____ and ____*Maggy Pearson*____, being duly sworn say:

We are acquainted with JANE SMITH. The signature at the end of the instrument dated February 25, 2012, declared by her to be her Last Will, was made by her at City of Sample, State of Sample State, in the presence of each of the undersigned.

At the time of signing Will, JANE SMITH declared the instrument to which her signature had been affixed to be her Will and we, and each of us, signed our names thereto at the end thereof at that time and at her request and in her presence.

At the time of the execution of the instrument JANE SMITH was over the age of 18 years, of sound mind and memory, and not under any restraint and competent in every respect to make a Will.

At the time of execution, JANE SMITH could read, write and converse in the English language, and was not suffering from defects of sight, hearing, or speech or any other physical or mental impairment that could affect her capacity to make a valid Will.

The Will was not executed in counterparts.

Michael Pearson
_____
Witness

Maggy Pearson
_____
Witness

STATE OF SAMPLE STATE   }
COUNTY OF SAMPLE COUNTY   } ss:

On the *25th* day of *February* in the year 2011 before me, the undersigned, a Notary Public in and for said State, personally appeared *Michael Pearson* and *Maggy Pearson*, the subscribing witnesses to the foregoing instrument, with whom I am personally acquainted, who being by me duly sworn, did depose and say that *Michael Pearson* resides at *1001 Reed Drive*, Sample State and *Maggy Pearson* resides at *1001 Reed Drive*, Sample State; that they know JANE SMITH to be the individual described in and who executed the foregoing instrument; that said subscribing witnesses were present and saw said JANE SMITH execute the same; and that said witnesses at the same time subscribed their names as witnesses thereto, and

Figure 9.1 (continued)

acknowledged to me that they executed the same in their capacities, and that by their signatures on the instrument, the individual(s) or the person upon behalf of which the individual(s) acted, executed the instrument.

Lila P. Legal
_____
Notary Public

> LILA P. LEGAL
> Notary Public, State of Sample
> Sample County
> My Commission Expires May 10, 2012

The will depicted in Figure 9.1 leaves the testatrix's estate in equal shares to her children and her nephew, reflecting the unique circumstances of the affected members of the Hypothetical Family. As you will see from reviewing the intestacy statutes that follow, Jane Smith's nephew would *not* inherit from her estate if she died intestate.

■ INTESTATE SUCCESSION

A decedent who dies without a valid will is said to die **intestate**. When a person dies intestate, their property passes according to their state's intestacy laws, called **intestate succession statutes**. It is generally preferable to choose who will inherit from one's estate, rather than let the state's default provisions apply. This is one very good reason to execute a valid will.

Many intestacy statutes follow the following basic pattern: to spouse, then children, then issue of children, then parents, then brothers and sisters, then issue of brothers and sisters, then grandparents, then issue of grandparents. "**Issue**" is a legal term that includes a person's children or other lineal descendants such as grandchildren and great-grandchildren in the direct bloodline. Consult with your state statutes to determine those lineal descendants who are included in the term "issue" in your state.

Determining Who Inherits Under Intestacy Law

Consanguinity (from the Latin word consanguinitas, *meaning* "blood relation") is the quality of being descended from the same ancestor as another person. Consanguinity is an important legal concept in that the laws of many jurisdictions consider consanguinity as a factor in deciding whether two individuals may be married, and whether a given person inherits property when a deceased person has not left a will (dies intestate). (With respect to marriage, consanguinity laws are linked to a jurisdiction's laws regarding incest, so that couples in an incestuous relationship will not be allowed to marry. Some United States jurisdictions forbid first cousins to marry, while others limit the prohibition to brothers, sisters, mothers, fathers, aunts, and uncles.) Consanguinity is not the same as **affinity**, which is a close relationship based on marriage rather than on common ancestry.

Consanguinity is relevant in issues of inheritance when a person dies without a will. Under Uniform Probate Code §2-103, when a person dies intestate, after a surviving spouse receives his or her share, the descendants (which, depending on the

PARALEGAL PRACTICE TIPS

- *When interviewing a client regarding a decedent who died intestate, it is essential that you get a complete family tree of relatives on both sides of the decedent's family.*

- *Getting a complete family tree includes finding out about the family members who predeceased the decedent and whether or not they had children. If they had children, record information about those children, as they may inherit in place of their deceased parent under intestacy law.*

Intestate Succession Statutes
State laws that determine who will inherit the property of a person who dies without a valid will.

Issue
A person's children or other lineal descendants in the direct bloodline, such as grandchildren and great-grandchildren.

Consanguinity
(from the Latin word consanguinitas, meaning "blood relation"): The quality of being descended from the same ancestor as another person.

Affinity
A close relation based on marriage rather than on common ancestry.

circumstances, may include children, grandchildren, or great-grandchildren, either biological or adopted) receive the remainder of the intestate estate. If there are no children, the decedent's parent(s) receive the remainder of the estate. If there are neither descendants nor parents, the decedent's estate is distributed to descendants of the decedent's parents (again, depending on the circumstances, brothers and sisters, nieces and nephews, grandnieces and grandnephews, and great-grandnieces and great-grandnephews). If there are no descendants, parents, or descendants of parents, the deceased's property passes to descendants of the grandparents of the decedent (uncles and aunts, first cousins, or first cousins once, twice, or thrice removed).

The **Uniform Probate Code** is a model code promulgated by the National Conference of Commissioners on Uniform State Laws and is not binding on any state. States have the choice of whether to adopt the Uniform Probate Code, in whole or in part. So far, at least eighteen states have adopted at least part of the Uniform Probate Code.

The degree of relative consanguinity can be illustrated with a consanguinity table, in which each level of lineal consanguinity (i. e., generation) appears as a row, and individuals with a collaterally consanguineous relationship share the same row. *Lineal consanguinity* is the relation in a direct line—such as between parent, child, and grandparent. It may be determined either upward—as in the case of son, father, grandfather—or downward—as in son, grandson, great-grandson. *Collateral consanguinity* is a more remote relationship describing people who are related by a common ancestor but do not descend from each other—such as cousins who have the same grandparents.

Table 9.1 displays the relationships among relatives. Note that family members who appear alongside one another in the chart are members of the same generation. For example, self, brother, sister, first cousin, second cousin, and third cousin would all be part of the same generation.

Table 9.1 Table of Relationships

				Great-Great-Grandfather	Great-Great-Grandmother
			Great-Grandfather	Great-Grandmother	Great-Great-Uncle/Aunt
		Grandfather	Grandmother	Great-Uncle/Aunt	First Cousin Twice Removed
	Father	Mother	Uncle/Aunt	First Cousin Once Removed	Second Cousin Once Removed
	Brother/Sister	SELF	First Cousin	Second Cousin	Third Cousin
	Niece/Nephew	Son/Daughter	First Cousin Once Removed	Second Cousin Once Removed	Third Cousin Once Removed
	Grandniece/-nephew	Grandson/-daughter	First Cousin Twice Removed	Second Cousin Twice Removed	Third Cousin Twice Removed

Determining How Much Heirs Inherit Under Intestacy Law

Most intestate succession statutes reference either the term "per capita" or the term "per stirpes." **Per capita** is Latin for "by head" and indicates that succession is to be determined by the number of people in a class or group. **Per stirpes** is Latin for "by roots" and indicates succession by right of representation, share and share alike. Consider the following examples to illustrate the difference between these two terms.

In Example 1, the result is the same under either a per capita or a per stirpes distribution. Now, consider Example 2.

Figure 9.2 contains the intestacy statutes from the State of Maine, for purposes of example and discussion.

Per Capita
Latin for "by head"; indicates that succession is to be determined by the number of people in a class or group.

Per Stirpes
Latin for "by roots"; indicates succession by right of representation, share and share alike.

EXAMPLE 1

Grandma Jane had three children: Ralph, Sam, and Susan. Ralph had one child: Ralph, Jr. Sam had two children: Mark and Ryan. Susan had three children: Adam, Beth, and Connie. Ralph predeceased Grandma Jane. Determine who will inherit from Grandma Jane's estate and in what proportions.

Per capita: Had all of her children survived, Grandma Jane's estate would have passed in equal shares to Ralph, Sam, and Susan. Since Ralph predeceased Grandma Jane, there are two classes of survivors entitled to inherit from Jane's estate: children, and children of

deceased children. There is only one individual in the latter class: Ralph, Jr. So, Ralph, Jr., will inherit his deceased father's one-third share of the estate, Sam will inherit one-third, and Susan will inherit one-third.

Per stirpes: A per stirpes distribution passes by bloodline. Grandma Jane had three children in her bloodline. Each of those lines, or "stirpes," is entitled to one-third of Grandma Jane's estate. Since Ralph predeceased Grandma Jane, Ralph, Jr., inherits his father's one-third of the estate.

EXAMPLE 2

Grandma Jane had three children: Ralph, Sam, and Susan. Ralph had one child, Ralph, Jr. Sam had two children: Mark and Ryan. Susan had three children: Adam, Beth, and Connie. Both Ralph and Sam have predeceased Grandma Jane. Determine who will inherit from Grandma Jane's estate and in what proportions.

Per capita: Had all of her children survived, Grandma Jane's estate would have passed in equal shares to Ralph, Sam, and Susan. There are two classes of survivors entitled to inherit from Jane's estate: children, and children of deceased children. Susan, the surviving child, is entitled to one-third of the estate. The shares of the deceased children, Ralph and Sam, are combined to comprise two-thirds of Jane's estate. The two-thirds is then divided among the total number of children of deceased children. Therefore, Ralph, Jr., Mark, and Ryan, who are the children of the deceased children, will each inherit an equal share of this two-thirds of the estate. The

amount each heir will inherit was calculated by first determining how many heads were in the group.

Per stirpes: A per stirpes distribution passes by bloodline. Grandma Jane had three children to pass down her bloodline. Each of those lines, or stirpes, is entitled to one-third of Grandma Jane's estate. Therefore, Susan will inherit one-third of the estate; Ralph, Jr., will inherit his father's one-third of the estate; and Mark and Ryan will each inherit half of Sam's one-third of the estate. Per stirpes is also known as "by representation" because children of a deceased parent step into the shoes of that parent to represent that parent's share.

The language of state intestacy statutes directs not only which individuals are issue entitled to inherit from an intestate estate, but also whether the distribution will be per capita or per stirpes. The designation of distribution being per capita or per stirpes amounts to a direction of *how much* the heirs are each entitled to inherit.

Figure 9.2 Maine Revised Statutes

§2-101§2-103
Title 18-A: PROBATE CODE
Article 2: INTESTATE SUCCESSION AND WILLS
Part 1: INTESTATE SUCCESSION

§2-101. Intestate estate

Any part of the estate of a decedent not effectively disposed of by his will passes to his heirs as prescribed in the following sections of this Code.

§2-102. Share of spouse or registered domestic partner

The intestate share of the surviving spouse or surviving registered domestic partner is:

(1) If there is no surviving issue or parent of the decedent, the entire intestate estate;

(2) If there is no surviving issue but the decedent is survived by a parent or parents, the first $50,000, plus 1/2 of the balance of the intestate estate;

(3) If there are surviving issue all of whom are issue of the surviving spouse or surviving registered domestic partner also, the first $50,000, plus 1/2 of the balance of the intestate estate; or

(4) If there are surviving issue one or more of whom are not issue of the surviving spouse or surviving registered domestic partner, 1/2 of the intestate estate.

> Maine recognizes same sex unions through registered domestic partnerships. Maine's intestacy statute confers identical intestacy rights on surviving spouses and surviving registered domestic partners.

§2-103. Share of heirs other than surviving spouse or surviving registered domestic partner

The part of the intestate estate not passing to the surviving spouse or surviving registered domestic partner under section 2-102, or the entire estate if there is no surviving spouse or surviving registered domestic partner, passes as follows:

(1) To the issue of the decedent; to be distributed per capita at each generation as defined in section 2-106;

(2) If there is no surviving issue, to the decedent's parent or parents equally;

(3) If there is no surviving issue or parent, to the issue of the parents or either of them to be distributed per capita at each generation as defined in section 2-106;

(4) If there is no surviving issue, parent or issue of a parent, but the decedent is survived by one or more grandparents or issue of grandparents, half of the estate passes to the paternal grandparents if both survive, or to the surviving paternal grandparent, or to the issue of the paternal grandparents if both are deceased to be distributed per capita at each generation as defined in section 2-106; and the other half passes to the maternal relatives in the same manner; but if there is no surviving grandparent or issue of grandparents on either the paternal or maternal side, the entire estate passes to the relatives on the other side in the same manner as the half; or

(5) If there is no surviving issue, parent or issue of a parent, grandparent or issue of a grandparent, but the decedent is survived by one or more great-grandparents or issue of great-grandparents, half of the estate passes to the paternal great-grandparents who survive, or to the issue of the paternal great-grandparents if all are deceased, to be distributed per capita at each generation as defined in section 2-106; and the other half passes to the maternal relatives in the same manner; but if there is no surviving great-grandparent or issue of a great-grandparent on either the paternal or maternal side, the entire estate passes to the relatives on the other side in the same manner as the half.

> Interestingly, in Maine, surviving parents are entitled to inherit from a decedent child even when that child had a surviving spouse or registered domestic partner. Most states do not leave anything to a surviving parent unless there is no surviving spouse or surviving issue.

Maine's intestacy statute treats surviving spouses and surviving registered domestic partners equally. [The majority of states does not recognize same-sex marriages and do not include same-sex partners under the provisions of the intestacy statutes. Therefore, estate planning is especially essential in states that do not provide for same-sex couples under the law.] In Maine, if there is no surviving parent or issue of the decedent, the surviving spouse or partner inherits the entire estate. If there are one or more surviving parents but no issue, the surviving spouse or partner only inherits the first $50,000 plus one-half of the balance of the estate. If there are surviving issue, and all are issue of both the decedent and the surviving spouse or partner, the survivor gets the first $50,000 plus one-half of the balance of the estate. Finally, if the decedent was survived by one or more issue who are not also the issue of the spouse or partner, the surviving spouse or partner loses the $50,000 and only inherits one-half of the estate. Maine's statute differs from some other states' laws in that it includes surviving parents in the equation to inherit when there is a surviving spouse. The majority of intestacy statutes only look to whether there are surviving issue of the spouses or, sometimes, to whether there are issue of the decedent who are not also issue of the surviving spouse.

Now, compare and contrast Maine's intestacy statutes with Arizona's intestacy statutes in Figure 9.3. Note that, among other differences, Maine directs

Figure 9.3 Arizona Revised Statutes §§14-2101–14-2013

14-2101. <u>Intestate estate; modification by will</u>

A. Any part of a decedent's estate not effectively disposed of by will passes by intestate succession to the decedent's heirs as prescribed in this chapter, except as modified by the decedent's will.

B. A decedent by will may expressly exclude or limit the right of a person or class to succeed to property of the decedent that passes by intestate succession. If that person or a member of that class survives the decedent, the share of the decedent's intestate estate to which that person or class would have succeeded passes as if that person or each member of that class had disclaimed that person's intestate share.

14-2102. <u>Intestate share of surviving spouse</u>

The following part of the intestate estate, as to both separate property and the one-half of community property that belongs to the decedent, passes to the surviving spouse:

1. If there is no surviving issue or if there are surviving issue all of whom are issue of the surviving spouse also, the entire intestate estate.

2. If there are surviving issue one or more of whom are not issue of the surviving spouse, one-half of the intestate separate property and no interest in the one-half of the community property that belonged to the decedent.

14-2103. <u>Heirs other than surviving spouse; share in estate</u>

Any part of the intestate estate not passing to the decedent's surviving spouse under section 14-2102 or the entire intestate estate if there is no surviving spouse passes in the following order to the following persons who survive the decedent:

1. To the decedent's descendants by representation.

2. If there is no surviving descendant, to the decedent's parents equally if both survive or to the surviving parent.

3. If there is no surviving descendant or parent, to the descendants of the decedent's parents or either of them by representation.

4. If there is no surviving descendant, parent or descendant of a parent, but the decedent is survived by one or more grandparents or descendants of grandparents, half of the estate passes to the decedent's paternal grandparents equally if both survive or to the surviving paternal grandparent or the descendants of the decedent's paternal grandparents or either of them if both are deceased with the descendants taking by representation. The other half passes to the decedent's maternal relatives in the same manner. If there is no surviving grandparent or descendant of a grandparent on either the paternal or the maternal side, the entire estate passes to the decedent's relatives on the other side in the same manner as the half.

Questions and Discussion Points for Figure 9.3

1. What does ARS §14-2101 provide?

2. Pursuant to ARS §14-2102, what does a surviving spouse inherit if he or she has no children or if his or her children are all also children of the decedent?

3. Pursuant to ARS §14-2103, who is first in line to inherit if an intestate decedent has no surviving spouse or children?

a per capita distribution, whereas Arizona directs that the distribution be "by representation," which is the same as per stirpes.

Arizona is a community property state. Recall from Chapter 2 that in a community property state, property acquired during the marriage (other than gifts, bequests, and inheritances) is owned jointly and equally by each spouse and is divided upon divorce, annulment or death. In Arizona, the surviving spouse of an intestate decedent with only children in common (i. e., no children from a prior marriage) inherits the whole intestate estate from the decedent. By contrast, in Maine the same person would only inherit the first $50,000 plus one-half of the intestate estate. Compare and contrast Arizona's intestacy law with that of Texas, which is in Figure 9.4.

Figure 9.4 Texas Probate Code, Chapter II, Descent and Distribution, §38

Text of article effective until January 01, 2014

Sec. 38. PERSONS WHO TAKE UPON INTESTACY. (a) Intestate Leaving No Husband or Wife. Where any person, having title to any estate, real, personal or mixed, shall die intestate, leaving no husband or wife, it shall descend and pass in parcenary to his kindred, male and female, in the following course:

1. To his children and their descendants.

2. If there be no children nor their descendants, then to his father and mother, in equal portions. But if only the father or mother survive the intestate, then his estate shall be divided into two equal portions, one of which shall pass to such survivor, and the other half shall pass to the brothers and sisters of the deceased, and to their descendants; but if there be none such, then the whole estate shall be inherited by the surviving father or mother.

3. If there be neither father nor mother, then the whole of such estate shall pass to the brothers and sisters of the intestate, and to their descendants.

4. If there be none of the kindred aforesaid, then the inheritance shall be divided into two moieties, one of which shall go to the paternal and the other to the maternal kindred, in the following course: To the grandfather and grandmother in equal portions, but if only one of these be living, then the estate shall be divided into two equal parts, one of which shall go to such survivor, and the other shall go to the descendant or descendants of such deceased grandfather or grandmother. If there be no such descendants, then the whole estate shall be inherited by the surviving grandfather or grandmother. If there be no surviving grandfather or grandmother, then the whole of such estate shall go to their descendants, and so on without end, passing in like manner to the nearest lineal ancestors and their descendants.

(b) Intestate Leaving Husband or Wife. Where any person having title to any estate, real, personal or mixed, other than a community estate, shall die intestate as to such estate, and shall leave a surviving husband or wife, such estate of such intestate shall descend and pass as follows:

1. If the deceased have a child or children, or their descendants, the surviving husband or wife shall take one-third of the personal estate, and the balance of such personal estate shall go to the child or children of the deceased and their descendants. The surviving husband or wife shall also be entitled to an estate for life, in one-third of the land of the intestate, with remainder to the child or children of the intestate and their descendants.

2. If the deceased have no child or children, or their descendants, then the surviving husband or wife shall be entitled to all the personal estate, and to one-half of the lands of the intestate, without remainder to any person, and the other half shall pass and be inherited according to the rules of descent and distribution; provided, however, that if the deceased has neither surviving father nor mother nor surviving brothers or sisters, or their descendants, then the surviving husband or wife shall be entitled to the whole of the estate of such intestate.

Acts 1955, 54th Leg. , p. 88, ch. 55, eff. Jan. 1, 1956.

Questions and Discussion Points for Figure 9.4

1. To whom does Texas Probate, Chapter II, § 38 apply?

2. If a Texan died intestate and his closest living heirs were his mother, brother, and sister, who would inherit and in what percentages?

3. If a Texan died intestate, leaving behind only a maternal grandmother and two paternal cousins, who would inherit and in what percentages?

In Texas, the surviving spouse of an intestate decedent with surviving children or descendants of children inherits only one-third of the personal estate of the decedent, plus a life estate in one-third of the land of the intestate. Take a minute to really consider what this means. Typically, when married people execute wills, they leave their *entire estate* first to their surviving spouse, and then to their children or other heirs upon the death of the surviving spouse. However, under Texas intestacy law, the children are entitled to two-thirds of an intestate decedent's personal property, so the surviving spouse is left with a mere one-third. Imagine a poor widow watching two-thirds of the furniture being removed from her family home because it belonged to her intestate husband! Do you think that the widow's husband would have intended to leave only one-third of his personal effects to his wife? In most instances, the directions of the intestacy statutes do not match the lifetime intentions of an intestate decedent. This illustrates the value of executing a will to express one's intentions with respect to property distribution upon death.

Be sure to research your state's intestacy law and familiarize yourself with its terms. As a paralegal practicing in this field, you will frequently encounter intestate estates where a determination will have to be made as to who is legally entitled to inherit from the decedent.

■ LINKS TO STATE INTESTACY STATUTES

*Use the links in **Table 9.2** to access the statute or code of your state. From there, locate the chapter and section pertaining to your area of research. Please note that the links provided below were current when this chart was compiled but are subject to change. The chart in **Table 9.2** will be posted as an online resource where links will be monitored and updated. However, if the link is no longer valid, perform a search for your state's statutes.*

Table 9.2 State Intestacy Statutes

State	Link	Instructions
Alabama	http://alisondb.legislature.state.al.us/acas/ACASLogin.asp	
Alaska	http://www.legis.state.ak.us/basis/folio.asp	
Arizona	http://www.azleg.gov/ArizonaRevisedStatutes.asp	
Arkansas	http://www.arkleg.state.ar.us/assembly/2011/2011R/Pages/Home.aspx	Click on "Search/ View Arkansas Code"
California	www.leginfo.ca.gov/	
Colorado	http://www.michie.com/colorado/lpext.dll?f=templates&fn=main-h .htm&cp=	
Connecticut	http://www.cga.ct.gov/lco/statute_Web_Site_LCO.htm	
Delaware	http://delcode.delaware.gov/	
District of Columbia	http://www.justice.gov/archive/victimcompensation/law_dc.pdf	(Summary Table)
Florida	http://www.leg.state.fl.us/statutes/	

(continued)

Table 9.2 (continued)

Georgia	http://www.lexisnexis.com/hottopics/gacode/Default.asp	
Hawaii	http://www.capitol.hawaii.gov/site1/hrs/default.asp	
Idaho	http://www.legislature.idaho.gov/idstat/Title15/T15CH2PT1.htm	
Illinois	http://www.ilga.gov/search/iga_search.asp?scope=ilcs	
Indiana	http://www.in.gov/legislative/ic/code/	
Iowa	http://www.legis.state.ia.us/IACODE/1999/633/	Scroll down to "Rules of Inheritance"
Kansas	http://kansasstatutes.lesterama.org/Chapter_59/Article_5/#59-514	
Kentucky	http://www.lrc.ky.gov/krs/391-00/CHAPTER.HTM	
Louisiana	http://www.legis.state.la.us/lss/lss.asp?folder=68	CCP 3001 et.seq.
Maine	http://www.mainelegislature.org/legis/statutes/	
Maryland	http://www.michie.com/maryland/lpext.dll?f=templates&fn=main-h.htm&2.0	
Massachusetts	http://www.malegislature.gov/Laws/GeneralLaws/	
Michigan	http://www.legislature.mi.gov/(S(3mftci45b0oxcx3zvfmtaa45))/mileg.aspx?page=home	
Minnesota	https://www.revisor.mn.gov/bin/getpub.php?pubtype=STAT_CHAP_SEC&year=2006&section=524.2-101	
Mississippi	http://www.mscode.com/free/statutes/91/005/index.htm	
Missouri	http://www.moga.mo.gov/statutes/c400-499/4740000010.htm	
Montana	http://law.justia.com/montana/codes/2009/72/72_2/72_2_1/72_2_1.html	
Nebraska	http://nebraskalegislature.gov/laws/statutes.php?statute=30-2209	
Nevada	http://www.leg.state.nv.us/nrs/NRS-134.html	
New Hampshire	http://www.gencourt.state.nh.us/rsa/html/LVI/561/561-1.htm	
New Jersey	http://lis.njleg.state.nj.us/cgi-bin/om_isapi.dll?clientID=147937544&depth=2&expandheadings=off&headingswithhits=on&infobase=statutes.nfo&softpage=TOC_Frame_Pg42	
New Mexico	http://www.conwaygreene.com/nmsu/lpext.dll?f=templates&fn=main-h.htm&2.0	
New York	http://public.leginfo.state.ny.us/LAWSSEAF.cgi?QUERYTYPE=LAWS+&QUERYDATA=@SLEPT0A4P1+&LIST=LAW+&BROWSER=EXPLORER+&TOKEN=24113789+&TARGET=VIEW	
North Carolina	http://www.ncga.state.nc.us/gascripts/Statutes/StatutesTOC.pl?Chapter=0029	
North Dakota	http://www.legis.nd.gov/information/statutes/cent-code.html	Go to "Succession and Wills"

Table 9.2 (continued)

Ohio	http://codes.ohio.gov/orc/2105.06	
Oklahoma	http://www.lsb.state.ok.us/	
Oregon	http://www.leg.state.or.us/ors/112.html	
Pennsylvania	http://law.onecle.com/pennsylvania/decedents-estates-and-fiduciaries/00.021.001.000.html	
Rhode Island	http://www.rilin.state.ri.us/Statutes/TITLE33/33-1/INDEX.HTM	
South Carolina	http://www.scstatehouse.gov/code/t62c002.htm	
South Dakota	http://legis.state.sd.us/statutes/DisplayStatute.aspx?Type=Statute&Statute=29A-2	
Tennessee	http://www.lawserver.com/law/state/tennessee/tn-code/tennessee_code_title_31_chapter_2	
Texas	http://www.statutes.legis.state.tx.us/	
Utah	http://le.utah.gov/~code/TITLE75/75_02.htm	
Vermont	http://law.justia.com/vermont/codes/2009/title-14/chapter-42/301/	
Virginia	http://leg1.state.va.us/000/lst/LS594853.HTM	
Washington	http://apps.leg.wa.gov/rcw/default.aspx?cite=11.04	
West Virginia	http://www.legis.state.wv.us/WVCODE/Code.cfm?chap=42&art=1	
Wisconsin	http://legis.wisconsin.gov/statutes/Stat0852.pdf	
Wyoming	https://secure.ssa.gov/poms.nsf/lnx/1501005056	

■ WHAT HAPPENS WHEN THERE ARE NO SURVIVING HEIRS

If and only if a decedent dies intestate and there are no living relatives qualified to inherit pursuant to a state's intestacy statute, the estate will escheat to the state. **Escheat** takes place only when there are no heirs, descendants, or named beneficiaries to take property upon the death of the last known owner. It is the misconception of some that if you don't have a will at your death, the government will take your property. As you can see from the definition of escheat and the sample intestacy statutes included in this chapter, it is actually quite unlikely that escheat will occur, because even in intestacy, escheat requires that the decedent have no living heirs of a close enough degree to inherit. Many states cut off inheritance rights at the second or third cousin of the decedent.

Escheat
Vesting of property in the state; occurs only when there are no heirs, descendants, or named beneficiaries to take property upon the death of the last known owner.

■ UNCLAIMED PROPERTY

Sometimes property is unclaimed following an individual's death because beneficiaries or heirs are not aware that the decedent owned it. This often occurs with bank accounts. Every state in the United States has some sort of unclaimed funds program, and most programs can be accessed online at their individual websites. All of the states are members of the National Association of Unclaimed Property Administrators, which is a nonprofit organization that helps to educate people about unclaimed property and to facilitate the search process. The NAUPA has a website located at http://www.naupa.org that can be very helpful when you are learning about unclaimed property. The site can also direct you to state websites.

As a paralegal assisting with probate cases, it is a good idea to familiarize yourself with these resources so that you can perform searches for unclaimed property on behalf of your clients. Of course, always wait for the direction of your supervising attorney before doing an unclaimed property search.

■ CONCLUSION

Individuals who die intestate die without leaving behind a valid will. In contrast, those who leave a valid will die testate, and their assets are disposed of pursuant to their wishes expressed in the will. In order to execute a will, a person must have capacity and be of sound mind. Each state has its own requirements for the proper execution of a will.

Each state has its own intestacy statutes that dictate how assets pass under intestacy. An intestate estate passes to the issue of the decedent. The manner in which the estate is divided may be per capita or per stirpes. In a per capita distribution, intestate shares are combined and then divided so that the issue (children) of deceased issue (children) inherit in equal shares. For example, if Grandpa Joe died leaving no surviving children and four grandchildren but three are from one deceased parent and one is from another deceased parent, the deceased parents' shares would be combined and then divided into four equal shares. Under a per stirpes distribution, the only child would inherit 50% of Grandpa Joe's estate (his parent's 50% share), while the other three grandchildren would each inherit one-third of their parent's 50% share of the estate. Intestacy statutes extend fairly far down the bloodline, so it is only in extreme circumstances where there are no surviving beneficiaries or heirs that an estate will escheat to the state.

CONCEPT REVIEW AND REINFORCEMENT

KEY TERMS

Will 260	Intestate 260	Consanguinity 263
Executor 260	Beneficiary 260	Affinity 263
Testator 260	Simple Will 260	Per Capita 265
Testatrix 260	Testamentary Trust 260	Per Stirpes 265
Executrix 260	Intestate Succession Statute 263	Escheat 271
Testate 260	Issue 263	

REVIEW QUESTIONS

1. What is a "simple will?"
2. What are some of the advantages of dying testate?
3. Discuss the function of an intestate succession statute.
4. What is consanguinity?
5. Describe how property passes under a per capita distribution.
6. Describe how property passes under a per stirpes distribution.

7. What are unclaimed funds and how are they recovered?

8. What does escheat mean and when does it occur?

9. What does affinity mean?

10. Why is the probate process generally simpler when the decedent had a will?

BUILDING YOUR PARALEGAL SKILLS

CRITICAL THINKING EXERCISES

1. Under Figure 9.1, Jane Smith from the Hypothetical Family executed a will leaving everything to her children and her nephew, Mark Smith, Jr. Create a chart that reflects 1) who inherits under her current will; and 2) who would inherit from Jane's estate if she died intestate in Maine, Arizona, and Texas. Refer to Figures 9.2–9.4 to complete this assignment.

2. Research your state's intestacy statute and determine what would happen to your estate if you were to die intestate. Are your heirs at law the same people you would choose to leave your estate to under your will?

3. Do you agree with your state's intestacy statute? Why or why not? What would you change if you were a legislator?

PARALEGAL PRACTICE

Review each memorandum directed from the supervising attorney to you, the paralegal. Each memorandum will discuss a situation with a client and request your assistance in researching the matter. You must then report back with your findings, as directed in the memorandum.

1. _____

MEMORANDUM
To: Paralegal
From: Supervising Attorney
Client: Estate of Betsy Ford
Re: Escheat?

Today I met with a client named Rose Parks, who was neighbors with the decedent, Betsy Ford, for thirty years. Betsy Ford passed away two weeks ago and did not leave a will. Rose Parks wants to make sure that Betsy's estate is handled properly, and is concerned it will escheat to the state. Betsy had some cousins living in Pennsylvania, but they were older than Betsy and may have passed away. At least one of those cousins had children, because Betsy has photographs of them on her wall.

Please research your state's law to determine whether Betsy's cousins or second cousins will be able to inherit, or whether Betsy's estate will escheat to the state. Report your findings and your conclusion in the form of a return memorandum to the supervising attorney.

2. _____

MEMORANDUM
To: Paralegal
From: Supervising Attorney
Client: Chelsea Jones
Re: Simple Will

Today I met with Chelsea Jones, who is a widow with two children, Chad and Michael Jones. Both children are over eighteen. Chelsea wants to leave everything to her children with the right of survivorship. She wants to appoint Chad and Michael as co-executors. She wants to appoint Chad, alone, as guardian of her person, and Michael as alternate. Please draft the will for my review.

3. _____

MEMORANDUM
To: Paralegal
From: Supervising Attorney
Client: YOU
Re: Unclaimed Property Search

Perform an unclaimed property search online for yourself or one of your family members and report the findings in the form of a memorandum. Be certain to discuss what website(s) you used, what name(s) you searched, and your findings.

ONLINE RESOURCES

The Pearson Course Companion website contains the following additional resources:
- **Forms for Paralegal Practice Activities**
- Chapter Objectives

- Online Study Guide (Containing Multiple Choice and True/False Questions)
- Web Exercises www.pearsonhighered.com/careers

CASE FOR CONSIDERATION

CASE #1:

In the Matter of the ESTATE of MESSER, Deceased.

118 Ariz. 291; 576 p. 2d 150
February 21, 1978

OPINION BY: JACOBSON

OPINION

The primary issue on appeal is the effect of an amended judgment for separate maintenance on the rights of a surviving spouse and surviving children to an allowance in lieu of homestead, exempt property allowance, and family allowance pursuant to A. R. S. §§ 14-2401, 14-2402, 14-2403, respectively.

Elmer Jesse Messer died on July 28, 1975 leaving a will which devised all his property to appellee, June B. Miner, and appointed appellee, Thomas Aranda, Jr., as personal representative. The appellants are Mary Elizabeth Messer, Elmer's surviving spouse, and his four children who were minors at the time of his death. The appellants filed a petition in the probate court asking for statutory allowances. Following a hearing, the court entered an order on June 1, 1976 which provided a $4,000.00 lump sum settlement to Mrs. Messer for "all support claims, including future support claims, of the three minor children. . . ."(One child became eighteen years of age after her father's death but prior to the hearing.) At the time of Mr. Messer's death, the total value of the estate was approximately $13,400.00.

Mary E. Messer and the deceased had been married for nearly 33 years. In 1964, a decree of separate maintenance had been entered by the Superior Court of Maricopa County. An attempted reconciliation failed and the couple did not live together after 1965.

The original decree of separate maintenance required Mr. Messer to pay $475.00 a month for the support of his wife and at that time, nine minor children. Mr. Messer filed a petition for dissolution of the marriage in January, 1975, at which time he was approximately $36,000.00 in arrears for support payments under the separate maintenance decree. Through their attorneys, Mr. and Mrs. Messer joined in a stipulation to amend the 1964 judgment.[1] The order entering the amended judgment was signed by the court on January 21, 1975. The legal consequences of this amended judgment are at issue on this appeal. Appellees contended, apparently successfully, that this amended judgment was a complete property settlement under the provisions of A. R. S. § 14-2204[2] thus prohibiting Mrs. Messer and the minor children from collecting an allowance in lieu of homestead or exempt property allowance from the estate. The parties concede that the statutory basis for a lump sum settlement of $4,000.00 was made pursuant to the discretionary powers of the court under A. R. S. § 14-2403. (family allowance.)

[1]The stipulation also provided that neither party would file a petition for dissolution for at least one year. Both parties were apparently concerned with the effect of dissolution on various military benefits being received by Mrs. Messer and the children.

[2]A. R. S. § 14. 2204 provides in part: ". . . [HN1] a complete property settlement entered into after . . . legal separation . . . is a waiver of all rights to an allowance in lieu of homestead, exempt property and family allowance by each spouse in the property of the other . . . . "

There is no factual dispute over the terms of the amended judgment. It contained five major provisions: (1) Both parties were to live separately; (2) Mr. Messer was released from his indebtedness for past due support payments; (3) Mrs. Messer received the family home, household furnishings, and automobiles as her sole and separate property; (4) Mrs. Messer received custody of the four minor children; and (5) Mr. Messer would pay $110.00 a month as child support.[3] Had there been any evidence at trial that all community property was distributed, we would be compelled to accept as true the evidence which most strongly supports the trial court's holding that a complete property settlement had been made. See Feffer v. Newman, 17 Ariz. App. 273, 497 P. 2d 389 (1972). However, we need not disregard uncontradicted evidence that undermines the trial court's conclusion. See, Tena v. Yorgulez, 24 Ariz. App. 311, 538 P. 2d 398 (1975).

[3]Evidence was presented to show that the primary difference between this order and the 1964 decree was to reduce support payments, forgive arrearages, and to establish the family home as Mrs. Messer's property. The home had been paid for largely by Mrs. Messer's parents and the automobiles were gifts from Mrs. Messer's parents.

The uncontradicted evidence in the record is that the 1975 judgment contains no express language to the effect that it was intended to be a property settlement, and substantial assets which are presumptively community property were not included within the judgment.

Mr. Messer was the insured on five life insurance policies purchased during his marriage to Mary Messer and prior to their separation. Assets acquired during marriage are presumptively community property. See, A. R. S. § 25-211; Guerrero v. Guerrero, 18 Ariz. App. 400, 502 P. 2d 1077 (1972); Musker v. Gil Haskins Auto Leasing, Inc., 18 Ariz. App. 104, 500 P. 2d 635 (1972). No evidence was presented to the probate court to rebut this presumption. Although the value of most of these properties was minimal because Mr. Messer had borrowed against their value, one policy for $10,000 constitutes the bulk of the estate now being litigated.

During the time that the Messers lived separately, Mr. Messer purchased a truck and was making payments on a mobile home. The record is not clear whether the truck or mobile home were purchased before or after the amended judgment. Property acquired with the earnings[4] of a husband during a period of legal separation is community property. See, Guerrero, supra.[5] Appellee did not offer evidence to show that the truck or mobile home were acquired with other than community funds. If the purchases were initiated before the January 21, 1975 judgment, this property was also community property not disposed of by the judgment. However, we cannot make that determination from the record before us.

[4]Although Mr. Messer was apparently receiving no wages or salary during the years immediately prior to his death, he was receiving military retirement benefits which are considered earnings for purposes of community property. See, Van Loan v. Van Loan, 117 Ariz. 272, 569 P. 2d 214 (1977).

[5][HN5] A 1973 amendment to A. R. S. § 25-211 removed the distinction between wives' and husbands' earnings during legal separation. The earnings of either spouse during legal separation are now considered community property.

Appellee correctly argues that once a complete property settlement has been reached, A. R. S. § 14-2204 presumes a waiver of allowance in lieu of homestead, exempt property allowance and family allowance. However, that presumption is reached only after a determination that a complete property settlement has been made. Because there is uncontradicted evidence that five insurance policies which constituted a substantial portion of community assets were not covered by the 1975 amended judgment, we find it clearly erroneous for the trial court to have concluded that there had been a complete property settlement. Consequently, Mary E. Messer is entitled to an allowance in lieu of homestead, exempt property allowance, and family allowance as the surviving spouse of Elmer Jesse Messer.

We also note that even if the judgment were in fact a complete property settlement, as to Mrs. Messer, it would not have defeated the rights of decedent's four minor children to their statutory allowances. A. R. S. § 14-2802 provides the definition of "surviving spouse" to be used in construing A. R. S. §§ 14-2401, 14-2402 and 14-2403.[6]

"B . . . a surviving spouse does *not* include:

* * *

"³A person who was a party to a valid proceeding concluded by an order purporting to terminate all marital property rights." (Emphasis added.)

Therefore, under A. R. S. §§ 14-2401, 14-2402 and 14-2403, if Mrs. Messer had been a party to a complete property settlement, there would have been no surviving spouse and the four children who were minors when Mr. Messer died would have been entitled to the allowances.

[6] These statutes provide as follows:

A. R. S. § 14-2401. Allowance in lieu of homestead.

". . . If there is no surviving spouse, each dependent child of the decedent is entitled to an allowance of six thousand dollars divided by the number of dependent children of the decedent. . . . "

A. R. S. § 14-2402. Exempt property.

"In addition to the allowance in lieu of homestead the surviving spouse of a decedent who was domiciled in this state is entitled from the estate to value not exceeding three thousand five hundred dollars in excess of any security interests therein in household furniture, automobiles, furnishings, appliances and personal effects. If there is no surviving spouse, dependent children of the decedent are entitled jointly to the same value. . . . "

A. R. S. § 14-2403. Family allowance.

". . . It is payable to the surviving spouse, for the use of the surviving spouse and dependent children. If the spouse is not living the allowance is payable to the children or persons having their care and custody."

We reverse and remand this matter to the trial court to grant the allowance in lieu of homestead and the exempt property allowance to appellant, Mary E. Messer, in accordance with this opinion and to dispose of any remaining portion of this estate as either family allowance pursuant to A. R. S. § 14-2403 or under the terms of decedent's will.

Judgment reversed.

Case Questions

1. Who were the decedent's heirs in this case?
2. What was the issue before the court?
3. What was this court's holding, and what was the reason for its holding?

FORMS TO ACCOMPANY PARALEGAL PRACTICE

Disclaimer: The forms provided to aid students in completing the Paralegal Practice activities assigned in each chapter have been modified as samples to familiarize students with what each form commonly looks like and are not intended to be used as actual forms for any state

INSTRUCTIONS: The forms are provided in Microsoft Word format and employ the use of Stop Codes (such as SC1, SC2, SC3, and so on). Stop Codes are used in place of the form sections that must be updated with case-by-case information, such as SC1 for the client's name, SC3 for the client's address, and so on.

What each Stop Code represents can be inferred by reading the surrounding text on the form. By using the FIND & REPLACE tool on the Microsoft toolbar, the students can replace the Stop Codes with the information provided in the Paralegal Practice activity to complete each assignment. Students must also fill in any blank lines on each form with the appropriate information from the activity and then proofread the document prior to turning in their work.

The following forms are included following this section and will be posted online for students to access to complete the Paralegal Practice activities for this chapter:

- PP Form 9.1—Chart Containing Links to State Intestacy Statutes
- PP Form 9.2—Simple Will for Single Female

PP Form 9.1—Chart Containing Links to State Intestacy Statutes

State	Link	Instructions
Alabama	http://alisondb.legislature.state.al.us/acas/ACASLogin.asp	
Alaska	http://www.legis.state.ak.us/basis/folio.asp	
Arizona	http://www.azleg.gov/ArizonaRevisedStatutes.asp	
Arkansas	http://www.arkleg.state.ar.us/assembly/2011/2011R/Pages/Home.aspx	Click on "Search/View Arkansas Code"
California	www.leginfo.ca.gov/	
Colorado	http://www.michie.com/colorado/lpext.dll?f=templates&fn=main-h.htm&cp=	
Connecticut	http://www.cga.ct.gov/lco/statute_Web_Site_LCO.htm	
Delaware	http://delcode.delaware.gov/	
District of Columbia	http://www.justice.gov/archive/victimcompensation/law_dc.pdf	(Summary Table)
Florida	http://www.leg.state.fl.us/statutes/	
Georgia	http://www.lexisnexis.com/hottopics/gacode/Default.asp	
Hawaii	http://www.capitol.hawaii.gov/site1/hrs/default.asp	
Idaho	http://www.legislature.idaho.gov/idstat/Title15/T15CH2PT1.htm	
Illinois	http://www.ilga.gov/search/iga_search.asp?scope=ilcs	
Indiana	http://www.in.gov/legislative/ic/code/	
Iowa	http://www.legis.state.ia.us/IACODE/1999/633/	Scroll down to "Rules of Inheritance"
Kansas	http://kansasstatutes.lesterama.org/Chapter_59/Article_5/#59-514	
Kentucky	http://www.lrc.ky.gov/krs/391-00/CHAPTER.HTM	
Louisiana	http://www.legis.state.la.us/lss/lss.asp?folder=68	CCP 3001 et. seq.
Maine	http://www.mainelegislature.org/legis/statutes/	

(continued)

Maryland	http://www.michie.com/maryland/lpext.dll?f=templates&fn=main-h.htm&2.0	
Massachusetts	http://www.malegislature.gov/Laws/GeneralLaws/	
Michigan	http://www.legislature.mi.gov/(S(3mftci45b0oxcx3zvfmtaa45))/mileg.aspx?page=home	
Minnesota	https://www.revisor.mn.gov/bin/getpub.php?pubtype=STAT_CHAP_SEC&year=2006&section=524.2-101	
Mississippi	http://www.mscode.com/free/statutes/91/005/index.htm	
Missouri	http://www.moga.mo.gov/statutes/c400-499/4740000010.htm	
Montana	http://law.justia.com/montana/codes/2009/72/72_2/72_2_1/72_2_1.html	
Nebraska	http://nebraskalegislature.gov/laws/statutes.php?statute=30-2209	
Nevada	http://www.leg.state.nv.us/nrs/NRS-134.html	
New Hampshire	http://www.gencourt.state.nh.us/rsa/html/LVI/561/561-1.htm	
New Jersey	http://lis.njleg.state.nj.us/cgi-bin/om_isapi.dll?clientID=147937544&depth=2&expandheadings=off&headingswithhits=on&infobase=statutes.nfo&softpage=TOC_Frame_Pg42	
New Mexico	http://www.conwaygreene.com/nmsu/lpext.dll?f=templates&fn=main-h.htm&2.0	
New York	http://public.leginfo.state.ny.us/LAWSSEAF.cgi?QUERYTYPE=LAWS+&QUERYDATA=@SLEPT0A4P1+&LIST=LAW+&BROWSER=EXPLORER+&TOKEN=24113789+&TARGET=VIEW	
North Carolina	http://www.ncga.state.nc.us/gascripts/Statutes/StatutesTOC.pl?Chapter=0029	
North Dakota	http://www.legis.nd.gov/information/statutes/cent-code.html	Go to "Succession and Wills"
Ohio	http://codes.ohio.gov/orc/2105.06	
Oklahoma	http://www.lsb.state.ok.us/	
Oregon	http://www.leg.state.or.us/ors/112.html	
Pennsylvania	http://law.onecle.com/pennsylvania/decedents-estates-and-fiduciaries/00.021.001.000.html	
Rhode Island	http://www.rilin.state.ri.us/Statutes/TITLE33/33-1/INDEX.HTM	
South Carolina	http://www.scstatehouse.gov/code/t62c002.htm	
South Dakota	http://legis.state.sd.us/statutes/DisplayStatute.aspx?Type=Statute&Statute=29A-2	
Tennessee	http://www.lawserver.com/law/state/tennessee/tn-code/tennessee_code_title_31_chapter_2	
Texas	http://www.statutes.legis.state.tx.us/	

Utah	http://le.utah.gov/~code/TITLE75/75_02.htm	
Vermont	http://law.justia.com/vermont/codes/2009/title-14/chapter-42/301/	
Virginia	http://leg1.state.va.us/000/lst/LS594853.HTM	
Washington	http://apps.leg.wa.gov/rcw/default.aspx?cite=11.04	
West Virginia	http://www.legis.state.wv.us/WVCODE/Code.cfm?chap=42&art=1	
Wisconsin	http://legis.wisconsin.gov/statutes/Stat0852.pdf	
Wyoming	https://secure.ssa.gov/poms.nsf/lnx/1501005056	

PP Form 9.2—Simple Will for Single Female

LAST WILL AND TESTAMENT OF SC1

I, **SC1**, of the CITY OF SAMPLE, COUNTY OF SAMPLE, STATE OF SAMPLE, do hereby make, publish and declare the following to be my Last Will and Testament, hereby revoking all former Wills and Codicils made by me.

I. I direct that all my just legal debts and funeral expenses be paid, and I further authorize my Personal Representative, in its discretion, to prepay any mortgage or other installment indebtedness.

II. I give and bequeath to my children, SC2 (hereinafter referred to as "my children"), all of my clothing, jewelry, personal effects, household goods, furniture, furnishings, automobiles, and all other tangible personal property which I may own at the time of my death, to be divided among them as they shall agree. If my children are unable to agree as to the recipient of any article, that article, along with any articles not selected, shall be sold and the proceeds added to my residuary estate.

III. All the rest, residue and remainder of my property, real, personal and mixed, of every name and nature and wheresoever situate, I give, devise and bequeath in equal shares to my children, SC2, or all to the survivor(s) of them.

IV. I give to my Personal Representative, hereinafter named, and to the successor, the following powers and discretions, in addition to those vested in or imposed upon them or either of them by law:

A. To mortgage, sell, convey, exchange or otherwise deal with or dispose of any real or personal property for cash or on credit (including the right to accept a purchase money mortgage as part of the purchase price); to retain as part of the estate any and all securities and property in the form originally received, whether or not it is then income producing and regardless of any rule requiring diversification of investments; to invest and reinvest in any stocks, bonds, shares in mutual funds or authorized common trust funds, or other securities or property, whether real or personal, which my Personal Representative may deem safe and for the best interests of the estate, without being limited to investments authorized by law for the investment of trust funds; to hold title to any and all securities and other investments either in my Personal Representative's name or in the name of a nominee; to borrow money from itself or others on terms my Personal Representative may deem best, and to pledge any property of the estate as security for the repayment thereof; and to make distributions in cash or in kind, or partly in each, to the beneficiaries entitled thereto.

B. If any beneficiary or legatee entitled to receive a part of my estate shall be under twenty-one (21) years of age, I authorize and empower my Personal Representative to designate his or her parent, or some other appropriate adult person, or trust company, as custodian for the beneficiary or legatee under the Sample Uniform Transfers to Minors Act until the beneficiary or legatee reaches age twenty-one (21), and to distribute the share of the beneficiary or legatee to the designated custodian. A receipt from the custodian shall fully release my Personal Representative from all liability and accountability to the legatee or beneficiary.

V. I direct that all inheritance, succession, and estate taxes of every kind payable with respect to any property includable in my gross taxable estate, whether or not passing under this my Will, shall be paid out of my residuary estate and shall not be apportioned.

(continued)

VI. I hereby nominate, constitute, and appoint SC3 Personal Representative of this my Last Will and Testament; but if SC3 fails to survive me, or renounces, or fails to qualify, or upon his death, resignation or disqualification, I nominate and appoint SC4 as Personal Representative hereof. If both SC3 and SC4 are unwilling or unavailable to serve, I nominate, constitute and appoint SC5 as alternate Personal Representative hereof. I direct that no bond or other security shall be required of my Personal Representative.

VII. I hereby nominate, constitute and appoint SC6 as the Guardian of my Person. In the event that SC6 is unable or unwilling to so serve in this capacity, then I hereby nominate, constitute and appoint SC7 as my Alternate Guardian. *No bond shall be required of any Guardian.*

VIII. The masculine gender, whenever used herein, shall include the feminine; the feminine shall include the masculine; the neuter shall include both the masculine and feminine; and the singular shall include the plural, wherever necessary or appropriate.

IN WITNESS WHEREOF, I have hereunto subscribed my name this _____ day of _____, 2014.

_____
SC1

I, SC1, the Testatrix, sign my name to this instrument this _____ day of _____, 2014, and being first duly sworn, do declare to the undersigned authority that I sign and execute this instrument as my will and that I sign it willingly, or willingly direct another to sign for me, that I execute it as my free and voluntary act for the purposes expressed in that document and that I am eighteen years of age or older, of sound mind and under no constraint or undue influence.

_____
Testatrix

We, _____, _____, the witnesses, sign our names to this instrument being first duly sworn and do declare to the undersigned authority that the testator signs and executes this instrument as his/her will and that he/she signs it willingly, or willingly directs another to sign for him/her, and that each of us, in the presence and hearing of the testator, signs this will as witness to the testator's signing and that to the best of our knowledge the testator is eighteen years of age or older, of sound mind and under no constraint or undue influence.

_____
Witness

_____
Witness

The State of Sample}

County of Sample}

Subscribed, sworn to and acknowledged before me by SC1, the Testatrix, and subscribed and sworn to before me by _____ and _____, witnesses, this _____ day of _____, 2014.

_____
Notary Public

My Commission Expires:

Introduction to Estate Administration

CHAPTER **10**

A REAL-LIFE SCENARIO

Mr. Smith had three grown children and was married to his third wife at the time of his death. He died leaving a valid Florida will that left most of his assets to his wife. In addition to his home and assets in Florida, Mr. Smith also had parcels of land in Michigan, Arizona, and California. He left the land to his children. Although the main probate proceeding was in Florida, ancillary probate proceedings were necessary in the other three states to get the land transferred to Mr. Smith's children. Since the land in Arizona was of very small value, it could have potentially been transferred by a small estate proceeding called an affidavit of succession to real property. However, other statutory requirements for a small estate were not met, so a regular probate proceeding was required to transfer the Arizona property to Mr. Smith's son.

CHAPTER OBJECTIVES:

1. Understand the terminology and the various players in probate proceedings.

2. List and describe the different types of probates.

3. Examine statutory requirements for small estate settlement.

4. Identify which type of proceeding should be brought for given hypothetical scenarios.

■ INTRODUCTION

The foregoing scenario illustrates the complications that can arise when an individual owns property in multiple states at the time of death. Although the value of the property in the ancillary state was small, the requirements for a small estate proceeding were not met due to the total value of assets in other states.

Key Terms and Definitions

Probate has multiple definitions. One definition of **probate** is "to prove and have allowed by the court." **Probate** is also the process of proving a **will** is valid and thereafter administering the estate in accordance with the terms of the will. An alternate definition of **probate** is the general process of administration of estates of dead persons, including those without wills, with court supervision. Notice that a probate proceeding may be required whether or not a decedent had a will, depending on the circumstances. However, testate probates generally go more smoothly and quickly than intestate probates. Therefore, it is advisable for clients to execute wills expressing their intentions prior to death.

An **ancillary probate** is a probate proceeding in a state other than the venue of the main probate proceeding, which is conducted in the decedent's state of domicile. An **ancillary administrator** is a person appointed by the court to handle the affairs of a decedent in a foreign state. An **administrator** is a male appointed by the court to administer the estate of an intestate decedent. A **decedent** is the deceased person, referred to as having died **testate** or intestate. An **administratrix** is a female appointed by the court to administer the estate of an intestate decedent. **Intestate** means one had no valid will at death.

A **fiduciary** is a person in a position of trust, such as an executor, administrator, guardian, or trustee. An **executor** is a male nominated in the will of a decedent to carry out the terms of the will; a personal representative of an estate. An **executrix** is a female nominated in the will of a decedent to carry out the terms of the will; a personal representative of an estate. A **personal representative** is the executor or administrator of a deceased person.

■ A TIME OF GRIEF

The death of a loved one is a time of grief and sorrow. Probate attorneys and paralegals must exercise great delicacy, sensitivity, and patience when interacting with grieving clients. It is not uncommon for a surviving spouse or partner to be too distraught for weeks or even months following the death of a loved one to begin the process of estate administration. Every person is different, and it is important to allow clients the time they need to bury their loved one and mourn. Generally speaking, and barring pressing issues and circumstances, it is not imperative that the probate process begin right away, and clients should be encouraged to take the time they need and begin when they are ready. As such, this is a situation where legal professionals should take their cue from their clients and work around their timelines. However, expressing sympathy and concern is appropriate and customary.

Notification of Client's Death

When a client has passed away, the law firm will likely send a sympathy card and possibly flowers to the family of the deceased. If there was a close relationship

---

Probate
A general term for the entire process of administration of estates of dead persons, including those without wills, with court supervision.

Will
A written document that leaves the estate of the individual who signed the will to the named persons or entities.

Ancillary Probate
A probate proceeding in a state other than the venue of the main probate proceeding, which is conducted in the decedent's state of domicile.

Ancillary Administrator
A person appointed by the court to handle the affairs of a decedent in a foreign state.

Administrator
A male appointed by the court to administer the estate of an intestate decedent.

Administratrix
A female appointed by the court to administer the estate of an intestate decedent.

Testate
To die with a valid will.

Intestate
To die without a valid will.

Fiduciary
A person in a position of loyalty and trust, such as an executor, administrator, guardian, attorney-in-fact, or trustee; also a person to whom property or power is entrusted for the benefit of another.

Executor
A male nominated in a will of a decedent to carry out the terms of the will; a personal representative of the estate.

Executrix
A female nominated in a will to carry out the terms of the will; a personal representative of the estate.

Personal Representative
The executor or administrator of a deceased person. Whether the estate representative is referred to as an "executor" or a "personal representative" is dictated by the laws and customs of the jurisdiction; however, for all intents and purposes, the terms may be used interchangeably.

between the attorney and the client, the attorney may also attend the funeral to display sympathy for the loss. While the concept may seem morose if it is new to you, it is not unusual for a law firm that does extensive estate planning and probate work to charge a member of the professional staff with the task of reading the daily obituaries to see if any clients have passed away. It can be embarrassing for the firm if a valued longtime client has lost a spouse but does not call for several months. At that point, displays of sympathy are untimely. Accordingly, it is customary for some law firms to read the obituaries to be sure to send condolences when a client passes away.

If the firm has possession of the client's original will (stored in a fireproof vault), the client's next-of-kin must be notified of that fact. However, the deceased client's family is under no obligation to use the same law firm to handle the probate proceeding. It is entirely up to the party seeking appointment as personal representative to select an attorney to provide guidance through the probate process.

■ INTERVIEWING THE CLIENT

If the decedent's estate plan was drafted by the firm, it may already have a lot of information on file to assist with the probate. However, you cannot assume that the information did not change between the time the documents were drafted and the time of the decedent's death. Therefore, as with estate planning, attorneys often have clients fill out an intake sheet covering necessary and pertinent information prior to conducting a probate consultation. Law firms may also utilize a checklist during the consultation to make sure that all important topics are covered. Since many states have different types of probate proceedings depending on the size of the estate, it is very important to ascertain the total value of the decedent's estate. Figure 10.1 is a very basic probate intake sheet designed to get an overview of the situation from the client before the consultation.

Figure 10.1

PROBATE INTAKE SHEET

DATE:_____

Full Name: _____

Spouse's Name: _____ or N/A

Address: _____

_____

Home Phone: ( )_____

Cell Phone: ( ) _____

Email Address: _____ @ _____

Please answer the following questions prior to your consultation.

1. What was the decedent's full name? _____
2. What was the decedent's marital status?
   Married or Single or Divorced or Widowed
3. Was the decedent a resident of this State? Yes or No

(continued)

Figure 10.1 (continued)

4. What was the decedent's date of death? _____

5. Did the decedent have a Will?   Yes   or   No

6. What is your relationship to the decedent?

   Spouse   Child   Grandchild   Niece/Nephew   Other

7. How many children did the decedent have?   0   1   2   3   4   5+

8. List the name and age of each child.

Name of Child	Date of Birth

6. Provide any additional information you think we should know.

_____

_____

_____

PROBATE INTAKE SHEET
DATE:_____

Consultation Checklist:

- Real Property: _____
- Doe client have original will?_____
- Are there Creditors? _____ (If so, need list from client) _____
- Is anyone likely to contest the probate? _____
- Has anyone been disinherited? _____
- Other Assets: _____

Notes:

■ DETERMINE WHETHER A PROBATE IS NEEDED

As was discussed in earlier chapters, a probate proceeding is not always required when a person dies. Assets that are titled in joint name pass to the surviving owner or owners. Assets for which a beneficiary designation was made pass automatically by operation of law to the beneficiary following the owner's death. For example, a life insurance policy will pass to the designated beneficiaries following the death of the insured. No probate is necessary to effectuate the payout from the life insurance company. Usually an original death certificate must be submitted to the insurance company and possibly some forms, but little else is required. Therefore, if all of the decedent's assets are titled jointly or pass by beneficiary designation, no probate will be required, even if the decedent had a will.

If a decedent executed a valid revocable **living trust** prior to death and transferred all of his or her assets into the trust, no probate proceeding will be required. Under ordinary circumstances, the trustee will be able to distribute the

Living Trust
Also called an *inter vivos* trust, which is Latin for "within one's life," is a trust that is created and becomes effective during the lifetime of the trustor(s) [also called settlor(s)].

assets in accordance with the terms of the trust without assistance from the court. However, if a decedent has assets titled solely in his or her name at death, some sort of probate proceeding will be required in order to transfer the assets to the beneficiaries or heirs at law.

Probate Assets

Even when a person dies and a probate is required, it is possible that not all of the decedent's assets will go through probate. **Probate assets** are those assets that are distributed through a probate proceeding in a court of law. Generally speaking, probate assets are assets that are in the sole name of the decedent at the time of death. Common examples of property that would pass through probate are a separate bank account, titled solely in the name of the decedent, and a car titled only in the decedent's name. If the decedent had a will, the probate assets will pass as directed under the will. If the decedent did not have a will, the assets will pass to the decedent's heirs under the state's intestacy statutes, as was discussed in Chapter 9.

Probate Assets
The property of the decedent that must be distributed through a probate proceeding in a court of law.

Non-Probate Assets

In contrast with probate assets, **non-probate assets** pass to the intended beneficiary by operation of law independent of the provisions of a will or a probate proceeding. The most common ways this happens is by title or by beneficiary designation.

Non-Probate Assets
Property that passes to a decedent's intended beneficiaries by operation of law, independent of the provisions of a will or a probate proceeding.

By Title

An asset that is held in joint title will generally pass to the survivor at the first death. For example, if John and Sue are co-owners of a joint bank account and John passes away, the bank account legally belongs to Sue. Therefore, if a probate proceeding is initiated to administer John's estate, the joint bank account will not be a part of it because it is a non-probate asset. Further, if John has a will directing that the account pass to Sally, that provision will have no effect on the account, which will still pass by title to Sue.

By Beneficiary Designation

Some types of property allow the owner to appoint a **beneficiary** to receive the property upon the owner's death. Life insurance is one of the most common assets to pass by beneficiary designation. The beneficiary appointed to receive the life insurance upon the principal's death receives the proceeds by operation of law (via the beneficiary designation); thus, the insurance proceeds are a non-probate asset. Pay-on-death (POD) and transfer-on-death (TOD) accounts are other examples of non-probate assets that pass by beneficiary designation. Upon the death of the owner, these types of bank accounts pass to the beneficiary designated to receive the account. Finally, retirement accounts also pass by beneficiary designation and so are non-probate assets.

Beneficiary
(of a will): A person entitled to receive property under a will or to whom the decedent's property is given or distributed.

The only exception to the general rule that property that passes by beneficiary designation is a non-probate asset is when the beneficiary appointed is the decedent's estate. The owner of the asset may choose to appoint the estate as beneficiary if he or she wants the asset to pass pursuant to the will and go through probate. For example, the owner of a life insurance policy may direct that the life insurance be paid to his estate and then direct under his will that the proceeds of the policy be used to pay off the mortgage on a parcel of real property before the property is distributed to the beneficiary.

EXAMPLE 1

Ned Jones passed away and owned the following at the time of his death:

- Checking account (1255) containing $10,510.00, POD to Sandra Jones.
- Savings account (1288) in Ned's name containing $2,287.22.
- 2005 Corvette titled in Ned's name, worth $35,000.00.
- State Farm life insurance policy for $20,000.00, beneficiary Sandra Jones.
- 1987 Kawasaki motorcycle worth $500.00, titled jointly with Robert Jones.

- General Motors retirement account in the amount of $66,997.02 with no beneficiary designation made.

The following assets are subject to probate administration:

- Savings account (1288) in Ned's name containing $2,287.22.
- 2005 Corvette, titled in Ned's name worth $35,000.00.
- General Motors retirement account in the amount of $66,997.02 with no beneficiary designation made.

EXAMPLE 2

Sarah Marks passed away and owned the following at the time of her death:

- Checking account (9280) containing $3,610.00.
- Joint checking account (1223) with Ryan Marks containing $933.05.
- 2010 Honda Civic titled jointly with Ryan Marks, worth $12,000.00.
- Textbook royalty check in the amount of $5,000.00.
- Home located at 120 First Street titled as tenants in common with Ryan Marks (value $120,000.00).

The following assets are subject to probate administration:

- Checking account (9280) containing $3,610.00.
- Textbook royalty check in the amount of $5,000.00.
- Home located at 120 First Street titled as tenants in common with Ryan Marks (value $120,000.00). (For a review of this type of property ownership, see Chapter 2)

EXAMPLE 3

Michael Mathews passed away and left the following property at the time of his death:

- Joint checking account (1223) with Shawn Lucas containing $59,833.05.
- 2012 Ford F350 truck titled in Michael's name and valued at $28,000.00.
- Tax refund check in the amount of $129.00.
- Home located at 55 Smart Way titled as joint tenants with rights of survivorship with Shawn Lucas (value $120,000.00).

- Art gallery owned solely by Michael d/b/a (doing business as) Michael's Masterpieces, valued at $1 million.

The following assets are subject to probate administration:

- 2012 Ford F350 truck titled in Michael's name and valued at $28,000.00.
- Tax refund check in the amount of $129.00.
- Art museum owned solely by Michael d/b/a (doing business as) Michael's Masterpieces, valued at $1 million.

For Review:

Probate Assets	Non-Probate Assets
• Check payable to decedent • Real property titled solely in decedent's name • Real property held as tenants in common with two or more owners • Bank account solely in the decedent's name • Vehicle titled solely in the decedent's name • Life insurance payable to decedent's estate	• Property titled in the name of a trust • Joint bank account • Life insurance payable to a beneficiary • Real property titled as joint tenants with rights of survivorship • Retirement account • POD or TOD account

Determine What Type of Proceeding Is Necessary

Once you determine that a probate is required in order to transfer the decedent's assets to the beneficiaries or heirs, the next step is to determine which type of proceeding is necessary and which court has jurisdiction over the case. The value of the estate and the circumstances will dictate whether the appropriate process will be small estate settlement, an informal probate, a formal probate, and/or an ancillary probate.

■ TYPES OF PROBATE

In addition to small estate settlement, there are informal probates, formal probates, and ancillary probates. In states that use the foregoing distinctions (primarily the western states), the vast majority of probates are informal probates. **Informal probates** are uncontested probates that generally require minimal court supervision. **Formal probates** are contested probates where one or more heirs oppose or contest the probate of the will, the appointment of the personal representative, or both. A court hearing will be required and a judge will make the final determination about the validity of the proffered will and the priority of the petitioner for appointment as personal representative. The distinction between informal and formal probate does not exist in the eastern states, where the process is simply known as "probate."

Ancillary probates are secondary probates brought in another jurisdiction, most commonly to transfer a parcel of real property that is outside the state of the main probate proceeding. Depending on the law in the state of the ancillary probate, the proceeding may or may not be simplified compared to a regular (informal) probate proceeding.

Informal Probates
They are uncontested probates that generally require minimal court supervision.

Formal Probates
They are contested probates where one or more heirs oppose or contest the probate of the will, the appointment of the personal representative, or both.

The Probate Process

The details of the probate process vary from state to state. No two states have identical rules and requirements. This textbook provides you with a general overview in order to familiarize you with the probate process. As a paralegal, it is essential that you learn to conduct legal research and familiarize yourself with the resources that are available in your state, as well as in your particular jurisdiction.

In order to present the probate process in a logical and orderly fashion, this text has divided the probate process into main parts, beginning with Chapter 11. The designation of the probate part numbers may or may not be a distinction that you will come across in your career as a paralegal. However, the general order and steps depicted should be similar to the process required in most states. The remainder of this chapter covers small estate settlement.

SMALL ESTATE SETTLEMENT

Small Estate Settlement
A provision in some states allowing for probate assets below a certain value to be transferred by a simple affidavit when a variety of other conditions are met.

Many states have provisions for shortened proceedings where the value of estate assets is small and a variety of other conditions are met. Often, state statutes permit the transfer of probate assets of small value by **affidavit**. The affidavit describes the asset(s) being transferred, by whom, and to whom, and sets forth that all of the statutory requirements for such a transfer have been met. Statutory requirements may include, among other things, that the value of the estate is below a set amount, that a certain amount of time has passed since the decedent's death, and that no other probate proceeding is pending in another jurisdiction.

Figures 10.2–10.5 display the statutes setting forth the requirements for small estate settlement in Arizona, California, North Carolina, and Nevada. The exercises following these figures require that you analyze the statutes carefully to determine their requirements.

Figure 10.2 Arizona's Statute Providing for Collection of Personal Property and Real Property by Affidavit

A.R.S. § 14-3971 (2009)

§ 14-3971. Collection of personal property by **affidavit;** ownership of vehicles; **affidavit** of succession to **real property**

A. At any time after the death of a decedent, any employer owing wages, salary or other compensation for personal services of the decedent shall pay to the surviving spouse of the decedent the amount owing, not in excess of five thousand dollars, on being presented an **affidavit** made by or on behalf of the spouse stating that the affiant is the surviving spouse of the decedent, or is authorized to act on behalf of the spouse, and that no application or petition for the appointment of a personal representative is pending or has been granted in this state or, if granted, the personal representative has been discharged or more than one year has elapsed since a closing statement has been filed.

B. Thirty days after the death of a decedent, any person indebted to the decedent or having possession of tangible personal property or an instrument evidencing a debt, obligation, stock or chose in action belonging to the decedent shall make payment of the indebtedness or deliver the tangible personal property or an instrument evidencing a debt, obligation, stock or chose in action to a person claiming to be the successor of the decedent upon being presented an **affidavit** made by or on behalf of the successor and stating that all of the following are true:

   1. Thirty days have elapsed since the death of the decedent.
   2. Either:
      a. An application or petition for the appointment of a personal representative is not pending and a personal representative has not been appointed in any jurisdiction and the value of all personal property in the decedent's estate, wherever located, less liens and encumbrances, does not exceed fifty thousand dollars as valued as of the date of death.
      b. The personal representative has been discharged or more than one year has elapsed since a closing statement has been filed and the value of all personal property in the decedent's estate, wherever located, less liens and encumbrances, does not exceed fifty thousand dollars as valued as of the date of the **affidavit.**
   3. The claiming successor is entitled to payment or delivery of the property.

Figure 10.2 (continued)

C. A transfer agent of any security shall change the registered ownership on the books of a corporation from the decedent to the successor or successors on presentation of an **affidavit** pursuant to subsection B of this section.

D. The motor vehicle division shall transfer title of a motor vehicle from the decedent to the successor or successors on presentation of an **affidavit** as provided in subsection B of this section and on payment of the necessary fees.

E. No sooner than six months after the death of a decedent, a person or persons claiming as successor or successors to the decedent's interest in **real property,** including any debt secured by a lien on **real property,** may file in the court in the county in which the decedent was domiciled at the time of death, or if the decedent was not domiciled in this state then in any county in which **real property** of the decedent is located, an **affidavit** describing the **real property** and the interest of the decedent in that property and stating that all of the following are true and material and acknowledging that any false statement in the **affidavit** may subject the person or persons to penalties relating to perjury and subornation of perjury:

  1. Either:

    a. An application or petition for the appointment of a personal representative is not pending and a personal representative has not been appointed in any jurisdiction and the value of all **real property** in the decedent's estate located in this state, less liens and encumbrances against the **real property,** does not exceed seventy-five thousand dollars as valued at the date of death. The value of the decedent's interest in that **real property** shall be determined from the full cash value of the property as shown on the assessment rolls for the year in which the decedent died, except that in the case of a debt secured by a lien on **real property** the value shall be determined by the unpaid principal balance due on the debt as of the date of death.

    b. The personal representative has been discharged or more than one year has elapsed since a closing statement has been filed and the value of all **real property** in the decedent's estate, wherever located, less liens and encumbrances, does not exceed seventy-five thousand dollars as valued as of the date of the **affidavit.** The value of the decedent's interest in that **real property** is determined from the full cash value of the property as shown on the assessment rolls for the year in which the **affidavit** is given, except that if a debt is secured by a lien on **real property,** the value is determined by the unpaid principal balance due on the debt as of the date of the **affidavit.**

  2. Six months have elapsed since the death of the decedent as shown in a certified copy of the decedent's death certificate attached to the **affidavit.**

  3. Funeral expenses, expenses of last illness, and all unsecured debts of the decedent have been paid.

  4. The person or persons signing the **affidavit** are entitled to the **real property** by reason of the allowance in lieu of homestead, exempt property or family allowance, by intestate succession as the sole heir or heirs, or by devise under a valid last will of the decedent, the original of which is attached to the **affidavit** or has been probated.

  5. No other person has a right to the interest of the decedent in the described property.

  6. No federal or Arizona estate tax is due on the decedent's estate.

F. The normal filing fee shall be charged for the filing of an **affidavit** under subsection E of this section unless waived by the court as provided by section 12-301 or 12-302. On receipt of the **affidavit** and after determining that the **affidavit** is complete, the registrar shall cause to be issued a certified copy of the **affidavit** without attachments, and the copy shall be recorded in the office of the recorder in the county where the **real property** is located.

G. This section does not limit the rights of heirs and devisees under section 14-3901.

> ### Figure 10.2: Statutory Review- √ your Understanding
> 1. What two types of affidavits are provided for in this statute?
> 2. How much time must have elapsed since the decedent's death to use a personal property affidavit?
> 3. How much time must have elapsed since the decedent's death to use a real property affidavit?
> 4. What is the limit on the value of real property that may be transferred by affidavit?
> 5. What procedure must be followed for a real property affidavit?

Figure 10.3 California's Statute Providing for Collection of Real Property by Affidavit

Cal Probate Code § 13200 (2009)

§ 13200. Filing affidavit in superior court; Inventory and appraisement

(a) No sooner than six months from the death of a decedent, a person or persons claiming as successor of the decedent to a particular item of property that is **real property** may file in the superior court in the county in which the decedent was domiciled at the time of death, or if the decedent was not domiciled in this state at the time of death, then in any county in which **real property** of the decedent is located, an **affidavit** in the form prescribed by the Judicial Council pursuant to Section 1001 stating all of the following:

   (1)   The name of the decedent.

   (2)   The date and place of the decedent's death.

   (3)   A legal description of the **real property** and the interest of the decedent therein.

   (4)   The name and address of each person serving as guardian or conservator of the estate of the decedent at the time of the decedent's death, so far as known to the affiant.

   (5)   "The gross value of all **real property** in the decedent's estate located in California, as shown by the inventory and appraisal attached to this **affidavit,** excluding the **real property** described in Section 13050 of the California Probate Code, does not exceed twenty thousand dollars ($20,000)."

   (6)   "At least six months have elapsed since the death of the decedent as shown in a certified copy of decedent's death certificate attached to this **affidavit.**"

   (7)   Either of the following, as appropriate:

      (A) "No proceeding is now being or has been conducted in California for administration of the decedent's estate."

      (B) "The decedent's personal representative has consented in writing to use of the procedure provided by this chapter."

   (8)   "Funeral expenses, expenses of last illness, and all unsecured debts of the decedent have been paid."

   (9)   "The affiant is the successor of the decedent (as defined in Section 13006 of the Probate Code) and to the decedent's interest in the described property, and no other person has a superior right to the interest of the decedent in the described property."

  (10)   "The affiant declares under penalty of perjury under the law of the State of California that the foregoing is true and correct."

(b) For each person executing the **affidavit, the affidavit** shall contain a notary public's certificate of acknowledgment identifying the person.

(c) There shall be attached to the **affidavit** an inventory and appraisal of the decedent's **real property** in this state, excluding the **real property** described in Section 13050. The inventory and appraisal of the **real property** shall be made as provided in Part 3 (commencing with Section 8800) of Division 7. The appraisal shall be made by a probate referee selected by the affiant from those probate referees appointed by the Controller under Section 400 to appraise property in the county where the **real property** is located.

(d) If the affiant claims under the decedent's will and no estate proceeding is pending or has been conducted in California, a copy of the will shall be attached to the **affidavit.**

(e) A certified copy of the decedent's death certificate shall be attached to the **affidavit.** If the decedent's personal representative has consented to the use of the procedure provided by this chapter, a copy of the consent and of the personal representative's letters shall be attached to the **affidavit.**

(f) The affiant shall mail a copy of the **affidavit** and attachments to any person identified in paragraph (4) of subdivision (a).

Figure 10.3: Statutory Review- √ Your Understanding

  1. What type of affidavit is provided for in this statute?

  2. How much time must have elapsed since the decedent's death to use this affidavit?

  3. What is the limit on the value of property that may be transferred by affidavit?

  4. What procedure must be followed for this affidavit?

Figure 10.4 North Carolina's Statute Providing for Collection of Personal Property by Affidavit

N.C. Gen. Stat. § 28A-25-1.1 (2009)

§ 28A-25-1.1. Collection of property by **affidavit** when decedent dies testate

(a) When a decedent dies testate leaving personal property, less liens and encumbrances thereon, not exceeding twenty thousand dollars ($ 20,000) in value, at any time after 30 days from the date of death, any person indebted to the decedent or having possession of tangible personal property or an instrument evidencing a debt, obligation, stock or chose in action belonging to the decedent shall make payment of the indebtedness or deliver the tangible personal property or an instrument evidencing a debt, obligation, stock or chose in action to a person claiming to be the public administrator appointed pursuant to G.S. 28A-12-1, a person named or designated as executor in the will, devisee, heir or creditor, of the decedent, not disqualified under G.S. 28A-4-2, upon being presented a certified copy of an **affidavit** filed in accordance with subsection (b) and made by or on behalf of the heir, the person named or designated as executor in the will of the decedent, the creditor, the public administrator, or the devisee, stating:

(1) The name and address of the affiant and the fact that he is the public administrator, a person named or designated as executor in the will, devisee, heir or creditor, of the decedent;

(2) The name of the decedent and his residence at time of death;

(3) The date and place of death of the decedent;

(4) That 30 days have elapsed since the death of the decedent;

(5) That the decedent died testate leaving personal property, less liens and encumbrances thereon, not exceeding twenty thousand dollars ($ 20,000) in value;

(6) That the decedent's will has been admitted to probate in the court of the proper county and a duly certified copy of the will has been recorded in each county in which is located any **real property** owned by the decedent at the time of his death;

(7) That a certified copy of the decedent's will is attached to the **affidavit;**

(8) That no application or petition for appointment of a personal representative is pending or has been granted in any jurisdiction;

(9) The names and addresses of those persons who are entitled, under the provisions of the will, or if applicable, of the Intestate Succession Act, to the property of the decedent; and their relationship, if any, to the decedent; and

(10) A description sufficient to identify each tract of **real property** owned by the decedent at the time of his death.

In those cases in which the affiant is the surviving spouse, is entitled to all of the property of the decedent, and is not disqualified under G.S. 28A-4-2, the property described in this subsection that may be collected pursuant to this section may exceed twenty thousand dollars ($ 20,000) in value but shall not exceed thirty thousand dollars ($ 30,000) in value. In such cases, the **affidavit** shall state: (i) the name and address of the affiant and the fact that he or she is the surviving spouse and is entitled, under the provisions of the decedent's will, or if applicable, of the Intestate Succession Act, to all of the property of the decedent; (ii) that the decedent died testate leaving personal property, less liens and encumbrances thereon, not exceeding thirty thousand dollars ($ 30,000); and (iii) the information required under subdivisions (2), (3), (4), (6), (7), (8), and (10) of this subsection.

(b) Prior to the recovery of any assets of the decedent, a copy of the **affidavit** described in subsection (a) shall be filed in the office of the clerk of superior court of the county where the decedent had his domicile at the time of his death. The **affidavit** shall be filed by the clerk upon payment of the fee provided in G.S. 7A-307, shall be indexed in the index to estates, and a copy shall be mailed by the clerk to the persons shown in the **affidavit** as entitled to the property.

(c) The presentation of an **affidavit** as provided in subsection (a) shall be sufficient to require the transfer to the affiant or his designee of the title and license to a motor vehicle registered in the name of the decedent owner; the ownership rights of a savings account or checking account in a bank in the name of the decedent owner; the ownership rights of a savings account or share certificate in a credit union, building and loan association, or savings and loan association in the name of the decedent owner; the ownership rights in any stock or security registered on the books of a corporation in the name of a decedent owner; or any other property or contract right owned by decedent at the time of his death.

(continued)

Figure 10.4 (continued)

> **Figure 10.4: Statutory Review-√ Your Understanding**
> 1. What type of affidavit is provided for in this statute?
> 2. How much time must have elapsed since the decedent's death to use this affidavit?
> 3. What is the limit on the value of property that may be transferred by affidavit?
> 4. What procedure must be followed for this affidavit?

Figure 10.5 Nevada's Statute Providing for Collection of Personal Property by Affidavit

Nev. Rev. Stat. Ann. § 146.080 (2009)

146.080. Estates not exceeding $20,000: Transfer of assets without issuance of letters of administration or probate of will; affidavit showing right to assets.

1. If a decedent leaves no **real property,** nor interest therein, nor mortgage or lien thereon, in this state, and the gross value of the decedent's property in this state, over and above any amounts due to the decedent for services in the Armed Forces of the United States, does not exceed $20,000, a person who has a right to succeed to the property of the decedent pursuant to the laws of succession for a decedent who died intestate or pursuant to the valid will of a decedent who died testate, on behalf of all persons entitled to succeed to the property claimed, or the Director of the Department of Health and Human Services or public administrator on behalf of the State or others entitled to the property, may, 40 days after the death of the decedent, without procuring letters of administration or awaiting the probate of the will, collect any money due the decedent, receive the property of the decedent, and have any evidences of interest, indebtedness or right transferred to the claimant upon furnishing the person, representative, corporation, officer or body owing the money, having custody of the property or acting as registrar or transfer agent of the evidences of interest, indebtedness or right, with an **affidavit** showing the right of the affiant or affiants to receive the money or property or to have the evidence transferred.

2. An **affidavit** made pursuant to this section must state:

    (a) The affiant's name and address, and that the affiant is entitled by law to succeed to the property claimed;

    (b) The date and place of death of the decedent;

    (c) That the gross value of the decedent's property in this state, except amounts due the decedent for services in the Armed Forces of the United States, does not exceed $20,000, and that the property does not include any **real property** nor interest therein, nor mortgage or lien thereon;

    (d) That at least 40 days have elapsed since the death of the decedent, as shown in a certified copy of the certificate of death of the decedent attached to the **affidavit;**

    (e) That no petition for the appointment of a personal representative is pending or has been granted in any jurisdiction;

    (f) That all debts of the decedent, including funeral and burial expenses, and money owed to the Department of Human Resources as a result of the payment of benefits for Medicaid, have been paid or provided for;

    (g) A description of the personal property and the portion claimed;

    (h) That the affiant has given written notice, by personal service or by certified mail, identifying the affiant's claim and describing the property claimed, to every person whose right to succeed to the decedent's property is equal or superior to that of the affiant, and that at least 14 days have elapsed since the notice was served or mailed;

    (i) That the affiant is personally entitled, or the Department of Human Resources is entitled, to full payment or delivery of the property claimed or is entitled to payment or delivery on behalf of and with the written authority of all other successors who have an interest in the property; and

    (j) That the affiant acknowledges an understanding that filing a false **affidavit** constitutes a felony in this state.

Figure 10.5 (continued)

3. If the affiant:

   (a) Submits an **affidavit** which does not meet the requirements of subsection 2 or which contains statements which are not entirely true, any money or property the affiant receives is subject to all debts of the decedent.

   (b) Fails to give notice to other successors as required by subsection 2, any money or property the affiant receives is held by the affiant in trust for all other successors who have an interest in the property.

4. A person who receives an **affidavit** containing the information required by subsection 2 is entitled to rely upon that information, and if the person relies in good faith, the person is immune from civil liability for actions based on that reliance.

5. Upon receiving proof of the death of the decedent and an **affidavit** containing the information required by this section:

   (a) A transfer agent of any security shall change the registered ownership of the security claimed from the decedent to the person claiming to succeed to ownership of that security.

   (b) A governmental agency required to issue certificates of title, ownership or registration to personal property shall issue a new certificate of title, ownership or registration to the person claiming to succeed to ownership of the property.

6. If any property of the estate not exceeding $20,000 is located in a state which requires an order of a court for the transfer of the property, or if the estate consists of stocks or bonds which must be transferred by an agent outside this state, any person qualified pursuant to the provisions of subsection 1 to have the stocks or bonds or other property transferred may do so by obtaining a court order directing the transfer. The person desiring the transfer must file a petition, which may be ex parte, containing:

   (a) A specific description of all the property of the decedent.

   (b) A list of all the liens and mortgages of record at the date of the decedent's death.

   (c) An estimate of the value of the property of the decedent.

   (d) The names, ages of any minors and residences of the decedent's heirs and devisees.

   (e) A request for the court to issue an order directing the transfer of the stocks or bonds or other property if the court finds the gross value of the estate does not exceed $20,000.

   (f) An attached copy of the executed **affidavit** made pursuant to subsection 2.

If the court finds that the gross value of the estate does not exceed $20,000 and the person requesting the transfer is entitled to it, the court may enter an order directing the transfer.

Figure 10.5: Statutory Review- √ Your Understanding

1. What type of affidavit is provided for in this statute?
2. How much time must have elapsed since the decedent's death to use this affidavit?
3. What is the limit on the value of property that may be transferred by affidavit?
4. What procedure must be followed for this affidavit?

■ COURTS

A law firm representing a client must be certain to begin a probate proceeding in the proper court. Generally speaking, the probate will be brought in the jurisdiction where the decedent was domiciled at the time of death. **Domicile** is a person's principal place of abode; the place to which, whenever one is absent, one has the present intent of returning. A probate may also be necessary in a jurisdiction where the decedent owns real property. Sometimes, more than one probate proceeding is required. When a second probate proceeding must be started in another jurisdiction, that probate is known an **ancillary probate** proceeding.

Domicile
A person's principal place of abode; the place to which, whenever one is absent, one has the present intent of returning.

Jurisdiction
The power or authority that a court has to hear a case.

Probate and Family Court
A name given in some states to the court that exercises the function of settling decedents' estates. Other states simply call this court the "Probate Court" or the "Surrogate's Court." Finally, some states have trial courts of general jurisdiction that have authority to settle decedents' estates within their jurisdiction.

Jurisdiction is the power or authority that a court has to hear a case. The court in which the probate is initiated must have authority to hear probate cases. **Probate and Family Court** is a name given in some states to the court that exercises the function of settling decedents' estates. Other states simply call this court "Probate Court." Finally, some states have trial courts of general jurisdiction that have authority to settle decedents' estates within their jurisdiction.

Identifying the proper court in which to initiate a probate proceeding requires identifying both the state and the county of domicile (or the state and county in which real property is located).

■ LINKS TO STATE PROBATE FORMS

Use the links in Table 10.1 to access the model or sample probate forms that are available for your state. Please note that the links provided were current when this table was compiled but are subject to change. If a link is no longer valid, perform a search for your state's probate forms.

Table 10.1

State	Link	Instructions
Alabama	http://eforms.alacourt.gov/	Limited forms are available. Search your local court's website.
Alaska	http://www.courts.alaska.gov/forms.htm	
Arizona	No general probate forms are posted at this time.	Search your local superior court's website to locate probate forms.
Arkansas	https://courts.arkansas.gov/aoc/forms.cfm	Scroll down to "Circuit Court-Probate Division"
California	http://www.courtinfo.ca.gov/cgi-bin/forms.cgi	Select "Probate-Decedent's Estates" from the drop box.
Colorado	http://www.courts.state.co.us/Forms/SubCategory.cfm?Category=Probate	
Connecticut	http://www.jud.ct.gov/probate/faq3.html	
Delaware	No general probate forms are posted at this time.	Search your local court's website for probate forms.
District of Columbia	http://www.dcsc.gov/dccourts/superior/probate/forms.jsp	

Table 10.1

Florida	No general probate forms are posted at this time.	Search your local court's website for probate forms.
Georgia	http://www.gaprobate.org/forms.php	
Hawaii	No general probate forms are posted at this time.	Search your local court's website for probate forms.
Idaho	http://www.courtselfhelp.idaho.gov/	Some probate forms are available.
Illinois	No general probate forms are posted at this time.	Search your local court's website for probate forms.
Indiana	No general probate forms are posted at this time.	Search your local court's website for probate forms.
Iowa	http://www.iowacourtsonline.org/Court_Rules_and_Forms/Probate_Forms/	
Kansas	http://www.kansasjudicialcouncil.org/legal_forms.shtml	Only a few probate forms are posted. Search your local court's website.
Kentucky	http://courts.ky.gov/forms/formslibrarybycategory.htm	Scroll down to the probate section.
Louisiana	No general probate forms are posted at this time.	Search your local court's website for probate forms.
Maine	http://www.maineprobate.net/forms.html	
Maryland	http://registers.maryland.gov/main/forms.html	
Massachusetts	http://www.mass.gov/courts/courtsandjudges/courts/probateandfamilycourt/forms.html#probate	
Michigan	http://courts.michigan.gov/scao/courtforms/probate/gpindex.htm	
Minnesota	http://www.mncourts.gov/selfhelp/?page=338	
Mississippi	No general probate forms are posted at this time.	Search your local county court's website.
Missouri	http://www.courts.mo.gov/page.jsp?id=662	
Montana	http://courts.mt.gov/library/topic/end_life.mcpx	

(continued)

Table 10.1

Nebraska	http://court.nol.org/forms/	Scroll down to "County Court Forms" and then "Probate."
Nevada	No general probate forms are posted at this time.	Search your local county court's website.
New Hampshire	http://www.courts.state.nh.us/probate/pcforms/forms.htm#estate	
New Jersey	http://www.njsurrogates.com/	Select your county and then "forms."
New Mexico	http://www.bernco.gov/upload/images/probate/nmsupreme_formslink.htm	
New York	http://www.nycourts.gov/forms/surrogates/probate.shtml	
North Carolina	http://www.nccourts.org/Forms/FormSearch.asp	Select "Estate" forms from the drop-down Category box.
North Dakota	http://www.ndcourts.gov/court/forms/probate/forms.htm	
Ohio	http://www.probatect.org/ohioprobatecourts/ohio_courts_standardforms.html	
Oklahoma	No general probate forms are available at this time.	Search for probate forms at your county court's website.
Oregon	No general probate forms are available at this time.	Search for probate forms at your county court's website.
Pennsylvania	No general probate forms are available at this time.	Search your local court's website for probate forms.
Rhode Island	http://sos.ri.gov/library/probate/	
South Carolina	http://www.sccourts.org/forms/searchType.cfm	Probate forms are mixed in with all court forms, which are posted in alphabetical order.
South Dakota	http://www.sdjudicial.com/cc/circuithome.aspx	Select your circuit and then search for probate forms.
Tennessee	No general probate forms are available at this time.	Search your local court's website for probate forms.

Table 10.1

Texas	No general probate forms are available at this time.	Search your local court's website for probate forms.
Utah	http://www.utcourts.gov/howto/wills/#Forms	Scroll down to "Commonly Used Probate Forms." Limited forms are available. Search your local court's website.
Vermont	http://vermontjudiciary.org/MasterPages/Court-Forms-Probate-All.aspx	
Virginia	http://www.courts.state.va.us/forms/circuit/fiduciary.html	
Washington	No general probate forms are posted at this time.	Search your local court's website for probate forms.
West Virginia	No general probate forms are posted at this time.	Search your local court's website for probate forms.
Wisconsin	http://www.wicourts.gov/forms1/circuit/ccform.jsp?FormName=&FormNumber=&beg_date=10/07/2010&end_date=10/07/2010&StatuteCite=&Category=26	
Wyoming	No general probate forms are posted at this time.	Search your local court's website for probate forms.

■ CONCLUSION

A probate proceeding is not always necessary when a person dies. The necessity of a probate depends on how the decedent's assets are titled at the time of death. When assets are titled solely in the name of the decedent, some type of proceeding will be required. If the assets are below a certain dollar amount, many states have provisions for small estate settlement that allow the assets to be transferred to the heirs or beneficiaries using an affidavit. Some states make a distinction between formal and informal probates. In those states that make this distinction, most probate estates proceed as informal probates and must go through a set court procedure, but are not contested by heirs. However, when someone contests the probate of a will or the appointment of a personal representative, the probate becomes a formal (contested) probate proceeding. Finally, when a decedent owns property in more than one state, an ancillary probate may be required to transfer the out-of-state property. Some states have special procedures for ancillary probates, whereas other states do not.

PARALEGAL PRACTICE TIP

- Clients may assume that whenever a loved one passes away, a probate will be needed. Even where there has not been estate planning, a probate is not always needed. For example, many spouses hold all assets jointly. When that is the case, a probate is not needed at the death of the first spouse because all of the joint assets pass to the surviving owner.

CONCEPT REVIEW AND REINFORCEMENT

KEY TERMS

Probate 282
Will 282
Ancillary Probate 282
Ancillary Administrator 282
Administrator 282
Administratrix 282
Testate 282
Intestate 282

Fiduciary 282
Executor 282
Executrix 282
Personal Representative 282
Living Trust 284
Probate Assets 285
Non-Probate Assets 285
Beneficiary 285

Informal Probates 287
Formal Probates 287
Small Estate Settlement 288
Domicile 293
Jurisdiction 294
Probate and Family Court 294

REVIEW QUESTIONS

1. Is a probate proceeding always necessary when someone dies? Why or why not? Explain your answer.
2. What is the purpose of a probate intake sheet?
3. Why do some law firms task a member of the legal team with checking the daily obituaries?
4. Whose decision is it whether or not to retain a law firm to administer an estate?
5. Describe what is meant by the term "small estate."
6. What is the purpose of an ancillary probate?
7. Discuss what is meant by the term "formal probate."
8. When might it be necessary to have more than one probate proceeding for a decedent?
9. Compare probate assets with non-probate assets.
10. What is meant by the term "domicile?"

BUILDING YOUR PARALEGAL SKILLS

CRITICAL THINKING EXERCISES

1. Jesse Johnson died in the State of North Carolina owning the following: a Buick worth $2,000, a bank account containing $556, a dirt bike (with a title) worth $1100, and miscellaneous personal effects and home furnishings. He died just over two months ago. Review the statute in Figure 10.3 and determine whether it applies to Mr. Johnson. Is there any additional information that you need to know?

2. Tyler Worthless died in the State of Nevada six months ago. He owned a trailer on a small piece of land in Nevada worth $20,000 but with a lien attached in the amount of $25,000. Mr. Worthless also owned a 2000 Dodge Neon (no lien) and a bank account with $3,334 in it. Review Figure 10.4 to determine whether the statute applies. Is there any additional information that you need to know?

PARALEGAL PRACTICE

Review the memorandum directed from the supervising attorney to you, the paralegal. The memorandum will discuss a situation with a client and request your assistance in researching the matter. You must then report back with your findings, as directed in the memorandum.

1. _____

MEMORANDUM
To: Paralegal
From: Supervising Attorney
Client: Shirley Smalls
Re: Affidavit of Succession to Real Property
_____

Shirley passed away about 7 months ago and owned a small home worth about $85,000 with a $20,000 mortgage remaining. Shirley left a valid will leaving her home to her daughter, Maggy Smalls. She owned no other real property and had very few personal effects, which were of small value. Please draft an Affidavit of Succession to Real Property. Fill in any missing information as you see fit.

ONLINE RESOURCES

The Pearson Course Companion website contains the following additional resources:
- **Forms for Paralegal Practice Activities**
- Chapter Objectives

- Online Study Guide (Containing Multiple Choice and True/False Questions)
- Web Exercises

www.pearsonhigher.com/careers

CASE FOR CONSIDERATION

CASE #1:

VINCENT OTTICE SIMMONS, APPELLANT V. DOROTHY CLEMONS SIMMONS, APPELLEE

98 Ark. App. 12; 249 S.W.3d 843; 2007 Ark. App. LEXIS 107
February 14, 2007, Decided

OPINION BY: SAM BIRD

OPINION

SAM BIRD, Judge

This appeal arises out of the trial court's division of property in a divorce case. Vincent Simmons appeals from the trial court's order awarding to his wife, Dorothy Simmons, a one-half interest in land that he inherited from his parents. Vincent contends that the land is non-marital property and, consequently, should have remained his separate property. We agree, and we reverse and remand.

Vincent and Dorothy Simmons were married on October 9, 1976. On April 11, 1995, Vincent's mother, Louise Simmons, executed The Louise B. Simmons Trust in order to convey certain land in Florida to her children, Vincent and his sister, upon her death. Louise

Simmons died on April 1, 1999, but the land remained in trust for several years after her death. After Louise died, Dorothy became concerned that she would not receive an interest in the Florida land if Vincent died before the trust was distributed, so she hired an attorney in Monticello, David Chambers, to prepare a document to protect her interest. After speaking with Dorothy, Mr. Chambers drafted an affidavit to be executed by Vincent, which stated in pertinent part as follows:

1. My name is Vincent Simmons, of Monticello, Drew County, Arkansas, and I am over the age of eighteen years.
2. I am a beneficiary, along with my sister, Ella Kay Simmons (Tabb), of the Louise B. Simmons Trust. Louise B. Simmons is my mother and she has been deceased for a few years. At least part of the corpus of said Trust is certain real property located in the State of Florida, more particularly described as

the northwest corner of Highway 39 and Trapnell Road, south of Plant City, Hillsborough County, Florida, consisting of approximately 28 acres.

3. I have been married to my wife, Dorothy Simmons, for 25 years. It is my intention, through this affidavit, to convey to my said wife marital interest in said real property. If I should die prior to the above-stated Trust being dissolved, then my said wife shall receive my share of said real property as her own property. Otherwise, if said Trust is dissolved prior to my death, then my wife shall be entitled to her legal marital interest in said real property.

On June 11, 2002, Dorothy and Vincent went to Mr. Chambers's office in order for Vincent to sign the affidavit, which he did. The trust property was distributed to Vincent and his sister on November 1, 2002. On February 11, 2003, Dorothy filed a complaint for divorce. The parties reached agreement regarding the division of all property except for the Florida land. The trial court held a hearing regarding the character of this land as marital or non-marital on October 31, 2005.

On December 7, 2005, the trial court sent a letter to the parties' attorneys, stating that the letter was submitted as the court's findings on the issue of ownership of the land in Florida. While the trial court recognized that a person in a divorce action is not entitled to any interest in property inherited by his or her spouse, the court noted that this law can be negated by the inheriting spouse—that is, the inheriting spouse can convey the property to the non-inheriting spouse. The trial court found that, by signing the affidavit, Vincent conveyed one-half of his interest in the Florida land to Dorothy. The trial court determined that "[t]his was done in consideration of twenty-five years of marriage, and is found to be binding." The court entered an order incorporating its findings on January 9, 2006.

On appeal, Vincent argues that the trial court erred in finding that his affidavit constituted a contract to convey an interest in the Florida land to Dorothy. He argues, first, that there is a total absence of consideration to support a contract in this case. Second, he claims that the affidavit lacks the mutuality of obligation necessary to support a contract. He also contends that, because one cannot determine from the affidavit what is meant by the terms "marital interest" and "legal marital interest," a person is left to speculate whether the terms refer to dower, homestead, personal allowances, or something else.

Dorothy responds, arguing that her ongoing marriage to Vincent constituted adequate consideration to support the contract. She also contends that Vincent's obligation to convey land and her obligation to be Vincent's wife constituted mutual obligations. Dorothy does not argue that the Florida land was marital property prior to Vincent's purported transfer to her by affidavit.

Although we review domestic-relations cases de novo on the record, we will not reverse a finding of fact by the trial court unless it is clearly erroneous. *Scott v. Scott*, 86 Ark. App. 120, 125, 161 S.W.3d 307, 310 (2004); *see also Stewart v. Combs*, _S.W.3d_, 368 Ark. 121, 243 S.W.3d 294, 2006 Ark. LEXIS 562 (Nov. 16, 2006) (court reviewed validity of postnuptial agreement under clearly erroneous standard). A finding is clearly erroneous when, although there is evidence to support it, the reviewing court is left with the definite and firm conviction that a mistake has been committed. *Id.*

The trial court treated Vincent's affidavit as a contract, or postnuptial agreement. A postnuptial agreement is an agreement entered into during marriage to define each spouse's property rights in the event of death or divorce. The term commonly refers to an agreement made at a time when separation or divorce is not imminent. *Black's Law Dictionary* 1206 (8th ed. 1999). The Arkansas Supreme Court recently addressed the validity of postnuptial agreements and held that they should be analyzed under the basic principles of contract law. *Stewart*, Ark. at, S.W.3d at, 2006 Ark. LEXIS 562 at *8. The court also noted that postnuptial agreements are subject to close scrutiny to ensure that they are fair and equitable, as "the confidential relationship between a husband and a wife keeps them from dealing at arm's length." *Id.* (citing *Bratton v. Bratton*, 136 S.W.3d 595 (Tenn. 2004); *Peirce v. Peirce*, 2000 UT 7, 994 P.2d 193 (Utah 2000); *In re Estate of Gab*, 364 N.W.2d 924 (S.D. 1985)).

We turn to the law governing contracts in Arkansas to determine the contractual validity of Vincent's affidavit. The essential elements of a contract are (1) competent parties, (2) subject matter, (3) legal consideration, (4) mutual agreement, and (5) mutual obligations. *Id.* As neither of the parties appears to contest that this "contract" included competent parties, subject matter, and mutual agreement, we will not address those elements here. The parties do disagree about whether Vincent's expressed intention to convey an interest in the Florida land to Dorothy was supported by legal consideration and whether the affidavit contained mutual obligations.

Dorothy argues—and the trial court agreed with her argument—that the agreement was made in consideration of Dorothy's twenty-five years of marriage to Vincent. Vincent claims that a marriage is past consideration and therefore does not constitute legal consideration. While the issue of whether the marriage itself is adequate consideration to support a postnuptial agreement has not been specifically addressed in Arkansas, it has long been the law in Arkansas that past consideration will not support a current promise and is not adequate legal consideration. *See, e.g., Wilson Bros. Lumber Co. v. Furqueron*, 204 Ark. 1064, 166 S.W.2d 1026 (1942); *Ford v. Ward*, 26 Ark. 360 (1870); *Rohrscheib v. Helena Hosp. Ass'n*, 12 Ark. App. 6, 670 S.W.2d 812 (1984). Other jurisdictions that have addressed this issue have held that an existing marriage is past consideration and will not support a postnuptial agreement. In *Bratton*, relied upon by the Arkansas Supreme Court in *Stewart*, the Tennessee Supreme Court stated that "the marriage itself cannot act as sufficient consideration because past consideration cannot support a current promise." *Bratton*, 136 S.W.3d at 600; *accord Whitmore v. Whitmore*, 8 A.D.3d 371, 778 N.Y.S.2d 73 (N.Y. App. Div. 2004); *Marty v. Marty*, 111 Kan. 120, 206 p. 324 (Kan. 1922); and *Clow v. Brown*, 37 Ind. App. 172, 72 N.E. 534 (Ind. App. 1904). Following the guidance of the Tennessee Supreme Court in *Bratton* and our own case law holding that past consideration will not support a current

promise, we hold that the parties' marriage is not adequate legal consideration to support this agreement.

Finally, the element of mutual obligations does not exist in this agreement. "[M]utuality of contract means that an obligation must rest on each party to do or permit to be done something in consideration of the act or promise of the other; thus, neither party is bound unless both are bound." *Tyson Foods, Inc. v. Archer*, 356 Ark. 136, 142, 147 S.W.3d 681, 684 (2004). In finding that the mutual release by each party of his or her interest in property owned by the other constituted mutual obligations to support a postnuptial agreement in *Stewart v. Combs*, the supreme court said that "mutual promises may constitute consideration as long as each promise places a *real liability* on the other party." *Stewart*, __ Ark. at __ , __ S.W.3d at __, 2006 Ark. LEXIS 562 at *13. (emphasis added). In the case before us, there is no obligation or real liability upon Dorothy to do anything in consideration of Vincent's promise to convey an interest in the Florida land to her.

Because we hold that the affidavit is not supported by adequate legal consideration or mutual obligations, we do not address Vincent's argument that the terms "marital interest" and "legal marital interest" are not sufficiently defined in the affidavit to form a binding contract. We reverse the trial court's order finding that the Florida land is marital property and awarding a one-half interest in the land to Dorothy. We remand to the trial court to enter an order consistent with this opinion.

Reversed and remanded.

GLADWIN and BAKER, JJ., agree.

Case Questions

1. Why did Dorothy hire an attorney?
2. What type of document did Vincent execute and what was the purpose of the document?
3. What was the trial court's holding?
4. What was this court's holding, and what was the reason for its holding?

FORMS TO ACCOMPANY PARALEGAL PRACTICE

Disclaimer: The forms provided to aid students in completing the Paralegal Practice activities assigned in each chapter have been modified as samples to familiarize students with what each form commonly looks like and are not intended to be used as actual forms for any state.

INSTRUCTIONS: The forms are provided in Microsoft Word format and employ the use of Stop Codes (such as SC1, SC2, SC3, and so on). Stop Codes are used in place of the form sections that must be updated with case-by-case information, such as SC1 for the client's name, SC3 for the client's address, and so on. What each Stop Code represents can be inferred by reading the surrounding text on the form. By using the FIND & REPLACE tool on the Microsoft toolbar, the students can replace the Stop Codes with the information provided in the Paralegal Practice activity to complete each assignment. Students must also fill in any blank lines on each form with the appropriate information from the activity and then proofread the document prior to turning in their work.

The listed forms are included following this section and will be posted online for students to access to complete the Paralegal Practice activities for this chapter:

- PP Form 10.1—Affidavit of Succession to Real Property

PP Form 10.1—Affidavit of Succession to Real Property

Pearson & Pearson, Attorneys-At-Law
1001 Reed Drive
Sample County, Sample State 12345
(928) 788-1234
(928) 788-1235 (Facsimile)
michael.pearson@pearsonlaw.com
Attorney for Affiant

IN THE SUPERIOR COURT OF THE STATE OF SAMPLE
IN AND FOR THE COUNTY OF SAMPLE

In the Matter of the Estate of:	)	Case No.: PB-2014-_____
SC1, Deceased.	)))))))	**AFFIDAVIT OF SUCCESSION TO REAL PROPERTY**

STATE OF SAMPLE	)
	) ss.
County of	)

SC2, being first duly sworn on oath deposes and says,

1. SC1 died on DOD in the County of Sample, State of Sample, more than six months prior to the filing of this Affidavit as evidenced by the certified copy of decedent's death certificate attached to the Affidavit. *See* Exhibit 1.

2. At the time of death, Decedent SC1 was domiciled in Sample and owned an interest in real property located in this county.

3. The value of all real property, including any debt secured by a lien on real property, in decedent's remaining estate located in Sample, less liens and encumbrances as of the date of death, does not exceed $75,000.00, as determined by the unpaid principal balance due as of the date of death of the decedent, in the case of a debt secured by a lien on real property.

4. The property is located at **SC4**

   The parcel number is _____

   The legal description of the property is _____

5. Decedent's interest in the property is fee simple.

6. No pending application or petition for the appointment of a personal representative is pending or has been granted in any jurisdiction.

7. Funeral expenses, expenses of last illness, and all unsecured debts of the decedent have been paid.

8. No federal or Sample estate tax is due on decedent's estate.

9. The Affiant is entitled to the real property by reason of a devise under a valid Last Will of the decedent, the original of which is attached to this affidavit. *See* Exhibit 2.

10. When recorded, please mail all future tax statements as follows:

SC2
Address2

   The affiant affirms that all statements in this Affidavit are true and material and further acknowledges that any false statements may subject the person or persons to penalties relating to perjury and subornation of perjury.

_____

Date

_____

Affiant's Signature

_____

Affiant's Printed Name

SUBSCRIBED, SWORN TO AND ACKNOWLEDGED before me on _____, 2014 by SC2.

_____

Notary Public

My Commission Expires: _____

Probate Part 1: Appointment of Personal Representative

CHAPTER 11

A REAL-LIFE SCENARIO

Eighty-five-year-old Roberta Nelson passed away peacefully in her sleep in a nursing home in Idaho. Sadly, during her two-year stay at Shady Pines, Roberta did not have any visitors. Further, she suffered from dementia and remembered very little about herself or her past. As a result, the nursing home staff knew very little about her and no one realized that she was, in fact, very wealthy.

After Roberta's death, the nursing home director called the only contact person listed on Roberta's entrance application—Betsy Smith. Betsy turned out to be Roberta's younger cousin. Betsy herself was eighty-two years old. She knew that Roberta had executed a will and that she had left the will in a safe deposit box. Roberta had made Betsy a joint owner of the safe deposit box and had given her a key.

Betsy was no longer able to get around very well herself. However, Betsy's daughter brought her to the bank and Betsy was able to retrieve the will. Under the will, Roberta appointed Betsy as personal

© Mesut Dogan/Shutterstock

CHAPTER OBJECTIVES:

1. List and discuss the information that must be gathered during the initial client conference.

2. Create a family tree.

3. List the documents that are commonly included in Probate Part 1.

4. Discuss the probate issues that arise when a decedent dies intestate.

5. Prepare Part 1 probate documents.

representative to administer her estate. Roberta also left her entire estate to Betsy, as her closest living relative. Betsy was shocked and honored to learn that her closest cousin had thought so highly of her. However, she was also immediately concerned. How could she, at age eighty-two, serve as personal representative of the estate?

■ INTRODUCTION

The loss of a loved one is a very difficult time for most people. However, the bills continue to come in, the mortgage still needs to be paid, and the funeral expenses must be tendered. After the initial shock and grief subsides, the loved ones who were left behind realize that the decedent's estate must be administered. It is at this point that most people consult with an attorney to determine what steps must be taken to get the probate started.

As the foregoing real-life scenario indicates, even when there is a will, the person who the decedent appointed to serve as personal representative may or may not be in a position to serve. The personal representative must be capable and able-bodied to perform the many functions required of a fiduciary. However, Betsy would not automatically be disqualified simply because of her age. If she was still of sound mind and able and willing to perform the duties required of a personal representative, she could be appointed by the court to serve. If she was not capable of performing the duties or was unwilling to serve, she could renounce her appointment and the person appointed as successor personal representative under the will would be next in line to serve. In this chapter, we will learn about the process of how a personal representative is appointed by the court, as well as some of the duties personal representatives have in connection with their appointment.

Key Terms and Definitions

A **fiduciary** is a person in a position of trust, such as an executor, administrator, guardian, or trustee. An **executor** is a male nominated in the will of a decedent to carry out the terms of the will and act as the personal representative of an estate. An **executrix** is a female nominated in the will of a decedent to carry out the terms of the will and act as the personal representative of an estate. A **personal representative** is the executor or administrator of a deceased person. Whether the estate representative is referred to as an "executor" or a "personal representative" is dictated by the laws and customs of the jurisdiction; however, for all intents and purposes, the terms may be used interchangeably. An appointed personal representative who is unwilling or unable to serve can **renounce**, or reject, the appointment, leaving the alternate appointee to serve.

An **administrator** is a male appointed by the court to administer the estate of an intestate decedent. An **administratrix** is a female appointed by the court to administer the estate of an intestate decedent. **Intestate** means having no valid will at death. Probate has multiple definitions. One definition of **probate** is to prove and have allowed by the court. **Probate** is also the process of proving a will is valid and thereafter administering the estate in accordance with the terms of the will. An alternate definition of **probate** is the general process of administration of estates of dead persons, including those without wills, with court supervision. Notice that a probate proceeding may be required whether or not a decedent had a will, depending on the circumstances.

Fiduciary
A person in a position of loyalty and trust, such as an executor, administrator, guardian, attorney-in-fact, or trustee; also a person to whom property or power is entrusted for the benefit of another.

Executor
A male nominated in the will of a decedent to carry out the terms of the will; a personal representative of an estate.

Executrix
A female nominated in the will of a decedent to carry out the terms of the will; a personal representative of an estate.

Personal Representative
The executor or administrator of a deceased person. Whether the estate representative is referred to as an "executor" or a "personal representative" is dictated by the laws and customs of the jurisdiction; however, for all intents and purposes, the terms may be used interchangeably.

Renounce
The rejection of a nomination under a will or other legal document.

Administrator
A male appointed by the court to administer the estate of an intestate decedent.

Administratrix
A female appointed by the court to administer the estate of an intestate decedent.

Intestate
Having no valid will at death.

Probate
A general term for the entire process of administration of estates of dead persons, including those without wills, with court supervision.

An **ancillary probate** is a probate proceeding in a state other than the main probate proceeding, which is conducted in the decedent's state of domicile. **Domicile** is a person's principal place of abode—the place to which, whenever one is absent, one has the present intent of returning. A probate may also be necessary in a jurisdiction where the decedent owns real property. Sometimes, more than one probate proceeding is required. When a second probate proceeding must be started in another jurisdiction, that probate is known an **ancillary probate** proceeding. An **ancillary administrator** is a person appointed by the court to handle the affairs of a decedent in a foreign state.

Jurisdiction is the power or authority that a court has to hear a case. The court in which the probate is initiated must have authority to hear probate cases. **Probate and Family Court** is a name given in some states to the court that exercises the function of settling decedents' estates. Other states simply call this court "Probate Court" or the "Surrogate's Court." Finally, some states have trial courts of general jurisdiction that have authority to settle decedents' estates within their jurisdiction.

■ THE INITIAL CLIENT CONFERENCE

Who is your client? If you are initiating the probate proceeding, your client is the individual seeking appointment as personal representative or executor of the estate. The individual will be known as the petitioner until appointed by the court as personal representative or executor.

To ensure quality representation and a smooth probate proceeding, it is essential to obtain as much information as you possibly can at the initial client meeting. It is also essential that you compile the information in a way that you can easily access it afterward. Clients can become very irritated when their attorney requests information that they have already provided to the firm. The following paragraphs discuss what information must be gathered at the initial client conference in greater detail. (At this point, we will assume that you have determined that a probate is necessary and that the size of the estate exceeds the amount that can be transferred by affidavit in the appropriate jurisdiction.)

Determine Heirs or Beneficiaries

Regardless of whether the decedent dies testate or intestate, it is essential to obtain complete family information in order to anticipate any issues that might arise in the case. For example, if the decedent died with a valid will leaving everything to Child A but the decedent actually had two additional children who were not mentioned in the will—Child B and Child C—there is a strong chance that the latter two children will contest the probate of the will. This information will not only factor into the advice the attorney will give to the clients, but also into the structure of the fee agreement and the anticipated cost of the probate proceeding. Further, it will impact the type of case that must be filed with the court.

Types of Probate Proceedings

✓ By way of review, in addition to small estate settlement, there are informal probates, formal probates, and ancillary probates. In states that distinguish between formal and informal probates, the majority of proceedings are informal probates. Informal probates are uncontested probates that generally require minimal court supervision. Formal probates are contested probates where one or more heirs oppose or contest the probate of the will, the

Ancillary Probate
An additional probate proceeding conducted in a state other than the main probate proceeding in the decedent's state of domicile.

Domicile
A person's principal place of abode; the place to which, whenever one is absent, one has the present intent of returning.

Ancillary Administrator
A person appointed by the court to handle the affairs of a decedent in a foreign state.

Jurisdiction
The power or authority that a court has to hear a case.

Probate and Family Court
A name given in some states to the court that exercises the function of settling decedents' estates. Other states simply call this court the "Probate Court" or the "Surrogate's Court." Finally, some states have trial courts of general jurisdiction that have authority to settle decedents' estates within their jurisdiction.

appointment of the personal representative, or both. A court hearing will be required and a judge will make the final determination about the validity of the proffered will and the priority of the petitioner for appointment as personal representative. **Ancillary probates** are secondary probates brought in another jurisdiction, most commonly to transfer a parcel of real property that is outside the state of the main probate proceeding. Depending on the law in the state of the ancillary probate, the proceeding may or may not be simpler than a regular probate proceeding.

Compile a Family Tree

It may be necessary to compile information about the decedent's heirs, as well as ancestors, depending on whether the decedent died testate or intestate and who has survived the decedent. After getting the information from your client, organize the information using a flow chart or family tree as a visual aid and include it in your client's file for easy reference.

EXAMPLE 1 _____

The decedent, Richard Smith, died leaving a wife, Nichole Smith, and three children, Alice Smith, Bert Smith, and Charles Smith. Richard left everything to his wife, or if she failed to survive, equally to his three children. Alice has one child, Derek Smith, born out of wedlock. The family tree could be drawn as follows:

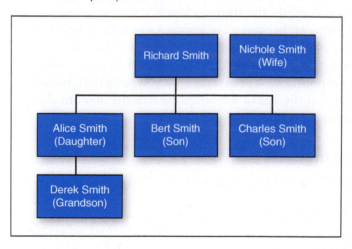

The foregoing example is very simple and straightforward. However, in a situation where a decedent died intestate and did not leave behind descendants, it becomes necessary to gather information about parents, siblings, grandparents, and sometimes, even aunts, uncles and cousins. The family tree then becomes very useful as it is compared with the state intestacy statute to determine who is entitled to inherit from the decedent.

Compile Financial Information

In addition to family tree information, it is essential to gather data about the decedent's real and personal property in the initial consultation. The attorney can help the client to determine whether these assets are probate or non-probate assets. Non-probate assets will be transferred by operation of law outside of the probate proceeding. Therefore, they are excluded from the probate forms (but may be included on any necessary tax forms). Most law firms design their own client intake sheet for clients to fill out all of the necessary financial information at the initial consultation. Sample client intake sheets can be found in Chapter 10.

Prepare a Fee Agreement

Before beginning representation, it is important for attorneys and clients to agree on the terms and parameters, which can vary widely based on state and local custom. Many probates are done on an hourly basis, meaning that the attorney charges by the hour for representation through the duration of the probate case. Hourly fee attorneys generally require an up-front retainer in an amount close to their estimated fee for the case, and then bill hourly against the retainer. When a proceeding is expected to be simple and straightforward, some attorneys may offer clients a flat fee agreement where the total fee is paid in advance and is not subject to change if there is additional work. Some states, such as California and Nevada, have a statutory percentage fee that dictates how much attorneys earn for representation in probate proceedings. Finally, it is customary in some jurisdictions, such as New York State, to have a hybrid arrangement that includes both a small percentage fee based on the total estate, plus an hourly fee for services. Whatever the terms, it is necessary to come to an agreement with the client at the onset of representation.

Original Documents

If the decedent had a will, it will be necessary to file the original will with the court when opening the probate proceeding. In addition, the court will require an original, certified death certificate. Both of these items should be entrusted with the attorney at the initial client conference (if the client is retaining the attorney) for use when preparing the initial probate documents.

■ PREPARE COURT DOCUMENTS

Part One of a probate proceeding involves admitting the will to probate, if there is a will. If there is no will, it involves a judicial determination that the decedent died intestate, which in turn means that the estate will pass according to state intestacy law. Part One also involves the petitioner seeking appointment as personal representative of the estate.

Testate

If the decedent had a will, the goal is normally to prove that the will is valid and have it admitted to probate. In addition, the person appointed under the will as personal representative is usually seeking appointment by the court. If no one is expected to contest the probate of the will, the proceeding is known as an **informal probate** in those states that make this distinction.

The initial forms in Step One are likely to include variations of all of the following forms:

- ✓ Application for Informal Probate of Will and Appointment as Personal Representative
- ✓ Acceptance of Appointment as Personal Representative

✓ Statement of Informal Probate of Will and Appointment as Personal Representative

✓ Letters of Personal Representative

✓ Notice of Informal Probate of Will and Appointment as Personal Representative

✓ Proof of Mailing Notice of Informal Appointment of Will and Appointment as Personal Representative

Letters Testamentary
A document issued by the court as evidence of its authorization for the personal representative's to act on behalf of a deceased's estate.

The acceptance of appointment and letters of appointment, also known as **Letters Testamentary** and **Letters of Personal Representative**, are often combined into one form, with the acceptance being executed by the personal representative in advance of appointment in contemplation that the letters will later be issued by the court.

In some jurisdictions, in an informal proceeding a hearing is not required to admit the proffered will to probate and appoint the personal representative. The letters of personal representative giving the personal representative authority to act may be issued fairly easily and then, should the matter become contested, the letters can be revoked pending a judicial determination at an evidentiary hearing. Other jurisdictions do require notice and a hearing before the personal representative can be appointed by the court, whether or not a will contest, or contested probate, is anticipated.

Intestate

If the decedent died intestate, a hearing will be required in most jurisdictions before the Personal Representative can be appointed. Notice of the hearing must be sent to all heirs, and may be required to be published in a newspaper of general circulation in the jurisdiction, as well. The process is otherwise similar to the steps described above, except that the application is instead replaced by a Petition for Adjudication of Intestacy and Appointment of Personal Representative. The ability of the petitioner to be appointed successfully will depend on priority for appointment under state statute, as well as on whether other individuals with equal or greater priority for appointment contest the petitioner's appointment or support it. Under common statutes regarding priority for appointment, spouses may come first, followed by children. Therefore, if one child is seeking appointment as personal representative and another child also wants the job, the court will have to decide who is most qualified or deserving, given the parties' equal status with respect to priority. Of course, if the children get along, they can seek appointment as co-personal representatives instead.

■ THE HYPOTHETICAL FAMILY

Your client Susan Smith-Thompson calls the office and tearfully informs the receptionist that her mother, Jane Smith, died in her home while in hospice care on January 2, 2014. She passed away peacefully, in her sleep, after a long battle with cancer. An appointment is set for a probate consultation the very next day.

The Client Meeting

Susan Smith-Thompson and John Smith attend the consultation together. You (the paralegal) and the supervising attorney both meet with them. Each appears to have an original will in hand.

Recall that in Figure 5.1 (also duplicated in Figure 9.1), Jane Smith executed a will dated February 25, 2012, leaving her estate in equal shares to John Smith, Susan Smith, and Mark Smith, or all to the survivors of them. She appointed John as executor and Susan as alternate executrix. It is this will that Susan Smith thrusts forward:

LAST WILL AND TESTAMENT

I, **JANE SMITH**, of the CITY OF SAMPLE, COUNTY OF SAMPLE COUNTY, STATE OF SAMPLE STATE, do hereby make, publish and declare the following to be my Last Will and Testament, hereby revoking all former Wills and Codicils made by me.

I. I direct that all my debts and funeral expenses be paid and I further authorize my Executor, in its discretion, to prepay any mortgage or other installment indebtedness.

II. I give and bequeath to my children, JOHN SMITH and SUSAN SMITH, and my nephew, MARK SMITH, JR., all of my clothing, jewelry, personal effects, household goods, furniture, furnishings, automobiles and all other tangible personal property which I may own at the time of my death, to be divided among them as they shall agree. If my beneficiaries are unable to agree as to the recipient of any article, that article, as well as any articles not selected, shall be sold and the proceeds added to my residuary estate.

III. All the rest, residue and remainder of my property, real, personal and mixed, of every name and nature, and wheresoever situate, I give, devise and bequeath in equal shares to JOHN SMITH, SUSAN SMITH, and MARK SMITH, JR., or all to the survivors of them.

IV. I give to my Executor hereinafter named, and to the successor, the following powers and discretions, in addition to those vested in or imposed upon them or either of them by law:

A. To mortgage, sell, convey, exchange or otherwise deal with or dispose of any real or personal property for cash or on credit (including the right to accept a purchase money mortgage as part of the purchase price); to retain as part of the estate any and all securities and property in the form originally received, whether or not it is then income producing and regardless of any rule requiring diversification of investments; to invest and reinvest in any stocks, bonds, shares in mutual funds or authorized common trust funds, or other securities or property, whether real or personal, which my Executor may deem safe and for the best interests of the estate, without being limited to investments authorized by law for the investment of trust funds; to hold title to any and all securities and other investments either in my Executor's name or in the name of a nominee; to borrow money from itself or others on terms my Executor may deem best, and to pledge any property of the estate as security for the repayment thereof; and to make distributions in cash or in kind, or partly in each to the beneficiaries entitled thereto.

B. If any beneficiary or legatee entitled to receive a part of my estate shall be under twenty-one (21) years of age, I authorize and empower my Executor to designate his or her parent, or some other appropriate adult person, or trust company, as custodian for the beneficiary or legatee under the Sample State Uniform Transfers to Minors Act until age twenty-one (21), and to distribute the share of the beneficiary or legatee to the designated custodian. A receipt from the custodian shall fully release my Executor.

V. I direct that all inheritance, succession and estate taxes of every kind payable with respect to any property includable in my gross taxable estate, whether or not passing under this my Will, shall be paid out of my residuary estate, and shall not be apportioned.

VI. I hereby nominate, constitute and appoint JOHN SMITH as Executor of this my Last Will and Testament, but if he fails to survive me, or renounces, or fails to qualify, or upon his death, resignation or disqualification, I nominate and appoint SUSAN SMITH as Executrix. I direct that no bond or other security shall be required of my Executor.

VII. The masculine gender, whenever used herein, shall include the feminine, the feminine shall include the masculine; the neuter shall include both the masculine and feminine; and the singular shall include the plural wherever necessary or appropriate.

IN WITNESS WHEREOF, I have hereunto subscribed my name and affixed my seal this <u>25th</u> day of <u>February</u>, 2012.

Jane Smith

_____

JANE SMITH

We, whose names are hereto subscribed, do certify that on the 25th day of February, 2012, the Testatrix, JANE SMITH, subscribed her name to this instrument, in our presence and in the presence of each of us, and at the same time in our presence and hearing, declared the same to be her Last Will and Testament, and requested us, and each of us, to sign our names thereto as witnesses to the execution thereof, which we hereby do in the presence of the Testatrix and of each other.

*Michael Pearson*_____ residing at *1001 Reed Drive, Sample City, Sample State 12345* _____

*Maggy Pearson*_____ residing at *1001 Reed Drive, Sample City, Sample State 12345* _____

AFFIDAVIT OF ATTESTING WITNESSES

STATE OF SAMPLE STATE)
COUNTY OF SAMPLE COUNTY) SS:

____*Michael Pearson*____ and ____*Maggy Pearson*____, being duly sworn say:

We are acquainted with JANE SMITH. The signature at the end of the instrument dated February 25, 2012, and declared by her to be her Last Will, was made by her at City of Sample, State of Sample State, in the presence of each of the undersigned.

At the time of signing this Will, JANE SMITH declared the instrument to which her signature had been affixed to be her Will and we, and each of us, signed our names thereto at the end thereof at that time and at her request and in her presence.

At the time of the execution of the instrument JANE SMITH was over the age of 18 years, of sound mind and memory, and not under any restraint and competent in every respect to make a Will.

At the time of execution, JANE SMITH could read, write and converse in the English language, and was not suffering from defects of sight, hearing, or speech or any other physical or mental impairment that could affect her capacity to make a valid Will.

The Will was not executed in counterparts.

*Michael Pearson*_____
Witness

*Maggy Pearson*_____
Witness

STATE OF SAMPLE STATE}
COUNTY OF SAMPLE COUNTY} ss:

On the 25th day of February in the year 2011 before me, the undersigned, a Notary Public in and for said State, personally appeared Michael Pearson and Maggy Pearson, the subscribing witnesses to the foregoing instrument, with whom I am personally acquainted, who being by me duly sworn, did depose and say that Michael Pearson resides at 1001 Reed Drive, Sample State and Maggy Pearson resides at 1001 Reed Drive, Sample State; that they know JANE SMITH to be the individual described in and who executed the foregoing instrument; that said subscribing witnesses were present and saw said JANE SMITH execute the same; and that said witnesses at the same time subscribed their names as witnesses thereto, and acknowledged to me that they executed the same in their capacities, and that by their signatures on the instrument, the individual(s) or the person upon behalf of which the individual(s) acted, executed the instrument.

*Lila P. Legal*_____
Notary Public

> **LILA P. LEGAL**
> Notary Public, State of Sample
> Sample County
> My Commission Expires May 10, 2012

However, earlier, in Figure 1.1, Jane Smith had executed a will dated December 27, 2011, leaving everything to her two children, John Smith and Susan Smith-Thompson. She appointed John as executor and Susan as alternate executrix. John Smith has this will in hand. He does not appear to be very happy about the newer will, since it leaves a share of the estate to Mark Smith.

Which will is valid? John and Susan want to know.

The later will contains a revocation clause, which is duplicated here.

> I, **JANE SMITH,** of the CITY OF SAMPLE, COUNTY OF SAMPLE COUNTY, STATE OF SAMPLE STATE, do hereby make, publish and declare the following to be my Last Will and Testament, **hereby revoking all former Wills and Codicils made by me.**

Therefore, the will dated February 25, 2012 is the Last Will and Testament of Jane Smith and the one that must be presented to probate.

During your interview with the grief-stricken children, you collect the following information:

- ✓ Date of Death: January 2, 2014.
- ✓ Date of Birth: December 22, 1951.
- ✓ Shirley Smith is still alive and still resides at 121 Oak Street, Sample City, Sample State 12345.
- ✓ John Smith still resides at 234 Sunny Lane, Sample City, Sample State 12345.
- ✓ Susan Smith-Thompson resides at 345 Maple Street, Sister City, Sample State 12346.
- ✓ Mark Smith, Jr. is now an adult but still resides at 123 Oak Street, Sample City, Sample State 12345.
- ✓ John Smith wants to serve as executor and will not renounce his position. This makes him the client.
- ✓ Shirley Smith had both real and personal property, as depicted in Table 11.1. All of the property was titled solely in her name.

Table 11.1 Property of Shirley Smith

REAL PROPERTY:	123 Oak Street, Sample City, Sample State 12345 (No Mortgage)	$200,000
PERSONAL PROPERTY:	2012 Ford Expedition (Subject to $5,000 Lien)	$15,000
	First Bank Checking Account	$5,110
	First Bank Savings Account	$18,050
	Sample Community Bank Brokerage Account	$33,225
	Personal Property and Household Goods	$4,000
TOTAL GROSS ESTATE:		$275,385

Based on the information provided, your supervising attorney informs the client that a probate proceeding is necessary to transfer the assets in Jane's estate to the three beneficiaries. John, as the appointed executor, decides to hire your firm and agrees to the attorney's proposed fee agreement. Figure 11.1 depicts the signed fee agreement, which is in accordance with the attorney's fees set by statute based on the size of the gross estate.

Figure 11.1

FEE AGREEMENT FOR SAMPLE PROBATE PROCEEDING-BASED ON VALUE OF ESTATE PURSUANT TO SRS 150.060(4)

Pearson & Pearson,
Attorneys-At-Law
1001 Reed Drive
Sample City, Sample State 12345
(928) 788-1234
(928) 788-1235 (Facsimile)
michael.pearson@pearsonlaw.com

CONFIDENTIAL AND PRIVILEGED INFORMATION

February 18, 2014

Mr. John Smith

234 Sunny Lane

Sample City, Sample State 12345

RE: Estate of Jane Smith

Dear Mr. Smith:

I am writing to confirm the terms under which Pearson & Pearson (the "Firm") proposes to represent you (the "Client") in connection with a Sample probate proceeding for your mother's estate. I appreciate your decision to retain the Firm in this matter. So that we all clearly understand the basis upon which we have agreed to represent you, I have prepared this letter.

1. <u>Staffing</u>. I will have primary responsibility for the matter. Particularly at the outset, I expect to perform the bulk of the work. I also may utilize other attorneys, paralegals and litigation/clerical assistants where appropriate. Staffing decisions will be made by me, with the objective of rendering services on an efficient and cost-effective basis.

   Our representation is effective as of the date we first begin providing services to you as a result of the requested representation. We will undertake your representation and work with you to achieve the desired objectives by using our best judgment and skill in representing you. You understand that we cannot and have not made any guarantee regarding the outcome of the matter.

2. <u>Attorney's Fee</u>. The fee shall be calculated as a percentage of the gross estate, pursuant to SRS 150.060(4), as follows:

   SRS 150.060 Attorneys for personal representatives and minor, absent, unborn, incapacitated or nonresident heirs: General compensation.

   4. If the attorney is requesting compensation based on the value of the estate accounted for by the personal representative, the allowable compensation of the attorney for ordinary services must be determined as follows:

   (a) For the first $100,000, at the rate of 4 percent;

   (b) For the next $100,000, at the rate of 3 percent;

   (c) For the next $800,000, at the rate of 2 percent;

   (d) For the next $9,000,000, at the rate of 1 percent;

   (e) For the next $15,000,000, at the rate of 0.5 percent; and

   (f) For all amounts above $25,000,000, a reasonable amount to be determined by the court.

3. <u>Costs</u>. A cost retainer is needed to cover out-of-pocket expenses that must be paid prior to and during the probate proceeding. Clients will be responsible for all out-of-pocket disbursements that we incur on their behalf. Typical costs include filing fees, publication fees, travel expenses, long-distance telephone calls, long distance outgoing faxes (at ten cents per page), Federal Express, courier services, and delivery charges, and large photocopying jobs (at ten cents per page). We anticipate making advances to cover out-of-pocket costs incurred but reserve the right to forward to Clients any larger items with the request that they pay them directly to the service providers.

   The total cost retainer requested at this time is $1,500.00. This is an estimate of the total costs, but the actual may be more or less.

Figure 11.1 (continued)

4. <u>Clients' Responsibilities.</u> Recognizing that the Firm cannot effectively represent Clients without their cooperation and assistance, Clients agree to cooperate fully with the Firm and to provide promptly all information known or available to Clients relevant to the Firm's representation, including providing information and documents requested in a timely fashion; assisting in discovery, disclosure and trial preparation; cooperating in scheduling and related matters; responding to telephone calls and correspondence in a timely manner; and informing the Firm of changes in Clients' address and telephone numbers.

5. <u>Advance Waiver of Conflicts.</u> As we have discussed, the Firm represents many other companies and individuals. It is possible, if not probable, that some of our present or future clients could have disputes or transactions with Clients. Therefore, as a condition to our undertaking this matter, Clients must agree that the Firm may continue to represent or may undertake in the future to represent existing or new clients in any matter that is not substantially related to our work for Clients, even if the interests of such entities in those other matters are directly adverse to Clients. We agree, however, that Clients' prospective consent to conflicting representation contained in this paragraph shall not apply in any instances where, as a result of our representation of Clients, we have obtained privileged, proprietary or other confidential information of a nonpublic nature that, if known to such other entity, could be used in any such other matter by such entity to Clients' material disadvantage.

6. <u>Document Retention.</u> During the course of our representation of Clients, they may have occasion to provide us with documents and other materials from their files. At the end of our engagement, we will return the documents and materials to Clients in care of your office, or retain them as Clients direct. If we receive no such direction from Clients, and the documents and materials are not returned to Clients, we would like Clients' agreement that the documents may be destroyed at such time as the file itself is destroyed in accordance with our document retention policy. Currently, it is our policy to destroy files after they have been closed for five (5) years. *Client files that do not contain original client documents (such as original deeds, titles, or Last Wills and Testaments) may be stored solely in electronic format.* We will deem Clients' acknowledgement of our engagement as an assent to the handling of Clients' documents in this respect.

7. <u>Termination of Engagement and Post-Engagement Matters.</u> Either of us may terminate the engagement at any time for any reason by written notice, subject on our part to applicable rules of professional conduct. In the event that we terminate the engagement, we will take such steps as are reasonably practicable to protect Clients' interests in this matter and, if you so request, we will suggest to you possible successor counsel and provide successor counsel of your choosing with whatever papers you have provided to us. Unless previously terminated, our representation of Clients will terminate upon our sending our final statement for services rendered. Clients are engaging the Firm to provide legal services in connection with a specific matter. After completion of the matter, changes may occur in laws or regulations that are applicable to Clients that could have an impact upon their future rights and liabilities. Unless Clients continue to engage us to provide additional advice, this Firm will assume that it has no continuing obligation to advise Clients with respect to future legal developments.

9. <u>Arbitration.</u> If a dispute arises between the Firm and Clients regarding attorneys' fees or the services provided in the engagement, the parties agree to resolve that dispute through mediation followed by arbitration through an arbitration service to be agreed upon by the parties.

10. <u>No Advice Regarding This Fee Agreement.</u> The Firm is not acting as Clients' counsel in advising them with respect to this letter, as we would have a conflict of interest in doing so. If Clients, or any of them, wish to be advised by independent counsel on the question of whether they should be so represented, we recommend that they consult with independent counsel of their choice. In addition, if they have any questions or would like additional information, we would be happy to discuss this matter with any of them.

If the foregoing correctly states our understanding regarding the Firm's representation of Clients, please sign the original in the space provided and return it to me with the retainer at your earliest convenience. There is also a second copy for your records.

Very truly yours,

Michael Pearson, Esq.

**THE TERMS OF THE ENGAGEMENT OF THE FIRM AS STATED
ABOVE ARE ACCEPTED AND APPROVED BY**

John Smith

Date: 2/18/2014

You then prepare the following documents to initiate the probate proceeding and get John appointed as executor of Jane's estate. The attorney approves them, the client signs them, and they are filed with the court.

Figure 11.2 depicts the initial application for informal probate of will and appointment of personal representative for the Estate of Jane Smith. John Smith has filed the application, by and through his counsel, Pearson & Pearson, petitioning the court to be appointed as personal representative of Jane's estate and to admit the will to probate.

Figure 11.2

Pearson & Pearson, Attorneys-At-Law
1001 Reed Drive
Sample City, Sample State 12345
(928) 788-1234
(928) 788-1235 (Facsimile)
michael.pearson@pearsonlaw.com
Attorney for Petitioner

IN THE SUPERIOR COURT OF THE STATE OF SAMPLE OF SAMPLE
IN AND FOR THE COUNTY OF SAMPLE

In the Matter of the Estate of JANE SMITH Deceased,	Case No. PB-2014-0007 APPLICATION FOR INFORMAL PROBATE OF WILL AND APPOINTMENT OF PERSONAL REPRESENTATIVE

1. This Application is made by JOHN SMITH, who is entitled to file this Application under S.R.S. §14-3301 because he is the son of the Decedent and was appointed as executor under the will.

2. Decedent died on January 2, 2014, at the age of 62 years. At the time of death, decedent was domiciled in Sample County, State of Sample.

3. The original of decedent's Will, dated February 25, 2012 is being filed with this Application.

4. Decedent left surviving the following persons who are the surviving spouse, children, heirs and devisees of decedent:

Name and Address	Age (if minor)	Heir or Devisee	Relationship (To Decedent)
John Smith 234 Sunny Lane Sample City, Sample State 12345	Heir/Devisee		Son
Susan Smith-Thompson 345 Maple Street Sister City, Sample State 12346	Heir/Devisee		Daughter
Mark Smith, Jr. 123 Oak Street Sample City, Sample State 12345	Devisee		Nephew

5. Venue for this proceeding is in this county because decedent was a domiciliary of this state and owned property located in this county at the time of death.

6. No personal representative for decedent's estate has been appointed in this state or elsewhere.

7. Applicant has not received a demand for notice and is not aware of any demand for notice by any interested person of any proceedings concerning decedent in this state or elsewhere.

8. Applicant believes that the Will, dated February 25, 2012, was validly executed and is decedent's last Will and, after the exercise of reasonable diligence, Applicant is unaware of any instrument revoking the Will.

9. The time for informal probate and appointment has not expired under S.R.S. §14-3108 because less than two years have passed since decedent's death.

Figure 11.2 (continued)

10. Applicant states that John Smith of 234 Sunny Lane, Sample City, Sample State 12345, has priority for appointment as Personal Representative under the Will pursuant to the provisions of S.R.S. §14-3203 because he was appointed as executor under the will.

11. Bond is not required of the Personal Representative under S.R.S. §14-3603 because it has been waived in the Will.

12. Applicant's best estimate of the value of property owned by decedent and subject to the probate jurisdiction of the Court is as follows:

Personal property	$75,385.00
Real property (less encumbrances thereon)	$200,000.00
Expected annual income of Estate	$0.00
TOTAL	**$275,385.00**

13. Applicant requests that decedent's last Will be admitted to informal probate and that John Smith be appointed as the Personal Representative to administer decedent's Estate without bond.

Dated this <u>20th</u> day of <u>February</u>, 2014.

John Smith
_____
JOHN SMITH
234 Sunny Lane
Sample City, Sample State 12345

STATE OF SAMPLE)
County of SAMPLE)   )ss.

JOHN SMITH, being duly sworn, states as follows:

That he is the son of the Decedent and the Applicant in the foregoing Application, and that the statements in the Application are accurate and complete to the best of his knowledge and belief.

John Smith
_____
JOHN SMITH

    SUBSCRIBED AND SWORN TO before me, the undersigned Notary Public, this <u>20th</u> day of <u>February</u>, 2014, by JOHN SMITH.

Lila P. Legal
_____
Notary Public

LILA P. LEGAL Notary Public, State of Sample Sample County My Commission Expires May 10, 2016

Figure 11.3 contains the statement of informal probate of will and appointment of personal representative for the Estate of Jane Smith. The form is filed with the court along with the initial application for completion by the probate registrar.

Figure 11.4 contains the letters of appointment of personal representative and acceptance of appointment for the Estate of Jane Smith. Notice that the acceptance was completed by John Smith at the time he completed the application and was then filed with the court in contemplation of the court approving the application and issuing the letters. The completed letters are evidence of the personal representative's authority to act on behalf of the estate.

Figure 11.3

Pearson & Pearson, Attorneys-At-Law
1001 Reed Drive
Sample City, Sample State 12345
(928) 788-1234
(928) 788-1235 (Facsimile)
michael.pearson@pearsonlaw.com
Attorney for Petitioner

IN THE SUPERIOR COURT OF THE STATE OF SAMPLE
IN AND FOR THE COUNTY OF SAMPLE

In the Matter of the Estate of **JANE SMITH** Deceased.	**Case No. PB-2014-0007** STATEMENT OF INFORMAL PROBATE OF WILL AND APPOINTMENT OF PERSONAL REPRESENTATIVE

An Application for Informal Probate of Will and Appointment of Personal Representative has been submitted by JOHN SMITH, requesting admission to probate of the Will of decedent dated February 25, 2012, and the appointment of JOHN SMITH as the Personal Representative to administer decedent's Estate.

The undersigned has found compliance with S.R.S. §§ 14-3303 and 14-3308 and is satisfied that said Will is entitled to probate and that JOHN SMITH is entitled to appointment as Personal Representative under all applicable provisions of S.R.S. Title 14, Chapter 3, Article 3.

THEREFORE, the Will of JANE SMITH, dated February 25, 2012 is admitted to informal probate.

FURTHER, JOHN SMITH is appointed as personal representative of decedent's Estate without bond and letters shall be issued upon said personal representative accepting this appointment.

FURTHER, the Personal Representative shall immediately notify the Court in these proceedings of any change in address and shall be responsible for all costs resulting from failure to do so.

DATED this <u>28th</u> day of <u>February</u>, 2014.

Christina Courte
—————————————————
Probate Registrar

Figure 11.4

Pearson & Pearson, Attorneys-At-Law
1001 Reed Drive
Sample City, Sample State 12345
(928) 788-1234
(928) 788-1235 (Facsimile)
michael.pearson@pearsonlaw.com
Attorney for Petitioner

IN THE SUPERIOR COURT OF THE STATE OF SAMPLE
IN AND FOR THE COUNTY OF SAMPLE

In the Matter of the Estate of **JANE SMITH** Deceased.	**Case No. PB-2014-0007** LETTERS OF APPOINTMENT OF PERSONAL REPRESENTATIVE AND ACCEPTANCE OF APPOINTMENT AS PERSONAL REPRESENTATIVE

LETTERS OF PERSONAL REPRESENTATIVE

JOHN SMITH is hereby appointed as Personal Representative of this Estate without restriction.

WITNESS: <u>February 28, 2014</u>

Figure 11.4 (continued)

Clerk of the Superior Court

By ___Simon Clerky___

Deputy Clerk

ACCEPTANCE OF APPOINTMENT

STATE OF SAMPLE)

COUNTY OF SAMPLE)) ss.

I hereby accept the duties of personal representative of the Estate of the above-named decedent and do solemnly swear that I will perform, according to law, the duties of such fiduciary.

DATED this <u>20th</u> day of <u>February</u>, 2014.

John Smith
JOHN SMITH

SUBSCRIBED AND SWORN TO before me, the undersigned Notary Public, this <u>20th</u> day of <u>February</u>, 2014, by JOHN SMITH.

Lila P. Legal
Notary Public

> **LILA P. LEGAL**
> Notary Public, State of Sample
> Sample County
> My Commission Expires May 10, 2016

Figure 11.5 contains the order to personal representative and acknowledgment and information to heirs for the Estate of Jane Smith. Once again, John Smith was required to sign the order in advance of it being approved by the court. After the judge signed the order, a copy of it had to be sent to each of the heirs and/or beneficiaries of the estate.

Figure 11.5

Pearson & Pearson, Attorneys-At-Law
1001 Reed Drive
Sample City, Sample State 12345
(928) 788-1234
(928) 788-1235 (Facsimile)
michael.pearson@pearsonlaw.com
Attorney for Petitioner

IN THE SUPERIOR COURT OF THE STATE OF SAMPLE
IN AND FOR THE COUNTY OF SAMPLE

In The Matter of the Estate of **JANE SMITH**, Deceased.	))))))))	**Case No.: PB-2012-0007** ORDER TO PERSONAL REPRESENTATIVE AND ACKNOWLEDGMENT AND INFORMATION TO HEIRS

(continued)

Figure 11.5 (continued)

> WARNING: This is only an outline of some of your duties as Personal Representative. This Order does not describe all of your duties and is not a substitute or obtaining professional legal advice. This is general outline of your duties only. If you have any questions as Personal Representative, before taking any action you should contact an attorney who handles probate estates to find out what to do.

The best interest of this estate is of great concern to this Court. As Personal Representative, you are subject to the power of the Court. Therefore, to help avoid problems and to assist you in your duties, this order is entered. You are required by the Order and to obey it.

Unless an interested party files a written request to the Court, this Court will not review or supervise your actions as Personal Representative. In Sample, if you are a beneficiary of an estate, you are expected to protect your own interests in the estate. The Personal Representative is required to provide sufficient information to the beneficiary to permit the beneficiary to protect his or her interests. The Court may hold a Personal Representative personally liable and responsible for any damage or loss to the estate resulting from a violation of the Personal Representative's duties. The following is an outline of some of your duties as Personal Representative:

DUTIES OF THE PERSONAL REPRESENTATIVE: The duties of the Personal Representative are found in Chapter 3, Title 14 of the Sample Revised Statutes. You are responsible for knowing and doing your duties according to these statutes. Some of the duties are the following:

1. **GATHER, CONTROL AND MANAGE ESTATE ASSETS.** As Personal Representative you have the duty to gather and control all assets that belonged to the decedent (the person who had died) at the time of his or her death. After the valid debts and expenses are paid, you have the duty to distribute any remaining assets according to the decedent's Will or, if there is no Will, to the intestate heirs of the decedent. As Personal Representative, you have the authority to manage the estate assets, but you must manage the estate assets for the benefit of those interested in the estate.

2. **FIDUCIARY DUTIES.** As Personal Representative you are a fiduciary. This means you have legal duty of undivided loyalty to the beneficiaries and the creditors of the estate. You must be cautious and prudent in dealing with estate assets. As Personal Representative, the estate assets do not belong to you and must never be used for your benefit or mixed with your assets or anyone else's assets. Sample law prohibits a Personal Representative from participating in transactions that are a conflict of interest between you, as Personal Representative from participating in transactions that are a conflict of interest between you, as Personal Representative, and you as an individual. Other than receiving reasonable compensation for your services as Personal Representative, you may not profit from dealing with estate assets.

3. **PROVIDE NOTICE OF APPOINTMENT.** Within 30 (thirty) days after your Appointment as Personal Representative, you must mail notice of your appointment to the heirs and devisees whose addresses are reasonably available to you. If your appointment is made in a formal proceeding, you need not give notice to those persons previously noticed of a formal appointment proceeding. See S.R.S. §14-3705.

4. **PROVIDE NOTICE OF ADMISSION OF WILL TO PROBATE.** Within 30 days of the admission of the Will to informal probate, you must give written notice to all heirs and devisees of the admission of the Will to probate, together with a copy of the Will. You must notify the heirs that they have 4 (four) months to contest the probate. See S.R.S. §14-3306.

5. **MAIL COPIES OF THIS ORDER TO PERSONAL REPRESENTATIVE.** WITHIN 30 DAYS OF YOUR APPOINTMENT, YOU MUST MAIL A COPY OF THIS ORDER TO PERSONAL REPRESENTATIVE AND ACKNOWLEDGE AND INFORMATION TO HEIRS, TO ALL THE HEIRS AND DEVISEES OF THE ESTATE, AND TO ANY OTHER PERSONS WHO HAVE FILED A DEMAND FOR NOTICE. See S.R.S. §14-3705.

6. **FILE PROOF OF COMPLIANCE.** Within forty-five days of your appointment as Personal Representative, you must file with the Court a notarized statement swearing that a copy of this Order was mailed to each devisee, to each heir in intestate (no will) estates and to any other persons who have filed a demand for notice.

7. **PUBLISH NOTICE.** After your appointment as Personal Representative, you must publish a notice once a week for three consecutive weeks in a Sample County newspaper of general circulation that announces your appointment as Personal Representative and tells creditors of the estate that unless they present their claims against the estate within the prescribed time limit, the claims will not be paid. In addition, you must mail a similar notice to all persons you know are creditors and to all persons you can reasonably find out are creditors of the estate. See S.R.S. §14-3801.

8. **PROTECT ASSETS.** You must immediately find, identify, and take possession of the estate assets and make proper arrangements to protect them. See S.R.S. §14-3709. All property must be re titled to show ownership in the

Figure 11.5 (continued)

name of the estate- such as "Estate of (decedent's name), your name, as Personal Representative." Do not put the estate assets into your name, anyone else's name, joint accounts, trust accounts ("in trust for"), or payable on death ("POD") accounts. Do not list yourself or any other person as joint owner or beneficiary on any bank accounts or other assets belonging to the estate. Do not mix any estate assets with your own assets or anyone else's assets.

If the Court has limited your authority as Personal Representative, you must promptly protect the estate assets as ordered, and file a Proof of Restricted Assets with the Court. You may not sell, encumber, distribute, withdraw, or otherwise transfer restricted assets without first obtaining permission from the Court.

9. **DETERMINE STATUTORY ALLOWANCES.** It is your responsibility to determine whether any individuals are entitled to statutory allowances under S.R.S. §14-2402, 2403, and 2404. Statutory allowances include a homestead allowance, exempt property allowance, and a family allowance.

10. **INVENTORY ASSETS.** Within 90 days after your appointment as Personal Representative, you must prepare an inventory or list of the decedent's probate assets and their values as of the date of death. See S.R.S. §14-306. The inventory must be either (1) filed with the Court and mailed to all interested persons who request it; or (2) not filed with the Court, but mailed to all heirs, devisees, and other interested persons who have requested it.

11. **STANDARD OF CARE.** In administering estate assets, you must observe the standards of care applicable to a trustee, including the prudent investor act. See S.R.S. §§ 14-7301 et seq., and 14-7601 et seq.

12. **KEEP DETAILED RECORDS.** You must keep detailed records of all receipts and expenses of the estate. You are required to provide an accounting of your administration of the estate to all persons affected by the administration. See S.R.S. §14-3933.

13. **PAY VALID DEBTS AND EXPENSES.** You must determine which claims and expenses of the estate are valid and should be paid. You must provide to any creditor whose claims are not allowed prompt written notification that they will not be paid or will not be paid in full. See S.R.S. §14-3806. To the extent there are enough assets in the estate, you are responsible for the payment of any estate debts and/ or expenses you know about or can find out about. If there are not enough estate assets to pay all debts and expenses, you must determine which debt and expenses should be paid according to the law. See S.R.S. §14-3805. You may be personally liable if you pay a debt or expense that should not be paid.

14. **PAY TAXES.** It is your responsibility to determine that all taxes are paid and that all tax returns for the decedent and the estate are prepared and filed.

15. **DISTRIBUTE REMAINING ASSETS.** After payment of all debts and expenses of the estate, you must distribute estate assets as directed in the Will or, if there is not a Will, to the intestate heirs. If there are not enough assets in the estate to make the gifts as set forth in the Will, it is your responsibility to determine how the distribution should be made as required by law. See S.R.S. §§14-3902 and 14-3907. You may be personally liable if you make an improper distribution of estate assets.

16. **CHANGE OF ADDRESS.** Until the probate is closed and you are discharged as Personal Representative, you must notify the Court in writing if you change your home or mailing address.

17. **PAYMENT AS PERSONAL REPRESENTATIVE.** As Personal Representative, you are entitled to reasonable compensation. See Sample County. Sample statutes do not designate percentage fees for your work or say how much a Personal Representative should be paid. You must keep receipts to prove out-of-pocket expenses. In determining whether a fee is reasonable, the following factors will be considered:

  a. The time required (as supported by detailed time records), the novelty and difficulty of the issues involved, and the skill required to do the service properly;

  b. The likelihood that your acceptance as Personal Representative will preclude other employment;

  c. The fee normally charged in the area for similar services;

  d. The nature and value of estate assets, the income earned by the estate, and the responsibilities and potential liability assumed by you as Personal Representative;

  e. The results obtained for the estate;

  f. The time limitations imposed by the circumstances;

  g. The experience, reputation, diligence and ability of the person performing the services;

  h. The reasonableness of the time spent and service performed under the circumstances; and,

  i. Any other relevant factors.

18. **COURT INVOLVEMENT.** Usually, to reduce estate expenses, estates are administered and estate claims and expenses are paid, including the fees to the attorney and Personal Representative, with little Court involvement.

Figure 11.5 (continued)

The Court does not supervise informal probates or the conduct of a Personal Representative. However, if any interested party believes that the estate has not been properly handled of that the fees charged by the attorney or Personal Representative are not reasonable under the circumstances, that party may request that the court review the accounting for the Personal Representative's administration of the estate. Any additional Court involvement may result in additional delay and expenses. If appropriate, the Court may assess the additional expense against the estate or the non-prevailing party.

19. **CLOSE THE ESTATE.** After distribution of the estate has been completed, the estate must be closed, either formally or informally. In an informal closing, a copy of the Closing Statement is filed with the Court and must be sent to all persons receiving a distribution from the estate. See S.R.S. §14-3933. For a formal closing, see S.R.S. §§14-3931 and 14-3932. Usually, the Court expects the estate to be completely administered and closed within six (6) months to one (1) year of the initial appointment of the Personal Representative.

Failure to obey a Court Order and the statutory provisions relating to this estate may result in your removal as Personal Representative and other penalties. In some circumstances, you may be held in contempt of court, punished by confinement in jail, fine or both. In addition, if you violate any of your fiduciary duties, you could be held personally liable for any losses for which you are responsible.

Dated: <u>February 28, 2014</u>

Honorable Ralph Peterson
Judge

ACKNOWLEDGMENT

The undersigned acknowledges receiving a copy of this order and agrees to be bound by its provisions, whether or not he or she read it before signing, as long as he or she is Personal Representative.

John Smith

JOHN SMITH

<u>February 20, 2014</u>

Date

After the application was approved by the court, John Smith was required to notify all of the heirs and beneficiaries of the estate. Figure 11.6 depicts the notice of informal probate of will and appointment of personal representative.

Figure 11.6

Pearson & Pearson, Attorneys-At-Law
1001 Reed Drive
Sample City, Sample State 12345
(928) 788-1234
(928) 788-1235 (Facsimile)
michael.pearson@pearsonlaw.com
Attorney for Petitioner

IN THE SUPERIOR COURT OF THE STATE OF SAMPLE
IN AND FOR THE COUNTY OF SAMPLE

In the Matter of the Estate of **JANE SMITH** Deceased.	**Case No. PB-2014-0007** NOTICE OF INFORMAL PROBATE OF WILL AND APPOINTMENT OF PERSONAL REPRESENTATIVE

Figure 11.6 (continued)

YOU ARE HEREBY NOTIFIED THAT:

1. This Notice is being sent to those persons who have, or may have, some interest in the Estate of decedent.

2. Decedent died on January 2, 2014.

3. JOHN SMITH filed an Application for Informal Probate of Will and Appointment of Personal Representative in the above-named court, requesting that the Will of decedent executed on February 25, 2012, be admitted to informal probate and that JOHN SMITH be appointed Personal Representative of the Estate of decedent.

4. On February 28 , 2014, the Registrar admitted the Will to informal probate and appointed JOHN SMITH as Personal Representative of the Estate.

5. Bond is not required.

6. An heir of decedent wishing to contest the probate has four months from the receipt of this Notice to commence a formal testacy proceeding.

7. Papers relating to the Estate are on file with the Court and are available for your inspection.

DATED this 5th day of March, 2014.

John Smith
_____
JOHN SMITH
234 Sunny Lane
Sample City, Sample State 12345

After sending out the Notice of Informal Probate of Will and Appointment of Personal Representative, Pearson & Pearson filed the required Proof of Mailing with the court. The Proof of Mailing Notice of Informal Probate of Will and Appointment of Personal Representative is depicted in Figure 11.7.

Figure 11.7

Pearson & Pearson, Attorneys-At-Law
1001 Reed Drive
Sample City, Sample State 12345
(928) 788-1234
(928) 788-1235 (Facsimile)
michael.pearson@pearsonlaw.com
Attorney for Petitioner

IN THE SUPERIOR COURT OF THE STATE OF SAMPLE

IN AND FOR THE COUNTY OF SAMPLE

In the Matter of the Estate of **JANE SMITH** Deceased.	**Case No. PB-2014-0007** PROOF OF MAILING NOTICE OF INFORMAL PROBATE OF WILL AND APPOINTMENT OF PERSONAL REPRESENTATIVE

STATE OF SAMPLE   )
County of Sample)   ) ss.

(continued)

Figure 11.7 (continued)

The undersigned, SAMMY STUDENT, states that a copy of the Notice of Informal Probate of Will and Appointment of Personal Representative and a copy of the Will were both mailed on <u>March 6, 2014</u>, to the following persons:

Shirley Smith
121 Oak Street
Sample City, Sample State 12345

Susan Smith-Thompson
345 Maple Street
Sister City, Sample State 12346

Mark Smith, Jr.
123 Oak Street
Sample City, Sample State 12345

DATED this <u>6th</u> day of <u>March</u> , 2014.

Sammy Student
Sammy Student

    SUBSCRIBED AND SWORN TO before me, the undersigned Notary Public, this <u>6th</u> day of <u>March</u>, 2014, by SAMMY STUDENT.

Lila P. Legal
Notary Public

> **LILA P. LEGAL**
> Notary Public, State of Sample
> Sample County
> My Commission Expires May 10, 2016

PARALEGAL PRACTICE TIP

- Prior to being appointed by the court, the person appointed as personal representative or seeking appointment is known as the Petitioner. This person does not become the Personal Representative of the estate until the Letters Testamentary have been issued.

- Be sure to have your client sign as many of the required legal forms as possible in each client conference. This saves time and billable hours for the client and will help to foster trust and a good attorney–client relationship.

Once again, the order to personal representative depicted in Figure 11.5 outlines the duties a personal representative has in connection with estate administration. Among other things, some of the main duties are to collect the decedent's assets and distribute them in accordance with the directions in the will and to file the decedent's final tax returns, as well as any estate and fiduciary tax returns which may be required under federal and state law. A personal representative can be responsible for the administration of the estate while getting help from others to complete the work. Accordingly, the elderly woman in the Real-Life Scenario at the beginning of the chapter could potentially serve as the Personal Representative even with her physical limitations.

Personal Representative's Fees

As you may have surmised, being a personal representative is time consuming and often requires a great deal of work. Accordingly, personal representatives are entitled to be compensated for their time and service. Occasionally, a testator will specify in the will that the personal representative is required to serve without compensation. In that case, the personal representative must be willing to serve for free. Other times, a will may specify the amount of compensation the personal representative is to receive. Most often, wills are silent with respect to the issue of compensation. In that event, state statute controls and the representative will be entitled to receive whatever compensation is directed by law.

■ CONCLUSION

Representation of a probate client begins during the initial client interview. It is essential to gather complete and detailed information regarding the decedent's family, finances, and assets. Further, it is necessary to enter into a fee agreement memorializing the agreed-upon terms for payment. The firm initiating the probate proceeding typically represents the personal representative—not the beneficiaries or heirs of the estate. This chapter discusses the first step, or Part One, of a probate proceeding, which focuses on getting the will admitted to probate and the personal representative appointed in a testate proceeding. In an intestate proceeding, the goal is to have the court adjudicate the decedent as intestate and to appoint the petitioner as personal representative. The next chapter discusses what needs to be done immediately after the personal representative is appointed.

CONCEPT REVIEW AND REINFORCEMENT

KEY TERMS

Fiduciary 306	Administrator 306	Domicile 307
Executor 306	Administratrix 306	Ancillary Administrator 307
Executrix 306	Intestate 306	Jurisdiction 307
Personal Representative 306	Probate 306	Probate and Family Court 307
Renounce 306	Ancillary Probate 307	Letters Testamentary 310

REVIEW QUESTIONS

1. List some of the common names for a court having jurisdiction to settle a decedent's estate.
2. What is the title of a person seeking appointment as personal representative by the court?
3. If an appointee under a will is unable or unavailable to serve, what can the appointee do?
4. List some of the duties of a personal representative.
5. Is there an age limit for a person to serve as personal representative?
6. What is an ancillary probate proceeding?
7. If the decedent died intestate, will a hearing be required before a personal representative can be appointed?
8. Are personal representatives entitled to compensation for their services? Explain your answer.
9. Who enters the fee agreement with the law firm handling a given probate?
10. What are some of the common types of fee agreements for probate proceedings?

BUILDING YOUR PARALEGAL SKILLS

CRITICAL THINKING EXERCISES

1. WEB WORK: Visit the following website and review the Florida statute regarding appropriate compensation for attorneys representing personal representatives:
   http://www.leg.state.fl.us/Statutes/index.cfm?App_mode=Display_Statute&Search_String=&URL=Ch0733/SEC6171.HTM&Title=->2006->Ch0733->Section%206171. If the link is no longer active, do a search for "Florida Probate Code **733.6171**." Summarize the provisions of this Florida Code section and list the various levels of compensation for attorneys.

2. WEB WORK: Visit the following website and review the California statute regarding appropriate compensation for attorneys representing personal representatives: http://www.leginfo.ca.gov/.html/prob_table_of_contents.html. If the link is no longer active, do a search for "California Probate Code." Locate the section that applies to attorney's fees. Cite the code section and discuss how California probate attorneys are to be paid from the estate.

3. Compare and contrast the Florida and California attorney compensation statutes.

   a. How much compensation would an attorney receive in each state for an estate in the amount of $20,000?

   b. How much compensation would an attorney receive in each state for an estate worth $100,000?

   c. How much compensation would an attorney receive in each state for an estate worth $200,000?

4. Challenge Question: Locate your state's probate code to determine whether attorney's fees are set by statute. If not, review your state bar's website to see if there are any guidelines pertaining to attorney's fees in probate cases. Summarize your findings and be sure to provide citations to applicable statute sections and URLs.

PARALEGAL PRACTICE

Review the memorandum directed from the supervising attorney to you, the paralegal. The memorandum will discuss a situation with a client and request your assistance in researching the matter. You must then report back with your findings, as directed in the memorandum.

1. _____

MEMORANDUM

To: Paralegal
From: Supervising Attorney
Client: Nichole Smith
Re: Part One Probate Documents

Today I met with Nichole Smith regarding her husband's estate. Richard Smith passed away on December 1, 2010. He is survived by our client and their three children, Alice Smith, Bert Smith, and Charles Smith. Alice has one child, Derek Smith, born out-of-wedlock. Richard left everything to his wife, or if she failed to survive, equally to his three children. He appointed Nichole as Personal Representative. His assets are as follows:

1. The family residence located at 2345 Oak Street, Sample City, Sample State 45678. The value of the house is $150,000 and there is no mortgage. The family residence was solely in Richard's name.
2. A 2008 Pontiac Vibe in joint name with Nichole.
3. A 2005 Lincoln Navigator in Richard's name.
4. A joint checking account with $22,205 in it as of the date of death.
5. A separate savings account with $3,250 in it as of the date of death.

Prepare the Part One Probate documents for Richard Smith's estate.

Tip: Sort the assets into probate and non-probate assets before you begin.

2. _____

MEMORANDUM

To: Paralegal
From: Supervising Attorney

Client: Matthew Meyers
Re: Family Tree

Today I met with Matthew Meyers regarding his brother's estate. Matthew's brother was Thomas S. Meyers, and his date of death was November 12, 2010. Thomas died without a will. Thomas was divorced and had no children. He is survived by three siblings: Sally Meyers-Smith, Sandra Jacobsen, and our client. There was one predeceased brother: Mark Meyers. Mark Meyers had two children: Seth Meyers and Tabatha Jones. Our client has one son: Matthew Meyers, Jr. Sally and Sandra have no children.

Prepare a family tree for Thomas S. Meyers.

3. _____   State Challenge   _____

MEMORANDUM
To: Paralegal
From: Supervising Attorney
Client: Matthew Meyers
Re: Determine Heirs

The sole asset in Thomas's estate was a brokerage account containing assets equal to $200,000. Locate your state's intestacy statute and print a copy for the file. Compare the family tree that you prepared under Memorandum #2 to the intestacy statute to determine who will inherit from the estate and in what amounts.

ONLINE RESOURCES

The Pearson Course Companion website contains the following additional resources:
- **Forms for Paralegal Practice Activities**
- Chapter Objectives

- Online Study Guide (Containing Multiple Choice and True/False Questions)
- Web Exercises www.pearsonhighered.com/careers

FORMS TO ACCOMPANY PARALEGAL PRACTICE

Disclaimer: The forms provided to aid students in completing the Paralegal Practice activities assigned in each chapter have been modified as samples to familiarize students with what each form commonly looks like and are not intended to be used as actual forms for any state.

INSTRUCTIONS: The forms are provided in Microsoft Word format and employ the use of Stop Codes (such as SC1, SC2, SC3, and so on). Stop Codes are used in place of the form sections that must be updated with case-by-case information, such as SC1 for the client's name, SC3 for the client's address, and so on. What each Stop Code represents can be inferred by reading the surrounding text on the form. By using the FIND & REPLACE tool on the Microsoft toolbar, the students can replace the Stop Codes with the information provided in the Paralegal Practice activity to complete each assignment. Students must also fill in any blank lines on each form with the appropriate information from the activity and then proofread the document prior to turning in their work.

These forms are included following this section and will be posted online for students to access to complete the Paralegal Practice activities for this chapter:

- PP Form 11.1—Application for Informal Probate of Will and Appointment of Personal Representative
- PP Form 11.2—Acceptance of Personal Representative
- PP Form 11.3—Statement of Informal Probate and Appointment of Personal Representative
- PP Form 11.4—Letters of Appointment
- PP Form 11.5—Notice of Informal Probate of Will and Appointment of Personal Representative
- PP Form 11.6—Proof of Mailing Notice of Informal Probate of Will and Appointment of Personal Representative

PP Form 11.1—Application for Informal Probate of Will and Appointment of Personal Representative

Pearson & Pearson, Attorneys-At-Law
1001 Reed Drive
Sample City, Sample State 12345
(928) 788-1234
(928) 788-1235 (Facsimile)
michael.pearson@pearsonlaw.com
Attorney for Petitioner

IN THE SUPERIOR COURT OF THE STATE OF SAMPLE STATE
IN AND FOR THE COUNTY OF SAMPLE

In the Matter of the Estate of **SC1** Deceased,	**Case No. PB-2014-_____** **APPLICATION FOR INFORMAL PROBATE OF WILL AND APPOINTMENT OF PERSONAL REPRESENTATIVE**

1. This Application is made by SC2, who is entitled to file this Application under SAMPLE STATUTE §14-3301 because _____
_____.

2. Decedent died on _____, 20_____, at the age of _____ years. At the time of death, decedent was domiciled in _____ County, State of _____.

3. [The original/A certified copy, the original of which has been probated in_____,] of decedent's Will, dated _____ , _____, [is filed with this Application. /is in the possession of the Court.]

4. Decedent left surviving the following persons who are the surviving spouse, children, heirs and devisees of decedent:

	Age	Heir or	Relationship
Name and Address	(if minor)	Decedent	To Devisee

5. Venue for this proceeding is in this county because decedent [was a domiciliary of/was not domiciled in this state and owned property located in] this county at the time of death.

6. [No Personal Representative for decedent's Estate has been appointed in this state or elsewhere./_____ was appointed Personal Representative of decedent's Estate in the State of _____.]

7. Applicant has not received a demand for notice and is not aware of any demand for notice by any interested person of any proceedings concerning decedent in this state or elsewhere.

8. Applicant believes that the Will, dated _____, _____, was validly executed and is decedent's last Will and, after the exercise of reasonable diligence, Applicant is unaware of any instrument revoking the Will.

9. The time for informal probate and appointment has not expired under SAMPLE STATUTE §14-3108 because [less than two years have passed since decedent's death.]

10. Applicant states that _____, of _____, City of _____, State of _____, has priority for appointment as Personal Representative under the Will pursuant to the provisions of SAMPLE STATUTE §14-3203 because _____
_____.

11. [Bond is not required of the Personal Representative under SAMPLE STATUTE §14-3603 because (it has been waived in the Will/all the devisees have filed written waivers of bond./_____
_____)] [Bond is required of the Personal Representative.]

Applicant's best estimate of the value of property owned by decedent and subject to the probate jurisdiction of the Court is as follows:

Personal property	$_____
Real property (less encumbrances thereon)	$_____
Expected annual income of Estate	$_____
TOTAL	$_____]

12. Applicant requests that decedent's last Will be admitted to informal probate and that _____ be appointed as the Personal Representative to administer decedent's Estate [without bond./with such bond as may be required.]

DATED this _____ day of _____, 2014.

_____
SC2

STATE OF _____)
County of _____)   )ss.

SC2, being duly sworn, states as follows:

That [he/she] is [the _____ of _____,] the Applicant in the foregoing Application; and that the statements in the Application are accurate and complete to the best of [his/her] knowledge and belief.

_____
SC2

SUBSCRIBED AND SWORN TO before me, the undersigned Notary Public, this _____ day of _____, 2014, by SC2.

_____
Notary Public

My Commission Expires:
_____

PP Form 11.2—Acceptance of Appointment as Personal Representative

Pearson & Pearson, Attorneys-At-Law
1001 Reed Drive
Sample City, Sample State 12345
(928) 788-1234
(928) 788-1235 (Facsimile)
michael.pearson@pearsonlaw.com
Attorney for Petitioner

IN THE SUPERIOR COURT OF THE STATE OF SAMPLE STATE
IN AND FOR THE COUNTY OF SAMPLE

In the Matter of the Estate of **SC1** Deceased.	Case No. PB-2014-_____ **ACCEPTANCE OF APPOINTMENT AS PERSONAL REPRESENTATIVE**

STATE OF_____)
County of _____)   ) ss.

I hereby accept the duties of Personal Representative of the Estate of the above-named decedent and do solemnly swear that I will perform, according to law, the duties of such fiduciary.

DATED this ___ day of _____, 2014.

_____
SC2

SUBSCRIBED AND SWORN TO before me, the undersigned Notary Public, this ___ day of _____2014, by SC2.

_____
Notary Public

My Commission Expires:

_____

PP Form 11.3—Statement of Informal Probate of Will and Appointment of Personal Representative

Pearson & Pearson, Attorneys-At-Law
1001 Reed Drive
Sample City, Sample State 12345
(928) 788-1234
(928) 788-1235 (Facsimile)
michael.pearson@pearsonlaw.com
Attorney for Petitioner

IN THE SUPERIOR COURT OF THE STATE OF SAMPLE STATE
IN AND FOR THE COUNTY OF SAMPLE

In the Matter of the Estate of **SC1** Deceased.	**Case No. PB-2014-_____** **STATEMENT OF INFORMAL PROBATE OF WILL AND APPOINTMENT OF PERSONAL REPRESENTATIVE**

An Application for Informal Probate of Will and Appointment of Personal Representative has been submitted by SC2, requesting admission to probate of the Will of decedent dated _____, and the appointment of SC2 as the Personal Representative to administer decedent's Estate.

The undersigned has found compliance with SAMPLE STATUTE §§ 14-3303 and 14-3308 and is satisfied that said Will is entitled to probate and that SC2 is entitled to appointment as Personal Representative under all applicable provisions of SAMPLE STATUTE Title 14, Chapter 3, Article 3.

THEREFORE, the Will of SC1, dated _____ is admitted to informal probate.

FURTHER, SC2 is appointed as Personal Representative of decedent's Estate [without bond] and Letters shall be issued upon said Personal Representative accepting [and filing an approved bond in the amount of $_____].

[FURTHER, the Personal Representative shall immediately notify the Court in these proceedings of any change in address and shall be responsible for all costs resulting from failure to do so.]

DATED this ___ day of _____, 2014.

_____
Registrar

PP Form 11.4—Letters of Personal Representative

Pearson & Pearson, Attorneys-At-Law
1001 Reed Drive
Sample City, Sample State 12345
(928) 788-1234
(928) 788-1235 (Facsimile)
michael.pearson@pearsonlaw.com
Attorney for Personal Representative

IN THE SUPERIOR COURT OF THE STATE OF SAMPLE STATE
IN AND FOR THE COUNTY OF SAMPLE

In the Matter of the Estate of **SC1** Deceased.	**Case No. PB-2014-_____** **LETTERS OF PERSONAL REPRESENTATIVE**

SC2 is hereby appointed as Personal Representative of this Estate [without restriction/without restriction except the following: _____

_____.]

WITNESS: _____, 2014
Clerk of the Superior Court

By _____
Deputy Clerk

PP Form 11.5—Notice of Informal Probate of Will and Appointment of Personal Representative

Pearson & Pearson, Attorneys-At-Law
1001 Reed Drive
Sample City, Sample State 12345
(928) 788-1234
(928) 788-1235 (Facsimile)
michael.pearson@pearsonlaw.com
Attorney for Personal Representative

IN THE SUPERIOR COURT OF THE STATE OF SAMPLE STATE
IN AND FOR THE COUNTY OF SAMPLE

In the Matter of the Estate of **SC1** Deceased.	Case No. PB-2014-_____ **NOTICE OF INFORMAL PROBATE OF WILL AND** **APPOINTMENT OF PERSONAL REPRESENTATIVE**

YOU ARE HEREBY NOTIFIED that:

1. This Notice is being sent to those persons who have, or may have, some interest in the Estate of decedent.

2. Decedent died on _____.

3. SC2 filed an Application for Informal Probate of Will and Appointment of Personal Representative in the above-named court, requesting that the Will of decedent executed on _____, be admitted to informal probate and that SC2 be appointed Personal Representative of the Estate of decedent.

4. On _____, 2014, the Registrar admitted the Will to informal probate and appointed SC2 as Personal Representative of the Estate [with bond in the amount of $_____].

5. Bond [has been filed with the Court./is not required.]

6. An heir of decedent wishing to contest the probate has four months from the receipt of this Notice to commence a formal testacy proceeding.

7. Papers relating to the Estate are on file with the Court and are available for your inspection.

DATED this day ____ of _____, 2014.

_____

SC2

PP Form 11.6—Proof of Mailing Notice of Informal Probate of Will and Appointment of Personal Representative

Pearson & Pearson, Attorneys-At-Law
1001 Reed Drive
Sample City, Sample State 12345
(928) 788-1234
(928) 788-1235 (Facsimile)
michael.pearson@pearsonlaw.com
Attorney for Personal Representative

IN THE SUPERIOR COURT OF THE STATE OF SAMPLE STATE
IN AND FOR THE COUNTY OF SAMPLE

In the Matter of the Estate of **SC1** Deceased.	Case No. PB-2014-_____ **PROOF OF [MAILING/ DELIVERING] NOTICE OF INFORMAL [PROBATE OF WILL AND] APPOINTMENT OF PERSONAL REPRESENTATIVE**

STATE OF SAMPLE STATE   )
County of _____)   ) ss.

    The undersigned, SC3, states that a copy of the Notice of Informal [Probate of Will and] Appointment of Personal Representative [and a copy of the Will] [was/were] [mailed/delivered] on _____, 2014, to the following persons:

Name	Address

DATED this ____ day of _____, 2014.

_____

SC3

SUBSCRIBED AND SWORN TO before me this ____ day of_____, 2014, by SC3.

_____

Notary Public

My Commission Expires:

_____

Probate Part 2: Inventory and Appraisal

CHAPTER 12

A REAL-LIFE SCENARIO

Betsy Smith was appointed by the court as executrix to administer the estate of her favorite cousin, Roberta Nelson. Betsy thought it only right that she do the work, since she was the sole beneficiary of the estate under the will.

The logistics were a little bit difficult, but with her daughter's help making phone calls and transporting her around, Betsy was able to serve and carry out her duties. Gathering information about Roberta's assets was a little bit challenging. There was an old deed in the safe deposit box, along with a list of bank accounts (names and account numbers). There was also a forty-two-year-old life insurance policy naming Roberta's parents (long deceased) as beneficiaries.

Using her letters testamentary to prove her authority to act on behalf of the estate, Betsy went to the various banks named and began collecting current bank account information with date-of-death values to report on the inventory that she was required to file with the court. Some of the bank accounts on the list had been closed, but others contained healthy balances. Likewise, she was able to find out about the current value of the life insurance and learned that the policy was still valid. Since the beneficiaries named on the policy were deceased, the life insurance was subject to probate.

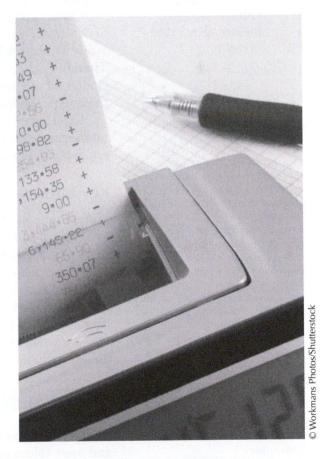

© Workmans Photos/Shutterstock

CHAPTER OBJECTIVES:

1. Understand the purpose of an inventory and appraisal.

2. Prepare an inventory and appraisal.

3. Discuss the importance of notifying the other parties of the inventory and appraisal.

4. Discuss how to determine the value of various estate assets.

Finally, some phone calls and a public records search revealed that Roberta owned a beautiful log cabin in the woods (she had never said a word about it to Betsy!). All of these assets were listed on the inventory that Betsy filed with the court.

INTRODUCTION

Once the personal representative is appointed, he or she is faced with the immediate task of compiling an inventory of all of the decedent's assets. States generally impose a statutory time frame within which the inventory must be filed with the court. The time generally ranges from thirty to ninety days.

The letters testamentary give the personal representative the legal authority to gather financial information from banks and other sources, as well as to act on behalf of the estate.

Once a complete list of assets has been compiled, the firm can help the client to determine whether the assets are probate or non-probate assets. Non-probate assets will be transferred by operation of law outside of the probate proceeding. Therefore, they are normally excluded from the probate forms but may be included on any necessary tax forms. (Be sure to check your state law regarding these requirements.)

In addition, in community property states, the assets must be further divided into **separate property** and **community property** categories. This distinction does not apply in non-community property states.

Key Terms and Definitions

Separate Property
In community property states, all property that is not community property; usually includes property owned before marriage and gifts, bequests, and inheritances received after marriage.

Community Property
A method of holding property acquired during marriage in which each spouse owns one-half of the property outright. Community property is currently valid in: Alaska, Arizona, California, Idaho, Louisiana, New Mexico, Nevada, Texas, and Washington. Wisconsin has a similar law known as "marital property law."

Letters Testamentary
A document issued by the court as evidence of its authorization for the personal representative's to act on behalf of a deceased's estate.

Inventory and Appraisal ("Inventory")
A detailed list of articles of property in an estate, made by the executor or administrator thereof.

Letters testamentary are the court's authorization of the personal representative's right to act on behalf of a deceased's estate. An **inventory** is a detailed list of articles of property in an estate, made by its executor or administrator. **Community property** is a method of holding property acquired during the marriage in which each spouse owns one-half of the property outright. Community property is only valid in the following ten states: Alaska, Arizona, Colorado, Idaho, Louisiana, Nevada, New Mexico, Texas, Washington, and Wisconsin. In community property states, **separate property** is all property that is not community property and usually includes gifts, bequests, and inheritances.

PREPARING THE INVENTORY AND APPRAISAL

In order to prepare the inventory and appraisal, you will need account balances and asset values as of the date of the decedent's death. The date-of-death value is used on the inventory even if weeks, months, or years have since passed. Part of the personal representative's job is to account for what happens to the estate assets from the date of death through the date of distribution to the beneficiaries or heirs. Therefore, the starting figures to be used on the inventory must be the date-of-death values.

Personal Property

Personal property must be listed with its fair market value as of the date of death. These values may be obtained in a variety of ways, depending on the type of property.

Automobiles

Valuation of automobiles may be done using sources such as the Kelley Blue Book and the National Automobile Dealers Association (NADA). Both offer free automobile valuation online. Kelley Blue Book's official website is www.kbb.com. NADA's website is www.nada.com. In order to obtain the approximate value of the vehicle, you will need, at a minimum, the following information:

- Year
- Make
- Model
- Mileage
- Condition of vehicle
- Vehicle attributes (such as number of doors, whether manual or automatic, presence or absence of other available features)
- Zip code

Bank Accounts, Brokerage Accounts, and Other Financial Accounts

If not already in the possession of the personal representative, account statements may be obtained from financial institutions using the letters testamentary as evidence of authority to act on behalf of the estate. The personal representative will need to get statements from each account for the period including the decedent's date of death. The proceeds from these accounts must be placed into new, separate accounts titled in the name of the estate.

Furniture, Furnishings and Personal Effects

It is difficult to value home furnishings because there is not usually much of a market or demand for used furniture. Therefore, for ordinary, run-of-the-mill furnishings, an educated estimation of the fair market value is usually sufficient for purposes of the inventory. The same is true for wearing apparel and personal effects.

Antiques and Memorabilia

On the other hand, if there are antiques or other items of value, the personal representative should have those items appraised to determine the appropriate fair market value, for purposes of the inventory and for the purpose of ensuring fair and equitable distribution to the beneficiaries or heirs.

Real Property

The requirements for the valuation of real property vary depending on state law. Some states, such as California, require that a formal real property appraisal be done. Other states do not. In states that do not require an appraisal, the personal representative can generally consult with a real estate agent. The agent would likely use comparables to determine the fair market value of the decedent's real property, similar to the way that any homeowner would arrive at a listing price for his or her property. Finally, if the real property is being distributed to beneficiaries or heirs, rather than sold, the property tax bill may be a sufficient starting point for valuation, depending on state law and local court rules.

Compiling the Information

In addition to the property values, the personal representative will need to get date-of-death lien values for any liens or mortgages on the property. The complete asset and lien information must then be compiled into the format of the inventory and appraisal for filing with the court.

■ NOTIFYING THE PARTIES

In addition to filing the inventory with the court, the personal representative has a duty to send a copy of the inventory to all of the beneficiaries and heirs of the estate, as well as any other interested parties. After doing so, the personal representative must file a Proof of Mailing Inventory and Appraisal, or a comparable local form, as evidence that the necessary parties have been notified.

■ AMENDING THE INVENTORY

It is not uncommon for the personal representative to find additional assets after the initial inventory is filed. Sometimes the new assets are discovered when the family goes through the decedent's personal effects and filing cabinets. Other times, letters and even bills that arrive in the mail tip the personal representative off to additional, previously unknown property. Finding additional assets is generally a good thing, since the more assets there are, the more the beneficiaries will inherit. Each state has a statutory time frame within which the personal representative must file an amended inventory with the court. Generally speaking, the time frame ranges from thirty to sixty days after the new asset is discovered. When an amended inventory is filed, it must be served on the interested parties; a new Proof of Mailing must also be filed with the court at that time.

■ THE HYPOTHETICAL FAMILY

John worked with his attorney to prepare an inventory and appraisal to file with the court.

Figure 12.1 depicts the inventory and appraisal signed by John Smith.

Figure 12.1

Pearson & Pearson, Attorneys-At-Law
1001 Reed Drive
Sample City, Sample State 12345
(928) 788-1234
(928) 788-1235 (Facsimile)
michael.pearson@pearsonlaw.com
Attorney for Personal Representative

IN THE SUPERIOR COURT OF THE STATE OF SAMPLE
IN AND FOR THE COUNTY OF SAMPLE

In the Matter of the Estate of **JANE SMITH,** Deceased.	Case No. PB-2014-0007 **INVENTORY AND APPRAISAL**

Figure 12.1 (continued)

JOHN SMITH, Personal Representative of the above Estate, states that the Inventory annexed hereto as Exhibit 1 contains a true statement of all the property owned by decedent at the time of decedent's death which has come to the knowledge of the Personal Representative and is subject to probate; indicates the fair market value of the property as of the date of decedent's death and its nature as separate or community; and discloses the type and amount of all encumbrances relating to each item.

DATED this 25th day of March, 2014.

John Smith
_____

JOHN SMITH
234 Sunny Lane
Sample City, Sample State 12345

INVENTORY

Real Property	Value	Encumbrances
123 Oak Street, Sample City, Sample State 12345	$200,000	-0-
Total Net Real Property	**$200,000**	

Personal Property	Value	Encumbrances
2012 Ford Expedition	$15,000	<$5,000>
First Bank Checking Account	$5,110	-0-
First Bank Savings Account	$18,050	-0-
Sample Community Bank Brokerage Account	$33,225	-0-
Personal Property & Household Goods	$4,000	-0-
Total Net Personal Property	**$70,385**	
Total Net Property of Decedent	**$270,385**	

EXHIBIT 1

After mailing out a copy of the inventory to each party entitled to notice, Pearson & Pearson filed the required proof of mailing with the court. The Proof of Mailing of Inventory and Appraisal form is depicted in Figure 12.2.

About a month after the inventory was filed, John Smith was going through an old filing cabinet in his mother's house when he found a very old executor's deed from the Estate of Jane Wildridge to Jane Smith. Jane Wildridge was the decedent's great-aunt. John looked up the address, drove out to the property, and found that it was a very beautiful parcel of wooded, vacant land near a lake. He then contacted a real estate agent and got an appraisal for the property, which set the market value at $25,000. Finally, he contacted Pearson & Pearson to let them know about the newfound asset.

Figure 12.3 depicts the First Amended Inventory and Appraisal.

Figure 12.2

Pearson & Pearson, Attorneys-At-Law
1001 Reed Drive
Sample City, Sample State 12345
(928) 788-1234
(928) 788-1235 (Facsimile)
michael.pearson@pearsonlaw.com
Attorney for Personal Representative

IN THE SUPERIOR COURT OF THE STATE OF SAMPLE
IN AND FOR THE COUNTY OF SAMPLE

In the Matter of the Estate of **JANE SMITH,** Deceased.	Case No. PB-2014-0007 **PROOF OF MAILING OF INVENTORY AND APPRAISAL**

STATE OF SAMPLE   )
) ss.

County of Sample   )

The undersigned, SAMMY STUDENT, states that a copy of the Inventory and Appraisal was mailed on March 26, 2014, to the following persons:

Shirley Smith
121 Oak Street
Sample City, Sample State 12345

Susan Smith-Thompson
345 Maple Street
Sister City, Sample State 12346

Mark Smith, Jr.
123 Oak Street
Sample City, Sample State 12345

DATED this <u>26th</u> day of <u>March</u> 2014.

Sammy Student
_____
SAMMY STUDENT

SUBSCRIBED AND SWORN TO before me, the undersigned Notary Public, this <u>26th</u> day of <u>March</u>, 2014, by SAMMY STUDENT.

Lila P. Legal
_____
Notary Public

LILA P. LEGAL
Notary Public, State of Sample
Sample County
My Commission Expires May 10, 2016

Figure 12.3

Pearson & Pearson, Attorneys-At-Law
1001 Reed Drive
Sample City, Sample State 12345
(928) 788-1234
(928) 788-1235 (Facsimile)
michael.pearson@pearsonlaw.com
Attorney for Personal Representative

IN THE SUPERIOR COURT OF THE STATE OF SAMPLE
IN AND FOR THE COUNTY OF SAMPLE

In the Matter of the Estate of **JANE SMITH** Deceased.	Case No. PB-2014-0007 **FIRST AMENDED INVENTORY AND APPRAISAL**

JOHN SMITH, Personal Representative of the above Estate, states that the Inventory annexed hereto as <u>Exhibit 1</u> contains a true statement of all the property owned by decedent at the time of decedent's death which has come to the knowledge of the Personal Representative and is subject to probate; indicates the fair market value of the property as of the date of decedent's death and its nature as separate or community; and discloses the type and amount of all encumbrances relating to each item.

DATED this <u>6th</u> day of <u>May</u>, 2014.

John Smith
_____
JOHN SMITH
234 Sunny Lane
Sample City, Sample State 12345

INVENTORY

Real Property	Value	Encumbrances
123 Oak Street, Sample City, Sample State 12345	$200,000	-0-
22 Old Woods Road, Nearby City, Sample State 12989	$25,000	-0-
Total Net Real Property	**$225,000**	

Personal Property	Value	Encumbrances
2012 Ford Expedition	$15,000	<$5,000>
First Bank Checking Account	$5,110	-0-
First Bank Savings Account	$18,050	-0-
National Bank Brokerage Account	$33,225	-0-
Personal Property & Household Goods	$4,000	-0-
Total Net Personal Property	**$70,385**	

Total Net Property of Decedent	**$295,385**	

EXHIBIT 1

■ CONCLUSION

Preparing the inventory and appraisal is one of the personal representative's most important jobs because it lays the foundation upon which the rest of the proceeding is based. The list of assets must be complete and accurate so that it is easy to account to the beneficiaries and the court regarding the administration of those assets through the probate proceeding. If an asset is later discovered, the personal representative can file an amended inventory and appraisal and then will have to notify the beneficiaries of the same. The inventory must be filed with the court within the statutory time limit. The paralegal often plays an integral role by helping the personal representative to compile the asset information and drafting the forms for the attorney's approval.

CONCEPT REVIEW AND REINFORCEMENT

KEY TERMS

Separate Property 334   Letters Testamentary 334   Inventory 334
Community Property 334

REVIEW QUESTIONS

1. Within what time frame do most states require a personal representative to prepare and file an inventory with the court?
2. What is the date that must be referred to when listing the values of assets on an inventory?
3. What document serves as proof of a personal representative's authority to act on behalf of the estate?
4. What websites can be used to ascertain the fair market value of vehicles owned by the decedent?
5. List the attributes that are required in order to obtain valuation of a vehicle.
6. When an additional asset is discovered after the initial inventory is filed, what document must be prepared?
7. Who is entitled to a copy of the Inventory and Appraisal?
8. How are furniture, furnishings, and personal effects valued?
9. What are the various ways in which proof of real property value may be proven?
10. What document serves as proof that the inventory was mailed to all interested parties?

BUILDING YOUR PARALEGAL SKILLS

CRITICAL THINKING EXERCISES

1. WEB WORK: Obtain a Kelley Blue Book value for the following vehicle: 2002 Ford Expedition XLT, 130,000 miles, automatic transmission; power windows and door locks, air conditioning; good condition; zip code 86442.
2. WEB WORK: Obtain a NADA value for the following vehicle: 2003 Ford F250 SPDTY, 100,000 miles, automatic transmission, no power windows or door locks, air conditioning; good condition; zip code 14606.
3. WEB WORK: Visit the following website, which contains the index of the California Probate Code: http://www.leginfo.ca.gov/.html/prob_table_of_contents.html. If the address is no longer valid, do a search for "California Probate Code." Locate the section that applies to the preparation of an

inventory. How long does a personal representative have to file an inventory with the court? Be sure to cite the code sections where you found your answer.

4. WEB WORK: Visit the following website, which contains the index of the California Probate Code: http://www.leginfo.ca.gov/.html/prob_table_of_contents.html. If the address is no longer valid, do a search for "California Probate Code." Locate the section that applies to the appraisal of assets for the inventory. Discuss how the decedent's personal property and real property must be appraised. Be sure to cite the code sections where you found your answers.

5. Challenge Question: Locate your state's probate code and determine whether there are specific rules related to the preparation of the inventory. When is the inventory due? Does the real property have to be formally appraised? Summarize your findings and be sure to provide citations to applicable statute sections and URLs.

PREPARE DOCUMENTS

1. _____

MEMORANDUM
To: Paralegal
From: Supervising Attorney
Client: Nichole Smith
Re: Part Two Probate Documents for The Estate of Richard Smith

Prepare an inventory for the Estate of Richard Smith. As a reminder, the assets and date-of-death values are as follows:

1. The family residence located at 2345 Oak Street, Sample City, Sample State 45678. The value of the house is $150,000 and there is no mortgage. The family residence was solely in Richard's name.
2. A 2008 Pontiac Vibe in joint name with Nichole.
3. A 2005 Lincoln Navigator in Richard's name.
4. A joint checking account with $22,205 in it as of the date of death.
5. A separate savings account with $3,250 in it as of the date of death.

The parties entitled to notice are the decedent's adult children: Alice Smith, Bert Smith, and Charles Smith. Here are their addresses:

Alice Smith
2347 Oak Street
Sample City, Sample State 45678

Bert Smith
200 Second Street
Sample City, Sample State 45678

Charles Smith
15½ Scenic Circle
Sample City, Sample State 45679

Remember that Nichole will sign these forms as the personal representative. Assume that you will be the notary public notarizing the Proof of Mailing.

2. _____

MEMORANDUM
To: Paralegal
From: Supervising Attorney
Client: Matthew Meyers
Re: Prepare Inventory and Appraisal

Our firm's client, Matthew Meyers, has been appointed as personal representative of his brother's estate.

Recall that Thomas S. Meyers died on November 12, 2010 and was survived by three siblings: Sally Meyers-Smith, Sandra Jacobsen, and our client. There was one predeceased brother: Mark Meyers. Mark Meyers had two children: Seth Meyers and Tabatha Jones. Our client has one son: Matthew Meyers, Jr. Sally and Sandra have no children.

The sole asset in Thomas' estate was a brokerage account containing $200,000. Please prepare an Inventory and Appraisal.

ONLINE RESOURCES

The Pearson Course Companion website contains the following additional resources:
- **Forms for Paralegal Practice Activities**
- Chapter Objectives

- Online Study Guide (Containing Multiple Choice and True/False Questions)
- Web Exercises
- Hypothetical Family and Accompanying Project Worksheet www.pearsonhighered.com/careers

FORMS TO ACCOMPANY PARALEGAL PRACTICE

Disclaimer: The forms provided to aid students in completing the Paralegal Practice activities assigned in each chapter have been modified as samples to familiarize students with what each form commonly looks like and are not intended to be used as actual forms for any state.

INSTRUCTIONS: The forms are provided in Microsoft Word format and employ the use of Stop Codes (such as SC1, SC2, SC3, and so on). Stop Codes are used in place of the form sections that must be updated with case-by-case information, such as SC1 for the client's name, SC3 for the client's address, and so on. What each Stop Code represents can be inferred by reading the surrounding text on the form. By using the FIND & REPLACE tool on the Microsoft toolbar, the students can replace the Stop Codes with the information provided in the Paralegal Practice activity to complete each assignment. Students must also fill in any blank lines on each form with the appropriate information from the activity and then proofread the document prior to turning in their work.

The following forms are included following this section and will be posted online for students to access to complete the Paralegal Practice activities for this chapter:

- PP Form 12.1—Inventory and Appraisal
- PP Form 12.2—Proof of Mailing Inventory and Appraisal

PP Form 12.1—Inventory and Appraisal

Pearson & Pearson, Attorneys-At-Law
1001 Reed Drive
Sample City, Sample State 12345
(928) 788-1234
(928) 788-1235 (Facsimile)
michael.pearson@pearsonlaw.com
Attorney for Personal Representative

**IN THE SUPERIOR COURT OF THE STATE OF SAMPLE STATE
IN AND FOR THE COUNTY OF SAMPLE**

In the Matter of the Estate of **SC1,** Deceased.	Case No. PB-2014-_____ **INVENTORY AND APPRAISAL**

SC2, Personal Representative of the above Estate, states that the Inventory annexed hereto as Exhibit 1 contains a true statement of all the property owned by decedent at the time of decedent's death which has come to the knowledge of the Personal Representative and is subject to probate; indicates the fair market value of the property as of the date of decedent's death and its nature as separate or community; and discloses the type and amount of all encumbrances relating to each item.

DATED this ____day of _____, 2014.

_____

SC2

INVENTORY

(NOTE: This inventory is for a community property state. A non-community property state would not categorize property as community and separate.)

Real Property	Value	Encumbrances
Community Property		
Separate Property		
Total Real Property	$	
Personal Property		
Community Property		
Separate Property		
Total Personal Property	$	
Total Net Property of Decedent	$	

EXHIBIT 1

PP Form 12.2—Proof of Mailing Inventory

Pearson & Pearson, Attorneys-At-Law
1001 Reed Drive
Sample City, Sample State 12345
(928) 788-1234
(928) 788-1235 (Facsimile)
michael.pearson@pearsonlaw.com
Attorney for Personal Representative

**IN THE SUPERIOR COURT OF THE STATE OF SAMPLE STATE IN
AND FOR THE COUNTY OF SAMPLE**

In the Matter of the Estate of **SC1,** Deceased.	Case No. PB-2014-_____ **PROOF OF MAILING OF INVENTORY AND APPRAISAL**

STATE OF SAMPLE STATE   )
) ss.
County of Sample   )

The undersigned, SC3, states that a copy of the Inventory and Appraisal was mailed on , 2014, to the following persons:

Name	Address

DATED this __ day of _____, 2014.

_____
SC3

SUBSCRIBED AND SWORN TO before me this _____ day of _____, 2014, by SC3.

_____
Notary Public

My Commission Expires:

CHAPTER 13

Probate Part 3: Creditors' Claims

A REAL-LIFE SCENARIO

The only bill that Betsy Smith received for the Estate of Roberta Nelson was a final bill from the nursing home. Roberta's funeral arrangements had been prepaid and there was no evidence that she had any credit card debt. However, Betsy's attorney accurately explained that the estate was still legally required to publish a notice to creditors in a newspaper of general circulation in the county to let any potential creditors know how to file claims. Not surprisingly, no claims were filed against the Estate of Roberta Nelson.

© Brian Jackson/Fotolia

■ INTRODUCTION

Unlike Roberta Nelson in the real-life scenario, most individuals die with at least a few outstanding bills. Many people have outstanding loans, credit cards, utilities, and other bills when they die. In most cases, those debts must be paid; and in all cases, the debts must be administered during the probate proceeding.

CHAPTER OBJECTIVES:

1. Understand the process of notifying creditors of the estate and assessing claims against the estate.

2. Prepare a Notice to Creditors.

3. Discuss some of the reasons why a claim may be disallowed.

Creditors
People or entities to whom money is owed.

Secured Creditor
One who holds some special monetary assurance of payment of a debt owed, such as a mortgage, collateral, or lien.

Unsecured Creditor
A creditor other than a preferential creditor that does not have the benefit of any security interests in the assets of the debtor (the decedent).

Claim
A right to payment.

Creditor's Claim
A written document by a creditor alleging that it is owed money by the estate. The claim must be delivered to the personal representative within the statutory time frame or it may be disallowed.

Disallowance of Claim
A document filed by a personal representative notifying the creditor that the claim is not being allowed and providing the legal grounds for the disallowance.

After the personal representative is appointed, he or she must notify all known creditors and provide instructions for filing claims against the estate. In addition, a notice must be published in a newspaper in order to notify any potential unknown creditors of how to file claims against the estate. This process is known as the third step or part of probate; however, it is wise for the personal representative to notify the creditors immediately following appointment in order to expedite the probate proceeding process. Many attorneys will notify the creditors at the same time the inventory and appraisal is prepared so that the proceeding can advance as quickly as possible.

Key Terms and Definitions

Creditors are people or entities to whom money is owed. A **secured creditor** is one who holds some special monetary assurance of payment of a debt owed, such as a mortgage, collateral, or lien. An **unsecured creditor** is a creditor other than a preferential creditor that does not have the benefit of any security interests in the assets of the debtor (the decedent). A **claim** is a right to payment. A **creditor's claim** is a written document delivered by a creditor alleging that it is owed money by the estate. The claim must be delivered to the personal representative within the statutory time frame or it may be disallowed. A **disallowance of claim** is a document filed by a personal representative notifying the creditor that the claim is not being allowed and providing the legal grounds for the disallowance.

■ KNOWN CREDITORS

It is the responsibility of the personal representative to send a Notice to Creditors to all known creditors of the decedent. Practically speaking, known creditors are likely to include mortgage holders, lien holders, credit card issuers, medical providers for the decedent's last illness, and funeral service providers. Any other known creditors must also be notified. The Notice to Creditors is usually mailed to the known creditors and also filed with the court. Included on the notice is the statutory time period within which the creditors must file their claims against the estate. The statutory time frame is commonly sixty to ninety days from receipt of the notice.

After the Notice to Creditors is sent out, the personal representative must also file a Proof of Mailing Notice to Creditors listing which creditors were notified, the method of notification, and the date of notification.

■ UNKNOWN CREDITORS

In addition to notifying all known creditors, all unknown creditors must be contacted. You may be wondering at this point how it is possible to notify creditors when you don't know who they are, where they are, or if they even exist. The method by which unknown creditors is contacted is publication. The Notice to Creditors for Publication must be published a certain number of times in a newspaper of general circulation in the county in which the probate proceeding is being administered. For example, in Arizona, the notice must be published once a week for three consecutive weeks. In other jurisdictions, the requirement is often three consecutive publications (meaning that it is printed three days in a row). The exact requirements vary by state. *Check your state statute to determine the exact publication requirements in your jurisdiction.*

After the publication is complete, the publisher must execute an Affidavit of Publication to file with the court as evidence that the publication requirement is complete.

RECEIPT OF CLAIMS

As a result of the notices that are mailed and published, the personal representative will normally receive a number of claims in the mail. It is his or her job, with the assistance of counsel, to determine how each claim should be treated. Practically speaking, this means determining whether or not each claim will be paid. An **allowed claim** is paid; a **disallowed claim** is not paid.

As a paralegal, it is likely that you will be the one sorting the claims and making an initial determination regarding the treatment of the claims while under the supervision of an attorney. If there are many creditors, it may be useful to create a spreadsheet or a checklist to make sure that each creditor has been properly dealt with and that no creditor is omitted.

Allowed Claim
A creditor's claim that is accepted to be paid from the estate.

Disallowed Claim
A creditor's claim that is rejected and will not be paid from the estate.

DISALLOWANCE OF CLAIMS

There are some circumstances under which otherwise just debts may be disallowed as creditor's claims. One reason for disallowance may be *insolvency*: if the estate is insolvent, there may be no funds with which to pay creditors. Another reason for disallowance may be that the claim was presented after the expiration of the claims period. There may be a variety of other valid reasons to disallow a claim, including that the claim is incorrect, invalid, void, or unenforceable. It is also important to note that *secured creditors* must be paid in order for the estate to keep the collateral, regardless of whether or not a claim is filed. For example, the mortgage on a decedent's house must be paid or the bank has the right to foreclose on the house. It is the personal representative's job to make an accurate determination regarding the treatment of each claim.

After the disallowance is filed, the creditor may file an objection with the court. If the creditor files an objection to disallowance of claim, the personal representative will likely need to file a response. If the matter cannot be resolved between the parties, a court hearing will likely be required to determine the validity of the claim.

Figure 13.1 is the statute pertaining to the creditor claim process in the State of Ohio.

Figure 13.1 Ohio Revised Code, Title 21, 2117.06 Presentation and allowance of creditor's claims—pending action against decedent.

(A) All creditors having claims against an estate, including claims arising out of contract, out of tort, on cognovit notes, or on judgments, whether due or not due, secured or unsecured, liquidated or unliquidated, shall present their claims in one of the following manners:

  (1) After the appointment of an executor or administrator and prior to the filing of a final account or a certificate of termination, in one of the following manners:

    (a) To the executor or administrator in a writing;

    (b) To the executor or administrator in a writing, and to the probate court by filing a copy of the writing with it;

    (c) In a writing that is sent by ordinary mail addressed to the decedent and that is actually received by the executor or administrator within the appropriate time specified in division (B) of this section. For purposes of this division, if an executor or administrator is not a natural person, the writing shall be considered as being actually received by the executor or administrator only if the person charged with the primary responsibility of administering the estate of the decedent actually receives the writing within the appropriate time specified in division (B) of this section.

(continued)

Figure 13.1 (continued)

(2) If the final account or certificate of termination has been filed, in a writing to those distributees of the decedent's estate who may share liability for the payment of the claim.

(B) Except as provided in section 2117.061 of the Revised Code, all claims shall be presented within six months after the death of the decedent, whether or not the estate is released from administration or an executor or administrator is appointed during that six-month period. Every claim presented shall set forth the claimant's address.

(C) Except as provided in section 2117.061 of the Revised Code, a claim that is not presented within six months after the death of the decedent shall be forever barred as to all parties, including, but not limited to, devisees, legatees, and distributees. No payment shall be made on the claim and no action shall be maintained on the claim, except as otherwise provided in sections 2117.37 to 2117.42 of the Revised Code with reference to contingent claims.

(D) In the absence of any prior demand for allowance, the executor or administrator shall allow or reject all claims, except tax assessment claims, within thirty days after their presentation, provided that failure of the executor or administrator to allow or reject within that time shall not prevent the executor or administrator from doing so after that time and shall not prejudice the rights of any claimant. Upon the allowance of a claim, the executor or the administrator, on demand of the creditor, shall furnish the creditor with a written statement or memorandum of the fact and date of the allowance.

(E) If the executor or administrator has actual knowledge of a pending action commenced against the decedent prior to the decedent's death in a court of record in this state, the executor or administrator shall file a notice of the appointment of the executor or administrator in the pending action within ten days after acquiring that knowledge. If the administrator or executor is not a natural person, actual knowledge of a pending suit against the decedent shall be limited to the actual knowledge of the person charged with the primary responsibility of administering the estate of the decedent. Failure to file the notice within the ten-day period does not extend the claim period established by this section.

(F) This section applies to any person who is required to give written notice to the executor or administrator of a motion or application to revive an action pending against the decedent at the date of the death of the decedent.

(G) Nothing in this section or in section 2117.07 of the Revised Code shall be construed to reduce the periods of limitation or periods prior to repose in section 2125.02 or Chapter 2305. of the Revised Code, provided that no portion of any recovery on a claim brought pursuant to that section or any section in that chapter shall come from the assets of an estate unless the claim has been presented against the estate in accordance with Chapter 2117. of the Revised Code.

(H) Any person whose claim has been presented and has not been rejected after presentment is a creditor as that term is used in Chapters 2113. to 2125. of the Revised Code. Claims that are contingent need not be presented except as provided in sections 2117.37 to 2117.42 of the Revised Code, but, whether presented pursuant to those sections or this section, contingent claims may be presented in any of the manners described in division (A) of this section.

(I) If a creditor presents a claim against an estate in accordance with division (A)(1)(b) of this section, the probate court shall not close the administration of the estate until that claim is allowed or rejected.

(J) The probate court shall not require an executor or administrator to make and return into the court a schedule of claims against the estate.

(K) If the executor or administrator makes a distribution of the assets of the estate pursuant to section 2113.53 of the Revised Code and prior to the expiration of the time for the presentation of claims as set forth in this section, the executor or administrator shall provide notice on the account delivered to each distributee that the distributee may be liable to the estate if a claim is presented prior to the filing of the final account and may be liable to the claimant if the claim is presented after the filing of the final account up to the value of the distribution and may be required to return all or any part of the value of the distribution if a valid claim is subsequently made against the estate within the time permitted under this section.

Effective Date: 04-08-2004; 04-07-2005

FIGURE 13.1: STATUTORY REVIEW- √ YOUR UNDERSTANDING

1. List the different manners in which a creditor may file a claim against an estate in Ohio.
2. How long do creditors have to file claims in Ohio?
3. How long after presentment does an executor have to allow or reject claims?

■ THE HYPOTHETICAL FAMILY

John Smith has just been appointed personal representative for the estate of his mother, Jane Smith. Around the same time that John Smith signed the initial inventory and appraisal, Pearson & Pearson prepared a Notice to Creditors to be published in Sample County.

Figure 13.2 depicts the notice to creditors that was both filed with the court and published three consecutive times in Sample County.

Figure 13.2

Pearson & Pearson, Attorneys-At-Law
1001 Reed Drive
Sample City, Sample State 12345
(928) 788-1234
(928) 788-1235 (Facsimile)
michael.pearson@pearsonlaw.com
Attorney for Personal Representative

IN THE SUPERIOR COURT OF THE STATE OF SAMPLE
IN AND FOR THE COUNTY OF SAMPLE

In the Matter of the Estate of **JANE SMITH** Deceased.	Case No. PB-2014-0007 **NOTICE TO CREDITORS** **(For Publication)**

   NOTICE IS HEREBY GIVEN that JOHN SMITH has been appointed Personal Representative of this Estate. All persons having claims against the Estate are required to present their claims within four months after the date of the first publication of this notice or the claims will be forever barred. Claims must be presented by delivering or mailing a written statement of the claim to the Personal Representative at the following address:

c/o **Pearson & Pearson, Attorneys-At-Law**
1001 Reed Drive
Sample County, Sample State 12345

DATED this <u>29th</u> day of March, 2014.

Michael Pearson
_____
Michael Pearson, Esq.

Recall from the inventory that the only known creditor for the estate of Jane Smith listed on the Inventory and Appraisal was the lien holder for her Ford Expedition. John Smith provided his attorney with a copy of the bill and then Pearson & Pearson prepared a Notice to Known Creditors, which is depicted in Figure 13.3.

After Pearson & Pearson mailed the Notice to Known Creditors to the lien holder for the Ford Expedition, they prepared the Proof of Mailing Notice to Known Creditors depicted in Figure 13.4.

It was proper for Pearson & Pearson to mail a notice to Ford Financing Company as a known creditor of the Estate of Jane Smith. However, since Ford had a valid lien on the Expedition, and could repossess the collateral for nonpayment, John Smith rightfully intended to pay Ford whether or not it filed a claim against the estate. After all, one of a personal representative's main jobs is to secure and preserve estate assets for later distribution to the beneficiaries.

Figure 13.3

Pearson & Pearson, Attorneys-At-Law
1001 Reed Drive
Sample County, Sample State 12345
(928) 788-1234
(928) 788-1235 (Facsimile)
michael.pearson@pearsonlaw.com
Attorney for Personal Representative

IN THE SUPERIOR COURT OF THE STATE OF SAMPLE
IN AND FOR THE COUNTY OF REED

In the Matter of the Estate of **JANE SMITH** Deceased.	Case No. PB-2014-0007 **NOTICE TO CREDITORS** **(For Mailing to Known Creditors)**

NOTICE IS HEREBY GIVEN that JOHN SMITH has been appointed Personal Representative of this Estate. A Notice to Creditors was first published on March 30, 2014. All persons having claims against the Estate are required to present their claims within four months after the published notice, if notice is given as provided in S.R.S. §3801A, or within 60 days after mailing or other delivery of this notice, whichever is later, or the claims will be forever barred. (See S.R.S. §14-3803(A), copy attached). Claims must be presented by delivering or mailing a written statement of the claim to the Personal Representative at the following address:

    c/o **Pearson & Pearson, Attorneys-At-Law**
    1001 Reed Drive
    Sample County, Sample State 12345

DATED this <u>1st</u> day of <u>April</u>, 2014.

Sammy Student
_____
SAMMY STUDENT

Figure 13.4

Pearson & Pearson, Attorneys-At-Law
1001 Reed Drive
Sample City, Sample State 12345
(928) 788-1234
(928) 788-1235 (Facsimile)
michael.pearson@pearsonlaw.com
Attorney for Personal Representative

IN THE SUPERIOR COURT OF THE STATE OF SAMPLE
IN AND FOR THE COUNTY OF REED

In the Matter of the Estate of **JANE SMITH**, Deceased.	Case No. PB-2014-0007 **PROOF OF MAILING NOTICE TO KNOWN** **CREDITORS**

STATE OF SAMPLE   )
) ss.
County of Reed   )

Figure 13.4 (continued)

The undersigned, SAMMY STUDENT, states that a copy of the Notice to Creditors of the above Estate was mailed to the following persons, on the date indicated:

FORD FINANCING COMPANY
1888 Expedition Drive
Sample City, Sample State 12366

DATED this 29th day of March , 2014.

Sammy Student
SAMMY STUDENT

SUBSCRIBED AND SWORN TO before me, the undersigned Notary Public, this 29th day of March, 2014, by SAMMY STUDENT.

Lila P. Legal
Notary Public

> **LILA P. LEGAL**
> Notary Public, State of Sample
> Sample County
> My Commission Expires May 10, 2016

On August 10, 2014, Pearson & Pearson received a claim against the Estate of Jane Smith from a local cable company. The claim alleged that the decedent owed $336.13 from an unpaid final bill back in 2006. John Smith did not recognize the name of the cable company or believe that his mother owed the bill. Further, Pearson & Pearson advised that the statute of limitations to collect on this type of bill was six years in Sample State. Further still, the claim was filed after the expiration date based on the publication of the Notice to Creditors..

Figure 13.5 depicts the Disallowance of Claim prepared by Pearson & Pearson on behalf of John Smith as personal representative.

Figure 13.5

Pearson & Pearson, Attorneys-At-Law
1001 Reed Drive
Sample City, Sample State 12345
(928) 788-1234
(928) 788-1235 (Facsimile)
michael.pearson@pearsonlaw.com
Attorney for Personal Representative

IN THE SUPERIOR COURT OF THE STATE OF SAMPLE
IN AND FOR THE COUNTY OF REED

In the Matter of the Estate of **JANE SMITH,** Deceased.	Case No. PB-2014-0007 **NOTICE OF DISALLOWANCE OF CLAIM TO SOUTHWEST CABLE CORPORATION**

Figure 13.5 (continued)

TO: **SOUTHWEST CABLE CORPORATION**
Bankruptcy Desk
PO Box 1498
Victorville, SAMPLE 92393-1498

Your claim against the above Estate in the amount of $336.13 has been **disallowed** in full for the following reasons:
1) it was filed after the expiration date for filing claims; 2) the debt's validity is disputed by the Personal Representative;
and 3) the time to collect on the debt, if originally valid, has legally expired.

DATED this 15th day of August, 2014.

Michael Pearson
———————————————
Michael Pearson, Esq.
Attorney for Personal Representative

Original plus two (2) copies filed with the
Court and a copy thereof mailed this
15th day of August, 2014 to

SOUTHWEST CABLE CORPORATION
Bankruptcy Desk
P.O. Box 1498
Victorville, SAMPLE 92393-1498

By: *Sammy Student*
———————————————
An employee of Pearson & Pearson

■ CONCLUSION

Part Three of the probate process is the stage at which the personal representative notifies the creditors, both known and unknown, regarding the time in which they may file a claim against the estate. After the claims are filed, the personal representative must assess the validity of the claims and determine whether or not they should be paid. If a claim is not going to be paid, the personal representative must file a Disallowance of Claim with the court and send a copy to the creditor. The Disallowance of Claim must provide the reason why the claim is not being paid. If the creditor objects to the disallowance, the personal representative must either work it out with the creditor or seek the assistance of the court to make a final determination. It is essential that all claims be dealt with to avoid any liability falling on the heirs of the estate in the future.

CONCEPT REVIEW AND REINFORCEMENT

KEY TERMS

REVIEW QUESTIONS

1. Explain what steps take place in Part 3 of a probate proceeding, as described in this chapter.
2. Describe what it means to be a secured creditor, and provide an example.
3. Describe what it means to be an unsecured creditor, and provide an example.
4. List some reasons why a creditor's claim may be disallowed.
5. Explain why secured claims need to be paid whether or not a claim is filed.

BUILDING YOUR PARALEGAL SKILLS

CRITICAL THINKING EXERCISES

1. WEB WORK: Visit the following link to the California Probate Code: http://www.leginfo.ca.gov/.html/prob_table_of_contents.html. If the link is no longer active, do a search for "California Probate Code." Locate the section that applies to notifying creditors how to file claims against the estate. How long does a creditor have to file a claim against the estate? What is the procedure for filing a claim? Be sure to answer these questions and cite the code sections where you found your answers.
2. WEB WORK: Visit the following link to the Rhode Island Probate Code: http://webserver.rilin.state.ri.us/Statutes/TITLE33/INDEX.HTM. If the link is no longer active, do a search for "Rhode Island Probate Code." Locate the section that applies to notifying creditors of how to file claims against the estate. How long does a creditor have to file a claim against the estate? What is the procedure for filing a claim? Be sure to answer these questions and cite the code sections where you found your answers.
3. Challenge Question: Locate your state's probate code to determine the rules related to creditors' claims. What are the requirements for publication? How long does a creditor have to file a claim against the estate? Summarize your findings and be sure to provide citations to applicable statute sections and URLs.

PARALEGAL PRACTICE

1. _____

MEMORANDUM

To: Paralegal
From: Supervising Attorney
Client: Nichole Smith
Re: Part Three Probate Documents

Ms. Smith just came into the office, very upset, credit card bills in hand. She cannot believe that Richard had three credit cards that she did not know about! The bills are from the following issuers:

FIRST BANK
123 MONEY STREET
SAMPLE CITY, SAMPLE STATE 12340

SECOND BANK
887 BILLING WAY
SAMPLE CITY, SAMPLE STATE 12355

THIRD BANK
4567 OUCH DRIVE
SAMPLE CITY, SAMPLE STATE 12988

Please prepare notices to creditors for these three banks. Also prepare a notice to creditors for publication and a proof of mailing the notices to the three banks.

Remember that Nichole will sign these forms as the personal representative. Assume that you will be the notary public notarizing the proof of mailing.

2. _____

MEMORANDUM
To: Paralegal
From: Supervising Attorney
Client: Matthew Meyers
Re: Third Bank Claim
_____

Matthew Meyers just received a credit card statement in the mail for his brother, Thomas. Matthew was very surprised to learn that Thomas had a card with such a high outstanding balance! The card was issued by Third Bank, and has a balance of $20,000. The bank's address is as follows:

THIRD BANK
PO BOX 988
SAMPLE CITY, SAMPLE STATE 12988

Prepare a notice to creditor for Third Bank, a notice to creditors for publication, and a proof of mailing the notice to Third Bank.

3. _____

MEMORANDUM
To: Paralegal
From: Supervising Attorney
Client: Nichole Smith
Re: Part Three Probate Documents
_____

The statutory time has elapsed for the creditors to file claims. First Bank filed a claim in the amount of $10,500. Second Bank did not file a claim. Third Bank filed a claim for $1250. Nichole does not disagree with the amounts of the two filed claims.

Prepare a disallowance of claim to Second Bank. The address is

SECOND BANK
887 BILLING WAY
SAMPLE CITY, SAMPLE STATE 12355

The basis for your disallowance should be that no claim was filed within the statutory time frame.

ONLINE RESOURCES

The Pearson Course Companion website contains the following additional resources:
- **Forms for Paralegal Practice Activities**
- Chapter Objectives

- Online Study Guide (Containing Multiple Choice and True/False Questions)
- Web Exercises
- Hypothetical Family and Accompanying Project Worksheet www.pearsonhighered.com/careers

CASE FOR CONSIDERATION

CASE #1:

SUPERIOR COURT OF THE STATE OF ARIZONA,
in and for the County of Maricopa, Respondent Judge,
JACK DAVID AND SHANNON DAVID, Real Parties in Interest.

208 Ariz. 229; 92 P.3d 859; 430 Ariz. Adv. Rep. 19

OPINION BY: Andrew D. Hurwitz

OPINION

EN BANC

HURWITZ, Justice

The issue in this case is whether life insurance proceeds paid to a decedent's spouse are exempt from claims of creditors of the estate. We hold the proceeds are exempt from creditors' claims pursuant to Arizona Revised Statutes ("A.R.S.") §20-1131 (2002).

I

Nancy May survived her husband James Edward May, who died on April 21, 2002. Nancy petitioned the superior court to probate her late husband's estate and was appointed personal representative. She subsequently filed an estate inventory, revealing that the estate contained no assets. At the time of James May's death, a civil suit was pending against the Mays in superior court. The suit, filed by Jack and Shannon David, alleged that the Mays engaged in fraud and odometer rollback when selling them an automobile.

The Davids filed a claim against the estate in the probate proceeding. The superior court allowed the claim, contingent upon the determination that James was liable to the Davids. Relying on A.R.S. §14-6102 (Supp. 2003), which restricts a non-probate transferee's claim to certain assets in favor of the decedent's creditors, the Davids filed a motion in the probate court requesting disclosure of James's non-probate assets. The court ordered Nancy to file an amended inventory, including non-probate assets. The amended inventory revealed two life insurance policies, each in the amount of $500,000. Nancy was the named beneficiary on each policy.

The Davids filed a motion to restrict or bond the life insurance policy proceeds. The superior court granted the motion. Nancy, however, had already exhausted the policy proceeds. The court then found Nancy in contempt and ordered her to provide an accounting of her expenditures, warning her that failure to provide a proper accounting could result in her removal as personal representative and incarceration.

In November 2003, Nancy filed an unaudited accounting of her expenditures. On December 3, 2003, the superior court nonetheless reaffirmed its contempt order and took under advisement the issue of whether a forensic accounting was necessary.[1] On December 12, Nancy filed a special action in the court of appeals, which declined jurisdiction. Nancy then petitioned this court for review of the order of the court of appeals declining special action jurisdiction, asking us to decide whether, under A.R.S. §14-6102(A), the proceeds from the two life insurance policies can be used to pay her late husband's creditors or whether, under A.R.S. §20-1131(A), these proceeds are beyond the creditors' reach.

We granted review of this purely legal question because the issue is one of first impression and is of statewide importance. The court has jurisdiction pursuant to Article 6, Section 5(3) of the Arizona Constitution, Arizona Rule of Civil Appellate Procedure 23, and A.R.S. §12-120.24 (2003).

II

Since 1954, Arizona law has provided that proceeds of life insurance policies payable to beneficiaries other than the decedent are exempt from claims against the decedent's estate:

> [HN1] When a policy of life insurance is effected by any person on his own life or on another life in favor of some person other than himself having an insurable interest therein . . . the lawful beneficiary thereof . . . shall be entitled to its proceeds against the creditors and representatives of the person effecting the same.

---

[1] At a status conference in January 2004, the superior court ordered Nancy to provide a forensic accounting.

A.R.S. §20-1131(A) (added by 1954 Ariz. Sess. Laws, ch. 64, §31). Notwithstanding A.R.S. §20-1131(A), the superior court apparently concluded that this case was controlled instead by A.R.S. §14-6102(A), enacted as part of an amendment of the Arizona probate code to conform with certain 1998 revisions in the Uniform Probate Code ("UPC"), 2001 Ariz. Sess. Laws, ch. 44, § 12. Section 14-6102(A) provides:

> [HN2] Except as otherwise provided by law, a transferee of a nonprobate transfer is subject to liability to the decedent's probate estate for allowed claims against the decedent's probate estate and statutory allowances to the decedent's spouse and children to the extent the decedent's probate estate is insufficient to satisfy those claims and allowances.

See also A.R.S. §14-6101(A) (1995) (defining a "provision for a nonprobate transfer on death in any insurance policy" as "nontestamentary").

While the superior court did not explain its reasoning, it appears that the judge agreed with the argument advanced by the Davids that §14-6102(A), the later enacted statute, was meant to render the exemption in §20-1131(A) inapplicable to the extent that the assets in the decedent's estate were insufficient to satisfy creditors' claims. In advancing that argument, the Davids rely primarily on *UNUM Life Insurance Co. of America v. Craig*, 200 Ariz. 327, 26 P.3d 510 (2001).

UNUM involved a dispute over the proceeds of life insurance policies. As the court noted,

> there are currently in force two statutes governing distribution of insurance proceeds upon simultaneous or near-simultaneous deaths. The one [A.R.S. § 14-2702] requires survival by 120 hours; the other [A.R.S. § 20-1127] requires that the beneficiary meet a more subjective standard of proof with complex evidence that the beneficiary survived the insured if only by a few moments.

Id. at 333 P29, 26 P.3d at 516. Because the named beneficiary in *UNUM* survived the insured only by moments, the statutes were in irreconcilable conflict. *Id.* We therefore turned to the legislative history of the two provisions at issue. *Id.* at 330-33 PP14-27, 26 P.3d at 513-16. We concluded that in adopting the UPC, which contains the 120 hours requirement in § 14-2702, the legislature implicitly repealed the conflicting provision in § 20-1127. *Id.* at 333 P29, 26 P.3d at 516. We therefore held that § 14-2702, requiring survival by 120 hours, was "the applicable rule of survival for a designated beneficiary of an insurance policy." *Id.* at 335 P38, 26 P.3d at 518.

Although we concluded in *UNUM* that the two statutes could not be harmonized, we recognized that our first duty when confronted with such claims of conflict is to "adopt a construction that reconciles one with the other, giving force and meaning to all statutes involved." *Id.* at 333 P28, 26 P.3d at 516. In this case, we have no difficulty in doing so.

Section 14-6102(A), the UPC provision, begins with a critical phrase: "Except as otherwise provided by law." Thus, § 14-6102(A), which allows a decedent's creditors to look to non-probate transfers to satisfy their claims, only applies when there is no other "law" to the contrary. Section 20-1131(A) is precisely such a "law." It expressly provides that life insurance proceeds are not subject to creditors' claims. Therefore, life insurance proceeds are not among the non-probate transfers available to satisfy the claims of creditors under § 14-6102(A).

Because there is no facial conflict between §§ 14-6102(A) and 20-1131(A), the superior court erred in concluding that the former somehow implicitly repealed the latter. *See UNUM*, 200 Ariz. at 329 P11, 26 P.3d at 512 (noting our duty to "harmonize" the language of purportedly conflicting statutes in order "to give effect to each"). Indeed, the official comments to the UPC directly buttress this conclusion. The comment to UPC § 6-102, the counterpart of A.R.S. § 14-6102, expressly provides that

> the initial clause of subsection (b), "Except as otherwise provided by statute," is designed to prevent a conflict with and to clarify that this section does not supersede existing legislation protecting death benefits in life insurance, retirement plans or IRAs from claims by creditors.

UPC § 6-102 cmt. 2. When, as here, "a statute is based on a uniform act, we assume that the legislature intended to adopt the construction placed on the act by its drafters," and "commentary to such a uniform act is highly persuasive." *UNUM*, 200 Ariz. at 332 P25, 26 P.3d at 515 (internal citation omitted).

III

For the reasons above, we hold that the life insurance proceeds paid Nancy are not part of James's estate, and therefore are not subject to the Davids' claims. The superior court's orders requiring an accounting of those proceeds and its order of contempt are vacated, and this case is remanded for further proceedings consistent with this opinion.[2]

---

[2]The Davids seek attorneys' fees, citing A.R.S. § 14-1302(B) (Supp. 2003). Because they are not the prevailing parties, we deny the claim.

Case Questions

1. What was the issue in this case?
2. Could the life insurance proceeds be used to satisfy the creditors' claims? Why or why not?
3. What was the holding in this case?
4. Do you agree with the result in this case? Why or why not?

FORMS TO ACCOMPANY PARALEGAL PRACTICE

> **Disclaimer: The forms provided to aid students in completing the Paralegal Practice activities assigned in each chapter have been modified as samples to familiarize students with what each form commonly looks like and are not intended to be used as actual forms for any state.**

INSTRUCTIONS: The forms are provided in Microsoft Word format and employ the use of Stop Codes (such as SC1, SC2, SC3, and so on). Stop Codes are used in place of the form sections that must be updated with case-by-case information, such as SC1 for the client's name, SC3 for the client's address, and so on. What each Stop Code represents can be inferred by reading the surrounding text on the form. By using the FIND & REPLACE tool on the Microsoft toolbar, the students can replace the Stop Codes with the information provided in the Paralegal Practice activity to complete each assignment. Students must also fill in any blank lines on each form with the appropriate information from the activity and then proofread the document prior to turning in their work.

The following forms are included following this section and will be posted online for students to access to complete the Paralegal Practice activities for this chapter:

- PP Form 13.1—Notice to Creditors (For Mailing to Known Creditors)
- PP Form 13.2—Notice to Creditors (For Publication)
- PP Form 13.3—Proof of Mailing Notice to Known Creditors
- PP Form 13.4—Notice of Disallowance of Claim

PP Form 13.1—Notice to Creditors (For Mailing to Known Creditors)

Pearson & Pearson, Attorneys-At-Law
1001 Reed Drive
Sample City, Sample State 12345
(928) 788-1234
(928) 788-1235 (Facsimile)
michael.pearson@pearsonlaw.com
Attorney for Personal Representative

IN THE SUPERIOR COURT OF THE STATE OF SAMPLE STATE
IN AND FOR THE COUNTY OF SAMPLE

In the Matter of the Estate of **SC1** Deceased.	Case No. PB-2014-_____ **NOTICE TO CREDITORS** **(For Mailing to Known Creditors)**

NOTICE IS HEREBY GIVEN that SC2 has been appointed Personal Representative of this Estate. A Notice to Creditors was first published on _____. All persons having claims against the Estate are required to present their claims within four months after the published notice, if notice is given as provided in S.R.S.

§ 3801A, or within 60 days after mailing or other delivery of this notice, whichever is later, or the claims will be forever barred. (See S.R.S. §14-3803(A), copy attached). Claims must be presented by delivering or mailing a written statement of the claim to the Personal Representative at the following address:

Name
Address
City, State Zip Code

DATED this ____ day of _____, 2014.

_____
SC3, Employee

PP Form 13.2—Notice to Creditors (For Publication)

Pearson & Pearson, Attorneys-At-Law
1001 Reed Drive
Sample City, Sample State 12345
(928) 788-1234
(928) 788-1235 (Facsimile)
michael.pearson@pearsonlaw.com
Attorney for Personal Representative

IN THE SUPERIOR COURT OF THE STATE OF SAMPLE STATE
IN AND FOR THE COUNTY OF SAMPLE

In the Matter of the Estate of **SC1** Deceased.	Case No. PB-2014-_____ **NOTICE TO CREDITORS** **(For Publication)**

NOTICE IS HEREBY GIVEN that SC2 has been appointed Personal Representative of this Estate. All persons having claims against the Estate are required to present their claims within four months after the date of the first publication of this notice or the claims will be forever barred. Claims must be presented by delivering or mailing a written statement of the claim to the Personal Representative at the following address:

Name
Address
City, State Zip Code

DATED this ____ day of _____, 2014.

_____
SC2

PP Form 13.3—Proof of Mailing Notice to Known Creditors

Pearson & Pearson, Attorneys-At-Law
1001 Reed Drive
Sample City, Sample State 12345
(928) 788-1234
(928) 788-1235 (Facsimile)
michael.pearson@pearsonlaw.com
Attorney for Personal Representative

IN THE SUPERIOR COURT OF THE STATE OF SAMPLE STATE
IN AND FOR THE COUNTY OF SAMPLE

| In the Matter of the Estate of
SC1,
Deceased. | Case No. PB-2014-_____

PROOF OF MAILING NOTICE TO KNOWN CREDITORS |

STATE OF SAMPLE STATE)
County of Sample)) ss.

    The undersigned, SC3, states that a copy of the Notice to Creditors of the above Estate was mailed to the following persons, on the date(s) indicated:

Name	Address	Date Mailed

    DATED this _____ day of _____, 2014.

_____
SC3, Employee

STATE OF SAMPLE STATE)
County of Sample)) ss.

    SUBSCRIBED AND SWORN TO before me this _____ day of _____ , 2014, by SC3.

_____
Notary Public

My Commission Expires:

PP Form 13.4—Notice to Creditor of Disallowance of Claim

Pearson & Pearson, Attorneys-At-Law
1001 Reed Drive
Sample City, Sample State 12345
(928) 788-1234
(928) 788-1235 (Facsimile)
michael.pearson@pearsonlaw.com
Attorney for Personal Representative

IN THE SUPERIOR COURT OF THE STATE OF SAMPLE STATE
IN AND FOR THE COUNTY OF SAMPLE

| In the Matter of the Estate of
SC1
Deceased, | Case No. PB-2014-_____

NOTICE OF DISALLOWANCE OF CLAIM TO SC3 |

TO: SC3

[Insert Address]

[1. Your claim against the above Estate in the amount of $_____ has been (allowed/disallowed) in full.]

[1. Your claim against the above Estate in the amount of $_____ has been allowed in the amount of $_____ and disallowed in the amount of $_____.]

2. Your claim has been classified as follows:

$_____as a community claim payable out of community property.

$_____as a separate claim payable out of separate property and decedent's half of the community property.

DATED this _____ day of _____, 2014.

_____
SC2, *Personal Representative*

Original plus two (2) copies filed with the Court and a copy thereof mailed this

___ day of _____, 2014 to

SC3

[Insert Address]

By: _____

Probate Part 4: Closing the Estate

CHAPTER 14

A REAL-LIFE SCENARIO

Betsy Smith was both the executrix of the Estate of Roberta Nelson and the sole beneficiary of the estate. Nevertheless, she was required to follow the rules of probate procedure and complete all of the necessary forms. In her jurisdiction, this meant preparing and filing a Proposal for Distribution form indicating that she was to receive all of the assets in the estate, as well as a Closing Statement. She was not required to prepare an accounting since there were no other heirs or beneficiaries to account to.

© Andy Dean/Fotolia

■ INTRODUCTION

Part Four is the final stage of a typical probate proceeding. It is the part that all of the interested parties have been anxiously waiting for: the time when they finally get their inheritance.

The final stage requires the personal representative to make a determination of how the estate assets should be distributed. Great care must be taken to make all distributions in accordance with the last will and testament or the state's intestacy law, if the decedent died intestate. The personal representative must prepare

CHAPTER OBJECTIVES:

1. Understand the final steps of estate administration.

2. Determine how the assets of an estate should be distributed.

3. Prepare a Proposal for Distribution.

4. Prepare a Closing Statement.

a Proposal for Distribution notifying the parties exactly how the personal representative intends to distribute the estate assets. The other interested parties then have an opportunity to object to the Proposal for Distribution if they believe that something is incorrect. Often, the personal representative is also required to prepare an accounting for the interested parties to see how the estate was administered and what creditors' claims were paid. In some states, an accounting is not required unless the probate remains open for a certain length of time; for example, over one year. When an accounting is required, most jurisdictions require that the court approve the accounting. Finally, when all issues have been resolved and the estate has been fully distributed, the personal representative files a Closing Statement with the court.

Key Terms and Definitions

Proposal for Distribution
A document that is filed with the court and distributed to the heirs or beneficiaries outlining how the personal representative proposes to distribute the estate. The Proposal for Distribution also notifies recipients of the statutory time frame they have in which to file an objection.

Closing Statement
A document filed by a personal representative that notifies the court that the estate has been fully administered.

General Legacy
A gift of money out of the general assets of the estate.

Anti-Lapse Statutes
Laws designed to minimize the effect of lapse.

A **Proposal for Distribution** is a document that is filed with the court and distributed to the heirs or beneficiaries outlining how the personal representative proposes to distribute the estate. The Proposal for Distribution also notifies recipients of the statutory time frame they have in which to file an objection. An **Accounting** is a document that accounts for what happened to the estate assets from the date of death to the final distribution, and includes the beginning estate balance, gains, receipts, losses, disbursements, and ending balance. The ending balance should be zero after the estate is fully administered. A **Closing Statement** is a document filed by a personal representative that notifies the court that the estate has been fully administered.

A **general legacy** is a gift of money out of the general assets of the estate. A **specific legacy** is a gift by will of a particular article of personal property. A **demonstrative legacy** is a bequest of a certain sum of money with a direction that it be paid out of a particular fund. A **devise** is a gift of real property in a will.

Lapse is the failure of a gift made in a will because the person for whom the gift was intended predeceased the person making the will. **Anti-lapse statutes** are laws designed to minimize the effect of lapse.

■ PROPOSAL FOR DISTRIBUTION

After the time for creditors to file claims has expired, it is time for the personal representative to sit down and determine how to distribute the estate. The ease or difficulty of this task depends on several factors. First is whether the decedent died testate or intestate. If the decedent died testate (with a will), the personal representative must follow the intentions expressed in the will. If the decedent died intestate, the personal representative must be certain to follow the state's intestacy statute when proposing the distribution of the estate. Second, difficulty can arise when there are assets of differing values that have not been, or cannot be, liquidated by sale. If the beneficiaries are to inherit equally but the items to be distributed are of unequal value, what can be done? Third, when instructions were made in a will as to assets that are no longer in the estate at the decedent's death, the personal representative must determine what to do. Finally, the personal representative must determine what to do when a beneficiary predeceases the testator or dies after the testator but before the estate has been fully administered.

Some items, such as antiques and collectibles, may have great value but little or no market. The state of the economy during the probate proceeding can impact whether items can be sold and the proceeds distributed, or whether the items themselves must be distributed. In the latter circumstance, and particularly with respect to personal effects, it is best if all of beneficiaries or heirs can agree. However, absent such agreement, the personal representative must make a proposal for distribution that is as fair and equitable as possible under the circumstances. Practicality dictates that "equal shares" may not mean identical shares. Particularly when there are strange circumstances, it is advisable to send out a **Receipt and Release and Waiver of Notice**, or another comparable state form, to all beneficiaries so they can acknowledge receipt of the inheritance received and approve the personal representative's distribution.

The priority of gifts is dictated by their classification under the terms of the will. A **general legacy** is a gift of money out of the general assets of the estate. For example, "*I give and bequeath One Thousand Dollars ($1,000.00) to Catherine Jones*" is a general legacy, which would be satisfied out of the general estate assets. A **demonstrative legacy** is a bequest of a certain sum of money with a direction that it be paid out of a particular fund. For example, "*I give and bequeath One Thousand Dollars ($1,000.00) from my Bank One Savings Account (2331) to Catherine Jones*" is a demonstrative legacy, which would be satisfied from the specified account. A **specific legacy** is a gift by will of a particular article of personal property. For example, "*I give and bequeath my 1998 Corvette to Catherine Jones*" is a specific legacy. A **devise** is a gift of real property in a will. When it will not be possible to make all of the gifts directed under the will, it is necessary to review the law in your jurisdiction to determine the priority of the gifts for the purpose of distribution.

A challenge also arises when the intended recipient of a gift is no longer alive. **Lapse** is the failure of a gift made in a will because the person for whom the gift was intended predeceased the person making the will. **Anti-lapse statutes** are laws designed to minimize the effect of lapse, and generally apply to gifts made to individuals of a designated close familial relationship. For example, a state's anti-lapse statute may provide that a gift to a sibling that would have lapsed due to the sibling's death be saved by passing on to the sibling's surviving children.

When the Proposal for Distribution is complete, it should be filed with the court and mailed to all interested parties. The Proposal for Distribution should provide a time frame within which any Objections to Proposal for Distribution must be filed. The time frame to object is often thirty to sixty days, but varies by jurisdiction. If there is an objection, the court will most likely set a hearing date for the issue to be resolved. After the Proposal for Distribution is mailed, a **Proof of Mailing Proposal for Distribution** must be completed and filed with the court as evidence that the interested parties were notified.

■ ACCOUNTING

Depending on the jurisdiction and the complexity of the probate, an Accounting may be required. An **Accounting** is a document that accounts for what happened to the estate assets from the date of death to the final distribution, and includes the beginning estate balance, gains, receipts, losses, disbursements, and ending balance. The ending balance should be zero after the estate is fully administered. In some jurisdictions, the personal representative may simply account to the heirs. In other jurisdictions, the personal representative may need to file a *Petition for Approval of Accounting*, or a similar document, in order to seek court approval of the accounting prior to making the final distribution of the estate.

Receipt and Release and Waiver of Notice
A form executed by a beneficiary to acknowledge receipt of the inheritance received and to acknowledge and approve the personal representative's distribution of the estate.

Demonstrative Legacy
A bequest of a certain sum of money with a direction that it be paid out of a particular fund.

Specific Legacy
A gift by will of a particular article of personal property.
Devise
A gift of real property under a will.

Lapse
The failure of a gift made in a will as a result of the person to whom the gift was intended predeceasing the person making the will.

Accounting
A document that accounts for what happened to the estate assets from the date of death to the final distribution, and includes the beginning estate balance, gains, receipts, losses, disbursements, and ending balance.

Figure 14.1 is a sample First and Final Accounting for an estate that remained open for many years due to the terrible state of the decedent's financial affairs at the time of his death. The decedent had not filed tax returns for many years and it took a long time to file all of the back tax returns and otherwise administer the estate. In the end, there was little left to be distributed to the beneficiaries.

Figure 14.1

**First and Final Accounting for the Estate of RALPH W. CARLSON
for the Period March 20, 2006 to Present.
Case No.: PB-2006-9999**

CURRENT BOND LEVEL: $None

ACCOUNT SUMMARY

Beginning Balance (Schedule 1)	**$5,475.00**
Gains on Sales or Other Dispositions (Schedule 2)	**+ $18,439.21**
	$23,914.21
Receipts (Schedule 3)	**− $13,961.21**
	$9,953.00
Losses on Sales or Other Dispositions (Schedule 4)	**− $3,812.00**
Subtotal	**$6,141.00**
Disbursements (Schedule 5)	**− $6,141.00**
Ending Balance	**$0.00**
Consisting of:	
TOTAL	**$0.00**

SCHEDULE 1-BEGINNING BALANCE CONSISTING OF:

Real Property	Value
Community Property	
None.	
Separate Property	
None.	
Total Real Property	**$0.00**
Personal Property	
Community Property	
Miscellaneous Personal Effects	Unknown/Nominal
Separate Property	
2001 Cavco Park Model Home	
Desert Skies Resort/RV Park	$62,000.00
Less Encumbrances	− $44,600.00

Figure 14.1 (continued)

Net Value of 2001 Cavco Park Model Home**	$ Reflected as Gain Below
Wells Fargo Checking Account (1321)	
$442.79 Reflected on Inventory in Error–Joint Account	$0.00
Refund from Vision of the Seas Cruise*	$ Reflected as Gain Below
1974 Fiat X19-Vin #128AS0020670	$525.00
1999 Chevy Blazer 4 DSW	$4,950.00
Exotic Birds	Unknown
Total Personal Property	**$5,475.00**
Total	**$5,475.00**

SCHEDULE 2-GAINS ON SALES OR OTHER DISPOSITIONS

Date	Description	Amount
8/9/2006	Refund from Vision of the Seas Cruise.	$2,834.09*
9/19/2006	Deposit	$741.92
9/22/2006	Deposit	$165.00
2/26/2007	Deposit	$125.00
5/8/2007	Deposit: Wire transfer from Nevada State Bank for Proceeds from Sale of 2001 Cavco Park Model Home.	$14,375.00**
6/19/2007	Deposit	$186.09
12/31/2007	Deposit	$12.11
	Total:	**$18,439.21**

SCHEDULE 3-RECEIPTS

Date	Payee and Purpose	Amount
8/15/2006	Harland Checks (Estate Account Checks)	$19.95
8/17/2006	Check #2503 (Postmaster)	$4.25
8/23/2006	Check #2500 (Humboldt County Treasure)	$22.14
8/24/2006	Check #2501(The Spectrum)	$158.34
8/31/2006	Check #2504 The Hartford	$100.60
9/19/2006	Check #2508 USPS	$4.64
9/20/2006	Check #2505 Craig Warren	$73.39
9/20/2006	Check #2506 MVD	$137.27
9/21/2006	Check #2511USPS	$4.64
9/25/2006	Check #2512 USPS	$51.82
9/25/2006	Check #2513 USPS	$38.14
9/29/2006	Check #2514 VVD	$6.92
9/29/2006	Check #2509 First Detail	$2.86

(continued)

Figure 14.1 (continued)

10/4/2006	Check #2507 Pro Glass & Paint	$17.79
10/13/2006	Check #2510 Sample County Sheriff	$257.81
10/19/2006	Check #2515 Dixie Escalante Electric	$64.68
10/26/2006	Check #2518 USPS	$4.64
10/30/2006	Check #2519 The Hartford	$69.20
11/08/2006	Check #2517 Sample County Treasure	$307.86
11/22/2006	Check #2520 Dixie Escalante Electric	$155.55
11/29/2006	Check #2522 USPS	$4.55
12/11/2006	Check #2521 Desert Skies RV Resort	$500.00
12/22/2006	Check #2523Dixie Escalante Electric	$152.93
1/17/2007	Bank Originated Debit	$1.78
1/23/2007	Check #2524 Dixie Escalante Electric	$67.93
1/25/2007	Check #2525 Desert Skies Resort	$250.00
1/29/2007	Check #2526 Barney McKenna	$500.00
2/12/2007	Check #2529 Big "O" Tires	$309.40
2/16/2007	Check #2528 Pro Glass & Paint	$177.39
2/20/2007	Check #2527 Barbie Line	$350.00
2/21/2007	Overdraft Fee	$34.00
5/8/2007	Wire Transfer Fee	$10.00
5/17/2007	Check #2530 Barney McKenna	$606.26
5/17/2007	Check #2533 Robert Simpson Reimbursement	$2,700.00
6/14/2007	Check #2534 Robert Simpson	$929.78
8/12/2008	Check #2550- Property Tax for Nevada Mine	$11.01
8/12/2008	Check #2551- Property Tax for Nevada Mine	$11.01
8/20/2008	Withdrawal from The Hartford	$199.88
9/11/2008	Check #2553- Attorney's Fees	$2,000.00
1/23/2009	Withdrawal from The Hartford	$119.44
8/14/2009	Check #2555- Property Tax for Nevada Mine	$11.01
8/14/2009	Check #2556- Property Tax for Nevada Mine	$11.01
10/25/2010	Check #2557 Eastside Tax	$70.00
11/8/2010	Check #2558- Attorney's Fees	2,000.00
11/8/2010	Check #2559 USPS	$10.05
11/19/2010	Check #2560 Eastside Tax & Accounting	$50.00
4/29/2011	Check #2562 Eastside Tax & Accounting	$45.00
5/2/2011	Check #2561 United States Treasury	$739.98
5/23/2011	Check #2563 USPS	$6.23
6/6/2011	Check #2564 Eastside Tax & Accounting	$338.00
8/1/2011	Check #2567	$5.59
8/2/2011	Check #2565- Property Tax for Nevada Mine	$11.01
8/2/2011	Check #2566- Property Tax for Nevada Mine	$11.01

Figure 14.1 (continued)

2/27/2012	Check #2568 USPS-—Sample Department of Revenue—Cert. Mail	$11.90
2/27/2012	Check # 2569 Eastside Tax & Accounting 2007 1041 & AZ Return	$175.00
8/4/2012	Humboldt County Treasurer Black 1 Check #2570	$11.01
8/4/2012	Humboldt County Treasurer Black II Check #2571	$11.01
8/7/2012	USPS 2012-2013 Property Taxes Check #2572	$5.75
	Total:	**$13,961.21**

SCHEDULE 4-LOSSES ON SALES OR OTHER DISPOSITIONS

Date	Description	Loss or Decrease
	1974 Fiat X19-Vin #128AS0020670 $525.00	$525.00
	Depreciation of 1999 Chevrolet Blazer to current Kelley Blue Book value of $1,663.00	$3,287.00
	Total:	**$3,812.00**

SCHEDULE 5-DISBURSEMENTS

Recipient	Description	Value
Robert Simpson PO Box 353 Indiana, Sample 12990	1/3 Beneficiary of Estate	$2,047.00
Sheila Montana 13425 Prospector Ridge Road Monroe, Sample 12990	1/3 Beneficiary of Estate	$2,047.00
Jonathan Gallo 2115 14th Street Almira, Sample 12992	1/3 Beneficiary of Estate	$2,047.00

■ CLOSING STATEMENT

When the estate has been fully administered and all necessary federal and state tax returns have been filed, the personal representative must file a **Closing Statement** with the court. A copy of the Closing Statement should be sent to all interested parties to let them know that the estate has been fully administered.

■ THE HYPOTHETICAL FAMILY

John Smith did an excellent job as personal representative and his attorneys were highly competent and helpful. As a result, the probate proceeding for the Estate of Jane Smith went very smoothly. Susan Smith-Thompson decided that she really wanted to keep her mother's home located at 123 Oak Street, Sample City, Sample State 12345. The other two beneficiaries had no problem with Susan keeping the home. However, since the home was worth $200,000.00 and each beneficiary's share of the estate was under $100,000.00, Susan paid $102,871.67 to the estate in exchange for the real property.

Figure 14.2 depicts the Proposal for Distribution prepared by Pearson & Pearson, signed by John Smith, and filed with the court.

Figure 14.2

Pearson & Pearson, Attorneys-At-Law
1001 Reed Drive
Sample City, Sample State 12345
(928) 788-1234
(928) 788-1235 (Facsimile)
michael.pearson@pearsonlaw.com
Attorney for Personal Representative

IN THE SUPERIOR COURT OF THE STATE OF SAMPLE
IN AND FOR THE COUNTY OF REED

In the Matter of the Estate of **JANE SMITH** Deceased.	Case No. PB-2014-0007 **PROPOSAL FOR DISTRIBUTION**

The undersigned Personal Representative, JOHN SMITH, in order to close this Estate, proposes the following distribution of the property in the Estate:

Proposed Distributee	Description	Total
John Smith	1/3 of Personal Effects ($1,333.33) Cash Distribution: $97,128.33	$98,461.66
Susan Smith-Thompson	1/3 of Personal Effects ($1,333.33) 123 Oak Street, Sample City, Sample State 12345	$98,461.67 Net Value* *$102,871.67 to be paid to estate.
Mark Smith, Jr.	1/3 of Personal Effects ($1,333.33) 2012 Ford Expedition ($15,000) 22 Old Woods Road, Nearby City, Sample State 12989 ($25,000) Cash Distribution: $57,128.33	$98,461.67

If your objection to the proposed distribution in writing is not received by the undersigned within thirty days after mailing or delivering this proposal, your right to object will terminate.

DATED this 5th day of September, 2014.

John Smith
_____
JOHN SMITH
234 Sunny Lane
Sample City, Sample State 12345

Figure 14.3 depicts the Proof of Mailing Proposal for Distribution prepared by Pearson & Pearson and filed with the court.

In Sample State, an accounting is not required when probates are open for less than one year. Further, all of the beneficiaries in the Hypothetical

Figure 14.3

Pearson & Pearson, Attorneys-At-Law
1001 Reed Drive
Sample City, Sample State 12345
(928) 788-1234
(928) 788-1235 (Facsimile)
michael.pearson@pearsonlaw.com
Attorney for Personal Representative

IN THE SUPERIOR COURT OF THE STATE OF SAMPLE
IN AND FOR THE COUNTY OF REED

In the Matter of the Estate of **JANE SMITH** Deceased.	Case No. PB-2014- 0007 **PROOF OF MAILING PROPOSAL FOR DISTRIBUTION**

STATE OF SAMPLE   )
)ss
County of Reed   )

    The undersigned, SAMMY STUDENT, states that a copy of the Proposal for Distribution was mailed on September 5, 2014, to the following persons:

Shirley Smith
121 Oak Street
Sample City, Sample State 12345

Susan Smith-Thompson
345 Maple Street
Sister City, Sample State 12346

Mark Smith, Jr.
123 Oak Street
Sample City, Sample State 12345

DATED this 5th day of September, 2014.

Sammy Student
SAMMY STUDENT

    SUBSCRIBED AND SWORN TO before me, the undersigned Notary Public, this 5th day of September, 2014, by SAMMY STUDENT.

Lila P. Legal
Notary Public

LILA P. LEGAL Notary Public, State of Sample Sample County My Commission Expires May 10, 2016

Family got along and agreed on the math and the way the assets were distributed. Figure 14.4 depicts the Receipt and Release and Waiver of Notice signed by Susan Smith-Thompson.

    Mark Smith, Jr., likewise signed a Receipt and Release and Waiver of Notice, displayed in Figure 14.5.

Figure 14.4

Pearson & Pearson, Attorneys-At-Law
1001 Reed Drive
Sample City, Sample State 12345
(928) 788-1234
(928) 788-1235 (Facsimile)
michael.pearson@pearsonlaw.com
Attorney for Personal Representative

IN THE SUPERIOR COURT OF THE STATE OF SAMPLE
IN AND FOR THE COUNTY OF REED

In the Matter of the Estate of: **JANE SMITH** Deceased.	Case No. PB-2014-0007 **Receipt And Release And Waiver Of Notice By Susan Smith-Thompson**

The undersigned, SUSAN SMITH-THOMPSON, a distributee of the Estate, states as follows:

1. The undersigned acknowledges receipt of the following assets:

   - 1/3 of Personal Effects ($1,333.33)
   - 123 Oak Street, Sample City, Sample State 12345

2. The undersigned acknowledges receipt from JOHN SMITH, Personal Representative of the Estate, of a complete written account of the administration of the Estate.

3. The undersigned acknowledges that the distribution listed herein represents the entire share of this Estate to which the undersigned is entitled.

4. The undersigned releases JOHN SMITH, Personal Representative of the Estate, from further liability or accountability in connection with the administration of the Estate.

5. The undersigned hereby waives notice of all further filings and proceedings in the Estate.

   DATED this 7th day of October, 2014.

   Susan Smith-Thompson
   SUSAN SMITH-THOMPSON

STATE OF SAMPLE   )
) ss.
County of REED   )

SUBSCRIBED AND SWORN TO before me this 7th day of October, 2014, by SUSAN SMITH-THOMPSON.

Maya Notarie
Notary Public

MAYA NOTARIE Notary Public, State of Sample Sample County My Commission Expires July 12, 2016

PARALEGAL PRACTICE TIP

- Be sure to familiarize yourself with the anti-lapse statute in your jurisdiction to determine when gifts will and will not lapse.

When the estate was fully administered and after the distributions were made to the beneficiaries, Pearson & Pearson prepared a Closing Statement for John Smith to sign. The Closing Statement appears in Figure 14.6.

■ CONCLUSION

Part Four of the probate process is the final phase of the probate process in which the personal representative determines how the estate should be distributed and prepares

Figure 14.5

Pearson & Pearson, Attorneys-At-Law
1001 Reed Drive
Sample City, Sample State 12345
(928) 788-1234
(928) 788-1235 (Facsimile)
michael.pearson@pearsonlaw.com
Attorney for Personal Representative

IN THE SUPERIOR COURT OF THE STATE OF SAMPLE
IN AND FOR THE COUNTY OF REED

In the Matter of the Estate of: **JANE SMITH** Deceased.	Case No. PB-2014-0007 **RECEIPT AND RELEASE AND WAIVER OF NOTICE BY MARK SMITH, JR.**

The undersigned, MARK SMITH, JR., a distributee of the Estate, states as follows:

1. The undersigned acknowledges receipt of the following assets:

   - 1/3 of Personal Effects ($1,333.33)
   - 2012 Ford Expedition ($15,000)
   - 22 Old Woods Road, Nearby City, Sample State 12989 ($25,000)
   - Cash Distribution: $57,128.33

2. The undersigned acknowledges receipt from JOHN SMITH, Personal Representative of the Estate, of a complete written account of the administration of the Estate.

3. The undersigned acknowledges that the distribution listed herein represents the entire share of this Estate to which the undersigned is entitled.

4. The undersigned releases JOHN SMITH, Personal Representative of the Estate, from further liability or accountability in connection with the administration of the Estate.

5. The undersigned hereby waives notice of all further filings and proceedings in the Estate.

   DATED this 7th day of October, 2014.

   Mark Smith, Jr.
   _____
   MARK SMITH, JR.

STATE OF SAMPLE   )
) ss.
County of REED   )

   SUBSCRIBED AND SWORN TO before me this 7th day of October, 2014, by MARK SMITH, JR.

   Maya Notarie
   _____
   Notary Public

MAYA NOTARIE Notary Public, State of Sample Sample County My Commission Expires July 12, 2016

---

a written Proposal for Distribution. The heirs or beneficiaries then have a statutory time frame within which they may file any objections to the Proposal for Distribution. If an objection is filed, the court will have to rule on the objection and a hearing will likely be required. If there are no objections, the personal representative is usually free to distribute to the beneficiaries in accordance with the Proposal for Distribution.

Figure 14.6

Pearson & Pearson, Attorneys-At-Law
1001 Reed Drive
Sample City, Sample State 12345
(928) 788-1234
(928) 788-1235 (Facsimile)
michael.pearson@pearsonlaw.com
Attorney for Personal Representative

IN THE SUPERIOR COURT OF THE STATE OF SAMPLE
IN AND FOR THE COUNTY OF REED

In the Matter of the Estate of **JANE SMITH** Deceased.	Case No. PB-2014-0007 **CLOSING STATEMENT**

The undersigned Personal Representative states:

1. The undersigned was appointed as Personal Representative of this Estate on February 28, 2014, more than four months prior to this Statement.

2. The undersigned has determined that the time limit for presentation of creditor's claims has expired.

3. The Estate has been fully administered by making payment, settlement or other disposition of all claims that were presented, expenses of administration, and all taxes and claims that have accrued against the Estate.

4. All of the assets of the Estate have been distributed to the persons entitled thereto.

5. A copy of this Statement has been sent to all of the distributees of the Estate and to all creditors or other claimants of whom the undersigned is aware whose claims are neither paid nor barred.

6. The undersigned has furnished a full account in writing of the administration of the Estate to the distributees whose interests are affected thereby, including guardians ad litem, conservators and guardians.

DATED this <u>4th</u> day of <u>October</u>, 2014.

John Smith
_____
JOHN SMITH
234 Sunny Lane
Sample City, Sample State 12345

STATE OF SAMPLE)
)ss.
County of Reed)

    JOHN SMITH, being duly sworn, states as follows: That he is the Personal Representative for the above Estate and that the statements in the Closing Statement are accurate and complete to the best of his knowledge and belief.

John Smith
_____
Personal Representative

The foregoing Closing Statement was subscribed and sworn to before me this <u>4th</u> day of <u>October</u>, 2014, by JOHN SMITH.

Lila P. Legal
_____
Notary Public

LILA P. LEGAL Notary Public, State of Sample Sample County My Commission Expires May 10, 2016

The personal representative may also need to prepare an Accounting to account for how the estate assets were administered and eventually distributed to the heirs. Finally, when all is said and done, the personal representative must file a Closing Statement to notify the court and the parties that the estate has been fully administered.

CONCEPT REVIEW AND REINFORCEMENT

KEY TERMS

Proposal for Distribution   362
Closing Statement   362
General Legacy   362
Anti-Lapse Statutes   362

Receipt and Release and Waiver of
   Notice   363
Demonstrative Legacy   363
Specific Legacy   363

Devise   363
Lapse   363
Accounting   363

REVIEW QUESTIONS

1. What is the purpose of a Proposal for Distribution?
2. What should heirs do if they disagree with the Proposal for Distribution?
3. What happens if there are no objections to the Proposal for Distribution?
4. What is the purpose of an accounting?
5. What is a general legacy?
6. What is a specific legacy?
7. What is a devise?
8. What does it mean for a gift to lapse?
9. What is the purpose of an anti-lapse statute?
10. When should the Closing Statement be filed?

BUILDING YOUR PARALEGAL SKILLS

CRITICAL THINKING EXERCISES

1. **Web Work**: Visit the following link to the California Probate Code: http://www.leginfo.ca.gov/.html/prob_table_of_contents.html. If the link is no longer active, do a search for "California Probate Code." Locate the anti-lapse statute and determine the circumstances under which an otherwise lapsed gift will be saved. Summarize your findings and cite your sources.

2. **Challenge Question**: Locate your state's probate code to determine the rules related to anti-lapse in your jurisdiction. Summarize your findings and cite your sources.

PARALEGAL PRACTICE

1. _____

MEMORANDUM
To: Paralegal
From: Supervising Attorney
Client: Nichole Smith
Re: Probate Closing Documents

Assume from the last chapter that First Bank filed a claim in the amount of $10,500, Second Bank's claim was disallowed, and Third Bank filed a claim for $1,250. Nichole did not disagree with the amounts of the filed claims, so First and Third Bank were paid.

Prepare a Proposal for Distribution, Proof of Mailing Proposal for Distribution, and Closing Statement for this estate.

Remember that Nichole will sign these forms as the personal representative. Assume that you will be the notary public notarizing the Proof of Mailing.

2. _____

MEMORANDUM
To: Paralegal
From: Supervising Attorney
Client: Matthew Meyers
Re: Probate Closing Documents

Matthew Meyer, your client, is personal representative for the estate of Hannah Black, his godmother. Assume that Third Bank timely filed a creditor's claim and that the estate paid the $20,000 balance.

Prepare a Proposal for Distribution, Proof of Mailing Proposal for Distribution, and Closing Statement for this estate.

ONLINE RESOURCES

The Pearson Course Companion website contains the following additional resources:
- **Forms for Paralegal Practice Activities**
- Chapter Objectives

- Online Study Guide (Containing Multiple Choice and True/False Questions)
- Web Exercises
- Hypothetical Family and Accompanying Project Worksheet www.pearsonhighered.com/careers

CASE FOR CONSIDERATION

CASE #1:

IN THE MATTER OF THE ESTATE OF DOROTHY ANN LEIPER MCMURCHIE, Deceased.

2002 ML 4164; 2002 Mont. Dist. LEXIS 2395
November 20, 2002, Decided

OPINION BY: Gregory R. Todd

OPINION

COURT'S FINDINGS OF FACT AND CONCLUSIONS OF LAW

This matter came on for hearing before the Court on October 4 and 7, 2002, on the Personal Representative's Petition to Approve Accounting and Settlement and Distribution of a Testate Estate. Mary C. McMurchie ("Mary") filed objections to the accounting and the proposed distribution. The Personal Representative, David J. McMurchie ("David") appeared with counsel, Jeffrey A. Hunnes, Wright Tolliver Guthals, P.C. Mary appeared with counsel Robert L. Stephens, Jr., Cynthia R. Woods appeared as counsel for Samp Law Firm. The Court having heard testimony and received evidence, now makes the following:

Findings of Fact

1. Prior to the commencement of the hearing, the parties stipulated that the probate of the Estate of Boyd McMurchie ("Boyd Sr.") should be dismissed. The Court has entered a separate Order of Dismissal.
2. Prior to commencement of the hearing, Mary withdrew her objection with respect to payment of rent to Dorothy's Estate from the South Dakota farm property specifically devised by Boyd Sr. to David and Boyd Leiper McMurchie ("Boyd").
3. Prior to commencement of the hearing, counsel for Mary and the Samp Law Firm stipulated that funds distributable to Mary from the Estate, up to $15,843.72, would be deposited with the Court pending resolution of any claim of the Samp Law Firm for attorney's fees, in order to allow the Estate to otherwise be distributed and closed.
4. Dorothy Ann Leiper McMurchie ("Dorothy" or "Decedent") died testate on October 26, 1999. She was 93 years of age. At the time of death, Dorothy was domiciled in Billings, Yellowstone County, Montana.
5. Dorothy and Boyd Sr. had three children - Mary, Boyd, and David.
6. On November 30, 1999, Boyd filed a Petition for Formal Probate of Will, Appointment as Personal Representative and Appointment of Special Administrator in Dorothy's Estate. On January 19, 2000, Mary objected to Boyd's appointment as personal representative and to the appointment of the proposed special administrator.
7. Hearing was held on the Petition and Objection on June 20, 2001. On July 20, 2001, the Court entered a Memorandum and Order denying Mary's Objection and finding Boyd or David to be qualified and appropriate for appointment as Personal Representative.
8. On September 27, 2001, the Court entered an Order of Formal Probate of Will, Determination of Testacy and Heirs and Appointment of Petitioner as Personal Representative. The Decedent's Will was admitted to probate. Letters were issued to David on September 27, 2001, and he is the duly-appointed, qualified and acting Personal Representative of the Decedent's Estate.
9. At the time of Dorothy's death, Wells Fargo Bank had been appointed Conservator for Dorothy in Yellowstone County, cause number DG/C 99-058.
10. On December 10, 2001, the District Court terminated Dorothy's Conservatorship and directed Wells Fargo to transfer the residual assets of the Conservatorship to David as Personal Representative.
11. David has filed an Inventory and Appraisement of the property of the Estate.
12. David has given notice to creditors as required by law. The time for presenting claims has expired.
13. All debts of Dorothy and of her Estate, and all expenses of administration thus far incurred and all taxes that have been attached to or accrued against Dorothy and her Estate have been paid or are provided for payment in David's Proposed Distribution.
14. A Certificate from the Montana Department of Revenue has been filed stating that no inheritance taxes are due.
15. David filed an Accounting Under Oath on July 15, 2002, which detailed all receipts and disbursements during the administration of the Conservatorship and the Estate through July 15, 2002.
16. The Court reviewed David's Accounting and considered David's testimony and finds that the accounting is accurate and correct in all respects and that the Accounting should be approved and settled.

2608 Broadwater Expenses

17. David requests the Court to treat payments of expenses for the house at 2608 Broadwater Ave. in Billings as an advancement against Mary's share of the residue of Dorothy's Estate. These payments totaled $10,332.54 through July 31, 2002. Dorothy's house at 2608 Broadwater was specifically devised to Mary in Dorothy's Will. Mary has lived in the house since Dorothy's death. Wells Fargo Bank, as conservator, paid all the utilities, lawn and snow removal, property taxes and dwelling insurance for the house from funds of the Estate. David has continued to pay for certain of these expenses since his appointment including some expenses since July 15, 2002.
18. Mary did not dispute that she has resided in the house and had the benefits of the payment of these household expenses from the Estate. She contends, however, that she was financially unable to pay these expenses and that no one demanded that

she pay rent. David testified to requests made to Mary to assume these expenses which she refused.

19. The expenses for the house are properly charged against Mary's share of the residue of Dorothy's Estate. These expenses are directly attributable to the house that passed to Mary and she has enjoyed the benefit of occupancy of the house since Dorothy's death.

Attorney's Fees for Objection to Appointment

20. David requests the Court to approve payment of attorney's fees of $23,164.01 incurred in defending against Mary's objection to Boyd and David's appointment as personal representative of Dorothy's Estate.

21. On November 30, 1999, Boyd petitioned to be appointed personal representative of Dorothy's Estate and to have a special administrator appointed to represent the Estate in a South Dakota declaratory judgment action regarding ownership of joint tenancy bank accounts. Mary objected to Boyd or David's appointment claiming violation of fiduciary duties, misappropriation and conversion of assets, fraud, conflict of interest, undue influence and that Boyd Sr. lacked capacity.

22. Litigation followed with discovery requests, depositions, motion practice, a pretrial order, trial brief and proposed findings. A full day hearing was held on Mary's objections on June 20, 2001. On July 20, 2001, the Court denied Mary's objections and found Boyd or David to be qualified and appropriate for appointment as Personal Representative. Following the Court's decision, Mary filed a motion to amend or for a new hearing that was briefed, argued and denied by the Court.

23. David requests the Court to approve payment of these fees from Dorothy's Estate as administrative expenses. David is a sophisticated business person who operates a mortgage brokerage company. He testified that he believed the fees were reasonable, necessary and consistent with the fee agreement with Wright Tolliver Guthals. David testified that he and Boyd defended against the objections to their appointment in good faith, to uphold their mother's Will and to refute unjustified objections and allegations by Mary.

24. Jeff Hunnes, an attorney for David and Boyd, testified that attorney's fees were charged at Wright Tolliver Guthals' regular hourly rates and explained the firm's timekeeping and billing procedures: Mr. Hunnes testified that the fees requested for defense of the objection to appointment did not include fees for dispute in Dorothy's guardianship/conservatorship proceedings prior to David's appointment, costs, or for services directly related to Boyd Sr.'s probate or the South Dakota declaratory judgment action.

25. John Jones, an attorney with Moulton, Bellingham, Longo & Mather, testified that the fees requested by David for defending against the objection to appointment of personal representative were fair and reasonable. He stated that the hourly rates charged were reasonable and the fees were consistent with the fee agreement with Wright Tolliver Guthals. Mr. Jones testified that in his opinion, an hourly fee agreement for estate administration is the fairest arrangement to the client. He testified that the services were necessary and beneficial to the Estate and that the fees were reasonable given the complexity and the success of the defense.

26. The fees requested are properly attributable as an administrative expense of Dorothy's Estate. Mary argues that the fees for defending against the objection should be allocated equally between Dorothy and Boyd Sr.'s Estates. Mr. Hunnes testified that Wright Tolliver Guthals was hired to complete Dorothy's Estate in Montana and not complete Boyd Sr.'s Estate. Boyd Sr.'s Estate was probated and litigated in South Dakota by South Dakota counsel. By the time of Dorothy's death, Boyd Sr.'s Estate was already almost administered in South Dakota. Mary petitioned to probate Boyd Sr.'s Estate in Montana. Boyd and David requested dismissal of Boyd Sr.'s probate in Montana because it would be unnecessary and burdensome as there were no assets requiring probate in Montana. This Court's Memorandum and Order of July 20, 2001, stated that it did not appear that there were any assets in Boyd Sr.'s Estate remaining for probate in Montana. The often-stated purpose of Mary's objections was to protect Dorothy's or her Estate's interests by preventing Boyd or David's appointment. Mary's objections focused on Boyd or David's unsuitability to serve as personal representative of Dorothy's Estate.

27. Mary contends that the fees requested should not be approved because they relate to the South Dakota declaratory judgment action. Mary's objections to Boyd or David's appointment were serious

and substantial. Boyd and David had to prepare to defend against all grounds for objection raised by Mary, including theft, conversion, undue influence, fraud and incapacity. Mary accused her brothers of stealing from a safe deposit box. She specifically alleged unethical behavior by Boyd to the South Dakota Judicial Ethics Committee. Mary raised the same issues in South Dakota and Montana. Until the winter of 2001, it was not certain whether the South Dakota trial or the Montana hearing would be held first. Judgment was entered in the South Dakota action on June 15, 2001, and hearing was held in Montana on June 20, 2001. Although many of Mary's objections were resolved by the South Dakota declaratory judgment, Mary continued to raise these issues at the hearing in Montana. This required motions and briefing to limit the issues based on collateral estoppel or res judicata.

28. At David's request, Mr. Hunnes allocated attorney's fees between Dorothy's probate, Boyd Sr.'s probate and the South Dakota declaratory judgment action. He testified that there were many entries regarding communications with South Dakota counsel, Mr. Smith, because Mr. Smith acted as an intermediary with Boyd and David and it was necessary to track the status of the South Dakota action and coordinate the cases and issues being raised. Mr. Jones testified that it was appropriate and necessary for counsel to coordinate efforts in both states and that this was beneficial to the estate.

29. The allocation of fees between Dorothy's Estate, Boyd Sr.'s Estate and the South Dakota litigation was appropriate and consistent with David's instructions. The requested fees should be paid as an administrative expense of Dorothy's Estate. Mary's actions throughout the course of this litigation, and in particular the appointment of a personal representative, have mandated the actions and costs incurred.

Administrative Fees and Costs

30. David requests approval of payment of administrative fees and costs through July 31, 2002, consisting of attorney's fees of $20,370.12 and costs of $692.78.

31. David testified that he had reviewed the attorney's fees and costs and believed that the fees and costs were reasonable, necessary and consistent with the fee agreement with Wright Tolliver Guthals.

32. David testified to complications and obstacles in administration of the Estate, including termination of the conservatorship and transfer of assets from the conservatorship. On February 8, 2002, Mary filed a claim against Dorothy's Estate for $251,900.96 for care services for Dorothy. If successful, said claim would have totally consumed the Estate. David filed a Notice of Disallowance of Mary's claim and filed a Motion to Dismiss the claim as barred. On June 7, 2002, the Court entered an Order dismissing Mary's claim.

33. Mr. Hunnes testified to the basis for preparation of the statement of attorney's fees and costs and the fee agreement with David. Dorothy's Estate incurred extraordinary fees in part due to the work required to terminate the conservatorship and deal with Mary's creditor's claim. There were motions concerning preliminary distributions from the Estate that were briefed, argued and decided in David's favor. There were problems with obtaining information from Mary regarding identification of assets and the Broadwater house.

34. Mr. Jones testified that the attorney's fees requested by the Personal Representative for administration of the Estate through July 31, 2002, were fair and reasonable. He testified that the hourly rates charges were reasonable and that the fees were consistent with the fee agreement. Mr. Jones testified that the attorney's services warranted extraordinary compensation due to the amount and complexity of the work. He did not find any unnecessary duplication of services. Mr. Jones considered the successful defense against the creditor's claim and other motions as important considerations in his opinion.

35. Mr. Stephens testified that in his opinion some extraordinary fees were appropriate for administration of the Estate, however, the amount of fees sought was excessive. Mr. Stephens argued that there should be equal allocation estate administration and litigation for Dorothy's Estate and for Boyd Sr.'s Estate. This argument is not supported by the above findings. Knowledge of the South Dakota litigation was necessary in this Court because of Mary's arguments herein.

36. David's proposed distribution of the Estate, attached as Exhibit "G" to the Petition, is appropriate and correct and should be approved. The proposed distribution benefits Mary by distributing Dorothy's automobile, personal property, and jewelry to Mary without any

allocation of their value. In addition, the distribution benefits Mary by paying all dividends attributable to the Putnam account to her. The proposed distribution estimates accountant fees and costs and additional administrative expenses at $12,500 through closing of the Estate. David will file an additional petition for approval of final administrative expenses.

From the foregoing Findings of Fact, the Court now makes the following:

CONCLUSIONS OF LAW

1. The Court has jurisdiction over this matter.
2. The Accounting Under Oath through July15, 2002, should be allowed and approved as correct in all respects.
3. Upon the death of a person, her real and personal property devolves to the person to whom it is devised by the last Will, subject to allowances, rights of creditors, elective share and administration. § 72-3-101 (2), M.C.A. The house at 2608 Broadwater devolved to Mary on Dorothy's death, subject to administration of the Estate.
4. Specific devisees are entitled to the income from property specifically devised to them less taxes, ordinary repairs and other expenses of management and operation of the property that accrue during the period of administration. §72-34-406 (2)(a), M.C.A. Although Mary did not receive rent from the house, she also did not pay rent for her occupancy of the property. Mary continued to live in the house and to receive benefit of living in the house, therefore, she should be responsible for the ordinary expenses relating to her occupancy. All household expenses, including utilities, lawn care, snow removal, repairs, property taxes and dwelling insurance, which total $10,332.54 as of July 15, 2002, are properly treated as an advancement against Mary's distributable share of the residue of Dorothy's Estate.
5. A person nominated as personal representative who defends any proceeding in good faith, is entitled to receive his necessary expenses and disbursements, including reasonable attorney's fees, from the Estate. §72-3-632, M.C.A. The primary requirement is that the personal representative defend any action in good faith and in light of his fiduciary duty to the Estate. Hauck v. Seright, 964 P.2d 749 (1998).
6. Boyd and David acted in good faith in defending their appointment as personal representatives under Dorothy's Will. They were required to prepare for and respond to allegations of theft, conversion, undue influence, incapacity, fraud and conflict of interest. They prevailed in their defense to these objections. David and Boyd acted in good faith in upholding the instructions of Dorothy under her Will.
7. The attorney's fees in the sum of $23,164.01 were properly related to the defense of Mary's objections and that these fees should be paid as an administrative expense of Dorothy's Estate.
8. The Court has authority to approve payment of extraordinary attorney's fees in an estate. §72-3-633 (5), M.C.A. The review of attorney's fees is left to the sound discretion of the Court and will not be overturned absent a showing of abuse of discretion, and the Court's Findings of Fact will be upheld unless clearly erroneous. In Re Estate of Stone, 768, P.2d 334 (1989).
9. With regard to legal services, a reasonable fee should be ascertained by considering time spent, the nature of the service, and the skill and experience required. A crucial factor for determining the reasonableness of any challenged fee is whether the services rendered were beneficial to the Estate. In Re Estate of Stone, supra.
10. A fee agreement entered into by a personal representative is valid if it is fair and equitable. Fairness is determined by considering such relevant factors as good faith and full disclosure in the execution of the contract, the amount of the fee, and the client's maturity, intelligence and understanding of the transaction, in Re Estate of Magelssen, 597 P.2d 90 (1979).
11. The additional fees requested, over and above the statutory attorney's fees, should be approved. The administration of Dorothy's Estate required additional work and the attorney's services and fees were reasonably necessary. Administration of the Estate was complicated and required significant additional work due to the issues with the conservatorship, the Broadwater house, the $250,000 creditor's claim, motions for advancements and objections.
12. The requested attorney's fees of $20,370.12 and costs of $692.78 for administration of the Estate through July 31, 2002, should be paid as an administrative expense from Dorothy's Estate.
13. The Court should reserve determination of approval of final administrative expenses through closing of the Estate pending further petition by David.
14. David's Proposed Distribution as set forth in Exhibit "G" to his Petition should be approved.

DATED this 20th day of November, 2002.
Gregory R. Todd DISTRICT COURT JUDGE

PROPOSED DISTRIBUTION OF ESTATE OF DOROTHY ANN LEIPER MCMURCHIE

ASSETS ON HAND as of July 15, 2002 Available for Distribution:

A.	Real Estate - 2608 Broadwater Ave.	$81,000.00	
B.	First Citizens Bank Checking Account	36,507.42	
C.	First Citizens Bank Savings Account	91,003.76	
D.	Putnam Investments Account	5,147.93	
E.	1974 Ford LTD	500.00	
F.	7 Cemetery Lots	805.00	
G.	Personal Property	1,500.00	
H.	Costume Jewelry from Safe Deposit Box	668.00	
I.	1999 Income Tax Refund (not yet received)	2,233.00	
	TOTAL		$219,365.11

TOTAL ASSETS AVAILABLE FOR DISTRIBUTION 7/15/02 subject to payment of administrative expenses as follows:

Attorney's fees for probate dispute	$23,164.01	
Attorney's fees and costs in administration		
(to 7/31/02)	$21.062.90	
Accountant's fees and costs (estimate)	$2.500.00	
Estimated additional administrative expenses *	$10,000.00	
TOTAL ADMINISTRATIVE EXPENSES		($56,726.91)
* Balance of estate funds after payment of administrative expenses (including attorney's fees, costs and accounting fees) will be divided equally between Mary, Boyd, and David		
TOTAL ASSETS AVAILABLE FOR DISTRIBUTION		
AFTER ADMINISTRATIVE EXPENSES		$162,635.20
TOTAL CASH AVAILABLE FOR DISTRIBUTION		
AFTER ADMINISTRATIVE EXPENSES		$73.017.27
(Petitioner proses to distribute automobile, personal property and jewelry to Mary)		
FIRST RESIDUE (before distribution of grandchildren		
devises)		$73.017.27
Less grandchildren distributions:		
Mary K. Nordquist	$1,000.00	
Megan K. McMurchie	$1,000.00	
Shannon M. McMurchie	$1,000.00	
James D. McMurchie	$1,000.00	
Clayton B. Ward	$1,000.00	
Neil A. Ward	$1,000.00	

Corey S. Ward	$1,000.00	
TOTAL		($7,000.00)

SECOND RESIDUE (available for equal distribution to three children)		$66,017.27
Add: Expenses paid by Conservator and Estate on 2608 Broadwater - chargeable to Mary	$10,332.54	
Deduct: Putnam dividends received by Estate But payable to Mary	(399.26)	
RESIDUE AVAILABLE FOR DISTRIBUTION		$75,950.45
ONE-THIRD TO EACH DEVISEE		$25,316.82

PROPOSED DISTRIBUTION

Mary C. McMurchie

Real Estate - 2608 Broadwater Ave.		$81.000.00	
Putnam Investments Account		5,147.93	
1974 Ford LTD		500.00	
Personal Property		1,500.00	
Costume Jewelry from Safe Deposit Box		668.00	
3 Cemetery Lots		345.00	
One Third of Residue	$25,316.83		
Less: Expenses paid by Estate for 2608 Broadwater	(10,332.54)		
Add: Putnam divided	399,36		
Net Amount Payable to Mary		$15,383.65 *	
TOTAL			$104,544.58

* Balance of estate funds after payment of administrative expenses (including attorney's fees, costs and accounting fees) will be divided equally between Mary, Boyd and David.

Boyd Leiper McMurchie

2 Cemetery Lots		230.00	
One-Third of Residue	$25,316.82 *		
TOTAL			$25,546.82

* Balance of estate funds after payment of administrative expenses (including attorney's fees, costs and accounting fees) will be divided equally between Mary, Boyd, and David

David J. McMurchie

2 Cemetery Lots	230.00	
One-Third of Residue	$25,316.82*	
TOTAL		$25,546.82
* Balance of estate funds after payment of administrative expenses (including attorney's fees, costs and accounting fees) will be divided equally between Mary, Boyd, and David.		

RECONCILIATION

To Mary	$15,383.65	
To Boyd	$25,316.82	
To David	$25,316.82	
TOTAL CASH AVAILABLE		
FOR DISTRIBUTION		
AS ABOVE:		$66,017.29

Case Questions

1. What was the issue in this case?
2. What was the holding in this case?
3. What was the reason for the court's holding?

FORMS TO ACCOMPANY PARALEGAL PRACTICE

Disclaimer: The forms provided to aid students in completing the Paralegal Practice activities assigned in each chapter have been modified as samples to familiarize students with what each form commonly looks like and are not intended to be used as actual forms for any state.

INSTRUCTIONS: The forms are provided in Microsoft Word format and employ the use of Stop Codes (such as SC1, SC2, SC3, and so on). Stop Codes are used in place of the form sections that must be updated with case-by-case information, such as SC1 for the client's name, SC3 for the client's address, and so on. What each Stop Code represents can be inferred by reading the surrounding text on the form. By using the FIND & RE-PLACE tool on the Microsoft toolbar, the students can replace the Stop Codes with the information provided in the Paralegal Practice activity to complete each assignment. Students must also fill in any blank lines on each form with the appropriate information from the activity and then proofread the document prior to turning in their work.

The following forms are included following this section and will be posted online for students to access to complete the Paralegal Practice activities for this chapter:

- PP Form 14.1—Proposal for Distribution
- PP Form 14.2—Proof of Mailing Proposal for Distribution
- PP Form 14.3—Receipt and Release and Waiver of Notice
- PP Form 14.4—Closing Statement

PP Form 14.1—Proposal for Distribution

Pearson & Pearson, Attorneys-At-Law
1001 Reed Drive
Sample City, Sample State 12345
(928) 788-1234
(928) 788-1235 (Facsimile)
michael.pearson@pearsonlaw.com
Attorney for Personal Representative

IN THE SUPERIOR COURT OF THE STATE OF SAMPLE STATE
IN AND FOR THE COUNTY OF SAMPLE

In the Matter of the Estate of **SC1** Deceased.	Case No. PB-2014-_____ **PROPOSAL FOR DISTRIBUTION**

The undersigned Personal Representative, SC2, in order to close this Estate, proposes the following distribution of the property in the Estate, also in accordance with the accounting attached hereto as <u>Exhibit 1</u>:

Proposed Distributee	Assets

If your objection to the proposed distribution in writing is not received by the undersigned within thirty days after mailing or delivering this proposal, your right to object will terminate.

DATED this _____ day of _____, 2014.

_____
SC2

PP Form 14.2—Proof of Mailing Proposal for Distribution

Pearson & Pearson, Attorneys-At-Law
1001 Reed Drive
Sample City, Sample State 12345
(928) 788-1234
(928) 788-1235 (Facsimile)
michael.pearson@pearsonlaw.com
Attorney for Personal Representative

IN THE SUPERIOR COURT OF THE STATE OF SAMPLE STATE
IN AND FOR THE COUNTY OF SAMPLE

In the Matter of the Estate of **SC1** Deceased.	Case No. PB-2014-_____ **PROOF OF MAILING PROPOSAL FOR DISTRIBUTION**

STATE OF SAMPLE STATE   )
)ss
County of Sample   )

The undersigned, SC2, states that a copy of the Proposal for Distribution was mailed on _____, 2014, to the following persons:

Name	Address

DATED this _____ day of _____, 2014.

_____
SC2

SUBSCRIBED AND SWORN TO before me this _____ day of _____, 2014, by SC2.

_____
Notary Public

My Commission Expires:

PP Form 14.3—Receipt and Release and Waiver of Notice

Pearson & Pearson, Attorneys-At-Law
1001 Reed Drive
Sample City, Sample State 12345
(928) 788-1234
(928) 788-1235 (Facsimile)
michael.pearson@pearsonlaw.com
Attorney for Personal Representative

IN THE SUPERIOR COURT OF THE STATE OF SAMPLE STATE
IN AND FOR THE COUNTY OF SAMPLE

In the Matter of the Estate of **SC1** Deceased.	Case No. PB-2014-_____ **RECEIPT AND RELEASE AND WAIVER OF NOTICE**

The undersigned, SC5, a distributee of the Estate, states as follows:

1. The undersigned acknowledges receipt of the following asset[s]:

2. The undersigned acknowledges receipt from SC2, Personal Representative of the Estate, of a complete written account of the administration of the Estate.

3. The undersigned acknowledges that the distribution listed herein represents the entire share of this Estate to which the undersigned is entitled.

4. The undersigned releases SC2, Personal Representative of the Estate, from further liability or accountability in connection with the administration of the Estate.

5. The undersigned hereby waives notice of all further filings and proceedings in the Estate.

DATED this ___ day of _____, 2014.

_____

SC5

STATE OF _____)
) ss.
County of   )

SUBSCRIBED AND SWORN TO before me this ___ day of _____, 2014, by SC5.

_____

Notary Public

My Commission Expires:

PP Form 14.4—Closing Statement

Pearson & Pearson, Attorneys-At-Law
1001 Reed Drive
Sample City, Sample State 12345
(928) 788-1234
(928) 788-1235 (Facsimile)
michael.pearson@pearsonlaw.com
Attorney for Personal Representative

IN THE SUPERIOR COURT OF THE STATE OF SAMPLE STATE
IN AND FOR THE COUNTY OF SAMPLE

In the Matter of the Estate of **SC1** Deceased.	Case No. PB-2014- _____ **CLOSING STATEMENT**

The undersigned Personal Representative states:

1. The undersigned was appointed as Personal Representative of this Estate on _____, more than four months prior to this Statement.

2. The undersigned has determined that the time limit for presentation of creditors' claims has expired.

3. The Estate has been fully administered by making payment, settlement or other disposition of all claims that were presented, expenses of administration, and all taxes and claims that have accrued against the Estate.

4. All of the assets of the Estate have been distributed to the persons entitled thereto.

5. A copy of this Statement has been sent to all of the distributees of the Estate and to all creditors or other claimants of whom the undersigned is aware whose claims are neither paid nor barred.

6. The undersigned has furnished a full account in writing of the administration of the Estate to the distributees whose interests are affected thereby, including guardians ad litem, conservators and guardians.

DATED this _____ day of _____, 2014.

_____
Sc2

STATE OF SAMPLE STATE   )
) ss.
County of Sample   )

SC2, being duly sworn, states as follows: That he/she is the Personal Representative for the above Estate and that the statements in the Closing Statement are accurate and complete to the best of his/her knowledge and belief.

_____
Personal Representative

The foregoing Closing Statement was subscribed and sworn to before me this _____ day of _____, 2014, by SC2.

_____
Notary Public

My Commission Expires:

CHAPTER 15

Tax Considerations

© Brian Jackson/Fotolia

A REAL-LIFE SCENARIO

Ralph W. Carlson was not necessarily a bad man—he just didn't follow the rules. When Ralph passed away at age seventy, he left behind a meager estate consisting of a few small assets with nearly as much debt. Ralph also had not filed his personal tax returns in seven years, even though his income was high enough that he was required to do so.

After Ralph passed away, his nephew, Robert Simpson, was appointed as executor of the estate. Robert had a real mess on his hands. The decedent's personal property was left in a state of total disarray, with years and years of old records saved in no particular order. However, Ralph was required to file the decedent's back tax returns in conjunction with the estate administration. Needless to say, the estate took much longer to administer than normal and there was very little money to be paid out to the beneficiaries at the end.

CHAPTER OBJECTIVES:

1. Understand the tax responsibilities that a personal representative has.

2. List and describe the various types of tax returns that may need to be filed after a decedent's death.

3. Prepare basic tax forms.

4. Know where to locate further information regarding federal tax issues.

■ INTRODUCTION

In addition to all of the other responsibilities discussed in previous chapters, the executor or estate administrator has the duty to file any required tax returns with the Internal Revenue Service and the appropriate state tax authority. (The terms "executor" and personal representative" are used interchangeably herein.) Further, it is the executor's duty to pay any tax imposed. *See* IRC §2002.

Free information may be obtained from the IRS website at http://www.irs.gov/. Publication 559 outlines the duties of a personal representative with respect to filing tax returns and paying taxes.

See http://www.irs.gov/publications/p559/ar02.html#en_US_publink 100099488.

Two forms are generally required to be filed with the IRS, whether the estate is small or large. The first form that must be filed is Form 56, *Notice Concerning Fiduciary Relationship*. Next, the personal representative must apply for an Employer Identification Number (EIN) for the estate using Form SS-4, *Application for an Employer Identification Number*. This application can now be completed online at https://sa2.www4.irs.gov/modiein/individual/index.jsp

Notification of Decedent's Death to IRS

It is important for the personal representative to notify the IRS that the decedent has died. This is accomplished with a simple, one-page document known as Form 56, *Notice Concerning Fiduciary Relationship*. This form identifies the decedent and the personal representative and directs which notices should be sent to the personal representative's address. Form 56 saves time by ensuring that notices and communications regarding the decedent are sent directly to the personal representative instead of the decedent's old address. This not only saves time, but also helps to prevent the possibility that taxes are not paid on time and penalty and interest incurred.

Figure 15.1 displays Form 56, *Notice Concerning Fiduciary Relationship*.

Figure 15.1

Form **56**
(Rev. December 2011)
Department of the Treasury
Internal Revenue Service

Notice Concerning Fiduciary Relationship

(Internal Revenue Code sections 6036 and 6903)

OMB No. 1545-0013

Part I   Identification

Name of person for whom you are acting (as shown on the tax return) | Identifying number | **Decedent's social security no.**

Address of person for whom you are acting (number, street, and room or suite no.)

City or town, state, and ZIP code (If a foreign address, see instructions.)

Fiduciary's name

Address of fiduciary (number, street, and room or suite no.)

City or town, state, and ZIP code | Telephone number (optional)   (   )

Section A. Authority

1   Authority for fiduciary relationship. Check applicable box:
 a ☐ Court appointment of testate estate (valid will exists)
 b ☐ Court appointment of intestate estate (no valid will exists)

Figure 15.1 (continued)

c ☐ Court appointment as guardian or conservator
d ☐ Valid trust instrument and amendments
e ☐ Bankruptcy or assignment for the benefit or creditors
f ☐ Other. Describe ▶ _____

2a If box 1a or 1b is checked, enter the date of death ▶ _____
2b If box 1c—1f is checked, enter the date of appointment, taking office, or assignment or transfer of assets ▶ _____

Section B. Nature of Liability and Tax Notices

3 Type of taxes (check all that apply): ☐ Income ☐ Gift ☐ Estate ☐ Generation-skipping transfer ☐ Employment
☐ Excise ☐ Other (describe) ▶ _____

4 Federal tax form number (check all that apply): **a**☐ 706 series **b**☐ 709 **c**☐ 940 **d**☐ 941, 943, 944
e☐ 1040, 1040-A, or 1040-EZ **f** ☐ 1041 **g**☐ 1120 **h**☐ Other (list) ▶ _____

5 If your authority as a fiduciary does not cover all years or tax periods, check here . . . . ▶ ☐
and list the specific years or periods ▶ _____

6 If the fiduciary listed wants a copy of notices or other written communications (see the instructions) check this box . . . . ▶ ☐
and enter the year(s) or period(s) for the corresponding line 4 item checked. If more than 1 form entered on line 4h, enter the
form number.

Complete only if the line 6 box is checked.

If this item is checked:	Enter year(s) or period(s)	If this item is checked:	Enter year(s) or period(s)
4a		4b	
4c		4d	
4e		4f	
4g		4h:	
4h:		4h:	

For Paperwork Reduction Act and Privacy Act Notice, see the separate instructions.   Cat. No. 16375I   Form **56** (Rev. 12-2011)

Part II **Court and Administrative Proceedings**

Name of court (if other than a court proceeding, identify the type of proceeding and name of agency)	Date proceeding initiated

Address of court | Docket number of proceeding

| City or town, state, and ZIP code | Date | Time | ☐ a.m. ☐ p.m. | Place of other proceedings |

Part III **Signature**

Please Sign Here

I certify that I have the authority to execute this notice concerning fiduciary relationship on behalf of the taxpayer.

▶ _____   _____   _____
Fiduciary's signature   Title, if applicable   Date

Form **56** (Rev. 12-2011)

Application for Tax Identification Number

The second important form for the personal representative to fill out is Form SS-4, *Application for an Employer Identification Number*. Form SS-4 is simply an application for a tax identification number for the estate. All taxpayers in the United States are identified not by name, but by identification number. Human beings are assigned social security numbers. Other entities, such as corporations and limited liability companies, as well as anyone who has employees, have employer identification numbers (EINs) instead.

Estates, being taxable entities, must also have identification numbers to be used on all forms and correspondence sent to the IRS. The EIN should be applied for immediately after the personal representative is appointed by the state court and obtains Letters Testamentary, as an EIN is necessary to open an estate bank account as well as to file tax returns. Obtaining an EIN is a simple and easy process and can be done by fax, by mail, or online.

Figure 15.2 is Form SS-4, *Application for an Employer Identification Number*.

Figure 15.2

Form **SS-4** (Rev. January 2010) Department of the Treasury Internal Revenue Service	**Application for Employer Identification Number** (For use by employers, corporations, partnerships, trusts, estates, churches, government agencies, Indian tribal entities, certain individuals, and others.) ▶ See separate instructions for each line. ▶ Keep a copy for your records.	OMB No. 1545-0003 EIN

Type or print clearly.

1 Legal name of entity (or individual) for whom the EIN is being requested

2 Trade name of business (if different from name on line 1)	**3** Executor, administrator, trustee, "care of" name
4a Mailing address (room, apt., suite no. and street, or P.O. box)	**5a** Street address (if different) (Do not enter a P.O. box.)
4b City, state, and ZIP code (if foreign, see instructions)	**5b** City, state, and ZIP code (if foreign, see instructions)

6 County and state where principal business is located

7a Name of responsible party	**7b** SSN, ITIN, or EIN

8a Is this application for a limited liability company (LLC) (or a foreign equivalent)? ☐ Yes ☐ No	**8b** If 8a is "Yes," enter the number of LLC members ▶

8c If 8a is "Yes," was the LLC organized in the United States? ☐ Yes ☐ No

9a **Type of entity** (check only one box). **Caution.** If 8a is "Yes," see the instructions for the correct box to check.

☐ Sole proprietor (SSN) _____
☐ Partnership
☐ Corporation (enter form number to be filed) ▶_____
☐ Personal service corporation
☐ Church or church-controlled organization
☐ Other nonprofit organization (specify) ▶_____
☐ Other (specify) ▶

☐ Estate (SSN of decedent) _____
☐ Plan administrator (TIN) _____
☐ Trust (TIN of grantor) _____
☐ National Guard   ☐ State/local government
☐ Farmers' cooperative ☐ Federal government/military
☐ REMIC   ☐ Indian tribal governments/enterprises
Group Exemption Number (GEN) if any ▶

9b If a corporation, name the state or foreign country (if applicable) where incorporated	State	Foreign country

10 **Reason for applying** (check only one box)

☐ Started new business (specify type) ▶ _____
_____
☐ Hired employees (Check the box and see line 13.)
☐ Compliance with IRS withholding regulations
☐ Other (specify) ▶

☐ Banking purpose (specify purpose) ▶_____
☐ Changed type of organization (specify new type) ▶_____
☐ Purchased going business
☐ Created a trust (specify type) ▶ _____
☐ Created a pension plan (specify type) ▶ _____

11 Date business started or acquired (month, day, year). See instructions.	**12** Closing month of accounting year
13 Highest number of employees expected in the next 12 months (enter -0- if none). If no employees expected, skip line 14. Agricultural / Household / Other	**14** If you expect your employment tax liability to be $1,000 or less in a full calendar year **and** want to file Form 944 annually instead of Forms 941 quarterly, check here. (Your employment tax liability generally will be $1,000 or less if you expect to pay $4,000 or less in total wages.) If you do not check this box, you must file Form 941 for every quarter. ☐

15 First date wages or annuities were paid (month, day, year). **Note.** If applicant is a withholding agent, enter date income will first be paid to nonresident alien (month, day, year) . . . . ▶

16 Check **one** box that best describes the principal activity of your business.
☐ Construction ☐ Rental & leasing ☐ Transportation & warehouse ☐ Health care & social assistance ☐ Wholesale-agent/broker
☐ Real estate ☐ Manufacturing ☐ Finance & insurance ☐ Accommodation & food service ☐ Wholesale-other ☐ Retail
☐ Other (specify)

17 Indicate principal line of merchandise sold, specific construction work done, products produced, or services provided.

Figure 15.2 (continued)

18 Has the applicant entity shown on line 1 ever applied for and received an EIN? ☐ **Yes** ☐ **No**

If "Yes," write previous EIN here ▶

Third Party Designee	Complete this section **only** if you want to authorize the named individual to receive the entity's EIN and answer questions about the completion of this form.	
	Designee's name	Designee's telephone number (include area code) ( )
	Address and ZIP code	Designee's fax number (include area code) ( )

Under penalties of perjury, I declare that I have examined this application, and to the best of my knowledge and belief, it is true, correct, and complete.

Name and title (type or print clearly) ▶ | Applicant's telephone number (include area code) ( )

Signature ▶ | Date ▶ | Applicant's fax number (include area code) ( )

For Privacy Act and Paperwork Reduction Act Notice, see separate instructions. Cat. No. 16055N Form **SS-4** (Rev. 1-2010)

Do I Need an EIN?

File Form SS-4 if the applicant entity does not already have an EIN but is required to show an EIN on any return, statement, or other document.[1] See also the separate instructions for each line on Form SS-4.

IF the applicant...	AND...	THEN...
Started a new business	Does not currently have (nor expect to have) employees	Complete lines 1, 2, 4a–8a, 8b–c (if applicable), 9a, 9b (if applicable), and 10–14 and 16–18.
Hired (or will hire) employees, including household employees	Does not already have an EIN	Complete lines 1, 2, 4a–6, 7a–b (if applicable), 8a, 8b–c (if applicable), 9a, 9b (if applicable), 10–18.
Opened a bank account	Needs an EIN for banking purposes only	Complete lines 1–5b, 7a–b (if applicable), 8a, 8b–c (if applicable), 9a, 9b (if applicable), 10, and 18.
Changed type of organization	Either the legal character of the organization or its ownership changed (for example, you incorporate a sole proprietorship or form a partnership)[2]	Complete lines 1–18 (as applicable).
Purchased a going business[3]	Does not already have an EIN	Complete lines 1–18 (as applicable).
Created a trust	The trust is other than a grantor trust or an IRA trust[4]	Complete lines 1–18 (as applicable).
Created a pension plan as a plan administrator[5]	Needs an EIN for reporting purposes	Complete lines 1, 3, 4a–5b, 9a, 10, and 18.
Is a foreign person needing an EIN to comply with IRS withholding regulations	Needs an EIN to complete a Form W-8 (other than Form W-8ECI), avoid withholding on portfolio assets, or claim tax treaty benefits[6]	Complete lines 1–5b, 7a–b (SSN or ITIN optional), 8a, 8b–c (if applicable), 9a, 9b (if applicable), 10, and 18.
Is administering an estate	Needs an EIN to report estate income on Form 1041	Complete lines 1–6, 9a, 10–12, 13–17 (if applicable), and 18.
Is a withholding agent for taxes on non-wage income paid to an alien (i.e., individual, corporation, or partnership, etc.)	Is an agent, broker, fiduciary, manager, tenant, or spouse who is required to file Form 1042, Annual Withholding Tax Return for U.S. Source Income of Foreign Persons	Complete lines 1, 2, 3 (if applicable), 4a–5b, 7a–b (if applicable), 8a, 8b–c (if applicable), 9a, 9b (if applicable), 10, and 18.
Is a state or local agency	Serves as a tax reporting agent for public assistance recipients under Rev. Proc. 80-4, 1980-1 C.B. 581[7]	Complete lines 1, 2, 4a–5b, 9a, 10, and 18.
Is a single-member LLC	Needs an EIN to file Form 8832, Classification Election, for filing employment tax returns and excise tax returns, or for state reporting purposes[8]	Complete lines 1–18 (as applicable).
Is an S corporation	Needs an EIN to file Form 2553, Election by a Small Business Corporation[9]	Complete lines 1–18 (as applicable).

[1] For example, a sole proprietorship or self-employed farmer who establishes a qualified retirement plan, or is required to file excise, employment, alcohol, tobacco, or firearms returns, must have an EIN. A partnership, corporation, REMIC (real estate mortgage investment conduit), nonprofit organization (church, club, etc.), or farmers' cooperative must use an EIN for any tax-related purpose even if the entity does not have employees.

[2] However, do not apply for a new EIN if the existing entity only (a) changed its business name, (b) elected on Form 8832 to change the way it is taxed (or is covered by the default rules), or (c) terminated its partnership status because at least 50% of the total interests in partnership capital and profits were sold or exchanged within a 12-month period. The EIN of the terminated partnership should continue to be used. See Regulations section 301.6109-1(d)(2)(iii).

[3] Do not use the EIN of the prior business unless you became the "owner" of a corporation by acquiring its stock.

[4] However, grantor trusts that do not file using Optional Method 1 and IRA trusts that are required to file Form 990-T, Exempt Organization Business Income Tax Return, must have an EIN. For more information on grantor trusts, see the Instructions for Form 1041.

[5] A plan administrator is the person or group of persons specified as the administrator by the instrument under which the plan is operated.

[6] Entities applying to be a Qualified Intermediary (QI) need a QI-EIN even if they already have an EIN. See Rev. Proc. 2000-12.

[7] See also *Household employer* on page 4 of the instructions. **Note.** State or local agencies may need an EIN for other reasons, for example, hired employees.

[8] See *Disregarded entities* on page 4 of the instructions for details on completing Form SS-4 for an LLC.

[9] An existing corporation that is electing or revoking S corporation status should use its previously-assigned EIN.

Hire an Accountant

Most attorneys do not assist in the preparation of income or estate tax returns. Instead, many probate attorneys have a close working relationship with an accountant or accounting firm that handles all the firm's tax matters.

It is highly advisable (and may be absolutely necessary) for the personal representative to seek the assistance of a certified public accountant (CPA) to assist with the preparation of all of the necessary tax returns. If a personal representative fails to file the proper forms in a timely manner, he or she will be held personally liable for any interest and penalties assessed by the Internal Revenue Service. Likewise, if a personal representative distributes the decedent's estate to the beneficiaries before any taxes due are paid, he or she will be held personally liable for the unpaid taxes.

Depending on the size of the estate, the income of the decedent prior to death, and the current tax law, an executor may have to file some or all of the following returns:

✓ Federal individual income tax return
✓ State individual income tax return
✓ Federal estate (and generation-skipping transfer) tax return
✓ State estate tax return
✓ State inheritance tax return
✓ Federal fiduciary income tax return
✓ State fiduciary income tax return
✓ Federal gift (and generation-skipping transfer) tax return
✓ State gift tax return

Tax law is constantly in a state of change. Therefore, this chapter seeks only to outline some of the most basic principles involving decedent's tax concerns.

■ THE DECEDENT'S FINAL FEDERAL INCOME TAX RETURNS

Form 1040, U.S. Individual Income Tax Return

It is the duty of the executor to file the decedent's final federal income tax returns on or before the fifteenth day of the fourth month of the calendar year following the year in which the decedent passed away. In addition, it is the duty of the personal representative to file any returns not filed for previous years.

Figure 15.3 displays Form 1040, *U.S. Individual Tax Return*.

If the decedent is owed a refund, it will also be necessary for the representative to file Form 1310, *Statement of Person Claiming Refund Due a Deceased Taxpayer*, with the tax return.

Figure 15.4, shows Form 1310, *Statement of Person Claiming Refund Due a Deceased Taxpayer*.

To learn more about additional forms and requirements, visit the IRS website or consult with your tax advisor.

Figure 15.3

Form 1040 Department of the Treasury—Internal Revenue Service (99)

U.S. Individual Income Tax Return **20**12 OMB No. 1545-0074 | IRS Use Only—Do not write or staple in this space.

For the year Jan. 1–Dec. 31, 2012, or other tax year beginning , 2012, ending , 20 | **See separate instructions.**

Your first name and initial | Last name | **Your social security number**

If a joint return, spouse's first name and initial | Last name | **Spouse's social security number**

Home address (number and street). If you have a P.O. box, see instructions. | Apt. no. | ▲ **Make sure the SSN(s) above and on line 6c are correct.**

City, town or post office, state, and ZIP code. If you have a foreign address, also complete spaces below (see instructions).

Presidential Election Campaign
Check here if you, or your spouse if filing jointly, want $3 to go to this fund. Checking a box below will not change your tax or refund. □ You □ Spouse

Foreign country name | Foreign province/state/county | Foreign postal code

Filing Status

Check only one box.

1 □ Single
2 □ Married filing jointly (even if only one had income)
3 □ Married filing separately. Enter spouse's SSN above and full name here. ▶
4 □ Head of household (with qualifying person). (See instructions.) If the qualifying person is a child but not your dependent, enter this child's name here. ▶
5 □ Qualifying widow(er) with dependent child

Exemptions

6a □ **Yourself.** If someone can claim you as a dependent, **do not** check box 6a . . . . .
b □ **Spouse** . . . .

Boxes checked on 6a and 6b
No. of children on 6c who:
• lived with you
• did not live with you due to divorce or separation (see instructions)
Dependents on 6c not entered above

c **Dependents:**

(1) First name Last name	(2) Dependent's social security number	(3) Dependent's relationship to you	(4) ✓ If child under age 17 qualifying for child tax credit (see instructions)
			□
			□
			□
			□

If more than four dependents, see instructions and check here ▶ □

d Total number of exemptions claimed . . . .

Add numbers on lines above ▶

Income

Attach Form(s) W-2 here. Also attach Forms W-2G and 1099-R if tax was withheld.

If you did not get a W-2, see instructions.

Enclose, but do not attach, any payment. Also, please use Form 1040-V.

7 Wages, salaries, tips, etc. Attach Form(s) W-2 . . . . | 7
8a **Taxable** interest. Attach Schedule B if required . . . . | 8a
b **Tax-exempt** interest. **Do not** include on line 8a . . . | 8b
9a Ordinary dividends. Attach Schedule B if required . . . . | 9a
b Qualified dividends . . . . | 9b
10 Taxable refunds, credits, or offsets of state and local income taxes . . . . . | 10
11 Alimony received . . . . | 11
12 Business income or (loss). Attach Schedule C or C-EZ . . . . | 12
13 Capital gain or (loss). Attach Schedule D if required. If not required, check here ▶ □ | 13
14 Other gains or (losses). Attach Form 4797 . . . . | 14
15a IRA distributions . | 15a | b Taxable amount . . | 15b
16a Pensions and annuities | 16a | b Taxable amount . . | 16b
17 Rental real estate, royalties, partnerships, S corporations, trusts, etc. Attach Schedule E | 17
18 Farm income or (loss). Attach Schedule F . . . . | 18
19 Unemployment compensation . . . . | 19
20a Social security benefits | 20a | b Taxable amount . . | 20b
21 Other income. List type and amount | 21
22 Combine the amounts in the far right column for lines 7 through 21. This is your **total income** ▶ | 22

Adjusted Gross Income

23 Educator expenses . . . . | 23
24 Certain business expenses of reservists, performing artists, and fee-basis government officials. Attach Form 2106 or 2106-EZ | 24
25 Health savings account deduction. Attach Form 8889 . | 25
26 Moving expenses. Attach Form 3903 . . . . . | 26
27 Deductible part of self-employment tax. Attach Schedule SE . | 27
28 Self-employed SEP, SIMPLE, and qualified plans . | 28
29 Self-employed health insurance deduction . . | 29
30 Penalty on early withdrawal of savings . . . . | 30
31a Alimony paid **b** Recipient's SSN ▶ | 31a
32 IRA deduction . . . . | 32
33 Student loan interest deduction . . . . . | 33
34 Tuition and fees. Attach Form 8917 . . . . . | 34
35 Domestic production activities deduction. Attach Form 8903 | 35
36 Add lines 23 through 35 . . . . | 36
37 Subtract line 36 from line 22. This is your **adjusted gross income** . . . . . ▶ | 37

For Disclosure, Privacy Act, and Paperwork Reduction Act Notice, see separate instructions. | Cat. No. 11320B | Form **1040** (2012)

(continued)

Figure 15.3 (continued)

Tax and Credits

Standard Deduction for—

- People who check any box on line 39a or 39b **or** who can be claimed as a dependent, see instructions.
- All others:

Single or Married filing separately, $5,950

Married filing jointly or Qualifying widow(er), $11,900

Head of household, $8,700

38	Amount from line 37 (adjusted gross income)		38
39a	Check if: ☐ **You** were born before January 2, 1948, ☐ Blind. **Total boxes** ☐ **Spouse** was born before January 2, 1948, ☐ Blind. checked ► 39a		
b	If your spouse itemizes on a separate return or you were a dual-status alien, check here► 39b ☐		
40	**Itemized deductions** (from Schedule A) or your **standard deduction** (see left margin)		40
41	Subtract line 40 from line 38		41
42	**Exemptions.** Multiply $3,800 by the number on line 6d		42
43	**Taxable income.** Subtract line 42 from line 41. If line 42 is more than line 41, enter -0-		43
44	**Tax** (see instructions). Check if any from: **a** ☐ Form(s) 8814 **b** ☐ Form 4972 **c** ☐ 962 election		44
45	**Alternative minimum tax** (see instructions). Attach Form 6251		45
46	Add lines 44 and 45 ►		46
47	Foreign tax credit. Attach Form 1116 if required	47	
48	Credit for child and dependent care expenses. Attach Form 2441	48	
49	Education credits from Form 8863, line 19	49	
50	Retirement savings contributions credit. Attach Form 8880	50	
51	Child tax credit. Attach Schedule 8812, if required	51	
52	Residential energy credits. Attach Form 5695	52	
53	Other credits from Form: **a** ☐ 3800 **b** ☐ 8801 **c** ☐	53	
54	Add lines 47 through 53. These are your **total credits**		54
55	Subtract line 54 from line 46. If line 54 is more than line 46, enter -0- ►		55

Other Taxes

56	Self-employment tax. Attach Schedule SE		56
57	Unreported social security and Medicare tax from Form: **a** ☐ 4137 **b** ☐ 8919		57
58	Additional tax on IRAs, other qualified retirement plans, etc. Attach Form 5329 if required		58
59a	Household employment taxes from Schedule H		59a
b	First-time homebuyer credit repayment. Attach Form 5405 if required		59b
60	Other taxes. Enter code(s) from instructions		60
61	Add lines 55 through 60. This is your **total tax** ►		61

Payments

If you have a qualifying child, attach Schedule EIC.

62	Federal income tax withheld from Forms W-2 and 1099	62	
63	2012 estimated tax payments and amount applied from 2011 return	63	
64a	**Earned income credit (EIC)**	64a	
b	Nontaxable combat pay election	64b	
65	Additional child tax credit. Attach Schedule 8812	65	
66	American opportunity credit from Form 8863, line 8	66	
67	Reserved	67	
68	Amount paid with request for extension to file	68	
69	Excess social security and tier 1 RRTA tax withheld	69	
70	Credit for federal tax on fuels. Attach Form 4136	70	
71	Credits from Form: **a** ☐ 2439 **b** ☐ Reserved **c** ☐ 8801 **d** ☐ 8885	71	
72	Add lines 62, 63, 64a, and 65 through 71. These are your **total payments** ►		72

Refund

Direct deposit? See instructions.

73	If line 72 is more than line 61, subtract line 61 from line 72. This is the amount you **overpaid**		73
74a	Amount of line 73 you want **refunded to you.** If Form 8888 is attached, check here ► ☐		74a
► b	Routing number _____ ► c Type: ☐ Checking ☐ Savings		
► d	Account number _____		
75	Amount of line 73 you want **applied to your 2013 estimated tax** ► 75		

Amount You Owe

76	**Amount you owe.** Subtract line 72 from line 61. For details on how to pay, see instructions ►		76
77	Estimated tax penalty (see instructions)	77	

Third Party Designee

Do you want to allow another person to discuss this return with the IRS (see instructions)? ☐ **Yes.** Complete below. ☐ **No**

Designee's name ►

Phone no. ►

Personal identification number (PIN) ►

Sign Here

Under penalties of perjury, I declare that I have examined this return and accompanying schedules and statements, and to the best of my knowledge and belief, they are true, correct, and complete. Declaration of preparer (other than taxpayer) is based on all information of which preparer has any knowledge.

Joint return? See instructions. Keep a copy for your records.

Your signature | Date | Your occupation | Daytime phone number

Spouse's signature. If a joint return, **both** must sign. | Date | Spouse's occupation | If the IRS sent you an Identity Protection PIN, enter it here (see inst.)

Paid Preparer Use Only

Print/Type preparer's name | Preparer's signature | Date | Check ☐ if self-employed | PTIN

Firm's name ►

Firm's address ►

Firm's EIN ►

Phone no.

Form **1040** (2012)

Figure 15.4

Form 1310
(Rev. November 2005)
Department of the Treasury
Internal Revenue Service

**Statement of Person Claiming
Refund Due a Deceased Taxpayer**

▶ **See instructions below and on back.**

OMB No. 1545-0074

Attachment
Sequence No. **87**

Tax year decedent was due a refund:

Calendar year _____ , or other tax year beginning _____ , 20____ , and ending _____ , 20____

Please print or type	Name of decedent	Date of death / /	Decedent's social security number
	Name of person claiming refund		Your social security number
	Home address (number and street). If you have a P.O. box, see instructions.		Apt. no.
	City, town or post office, state, and ZIP code. If you have a foreign address, see instructions.		

Part I **Check the box that applies to you.** Check only one box. **Be sure to complete Part III below.**

A ☐ Surviving spouse requesting reissuance of a refund check (see instructions).

B ☐ Court-appointed or certified personal representative (defined below). Attach a court certificate showing your appointment, unless previously filed (see instructions).

C ☐ Person, **other** than A or B, claiming refund for the decedent's estate (see instructions). Also, complete Part II.

Part II **Complete this part only if you checked the box on line C above.**

	Yes	No
1 Did the decedent leave a will?		
2a Has a court appointed a personal representative for the estate of the decedent?		
b If you answered **"No"** to 2a, will one be appointed?		
If you answered **"Yes"** to 2a or 2b, the personal representative must file for the refund.		
3 As the person claiming the refund for the decedent's estate, will you pay out the refund according to the laws of the state where the decedent was a legal resident?		

If you answered **"No"** to 3, a refund cannot be made until you submit a court certificate showing your appointment as personal representative or other evidence that you are entitled under state law to receive the refund.

Part III **Signature and verification. All filers must complete this part.**

I request a refund of taxes overpaid by or on behalf of the decedent. Under penalties of perjury, I declare that I have examined this claim, and to the best of my knowledge and belief, it is true, correct, and complete.

Signature of person claiming refund ▶ _____ Date ▶ _____

General Instructions

Purpose of Form

Use Form 1310 to claim a refund on behalf of a deceased taxpayer.

Who Must File

If you are claiming a refund on behalf of a deceased taxpayer, you must file Form 1310 unless either of the following applies:

● You are a surviving spouse filing an original or amended joint return with the decedent, or

● You are a personal representative (defined on this page) filing an original Form 1040, Form 1040A, Form 1040EZ, or Form 1040NR for the decedent and a court certificate showing your appointment is attached to the return.

Example. Assume Mr. Green died on January 4 before filing his tax return. On April 3 of the same year, you were appointed by the court as the personal representative for Mr. Green's estate and you file Form 1040 for Mr. Green. You do not need to file Form 1310 to claim the refund on Mr. Green's

tax return. However, you must attach to his return a copy of the court certificate showing your appointment.

Where To File

If you checked the box on line A, you can return the joint-name check with Form 1310 to your local IRS office or the Internal Revenue Service Center where you filed your return. If you checked the box on line B or line C, then:

● Follow the instructions for the form to which you are attaching Form 1310, or

● Send it to the same Internal Revenue Service Center where the original return was filed if you are filing Form 1310 separately. If the original return was filed electronically, mail Form 1310 to the Internal Revenue Service Center designated for the address shown on Form 1310 above. See the instructions for the original return for the address.

Personal Representative

For purposes of this form, a personal representative is the executor or administrator of the decedent's estate, as appointed or certified by the court. A copy of the decedent's

For Privacy Act and Paperwork Reduction Act Notice, see page 2.   Cat. No. 11566B   Form **1310** (Rev. 11-2005)

(continued)

Figure 15.4 (continued)

will cannot be accepted as evidence that you are the personal representative.

Additional Information

For more details, see *Death of a Taxpayer* in the index to the Form 1040, Form 1040A, or Form 1040EZ instructions, or get Pub. 559, Survivors, Executors, and Administrators.

Specific Instructions

P.O. Box

Enter your box number only if your post office does not deliver mail to your home.

Foreign Address

If your address is outside the United States or its possessions or territories, enter the information in the following order: City, province or state, and country. Follow the country's practice for entering the postal code. Do not abbreviate the country name.

Line A

Check the box on line A if you received a refund check in your name and your deceased spouse's name. You can return the joint-name check with Form 1310 to your local IRS office or the Internal Revenue Service Center where you filed your return. A new check will be issued in your name and mailed to you.

Line B

Check the box on line B only if you are the decedent's court-appointed personal representative claiming a refund for the decedent on Form 1040X, Amended U.S. Individual Income Tax Return, or Form 843, Claim for Refund and Request for Abatement. You must attach a copy of the court certificate showing your appointment. But if you have already sent the court certificate to the IRS, complete Form 1310 and write "Certificate Previously Filed" at the bottom of the form.

Line C

Check the box on line C if you are not a surviving spouse claiming a refund based on a joint return and there is no court-appointed personal representative. You must also complete Part II. If you check the box on line C, you must have proof of death.

The proof of death is a copy of either of the following:
- The death certificate, or
- The formal notification from the appropriate government office (for example, Department of Defense) informing the next of kin of the decedent's death.

Do not attach the death certificate or other proof of death to Form 1310. Instead, keep it for your records and provide it if requested.

Example. Your father died on August 25. You are his sole survivor. Your father did not have a will and the court did not appoint a personal representative for his estate. Your father is entitled to a $300 refund. To get the refund, you must complete and attach Form 1310 to your father's final return. You should check the box on Form 1310, line C, answer all the questions in Part II, and sign your name in Part III. You must also keep a copy of the death certificate or other proof of death for your records.

Lines 1–3

If you checked the box on line C, you must complete lines 1 through 3.

Privacy Act and Paperwork Reduction Act Notice

We ask for the information on this form to carry out the Internal Revenue laws of the United States. This information will be used to determine your eligibility pursuant to Internal Revenue Code section 6012 to claim the refund due the decedent. Code section 6109 requires you to provide your social security number and that of the decedent. You are not required to claim the refund due the decedent, but if you do so, you must provide the information requested on this form. Failure to provide this information may delay or prevent processing of your claim. Providing false or fraudulent information may subject you to penalties. Routine uses of this information include providing it to the Department of Justice for use in civil and criminal litigation, to the Social Security Administration for the administration of Social Security programs, and to cities, states, and the District of Columbia for the administration of their tax laws. We may also disclose this information to other countries under a tax treaty, to federal and state agencies to enforce federal nontax criminal laws, or to federal law enforcement and intelligence agencies to combat terrorism.

You are not required to provide the information requested on a form unless the form displays a valid OMB control number. Books or records relating to a form or its instructions must be retained as long as their contents may become material in the administration of any Internal Revenue law. Generally, tax returns and return information are confidential, as required by Code section 6103.

The average time and expenses required to complete and file this form will vary depending on individual circumstances. For the estimated averages, see the instructions for your income tax return.

If you have suggestions for making this form simpler, we would be happy to hear from you. See the instructions for your income tax return.

■ DECEDENT'S FINAL STATE INCOME TAX RETURN

The personal representative must also file the decedent's final state income tax return on or before April 15th of the calendar year following the decedent's death. The authority for this requirement can be found in state statutory law. Excluded from this requirement are those states that do not have a state income tax. States that currently do not have state income tax are Alaska, Florida, Nevada, New Hampshire, South Dakota, Texas, Tennessee, Washington, and Wyoming.

See http://www.irs.gov/uac/States-Without-a-State-Income-Tax.

■ FEDERAL ESTATE TAX RETURN

U.S. Treasury Form 706, U.S. Estate (and Generation-Skipping Transfer) Tax Return

According to the Internal Revenue Service, **estate tax** is a tax on your right to transfer property at your death. It requires an accounting of everything a decedent owns or has certain interests in on the date of death.

A federal estate tax return (Form 706) must be filed within nine months of the decedent's death for every United States citizen whose gross estate exceeds the applicable exclusion amount. If it will be difficult or impossible to file Form 706 with the nine-month time limit, Form 4768, *Application for Extension of Time to File U.S. Estate Tax Return*, should be filed as soon as possible since the IRS must rule on the extension before Form 706 is due.

The **applicable exclusion amount** is the maximum value of property that can be transferred to others without incurring any estate tax or federal gift tax because of the applicable credit amount. The **applicable credit amount** is a credit against the federal unified transfer tax on gifts (prior to death) and estates (after death). This law is in a state of flux, so be sure to consult with your tax advisor regarding the applicable exclusion amount.

Federal estate tax is imposed by Internal Revenue Code §2001, which is displayed in Figure 15.5.

Estate Tax
A tax on the right to transfer property at death; based on an accounting of everything one owns or has certain interests in as of the date of death.

Applicable Exclusion Amount
The maximum value of property that can be transferred to others without incurring any estate tax or federal gift tax because of the applicable credit amount.

Applicable Credit Amount
A credit against the federal unified transfer tax on gifts (prior to death) and estates (after death).

Figure 15.5

26 USC §2001. Imposition and rate of tax

(a) Imposition
A tax is hereby imposed on the transfer of the taxable estate of every decedent who is a citizen or resident of the United States.

(b) Computation of tax
The tax imposed by this section shall be the amount equal to the excess (if any) of—

(1) a tentative tax computed under subsection (c) on the sum of—

    (A) the amount of the taxable estate, and
    (B) the amount of the adjusted taxable gifts, over

(2) the aggregate amount of tax which would have been payable under chapter 12 with respect to gifts made by the decedent after December 31, 1976, if the modifications described in subsection (g) had been applicable at the time of such gifts.
For purposes of paragraph (1)(B), the term "adjusted taxable gifts" means the total amount of the taxable gifts (within the meaning of section 2503) made by the decedent after December 31, 1976, other than gifts which are includible in the gross estate of the decedent.

(C) Rate schedule

If the amount with respect to which the tentative tax to be computed is:	The tentative tax is:
Not over $10,000	18 percent of such amount.
Over $10,000 but not over $20,000	$1,800, plus 20 percent of the excess of such amount over $10,000.
Over $20,000 but not over $40,000	$3,800, plus 22 percent of the excess of such amount over $20,000.
Over $40,000 but not over $60,000	$8,200 plus 24 percent of the excess of such amount over $40,000.
Over $60,000 but not over $80,000	$13,000, plus 26 percent of the excess of such amount over $60,000.

(continued)

Figure 15.5 (continued)

Over $80,000 but not over $100,000	$18,200, plus 28 percent of the excess of such amount over $80,000.
Over $100,000 but not over $150,000	$23,800, plus 30 percent of the excess of such amount over $100,000.
Over $150,000 but not over $250,000	$38,800, plus 32 percent of the excess of such amount over $150,000.
Over $250,000 but not over $500,000	$70,800, plus 34 percent of the excess of such amount over $250,000.
Over $500,000	$155,800, plus 35 percent of the excess of such amount over $500,000.

(d) Adjustment for gift tax paid by spouse
For purposes of subsection (b)(2), if—

(1) the decedent was the donor of any gift one-half of which was considered under section 2513 as made by the decedent's spouse, and

(2) the amount of such gift is includible in the gross estate of the decedent, any tax payable by the spouse under chapter 12 on such gift (as determined under section 2012(d)) shall be treated as a tax payable with respect to a gift made by the decedent.

(e) Coordination of sections 2513 and 2035
If—

(1) the decedent's spouse was the donor of any gift one-half of which was considered under section 2513 as made by the decedent, and

(2) the amount of such gift is includible in the gross estate of the decedent's spouse by reason of section 2035, such gift shall not be included in the adjusted taxable gifts of the decedent for purposes of subsection (b)(1)(B), and the aggregate amount determined under subsection (b)(2) shall be reduced by the amount (if any) determined under subsection (d) which was treated as a tax payable by the decedent's spouse with respect to such gift.

(f) Valuation of gifts

(1) In general
If the time has expired under section 6501 within which a tax may be assessed under chapter 12 (or under corresponding provisions of prior laws) on—

(A) the transfer of property by gift made during a preceding calendar period (as defined in section 2502(b)); or

(B) an increase in taxable gifts required under section 2701(d), the value thereof shall, for purposes of computing the tax under this chapter, be the value as finally determined for purposes of chapter 12.

(2) Final determination
For purposes of paragraph (1), a value shall be treated as finally determined for purposes of chapter 12 if—

(A) the value is shown on a return under such chapter and such value is not contested by the Secretary before the expiration of the time referred to in paragraph (1) with respect to such return;

(B) in a case not described in subparagraph (A), the value is specified by the Secretary and such value is not timely contested by the taxpayer; or

(C) the value is determined by a court or pursuant to a settlement agreement with the Secretary.
        For purposes of subparagraph (A), the value of an item shall be treated as shown on a return if the item is disclosed in the return, or in a statement attached to the return, in a manner adequate to apprise the Secretary of the nature of such item.

(g) Modifications to gift tax payable to reflect different tax rates
For purposes of applying subsection (b)(2) with respect to 1 or more gifts, the rates of tax under subsection (c) in effect at the decedent's death shall, in lieu of the rates of tax in effect at the time of such gifts, be used both to compute—

(1) the tax imposed by chapter 12 with respect to such gifts, and

(2) the credit allowed against such tax under section 2505, including in computing—

(A) the applicable credit amount under section 2505(a)(1), and

(B) the sum of the amounts allowed as a credit for all preceding periods under section 2505(a)(2).

As you can tell from reading IRC §2001, the year in which a decedent dies has a tremendous impact on the amount of federal estate tax that is owed. It may be free to die in one year and very expensive to die in another year, depending on the size of one's gross estate.

IRC §2031(a) defines *gross estate* as follows: "The value of the **gross estate** of the decedent shall be determined by including to the extent provided for in this part, the value at the time of his death of all property, real or personal, tangible or intangible, wherever situated." Figure 15.6 is a table containing the applicable exclusion amount schedule for estate transfers by year.

Gross Estate
The value at the time of a decedent's death of all of the decedent's property, real or personal, tangible or intangible, wherever situated.

Figure 15.6

Year	Exclusion Amount	Max/Top Tax Rate
2001	$675,000	55%
2002	$1 million	50%
2003	$1 million	49%
2004	$1.5 million	48%
2005	$1.5 million	47%
2006	$2 million	46%
2007	$2 million	45%
2008	$2 million	45%
2009	$3.5 million	45%
2010	Repealed	
2011	$5 million	35%
2012	$5.12 million	35%
2013	$5 million	40%

Figure 15.6 displays the amount of exemption an estate would expect depending on the year of death. Estates whose gross value exceeds these amounts would be subject to estate tax, but only for the amount above the exemption. Note that for 2013, the amount of the exemption was $5 million. On January 1, 2013, the *American Taxpayer Relief Act of 2012* was passed. It permanently establishes an exemption of $5 million per person with a maximum tax rate of 40% for the year 2013 and beyond. Therefore, the tax law is no longer in the state of flux that it was for several years prior to 2012, and tax planners and attorneys can now better assist their clients with estate planning based on the gross size of their client's estate. Since most decedents do not have $5 million at their death, the vast majority of estates do not actually pay an estate tax.

Figure 15.7 displays the first few pages of Form 706, United States Estate (and Generation-Skipping Transfer) Tax Return. Form 706 is a very long and complicated tax form consisting of over thirty pages.

Figure 15.7

Form 706 (Rev. August 2012)
Department of the Treasury
Internal Revenue Service

United States Estate (and Generation-Skipping Transfer) Tax Return

► Estate of a citizen or resident of the United States (see instructions). To be filed for decedents dying after December 31, 2011, and before January 1, 2013.
► Information about Form 706 and its separate instructions is at *www.irs.gov/form706.*

OMB No. 1545-0015

Part 1—Decedent and Executor

1a Decedent's first name and middle initial (and maiden name, if any)
1b Decedent's last name
2 Decedent's social security no.

3a County, state, and ZIP or foreign country and postal code, of legal residence (domicile) at time of death
3b Year domicile established
4 Date of birth
5 Date of death

6b Executor's address (number and street including apartment or suite no.; city, town, or post office; state; country; and ZIP or postal code) and phone no.

6a Name of executor (see instructions)

6c Executor's social security number (see instructions)

Phone no.

6d If there are multiple executors, check here ☐ and attach a list showing the names, addresses, telephone numbers, and SSNs of the additional executors.

7a Name and location of court where will was probated or estate administered
7b Case number

8 If decedent died testate, check here ► ☐ and attach a certified copy of the will. **9** If you extended the time to file this Form 706, check here ► ☐

10 If Schedule R-1 is attached, check here ► ☐ **11** If you are estimating the value of assets included in the gross estate on line 1 pursuant to the special rule of Reg. section 20.2010-2T(a) (7)(ii), check here ► ☐

Part 2—Tax Computation

1	Total gross estate less exclusion (from Part 5—Recapitulation, item 13)	**1**
2	Tentative total allowable deductions (from Part 5—Recapitulation, item 24)	**2**
3a	Tentative taxable estate (subtract line 2 from line 1)	**3a**
b	State death tax deduction	**3b**
c	Taxable estate (subtract line 3b from line 3a)	**3c**
4	Adjusted taxable gifts (see instructions)	**4**
5	Add lines 3c and 4	**5**
6	Tentative tax on the amount on line 5 from Table A in the instructions	**6**
7	Total gift tax paid or payable (see instructions)	**7**
8	Gross estate tax (subtract line 7 from line 6)	**8**
9a	Basic exclusion amount	**9a**
9b	Deceased spousal unused exclusion (DSUE) amount from predeceased spouse(s), if any (from Section D, Part 6—Portability of Deceased Spousal Unused Exclusion).	**9b**
9c	Applicable exclusion amount (add lines 9a and 9b)	**9c**
9d	Applicable credit amount (tentative tax on the amount in 9c from Table A in the instructions)	**9d**
10	Adjustment to applicable credit amount (May not exceed $6,000. See instructions.)	**10**
11	Allowable applicable credit amount (subtract line 10 from line 9d)	**11**
12	Subtract line 11 from line 8 (but do not enter less than zero)	**12**
13	Credit for foreign death taxes (from Schedule P). (Attach Form(s) 706-CE.)	**13**
14	Credit for tax on prior transfers (from Schedule Q)	**14**
15	Total credits (add lines 13 and 14)	**15**
16	Net estate tax (subtract line 15 from line 12)	**16**
17	Generation-skipping transfer (GST) taxes payable (from Schedule R, Part 2, line 10)	**17**
18	Total transfer taxes (add lines 16 and 17)	**18**
19	Prior payments (explain in an attached statement)	**19**
20	Balance due (or overpayment) (subtract line 19 from line 18)	**20**

Under penalties of perjury, I declare that I have examined this return, including accompanying schedules and statements, and to the best of my knowledge and belief, it is true, correct, and complete. Declaration of preparer other than the executor is based on all information of which preparer has any knowledge.

Sign Here

Signature of executor | Date

Signature of executor | Date

Paid Preparer Use Only

Print/Type preparer's name | Preparer's signature | Date | Check ☐ if self-employed | PTIN

Firm's name ►

Firm's address ► | Firm's EIN ►

Phone no.

For Privacy Act and Paperwork Reduction Act Notice, see instructions.

Cat. No. 20548R

Form **706** (Rev. 8-2012)

Figure 15.7 (continued)

Form 706 (Rev. 8-2012)

	Decedent's social security number

Estate of:

Part 3—Elections by the Executor

Note. For information on electing portability of the decedent's DSUE amount, including how to opt out of the election, see Part 6—Portability of Deceased Spousal Unused Exclusion.

Note. Some of the following elections may require the posting of bonds or liens.

	Please check "Yes" or "No" box for each question (see instructions).		Yes	No
1	Do you elect alternate valuation?	1		
2	Do you elect special-use valuation? If "Yes," you must complete and attach Schedule A-1	2		
3	Do you elect to pay the taxes in installments as described in section 6166? If "Yes," you must attach the additional information described in the instructions. **Note. By electing section 6166 installment payments, you may be required to provide security for estate tax deferred under section 6166 and interest in the form of a surety bond or a section 6324A lien.**	3		
4	Do you elect to postpone the part of the taxes due to a reversionary or remainder interest as described in section 6163?	4		

Part 4—General Information

Note. Please attach the necessary supplemental documents. **You must attach the death certificate.** (See instructions)

Authorization to receive confidential tax information under Reg. section 601.504(b)(2)(i); to act as the estate's representative before the IRS; and to make written or oral presentations on behalf of the estate:

Name of representative (print or type)	State	Address (number, street, and room or suite no., city, state, and ZIP code)

I declare that I am the ☐ attorney/ ☐ certified public accountant/ ☐ enrolled agent (check the applicable box) for the executor. I am not under suspension or disbarment from practice before the Internal Revenue Service and am qualified to practice in the state shown above.

Signature	CAF number	Date	Telephone number

1 Death certificate number and issuing authority (attach a copy of the death certificate to this return).

2 Decedent's business or occupation. If retired, check here ▶ ☐ and state decedent's former business or occupation.

3a Marital status of the decedent at time of death:

☐ Married ☐ Widow/widower ☐ Single ☐ Legally separated ☐ Divorced

3b For all prior marriages, list the name and SSN of the former spouse, the date the marriage ended, and whether the marriage ended by annulment, divorce, or death. Attach additional statements of the same size if necessary.

4a Surviving spouse's name	4b Social security number	4c Amount received (see instructions)

5 Individuals (other than the surviving spouse), trusts, or other estates who receive benefits from the estate (do not include charitable beneficiaries shown in Schedule O) (see instructions).

Name of individual, trust, or estate receiving $5,000 or more	Identifying number	Relationship to decedent	Amount (see instructions)

All unascertainable beneficiaries and those who receive less than $5,000 ▶

Total

	If you answer "Yes" to any of the following questions, you must attach additional information as described.	Yes	No
6	Is the estate filing a protective claim for refund? If "Yes," complete and attach two copies of Schedule PC for each claim.		
7	Does the gross estate contain any section 2044 property (qualified terminable interest property (QTIP) from a prior gift or estate)? (see instructions)		
8a	Have federal gift tax returns ever been filed? If "Yes," attach copies of the returns, if available, and furnish the following information:		
b	Period(s) covered	c Internal Revenue office(s) where filed	
9a	Was there any insurance on the decedent's life that is not included on the return as part of the gross estate?		
b	Did the decedent own any insurance on the life of another that is not included in the gross estate?		

(continued)

Figure 15.7 (continued)

Form 706 (Rev. 8-2012)

Estate of:	Decedent's social security number

Part 4—General Information *(continued)*

If you answer "Yes" to any of the following questions, you must attach additional information as described.	Yes	No
10 Did the decedent at the time of death own any property as a joint tenant with right of survivorship in which **(a)** one or more of the other joint tenants was someone other than the decedent's spouse, and **(b)** less than the full value of the property is included on the return as part of the gross estate? If "Yes," you must complete and attach Schedule E		
11a Did the decedent, at the time of death, own any interest in a partnership (for example, a family limited partnership), an unincorporated business, or a limited liability company; or own any stock in an inactive or closely held corporation?		
b If "Yes," was the value of **any** interest owned (from above) discounted on this estate tax return? If "Yes," see the instructions on reporting the total accumulated or effective discounts taken on Schedule F or G		
12 Did the decedent make any transfer described in sections 2035, 2036, 2037, or 2038? (see instructions) If "Yes," you must complete and attach Schedule G		
13a Were there in existence at the time of the decedent's death any trusts created by the decedent during his or her lifetime? . .		
b Were there in existence at the time of the decedent's death any trusts not created by the decedent under which the decedent possessed any power, beneficial interest, or trusteeship?		
c Was the decedent receiving income from a trust created after October 22, 1986, by a parent or grandparent? . . . . If "Yes," was there a GST taxable termination (under section 2612) on the death of the decedent?		
d If there was a GST taxable termination (under section 2612), attach a statement to explain. Provide a copy of the trust or will creating the trust, and give the name, address, and phone number of the current trustee(s).		
e Did the decedent at any time during his or her lifetime transfer or sell an interest in a partnership, limited liability company, or closely held corporation to a trust described in lines 13a or 13b? . . . . If "Yes," provide the EIN for this transferred/sold item. ▶		
14 Did the decedent ever possess, exercise, or release any general power of appointment? If "Yes," you must complete and attach Schedule H		
15 Did the decedent have an interest in or a signature or other authority over a financial account in a foreign country, such as a bank account, securities account, or other financial account?		
16 Was the decedent, immediately before death, receiving an annuity described in the "General" paragraph of the instructions for Schedule I or a private annuity? If "Yes," you must complete and attach Schedule I		
17 Was the decedent ever the beneficiary of a trust for which a deduction was claimed by the estate of a predeceased spouse under section 2056(b)(7) and which is not reported on this return? If "Yes," attach an explanation		

Part 5—Recapitulation.

Note. If estimating the value of one or more assets pursuant to the special rule of Reg. section 20.2010-2T(a)(7)(ii), enter on both lines 10 and 23 the amount noted in the instructions for the corresponding range of values. (See instructions for details.)

Item no.	Gross estate		Alternate value	Value at date of death
1	Schedule A—Real Estate	1		
2	Schedule B—Stocks and Bonds	2		
3	Schedule C—Mortgages, Notes, and Cash	3		
4	Schedule D—Insurance on the Decedent's Life (attach Form(s) 712)	4		
5	Schedule E—Jointly Owned Property (attach Form(s) 712 for life insurance) .	5		
6	Schedule F—Other Miscellaneous Property (attach Form(s) 712 for life insurance)	6		
7	Schedule G—Transfers During Decedent's Life (att. Form(s) 712 for life insurance)	7		
8	Schedule H—Powers of Appointment	8		
9	Schedule I—Annuities	9		
10	Estimated value of assets subject to the special rule of Reg. section 20.2010-2T(a)(7)(ii)	10		
11	Total gross estate (add items 1 through 10)	11		
12	Schedule U—Qualified Conservation Easement Exclusion	12		
13	Total gross estate less exclusion (subtract item 12 from item 11). Enter here and on line 1 of Part 2—Tax Computation	13		

Item no.	Deductions		Amount	
14	Schedule J—Funeral Expenses and Expenses Incurred in Administering Property Subject to Claims	14		
15	Schedule K—Debts of the Decedent	15		
16	Schedule K—Mortgages and Liens	16		
17	Total of items 14 through 16	17		
18	Allowable amount of deductions from item 17 (see the instructions for item 18 of the Recapitulation)	18		
19	Schedule L—Net Losses During Administration	19		
20	Schedule L—Expenses Incurred in Administering Property Not Subject to Claims	20		
21	Schedule M—Bequests, etc., to Surviving Spouse	21		
22	Schedule O—Charitable, Public, and Similar Gifts and Bequests	22		
23	Estimated value of deductible assets subject to the special rule of Reg. section 20.2010-2T(a)(7)(ii)	23		
24	Tentative total allowable deductions (add items 18 through 23). Enter here and on line 2 of the Tax Computation	24		

Figure 15.7 (continued)

Form 706 (Rev. 8-2012)

Decedent's social security number

Estate of:

Part 6—Portability of Deceased Spousal Unused Exclusion (DSUE)

Portability Election

A decedent with a surviving spouse elects portability of the deceased spousal unused exclusion (DSUE) amount, if any, by completing and timely-filing this return. No further action is required to elect portability of the DSUE amount to allow the surviving spouse to use the decedent's DSUE amount.

Section A. Opting Out of Portability

The estate of a decedent with a surviving spouse may opt out of electing portability of the DSUE amount. Check here and do not complete Sections B and C of Part 6 only if the estate opts **NOT** to elect portability of the DSUE amount. ☐

Section B. QDOT

	Yes	**No**
Are any assets of the estate being transferred to a qualified domestic trust (QDOT)?		

If "Yes," the DSUE amount portable to a surviving spouse (calculated in Section C, below) is preliminary and shall be redetermined at the time of the final distribution or other taxable event imposing estate tax under section 2056A. See instructions for more details.

Section C. DSUE Amount Portable to the Surviving Spouse (To be completed by the estate of a decedent making a portability election.)

Complete the following calculation to determine the DSUE amount that can be transferred to the surviving spouse.

1	Enter amount from line 9c, Part 2—Tax Computation	**1**	
2	Enter amount from line 7, Part 2—Tax Computation	**2**	
3	Divide amount on line 2 by 35% (0.35). (do not enter less than zero)	**3**	
4	Add lines 1 and 3	**4**	
5	Enter the amount from line 5, Part 2—Tax Computation	**5**	
6	Subtract line 5 from line 4 (do not enter less than zero)	**6**	
7	DSUE amount portable to the surviving spouse (Enter the lesser of line 6 or line 9a, Part 2—Tax Computation)	**7**	

Section D. DSUE Amount Received from Predeceased Spouse(s) (To be completed by the estate of a deceased surviving spouse with DSUE amount from predeceased spouse(s))

Provide the following information to determine the DSUE amount received from deceased spouses.

A Name of Deceased Spouse (dates of death after December 31, 2010, only)	B Date of Death (enter as mm/dd/yy)	C Portability Election Made?		D If "Yes," DSUE Amount Received from Spouse	E DSUE Amount Applied by Decedent to Lifetime Gifts	F Year of Form 709 Reporting Use of DSUE Amount Listed in col E	G Remaining DSUE Amount, if any (subtract col. E from col. D)
		Yes	No				
Part 1 — DSUE RECEIVED FROM LAST DECEASED SPOUSE							
Part 2 — DSUE RECEIVED FROM OTHER PREDECEASED SPOUSE(S) AND USED BY DECEDENT							

Total (for all DSUE amounts from predeceased spouse(s) applied) . . . . . .

Add the amount from Part 1, column D and the total from Part 2, column E. Enter the result on line 9b, Part 2—Tax Computation . . . . ▶ _____

■ FIDUCIARY TAX RETURNS

Form 1041, U.S. Income Tax Return for Estates and Trusts

In addition to filing the decedent's final tax returns, the personal representative must also file a federal fiduciary income tax return to report accrued income and any income earned after the decedent's death that was not included on the final individual return. *See* IRC §6012. However, this requirement currently applies when there is gross income for the taxable year of $600 or more, to some domestic trusts, and to estates that have a beneficiary who is a nonresident alien. *See* IRC §6012. Figure 15.8 is Form 1041, *U.S. Income Tax Return for Estates and Trusts.*

Figure 15.8

Form **1041**
Department of the Treasury—Internal Revenue Service
U.S. Income Tax Return for Estates and Trusts 2012
▶ Information about Form 1041 and its separate instructions is at *www.irs.gov/form1041.*
OMB No. 1545-0092

A Check all that apply:
☐ Decedent's estate
☐ Simple trust
☐ Complex trust
☐ Qualified disability trust
☐ ESBT (S portion only)
☐ Grantor type trust
☐ Bankruptcy estate-Ch. 7
☐ Bankruptcy estate-Ch. 11
☐ Pooled income fund

For calendar year 2012 or fiscal year beginning , 2012, and ending , 20

Name of estate or trust (If a grantor type trust, see the instructions.)

Name and title of fiduciary

Number, street, and room or suite no. (If a P.O. box, see the instructions.)

City or town, state, and ZIP code

C Employer identification number

D Date entity created

E Nonexempt charitable and split-interest trusts, check applicable box(es), see instructions.
☐ Described in sec. 4947(a)(1). Check here if not a private foundation . . . . ▶ ☐
☐ Described in sec. 4947(a)(2)

B Number of Schedules K-1 attached (see instructions) ▶

F Check applicable boxes:
☐ Initial return ☐ Final return ☐ Amended return ☐ Change in trust's name
☐ Change in fiduciary ☐ Change in fiduciary's name ☐ Change in fiduciary's address

G Check here if the estate or filing trust made a section 645 election . . . . . . ▶ ☐

Income	1	Interest income	1
	2a	Total ordinary dividends	2a
	b	Qualified dividends allocable to: **(1)** Beneficiaries _____ **(2)** Estate or trust _____	
	3	Business income or (loss). Attach Schedule C or C-EZ (Form 1040) . . .	3
	4	Capital gain or (loss). Attach Schedule D (Form 1041)	4
	5	Rents, royalties, partnerships, other estates and trusts, etc. Attach Schedule E (Form 1040)	5
	6	Farm income or (loss). Attach Schedule F (Form 1040)	6
	7	Ordinary gain or (loss). Attach Form 4797	7
	8	Other income. List type and amount _____	8
	9	**Total income.** Combine lines 1, 2a, and 3 through 8 . . . . . . ▶	9
Deductions	10	Interest. Check if Form 4952 is attached ▶ ☐	10
	11	Taxes	11
	12	Fiduciary fees	12
	13	Charitable deduction (from Schedule A, line 7)	13
	14	Attorney, accountant, and return preparer fees	14
	15a	Other deductions **not** subject to the 2% floor (attach schedule) . .	15a
	b	Allowable miscellaneous itemized deductions subject to the 2% floor . .	15b
	16	Add lines 10 through 15b . . . . ▶	16
	17	Adjusted total income or (loss). Subtract line 16 from line 9 . . . **17**	
	18	Income distribution deduction (from Schedule B, line 15). Attach Schedules K-1 (Form 1041)	18
	19	Estate tax deduction including certain generation-skipping taxes (attach computation) . . .	19
	20	Exemption	20
	21	Add lines 18 through 20 . . . . ▶	21
Tax and Payments	22	Taxable income. Subtract line 21 from line 17. If a loss, see instructions	22
	23	**Total tax** (from Schedule G, line 7)	23
	24	**Payments: a** 2012 estimated tax payments and amount applied from 2011 return	24a
	b	Estimated tax payments allocated to beneficiaries (from Form 1041-T)	24b
	c	Subtract line 24b from line 24a	24c
	d	Tax paid with Form 7004 (see instructions)	24d
	e	Federal income tax withheld. If any is from Form(s) 1099, check ▶ ☐ . .	24e
		Other payments: **f** Form 2439 _____ ; **g** Form 4136 _____ ; Total ▶	24h
	25	**Total payments.** Add lines 24c through 24e, and 24h . . . . . ▶	25
	26	Estimated tax penalty (see instructions)	26
	27	**Tax due.** If line 25 is smaller than the total of lines 23 and 26, enter amount owed . .	27
	28	**Overpayment.** If line 25 is larger than the total of lines 23 and 26, enter amount overpaid . .	28
	29	Amount of line 28 to be: **a Credited to 2013 estimated tax** ▶ _____ ; **b Refunded** ▶	29

Sign Here
Under penalties of perjury, I declare that I have examined this return, including accompanying schedules and statements, and to the best of my knowledge and belief, it is true, correct, and complete. Declaration of preparer (other than taxpayer) is based on all information of which preparer has any knowledge.

▶ _____ Signature of fiduciary or officer representing fiduciary Date ▶ _____ EIN of fiduciary if a financial institution

May the IRS discuss this return with the preparer shown below (see instr.)? ☐ Yes ☐ No

Paid Preparer Use Only

Print/Type preparer's name	Preparer's signature	Date	Check ☐ if self-employed	PTIN
Firm's name ▶			Firm's EIN ▶	
Firm's address ▶			Phone no.	

For Paperwork Reduction Act Notice, see the separate instructions. Cat. No. 11370H Form **1041** (2012)

Figure 15.8 (continued)

Schedule A	**Charitable Deduction.** Do not complete for a simple trust or a pooled income fund.	
1	Amounts paid or permanently set aside for charitable purposes from gross income (see instructions)	1
2	Tax-exempt income allocable to charitable contributions (see instructions)	2
3	Subtract line 2 from line 1	3
4	Capital gains for the tax year allocated to corpus and paid or permanently set aside for charitable purposes	4
5	Add lines 3 and 4	5
6	Section 1202 exclusion allocable to capital gains paid or permanently set aside for charitable purposes (see instructions)	6
7	**Charitable deduction.** Subtract line 6 from line 5. Enter here and on page 1, line 13	7

Schedule B	**Income Distribution Deduction**	
1	Adjusted total income (see instructions)	1
2	Adjusted tax-exempt interest	2
3	Total net gain from Schedule D (Form 1041), line 15, column (1) (see instructions)	3
4	Enter amount from Schedule A, line 4 (minus any allocable section 1202 exclusion)	4
5	Capital gains for the tax year included on Schedule A, line 1 (see instructions)	5
6	Enter any gain from page 1, line 4, as a negative number. If page 1, line 4, is a loss, enter the loss as a positive number	6
7	**Distributable net income.** Combine lines 1 through 6. If zero or less, enter -0-	7
8	If a complex trust, enter accounting income for the tax year as determined under the governing instrument and applicable local law ⋅ 8	
9	Income required to be distributed currently	9
10	Other amounts paid, credited, or otherwise required to be distributed	10
11	Total distributions. Add lines 9 and 10. If greater than line 8, see instructions	11
12	Enter the amount of tax-exempt income included on line 11	12
13	Tentative income distribution deduction. Subtract line 12 from line 11	13
14	Tentative income distribution deduction. Subtract line 2 from line 7. If zero or less, enter -0-	14
15	**Income distribution deduction.** Enter the smaller of line 13 or line 14 here and on page 1, line 18	15

Schedule G	**Tax Computation** (see instructions)		
1 **Tax: a**	Tax on taxable income (see instructions)	1a	
b	Tax on lump-sum distributions. Attach Form 4972	1b	
c	Alternative minimum tax (from Schedule I (Form 1041), line 56)	1c	
d	**Total.** Add lines 1a through 1c ▶		1d
2a	Foreign tax credit. Attach Form 1116	2a	
b	General business credit. Attach Form 3800	2b	
c	Credit for prior year minimum tax. Attach Form 8801	2c	
d	Bond credits. Attach Form 8912	2d	
3	**Total credits.** Add lines 2a through 2d ▶		3
4	Subtract line 3 from line 1d. If zero or less, enter -0-		4
5	Recapture taxes. Check if from: ☐ Form 4255 ☐ Form 8611		5
6	Household employment taxes. Attach Schedule H (Form 1040)		6
7	**Total tax.** Add lines 4 through 6. Enter here and on page 1, line 23 ▶		7

	Other Information	Yes	No
1	Did the estate or trust receive tax-exempt income? If "Yes," attach a computation of the allocation of expenses Enter the amount of tax-exempt interest income and exempt-interest dividends ▶ $ _____		
2	Did the estate or trust receive all or any part of the earnings (salary, wages, and other compensation) of any individual by reason of a contract assignment or similar arrangement?		
3	At any time during calendar year 2012, did the estate or trust have an interest in or a signature or other authority over a bank, securities, or other financial account in a foreign country?		
	See the instructions for exceptions and filing requirements for Form TD F 90-22.1. If "Yes," enter the name of the foreign country ▶ _____		
4	During the tax year, did the estate or trust receive a distribution from, or was it the grantor of, or transferor to, a foreign trust? If "Yes," the estate or trust may have to file Form 3520. See instructions		
5	Did the estate or trust receive, or pay, any qualified residence interest on seller-provided financing? If "Yes," see the instructions for required attachment		
6	If this is an estate or a complex trust making the section 663(b) election, check here (see instructions) ▶ ☐		
7	To make a section 643(e)(3) election, attach Schedule D (Form 1041), and check here (see instructions) ▶ ☐		
8	If the decedent's estate has been open for more than 2 years, attach an explanation for the delay in closing the estate, and check here ▶ ☐		
9	Are any present or future trust beneficiaries skip persons? See instructions		

Form **1041** (2012)

GIFT TAX

U.S. Treasury Form 709, the U.S. Gift (and Generation-Skipping Transfer) Tax Return

Form 709 must also be executed and filed whenever a donor makes a lifetime, or *inter vivos*, gift in any calendar year in excess of the set amount (indexed annually for inflation) to any one donee. As of 2012, the amount was $13,000. For the tax year 2012, if a donor did not give more than $13,000 to any one donee, the estate did not have to file Form 709. Further, as of 2012, the annual exclusion for gifts made to spouses who are not U.S. citizens was $139,000, and the top rate for gifts and generation-skipping transfers was 35%.

Figure 15.9 shows Form 709, U.S. Gift (and Generation-Skipping Transfer) Tax Return.

It is noteworthy that only *individuals* are required to file gift tax returns. If a trust, estate, partnership, or corporation makes a gift, the individual beneficiaries, partners, or stockholders are considered donors and may be liable for the gift and generation-skipping transfer taxes.

The donor is responsible for paying the gift tax. However, if the donor does not pay the tax, the person receiving the gift may have to pay the tax. If a donor dies before filing a return, the donor's executor must file the return.

Figure 15.9

Form **709**

Department of the Treasury
Internal Revenue Service

United States Gift (and Generation-Skipping Transfer) Tax Return

▶ Information about Form 709 and its separate instructions is at *www.irs.gov/form709*.

(For gifts made during calendar year 2012)

▶ See instructions.

OMB No. 1545-0020

2012

1 Donor's first name and middle initial	2 Donor's last name	3 Donor's social security number
4 Address (number, street, and apartment number)		5 Legal residence (domicile)
6 City, state, and ZIP or postal code		7 Citizenship (see instructions)

Part 1—General Information

		Yes	No
8	If the donor died during the year, check here ▶ ☐ and enter date of death ______ , ______ .		
9	If you extended the time to file this Form 709, check here ▶ ☐		
10	Enter the total number of donees listed on Schedule A. Count each person only once. ▶		
11a	Have you (the donor) previously filed a Form 709 (or 709-A) for any other year? If "No," skip line 11b		
b	Has your address changed since you last filed Form 709 (or 709-A)?		
12	**Gifts by husband or wife to third parties.** Do you consent to have the gifts (including generation-skipping transfers) made by you and by your spouse to third parties during the calendar year considered as made one-half by each of you? (see instructions.) (If the answer is "Yes," the following information must be furnished and your spouse must sign the consent shown below. **If the answer is "No," skip lines 13–18.**)		
13	Name of consenting spouse — 14 SSN		
15	Were you married to one another during the entire calendar year? (see instructions)		
16	If 15 is "No," check whether ☐ married ☐ divorced or ☐ widowed/deceased, and give date (see instructions) ▶		
17	Will a gift tax return for this year be filed by your spouse? (If "Yes," mail both returns in the same envelope.)		
18	**Consent of Spouse.** I consent to have the gifts (and generation-skipping transfers) made by me and by my spouse to third parties during the calendar year considered as made one-half by each of us. We are both aware of the joint and several liability for tax created by the execution of this consent.		

Consenting spouse's signature ▶ **Date ▶**

19	Have you applied a DSUE amount received from a predeceased spouse to a gift or gifts reported on this or a previous Form 709? If "Yes," complete Schedule C		

1	Enter the amount from Schedule A, Part 4, line 11	1	
2	Enter the amount from Schedule B, line 3	2	
3	Total taxable gifts. Add lines 1 and 2	3	
4	Tax computed on amount on line 3 (see *Table for Computing Gift Tax* in instructions)	4	
5	Tax computed on amount on line 2 (see *Table for Computing Gift Tax* in instructions)	5	
6	Balance. Subtract line 5 from line 4	6	

Figure 15.9 (continued)

Part 2—Tax Computation

Attach check or money order here.

7	Applicable credit amount. If donor has DSUE amount from predeceased spouse(s), enter amount from Schedule C, line 5; otherwise, see instructions	7
8	Enter the applicable credit against tax allowable for all prior periods (from Sch. B, line 1, col. C) .	8
9	Balance. Subtract line 8 from line 7. Do not enter less than zero	9
10	Enter 20% (.20) of the amount allowed as a specific exemption for gifts made after September 8, 1976, and before January 1, 1977 (see instructions)	10
11	Balance. Subtract line 10 from line 9. Do not enter less than zero	11
12	Applicable credit. Enter the smaller of line 6 or line 11	12
13	Credit for foreign gift taxes (see instructions)	13
14	Total credits. Add lines 12 and 13	14
15	Balance. Subtract line 14 from line 6. Do not enter less than zero	15
16	Generation-skipping transfer taxes (from Schedule D, Part 3, col. H, Total)	16
17	Total tax. Add lines 15 and 16	17
18	Gift and generation-skipping transfer taxes prepaid with extension of time to file	18
19	If line 18 is less than line 17, enter **balance due** (see instructions)	19
20	If line 18 is greater than line 17, enter **amount to be refunded**	20

Under penalties of perjury, I declare that I have examined this return, including any accompanying schedules and statements, and to the best of my knowledge and belief, it is true, correct, and complete. Declaration of preparer (other than donor) is based on all information of which preparer has any knowledge.

Sign Here

May the IRS discuss this return with the preparer shown below (see instructions)? ☐ Yes ☐ No

▶ _____
Signature of donor   Date

Paid Preparer Use Only

Print/Type preparer's name	Preparer's signature	Date	Check ☐ if self-employed	PTIN

Firm's name ▶ _____   Firm's EIN ▶ _____

Firm's address ▶ _____   Phone no. _____

For Disclosure, Privacy Act, and Paperwork Reduction Act Notice, see the instructions for this form.   Cat. No. 16783M   Form **709** (2012)

SCHEDULE A   **Computation of Taxable Gifts** (Including transfers in trust) (see instructions)

A   Does the value of any item listed on Schedule A reflect any valuation discount? If "Yes," attach explanation . . . . Yes ☐ No ☐

B   ☐ ◀ Check here if you elect under section 529(c)(2)(B) to treat any transfers made this year to a qualified tuition program as made ratably over a 5-year period beginning this year. See instructions. Attach explanation.

Part 1—Gifts Subject Only to Gift Tax. Gifts less political organization, medical, and educational exclusions. (see instructions)

A Item number	B • Donee's name and address • Relationship to donor (if any) • Description of gift • If the gift was of securities, give CUSIP no. • If closely held entity, give EIN	C	D Donor's adjusted basis of gift	E Date of gift	F Value at date of gift	G For split gifts, enter ½ of column F	H Net transfer (subtract col. G from col. F)
Gifts made by spouse —*complete **only** if you are splitting gifts with your spouse and he/she also made gifts.*							

Total of Part 1. Add amounts from Part 1, column H . . . . ▶

Part 2—Direct Skips. Gifts that are direct skips and are subject to both gift tax and generation-skipping transfer tax. You must list the gifts in chronological order.

A Item number	B • Donee's name and address • Relationship to donor (if any) • Description of gift • If the gift was of securities, give CUSIP no. • If closely held entity, give EIN	C 2632(b) election out	D Donor's adjusted basis of gift	E Date of gift	F Value at date of gift	G For split gifts, enter ½ of column F	H Net transfer (subtract col. G from col. F)

(continued)

Figure 15.9 (continued)

Gifts made by spouse —*complete **only** if you are splitting gifts with your spouse and he/she also made gifts.*

Total of Part 2. Add amounts from Part 2, column H . . . . ▶

Part 3—Indirect Skips. Gifts to trusts that are currently subject to gift tax and may later be subject to generation-skipping transfer tax. You must list these gifts in chronological order.

A Item number	B • Donee's name and address • Relationship to donor (if any) • Description of gift • If the gift was of securities, give CUSIP no. • If closely held entity, give EIN	C 2632(c) election	D Donor's adjusted basis of gift	E Date of gift	F Value at date of gift	G For split gifts, enter ¹/₂ of column F	H Net transfer (subtract col. G from col. F)

Gifts made by spouse —*complete **only** if you are splitting gifts with your spouse and he/she also made gifts.*

Total of Part 3. Add amounts from Part 3, column H . . . . ▶

(If more space is needed, attach additional statements.)

Form **709** (2012)

Part 4—Taxable Gift Reconciliation

1	Total value of gifts of donor. Add totals from column H of Parts 1, 2, and 3	**1**		
2	Total annual exclusions for gifts listed on line 1 (see instructions)	**2**		
3	Total included amount of gifts. Subtract line 2 from line 1	**3**		

Deductions (see instructions)

4	Gifts of interests to spouse for which a marital deduction will be claimed, based on item numbers _____ of Schedule A . .	**4**			
5	Exclusions attributable to gifts on line 4	**5**			
6	Marital deduction. Subtract line 5 from line 4	**6**			
7	Charitable deduction, based on item nos. _____ less exclusions .	**7**			
8	Total deductions. Add lines 6 and 7			**8**	
9	Subtract line 8 from line 3			**9**	
10	Generation-skipping transfer taxes payable with this Form 709 (from Schedule D, Part 3, col. H, Total) . .			**10**	
11	**Taxable gifts.** Add lines 9 and 10. Enter here and on page 1, Part 2—Tax Computation, line 1 . . .			**11**	

Terminable Interest (QTIP) Marital Deduction. (see instructions for Schedule A, Part 4, line 4)

If a trust (or other property) meets the requirements of qualified terminable interest property under section 2523(f), and:

a. The trust (or other property) is listed on Schedule A, and

b. The value of the trust (or other property) is entered in whole or in part as a deduction on Schedule A, Part 4, line 4,

then the donor shall be deemed to have made an election to have such trust (or other property) treated as qualified terminable interest property under section 2523(f).

If less than the entire value of the trust (or other property) that the donor has included in Parts 1 and 3 of Schedule A is entered as a deduction on line 4, the donor shall be considered to have made an election only as to a fraction of the trust (or other property). The numerator of this fraction is equal to the amount of the trust (or other property) deducted on Schedule A, Part 4, line 6. The denominator is equal to the total value of the trust (or other property) listed in Parts 1 and 3 of Schedule A.

If you make the QTIP election, the terminable interest property involved will be included in your spouse's gross estate upon his or her death (section 2044). See instructions for line 4 of Schedule A. If your spouse disposes (by gift or otherwise) of all or part of the qualifying life income interest, he or she will be considered to have made a transfer of the entire property that is subject to the gift tax. See *Transfer of Certain Life Estates Received From Spouse* in the instructions.

12 Election Out of QTIP Treatment of Annuities

☐ ◀Check here if you elect under section 2523(f)(6) **not** to treat as qualified terminable interest property any joint and survivor annuities that are reported on Schedule A and would otherwise be treated as qualified terminable interest property under section 2523(f). See instructions. Enter the item numbers from Schedule A for the annuities for which you are making this election ▶ _____

Figure 15.9 (continued)

SCHEDULE B	Gifts From Prior Periods

If you answered "Yes," on line 11a of page 1, Part 1, see the instructions for completing Schedule B. If you answered "No," skip to the Tax Computation on page 1 (or Schedules C or D, if applicable). Complete Schedule A before beginning Schedule B. See instructions for recalculation of the column C amounts. Attach calculations.

A Calendar year or calendar quarter (see instructions)	B Internal Revenue office where prior return was filed	C Amount of applicable credit (unified credit) against gift tax for periods after December 31, 1976	D Amount of specific exemption for prior periods ending before January 1, 1977	E Amount of taxable gifts

1   Totals for prior periods . . . . | **1** |

2   Amount, if any, by which total specific exemption, line 1, column D is more than $30,000 . . . . . . | **2** |

3   Total amount of taxable gifts for prior periods. Add amount on line 1, column E and amount, if any, on line 2. Enter here and on page 1, Part 2—Tax Computation, line 2 . . . . | **3** |

(If more space is needed, attach additional statements.)   Form **709** (2012)

SCHEDULE C	Deceased Spousal Unused Exclusion (DSUE) Amount

Provide the following information to determine the DSUE amount and applicable credit received from prior spouses. Complete Schedule A before beginning Schedule C.

A Name of Deceased Spouse (dates of death after December 31, 2010 only)	B Date of Death	C Portability Election Made? Yes / No	D If "Yes," DSUE Amount Received from Spouse	E DSUE Amount Applied by Donor to Lifetime Gifts (list current and prior gifts)	F Date of Gift(s) (enter as mm/dd/yy for Part 1 and as yyyy for Part 2)	G RESERVED
Part 1—DSUE RECEIVED FROM LAST DECEASED SPOUSE						
Part 2—DSUE RECEIVED FROM PREDECEASED SPOUSE(S)						
TOTAL (for all DSUE amounts applied for Part 1 and Part 2)						

1	Donor's basic exclusion amount (see instructions)	**1**
2	Total from column E, Parts 1 and 2	**2**
3	Reserved	**3**
4	Add lines 1 and 2	**4**
5	Applicable credit on amount in line 4 (See *Table for Computing Gift Tax* in the instructions). Enter here and on line 7, Part 2—Tax Computation	**5**
6	Reserved	**6**
7	Reserved	**7**
8	Reserved	**8**
9	Reserved	**9**
10	Reserved	**10**

SCHEDULE D	Computation of Generation-Skipping Transfer Tax

Note. Inter vivos direct skips that are completely excluded by the GST exemption must still be fully reported (including value and exemptions claimed) on Schedule D.

(continued)

Figure 15.9 (continued)

Part 1—Generation-Skipping Transfers

A Item No. (from Schedule A, Part 2, col. A)	B Value (from Schedule A, Part 2, col. H)	C Nontaxable Portion of Transfer	D Net Transfer (subtract col. C from col. B)
Gifts made by spouse (for gift splitting only)			

(If more space is needed, attach additional statements.)   Form **709** (2012)

Part 2—GST Exemption Reconciliation (Section 2631) and Section 2652(a)(3) Election

Check here ▶ ☐ if you are making a section 2652(a)(3) (special QTIP) election (see instructions)

Enter the item numbers from Schedule A of the gifts for which you are making this election ▶ -----------------------------

1	Maximum allowable exemption (see instructions)	1
2	Total exemption used for periods before filing this return	2
3	Exemption available for this return. Subtract line 2 from line 1	3
4	Exemption claimed on this return from Part 3, column C total, below	4
5	Automatic allocation of exemption to transfers reported on Schedule A, Part 3 (see instructions)	5
6	Exemption allocated to transfers not shown on line 4 or 5, above. **You must attach a "Notice of Allocation."** (see instructions)	6
7	Add lines 4, 5, and 6	7
8	Exemption available for future transfers. Subtract line 7 from line 3	8

Part 3—Tax Computation

A Item No. (from Schedule D, Part 1)	B Net Transfer (from Schedule D, Part 1, col. D)	C GST Exemption Allocated	D Divide col. C by col. B	E Inclusion Ratio (Subtract col. D from 1.000)	F Maximum Estate Tax Rate	G Applicable Rate (multiply col. E by col. F)	H Generation-Skipping Transfer Tax (multiply col. B by col. G)
					35% (.35)		
					35% (.35)		
					35% (.35)		
					35% (.35)		
					35% (.35)		
					35% (.35)		
Gifts made by spouse (for gift splitting only)							
					35% (.35)		
					35% (.35)		
					35% (.35)		
					35% (.35)		
					35% (.35)		
					35% (.35)		
Total exemption claimed. Enter here and on Part 2, line 4, above. May not exceed Part 2, line 3, above		**Total generation-skipping transfer tax.** Enter here; on page 3, Schedule A, Part 4, line 10; and on page 1, Part 2—Tax Computation, line 16					

(If more space is needed, attach additional statements.)   Form **709** (2012)

■ STATE ESTATE TAX

Some states impose a tax on the decedent's transfer of property to his or her beneficiaries, measured by the value of the property transferred. However, not all states have an estate tax. Research your state's tax law or seek the advice of an accountant regarding the law in your state. If state estate tax is due, it is the duty of the personal representative to file the appropriate tax return and to pay the tax.

■ INHERITANCE TAX

Some states impose an inheritance tax on beneficiaries who receive property from a decedent's estate. This may be instead of or in addition to a state estate tax. Not all states have an inheritance tax. Research your state tax law or seek the advice of an accountant regarding the law in your state. If state inheritance tax is due, it is the duty of the personal representative to file the appropriate tax return and to pay the tax.

■ CONCLUSION

This chapter provided only a brief overview of the different types of tax returns that may need to be filed by the personal representative. Tax law is complicated and ever changing. As a result, many probate firms employ a firm accountant or work very closely with a certified public accountant to ensure that their mutual clients meet all of their legal obligations both under probate law and to the federal and state taxing authorities. The personal representative must be sure that all appropriate tax returns are filed and any tax issues are resolved prior to the closing the probate estate.

CONCEPT REVIEW AND REINFORCEMENT

KEY TERMS

Estate Tax   397
Applicable Exclusion Amount   397

Applicable Credit
Amount   397

Gross Estate   399

REVIEW QUESTIONS

1. What are the first two forms that a personal representative should file with the Internal Revenue Service as soon as possible after being appointed?
2. What final tax return(s) must a personal representative file on behalf of the decedent as an individual?
3. What must be done if a decedent failed to file tax returns for years prior to the decedent's death?
4. Which states currently do not impose individual income tax?
5. When must a gift tax return be filed?
6. Which form is used to notify the Internal Revenue Service that the decedent passed away?
7. What form is used to obtain an identification number for the estate?
8. What is the purpose of Form 706?
9. What is the purpose of Form 1041?
10. What is the purpose of Form 709?

BUILDING YOUR PARALEGAL SKILLS

CRITICAL THINKING EXERCISES

1. Samantha Ford died in 2008. Her estate consisted of a mansion worth $700,000, a brokerage account with a date-of-death value of $1 million, and two vehicles with a combined value of $55,000. Will her personal representative be required to file Form 706? How much tax will be owed?

2. Now assume that Samantha Ford died in 2010. Her estate consisted of a mansion worth $700,000, a brokerage account with a date-of-death value of $1 million, and two vehicles with a combined value of $55,000. Will her personal representative be required to file Form 706? How much tax will be owed?

3. This time assume that Samantha Ford died in 2013. Her estate consisted of a mansion worth $700,000, a brokerage account with a date-of-death value of $1 million, and two vehicles with a combined value of $55,000. Will her personal representative be required to file Form 706? How much tax will be owed?

PARALEGAL PRACTICE

1. _____

MEMORANDUM

To: Paralegal
From: Supervising Attorney
Client: Samantha Ford
Re: Form 56

We were retained by Thomas Ford to represent him in connection with the estate of his mother, Samantha Ford. He has now been appointed by the court as personal representative. Please prepare Form 56 to notify the IRS about the decedent's death. Following is some of the information you will need regarding Samantha Ford:

- Address: 1278 First Street, Brownstone, Sample 12778
- Social Security Number: 121-1-1212
- Date of Death: 2/1/2013

2. _____

MEMORANDUM

To: Paralegal
From: Supervising Attorney
Client: Samantha Ford
Re: Form SS-4

Please also prepare Form SS-4. Our client's address is 81 Rose Avenue, Brownstone, Sample 12778. His Social Security Number is 988-90-9999.

ONLINE RESOURCES

The Pearson Course Companion website contains the following additional resources:

- **Forms for Paralegal Practice Activities**
- Chapter Objectives
- Online Study Guide (Containing Multiple Choice and True/False Questions)
- Web Exercises
- Hypothetical Family and Accompanying Project Worksheet www.pearsonhighered.com/careers

FORMS TO ACCOMPANY PARALEGAL PRACTICE

Disclaimer: The forms provided to aid students in completing the Paralegal Practice activities assigned in each chapter have been modified as samples to familiarize students with what each form commonly looks like and are not intended to be used as actual forms for any state.

INSTRUCTIONS: The forms are provided in Microsoft Word format and employ the use of Stop Codes (such as SC1, SC2, SC3, and so on). Stop Codes are used in place of the form sections that must be updated with case-by-case information, such as SC1 for the client's name, SC3 for the client's address, and so on. What each Stop Code represents can be inferred by reading the surrounding text on the form. By using the FIND & REPLACE tool on the Microsoft toolbar, the students can replace the Stop Codes with the information provided in the Paralegal Practice activity to complete each assignment. Students must also fill in any blank lines on each form with the appropriate information from the activity and then proofread the document prior to turning in their work.

The following forms are included following this section and will be posted online for students to access to complete the Paralegal Practice activities for this chapter:

- PP Form 15.1—IRS Form 56
- PP Form 15.2—IRS Form SS-4

Form 56
(Rev. December 2011)
Department of the Treasury
Internal Revenue Service

Notice Concerning Fiduciary Relationship
(Internal Revenue Code sections 6036 and 6903)

OMB No. 1545-0013

Part I   Identification

Name of person for whom you are acting (as shown on the tax return)	Identifying number	Decedent's social security no.

Address of person for whom you are acting (number, street, and room or suite no.)

City or town, state, and ZIP code (If a foreign address, see instructions.)

Fiduciary's name

Address of fiduciary (number, street, and room or suite no.)

City or town, state, and ZIP code	Telephone number (optional) ( )

Section A.   Authority

1   Authority for fiduciary relationship. Check applicable box:
a ☐ Court appointment of testate estate (valid will exists)
b ☐ Court appointment of intestate estate (no valid will exists)
c ☐ Court appointment as guardian or conservator
d ☐ Valid trust instrument and amendments
e ☐ Bankruptcy or assignment for the benefit or creditors
f ☐ Other. Describe ▶ _____
2a   If box 1a or 1b is checked, enter the date of death ▶ _____
2b   If box 1c–1f is checked, enter the date of appointment, taking office, or assignment or transfer of assets ▶ _____

Section B.   Nature of Liability and Tax Notices

3   Type of taxes (check all that apply): ☐ Income   ☐ Gift ☐ Estate ☐ Generation-skipping transfer   ☐ Employment
☐ Excise   ☐ Other (describe) ▶ _____

(continued)

4 Federal tax form number (check all that apply): **a** ☐ 706 series **b** ☐ 709 **c** ☐ 940 **d** ☐ 941, 943, 944 **e** ☐ 1040, 1040-A, or 1040-EZ **f** ☐ 1041 **g** ☐ 1120 **h** ☐ Other (list) ▶ _____

5 If your authority as a fiduciary does not cover all years or tax periods, check here . . . . ▶ ☐
and list the specific years or periods ▶ _____

6 If the fiduciary listed wants a copy of notices or other written communications (see the instructions) check this box . . . . ▶ ☐
and enter the year(s) or period(s) for the corresponding line 4 item checked. If more than 1 form entered on line 4h, enter the
form number.

Complete only if the line 6 box is checked.

If this item is checked:	Enter year(s) or period(s)	If this item is checked:	Enter year(s) or period(s)
4a		4b	
4c		4d	
4e		4f	
4g		4h:	
4h:		4h:	

For Paperwork Reduction Act and Privacy Act Notice, see the separate instructions.   Cat. No. 16375I   Form **56** (Rev. 12-2011)

Part II	**Court and Administrative Proceedings**

Name of court (if other than a court proceeding, identify the type of proceeding and name of agency)	Date proceeding initiated
Address of court	Docket number of proceeding

City or town, state, and ZIP code	Date	Time	☐ a.m. ☐ p.m.	Place of other proceedings

Part III	**Signature**

Please Sign Here	I certify that I have the authority to execute this notice concerning fiduciary relationship on behalf of the taxpayer.

▶ _____   _____   _____
Fiduciary's signature   Title, if applicable   Date

Form **56** (Rev. 12-2011)

Form **SS-4**
(Rev. January 2010)
Department of the Treasury
Internal Revenue Service

Application for Employer Identification Number
(For use by employers, corporations, partnerships, trusts, estates, churches, government agencies, Indian tribal entities, certain individuals, and others.)
▶ **See separate instructions for each line.**　▶ **Keep a copy for your records.**

OMB No. 1545-0003

EIN

Type or print clearly.

1	Legal name of entity (or individual) for whom the EIN is being requested

2 Trade name of business (if different from name on line 1)	**3** Executor, administrator, trustee, "care of" name

4a Mailing address (room, apt., suite no. and street, or P.O. box)	**5a** Street address (if different) (Do not enter a P.O. box.)
4b City, state, and ZIP code (if foreign, see instructions)	**5b** City, state, and ZIP code (if foreign, see instructions)

6	County and state where principal business is located

7a Name of responsible party	**7b** SSN, ITIN, or EIN

8a Is this application for a limited liability company (LLC) (or a foreign equivalent)? . . . . ☐ Yes ☐ No	**8b** If 8a is "Yes," enter the number of LLC members . . . ▶

8c If 8a is "Yes," was the LLC organized in the United States? . . . . ☐ Yes ☐ No

9a **Type of entity** (check only one box). **Caution.** If 8a is "Yes," see the instructions for the correct box to check.

☐ Sole proprietor (SSN) _____

☐ Partnership

☐ Corporation (enter form number to be filed) ▶ _____

☐ Personal service corporation

☐ Church or church-controlled organization

☐ Other nonprofit organization (specify) ▶ _____

☐ Other (specify) ▶ _____

☐ Estate (SSN of decedent) _____

☐ Plan administrator (TIN) _____

☐ Trust (TIN of grantor) _____

☐ National Guard ☐ State/local government

☐ Farmers' cooperative ☐ Federal government/military

☐ REMIC ☐ Indian tribal governments/enterprises

Group Exemption Number (GEN) if any ▶ _____

		State	Foreign country
9b	If a corporation, name the state or foreign country (if applicable) where incorporated		

10 **Reason for applying** (check only one box)

☐ Started new business (specify type) ▶ _____

☐ Hired employees (Check the box and see line 13.)

☐ Compliance with IRS withholding regulations

☐ Other (specify) ▶

☐ Banking purpose (specify purpose) ▶ _____

☐ Changed type of organization (specify new type) ▶ _____

☐ Purchased going business

☐ Created a trust (specify type) ▶ _____

☐ Created a pension plan (specify type) ▶ _____

11 Date business started or acquired (month, day, year). See instructions.

12 Closing month of accounting year

14 If you expect your employment tax liability to be $1,000 or less in a full calendar year **and** want to file Form 944 annually instead of Forms 941 quarterly, check here. (Your employment tax liability generally will be $1,000 or less if you expect to pay $4,000 or less in total wages.) If you do not check this box, you must file Form 941 for every quarter. ☐

13 Highest number of employees expected in the next 12 months (enter -0- if none).

If no employees expected, skip line 14.

Agricultural	Household	Other

15 First date wages or annuities were paid (month, day, year). **Note.** If applicant is a withholding agent, enter date income will first be paid to nonresident alien (month, day, year) . . . . ▶

16 Check **one** box that best describes the principal activity of your business. ☐ Health care & social assistance ☐ Wholesale-agent/broker

☐ Construction ☐ Rental & leasing ☐ Transportation & warehousing ☐ Accommodation & food service ☐ Wholesale-other ☐ Retail

☐ Real estate ☐ Manufacturing ☐ Finance & insurance ☐ Other (specify)

17 Indicate principal line of merchandise sold, specific construction work done, products produced, or services provided.

18 Has the applicant entity shown on line 1 ever applied for and received an EIN? ☐ Yes ☐ No

If "Yes," write previous EIN here ▶

Third Party Designee	Complete this section **only** if you want to authorize the named individual to receive the entity's EIN and answer questions about the completion of this form.	
	Designee's name	Designee's telephone number (include area code) ( )
	Address and ZIP code	Designee's fax number (include area code) ( )

Under penalties of perjury, I declare that I have examined this application, and to the best of my knowledge and belief, it is true, correct, and complete.

Applicant's telephone number (include area code) ( )

Name and title (type or print clearly) ▶

Applicant's fax number (include area code) ( )

Signature ▶   Date ▶

For Privacy Act and Paperwork Reduction Act Notice, see separate instructions.   Cat. No. 16055N   Form **SS-4** (Rev. 1-2010)

Do I Need an EIN?

File Form SS-4 if the applicant entity does not already have an EIN but is required to show an EIN on any return, statement, or other document.[1] See also the separate instructions for each line on Form SS-4.

IF the applicant...	AND...	THEN...
Started a new business	Does not currently have (nor expect to have) employees	Complete lines 1, 2, 4a–8a, 8b–c (if applicable), 9a, 9b (if applicable), and 10–14 and 16–18.
Hired (or will hire) employees, including household employees	Does not already have an EIN	Complete lines 1, 2, 4a–6, 7a–b (if applicable), 8a, 8b–c (if applicable), 9a, 9b (if applicable), 10–18.
Opened a bank account	Needs an EIN for banking purposes only	Complete lines 1–5b, 7a–b (if applicable), 8a, 8b–c (if applicable), 9a, 9b (if applicable), 10, and 18.
Changed type of organization	Either the legal character of the organization or its ownership changed (for example, you incorporate a sole proprietorship or form a partnership)[2]	Complete lines 1–18 (as applicable).
Purchased a going business[3]	Does not already have an EIN	Complete lines 1–18 (as applicable).
Created a trust	The trust is other than a grantor trust or an IRA trust[4]	Complete lines 1–18 (as applicable).
Created a pension plan as a plan administrator[5]	Needs an EIN for reporting purposes	Complete lines 1, 3, 4a–5b, 9a, 10, and 18.

(continued)

Is a foreign person needing an EIN to comply with IRS withholding regulations	Needs an EIN to complete a Form W-8 (other than Form W-8ECI), avoid withholding on portfolio assets, or claim tax treaty benefits [6]	Complete lines 1–5b, 7a–b (SSN or ITIN optional), 8a, 8b–c (if applicable), 9a, 9b (if applicable), 10, and 18.
Is administering an estate	Needs an EIN to report estate income on Form 1041	Complete lines 1–6, 9a, 10–12, 13–17 (if applicable), and 18.
Is a withholding agent for taxes on non-wage income paid to an alien (i.e., individual, corporation, or partnership, etc.)	Is an agent, broker, fiduciary, manager, tenant, or spouse who is required to file Form 1042, Annual Withholding Tax Return for U.S. Source Income of Foreign Persons	Complete lines 1, 2, 3 (if applicable), 4a–5b, 7a–b (if applicable), 8a, 8b–c (if applicable), 9a, 9b (if applicable), 10, and 18.
Is a state or local agency	Serves as a tax reporting agent for public assistance recipients under Rev. Proc. 80-4, 1980-1 C.B. 581 [7]	Complete lines 1, 2, 4a–5b, 9a, 10, and 18.
Is a single-member LLC	Needs an EIN to file Form 8832, Classification Election, for filing employment tax returns and excise tax returns, or for state reporting purposes [8]	Complete lines 1–18 (as applicable).
Is an S corporation	Needs an EIN to file Form 2553, Election by a Small Business Corporation [9]	Complete lines 1–18 (as applicable).

[1] For example, a sole proprietorship or self-employed farmer who establishes a qualified retirement plan, or is required to file excise, employment, alcohol, tobacco, or firearms returns, must have an EIN. A partnership, corporation, REMIC (real estate mortgage investment conduit), nonprofit organization (church, club, etc.), or farmers' cooperative must use an EIN for any tax-related purpose even if the entity does not have employees.

[2] However, do not apply for a new EIN if the existing entity only (a) changed its business name, (b) elected on Form 8832 to change the way it is taxed (or is covered by the default rules), or (c) terminated its partnership status because at least 50% of the total interests in partnership capital and profits were sold or exchanged within a 12-month period. The EIN of the terminated partnership should continue to be used. See Regulations section 301.6109-1(d)(2)(iii).

[3] Do not use the EIN of the prior business unless you became the "owner" of a corporation by acquiring its stock.

[4] However, grantor trusts that do not file using Optional Method 1 and IRA trusts that are required to file Form 990-T, Exempt Organization Business Income Tax Return, must have an EIN. For more information on grantor trusts, see the Instructions for Form 1041.

[5] A plan administrator is the person or group of persons specified as the administrator by the instrument under which the plan is operated.

[6] Entities applying to be a Qualified Intermediary (QI) need a QI-EIN even if they already have an EIN. See Rev. Proc. 2000-12.

[7] See also *Household employer* on page 4 of the instructions. **Note.** State or local agencies may need an EIN for other reasons, for example, hired employees.

[8] See *Disregarded entities* on page 4 of the instructions for details on completing Form SS-4 for an LLC.

[9] An existing corporation that is electing or revoking S corporation status should use its previously-assigned EIN.

Remedies for Improper Administration

CHAPTER 16

A REAL-LIFE SCENARIO

Fred Williams and his wife, Mary, moved from a busy city to a small town out West after retirement. After Mary passed away, Fred's health began to decline and he hired a housekeeper to do basic chores. The housekeeper became more than a housekeeper and, as Fred developed dementia, began taking over Fred's finances. She went to a stationery store, bought a will kit, and helped Fred to write her name in as the sole beneficiary of his estate. The housekeeper also hired a traveling notary to come to the home and had a couple of her friends come over to sign as witnesses. The traveling notary assumed that the housekeeper was Fred's daughter and didn't think anything of it. After Fred passed away, his children found out about the will and were outraged. They immediately sought legal advice from an attorney to find out what they could do.

© Africa Studio/Shutterstock

■ INTRODUCTION

In an ideal world, everyone would do the right thing all of the time. However, as the foregoing scenario illustrates, there are times when people engage in immoral and even illegal activity.

CHAPTER OBJECTIVES:

1. Understand the objections that may be filed at different stages of a probate proceeding.

2. Understand the remedy for improper trust administration.

3. Know how to draft an objection to a given example of improper administration.

When a testator signs a will under false pretenses or without having the requisite capacity to sign, family members may contest the validity of the will.

Further, in the context of estate administration, disagreements sometimes arise as to whether an executor should be appointed or whether an appointed executor or trustee has properly administered the estate or the trust. This chapter discusses the various options and remedies that are available to other interested parties.

Key Terms and Definitions

A **fiduciary** is a person in a position of trust, such as an executor, administrator, guardian, attorney-in-fact, or trustee. A **fiduciary** is also a person to whom property or power is entrusted for the benefit of another. **Fiduciary capacity** means a position of trust. A **will contest** is a lawsuit over the allowance or disallowance of a will.

Will Contest
A lawsuit over the allowance or disallowance of a will.

■ PROBATE PROCEEDING

Chapters 11–14 discussed the four parts of a probate proceeding. You may recall that all interested parties must be notified at each and every stage of a probate proceeding, and proof of that notification is evidenced by Proof of Mailing forms (or some other proof of service that is filed with the court). The various documents that are sent out to other parties outline their legal rights and their time to file any objections with the court.

Part One Probate Objections

When the petitioner first files the Application for Informal Probate of Will and Appointment as Personal Representative, or another comparable application or petition with the court, any notified party that disagrees with the application or petition must promptly object and state valid, legal reasons for their objection. The party may object to the appointment of the personal representative, to the probate of the will, or both.

Objection to Appointment as Personal Representative

There are a number of possible grounds to object to a petitioner's appointment as personal representative. Objections to appointment are more likely to be filed in intestacy proceedings (where the decedent died without a will), but can also occur when there was a will.

Priority for Appointment

One of the strongest possible objections is that the individual seeking appointment as personal representative does not have priority for appointment. Someone filing an objection on this ground (the "respondent") will allege that he or she has a greater priority, or legal right, for appointment than the petitioner. Priority for appointment is established by state law and is generally very logical and intuitive. A personal representative appointed under a will usually has first priority for appointment. That is the case in California, as is evidenced by the statutory provisions in Figure 16.1.

Next in line after a person nominated in a will are usually the decedent's family members, with highest priority given to the closest relatives. Figure 16.2 shows Arizona's law regarding priority for appointment.

Figure 16.1

> **California Probate Code §8420 states:**
>
> The person named as executor in the decedent's will has the right to appointment as personal representative.
>
> **California Probate Code §8421 states:**
>
> If a person is not named as executor in a will but it appears by the terms of the will that the testator intended to commit the execution of the will and the administration of the estate to the person, the person is entitled to appointment as personal representative in the same manner as if named as executor.

Figure 16.2

> **Arizona Revised Statute §14-3203,** *Priority among persons seeking appointment as personal representative,* **states in relevant part:**
>
> A. Whether the proceedings are formal or informal, persons who are not disqualified have priority for appointment in the following order:
>   1. The person with priority as determined by a probated will including a person nominated by a power conferred in a will.
>   2. The surviving spouse of the decedent who is a devisee of the decedent.
>   3. Other devisees of the decedent.
>   4. The surviving spouse of the decedent.
>   5. Other heirs of the decedent.
>   6. If the decedent was a veteran or the spouse or child of a veteran, the department of veterans' services.
>   7. Forty-five days after the death of the decedent, any creditor.
>   8. The public fiduciary.

The same Arizona statutory section goes on to discuss how objections to appointment may be made. By way of review, an informal probate proceeding is an uncontested proceeding. Once an objection is filed in the State of Arizona, the probate proceeding is deemed a formal proceeding from that point forward, as shown in Figure 16.3.

Figure 16.3

> **Arizona Revised Statute §14-3203 continues as follows:**
>
> A. An objection to an appointment can be made only in formal proceedings. In case of objection the priorities stated in subsection A of this section apply, except that:
>   1. If the estate appears to be more than adequate to meet exemptions and costs of administration but inadequate to discharge anticipated unsecured claims, the court, on petition of creditors, may appoint any qualified person.
>   2. In case of objection to appointment of a surviving spouse, other than one whose priority is determined by will, by an heir or devisee appearing to have a substantial interest in the estate, and the surviving spouse is found by the court to be unsuitable, the court may appoint a person who is acceptable to heirs and devisees, whose interests in the estate appear to be worth in total more than half of the probable distributable value or, in default of this accord, any suitable person.
>   3. In case of objection to appointment of a person who is not a surviving spouse, other than one whose priority is determined by will, by an heir or devisee appearing to have a substantial interest in the estate, the court may ap-

(continued)

Figure 16.3 (continued)

point a person who is acceptable to heirs and devisees whose interests in the estate appear to be worth in total more than half of the probable distributable value, or, in default of this accord any suitable person.

B. A person entitled to letters under subsection A, paragraphs 2 through 5 of this section and a person age fourteen and over who would be entitled to letters but for the person's age may nominate a qualified person to act as personal representative. Any person age eighteen and over may renounce the person's right to nominate or to an appointment by appropriate writing filed with the court. If two or more persons share a priority, those of them who do not renounce must concur in nominating another to act for them, or in applying for appointment.

C. Conservators of the estates of protected persons, or if there is no conservator, any guardian except a guardian ad litem of a minor or incapacitated person, may exercise the same right to nominate, to object to another's appointment, or to participate in determining the preference of a majority in interest of the heirs and devisees that the protected person or ward would have if qualified for appointment.

D. Formal proceedings are required to appoint a personal representative in any of the following situations:

   1. If there is a person with a higher order of priority who has not renounced or waived the person's right by appropriate writing filed with the court.

   2. If a priority is shared by two or more persons, as devisees under subsection A, paragraph 3 of this section, or as heirs under subsection A, paragraph 5 of this section, and one or more of them has not renounced or concurred in nominating the person whose appointment is applied for.

   3. If appointment is sought for a person who does not have any priority under this section, under this paragraph the court shall determine that those having priority do not object to the appointment, and that administration is necessary.

E. A person is not qualified to serve as a personal representative who is:

   1. Under the age of majority as defined in section 1–215.

   2. A person whom the court finds unsuitable in formal proceedings.

   3. A foreign corporation.

F. A personal representative appointed by a court of the decedent's domicile has priority over all other persons except if the decedent's will nominates different persons to be personal representative in this state and in the state of domicile. The domiciliary personal representative may nominate another, who shall have the same priority as the domiciliary personal representative.

G. This section governs priority for appointment of a successor personal representative but does not apply to the selection of a special administrator.

Of course, many states do not make a distinction between formal and informal probates. Figure 16.4 is the relevant section of the 2012 Florida Statutes regarding the priority for appointment of a representative.

Capacity or Suitability of Personal Representative

There are a variety of other reasons why interested parties may object to the petitioner's appointment. First, the petitioner may not have *capacity*, or legal competency, to act as personal representative. For example, a stubborn, 83-year-old widow may seek appointment as personal representative of her husband's estate, but her grown children may object on the ground that she no longer has capacity to do the job because she cannot pay her own bills or balance her own checkbook. Another ground for objection to appointment may be that the personal representative has a criminal background or other undesirable personality traits that make him or her unsuitable for the job. In addition, if the will does not waive bond, or if there is no will, the personal representative will usually be required to secure a bond. If the petitioner is unable to secure

Figure 16.4

733.301   Preference in appointment of personal representative. —

(1) In granting letters of administration, the following order of preference shall be observed:

   (a) In testate estates:

      1. The personal representative, or his or her successor, nominated by the will or pursuant to a power conferred in the will.

      2. The person selected by a majority in interest of the persons entitled to the estate.

      3. A devisee under the will. If more than one devisee applies, the court may select the one best qualified.

   (b) In intestate estates:

      1. The surviving spouse.

      2. The person selected by a majority in interest of the heirs.

      3. The heir nearest in degree. If more than one applies, the court may select the one best qualified.

(2) A guardian of the property of a ward who if competent would be entitled to appointment as, or to select, the personal representative may exercise the right to select the personal representative.

(3) In either a testate or an intestate estate, if no application is made by any of the persons described in subsection (1), the court shall appoint a capable person; but no person may be appointed under this subsection:

   (a) Who works for, or holds public office under, the court.

   (b) Who is employed by, or holds office under, any judge exercising probate jurisdiction.

(4) After letters have been granted in either a testate or an intestate estate, if a person who was entitled to, and has not waived, preference over the person appointed at the time of the appointment and on whom formal notice was not served seeks the appointment, the letters granted may be revoked and the person entitled to preference may have letters granted after formal notice and hearing.

(5) After letters have been granted in either a testate or an intestate estate, if any will is subsequently admitted to probate, the letters shall be revoked and new letters granted.

History.—s. 1, ch. 74-106; s. 62, ch. 75-220; s. 21, ch. 77-87; s. 1, ch. 77-174; s. 988, ch. 97-102; s. 98, ch. 2001-226.

Note.—Created from former s. 732.44.

a bond for financial or other personal reasons, the other parties may object to the appointment. This list is not exhaustive; there are no doubt a variety of other valid, legal grounds on which to object to a petitioner's appointment as personal representative.

Objection to Probate of Will

Another common objection that takes place seeks to prevent the proffered will from being admitted to probate. The respondent may allege that the will is invalid for a number of reasons, or may claim that the will was revoked by a later will. The result is a **will contest**, or a lawsuit over the allowance or disallowance of a will.

Recall that in order for a will to be valid, the signing party must have had capacity at the time the will was signed and the execution of the will must have complied with statutory requirements.

Lack of Capacity

In order to execute a will, a person must have legal capacity and be "of sound mind." **Legal capacity** is the age of majority, at which a person acquires the capacity to make a valid will. Majority age is eighteen (18) in most states, but is age twenty-one (21) in a minority of states. What it means to be "of **sound mind**"

Legal Capacity
The age of majority, at which a person acquires the capacity to make a valid will. Majority age is eighteen (18) in most states, but is age twenty-one (21) in a minority of states.

Sound Mind
To have the mental ability to make a valid will; the normal condition of the human mind, not impaired by insanity or other mental disorders.

is to have the mental ability to make a valid will. Sound mind is the normal condition of the human mind, not impaired by insanity or other mental disorders.

Improper Execution of Will

The requirements for due execution of a will vary by state, but most states require that, at a minimum, the will be written, signed and dated by the maker, and attested and signed by two witnesses. Some states require that there be three witnesses.

If the objecting party can prove that the decedent lacked testamentary capacity or failed to properly execute the proffered will, that party is likely to prevail. If there is no valid will, the estate will pass under intestacy.

Revocation by Later Will

One fairly common objection that can occur is on the ground that the will was revoked by a later will, in which case the objecting party requests that the later will be probated instead. If it is determined that the later will is valid and that it effectively revoked the first will, the later document will be admitted to probate.

■ PART THREE PROBATE OBJECTIONS

As was discussed in Chapter 13, **creditors** are people to whom money is owed. A **claim** is a right to payment. A **Creditor's Claim** is a written document submitted by a creditor alleging that it is owed money by the estate. The claim must be delivered to the personal representative within the statutory time frame or it may be disallowed. A **Disallowance of Claim** is a document filed by a personal representative notifying the creditor that the claim is not being allowed and providing the legal grounds for the disallowance. If a creditor disagrees with the reason that their claim is being disallowed, the creditor must file an Objection to Disallowance of Claim within the statutory time frame and state the legal basis for their objection. If the personal representative did not have a valid reason to disallow the claim, the court will likely order him or her to pay the creditor. Some personal representatives may disallow valid claims in hopes that the creditors will not timely object. This is an unethical practice, but it does happen.

Figure 16.5 depicts an Objection to Disallowance of Claim where a creditor filed a valid claim against an estate but the personal representative denied the claim.

Figure 16.6 is a Motion to Compel filed by one co-personal representative of an estate against the other co-representative. The party filing the motion was the second wife of the decedent and was alleging that the other co-personal representative, the grown son of the decedent from a prior marriage, was withholding important financial information and also not giving her the share she was entitled to. The parties were represented by separate legal counsel and became co-representatives as a compromise when both the second wife and the grown son petitioned for appointment as personal representative of the intestate estate. As you might expect, there were hard feelings between the parties and the case did not go smoothly. While complicated, the following motion illustrates several different types of disputes that have been discussed in this chapter.

Figure 16.5

Jasmine Attornie, Esq.
LAW OFFICE OF JASMINE ATTORNIE, PLLC
10011 Palma Road, Suite 1
Littletown, Sample 11123
(123) 456-7879
(123) 456-7870 (Facsimile)
Attorney for Respondent Leslie Adams

IN THE SUPERIOR COURT OF THE STATE OF SAMPLE
IN AND FOR THE COUNTY OF REED

In the Matter of the Estate of: JERRY B. DOWNEY, Deceased.	Case No.: PB-2010-5558 **OBJECTION TO DISALLOWANCE OF CLAIM**

Respondent LESLIE ADAMS, by and through undersigned counsel, the Law Office of Jasmine Attornie, PLLC, hereby objects to the disallowance of her creditor's claim, as follows:

The Minute Order dated November 13, 2010 stated as follows: "The Court further finds that the Respondent has an appropriate claim against the Estate to the extent of the joint credit card of which the Decedent's former roommates utilized and ran up charges against the same. Respondent is directed to file an appropriate claim against the estate in that regard." *See* Minute Order, p. 4. The Personal Representative attempted to deny Respondent's rights in the lodged Order, but the Court was kind enough to write in: "Leslie Adams has a claim against the Estate based on the joint credit card with decedent." *See* Minute Order dated December 1, 2010 and attached Order, p. 6, ¶7, initialed and dated by the Judge.

Respondent filed a Claim Against the Estate on January 8, 2010 for an estimated $27,000.00 with attached documentation. *See* Claim Against Estate. The Personal Representative filed a Notice of Disallowance dated February 24, 2010 that did not state any reason for the disallowance. *See* Notice of Disallowance of Claim; *See also* SRS §14-3806. The estate is not insolvent and Ms. Adams has a valid claim against the estate. The Personal Representative has no legal basis for the disallowance.

WHEREFORE, the Respondent respectfully requests the Court to order the payment of Ms. Adams's valid claim against the estate; and for such other further relief as the Court deems just and appropriate.

RESPECTFULLY SUBMITTED this 12th day of March, 2010.

LAW OFFICE OF JASMINE ATTORNIE, PLLC

S/ Jasmine Attornie
Jasmine Attornie, Esq.

Original plus two (2) copies filed with
the Court and a copy thereof mailed
this 12th day of March, 2010, to:

LAW OFFICES OF KEITH S. NUCKEL, P.C.
2153 Highway 95
Littletown, Sample 12222

By: S/Employee

An Employee of the Law Office of Jasmine Attornie, PLLC

Figure 16.6

Jasmine Attornie, Esq.
LAW OFFICE OF JASMINE ATTORNIE, PLLC
10011 Palma Road, Suite 1
Littletown, Sample 11123
(123) 456-7879
(123) 456-7870 (Facsimile)
Attorney for Petitioner

IN THE SUPERIOR COURT OF THE STATE OF SAMPLE
IN AND FOR THE COUNTY OF REED

In the Matter of the Estate of **JUAN HERNANDEZ,** Deceased.	Case No. PB-2009-9990 **MOTION TO COMPEL**

RAFAELA HERNANDEZ, by and through undersigned counsel, the Law Office of Jasmine Attornie, PLLC, hereby moves the Court to compel disclosure of the specifics of the assets that passed to the decedent's sons via non-probate transfers, based upon the following Memorandum of Points and Authorities:

Memorandum of Points and Authorities

Facts

The decedent had a Fidelity Retirement Savings Account that had a balance of $24,709.04. *See* Exhibit 1. Mrs. HERNANDEZ thought that she was the beneficiary of the account but was not; the sons of the decedent inherited the money and received the proceeds. Mrs. HERNANDEZ has requested the statements from opposing counsel on several occasions but has not received them.

The decedent also had life insurance through his employer in the amount of one year's salary, or approximately Thirty-Five Thousand Dollars ($35,000.00). This, too, was paid out to the decedent's two sons. Accordingly, upon information and belief, some Fifty-Nine Thousand Seven Hundred Nine ($59,709.00) has already passed to the decedent's sons through non-probate transfers.

The estate account balance as of April 30, 2010 was $27,425.64. There is also a parcel of land in Neartown, Sample that is listed for sale.

Mrs. HERNANDEZ filed a Claim Against the Estate for the Homestead, Exempt Property, and Family allowances on March 13, 2010. This claim was not disputed and cannot be disputed because she is the surviving spouse of the decedent.

Accordingly, the amount of the estate passing to the decedent's sons must be reduced by the non-probate transfers that they have already received, as more fully described below, and Mrs. HERNANDEZ is requesting an order compelling them to provide exact figures. Further, Mrs. HERNANDEZ may be entitled to reimbursement from them in order that she receives the amount she is entitled to.

Law

Share of Surviving Spouse

S.R.S. §14-2102, Intestate share of surviving spouse, paragraph (2), states that the following passes to the surviving spouse: "If there are surviving issue one or more of whom are not issue of the surviving spouse, one-half of the intestate separate property and no interest in the one-half of the community property that belonged to the decedent."

Homestead Allowance and Exempt Property

Pursuant to S.R.S. §14-2402(A), the surviving spouse is entitled to an Eighteen Thousand Dollar ($18,000.00) homestead allowance. In addition, the surviving spouse is entitled to exempt property totaling Seven Thousand Dollars ($7,000.00) in household furniture, automobiles, furnishings, appliances, and personal effects. *See* S.R.S. §14-2403.

Figure 16.6 (continued)

Sons of Decedent Liable for Nonprobate Transfers

S.R.S. §14-6102, Nonprobate transferees; liability for creditor claims and statutory allowances, provides:

> "A. Except as otherwise provided by law, a transferee of a nonprobate transfer is subject to liability to the decedent's probate estate for allowed claims against the decedent's probate estate and statutory allowances to the decedent's spouse and children to the extent the decedent's probate estate is insufficient to satisfy those claims and allowances. The liability of a nonprobate transferee may not exceed the value of nonprobate transfers received or controlled by that transferee."

Rules of Civil Procedure Apply

Sample Revised Statute §14-1304, Practice in Court, states:

"Unless specifically provided to the contrary in this title or unless inconsistent with its provisions, the rules of civil procedure including the rules concerning vacation of orders and appellate review govern formal proceedings under this title."

Motion to Compel

16 S.R.S. Rules of Civil Procedure, Rule 37(a), *Motion for Order Compelling Disclosure or Discovery*, provides that a party may motion the court for an order compelling disclosure or discovery that they are entitled to but which has not been disclosed in the proceeding.

Analysis

Mrs. HERNANDEZ is entitled to the Eighteen Thousand Dollar ($18,000.00) homestead allowance right off the top. *See* S.R.S. §14-2402(A). She is further entitled to the exempt property allowance for the personal property items. *See* S.R.S. §14-2403. After that, she is entitled to 50% of what remains, including probate and non-probate transfers. *See* S.R.S. §14-2102(2) & S.R.S. §14-6102. Further, the sons of the decedent are required to reimburse Mrs. HERNANDEZ to the extent they received more than their share, and it appears highly likely that they have, since all that remains in the probate estate is the estate account with Twenty-Seven Thousand Four Hundred Twenty-Five Dollars and Sixty-Four Cents ($27,425.64) in it and a parcel of land in Neartown that is not worth much—less than Sixteen Thousand Dollars ($16,000.00). *See* S.R.S. §14-6102.

Multiple requests have been made to the counsel for the sons, both oral and written, and the information has not been provided. *See* Exhibits 2–6.

Conclusion

WHEREFORE, Petitioner respectfully requests that the Court to compel the decedent's sons to produce the information about the non-probate transfers they have received and, if the Petitioner is entitled to the remainder of the estate, to order that it be distributed to her, as well as that she be reimbursed for any funds that she is entitled to from the decedent's sons.

RESPECTFULLY SUBMITTED this <u>20th</u> day of May, 2010.

_____
Jasmine Attornie, Esq.
Attorney for Rafaela Hernandez

Original plus two (2) copies filed with the
Court this 20th day of May, 2010:

Law Offices of Daniel Oppose
2001 Highway 95, Suite 15
Littletown, Sample 11123

By: <u>S/Employee</u>_____
An Employee of the Law Office of Jasmine Attornie, PLLC

■ TRUST MANAGEMENT

A more difficult situation can arise in the context of improper administration of a non-testamentary trust that is not being overseen by the court. A revocable living trust is a trust created by a written declaration during the lifetime of the creator. The fact that this type of trust is revocable means that the trustor reserves the right to amend or revoke the trust during his or her lifetime. With a revocable living trust, the trustor usually acts as trustee during his or her lifetime and is also the beneficiary of the trust during his or her lifetime. Upon the death of the trustor or settlor, a successor trustee takes over and the trust either terminates or continues for the benefit of the remainder beneficiaries. Problems may arise for the beneficiaries if the successor trustee does not do what he or she is told to do by the trust document.

A variety of problems can occur. Trustees may distribute assets improperly, fail to distribute when they are supposed to, or engage in acts of self-dealing. Recall that, like an executor, administrator, guardian, or attorney-in-fact, a trustee is a **fiduciary**, or a person to whom property or power is entrusted for the benefit of another. He or she has a **fiduciary duty** to uphold as the agent of the principal. The phrase "**fiduciary capacity**" means a position of trust.

Fiduciary
A person in a position of loyalty and trust, such as an executor, administrator, guardian, attorney-in-fact, or trustee; also a person to whom property or power is entrusted for the benefit of another.

Fiduciary Capacity
A position of trust; the legal capability of a person or institution (such as a bank) to act as a fiduciary.

Civil Lawsuit

If trust beneficiaries suspect or are certain of trustee misconduct and are unable to successfully resolve matters with the trustee, legal assistance will be necessary. The beneficiaries may then sue the trustee civilly to seek his or her removal as trustee and to seek damages for any wrongdoing. The primary cause of action will likely be *breach of fiduciary duty*, alleging that the trustee failed to meet the high ethical standards imposed on trustees in acting for the benefit of those whom they serve. If the trustee took assets from the trust for personal gain, there may be a cause of action for *conversion*. It will be necessary to fully discuss matters with the attorney to determine which causes of action are appropriate to include in a complaint against the trustee.

There are several downsides to this. A trust beneficiary may have to pay considerable sums out of pocket to fight for trust assets that he or she is entitled to but has not received. It is also difficult to recapture assets or funds that have been misappropriated or spent, even if a judgment has been obtained. However, it is certain that action should be taken to remove a dishonest trustee from appointment and to try to right matters through the court.

■ CONCLUSION

In conclusion, the remedies that are available to interested parties depend on a variety of factors. If there is a probate proceeding, parties may object to the appointment of another person as personal representative, to the probate of the will, or to both. While the probate proceeding is in progress, beneficiaries of the estate may object to the personal representative's Proposal for Distribution or other actions taken on behalf of the estate. In rare instances, co-personal representatives may disagree with each other about how to administer the estate and need judicial intervention. Finally, if a non-testamentary trust is being administered improperly, the remedy is to file a civil lawsuit against the trustee.

CONCEPT REVIEW AND REINFORCEMENT

KEY TERMS

Will Contest   418

Legal Capacity   421

Sound Mind   421

Fiduciary   426

Fiduciary Capacity   426

REVIEW QUESTIONS

1. What are some of the grounds for a will contest?
2. Explain the requirement of legal capacity.
3. If a creditor's claim is wrongfully disallowed, what document should the creditor file with the court?
4. What legal action can be taken by the beneficiaries of a revocable living trust when the trustee of the trust has engaged in wrongdoing?
5. What are two common causes of action that trust beneficiaries may have against the trustee?

BUILDING YOUR PARALEGAL SKILLS

CRITICAL THINKING EXERCISES

1. Challenge Question: Locate your state's probate code to determine the priority given to individuals seeking appointment as personal representative. Summarize your findings and cite your sources. Then, apply your state statute to the following hypothetical cases to determine who should be appointed as personal representative. Discuss whether there are other considerations beyond the priority in the statute.

   a. Decedent left a valid will appointing Betsy as personal representative and William as alternate. Betsy seeks appointment and William objects.

   b. Decedent died without a will and is survived by his wife, Wilma, and two sons from a previous marriage. Wilma seeks appointment as personal representative and the two sons object and seek appointment as co-personal representatives.

   c. Decedent died without a will and had no wife or children. Decedent was survived by a brother, Peter, and a sister, Samantha. Both wish to be appointed as personal representative. Both are upstanding citizens but they do not get along.

   d. Same as c, above, except that Peter has a criminal record with numerous convictions for crimes of fraud and moral turpitude.

PREPARE DOCUMENTS

1. _____

MEMORANDUM

To: Paralegal

From: Supervising Attorney

Client: Nichole Smith

Re: Objection to Disallowance of Claim.

Assume from the previous chapters that Nichole improperly denied Second Bank's creditor's claim without giving any grounds for the disallowance. Prepare an Objection to the Disallowance of Claim on behalf of Second Bank.

The Pearson Course Companion website contains the following additional resources:

- **Forms for Paralegal Practice Activities**
- Chapter Objectives
- Online Study Guide (Containing Multiple Choice and True/False Questions)

- Web Exercises
- Hypothetical Family and Accompanying Project Worksheet www.pearsonhighered.com/careers

CASES FOR CONSIDERATION

CASE #1:

IN THE MATTER OF THE ESTATE OF: MILDRED G. HORTON, Deceased

2002 Ohio 1377; 2002 Ohio App. LEXIS 1391
March 27, 2002, Decided

OPINION

Decision And Journal Entry

Dated: March 27, 2002

This cause was heard upon the record in the trial court. Each error assigned has been reviewed and the following disposition is made:

CARR, J.

This case involves two appeals from the Summit County Probate Court. Appellant, George A. Horton, Jr. ("Mr. Horton") has appealed from an order of the Summit County Probate Court finding him unsuitable to serve as executor of his mother's estate and appointing a third party. Appellant, Alma Horton (Mrs. Horton) has appealed from the denial of her application to serve as executor as well. This Court reverses in regard to Mr. Horton and dismisses Mrs. Horton's appeal as moot.

I

Mr. Horton is the only child and sole heir of Mildred G. Horton, who died, testate, on April 4, 1998. Mildred Horton's will named Mr. Horton to serve as the executor of her estate. The will also provided that,

if Mr. Horton predeceased her or was unable to serve, Alma Horton was to serve as the executor instead. On July 15, 1998, Mr. Horton filed an application to probate the will of his mother which was granted on the same day. The next day, Mr. Horton filed an application to release the estate from administration, pursuant to R.C. 2113.03. Included with the application was a statement of the assets and liabilities of the estate. In this statement was a notice regarding a potential claim by the Ohio Department of Human Services, nka the Ohio Department of Job and Family Services (ODJFS).

On August 6, 1998, the estate was released from administration. On October 1, 1998, the ODJFS filed a motion to vacate the entry releasing the estate from administration pursuant to Civ.R. 60(B) alleging that it had not been notified of Mr. Horton's application to release the estate from administration and that it had been omitted from the list of creditors filed by Mr. Horton. The trial court granted the ODJFS's Civ.R. 60(B) motion to vacate and appeal was taken to this Court. On August 2, 2000, this Court affirmed the trial court's decision.

On September 15, 2000, Mr. Horton filed an application for authority to administer estate pursuant to R.C. 2113.05 and 2113.07. ODJFS filed objections to Mr. Horton's appointment and requested the appointment of a third party instead. The matter was heard before a magistrate on April 2, 2001, who found that Mr. Horton was not a suitable person to serve as executor of the estate and denied his application. Mr. Horton filed objections to the magistrate's decision. After a hearing on the matter, the trial court adopted the magistrate's decision and found Mr. Horton unsuitable and ordered the appointment of a suitable, disinterested person as administrator with the will annexed. On July 18, 2001, the trial court then requested Robert H. McDowall to make application to administer the estate. On August 2, 2001, Mrs. Horton applied to administer the estate. The trial court denied Mrs. Horton's application. Mr. and Mrs. Horton timely appealed.

MR. HORTON'S ASSIGNMENT OF ERROR ONE

THE TRIAL COURT ERRED AS A MATTER OF LAW WHEN IT FAILED TO STRIKE THE OBJECTIONS OF THE OHIO DEPARTMENT OF JOB AND FAMILY SERVICES AND FOUND THAT ODJFS HAD STANDING TO OBJECT TO APPELLANT'S APPLICATION TO BE APPOINTED EXECUTOR PURSUANT TO R.C. 2113.06.

In his first assignment of error, Mr. Horton argues the trial court erred in finding that ODJFS had standing to object to his appointment as executor. This Court agrees.

A testator has the right to name his or her fiduciary and the law is very protective of a testator's choice. *In re Estate of Nagle* (1974), 40 Ohio App. 2d 40, 317 N.E.2d 242.

R.C. 2113.05 establishes the procedure for appointment of an executor named in a will. This statute provides in pertinent part:

When a will is approved and allowed, the probate court shall issue letters testamentary to the executor named in the will *** if he is suitable, competent, accepts the appointment, and gives bond if that is required.

Mr. Horton filed an application for authority to administer estate pursuant to R.C. 2113.05 and 2113.07 and ODJFS filed an objection to his appointment and a request for the court to appoint a disinterested, third party.

R.C. 2113.05 and R.C. 2133.07 do not expressly authorize anyone to file objections to an individual's application to be appointed executor. "Where the party does not rely on any specific statute authorizing invocation of the judicial process, the question of standing depends on whether the party has alleged * * * a 'personal stake in the outcome of the controversy.'" *Middletown v. Ferguson* (1986), 25 Ohio St. 3d 71, 75, 495 N.E.2d 380, quoting *Sierra Club v. Morton* (1972), 405 U.S. 727, 731-732, 31 L. Ed. 2d 636, 92 S. Ct. 1361.

ODJFS had the burden of establishing that it had standing to object to the appointment of the executor. See *Ohio Contractors Assn. v. Bicking* (1994), 71 Ohio St. 3d 318, 320, 643 N.E.2d 1088. To have standing, a person must demonstrate an immediate, pecuniary interest in the subject matter of the litigation. A future, contingent or speculative interest is not enough. *Tiemann v. Univ. of Cincinnati* (1999), 127 Ohio App. 3d 312, 325, 712 N.E.2d 1258, citing *City of Los Angeles v. Lyons* (1983), 461 U.S. 95, 75 L. Ed. 2d 675, 103 S. Ct. 1660. "A bare allegation that *** some injury will or may occur is insufficient to confer standing." *Id.*

At hearing ODJFS argued that it had standing as a creditor of the estate. It further argued that Mr. Horton's prior conduct in not specifically listing ODJFS as a creditor of the estate and his present indication that he would reject their claim gives it a present and compelling interest in Mr. Horton's appointment as executor. This Court disagrees.

At the time of filing its objection and request for appointment of a disinterested third party with Probate Court, ODJFS had not even filed a claim against the estate. Also, Mr. Horton's comments about rejecting any claim submitted by ODJFS were not made in his capacity as executor of the estate because he had not been appointed as executor at that point. What ODJFS basically attempted to do was to make a preemptive strike against Mr. Horton to prevent him from rejecting any claim it may submit if he was appointed executor. This Court can find no case law or statutory authority to empower an alleged creditor of an estate to take such action.

The very fact that there is no statutory authority to file this type of action is especially noteworthy since the state legislature has provided a complete statutory scheme for creditors of a decedent's estate to follow to protect their interests.

All creditors having claims against an estate, including claims arising out of contract, out of tort, on cognovit notes, or on judgments, whether due or not due, secured or unsecured, liquidated or unliquidated, shall present their claims in one of the following manners:

(1) To the executor or administrator in a writing[.]

R.C. 2117.06(B) states that all claims must be presented within one year after the death of the decedent or be forever barred. According to R.C. 2117.11, "an executor or administrator shall reject a creditor's claim *** by giving the claimant written notice of the disallowance thereof. *** A claim may be rejected in whole or in part." When a claim against an estate is rejected in whole or in part, and is not referred to referees, an action on the claim must be commenced within two months after rejection. R.C. 2117.12.

Palmentera v. Marino (Mar. 27, 1996), 1996 Ohio App. LEXIS 1129, Summit App. No. 17430, unreported.

The legislature has specifically conferred standing on a creditor in other probate proceedings. See, for example, R.C. 2109.50 (creditor of a person interested in a trust estate may file a complaint for concealed assets); R.C. 2109.59 (creditor may file a petition to enforce payment or distribution); 2113.06 (creditor may administer estate of an intestate decedent); R.C. 2117.13 (creditor may file written requisition on executor or administrator to reject claim); R.C. 2117.14 (creditor filing requisition under 2117.13 must be made party defendant to action on claim rejected on requisition); R.C. 2117.38 (creditor may bring action against the distributees of estate on allowed contingent claim); R.C. 2127.03 (creditor may move to compel the fiduciary to sell real property if the value of the personal property is not sufficient to pay legacy, debts, allowance to surviving spouse and minor children, and costs of administering estate); R.C. 2129.04 (creditor may apply for ancillary administration of the property of a nonresident decedent); 2129.08(B) (creditor may be appointed ancillary administrator of a nonresident intestate's estate).

Moreover, although R.C. 2133.05 and 2113.07 do not expressly authorize anyone to file objections, R.C. 2113.07 does require the person filing an application for appointment as executor to include the names and addresses of the surviving spouse and next of kin, suggesting that they will be given notice and an opportunity to be heard. R.C. 2113.18 expressly authorizes the surviving spouse, children, or other next of kin to file a motion to remove the executor after appointment. No such authority is given to those purporting to be creditors of the estate. "Under the general rule of statutory construction *expressio unius est exclusio alterius*, the expression of one or more items of a class implies that those not identified are to be excluded." *State v. Droste* (1998), 83 Ohio St. 3d 36, 39, 697 N.E.2d 620, citing *Thomas v. Freeman* (1997), 79 Ohio St. 3d 221, 224-225, 680 N.E.2d 997.

Consequently, this Court finds ODJFS lacked standing to file objections to Mr. Horton's appointment as executor and to request appointment of a disinterested third party to administer the estate. Since the ODJFS lacked standing, it was error for the trial court to consider evidence submitted by it. Therefore,

Mr. Horton's assignment of error number one is sustained.

MR. HORTON'S ASSIGNMENTS OF ERROR TWO AND THREE

THE TRIAL COURT'S FINDING THAT APPELLANT'S FAILURE TO LIST THE STATE AS A CREDITOR IN THE PRIOR RELEASE OF ADMINISTRATION PROCEEDING WAS AN ABUSE OF DISCRETION.

THE TRIAL COURT'S CONSIDERATION OF THE FACT THAT APPELLANT WOULD REQUIRE THE STATE TO SUPPORT ITS CLAIM AND, IF APPOINTED EXECUTOR, APPELLANT WOULD REJECT THE CLAIM, WERE MATTERS OUTSIDE THE JURISDICTION OF THE TRIAL COURT AND ERROR AS A MATTER OF LAW.

MRS. HORTON'S ASSIGNMENT OF ERROR

THE TRIAL COURT ERRED AS A MATTER OF LAW WHEN IT SUMMARILY DENIED APPELLANT'S APPLICATION TO BE APPOINTED EXECUTRIX OF THE ESTATE OF MILDRED HORTON.

This Court need not address Mr. Horton's last two assignments of error and Mrs. Horton's assignment of error as they have been rendered moot by this Court's disposition of Mr. Horton's assignment of error one. See App.R. 12(A)(1)(c).

Judgement reversed and cause remanded.

The Court finds that there were reasonable grounds for these appeals.

We order that a special mandate issue out of this Court, directing the Court of Common Pleas, County of Summit, State of Ohio, to carry this judgment into execution. A certified copy of this journal entry shall constitute the mandate, pursuant to App.R. 27.

Immediately upon the filing hereof, this document shall constitute the journal entry of judgment, and it shall be file stamped by the Clerk of the Court of Appeals at which time the period for review shall begin to run. App.R. 22(E). The Clerk of the Court of Appeals is instructed to mail a notice of entry of this judgment to the parties and to make a notation of the mailing in the docket, pursuant to App.R. 30.

Costs taxed to appellee.
Exceptions.
DONNA J. CARR
FOR THE COURT
BAIRD, P. J.
WHITMORE, J.
CONCUR

Case Questions

1. What was the issue in this case?
2. Did ODJFS have standing to file objections to Mr. Horton's appointment as executor and to request appointment of a disinterested third party to administer the estate? Why or why not?
3. What was the holding in this case?
4. As a matter of public policy, do you agree with the holding in this case? Why or why not?

CASE #2:

IN THE MATTER OF THE REVOCABLE TRUST OF NAOMI MARGOLIS

731 N.W.2d 539; 2007 Minn. App. LEXIS 65
May 22, 2007, Filed

OPINION

MINGE, Judge

Appellant-co-beneficiary of a trust challenges the district court's affirmation of respondent-co-**trustee's** accounting. Appellant argues that respondent's use of trust funds to pay for the beneficiary's medical care was barred by Minn. Stat. § 501B.14 (2006) and that by using trust funds in this way, respondent breached fiduciary duties. Appellant also maintains that the court clearly erred in finding that a $100,000 Norwest certificate of deposit (CD) was not trust property. Because the district court did not clearly err in finding that the Norwest CD was not trust property, we affirm that finding. But because the district court erred in its interpretation and application of Minn. Stat. § 501B.14, we reverse that portion of the decision. And because the district court did not adequately consider appellant's breach-of-fiduciary-duty claims, we remand for consideration of those claims, the appropriate remedy, and possible damages.

FACTS

Respondent Jack Margolis[1] and Naomi Margolis married in 1979. Both had been married previously, and both had children from their prior marriages. Appellant Barry Lorberbaum is one of Naomi's two children. Respondent brought greater wealth to the marriage, and the couple signed an antenuptial property agreement. In 1994, Naomi executed the Naomi Margolis Revocable Trust Agreement, displacing that antenuptial agreement.[2] The terms of the trust designated respondent and Naomi as co-trustees. Respondent and Naomi also delegated to each other all of their powers as co-trustee, and Naomi executed a short-form power of attorney designating respondent as her attorney-in-fact.

Article 2 of the trust governs the use of trust property for the support of Naomi. Section 2.1 of the trust requires that during her lifetime the trust distribute to Naomi such income and principal of the trust as she may request. Section 2.2 directs that if Naomi becomes incompetent, the trustees, in their discretion, are to provide for her support, maintenance, and health. Section 6.6 confirms this power.

Articles 3, 4, and 8 of the trust govern the distribution of trust property following Naomi's death. Section 3.1 provides for the use of trust property to pay for "[Naomi]'s just debts, [and] the expenses of [Naomi]'s last illness, funeral and burial, and the expenses of the administration of [Naomi]'s estate. . . ." Section 4.1 requires the remaining trust property to be distributed to Naomi's children and grandchildren in equal shares. Section 8.1 provides that if Naomi is unable to serve as trustee and fails to designate a successor trustee, appellant is to become her successor trustee.

---

[1]Although Jack Margolis died after the district court proceeding, his death does not affect the appeal, and we refer to respondent as an individual for simplicity in discussing the case.

[2]The record indicates that the trust assets had been transferred by respondent to Naomi several years prior to the creation of the trust. Respondent does not claim and the district court did not find that respondent's earlier ownership of the assets affected the merits of appellant's claims.

Although the trust agreement submitted in the record does not include a list of trust property, it is undisputed that the following assets were transferred to the trust:

Knollwood West Partnership Interest—12.619%
Rosewood Center Partnership Interest—7.5%
Ridgehill Partners Partnership Interest—8.33%
Northstar Bank Certificate of Deposit # 24842—$10,000
Northstar Bank Certificate of Deposit # 30740—$10,000
Northstar Bank Certificate of Deposit # 36392—$10,000
Piper Jaffray Account—beginning balance $19,316

A schedule in Naomi's handwriting also includes a Norwest CD in the amount of $100,000 in the list of assets transferred to the trust. Another note in her handwriting places respondent's name next to the $100,000 Norwest CD. From 1994 to 2000, Naomi received annual trust distributions between $5,000 and $50,000.

In 2001, Naomi's health declined. She had difficulty speaking, was unable to communicate effectively, and required assistance with physical activities. A physician advised respondent that Naomi could no longer live at their residence, and she was admitted to the Sholom Home, a long-term health-care facility. When Naomi was admitted, respondent signed an Admission Agreement with the Sholom Home. On the last page, respondent signed next to the heading "RESIDENT'S SPOUSE" and above the line which reads: "The spouse by signing above, acknowledges joint and several responsibility for payment of all charges." Naomi never signed the Agreement.

While Naomi resided at the Sholom Home, respondent used trust assets indirectly to pay for nursing-home services. Trust income was not deposited in a trust account. Rather, respondent deposited checks payable to the Naomi Margolis Revocable Trust and the proceeds from liquidation of the trust's three Northstar CD's directly into the couple's joint checking account. Respondent then drew on this joint account to make payments to the Sholom Home. According to Sholom Home records, respondent paid $194,089.85 for the uninsured cost of Naomi's care. According to respondent's accountant, respondent paid a total of $206,384 for Naomi's care in the Sholom Home and other medical expenses.

In November 2003, Naomi's death was imminent, and respondent sought legal advice to determine whether he could move the Ridgehill, Knollwood, and Rosewood partnership interests, then in Naomi's trust,

to his own trust. Relying on the advice of his lawyer, respondent transferred those assets to his trust, the Jack Margolis Revocable Trust. After the conveyance, his trust received cash distributions from the partnerships. But near the end of 2004, again on the advice of his lawyer, respondent transferred the partnership interests back to the Naomi Margolis Revocable Trust. While respondent held the partnership interests in his own trust, he received $29,263.65 in partnership distributions.

Naomi died in February of 2004. She was survived by her daughter and appellant. In August 2004, appellant petitioned the district court for removal of respondent as trustee of the Naomi Margolis Revocable Trust, for his own appointment as trustee, for redress for respondent's alleged breach of fiduciary duties, and for a full accounting of the trust's income, distributions, liabilities, and expenses. The district court granted appellant's requests for respondent's removal, his appointment, and an accounting, but it deferred the fiduciary issues to a subsequent hearing. Respondent then filed an accounting.

At trial, appellant claimed that respondent improperly used trust funds to pay for Naomi's medical expenses, that respondent's accounting failed to include the $100,000 Norwest CD as trust property, and that respondent breached fiduciary duties owed to the trust. Appellant sought restitution in the amount of $307,902.80 for the allegedly improper payment of Naomi's medical expenses ($206,384), and the $100,000 Norwest CD. The district court concluded that all of the trust distributions were used to pay for Naomi's medical care, that the expenditures were proper, and that appellant did not meet his burden to establish that the Norwest CD was trust property. The district court did not explicitly address appellant's fiduciary duty arguments. This appeal follows.

ISSUES

I. Did the district court err by affirming respondent's use of trust funds for Naomi Margolis's medical expenses?

II. Did the district court clearly err in finding that the $100,000 Norwest certificate of deposit was not trust property?

ANALYSIS

I

Appellant contends that the district court erred by affirming respondent's accounting because: (A) respondent's distributions for Naomi's medical care violated Minn. Stat. § 501B.14 (2006); (B) respondent's handling of funds breached fiduciary duties owed to the trust; and (C) respondent breached the terms of the trust by failing to consult a medical advisor and appoint a successor trustee upon Naomi's incapacitation.

A. Minn. Stat. § 501B.14

The first issue is whether respondent's use of trust funds to pay for Naomi's medical services was barred by Minn. Stat. § 501B.14, subd. 1(2). In relevant part, this statute provides:

> No trustee may exercise or participate in the exercise of any of the following powers: . . . (2) any power to make discretionary distributions of either principal or income to discharge any legal support or other obligations of the **trustee** to any person.

The interpretation and application of a statute to the undisputed facts of a case involves a question of law, and we review the district court's decision de novo. *O'Malley v. Ulland Bros.*, 549 N.W.2d 889, 892 (Minn. 1996). The goal of statutory interpretation is to "ascertain and effectuate" the legislature's intent. Minn. Stat. § 645.16 (2006). "When interpreting a statute, we first look to see whether the statute's language, on its face, is clear or ambiguous. A statute is only ambiguous when the language therein is subject to more than one reasonable interpretation." *Am. Family Ins. Group v. Schroedl*, 616 N.W.2d 273, 277 (Minn. 2000) (quotations omitted). If the statute is unambiguous, we give the language its plain meaning. *State v. J.R.A.*, 714 N.W.2d 722, 726 (Minn. App. 2006), *review denied* (Minn. Aug. 23, 2006). "If the language is ambiguous, however, we may consider other factors, such as the purpose of the statute and the consequences of a particular interpretation." *In re Estate of Sullivan*, 724 N.W.2d 532, 535 (Minn. App. 2006).

Initially, respondent argues that Minn. Stat. § 501B.14 is not applicable to this case because it was enacted solely for federal estate tax purposes. Even if the statute were prompted by estate-tax considerations, it contains no qualification or limitation regarding its application, and this claim is not an adequate reason to disregard its language. Moreover, subdivision 3 of the statute expressly governs the statute's application and states, in part:

> Except as provided in paragraph (b), this section applies to any exercise of any powers of the **trustee** after May [*544] 14, 1993, under any trust created before, on, or after May 14, 1993, unless the terms of the trust refer specifically to this section and provide that this section does not apply.

Minn. Stat. § 501B.14, subd. 3(a). The subdivision proceeds to list four instances in which the statute does not apply to a trustee. Minn. Stat. § 501B.14, subd. 3. Respondent makes no claim that this case falls within any of the four exceptions listed in subdivision 3, and the text of the trust agreement does not reference Minn. Stat. § 501B.14 or provide that the statute does not apply. Because the reach of the statute's application is unambiguous, we do not further consider respondent's argument regarding its tax purpose.

The question of whether respondent's allocation of trust funds to pay for Naomi's medical care was prohibited by Minn. Stat. § 501B.14, is more difficult. Minn. Stat. § 501B.14 was enacted in 1993, and since that date, the statute has been cited in only one Minnesota case, which is not directly on point. *See Morrison v. Doyle*, 582 N.W.2d 237, 241 (Minn. 1998). The question we must resolve is whether respondent "discharge[d] [a] legal support or other obligation[] of the trustee," within the meaning of Minn. Stat. § 501B.14, by paying for Naomi's medical care with trust funds.

Respondent urges this court to construe "legal support . . . obligation" as an obligation for which the trustee is *primarily* liable. According to respondent, the statute only prohibits a trustee from using trust funds to discharge a legal obligation when the obligation is *primarily* the trustee's and not also the beneficiary's. In contrast, appellant urges us to construe the phrase "legal support . . . obligation" according to its plain meaning. Appellant argues that by using trust funds to pay for Naomi's medical care, respondent unlawfully discharged his legal-support obligations pursuant to the nursing-home contract he signed and as her husband pursuant to Minn. Stat. § 519.05(a) (2006). By contract and by law, respondent was liable for Naomi's medical care.

Although we are sympathetic to respondent's argument, we find it unpersuasive. We acknowledge that trust provisions permitting spouse-trustees to make distributions for the support of the spouse-beneficiaries are commonplace. Also, we recognize that nursing homes and other care providers may regularly require spouses or others who may be trustees to assume liability for the expenses. But the statutory language does not accommodate respondent's reading of the statute. The statute prohibits a trustee's use of trust funds to discharge "*any* legal support or other obligations of the trustee to *any* person." Minn. Stat. § 501B.14, subd. 1(2) (emphasis added). The statute does not limit its prohibition to payment of the trustee's primary support obligations. Black's Law Dictionary defines an "obligation," in its popular sense, as "[a] legal . . . duty to do or not do something." *Black's Law Dictionary* 1104 (8th ed. 2004). In the more technical sense, "obligation" is defined as: "A formal, binding agreement or acknowledgment of a liability to pay a certain amount. . . ." *Id.* Both definitions encompass respondent's duty to pay for Naomi's care. The plain meaning of the statute's text does not admit the qualification advanced by respondent and the legislature can easily correct any problem it may have created. Absent a constitutional infirmity, judicial rewriting of an unambiguous statute is inappropriate.

Here, respondent had a contractual and statutory legal support obligation to provide for Naomi's healthcare and nursing-home expenses. And Minn. Stat. § 501B.14 plainly, and with no qualification, prohibits trustees from using trust funds to discharge their own legal support obligations. Respondent did so here, and in so doing violated that statute. Respondent argues that this interpretation produces a harsh, and even absurd, result. We disagree. Subdivision 2 of section 501B.14 allows a trustee to avoid the potential harshness of this result by obtaining court approval of expenditures, and subdivision 3 allows settlors to opt out of the reach of this statute "if the terms of the trust refer specifically to this section and provide that this section does not apply." Minn. Stat. § 501B.14, subds. 2, 3(a). Thus, prudent parties may work around the statute. Furthermore, as the ensuing discussion of remedies indicates, the result is tempered by the context.

Respondent's claim that the request is harsh is unpersuasive. Not only was respondent liable for Naomi's care, but the record indicates that they had joint accounts and that respondent had substantial, separate assets that could have been used to pay Naomi's bills. After her death, Naomi's children are the beneficiaries of her trust. Respondent was, or upon her death would be, the sole owner of the joint accounts, which his children would inherit from him. Thus, the choice of whether to pay bills out of her trust was not without significance. We conclude that the district court erred in determining that respondent's distribution was permissible under the statute.

Having determined that the statute proscribes the disbursements as made by respondent, we are faced with the question of how the statute is to be enforced. We note that the statute does not provide a remedy for its violation. Appellant seeks to impose absolute, personal liability on respondent. Although this is a possible remedy, section 8.8 of the trust agreement states:

> [No **trustee**] shall at any time be held liable for a mistake of law and/or fact, for an error of judgment, nor for any loss or injury coming to any trust estate

or to any beneficiary thereof . . . except as a result of actual fraud or willful misconduct. . . .

Although the per se standard is appropriate in instances of actual fraud/willful misconduct, we are not aware of an application of the per se standard when the trust agreement provides its own standard. Here, there should be appropriate findings of fact and conclusions of law on this issue. This is the function of the district court. The facts referenced in this and the next section are relevant to this undertaking. Accordingly, we remand to the district court with instructions to make factual findings pursuant to section 8.8 of the agreement and to determine the appropriate remedy and damages for respondent's failure to comply with the statute.

B. Breach-of-Fiduciary-Duty Claims

Appellant also argues that the district court erred in allowing respondent's accounting because respondent breached fiduciary duties owed to the trust. Under Minnesota law, trustees owe several fiduciary duties to trust beneficiaries. Most importantly, trustees owe a duty of loyalty to trust beneficiaries. The trustee's "primary duty [is] not to allow his interest as an individual even the opportunity of conflict with his interest as trustee." *Smith v. Tolversen*, 190 Minn. 410, 413, 252 N.W. 423, 425 (1934). A trustee can breach the duty of loyalty by acting for personal gain. *See In re Estate of Lee*, 214 Minn. 448, 9 N.W.2d 245 (1943). But there is no breach of the duty of loyalty where the transaction is explicitly authorized by the terms of the trust. Restatement (Second) of Trusts § 170 cmt. a (1959). Trustees also have a duty to act pursuant to the terms of the trust, and they commit a breach of trust when they fail to do so. *Id.* at § 201. Moreover, trustees owe beneficiaries a duty of full disclosure, *id.* at § 173, are prohibited from co-mingling trust funds with their own personal funds, *id.* at § 179, and have a responsibility to thoroughly maintain an accounting of their management of trust property, *id.* at § 172.

Here, the record indicates that respondent co-mingled trust funds with his own funds, failed to keep the beneficiaries reasonably informed of material facts, refused to respond to appellant's requests for information, failed to maintain an accurate accounting of his management of the trust funds, and failed to inform appellant that he was to serve as a successor trustee after Naomi became incapacitated, even though the trust expressly calls for that appointment. Further, appellant asserts that respondent expended funds from the trust, as opposed to other sources, so as to favor himself and his descendents at the expense of Naomi's children, that respondent attempted to claim the trust's limited partnership interests as his own property, and that respondent intentionally misrepresented the trust's assets. There is support in the record for these claims. But arguments and evidence notwithstanding, the district court made no findings or conclusions regarding appellant's breach-of-fiduciary-duty claims. Appellant's arguments were presented to the district court both in his initial petition and his memorandum of law.

Because the breach-of-fiduciary claims raise important fact issues that the district court did not address, we remand for their consideration. We direct the district court to make any findings of fact necessary to resolve this issue. Further, in the event the district court concludes that respondent breached his fiduciary duty to the trust beneficiaries, the district court should determine the proper remedy and damages for such a breach.

C. Consultation of a Medical Advisor and Appointment of a Successor Trustee

Appellant also argues that the court's affirmation of respondent's accounting was error because respondent did not follow the provisions of the trust agreement by consulting a medical advisor upon Naomi's incapacitation or appointing a successor trustee in accordance with the terms of the trust.

Section 2.2 of the trust agreement provides:

2.2 Payments in the event the Grantor becomes Incapacitated. At any time while the Grantor, in the opinion of the Trustees and a competent medical advisor, is incapacitated through illness or any other cause, the Trustees shall pay to or expend for the benefit of the Grantor, and the Grantor's issue such sum or sums from either the net income from or the principal of the Trust Estate as the Trustees, in the Trustee's discretion, may deem necessary or advisable to provide for the proper support, maintenance, and health of the Grantor, and the Grantor's issue.

Here, respondent never sought an independent medical advisor's opinion to establish Naomi's incapacitation. The district court reasoned that because "[t]here is no dispute that [Naomi] was incapacitated to the extent that she required nursing home care... the mere failure of [respondent] to obtain an independent medical opinion regarding her capacity is of no consequence." Based on the record in this case, we agree. Appellant does not challenge the district court's finding that Naomi was incapacitated at the time she entered the Sholom Home. In fact, appellant testified to her incapacity at trial, and appellant conceded such incapacitation from the outset of the litigation.

Additionally, appellant has not shown how respondent's failure to consult an independent medical advisor resulted in the misuse of trust assets. We affirm this portion of the district court's decision.

Appellant also contends that the district court erred in affirming respondent's accounting because respondent failed to bring to appellant's attention appellant's role as a successor trustee upon Naomi's incapacitation. The district court concluded that respondent's failure to do so was immaterial because "[h]ad [appellant] assumed the duties of successor trustee and had he objected to the payment of his mother's nursing home costs from her trust, the issue would have been brought before the court, which would have ordered payment from her trust." However, this conclusion ignores the conflict of interest respondent faced over whether to use resources from Naomi's trust or their joint accounts to pay her expenses. It further assumes that appellant or an independent, additional trustee either would have concurred that Naomi's trust should bear the primary expense of her care or would not have had any persuasive perspective on the question. The district court may have been presented with a different request if respondent was not the sole trustee. Because we remand for consideration of appellant's section 501B.14 and fiduciary-duty claims, we include in our remand an instruction to the district court to reconsider the adverse effect, if any, of respondent's failure to obtain a successor trustee.

II

Next, appellant argues that the district court clearly erred in finding that the $100,000 Norwest CD was not trust property. The question of whether property is trust property depends on whether the grantor was the owner of and intended to identify "a definite trust res wherein the trustee's title and estate is separated from the vested beneficial interest of the beneficiary." *Brooks v. Ramsey County Cmty. Human Servs. Dep't*, 405 N.W.2d 432, 435 (Minn. App. 1987). The existence of intent is a question of fact. *Dannheim Dev., Inc. v. Mogler*, 412 N.W.2d 398, 400 (Minn. App. 1987).

"Findings of fact . . . shall not be set aside unless clearly erroneous, and due regard shall be given to the opportunity of the trial court to judge the credibility of the witnesses. "Minn. R. Civ. p. 52.01. In applying Minn. R. Civ. p. 52.01, we view the record in the light most favorable to the district court's judgment and will not reverse merely because we view the evidence differently. *Rogers v. Moore*, 603 N.W.2d 650, 656 (Minn. 1999). The district court's factual findings must be clearly erroneous or "manifestly contrary to the weight of the evidence or not reasonably supported by the evidence as a whole" to warrant reversal. *Id.* (quotation omitted). "Findings of fact are clearly erroneous only if the reviewing court is left with the definite and firm conviction that a mistake has been made." *Fletcher v. St. Paul Pioneer Press,* 589 N.W.2d 96, 101 (Minn. 1999) (quotation omitted).

Here, appellant introduced two pages of Naomi's hand-written notes listing various assets held by her and respondent. There are two columns on the first page of the notes, each with headings for Naomi and for respondent. Listed on separate lines below the Naomi heading is: "North Star Bank," "Ridgehill," "Rosewood," "Knollwood," "Norwest CD 100,000 only," and "Piper Jaffray." The second column has the heading "Jack" and lists several assets. The following page of notes contains the notation: "Jack ?: Norwest # 1191946 CD... 100,000." Appellant did not present any evidence indicating whether the notes were written before or after execution of the trust. Respondent offered two documents from Norwest Bank in opposition to appellant's claim. Both documents indicate that the certificate number of the Northwest CD is 4101191946. The first document is a "notice of certificate maturity." This document attributes ownership of that $100,000 CD to "Jack Margolis or Naomi R Margolis," not the Naomi Margolis Revocable Trust. Similarly, the second document, a "CD/Retirement Disclosure," lists "Jack Margolis" as the depositor of the CD.

Appellant argues that Minnesota law employs a presumption that assets traced into the hands of a trustee are presumed to remain in trust, unless the trustee shows otherwise. By requiring a trustee to explain any ambiguity in accounting for trust property, the presumption operates to encourage clear and diligent accounting of trust property. Appellant's recitation of the presumption finds support in early Minnesota caselaw. *See Stein v. Kemp,* 132 Minn. 44, 47, 155 N.W. 1052, 1053 (1916); *Blythe v. Kujawa,* 175 Minn. 88, 92, 220 N.W. 168, 169 (1928).

But appellant's reliance on this presumption is misplaced. This presumption is grounded on the presupposition that the property in question is, in fact, trust property. And the presumption takes effect only after it is shown that the property in question was an asset of the trust at the trust's inception. Here, the district court found that appellant did not meet his evidentiary burden to show that the CD was a trust asset. Because the limited and conflicting evidence presented on the issue is adequate to support the district court's finding and because we defer to the district court's weighing of the conflicting evidence, we conclude that the district court did not clearly err in finding that the Norwest CD was not trust property.

DECISION

Because the district court did not clearly err in finding that the Norwest CD was not trust property, we affirm that finding. But because the district court erred in its interpretation and application of Minn. Stat. § 501B.14 (2006), and because the district court did not adequately consider appellant's breach-of-fiduciary-duty and replacement-trustee claims, we remand for consideration of those matters, the appropriate remedy, and damages.

Affirmed in part, reversed in part, and remanded.

Case Questions

1. What was the cause of action against the trustee?
2. What was the basis for the cause of action against the trustee?
3. What was the holding in this case?
4. What was the reason for the court's holding (the rationale) in this case?

FORMS TO ACCOMPANY PARALEGAL PRACTICE

Disclaimer: The forms provided to aid students in completing the Paralegal Practice activities assigned in each chapter have been modified as samples to familiarize students with what each form commonly looks like and are not intended to be used as actual forms for any state.

INSTRUCTIONS: The forms are provided in Microsoft Word format and employ the use of Stop Codes (such as SC1, SC2, SC3, and so on). Stop Codes are used in place of the form sections that must be updated with case-by-case information, such as SC1 for the client's name, SC3 for the client's address, and so on. What each Stop Code represents can be inferred by reading the surrounding text on the form. By using the FIND & REPLACE tool on the Microsoft toolbar, the students can replace the Stop Codes with the information provided in the Paralegal Practice activity to complete each assignment. Students must also fill in any blank lines on each form with the appropriate information from the activity and then proofread the document prior to turning in their work.

The following forms are included following this section and will be posted online for students to access to complete the Paralegal Practice activities for this chapter:

- PP Form 16.1—Objection to Disallowance of Claim

PP Form 16.1—Objection to Disallowance of Claim

Name
Address
City, State Zip Code
Phone Number
Fax Number
Respondent

IN THE SUPERIOR COURT OF THE STATE OF SAMPLE STATE
IN AND FOR THE COUNTY OF SAMPLE

In the Matter of the Estate of **SC1,** Deceased.	Case No. PB-2014-_____ **OBJECTION TO DISALLOWANCE OF CLAIM**

The undersigned, SC5 ("Respondent"), hereby objects to the Disallowance of Claim filed by the Personal Representative, as follows:

1. The undersigned filed a Creditor's Claim in the amount of $_____ on the following date: _____ (hereinafter referred to as "the claim").

2. The Personal Representative disallowed the claim on _____ for the following reason: _____.

3. The claim should be allowed for the following reasons: _____ _____.

WHEREFORE, the Respondent respectfully requests the Court to issue an order allowing the claim in the amount of $_____ and ordering the payment of the same, and for such other further relief as the Court deems just and appropriate under the circumstances.

RESPECTFULLY SUBMITTED this ___ day of _____, 2014.

_____
SC5, Respondent

GLOSSARY

Administrator   A male appointed by the court to administer the estate of an intestate decedent.

Administratrix   A female appointed by the court to administer the estate of an intestate decedent.

Advance Directives   Documents used to inform family, friends, and medical personnel about the kind of medical care and treatment a person desires if he or she becomes terminally ill or otherwise incapacitated and to appoint a person to make sure those wishes are carried out.

Affinity   A close relation based on marriage rather than on common ancestry.

Agent   A person or business authorized to act on another's behalf.

Allowed Claim   A creditor's claim that is accepted to be paid from the estate.

Ambulatory   Revocable or subject to change.

Ancillary Administrator   A person appointed by the court to handle the affairs of a decedent in a foreign state.

Ancillary Probate   An additional probate proceeding conducted in a state other than the main probate proceeding in the decedent's state of domicile.

Anti-Lapse Statutes   Laws designed to minimize the effect of lapse.

Applicable Credit Amount   A credit against the federal unified transfer tax on gifts (prior to death) and estates (after death).

Applicable Exclusion Amount   The maximum value of property that can be transferred to others without incurring any estate tax or federal gift tax because of the applicable credit amount.

Attestation   The act of witnessing a signature for the purpose of declaring that the will was properly signed and declared by the signer to be his or her signature.

Attorney-in-Fact   The person appointed under a power of attorney to act as the principal's agent.

Beneficiary   A beneficiary of a will is a person entitled to receive property under a will or to whom the decedent's property is given or distributed.

Beneficiary (of a will)   A person entitled to receive property under a will or to whom the decedent's property is given or distributed.

Beneficiary Deed   A deed executed while the grantor is alive that takes effect only upon the death of the grantor.

Bequest   A gift of personal property under a will.

Bill of Sale   A document used to transfer personal property, such as the contents of the trust creator's home, into the trust.

Breach of Fiduciary Duty   A failure by a fiduciary to act in the best interest of those being served.

Bypass Trust   An estate planning device whereby a designated portion of a deceased spouse's estate passes to a trust for the benefit of the surviving spouse, rather than passing outright to the surviving spouse, thereby reducing the likelihood that the surviving spouse's estate will be subject to federal estate tax.

Charitable Remainder Annuity Trust   A trust in which the beneficiary receives a fixed amount of income from the trust in at least annual installments and, after death, the balance is given to charity.

Charitable Remainder Trust   A trust in which the trustor or a beneficiary receives the income from the trust for a time period (usually for life) and then the remainder of the trust is given to charity.

Child Protective Services (CPS)   In many states of the United States, the name of a governmental agency that responds to reports of child abuse or neglect.

Claim   A right to payment.

Closing Statement   A document filed by a personal representative that notifies the court that the estate has been fully administered.

Codicil   A written amendment to a person's will, which must be executed with the same formalities as the original will (i.e. dated, signed and witnessed) and must reference the will it amends.

Community Property   A method of holding property acquired during marriage in which each spouse owns one-half of the property outright. Community property is currently valid in: Alaska, Arizona, California, Idaho, Louisiana, New Mexico, Nevada, Texas, and Washington. Wisconsin has a similar law known as "marital property law."

Conditional Bequest   A gift under a will which will take place only if a particular event has occurred by the time the maker of the will dies.

Consanguinity   (from the Latin word consanguinitas, *meaning* "blood relation"): The quality of being descended from the same ancestor as another person.

Conservator   One who legally has the care and management of the property, but not the person, of someone who is incompetent.

Conservatorship   The legal process by which a conservator is appointed.

Creditor's Claim   A written document by a creditor alleging that it is owed money by the estate. The claim must be delivered to the personal representative within the statutory time frame or it may be disallowed.

Creditors   People or entities to whom money is owed.

cy pres doctrine   When a testator or a trustor makes a gift to a charity under a will or trust and it subsequently becomes impossible or impracticable to apply the gift to the particular named charity, the equity court may order the gift to be applied to another charity "as near as possible" to the designated charity.

Decedent   A dead person.

Deed   A written document that transfers title or an interest in real property from one person to another person or persons.

Demonstrative Legacy   A bequest of a certain sum of money with a direction that it be paid out of a particular fund.

Devise   A gift of real property under a will.

Disallowance of Claim   A document filed by a personal representative notifying the creditor that the claim is not being allowed and providing the legal grounds for the disallowance.

Disallowed Claim   A creditor's claim that is rejected and will not be paid from the estate.

Domicile   A person's principal place of abode; the place to which, whenever one is absent, one has the present intent of returning.

Durable   Indicates that a power of attorney will remain in effect after the principal becomes incapacitated.

Elder Abuse   Any form of mistreatment that results in harm or loss to an older person

Escheat   Vesting of property in the state; occurs only when there are no heirs, descendants, or named beneficiaries to take property upon the death of the last known owner.

Estate Plan   A plan made to provide for the maker's physical and financial needs during lifetime, as well as the distribution of their estate upon death.

Estate Tax   A tax on the right to transfer property at death; based on an accounting of everything one owns or has certain interests in as of the date of death.

Executor   A male nominated in a will of a decedent to carry out the terms of the will; a personal representative of the estate.

Executory Bequest   A bequest which provides for a gift to a beneficiary upon the happening of a specified event, such as when the beneficiary graduates from college or marries.

Executrix   A female nominated in a will to carry out the terms of the will; a personal representative of the estate.

Fee Simple   The greatest and most absolute estate that anyone can have in land.

Fiduciary Capacity   A position of trust; the legal capability of a person or institution (such as a bank) to act as a fiduciary.

Fiduciary Duty   A duty or responsibility required of a fiduciary that arises out of a position of loyalty and trust.

Fiduciary   A person in a position of loyalty and trust, such as an executor, administrator, guardian, attorney-in-fact, or trustee; also a person to whom property or power is entrusted for the benefit of another.

Fixture   Personal property that is so permanently attached to real property that it becomes part of the real property.

General Legacy   A gift of money out of the general assets of the estate.

Grant Deed   A deed that transfers title to real property from a grantor to a grantee. A grant deed is generally a warranty deed.

Grantee   The person receiving the interest in the real property in a deed.

Grantor   The person making the transfer of real property in a deed.

Gross Estate   The value at the time of a decedent's death of all of the decedent's property, real or personal, tangible or intangible, wherever situated.

Guardian Ad Litem   A guardian appointed by a court to protect a minor who brings or defends a lawsuit.

Guardian   The one who legally has the care and management of the person, property, or both of a minor or incompetent person.

Guardianship   The legal process by which a guardian is appointed.

Health Care Power of Attorney   A power of attorney for medical decisions; in it, the principal appoints an agent to make medical decisions when the principal is incapacitated.

Health Care Proxy   A written statement authorizing an agent or surrogate to make medical treatment decisions for another in the event of the other's inability to do so.

Holographic Will   A will that is written completely in the handwriting of the testator and signed and dated by the maker. Witnesses may or may not be required, depending on state law.

Inter Vivos Trust (also known as a Living Trust)   A trust created by a written declaration during the lifetime of the creator.

Intestate Succession Statutes   State laws that determine who will inherit the property of a person who dies without a valid will.

Intestate   To die without a valid will.

Intestate   Having no valid will at death.

Inventory and Appraisal ("Inventory")   A detailed list of articles of property in an estate, made by the executor or administrator thereof.

Issue   A person's children or other lineal descendants in the direct bloodline, such as grandchildren and great-grandchildren.

Joint Tenancy   Title to property held by more than one person with a right of survivorship.

Jurisdiction   The power or authority that a court has to hear a case.

Lapse   The failure of a gift made in a will as a result of the person to whom the gift was intended predeceasing the person making the will.

Last Will and Testament (Will)   A written document that leaves the estate of the individual who signed the will to the named persons or entities.

Legacy   A gift of personal property or money to a beneficiary (legatee) of a will. A legacy technically does not include real property (which is a "devise"), but usually refers to any gift from the estate of one who died.

Legal Capacity   The age of majority at which a person acquires the capacity to make a valid will. Majority age is eighteen (18) in most states, but is age twenty-one (21) in a minority of states.

Letters Testamentary   A document issued by the court as evidence of its authorization for the personal representative's to act on behalf of a deceased's estate.

Life Estate   A tenancy that allows a person to own real property for his or her lifetime only.

Limited Power of Attorney   A power of attorney that limits the scope of the agent's authority and/or the length of time that the document remains in effect.

Living Trust   Also called an *inter vivos* trust, (*inter vivos* is Latin for "within one's life") is a trust that is created and becomes effective during the lifetime of the trustor(s) [also called settlor(s)].

Living Will and Health Care Proxy   A legal document that combines a living will with a health care proxy into one form by expressing the principal's wishes to be allowed to die a natural death and appointing an agent to make medical treatment decisions on the principal's behalf.

Living Will   A written expression of a person's wishes to be allowed to die a natural death and not be kept alive by heroic or artificial methods.

Malpractice   An act or continuing conduct of a professional that does not meet the standard of professional competence and results in provable damages to the professional's client. Such an error or omission may be through negligence, ignorance of something the professional should have known, or intentional wrongdoing.

No Contest Clause   Also called an *in terrorem clause*; a clause included in a will in order to prevent the disinherited individual from contesting the probate of the will, resulting in delays and additional administrative expenses for the estate.

Non-Probate Assets   Property that passes to a decedent's intended beneficiaries by operation of law, independent of the provisions of a will or a probate proceeding.

Nuncupative Will   A will that has been delivered orally to witnesses, as opposed to being written down and executed with the usual formalities.

Per capita   Latin for "by head"; indicates that succession is to be determined by the number of people in a class or group.

Per stirpes   Latin for "by roots"; indicates succession by right of representation, share and share alike.

Persistent Vegetative State (PVS)   A condition of patients with severe brain damage in whom a coma has progressed to a state of wakefulness without detectable awareness. It is a diagnosis of some uncertainty in that it deals with a syndrome.

Personal Property   Includes all moveable assets, or things, that are not classified as real property; includes both tangible and intangible property.

Personal Representative's Deed   A deed in which the personal representative of an estate is the grantor and is transferring real property to the decedent's heirs or devisees.

Personal Representative   The executor or administrator of a deceased person. Whether the estate representative is referred to as an "executor" or a "personal representative" is dictated by the laws and customs of the jurisdiction; however, for all intents and purposes, the terms may be used interchangeably.

Pet Trust   A trust established to provide for the care of one or more animals and which terminates upon the death of the last animal cared for under the trust; pet trusts are now legal in 45 states.

Pour-over Will   A will that leaves the testator's assets to a living trust, to be administered pursuant to the terms thereof.

Power of Attorney   A legal document that authorizes another person to act as the grantor's attorney-in-fact and agent; execution before a notary public is nearly always required.

Power   A legal ability, capacity, or authority.

Principal   A person who authorizes another, as an agent, to represent him or her.

Probate and Family Court   A name given in some states to the court that exercises the function of settling decedents' estates. Other states simply call this court the "Probate Court" or the "Surrogate's Court." Finally, some states have trial courts of general jurisdiction that have authority to settle decedents' estates within their jurisdiction.

Probate Assets   The property of the decedent that must be distributed through a probate proceeding in a court of law.

Probate   A general term for the entire process of administration of estates of dead persons, including those without wills, with court supervision.

Proposal for Distribution   A document that is filed with the court and distributed to the heirs or beneficiaries outlining how the personal representative proposes to distribute the estate. The Proposal for Distribution also notifies recipients of the statutory time frame they have in which to file an objection.

Quitclaim Deed   A deed to real property that transfers to the grantee only whatever interest the grantor has in the property.

Real Property   All land, structures, firmly attached and integrated equipment, anything growing on the land, and all interests in the property. Real property is immovable.

Receipt and Release and Waiver of Notice   A form executed by a beneficiary to acknowledge receipt of the inheritance received and to acknowledge and approve the personal representative's distribution of the estate.

Renounce   The rejection of a nomination under a will or other legal document.

Revocable Living Trust   A trust created by a written declaration during the lifetime of the creator that can be amended or revoked during the creator's lifetime.

Secured Creditor   One who holds some special monetary assurance of payment of a debt owed, such as a mortgage, collateral, or lien.

Separate Property   In community property states, all property that is not community property; usually includes property owned before marriage and gifts, bequests, and inheritances received after marriage.

Simple Will   A phrase used by legal professionals to indicate a will that does not include tax planning language.

Small Estate Settlement   A provision in some states allowing for probate assets below a certain value to be transferred by a simple affidavit when a variety of other conditions are met.

Sound Mind   Having the mental capacity to execute a document, such as a will. Sound mind is the normal condition of the human mind, not impaired by insanity or other mental disorders.

Sound Mind   To have the mental ability to make a valid will; the normal condition of the human mind, not impaired by insanity or other mental disorders.

Special Needs Trust   A trust created to ensure that a beneficiary who is disabled or mentally ill can enjoy the use of property that is intended to be held for his or her benefit while also preventing the beneficiary from losing access to essential government benefits.

Specific Bequest   A gift in a will of a specified article to a certain person or persons.

Specific Legacy   A gift by will of a particular article of personal property.

Spendthrift Clause   A provision in a trust or will that states that if a prospective beneficiary has pledged to turn over his or her inheritance to a third party, the trustee or executor shall not honor such a pledge.

Spendthrift Trust   A trust created to provide a fund for the maintenance of a beneficiary and at the same time to secure it against the beneficiary's improvidence or incapacity.

Springing Power of Attorney   A power of attorney that becomes effective upon the occurrence of a specific event at a future time.

Sprinkling trust (also called "spraying trust")   A trust in which the income or principal is distributed among members of a designated class in amounts and proportions determined by the trustee's discretion.

Tenancy by the Entirety   A form of property ownership shared by husbands and wives where both have the right to the entire property and, upon the death of one spouse, the surviving spouse enjoys title to the whole property by right of survivorship.

Tenancy in Common   Ownership in property by two or more persons in which each owner has an undivided interest in the property without right of survivorship.

Testimonium clause   Also called a signature clause, this clause appears immediately above the testator's signature to establish the end of the will by presenting the testator's signature and affixing the date of the will's execution.

Terminating Event   The event that triggers trust termination.

Testamentary Trust   A trust that is drafted as part of the testator's will and only becomes effective upon the testator's death.

Testate   To die with a valid will.

Testator   A man who executes a will.

Testatrix   A female who executes a will.

Trust Corpus (Latin for "body")   The principal of the trust, usually comprising money, securities, and other assets.

Trust for Minor(s)   A trust created for the benefit of one or more minor beneficiaries that is set to terminate after the designated beneficiary has attained a specified age.

Trustee   The person or entity who holds the assets (corpus) of the trust and manages the trust and its assets pursuant to the trust's terms.

Trustor, Donor, or Settlor   The creator of a trust.

Uniform Fiduciaries Act   An act drafted by the National Conference of Commissioners on Uniform State laws and approved and recommended for enactment in all states in 1922. "The general purpose of the Act is to establish uniform and definite rules in place . . . as to 'constructive notice' of breaches of fiduciary obligations . . . [and to] facilitate the performance by fiduciaries of their obligations, rather than to favor any particular class of persons dealing with fiduciaries."

Unsecured Creditor   A creditor other than a preferential creditor that does not have the benefit of any security interests in the assets of the debtor (the decedent).

Ward   A person who has been legally placed under the care of a guardian or a court.

Warranty Deed   A deed to real property which guarantees that the seller has clear title to the property, and that title can be transferred or conveyed to the buyer.

Will   A written document that leaves the estate of the individual who signed the will to the named persons or entities.

Will Contest   A lawsuit over the allowance or disallowance of a will.

CASE INDEX

SUBJECT INDEX